We are shaped and fashioned by what we love
Johann Wolfgang von Goethe

TO KNOW HISTORY
IS TO
LOVE HISTORY

Welcome to Prentice Hall's **T.L.C. Edition**.
That's **T**eaching and **L**earning **C**lassroom Edition.

Dear Student,

Your instructor already knows—and loves—history. *Do you?*

Welcome to the new and exciting TLC Edition—this is the book that will change the way you feel about history. Prentice Hall developed this text to bring history to you with more visual appeal than ever. This is the book that you will want to read because it is interesting. You will think about what you're reading because it has relevance to your life. With this book and the multimedia tools we crafted to accompany it, you will truly experience history's dramatic trials and passionate triumphs in a way that adds meaning to your own life. And you will score better on tests because preparation will be easier and less time—consuming than you ever dreamed possible.

Read on and find out why this book is just the T.L.C. you need to say "I DO" know—and love—history.

TO KNOW HISTORY
IS TO LOVE HISTORY

Imagine if you could make sense of all the names, dates, events, and people who made history? Imagine putting it all into a context that made you rethink your world, your life, yourself—with the fascinating perspective that only history provides? **All it takes is the T.L.C. you are now holding in your hand.**

Here's what makes this T.L.C. Edition different...

- You will be compelled to READ this dramatically different, vividly illustrated, less dense textbook because it is not at all overwhelming

- You will be inspired to THINK about *what you are reading as you are reading.*

- You will come to class READY to take notes with your automatically bundled, portable, and easy-to-use *HistoryNotes.*

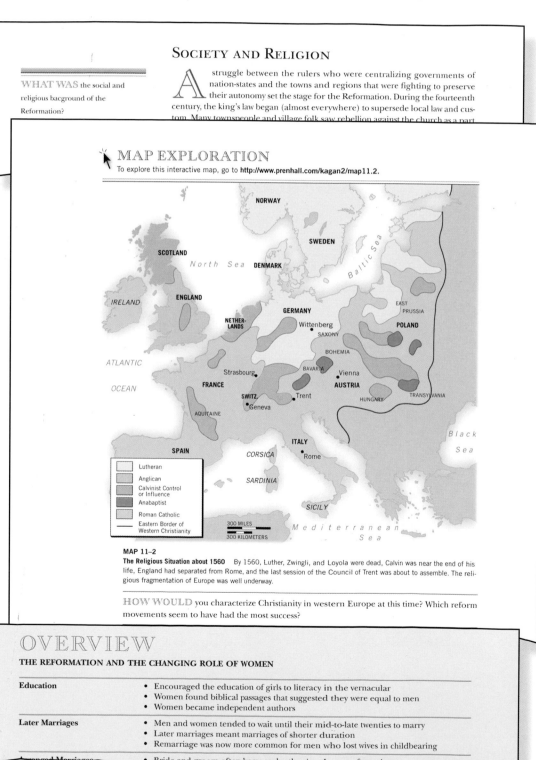

WHAT WAS the social and religious bacground of the Reformation?

SOCIETY AND RELIGION

A struggle between the rulers who were centralizing governments of nation-states and the towns and regions that were fighting to preserve their autonomy set the stage for the Reformation. During the fourteenth century, the king's law began (almost everywhere) to supersede local law and custom. Many townspeople and village folk saw rebellion against the church as a part

MAP EXPLORATION
To explore this interactive map, go to http://www.prenhall.com/kagan2/map11.2.

Lutheran
Anglican
Calvinist Control or Influence
Anabaptist
Roman Catholic
Eastern Border of Western Christianity

MAP 11–2

The Religious Situation about 1560 By 1560, Luther, Zwingli, and Loyola were dead, Calvin was near the end of his life, England had separated from Rome, and the last session of the Council of Trent was about to assemble. The religious fragmentation of Europe was well underway.

HOW WOULD you characterize Christianity in western Europe at this time? Which reform movements seem to have had the most success?

OVERVIEW
THE REFORMATION AND THE CHANGING ROLE OF WOMEN

Education	• Encouraged the education of girls to literacy in the vernacular • Women found biblical passages that suggested they were equal to men • Women became independent authors
Later Marriages	• Men and women tended to wait until their mid-to-late twenties to marry • Later marriages meant marriages of shorter duration • Remarriage was now more common for men who lost wives in childbearing
Arranged Marriages	• Bride and groom often knew each other in advance of marriage

To be able to be caught up into the world of thought—that is to be educated.
Edith Hamilton

◆ HISTORY'S VOICES ◆

A Sixteenth-Century Father Describes His One-Year-Old Son

On each of his son's birthdays, Christoph Scheurl, a resident of Nuremberg, wrote an account of the boy's development. The result is a unique glimpse into childhood and parenting in the sixteenth century.

GIVEN ITS historical era, is the father-son relationship Scheurl describes at all surprising?

This Sunday, April 19, my dear son Georg is one year old. So far, he is hearty, and apart from an episode of colic has remained healthy. Presently only his teeth, of which there are five and a half (the upper front two being great shovels) have caused him to run a temperature. [The milk] of his wet nurse has agreed with him throughout the year, and his physical growth and development have been good. He has a large, strong head, likes to laugh, and is a happy, high-spirited child. He can say "ka, ka" [meaning "da, da"], extend his little hand to Father, and point to birds in the bird house on the window. He also likes to go out into the open air. When he sees Father washing his hands, he must wash his too and splash about in the sink. He also takes after his father in liking horses. . . .

He is a fast eater and drinker. By no means will he sit or otherwise remain still in his chair, but he bends over double, as he struggles against it. Otherwise, he does not whine, nor is he willful. He freely allows the nurse to suckle him and points out the chair to her [when he is hungry]. He loves her very much, as she does him. And he goes happily to Father and loves him too. Moreover, he is Father's every joy, delight, and treasure.

Father will say to him: "Georg, be a bad one," and he then wrinkles up his nose and sneers. If Father coughs, he coughs too; and he can sit only beside Father. He can understand and duplicate an action [once it has been shown him]. In sum, Georg Scheurl, by his bearing, gestures, and role playing, presents himself at one year as a plucky, resolute child. He is learning to use his hands now and really likes to go through books, letters, and papers; he throws up his arms and shrieks with joy.

Reprinted from Steven Ozment, *Flesh & Spirit: Family Life in Early Modern Germany* (New York: Penguin, 1999), pp. 98–99.

one-half were dead by age twenty. Rare was the family at any social level that did not suffer the loss of children. Martin Luther fathered six children, two of whom

REVIEW QUESTIONS

1. What were the main problems of the church that contributed to the Protestant Reformation? On what did Luther and Zwingli agree? On what did they disagree? What about Luther and Calvin?

2. What was the Catholic Reformation? What were the major reforms instituted by the Council of Trent? Did the Protestant Reformation have a healthy effect on the Catholic Church?

3. Why did Henry VIII break with the Catholic Church? Did he establish a truly Protestant religion in England? What problems did his successors face as a result of his religious policies?

4. What impact did the Reformation have on women in the sixteenth and seventeenth centuries? What new factors and pressures affected relations between men and women, family size, and child care during this period?

KEY TERMS

Act of Supremacy (p. 00)   **Augsburg Confession** (p. 00)
Anabaptists (p. 00)   **indulgence** (p. 00)

For additional study resources for this chapter, go to:

With T.L.C. comes all the FREE resources you need to succeed in History.

Q: Wondering why *HistoryNotes* was bound free with your text?
A: BETTER TEST SCORES!

Having read and thought about the material in your text, you will come to class ready to take notes with *HistoryNotes*. This new tool replaces your traditional study guide, and offers you an incredible, portable system for taking and organizing notes, and for doing practice activities. Take *HistoryNotes* with you to class, and keep all of your notes in one place. *HistoryNotes* provides for every section of every chapter of this T.L.C. text:

■ Map exercises for you to complete during or after class.

■ Review/study activities for classroom collaboration or for individual review at home.

■ Practice tests to reinforce what you've learned in class.

■ Perforated pages with space on each page for note taking.

Map Exercise 6-C

Using the map on page 189, outline and label the approximate areas inhabited by the following Roman successors:

1. Frankish Kingdoms
2. Byzantine Empire
3. Kingdom of the Ostrogoths
4. Kingdom of the Vandals
5. Kingdom of the Sueves
6. Kingdom of the Thuringians
7. Kingdom of Burgundy

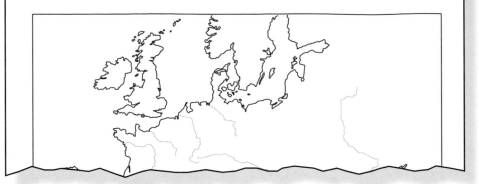

OneKey is your free, all-inclusive online resource for review and application of what you learn in this text and in class—and it is designed to simplify your test preparation so that your test performance will be better than ever. Think of **OneKey** as everything you need to succeed—all in one place—all designed to accompany this text, by chapter, including:

WEB-BASED ACTIVITIES

■ Automatically graded quizzes and essay questions that can be emailed to your professor

■ An online version of this text that automatically brings you to the page where you'll find the correct answers to any questions you may have answered incorrectly

■ Chat rooms, message boards, and dynamic Web links for further exploration

■ Interactive versions of the maps from your text

DRAMATIC MULTIMEDIA

■ Authentic Primary and Secondary Source Documents

■ Lively maps to illustrate the importance of the relationship between what happened and where it happened

■ Biographies of the people who had influence on the development of distinctively American character

■ Authentic live audio and video clips to animate key events throughout history.

RESEARCH MADE SIMPLE

OneKey offers you extensive help on finding and citing research with **Research Navigator**™ and its three exclusive databases of relevant, reliable source material including: EBSCO's *ContentSelect* Academic Journal Database; *The New York Times* Search by Subject Archive; and Best of the Web Link Library.

The Heritage of World Civilizations

TEACHING AND LEARNING CLASSROOM EDITION

BRIEF SECOND EDITION

VOLUME TWO: SINCE 1500

Albert M. Craig
HARVARD UNIVERSITY

William A. Graham
HARVARD UNIVERSITY

Donald Kagan
YALE UNIVERSITY

Steven Ozment
HARVARD UNIVERSITY

Frank M. Turner
YALE UNIVERSITY

PEARSON

Prentice
Hall

Upper Saddle River, NJ 07458

Library of Congress Cataloging-in-Publication Data

The heritage of world civilizations / Albert M. Craig ... [et al.].– Brief 2nd ed., Combined ed.
   p. cm.
   Includes bibliographical references and index.
   ISBN 0-13-150100-3
   1. Civilization–History.   I. Craig, Albert M.
   CB69.H45 2004
   909'—dc22

2003070692

VP, Editorial Director: Charlyce Jones Owen
Executive Editor: Charles Cavaliere
Associate Editor: Emsal Hasan
Media Editor: Deborah O'Connell
Editorial Assistant: Shannon Corliss
Editor-in-Chief, Development: Rochelle Diogenes
Development Editors: Roberta Meyer, Gerald Lombardi
**AVP, Director of Production
and Manufacturing:** Barbara Kittle
Managing Editor: Joanne Riker
Production Editor: Kathleen Sleys
Production Assistants: Marlene Gassler, Kristen Sleys
Prepress and Manufacturing Manager: Nick Sklitsis
Prepress and Manufacturing Buyer: Tricia Kenny
Director of Marketing: Beth Mejia
Executive Marketing Manager: Heather Shelstad

Creative Design Director: Leslie Osher
Interior and Cover Designer: Anne DeMarinis
Manager, Production, Formatting and Art: Guy Ruggiero
Cartographer: CartoGraphics
Electronic Artists: Maria Piper, Mirella Signoretto, Rosemary Ross, Bruce Killmer, Carey Davies
Director, Image Resource Center: Melinda Reo
Interior Image Specialist: Beth Boyd Brenzel
Cover Image Specialist: Karen Sanatar
Image Permission Coordinator: Michelina Viscusi
Photo Researcher: Elaine Soares
Color Scanning Services: Joe Conti, Greg Harrison, Cory Skidds, Rob Uibelhoer, Ron Walko
Compositor: Preparé, Inc.
Printer/Binder: Von Hoffman Corporation
Cover Printer: The Lehigh Press, Inc.

Cover Art: Japanese woman in Kimono. Michael Maslan Historic Photographs/CORBIS

Credits and acknowledgments borrowed from other sources and reproduced, with permission, in this textbook appear on appropriate page within text or on page C-1

Pearson Education Ltd., London
Pearson Education Australia Pty., Limited, Sydney
Pearson Education Singapore, Pte., Ltd.
Pearson Education North Asia Ltd., Hong Kong

Pearson Education Canada, Ltd., Toronto
Pearson Educación de Mexico, S.A. de C.V.
Pearson Education — Japan, Tokyo
Pearson Education Malaysia, Pte., Ltd.

10 9 8 7 6 5 4 3 2

ISBN 0-13-150098-8

4

VISUALIZING THE PAST

**Goddesses and the Female Form
in Ancient Art**   90

5

VISUALIZING THE PAST
The Divine in the Middle Ages   296

15

Europe to the Early 1500s: Revival, Decline, and Renaissance   296

PART 4
The World in Transition   328

16

The Age of Reformation and Religious Wars   330

17

18

19

20

European State-Building and Worldwide Conflict 434

21

European Society Under the Old Regime 456

22

The Last Great Islamic Empires (1500–1800)
476

VISUALIZING THE PAST
The "Other" in the Early Modern Period 490

PART 5
ENLIGHTENMENT AND REVOLUTION IN THE WEST 492

23

The Age of European Enlightenment 494

24

Revolutions in the Transatlantic World 510

25

*Political Consolidation in Nineteenth-Century
Europe and North America 1815–1880* 534

PART 6
INTO THE MODERN WORLD 564

26

*Northern Transatlantic Economy
and Society 1815–1914* 566

27

Latin America: From Independence to the 1940s   598

28

India, the Islamic Heartlands, and Africa: The Encounter with the Modern West (1800–1945)   616

29

Modern East Asia   636

VISUALIZING THE PAST

PART 7
GLOBAL CONFLICT AND CHANGE   664

30

Imperialism and World War I 666

31

*Depression, European Dictators,
and the American New Deal* 688

32

World War II 710

33

The West Since World War II 730

34

*East Asia in the Late Twentieth
Century* 754

35

The Emerging Nations of Africa, Asia, and Latin America Since 1945 768

VISUALIZING THE PAST
Imperialism and Race in Modern Art 790

HISTORY'S VOICES

MAPS

PREFACE

The events of September 11, 2001, as nothing in the immediate past, have brought upon the world a new awareness of human history in a global context. Prior to that day North American readers generally understood world history and globalism as academic concepts; they now understand them as realities shaping their daily lives and experience. The new, immediate pressures of the present draw us to seek a more certain and extensive understanding of the past.

The idea of globalization is now a pressing reality on the life of nations, affecting the domestic security of their citizens, their standard of living, and the environment. Whether, as Samuel Huntington, the distinguished Harvard political scientist, contends, we are witnessing a clash of civilizations, we have certainly entered a new era in which no active citizen or educated person can escape the necessity of understanding the past in global terms. Both the historical experience and the moral and political values of the different world civilizations now demand our attention and our understanding. It is our hope that in these new, challenging times The Heritage of World Civilizations will provide one path to such knowledge.

THE ROOTS OF GLOBALIZATION

Globalization—that is, the increasing interaction and interdependency of the various regions of the world—has resulted from two major historical developments: the closing of the European era of world history and the rise of technology.

From approximately 1500 to the middle of the twentieth century, Europeans gradually came to dominate the world through colonization (most particularly in North and South America), state-building, economic productivity, and military power. That era of European dominance ended during the third quarter of the twentieth century after Europe had brought unprecedented destruction on itself during World War II and as the nations of Asia, the Near East, and Africa achieved new positions on the world scene. Their new political independence, their control over strategic natural resources, and the expansion of their economies (especially those of the nations of the Pacific rim of Asia), and in some cases their access to nuclear weapons have changed the shape of world affairs.

Further changing the world political and social situation has been a growing discrepancy in the economic development of different regions that is often portrayed as a problem between the northern and southern hemispheres. Beyond the emergence of this economic disparity has been the remarkable advance of political Islam during the past forty years. In the midst of all these developments, as a result of the political collapse of the former Soviet Union, the United States has emerged as the single major world power.

The second historical development that continues to fuel the pace of globalization is the advance of technology, associated most importantly with transportation, military weapons, and electron communication. The advances in transportation over the past two centuries including ships, railways, and airplanes have made more parts of the world and its resources accessible to more people in ever shorter spans of time. Military weapons of increasingly destructive power over the past century and a half enabled Europeans and then later the United States to dominate other regions of the globe. Now, the spread of these weapons means that any nation with sophisticated military technology can threaten other nations, no matter how far away. Furthermore, technologies that originated in the West from the early twentieth century to the present have been turned against the West. More recently, the electronic revolution associated with computer technology has sparked unprecedented speed and complexity in global communications. It is astonishing to recall that personal computers have been generally available for less than twenty-five years and the rapid personal communication associated with them has existed for less than fifteen years.

Why not, then, focus only on new factors in the modern world, such as the impact of technology and the end of the European era? To do so would ignore the very deep roots that these developments have in the past. More important, the events of recent months and the response to them demonstrate, as the authors of this book have long contended, that the major religious traditions continue to shape and drive the modern world as well as the world of the past. The religious traditions link today's civilizations to their most ancient roots. We believe this emphasis on the great religious traditions recognizes not only a factor that has shaped the past, but one that is profoundly and dynamically alive in our world today.

STRENGTHS OF THE TEXT

Balanced and Flexible Presentation   In this edition, as in past editions, we have sought to present world history fairly, accurately, and in a way that does justice to its great variety. History has many facets, no one of which can account for the others. Any attempt to tell the story of civilization from a single perspective, no matter how timely, is bound to neglect or suppress some important part of that story.

Historians have recently brought a vast array of new tools and concepts to bear on the study of history. Our coverage introduces students to various aspects of social and intellectual history as well as to the more traditional political, diplomatic, and military coverage. We firmly believe that only through an appreciation of all pathways to understanding of the past can the real heritage of world civilizations be claimed.

The Heritage of World Civilizations, Teaching and Learning Classroom Edition, is designed to accommodate a variety of approaches to a course in world civilization, allowing teachers to stress what is most important to them. Some teachers will ask students to read all the chapters. Others will select among them to reinforce assigned readings and lectures.

Clarity and Accessibility Good narrative history requires clear, vigorous prose. Our goal has been to make our presentation fully accessible to students without compromising on vocabulary or conceptual level. We hope this effort will benefit both teachers and students.

Recent Scholarship As in previous editions, changes in this edition reflect our determination to incorporate the most recent developments in historical scholarship and the expanding concerns of professional historians.

The Teaching and Learning Classroom Edition includes greater discussion of the origins of humankind in Chapter 1, incorporation of new scholarship on Islam and East Asia, updated coverage of developments in Africa and Latin America, and analysis of globalization, terrorism, women's rights, and recent events in the Middle East.

Pedagogical Features This edition retains the pedagogical features of the last edition, helping to make the text accessible to students, reinforcing key concepts, and providing a global, comparative perspective.

- **Part Timelines** show the major events in five regions—Europe, the Near East and India, East Asia, Africa, and the Americas—side by side. Appropriate photographs enrich each timeline.

- **Chapter-Opening Questions**, organized by the main subtopics of each chapter, encourage careful consideration of important themes and developments. Each question is repeated at the appropriate place in the margin of the text.

- **Chronologies** within each chapter help students organize a time sequence for key events.

- **History's Voices**, including selections from sacred books, poems, philosophy, political manifestos, letters, and travel accounts, introduce students to the raw material of history, providing an intimate contact with the people of the past and their concerns. Questions accompanying the source documents direct students toward important, thought-

provoking issues and help them relate the documents to the material in the text. They can be used to stimulate class discussion or as topics for essays and study groups.

- **Map Explorations** and **Critical-Thinking Questions** prompt students to engage with maps, often in an interactive fashion. Each Map Exploration is found on the Companion Website for the text.

- **Visualizing the Past** essays, found at the end of selected chapters, analyze important aspects of world history through photographs, fine art, sculpture, and woodcuts. Focus questions and a running narrative guide students though a careful examination of the historical implication of each topic in question.

- **Chapter review** questions help students focus on and interpret the broad themes of a chapter. These questions can be used for class discussion and essay topics.

- **Overview Tables** in each chapter summarize complex issues.

- **Quick Reviews**, found at key places in the margins of each chapter, encourage students to review important concepts.

- **Comparative Perspectives** essays, located on the Companion Website for The Heritage of World Civilizations, examine technology and civilizations from a cross-cultural perspective.

Content and Organization The many changes in content and organization in this edition of The Heritage of World Civilizations reflect our ongoing effort to present a truly global survey of world civilization that at the same time gives a rich picture of the history of individual regions.

To better accomplish this, several significant changes to the book's organization have been carried out in this revision. Coverage of events during the European High Middle Ages and the Renaissance, which was formerly treated in two chapters, has been reconceived into a single chapter (Chapter 15) entitled, "Europe to the Early 1500s: Revival, Decline, and Renaissance." Coverage of Europe and North America in the nineteenth century, which formerly was addressed in four chapters, has been streamlined so that it is discussed in two new chapters (Chapters 25 and 26) that integrate discussion of the ideas, politics, society, and culture of the period. This consolidation of material on Europe provides for an even more balanced treatment of world history, a smoother narrative line, and a reduction of the total number of chapters from thirty-eight to thirty-five.

A Note on Dates and Transliterations We have used B.C.E. (before the common era) and C.E. (common era) instead of B.C. (before Christ) and A.D. (anno domini, the year of our Lord) to designate dates.

Until recently, most scholarship on China used the Wade-Giles system of romanization for Chinese names and terms. In order that students may move easily from the present text to the existing body of advanced scholarship on Chinese history, we have used the Wade-Giles system throughout. China today, however, uses another system known as pinyin. Virtually all Western newspapers have adopted it. Therefore, for Chinese history since 1949 we have included the pinyin spellings in parentheses after the Wade-Giles.

Also, we have followed the currently accepted English transliterations of Arabic words. For example, today Koran is being replaced by the more accurate Qur'an; similarly Muhammad is preferable to Mohammed and Muslim to Moslem. We have not tried to distinguish the letters 'ayn and hamza; both are rendered by a simple apostrophe (') as in shi'ite.

With regard to Sanskritic transliteration, we have not distinguished linguals and dentals, and both palatal and lingual s are rendered sh, as in Shiva and Upanishad.

ANCILLARY INSTRUCTIONAL MATERIALS

The Heritage of World Civilizations, TLC Edition, comes with an extensive package of ancillary materials.

PRINT SUPPLEMENTS

Instructor's Resource Binder This innovative, all-in-one resource organizes the instructor's manual, the Test-Item File, and the transparency pack by each chapter of *The Heritage of World Civilizations* to facilitate class preparation. The Instructor's Resource Binder also includes and **Instructor's Resource CD-ROM**, which contains all of the maps, graphs, and illustrations from the text in easily-downloadable electronic files.

Prentice Hall Test Generator Suitable for both Windows and Macintosh environments, this commerical-quality, computerized test-management program allows instructors to select items from the test-item file and design their own exams.

History Notes (Volumes I and II) Replacing a traditional study guide, History Notes provides students with practice tests, map exercises, and How? When? Where? Questions for each chapter of *The Heritage of World Civilizations*. Each new copy of the TLC edition comes bundled with History Notes.

Map Workbook Map Workbook helps students develop geographical knowledge. This workbook is free when bundled with the text.

Prentice Hall and Penguin Bundle Program Prentice Hall is pleased to provide adopters of *The Heritage of World Civilizations* with an opportunity to receive significant discounts when copies of the text are bundled with Penguin titles in world history. Contact your local Prentice Hall representative for details.

MULTIMEDIA SUPPLEMENTS

Companion Website Available at **http://www.prenhall.com/ craig** *The Heritage of World Civilizations Companion Website* offers students multiple choice, true-false, essay, identification, map labeling, and document questions based on material from the text, organized by the primary subtopics in each chapter. Additionally, the *Companion Website* provides numerous interactive maps tied to the text, source documents, and other interactive modules related to the content in each chapter. The Faculty Module contains materials for instructors, including the entire instructor's manual in PDF file, and downloadable presentations with maps, charts, graphs, summary tables, and illustrations.

World History Documents CD-ROM Bound in every new copy of *The Heritage of World Civilizations*, and organized according to the main periods in World history, the World History Documents CD-ROM contains over 200 primary sources in an easily-navigable PDF file. Each document is accompanied by essay questions that allow students to read important sources in world history via the CD-ROM and respond online via a dedicated website.

Evaluating Online Sources with Research Navigator, 2003 Edition This brief guide focuses on developing critical thinking skills necessary to evaluate and use online sources. It provides a brief introduction to navigating the Internet with comprehensive references to History web sites. It also provides an access code and instruction on using Research Navigator, a powerful research tool that provides access to three exclusive databases of reliable source material: ContentSelect Academic Journal Database, *The New York Times* Search by Subject Archive, and Link Library.

OneKey OneKey lets you in to the best teaching and learning resources all in one place. OneKey for *The Heritage of World Civilizations* is all your students need for out-of-class work conveniently organized by chapter to reinforce and apply what they've learned in class and from the text. Among the resources available for each chapter are: a complete media-rich, interactive e-book version of *The Heritage of World Civilizations*, quizzes organized by the main topics of each chapter, primary source documents, map labeling and interactive map quizzes. OneKey is all you need to plan and administer your course. All your instructor resources are in one place to maximize your effectiveness and minimize your time and effort. Instructor material includes: images and maps from *The Heritage of World Civilizations*, hundreds of documents, video and audio clips, interactive learning activities, and PowerPoint presentations.

ACKNOWLEDGMENTS

We are grateful to the many scholars and teachers whose thoughtful and often detailed comments helped shape this as well as previous editions of The Heritage of World Civilizations:

Wayne Ackerson, *Salisbury State University*
Jack Martin Balcer, *Ohio State University*
Charmarie J. Blaisdell, *Northeastern University*
Gayle Brunelle, *California State University, Fullerton*
Deborah Buffton, *University of Wisconsin at La Crosse*
Loretta Burns, *Mankato State University*
Chun-shu Chang, *University of Michigan, Ann Arbor*
Mark Chavalas, *University of Wisconsin at La Crosse*
Anthony Cheeseboro, *Southern Illinois University at Edwardsville*
William J. Courteney, *University of Wisconsin*
Samuel Willard Crompton, *Holyoke Community College*
James B. Crowley, *Yale University*
Bruce Cummings, *The University of Chicago*
Stephen F. Dale, *Ohio State University, Columbus*
Clarence B. Davis, *Marian College*
Raymond Van Dam, *University of Michigan, Ann Arbor*
Bill Donovan, *Loyola University of Maryland*
Wayne Farris, *University of Tennessee*
Suzanne Gay, *Oberlin College*
Robert Gerlich, *Loyola University*
Samuel Robert Goldberger, *Capital Community-Technical College*
Andrew Gow, *University of Alberta*
Katheryn L. Green, *University of Wisconsin, Madison*
David Griffiths, *University of North Carolina, Chapel Hill*
Louis Haas, *Duquesne University*
Joseph T. Hapak, *Moraine Valley Community College*

Hue-Tam Ho Tai, *Harvard University*
David Kieft, *University of Minnesota*
Frederick Krome, *Northern Kentucky University*
Lisa M. Lane, *Mira Costa College*
Richard Law, *Washington State University*
David Lelyveld, *Columbia University*
Jan Lewis, *Rutgers University, Newark*
James C. Livingston, *College of William and Mary*
Richard L. Moore Jr., *St. Augustine's College*
Beth Nachison, *Southern Connecticut State University*
Robin S. Oggins, *Binghamton University*
Louis A. Perez Jr., *University of South Florida*
Cora Ann Presley, *Tulane University*
Norman Raiford, *Greenville Technical College*
Norman Ravitch, *University of California, Riverside*
Philip F. Riley, *James Madison University*
Thomas Robisheaux, *Duke University*
David Ruffley, *United States Air Force Academy*
Dankwart A. Rustow, *The City University of New York*
James J. Sack, *University of Illinois at Chicago*
William Schell, *Murray State University*
Marvin Slind, *Washington State University*
Daniel Scavone, *University of Southern Indiana*
Charles C. Stewart, *University of Illinois*
Carson Tavenner, *United States Air Force Academy*
Truong-buu Lam, *University of Hawaii*
Harry L. Watson, *Loyola College of Maryland*
William B. Whisenhunt, *College of DuPage*
Paul Varley, *Columbia University*

Finally, we would like to thank the dedicated people who helped produce this revision: our acquisitions editor, Charles Cavaliere; our development editor, Gerald Lombardi; our photo researcher, Elaine Soares; Anne DeMarinis who created the exiting new design for this edition; Kathy Sleys, our production editor; Tricia Kenny, our manufacturing buyer.

A.M.C.
W.A.G.
D.K.
S.O.
F.M.T.

ABOUT THE AUTHORS

ALBERT M. CRAIG is the Harvard-Yenching Research Professor of History at Harvard University, where he has taught since 1959. A graduate of Northwestern University, he took his Ph.D. at Harvard University. He has studied at Strasbourg University and at Kyoto, Keio, and Tokyo universities in Japan. He is the author of *Choshu in the Meiji Restoration* (1961), *The Heritage of Chinese Civilization* (2001), and, with others, of *East Asia, Tradition and Transformation* (1989). He is the editor of *Japan, A Comparative View* (1973) and co-editor of *Personality in Japanese History* (1970). At present he is engaged in research on the thought of Fukuzawa Yukichi. For eleven years (1976–1987) he was the director of the Harvard-Yenching Institute. He has also been a visiting professor at Kyoto and Tokyo Universities. He has received Guggenheim, Fulbright, and Japan Foundation Fellowships. In 1988 he was awarded the Order of the Rising Sun by the Japanese government.

WILLIAM A. GRAHAM is Albertson Professor of Middle Eastern Studies and Professor of the History of Religion at Harvard University, and Master of Currier House at Harvard University. From 1990–1996 he directed Harvard's Center for Middle Eastern Studies. He has taught for twenty-six years at Harvard, where he received the A.M. and Ph.D. degrees. He also studied in Göttingen, Tübingen, and Lebanon. He is the author of *Divine World and Prophetic World in Early Islam* (1977), awarded the American Council of Learned Societies History of Religions book prize in 1978, and of *Beyond the Written Word: Oral Aspects of Scripture in the History of Religion* (1987). He has published a variety of articles in both Islamic studies and the general history of religion and is one of the editors of the *Encyclopedia of the Qur'an*. He serves currently on the editorial board of several journals and has held John Simon Guggenheim and Alexander von Humboldt research fellowships. *Three Faiths, One God*, co-authored with Jacob Neusner and Bruce Chilton, published in January 2003.

DONALD KAGAN is Sterling Professor of History and Classics at Yale University, where he has taught since 1969. He received the A.B. degree in history from Brooklyn College, the M.A. in classics from Brown University, and the Ph.D. in history from Ohio State University. During 1958–1959 he studied at the American School of Classical Studies as a Fulbright Scholar. He has received three awards for undergraduate teaching at Cornell and Yale. He is the author of a history of Greek political thought, *The Great Dialogue* (1965); a four-volume history of the Peloponnesian war, *The Origins of the Peloponnesian War* (1969); *The Archidamian War* (1974); *The Peace of Nicias and the Sicilian Expe-* dition (1981); *The Fall of the Athenian Empire* (1987); and a biography of Pericles, *Pericles of Athens and the Birth of Democracy* (1991); *On the Origins of War* (1995), and *The Peloponnesian War* (2003). He is coauthor, with Frederick W. Kagan of *While America Sleeps* (2000). With Brian Tierney and L. Pearce Williams, he is the editor of *Great Issues in Western Civilization,* a collection of readings. He was awarded the National Humanities Medal for 2002.

STEVEN OZMENT is McLean Professor of Ancient and Modern History at Harvard University. He has taught Western Civilization at Yale, Stanford, and Harvard. He is the author of nine books. *The Age of Reform,* 1250–1550 (1980) won the Schaff Prize and was nominated for the 1981 National Book Award. Five of his books have been selections of the History Book Club: *Magdalena and Balthasar: An Intimate Portrait of Life in Sixteenth Century Europe* (1986), *Three Behaim Boys: Growing Up in Early Modern Germany* (1990), *Protestants: The Birth of A Revolution* (1992), *The Burgermeister's Daughter: Scandal in a Sixteenth Century German Town* (1996), and *Flesh and Spirit: Private Life in Early Modern Germany* (1999). His most recent book is *Ancestors: The Loving Family of Old Europe* (2001). A history of Germany, *A Mighty Fortress: A New History of the German People,* published in January 2004.

FRANK M. TURNER is John Hay Whitney Professor of History at Yale University, where he served as University Provost from 1988 to 1992. He received his B.A. degree at the College of William and Mary and his Ph.D. from Yale. He has received the Yale College Award for Distinguished Undergraduate Teaching. He has directed a National Endowment for the Humanities Summer Institute. His scholarly research has received the support of fellowships from the National Endowment for the Humanities and the Guggenheim Foundation and the Woodrow Wilson Center. He is the author of *Between Science and Religion: The Reaction to Scientific Naturalism in Late Victorian England* (1974), *The Greek Heritage in Victorian Britain* (1981), which received the British Council Prize of the Conference on British Studies and the Yale Press Governors Award, *Contesting Cultural Authority: Essays in Victorian Intellectual Life* (1993), and *John Henry Newman: The Challenge to Evangelical Religion* (2002). He has also contributed numerous articles to journals and has served on the editorial advisory boards of *The Journal of Modern History, Isis,* and *Victorian Studies.* He edited *The Idea of a University,* by John Henry Newman (1996). Since 1996 he has served as a Trustee of Connecticut College. In 2003, Professor Turner was appointed Director of the Beinecke Rare Book and Manuscript Library at Yale University.

STUDENT TOOL KIT

When writing history, historians use maps, tables, graphs, and visuals to help their readers understand the past. What follows is an explanation of how to use the historian's tools that are contained in this book.

TEXT

Whether it is a biography of Gandhi, an article on the Ottoman Empire, or a survey of world history such as this one, the text is the historian's basic tool for discussing the past. Historians write about the past using narration and analysis. Narration is the story line of history. It describes what happened in the past, who did it, and where and when it occurred. Narration is also used to describe how people in the past lived, how they passed their daily lives and even, when the historical evidence makes it possible for us to know, what they thought, felt, feared, or desired. Using analysis, historians explain why they think events in the past happened the way they did and offer an explanation for the story of history. In this book, narration and analysis are interwoven in each chapter.

STUDY AIDS

A number of features in this book are designed to aid in the study of history. Each chapter begins with **Questions**, organized by the main subtopics of each chapter, that encourage careful consideration of important themes and developments. Each question is repeated at the appropriate place in the margin of the text.

THE POLITICS OF IMPERIAL JAPAN (1890–1945)

WHY DID Japan join the imperialist scramble for colonies?

Parliaments began in the West and have worked better there than in the rest of the world. Even so cautious a constitution as that of Meiji had no precedent outside the West at the time. How are we then to view the Japanese political experience after 1890?

One view is that because Japanese society was not ready for constitutional government, the militarism of the thirties was inevitable. From the perspective of an ideal democracy, Japanese society had many weaknesses: a small middle class, weak trade unions, an independent military under the emperor, a strong emperor-centered nationalism, and so on. But these weaknesses did not prevent the Diet from growing in importance, nor did they block the transfer of power from the bureaucratic

MAPS

Maps are important historical tools. They show how geography has affected history and concisely summarize complex relationships and events. Knowing how to read and interpret a map is important to understanding history. Map 11–1 from Chapter 11 shows Muslim conquests from 622–750 C.E. It has three features to help you read it: a **caption**, a **legend**, and a **scale**. The caption explains the rapid rise of Islam from its beginnings in Arabia to its domination of much of the Mediterranean and Persia.

The legend is situated on the bottom left corner of the map. The legend provides information for what each colored area of the map represents. The purple region is the Byzantine Empire. The dark orange represents Muhammad's conquests from 622–632. The areas in light orange were conquered in 632–661. The territories in brown were conquered between 661–750.

The scale, located on the top of the map, informs us that three-quarters of an inch equals 1000 miles (or about 1600 kilometers). With this information, estimates of distance between points on the map are easily made.

The map also shows the topography of the region—its mountains, rivers, and seas. This helps us understand the interplay between geography and history. For example, note how the spread of Islam stops at the Caucasus Mountains. Do you think the topography of this region played a role in limiting the Muslim advance?

Finally, a **critical-thinking question** asks for careful consideration of the spatial connections between geography and history.

MAP EXPLORATION

Interactive map: To explore this map further, go to **http://www.prenhall.com/craig2/map11.1**

Byzantine Empire
Conquests of Muhammad, 622-632
Conquests, 632-661
Conquests, 661-750

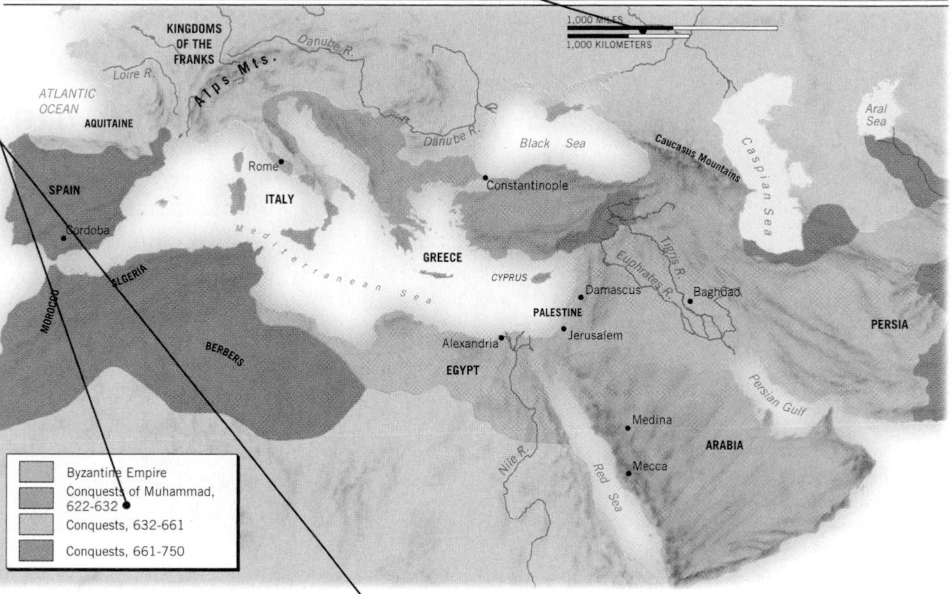

MAP 11–1

Muslim conquests and domination of the Mediterranean to about 750 C.E.   The rapid spread of Islam (both religion and political-military power) is shown here. Within 125 years of Muhammad's rise Muslims came to dominate Spain and all areas south and east of the Mediterranean.

WHY DID so many subject peoples welcome Islamic rule?

MAP EXPLORATIONS

Many of the maps in each chapter are provided in a useful interactive version on the text's Companion Website. These maps are easily identified by a bar along the top (see example above) that reads "**Map Exploration.**" An *interactive version of Muslim Conquests and Domination of the Mediterranean to 750 C.E. can be found at* **www.prenhall.com/craig2/map11.1**. The interactive version of this particular map provides an opportunity to move a timeline from left to right to see the spread of muslim conquests vividly.

Brazilian coffee being loaded onto a British ship. Most Latin American countries developed an export economy based on the exchange of agricultural products, raw materials, and semifinished goods for finished goods and services from abroad. From the 1890s onward, the coffee industry dominated both the political and economic life of Brazil.

Corbis-Bettmann

ANALYZING VISUALS

Visual images embedded throughout the text can provide as much insight into world history as the written word. Within photographs and pieces of fine art lies emotional and historical meaning. Captions also provide valuable information, such as in the example below. When studying the image, consider questions such as: "Who are these people?"; "What are they doing?"; and "What can we learn from the way the people are dressed?" Such analysis allows for a fuller understanding of the way people lived in the past.

VISUALIZING THE PAST

These essays, found at the end of selected chapters, analyze important aspects of world history through photographs, fine art, sculpture, and woodcuts. Focus questions and a running narrative guide students though a careful examination of the historical implications of each topic in question.

The Divine in the Middle Ages

HOW DID artists of different religions depict the divine? How did their differing conceptions of the divine, and rules within religions about how and whether, the divine should be depicted, shape religious art?

The Middle Ages (500 C.E.–1300 C.E.) witnessed the creation of a new world religion, Islam, and the expansion and consolidation of others, including Christianity, Buddhism, and Hinduism. Each of these religions fostered forms of religious art suited to its conception of the divine. Religious and secular leaders alike commissioned the art as objects or focuses of worship, teaching tools, and decorations. Secular leaders enhanced their status by associating themselves with the divine through patronage of religious art.

"Standing Parvati," India, Chola Period (880–1279), circa first quarter of the tenth century. This statue of the Hindu goddess Parvati hails from the Chola-ruled region of South India. Chola art, known for its exceptional grace and beauty, influenced Hindu art throughout south Asia. Hinduism is the only major polytheistic world religion of the medieval period and it also was the only one to retain female as well as male gods.
Indian, Tamil Nadu, Standing Parvati, Chola period (ca. 860–1279), ca. first quarter of 10th century, Copper alloy. H. 27 5/8 in. (69.5 cm). "The Metropolitan Museum of Art, Bequest of Cora Timken Burnett, 1956. (57.5.3). Photograph by Bruce White. © 1994 The Metropolitan Museum of Art"

This is a page from a vellum medieval Koran with a rosette in the margin, by the medieval Islamic School. Islam follows the Jewish tradition in prohibiting images of God (Allah). Because Islam also prohibits depicting the human form (although some Islamic artists did produce images of people and animals), as this picture shows, Islamic art tended to be highly abstract, and Islamic writing itself became an art form of great beauty and refinement.
Page from the Koran with a rosette in the margin by Islamic School Musee Conde, Chantilly, France, France/Bridgeman Art Library

294

Overviews

The **Overview** tables in this text are a special feature designed to highlight and summarize important topics within a chapter. The Overview table shown here, for example, summarizes the periods of Mesoamerican and Andean civilizations.

OVERVIEW

THE PERIODS OF MESOAMERICAN AND ANDEAN CIVILIZATIONS

Scholars divide the history of the Mesoamerican and Andean peoples into several distict periods.

MESOAMERICA

Period	Civilization
Archaic, 8000–2000 B.C.E.	agricultural villages; maize cultivation
Formative, 2000 B.C.E.–150 C.E.	Olmecs, Monte Alban; urban centers, writing, a calendar
Classic, 150–900 C.E.	Maya, Teotihuacán; sophisticated mathematics, astronomy, and calendar

Quick Reviews

Quick reviews, placed at key locations in the margins of each chapter, provide pinpoint summaries of important concepts.

QUICK REVIEW

Key Factors in "Scramble for Africa"

- Popular and commercial interest in Africa spurred by exploration
- Intra-European competition for power and prestige
- Technological and material superiority of Europe

Rise of Macedon

359–336 B.C.E.	Reign of Philip II
338 B.C.E.	Battle of Chaeronea; Philip conquers Greece; founding of League of Corinth
336–323 B.C.E.	Reign of Alexander III, the Great
334 B.C.E.	Alexander invades Asia
333 B.C.E.	Battle of Issus
331 B.C.E.	Battle of Gaugamela
330 B.C.E.	Fall of Persepolis
327 B.C.E.	Alexander reaches Indus Valley
323 B.C.E.	Death of Alexander

Chronologies

Each chapter includes **Chronologies** that list, in chronological order, key events discussed in the chapter. The chronology, shown here from Chapter 3, lists the dates of key events in the life of Alexander the Great. Chronologies provide a review of important events and their relationship to one another.

PRIMARY SOURCE DOCUMENTS

Historians find most of their information in written records, original documents that have survived from the past. These include government publications, letters, diaries, newspapers—whatever people wrote or printed, including many private documents never intended for publication. Each chapter in the book contains a feature called **History's Voices**—a selection from a primary source document. The example shown here is a description by Marco Polo of the city of Hangchow in China. Each **History's Voices** begins with a brief introduction followed by questions on what the document reveals.

•HISTORY'S VOICES•

MARCO POLO DESCRIBES THE CITY OF HANGCHOW

arco Polo was a Venetian. In 1300 Venice had a population of more than 100,000 and was one of the wealthiest Mediterranean city-states. But Polo was nonetheless unprepared for what he saw in China. Commenting on Hangchow, China's capital during the Southern Sung, he first noted its size (ten or twelve times larger than Venice), then its many canals and bridges, its streets "paved with stones and bricks," and its location between "a lake of fresh and very clear water" and "a river of great magnitude." He spoke of "the prodigious concourse of people" frequenting its ten great marketplaces and of its "capacious warehouses built of stone for the accommodation of merchants who arrive from India and other parts." He then described the life of its people.

EUROPEANS WHO read Marco Polo's account of

adapted to every description of person, insomuch that strangers who have once become so enchanted by their meretricious arts, that they can never divest themselves of the impression. Thus intoxicated with sensual pleasures, when they return to their homes they report that they have been in Kin-sai [Hangchow], or the celestial city, and pant for the time when they may be enabled to revisit paradise.

The inhabitants of the city are idolaters, and they use paper money as currency. The men as well as the women have fair complexions, and are handsome. The greater part of them are always clothed in silk, in consequence of the vast quantity of that material produced in the territory of Kin-sai, exclusively of what the merchants import from other provinces. Amongst the handicraft trades exercised in the place, there are twelve considered to be superior to the rest,

WORLD HISTORY DOCUMENT CD-ROM

2.4
Confucius: *Analects*

Bound into every new copy of this textbook is a free world. History Document CD-ROM. This is a powerful resource for research and additional reading that contains more than 200 primary source documents central to world History. Each document provides essay questions that are linked directly to a website where short-essay answers can be submitted online or printed out. Particularly relevant or interesting documents are called out at appropriate places in the margin of each chapter (see example). A complete list of documents on the CD-ROM is found at the end of the text.

SUMMARIES, REVIEW QUESTIONS, AND ADDITIONAL STUDY RESOURCES

At the end of each chapter **summaries** and **review questions** reconsider the main topics. The URL for the Companion Website ™ is also found at the end of each chapter; this is an excellent resource for additional study aids.

Feudal Society The Middle Ages were characterized by a chronic absence of central government and the constant threat of famine, disease, and invasion. Lords were those who could guarantee protection under these conditions. Feudal society was one in which a local lord is dominant and offers security in return for allegiance from his dependents or vassals. It was a system of mutual rights and responsibilities. Medieval vassals pledged fealty to their lord in return for a fief, or grant of land. They promised to support their "liege lord" with troops or money when he called upon them for aid.

The feudal economy was organized and controlled through agrarian villages known as manors, worked by free peasants, who had their own modest property and economic and legal rights, or by serfs, impoverished peasants who were bound to the land and obliged to provide their lords with an array of services, dues in kind, and products.

REVIEW QUESTIONS

1. How did the church become a political power in the western Roman Empire?
2. How did the Franks become the dominant force in western Europe? Why did Charlemagne's empire break apart?
3. How and why was the history of the eastern or Byzantine half of the Roman Empire so different from the western half?
4. What were the defining features of feudalism? Is a feudal society a "backward" society?

KEY TERMS

apostolic primacy (p. 246)
demesne (p. 251)
fealty (p. 255)
feudal society (p. 253)

fief (p. 247)
Magyars (p. 253)
manor (p. 250)
Papal States (p. 248)

plenitude of power (p. 246)
serfs (p. 252)
three-field system (p. 252)
vassal (p. 254)

 For additional study resources for this chapter, go to:
www.prenhall.com/craig/chapter12

GLOSSARY/KEY TERMS

Significant historical terms are called out in heavy type throughout the text, defined in the margin, and listed at the end of each chapter with appropriate page numbers. These are listed alphabetically and defined in a glossary at the end of the book.

The University of Bologna in central Italy was distinguished as the center for the revival of Roman law. This carving on the tomb of a Bolognese professor of law shows students attending one of his lectures. Museo Civico, Bologna, Italy

15

EUROPE TO THE EARLY 1500s
Revival, Decline, and Renaissance

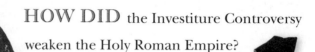

HOW DID the Investiture Controversy weaken the Holy Roman Empire?

WHAT WERE the three basic social groups in medieval society?

HOW DID England and France develop strong royal governments by the thirteenth century?

WHAT WERE the causes of the political and social breakdown that occurred during the fourteenth century?

WHY WAS the Renaissance a transition from the medieval to the modern world?

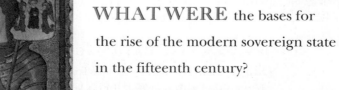

WHAT WERE the bases for the rise of the modern sovereign state in the fifteenth century?

IMAGE KEY

Image Key for pages 296–297
is on page 326.

The High Middle Ages (from the eleventh through the thirteenth centuries) were a period of both political expansion and consolidation and intellectual flowering and synthesis. The Latin, or Western, church established itself as a spiritual authority independent of secular monarchies, which themselves became more powerful and self-aggrandizing. The parliaments and popular assemblies that accompanied the rise of these monarchies laid the foundations of modern representative institutions.

The High Middle Ages saw a revolution in agriculture that increased food supplies and populations. Trade and commerce revived, towns expanded, protomodern forms of banking and credit developed, and a "new rich" merchant class became ascendant in Europe's cities. Universities arose and contact with the Arab world led to the beginning of the recovery of the writings of the ancient Greek philosophers, which would in turn stimulate the great expansion of Western education and culture during the late Middle Ages and the Renaissance.

The late Middle Ages and the Renaissance (the fourteenth, fifteenth, and early sixteenth centuries) were a time of unprecedented calamity and of bold new beginnings in Europe. France and England grappled with each other in a bitter conflict known as the Hundred Years' War (1337–1453). Bubonic plague, known to contemporaries as the Black Death, killed as much as one third of the population in many regions between 1348 and 1350. A schism emerged within the church (1378–1417). In 1453 the Turks captured Constantinople and threatened the West. Western civilization seemed to be collapsing.

But the late Middle Ages also witnessed a rebirth that would continue into the seventeenth century. Scholars criticized medieval assumptions about the nature of God, humankind, and society. Italian and northern humanists made a full recovery of classical knowledge and languages and began cultural changes that would spread throughout Europe. The "divine art" of printing was invented. The vernacular, the local language, began to take its place alongside Latin. In the independent nation-states of Europe, patriotism and incipient nationalism became major forces.

REVIVAL OF EMPIRE, CHURCH, AND TOWNS

OTTO I AND THE REVIVAL OF THE EMPIRE

HOW DID the Investiture
Controversy weaken the Holy
Roman Empire?

The fortunes of both the old empire and the papacy began to revive when the Saxon Henry I ("the Fowler"; d. 936) became the first non-Frankish king of Germany in 918. Henry rebuilt royal power and left his son and successor Otto I (r. 936–973) in a strong territorial position. Otto maneuvered his own kin into power in Bavaria, Swabia, and Franconia and invaded Italy and proclaimed himself its king in 951. In 955 he defeated the Hungarians at Lechfeld, which secured German borders against new barbarian attacks and earned Otto the title "the Great."

As part of a careful rebuilding program, Otto enlisted the church. Bishops and abbots, men who possessed a sense of universal empire yet did not marry and found competitive dynasties, were made royal princes and agents of the king. In 961 Otto, who had long aspired to the imperial crown, responded to a call for help from Pope John XII (955–964), in return for which John crowned him emperor on February 2, 962. The church was now more than ever under royal control. Under Otto I popes ruled at the emperor's pleasure.

THE REVIVING CATHOLIC CHURCH

Otto thus shifted the royal focus from Germany to Italy. His successors became so preoccupied with Italy that their German base began to disintegrate. As the revived empire began to crumble in the eleventh century, the church, long unhappy with imperial domination, prepared to declare its independence to a new force for reform within the church itself.

Cluny Reform Movement   In a great monastery at Cluny, founded in 910 in east-central France, a reform movement was born. The reformers of Cluny were aided in their efforts by popular respect for the church that found expression in both religious fervor among laypersons and generous baronial patronage of religious houses. People admired clerics and monks because the church was medieval society's most democratic institution as far as lay participation was concerned. In the Middle Ages any man could theoretically become pope, since the pope was supposed to be elected by the people and the clergy of Rome. All people were candidates for the church's grace and salvation. The church promised a better life to come to the great mass of ordinary people, who found their present existence brutish and without hope.

Otto I presents the Magdeburg Cathedral to Christ, as the pope (holding the keys to the kingdom of heaven) watches, a testimony to Otto's guardianship of the church.

Metropolitan Museum of Art, bequest of George Blumenthal, 1941 (41.300.157). Photograph © 1986 The Metropolitan Museum of Art

The Cluny reformers rejected the subservience of the clergy to royal authority. They taught that the pope in Rome was sole ruler over all the clergy. They further denounced the transgression of ascetic piety by "secular" parish clergy, who maintained concubines in a relationship akin to marriage. The distinctive Western separation of church and state and the celibacy of the Catholic clergy had their definitive origins in the Cluny reform movement. From Cluny, reformers were dispatched throughout France and Italy, and in the late eleventh century the papacy embraced their reforms.

Investiture Struggle: Gregory VII and Henry IV   In 1075 Pope Gregory VII (r. 1073–1085), a fierce advocate of church reform, condemned under penalty of excommunication the lay investiture of clergy at any level. He had primarily in mind the emperor's well-established custom of installing bishops by presenting them with the ring and staff that symbolized episcopal office. Henry IV considered Gregory's action a direct challenge to his authority. The territorial princes, on the other hand, eager to see the emperor weakened, fully supported Gregory's edict.

The lines of battle were quickly drawn. Henry assembled his loyal German bishops at Worms in January 1076 and had them proclaim their independence from Gregory. Gregory promptly excommunicated Henry and absolved all Henry's subjects from loyalty to him. The German princes were delighted, and Henry faced a general revolt. He had to come to terms with Gregory. In a famous scene, Henry prostrated himself outside Gregory's castle retreat at Canossa in northern Italy on January 25, 1077. There he reportedly stood barefoot in the snow off and on for three days before the pope absolved him. Papal power had reached a pinnacle.

The investiture controversy was finally settled in 1122 with the Concordat of Worms. Emperor Henry V (r. 1106–1125) formally renounced his power to invest bishops with ring and staff. In exchange, Pope Calixtus II (r. 1119–1124) recognized the emperor's right to be present and to invest bishops with fiefs before or after their investment with ring and staff by the church. The emperor also effectively retained the right to nominate or veto a candidate.

QUICK REVIEW

Church and State
- Investiture crisis centered on authority to appoint and control clergy
- Pope Gregory excommunicated Henry IV when he proclaimed his independence from papacy
- Crisis settled in 1122 with Concordat of Worms

A twelfth-century German manuscript portrays the struggle between Emperor Henry IV and Pope Gregory VII. In the top panel, Henry installs the puppet pope Clement III and drives Gregory from Rome. Below, Gregory dies in exile. The artist was a monk; his sympathies were with Gregory, not Henry.

Thuringer Universities and Landesbibliothek, Jena

7.6
Launching the Crusades
(1095): "It Is the Will of God!"

Crusades   Religious wars directed by the church against infidels and heretics.

The Gregorian party secured the independence of the clergy, but at the price of encouraging the divisiveness of the political forces within the empire. The pope had made himself strong by making imperial authority weak. In the end, the local princes profited most from the investiture controversy.

THE FIRST CRUSADES

If an index of popular piety and support for the pope in the High Middle Ages is needed, the **Crusades** amply provide it. What the Cluny reform was to the clergy, the First Crusade to the Holy Land was to the laity: an outlet for the heightened religious zeal of the late eleventh and the twelfth centuries, Europe's most religious period before the Protestant Reformation.

Late in the eleventh century, the Byzantine Empire was under severe pressure from the Seljuk Turks, and Emperor Alexius I Comnenus (r. 1081–1118) appealed for Western aid. (See Chapter 12.) At the Council of Clermont in 1095, Pope Urban II (r. 1088–1099) responded by launching the First Crusade.

Religion was not the only motive inspiring the Crusaders; hot blood and greed were equally influential. But unlike the later Crusades, undertaken for patently mercenary reasons, the early Crusades were inspired by genuine religious piety and were carefully orchestrated by the revived papacy. Popes promised participants in the First Crusade a plenary indulgence should they die in battle–that is, a complete remission of any outstanding temporal punishment for their unrepented mortal sins and hence release from suffering for them in purgatory. In addition to this direct spiritual reward, the Crusaders were also impelled by their enthusiasm for a Holy War against the hated infidel and by the romance of a pilgrimage to the Holy Land. Crusading zeal also sparked anti-Jewish riots and massacres in Europe, an expression of intolerance to Jews that became an enduring feature of militant Christianity.

These fanatical Crusaders defeated one Seljuk army after another in a steady advance toward Jerusalem, which fell to them on July 15, 1099. They divided the conquered territory into "states," which they held as alleged fiefs from the pope.

However, the Latin presence in the East soon began to crumble. A Second Crusade, preached by Saint Bernard of Clairvaux (1091–1153), Christendom's most powerful monastic leader, was a dismal failure. In October 1187 Jerusalem itself was reconquered by Saladin (r. 1138–1193), king of Egypt and Syria.

A Third Crusade in the twelfth century (1189–1192) attempted yet another rescue, enlisting as its leaders the most powerful Western rulers: Emperor Frederick Barbarossa (r. 1152–1190); Richard the Lion-Hearted, king of England (r. 1189–1199); and Philip Augustus, king of France (r. 1179–1223). But it, too, was a failure. The Holy Land remained as firmly Muslim as ever.

However, the Crusades did stimulate Western trade and cultural interaction with the East. Italian merchants followed the Crusaders' cross to lucrative new markets. The need to resupply the new Christian settlements in the Near East not only reopened old trade routes that had long been closed by Arab domination of the Mediterranean, but also opened new ones.

The Crusades	
1095	Pope Urban II launches the First Crusade
1099	The Crusaders take Jerusalem
1147–1149	The Second Crusade
1187	Jerusalem retaken by the Muslims
1189–1192	Third Crusade
1202–1204	Fourth Crusade

TOWNS AND TOWNSPEOPLE

In the eleventh and twelfth centuries, most towns were small and held only about 5 percent of western Europe's population. But they contained the most creative segments of medieval society.

The Chartering of Towns   Towns were originally dominated by feudal lords, both lay and clerical, who granted charters to those who would agree to live and work within them. The charters guaranteed the towns' safety and gave their inhabitants an independence unknown to peasants who worked the land. The purpose was originally to concentrate skilled laborers who could manufacture the finished goods desired by lords and bishops.

As towns grew and beckoned, many serfs took their skills to the new urban centers. There they found the freedom and profits that could lift an industrious craftsperson into higher social ranks. As this migration of serfs to the towns accelerated, the lords in the countryside offered serfs more favorable terms of tenure to keep them on the land. The growth of towns thus improved the lot of serfs generally.

The Rise of Merchants   Rural society not only gave the towns their craftspeople and day laborers, but the first merchants themselves may also have been enterprising serfs. Certainly, some of the long-distance traders were people who had nothing to lose and everything to gain from the enormous risks of foreign trade.

They traveled together in armed caravans and convoys, buying goods and products as cheaply as possible at the source, and selling them for all they could get in western ports.

At first the merchants were disliked because they were outside the traditional social groups of nobility, clergy, and peasantry. Over time, however, the powerful grew to respect the merchants, and the weak always tried to imitate them, because the merchants left a trail of wealth behind them.

As the traders established themselves in towns, they grew in wealth and numbers, formed their own protective associations, and soon found themselves able to challenge traditional seigneurial authority. Merchants especially wanted to end the arbitrary tolls and tariffs regional magnates imposed over the surrounding countryside. Such regulations hampered the flow of commerce on which both merchant and craftsman in the growing urban export industries depended.

Townspeople needed simple and uniform laws and a government sympathetic to their new forms of business activity, not the fortress mentality of the lords of the countryside. The result was often a struggle with the old nobility within and outside the towns. This conflict led towns in the High and late Middle Ages to form their own independent communes and to ally themselves with kings against the nobility in the countryside, a development that would eventually rearrange the centers of power in medieval Europe and dissolve classic feudal government.

Because the merchants were the engine of the urban economy, small shopkeepers and artisans identified far more with them than with aloof lords and bishops, who had been medieval society's traditional masters. The lesser nobility (small knights) outside the towns also recognized the new mercantile economy as the wave of the future. During the eleventh and twelfth centuries, the burgher upper classes increased their economic strength and successfully challenged the old noble urban lords for control of the towns.

New Models of Government   With urban autonomy came new models of self-government. Around 1100 the old urban nobility and the new burgher upper class merged into an urban patriciate. It was a marriage between those wealthy by birth (inherited property) and those who made their fortunes in long-distance trade. From this new ruling class was born the aristocratic town council, which henceforth governed towns.

Enriching and complicating the situation, small artisans and craftspeople also slowly developed their own protective associations or **guilds** and began to gain a voice in government. The towns' opportunities for the "little person" had created the slogan "Town air brings freedom." Within town walls people thought of themselves as citizens with basic rights, not subjects liable to their masters' whim.

Towns and Kings   By providing kings with the resources they needed to curb factious noblemen, towns became a major force in the transition from feudal societies to national governments. Towns were a ready source of educated bureaucrats and lawyers who knew Roman law, the tool for running the state. Money was also to be found in the towns in great quantity, enabling kings to hire their own armies and free themselves from dependence on the nobility. In turn, towns won royal political recognition and had their constitutions guaranteed. In France, towns became integrated early into royal government. In Germany, they fell under ever-tighter control by the princes. In Italy, uniquely, towns became genuine city-states during the Renaissance.

Jews in Christian Society   Towns also attracted Jews who plied trades in small businesses. Many became wealthy as moneylenders to kings, popes, and businesspeople. Jewish intellectual and religious culture both dazzled and threatened

guild An association of merchants or craftsmen that offered protection to its members and set rules for their work and products.

Christians. These various factors encouraged suspicion and distrust among Christians, and led to an unprecedented surge in anti-Jewish sentiment in the late twelfth and early thirteenth centuries.

Schools and Universities   In the twelfth century, Byzantine and Spanish Islamic scholars made it possible for the philosophical works of Aristotle, the writings of Euclid and Ptolemy, the texts of Greek physicians and Arab mathematicians, and the corpus of Roman law to circulate among western scholars. Islamic scholars wrote thought-provoking commentaries on Greek texts that were translated into Latin and made available to western scholars and students. The resulting intellectual ferment gave rise to western universities.

The first important western university was established in 1158 in Bologna, a town famous for the revival of Roman law, and became the model for the universities of Spain, Italy, and southern France. Paris became the model for northern European universities and the study of theology.

The Curriculum   In the High Middle Ages the learning process was basic. People assumed that truth was already known and only needed to be properly organized, elucidated, and defended. Students wrote commentaries on authoritative texts, especially those of Aristotle and the church fathers. Teachers did not encourage students to strive independently for undiscovered truth. Students rather learned to organize and harmonize the accepted truths of tradition, which were drilled into them.

This method of study, was known as **Scholasticism**. Students summarized the traditional authorities in their field, elaborated traditional arguments pro and con, and then drew conclusions. Logic and dialectic were the tools to discipline knowledge and thought. Dialectic is the art of discovering a truth by finding the contradictions in arguments against it. Astonishingly, medical students did no practical medical work; they studied and debated the authoritative texts in their field just as the law and theology students did in theirs.

Scholasticism   Method of study based on logic and dialectic that dominated the medieval schools. It assumed that truth already existed; students had only to organize, elucidate, and defend knowledge learned from authoritative texts, especially those of Aristotle and the Church Fathers.

SOCIETY

THE ORDER OF LIFE

In the art and literature of the Middle Ages, three basic social groups were represented: those who fought as mounted knights (the landed nobility), those who prayed (the clergy), and those who labored in fields and shops (the peasantry and village artisans). After the revival of towns in the eleventh century, a fourth social group emerged: the long-distance traders and merchants.

WHAT WERE the three basic social groups in medieval society?

Nobles   By the late Middle Ages, a distinguishable higher and lower nobility had evolved, living in both town and country. The higher were the great landowners and territorial magnates, long the dominant powers in their regions; the lower were petty landlords, the descendants of minor knights, newly rich merchants, or wealthy farmers.

Arms were the nobleman's profession; waging war was his sole occupation. In the eighth century the adoption of stirrups made mounted warriors the key ingredient of a successful army. The nobility accordingly celebrated the physical strength, courage, and constant activity of warfare. Warring gave them both new riches and an opportunity to gain honor and glory. Peace meant economic stagnation and boredom.

OVERVIEW

MEDIEVAL UNIVERSITIES

In the twelfth century, Latin translations of of ancient texts in law, astronomy, philosophy, and mathematics, and of learned commentaries on them by Islamic and Byzantine scholars, reached the West. The resulting intellectual ferment gave rise to the medieval universities. The first university was established at Bologna in Italy in 1158. By 1500, there were almost fifty universities across Europe from Scotland to Poland. Universities helped bring wealth and prestige to towns; graduated professionals, such as lawyers, physicians, and theologians; and provided rulers with trained bureaucrats for their increasingly complex administrations. The following is a list of the medieval universities and the dates of their founding.

University	Country	Date of Founding	University	Country	Date of Founding
Paris	France	ca. 1150–1160	Erfurt	Germany	1379
Oxford	England	1167	Heidelberg	Germany	1385
Vicenza	Italy	1204	Ferrara	Italy	1391
Cambridge	England	1209	Wurzburg	Germany	1402
Salamanca	Spain	1218	Leipzig	Germany	1409
Padua	Italy	1222	St. Andrews	Scotland	1411
Naples	Italy	1224	Turin	Italy	1412
Toulouse	France	1229	Louvain	Belgium	1426
Rome	Italy	1244	Poitiers	France	1431
Siena	Italy	1247	Caen	France	1437
Piacenza	Italy	1248	Bourdeaux	France	1441
Montpellier	France	1289	Barcelona	Spain	1450
Lisbon	Portugal	1290	Trier	Germany	1450
Avignon	France	1303	Glasgow	Scotland	1451
Orleans	France	1305	Freiburg	Germany	1455
Perugia	Italy	1308	Ingolstadt	Germany	1459
Coimbra	Portugal	1308	Basel	Switzerland	1460
Grenoble	France	1339	Nantes	France	1463
Pisa	Italy	1343	Bourges	France	1465
Valladolid	Spain	1346	Ofen	Germany	1475
Prague	Bohemia	1348	Tubingen	Germany	1477
Pavia	Italy	1361	Uppsala	Sweden	1477
Vienna	Austria	1364	Copenhagen	Denmark	1479
Cracow	Poland	1364	Aberdeen	Scotland	1494

No medieval social group was absolutely uniform. Noblemen formed a broad spectrum—from minor vassals without subordinate vassals to mighty barons, the principal vassals of a king or prince, who had many vassals of their own. Dignity and status within the nobility were directly related to the exercise of authority over others; a chief with many vassals far excelled the small country nobleman who was lord over none but himself.

By the late Middle Ages, several factors forced the landed nobility into a steep economic and political decline from which it never recovered. Climatic changes and agricultural failures created large famines, while the great plague (to be discussed later) brought about unprecedented population losses. Changing military tactics occasioned by the use of infantry and heavy artillery during the Hundred Years' War made the noble cavalry nearly obsolete. And the alliance of wealthy towns with the king weakened the nobility within their own domains. After the fourteenth century, land and wealth counted for far more than lineage as qualification for entrance into the highest social class.

Clergy   Unlike the nobility and the peasantry, the clergy was an open estate: one was a cleric by religious training and ordination, not because of birth or military prowess.

There were two basic types of clerical vocation: regular and secular. The **regular clergy** comprised the orders of monks who lived according to a special ascetic rule (*regula*) in cloisters separated from the world. In the thirteenth century, two new orders—the Franciscans and the Dominicans—gained the sanction of the church. Their members went out into the world to preach the church's mission and to combat heresy.

The **secular clergy**, those who lived and worked directly among the laity in the world (*saeculum*), formed a vast hierarchy. At the top were the wealthy cardinals, archbishops, and bishops who were drawn almost exclusively from the nobility. Below them were the urban priests, the cathedral canons, and the court clerks. Finally, there was the great mass of poor parish priests, who were neither financially nor intellectually much above the common people they served.

regular clergy   Monks and nuns who belong to religious orders.

secular clergy   Parish clergy who did not belong to a religious order.

A fifteenth-century rendering of an eleventh- or twelfth-century marketplace. Medieval women were active in all trades, but especially in the food and clothing industries.

Scala/Art Resource, N.Y.

During most of the Middle Ages, the clergy were the first estate, and theology was the queen of the sciences. How did the clergy attain such prominence? A lot of it was self-proclaimed. However, there was also popular respect and reverence for the clergy's role as mediator between God and humanity. The priest brought the Son of God down to earth when he celebrated the sacrament of the Eucharist; his absolution released penitents from punishment for sin. It was declared improper for mere laypeople to sit in judgment on such a priest.

Peasants   The largest and lowest social group in medieval society was one on whose labor the welfare of all others depended: the agrarian peasantry. Many peasants lived and worked on the manors of the nobility, the vital cells of rural social life. The lord of the manor required a certain amount of produce (grain, eggs, and the like) and services from the peasant families and held both judicial and police powers. He owned and operated the machines that processed crops into food and drink. The lord also had the right to subject his tenants to exactions known as *banalities*. He could, for example, force them to breed their cows with his bull, and to pay for the privilege; to grind their bread grains in his mill; to bake their bread in his oven; to make their wine in his wine press; to buy their beer from his brewery; and even to surrender to him the choice parts of all animals slaughtered on his lands. The lord also collected as an inheritance tax a serf's best animal. Without the lord's permission, a serf could neither travel nor marry outside the manor in which he served.

However, the serfs' status was not chattel slavery. It was to a lord's advantage to keep his serfs healthy and happy; his welfare, like theirs, depended on a successful harvest. Serfs had their own dwellings and modest strips of land, and they

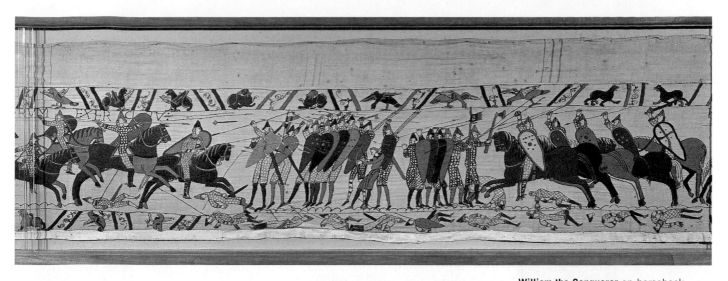

William the Conqueror on horseback urging his troops into combat with the English at the Battle of Hastings (October 14, 1066). From the Bayeux Tapestry, about 1073–1083.

Giraudon/Art Resource, N.Y.

lived off the produce of their own labor and organization. They could also market for their own profit any surpluses that remained after the harvest. And serfs could pass their property (their dwellings and field strips) on to their children, along with their worldly goods.

Two basic changes occurred in the evolution of the manor from the early to the later Middle Ages. The first was the increasing importance of the single-family holding. As family farms replaced manorial units, land and property remained in the possession of a single family from generation to generation. Second was the conversion of the serf's dues into money payments, a change made possible by the revival of trade and the rise of the towns. This development, completed by the thirteenth century, permitted serfs to hold their land as rent-paying tenants and to overcome their servile status.

By the mid-fourteenth century, a declining nobility in England and France, faced with the ravages of the great plague and the Hundred Years' War, tried to turn back the historical clock by increasing taxes on the peasantry and restricting their migration to the cities. The response was armed revolt. The revolts of the agrarian peasantry, like those of the urban proletariat, were brutally crushed. They stand out at the end of the Middle Ages as violent testimony to the breakup of medieval society. As growing national sentiment would break its political unity and heretical movements end its nominal religious unity, the peasantry's revolts revealed the absence of medieval social unity.

MEDIEVAL WOMEN

Although the male Christian clergy praised the ideal of a celibate life of chastity, poverty, and obedience and often depicted women as the physical, mental, and moral inferiors of men, most medieval women were workers in fields, trades, and businesses. Evidence suggests that they were respected and loved by their husbands, perhaps because they worked shoulder to shoulder and hour by hour with them. Between the ages of 10 and 15, girls were apprenticed in a trade, much like boys, and they learned a marketable skill. Women appeared in virtually every "blue-collar" trade, but were especially prominent in the food and clothing industries. They belonged to guilds and they could become craftmasters. In the late Middle Ages, townswomen often went to school and gained vernacular literacy although they were excluded from universities and the professions of scholarship, law, and medicine.

10.3
The Goodman of Paris

HOW DID England and France develop strong royal governments by the thirteenth century?

The portal of Reims Cathedral, where the kings of France were crowned. The cathedral was built in the Gothic style-emblematic of the High and late Middle Ages-that originated in France in the mid-twelfth century. The earlier Romanesque (Roman-like) style from which it evolved is characterized by fortresslike buildings pith thick stone walls, rounded arches and vaults, and few hindows. The Gothic style, in contrast, is characterized by soaring structures, their interiors flooded with colored light from vast expanses of stained glass. Distinctive features of the style include ribbed, crisscrossing vaulting; pointed rather than roudned arches; and prominent exterior flying buttresses.

Scala/Art Resource, NY

Magna Carta The "Great Charter" limiting royal power that the English nobility forced King John to sign in 1215.

GROWTH OF NATIONAL MONARCHIES

While stable governments developed in both England and France during the Middle Ages, the Holy Roman Empire, fragmented in disunity and blood feuding (see Map 15–1).

ENGLAND AND FRANCE: HASTINGS (1066) TO BOUVINES (1214)

The most important change in English political life was occasioned in 1066 by the death of the childless Anglo-Saxon ruler Edward the Confessor (r. 1042–1066), so named because of his reputation of piety. Edward's mother was a Norman princess, which gave Duke William of Normandy (d. 1087) a hereditary claim to the English throne. The Anglo-Saxon assembly, however, chose instead Harold Godwinsson (ca. 1022–1066). That defiant action brought the swift conquest of England by the powerful Normans. William's forces defeated Harold's army at Hastings on October 14, 1066, and William was crowned king of England in Westminster Abbey within weeks of the invasion.

Thereafter William established a strong monarchy but kept the Anglo-Saxon tax system, the practice of court writs (legal warnings) as a flexible form of central control over localities, and the Anglo-Saxon quasi-democratic tradition of frequent *parleying*—that is, the holding of conferences between the king and lesser powers who had vested interests in royal decisions. The result was a balancing of monarchical and parliamentary elements that remains true of English government today.

Popular Rebellion and Magna Carta   William's grandson, Henry II (r. 1154–1189), brought to the throne greatly expanded French holdings through inheritance from his father (Maine, Touraine, and Anjou) and his marriage to Eleanor of Aquitaine (1122–1204), a union that created the so-called Angevin or English-French empire. As Henry II acquired new lands abroad, he became more autocratic at home. The result was strong political resistance from both the nobility and the clergy.

Under Henry's successors, the brothers Richard the Lion-Hearted (r. 1189–1199) and John (r. 1199–1216), burdensome taxation in support of foreign Crusades and a failing war with France turned resistance into outright rebellion. With the full support of the clergy and the townspeople, English barons forced the king's grudging recognition of the **Magna Carta** ("Great Charter") in 1215.

This famous cornerstone of modern English law put limits on royal power and secured the rights of the privileged to be represented at the highest levels of government in important matters like taxation. The Great Charter enabled the English to avoid both a dissolution of the monarchy by the nobility and the abridgment of the rights of the nobility by the monarchy.

Philip II Augustus   Powerful feudal princes dominated France from the beginning of the Capetian dynasty (987) until the reign of Philip II Augustus (1180–1223). During this period the Capetian kings wisely concentrated their limited resources on securing the territory surrounding Paris known as the Île-de-France. By the time of Philip II, Paris had become the center of French government and culture, and the Capetian dynasty a secure hereditary monarchy. Thereafter, the kings of France were able to impose their will on the French nobles.

The Norman Conquest of England enabled the Capetian kings to establish a truly national monarchy. The Duke of Normandy, who after 1066 was master of England, was also a vassal of the French king in Paris. Capetian kings understandably watched with alarm as the power of their Norman vassal grew.

Philip Augustus faced both an internal and an international struggle, and he succeeded at both. His armies occupied all the English territories on the French

MAP EXPLORATION

Interactive map: To explore this map further, go to **http://www.prenhall.com/craig2/map15.1**

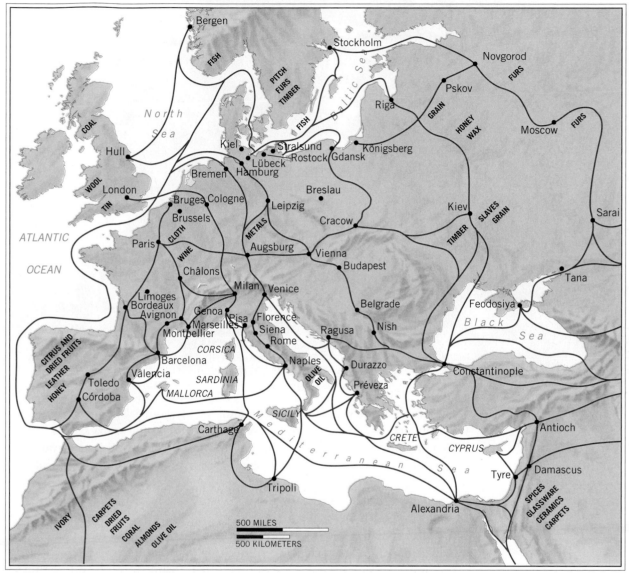

MAP 15–1

Medieval trade routes and regional products.   Trade in the West varied in intensity and geographical extent in different periods during the Middle Ages. The map shows some of the channels that came to be used in interregional commerce. Labels tell part of what was carried in that commerce.

WHICH REGION appears to have the most flourishing trade?

---

coast, except for Aquitaine. At Bouvines on July 27, 1214, the French won handily over the English and their German allies. The victory unified France around the monarchy and thereby laid the foundation for French ascendancy in the late Middle Ages.

FRANCE IN THE THIRTEENTH CENTURY: REIGN OF LOUIS IX

Louis IX (r. 1226–1270), the grandson of Philip Augustus, embodied the medieval view of the perfect ruler. He inherited a unified and secure kingdom.

Louis's greatest achievements lay at home. The efficient French bureaucracy became under him an instrument of order and fair play in local government.

Pope Innocent III depicted in an early thirteenth century fresco from the monastic church of Subiaco in Italy.

Scala/Art Resource, NY

He sent forth royal commissioners to monitor the royal officials responsible for local governmental administration and ensure justice. These royal ambassadors were received as genuine tribunes of the people. Louis further abolished private wars and serfdom within his own royal domain, gave his subjects the right of appeal from local to higher courts, and made the tax system more equitable. The French people came to associate their king with justice; and national feeling, the glue of nationhood, grew strong during his reign.

During Louis's reign, French society and culture became an example to all of Europe, a pattern that would continue into the modern period. Northern France became the showcase of monastic reform, chivalry, and Gothic art and architecture. Louis's reign also coincided with the golden age of Scholasticism, which saw the convergence of Europe's greatest thinkers on Paris, among them Saint Thomas Aquinas.

The Hohenstaufen Empire (1152–1272)

Frederick I Barbarossa (1152–1190), the first of the Hohenstaufens, reestablished imperial authority but also initiated a new phase in the contest between popes and emperors. Never have rulers and popes despised and persecuted one another more than they did during the Hohenstaufen dynasty. Frederick attempted to hold the empire together by stressing feudal bonds, but his reign ended with stalemate in Germany and defeat in Italy. In 1186 his son—the future Henry VI (r. 1190–1197)—married Constance, heiress to the kingdom of Sicily. That alliance became a fatal distraction for the Hohenstaufens. This union of the empire with Sicily left Rome encircled, thereby ensuring the undying hostility of a papacy already thoroughly distrustful of the emperor.

When Henry VI died in September 1197, chaos followed. Germany was thrown into anarchy and civil war. Meanwhile, Henry VI's four-year-old son, Frederick, who had a direct hereditary claim to the imperial crown, had for his own safety been made—fatefully, it would prove—a ward of Pope Innocent III (r. 1198–1215), who proclaimed and practiced as none before him the doctrine of the plenitude of papal power. Innocent had both the will and the means to challenge the Hohenstaufens.

Frederick II   Hohenstaufen support had meanwhile remained alive in Germany, where in December 1212 young Frederick, with papal support, became Emperor Frederick II. But Frederick soon disappointed papal hopes. He was Sicilian and only nine of his 38 years as emperor were spent in Germany. To secure the imperial title for himself and his sons, he gave the German princes what they wanted. The German princes became undisputed lords over their territories, petty kings.

Frederick had an equally disastrous relationship with the papacy, which excommunicated him four times and led the German princes against him, launching the church into European politics on a massive scale. This transformation of the papacy into a formidable political and military power soon made the church highly vulnerable to criticism from religious reformers and royal apologists.

When Frederick died in 1250, the German monarchy died with him. The princes established an electoral college in 1257 to pick the emperor, and the "king of the Romans" became their puppet. Between 1250 and 1272 the Hohenstaufen dynasty slowly faded into oblivion.

POLITICAL AND SOCIAL BREAKDOWN

The Causes of the Hundred Years' War   The Hundred Years' War, which began in May 1337 and lasted until October 1453, started when the English king Edward III (r. 1327–1377), the grandson of Philip the Fair of France (r. 1285–1314), claimed the French throne. But the war was more than a dynastic quarrel. England and France were territorial and economic rivals with a long history of prejudice and animosity between them. These factors made the Hundred Years' War a struggle for national identity.

Although France had three times the population of England, was far wealthier, and fought on its own soil, most of the major battles were stunning English victories. The primary reason for these French failures was internal disunity caused by endemic social conflicts. Unlike England, France was still struggling to make the transition from a fragmented feudal society to a centralized modern state.

France's defeats also resulted from incompetent leadership and English military superiority. The English infantry was more disciplined than the French, and English archers could fire six arrows a minute with enough force to pierce an inch of wood or the armor of a knight at 200 yards. Eventually, thanks in part to the inspiring leadership of Joan of Arc (1412–1431), and a sense of national identity and self-confidence, the French were able to expel the English from France. By 1453, all that remained to the English was their coastal enclave of Calais.

Charles forgot his liberator as quickly as he had embraced her. When the Burgundians captured Joan in May 1430, he could have secured her release but did not. The Burgundians and the English wanted her publicly discredited, believing this would demoralize French resistance. She was turned over to the Inquisition in English-held Rouen, where, after ten weeks of interrogation, she was executed on May 30, 1431.

The Hundred Years' War had lasting political and social consequences. It devastated France, but it also awakened French nationalism and hastened the country's transition from a feudal monarchy to a centralized state. In both France and England the burden of the war fell most heavily on the peasantry, who were forced to support it with taxes and services.

WHAT WERE the causes of the political and social breakdowns that occurred during the fourteenth century?

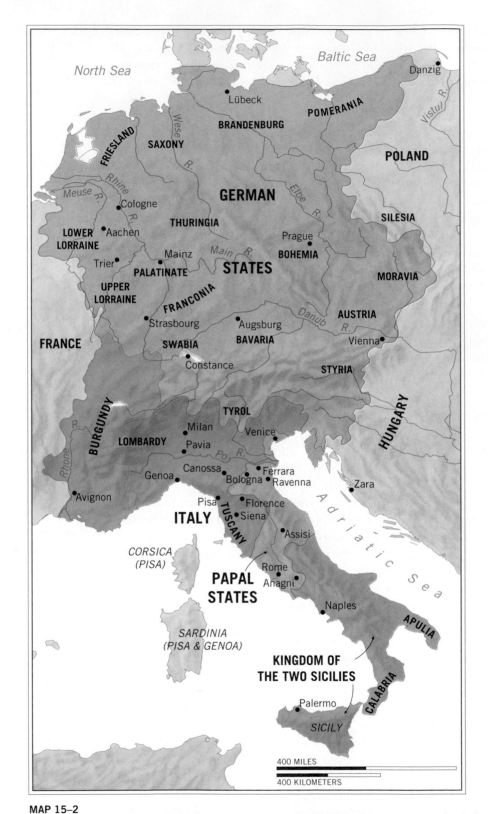

MAP 15–2

Germany and Italy in the Middle Ages.   Medieval Germany and Italy were divided lands. The Holy Roman Empire (Germany) embraced hundreds of independent territories that the emperor ruled only in name. The papacy controlled the Rome area and tried to enforce its will in the Romagna. Under the Hohenstaufens (mid-twelfth to mid-thirteenth centuries), internal German divisions and papal conflict reached new heights; German rulers sought to extend their power to southern Italy and Sicily.

WHY WERE the emperors unable to unite Germany and Italy in the Middle Ages?

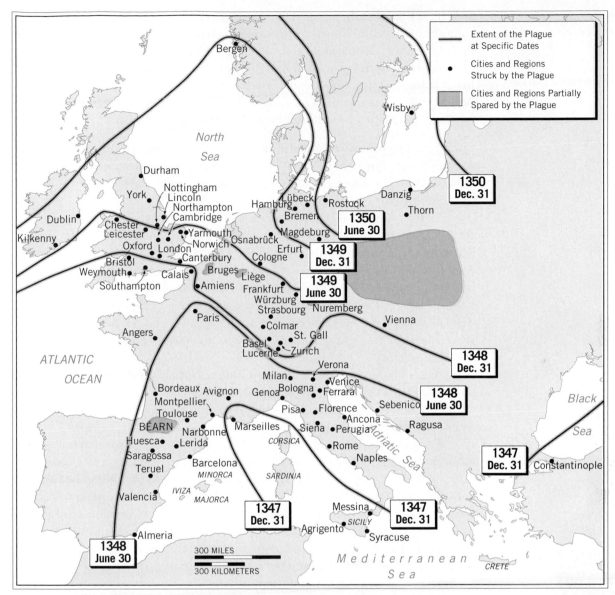

MAP 15–3

Spread of the Black Death.   Apparently introduced by sea-borne rats from areas around the Black Sea where plague-infested rodents have long been known, the Black Death had great human, social, and economic consequences. According to one of the lower estimates, it killed 25 million in Europe. The map charts the spread of the plague in the mid-14th century. Generally following trade routes, it reached Scandinavia by 1350, and some believe it then went on to Iceland and even Greenland. Areas off the main trade routes were largely spared.

WHAT WERE the social and economic consequences of the plague?

THE BLACK DEATH

Preconditions and Causes   In the late Middle Ages, improvements in agriculture increased both the food supply and the population. It is estimated that Europe's population doubled between the years 1000 and 1300, and then began to outstrip food production. There were now more people than food to feed them or jobs to employ them, and the average European faced the probability of famine at least once during his or her expected 35-year life-span. Decades of overpopulation, economic depression, famine, and bad health made Europe's population vulnerable to a virulent bubonic plague that struck with full force in 1348.

10.7
"A Most Terrible Plague:"
Giovanni Boccaccio

Black Death The bubonic plague that killed millions of Europeans in the fourteenth century.

This **Black Death**, so called because it discolored the body, followed the trade routes from Asia into Europe. Appearing in Sicily in late 1347, it entered Europe through Venice, Genoa, and Pisa in 1348, and from there it swept rapidly through Spain and southern France and into northern Europe. Areas that lay outside the major trade routes, like Bohemia, appear to have remained virtually unaffected. Bubonic plague reappeared in succeeding decades. By the early fifteenth century, it may have killed two-fifths of western Europe's population.

Social and Economic Consequences Whole villages vanished in the wake of the plague. Among the social and economic consequences of this depopulation were a shrunken labor supply and a decline in the value of the estates of the nobility.

As the number of farm laborers decreased, their wages increased, and those of skilled artisans soared. Many serfs now replaced their labor services with money payments or abandoned the farm altogether for jobs in the cities. Agricultural prices fell because of lowered demand, and the price of luxury and manufactured goods—the work of skilled artisans—rose. The noble landholders suffered the greatest decline in power from this new state of affairs. They were forced to pay more for finished products and for farm labor, but received less for their agricultural produce. Everywhere their rents declined after the plague.

Although the plague hit urban populations especially hard, the cities and their skilled industries eventually prospered from its effects. Cities had always protected their interests by regulating competition and immigration from rural areas. After the plague the reach of such laws was extended beyond the cities.

The omnipresence of death whetted the appetite for goods that only skilled urban industries could produce. Expensive cloths, jewelry, furs, and silks were in great demand. Faced with life at its worst, people insisted on having the best. Initially this new demand could not be met, as the first wave of plague transformed the already restricted supply of skilled artisans into a shortage almost overnight. As a result, the prices of manufactured and luxury items soared to new heights, but this in turn encouraged workers to migrate to the city to become artisans. As wealth poured into the cities and per capita income rose, urban dwellers paid less for agricultural products from the countryside.

There was also gain as well as loss for the church. Although it suffered losses as a great landholder and was politically weakened, it had received new revenues from the vastly increased demand for religious services for the dead and the dying and from the multiplication of gifts and bequests. Nonetheless, after 1350, and largely as a consequence of the plague, the two traditional "containers" of monarchy—the landed nobility and the church—were politically on the defensive.

ECCLESIASTICAL BREAKDOWN AND REVIVAL: THE LATE MEDIEVAL CHURCH

BONIFACE VIII AND PHILIP THE FAIR

By the fourteenth century, popes faced rulers far more powerful than the papacy. When Pope Boniface VIII (r. 1294–1303) issued a bull, *Clericis Laicos*, which forbade lay taxation of the clergy without prior papal approval, King Philip the Fair of France (r. 1285–1314) unleashed a ruthless antipapal campaign. Boniface made a last-ditch stand against state control of national churches on November 18, 1302,

Pope Boniface VIII (r. 1294-1303), who opposed the taxation of the clergy by the kings of France and England and issued one of the strongest declarations of papal authority, the bull Unam Sanctam. This statue is in the Museo Civico, Bologna, Italy.

when he issued the bull *Unam Sanctam*, which declared that temporal authority was "subject" to the spiritual power of the church.

The French, however, responded with force. Philip sent troops who beat the pope badly, and might even have executed him had not an aroused populace liberated the pope and returned him safely to Rome.

There was no papal retaliation. No pope ever again so seriously threatened kings and emperors. Future relations between Church and State would henceforth tilt toward state control of religion within particular monarchies.

THE GREAT SCHISM (1378–1417) AND THE CONCILIAR MOVEMENT TO 1449

After Boniface VIII's death, his successor, Clement V (r. 1305–1314), moved the papal court to Avignon on the southeastern border with France, where it remained until Pope Gregory XI (r. 1370–1378) reestablished the papacy in Rome in January 1377. His successor, Pope Urban VI (r. 1378–1389), proclaimed his intention to reform the **Curia**. This announcement alarmed the cardinals, most of whom were French. Not wanting to surrender the benefits of a papacy under French influence, the French king, Charles V (r. 1364–1380), supported a schism in the church and on September 20, 1378, 13 cardinals, all but one of whom was French, elected a cousin of the French king as Pope Clement VII (r. 1378–1397). Clement returned to Avignon. Thereafter allegiance to the two papal courts divided along political lines: England and its allies (the **Holy Roman Empire**, Hungary, Bohemia, and Poland) acknowledged Urban VI, whereas France and its orbit (Naples, Scotland, Castile, and Aragon) supported Clement VII. Only the Roman line of popes, however, is recognized as official by the church.

In 1409 a council at Pisa deposed both the Roman and the Avignon popes and elected its own new pope. But neither Rome nor Avignon accepted its action, so after 1409 there were three contending popes. This intolerable situation ended when the emperor Sigismund (r. 1410–1437) prevailed on the Pisan pope to summon a legal council of the church in Constance in 1414, a council also recognized by the reigning Roman pope Gregory XII (r. 1406–1415). After the three contending popes had either resigned or been deposed, the council elected a new pope, Martin V (r. 1417–1431), in November 1417, reuniting the church.

Under Pope Eugenius IV (r. 1431–1447), the papacy regained much of its prestige and authority, and in 1460 the papal bull *Execrabilis* condemned all appeals to councils as "completely null and void." But the conciliar movement had planted deep within the conscience of all western peoples the conviction that the leader of an institution must be responsive to its members and not act against their best interests.

Great Schism   The appearance of two and at times three rival popes between 1378 and 1415.

Curia   The papal government.

Holy Roman Empire   The revival of the old Roman Empire, based mainly in Germany and northern Italy, that endured from 870 to 1806.

THE RENAISSANCE IN ITALY (1375–1527)

Most scholars agree that the **Renaissance** was a transition from the medieval to the modern world. Medieval Europe, especially before the twelfth century, had been a fragmented feudal society with an agricultural economy, its thought and culture dominated by the church. Renaissance Europe, especially after the fourteenth century, was characterized by growing national consciousness and political centralization, an urban economy based on organized commerce and capitalism, and ever greater lay and secular control of thought and culture.

The distinctive features and achievements of the Renaissance are most strikingly revealed in Italy from roughly 1375 to 1527, the year of the infamous sack of Rome by imperial soldiers. What was achieved in Italy during these centuries also deeply influenced northern Europe.

WHY WAS the Renaissance a transition from the medieval to the modern world?

Renaissance   The revival of ancient learning and the supplanting of traditional religious beliefs by new secular and scientific values that began in Italy in the fourteenth and fifteenth centuries.

Cosimo de' Medici (1389–1464),
Florentine banker and statesman, in his
lifetime the city's wealthiest man and
most successfull politician. This portrait
is by Jacopo da Pontormo (1494–1556).

Erich Lessing/Art Resource, NY

humanism   The study of the Latin
and Greek classics and of the
Church Fathers both for their own
sake and to promote a rebirth of
ancient norms and values.

studia humanitatis   During the Renaissance, a liberal arts program of study
that embraced grammar, rhetoric, poetry, history, philosophy, and politics.

THE ITALIAN CITY-STATE: SOCIAL CONFLICT AND DESPOTISM

Renaissance society took distinctive shape within the
cities of late medieval Italy. Italy was the natural gateway between East and West. Venice, Genoa, and Pisa
traded uninterruptedly with the Near East throughout the Middle Ages, and maintained vibrant urban
societies. During the thirteenth and fourteenth centuries, the trade-rich Italian cities became powerful
city-states, dominating the political and economic
life of the surrounding countryside. By the fifteenth
century, the great Italian cities had become the
bankers for much of Europe. There were five such
major, competitive states in Italy: the duchy of Milan,
the republics of Florence and Venice, the Papal
States, and the kingdom of Naples.

Social strife and competition for political power
were so intense within the cities that for survival's
sake, most had evolved into despotisms by the fifteenth century. Venice, ruled by a successful merchant oligarchy, was the notable exception.
Elsewhere, the new social classes and divisions within society produced by rapid urban growth fueled
chronic, near-anarchic conflict.

In Florence, these social divisions produced
conflict at every level of society. True stability was not
established until the ascent to power in 1434 of
Cosimo de' Medici (1389–1464). The wealthiest
Florentine and a most astute statesman, Cosimo
controlled the city internally from behind the
scenes, skillfully manipulating the constitution and influencing elections. His
grandson Lorenzo the Magnificent (1449–1492, r. 1478–1492) ruled Florence in
almost totalitarian fashion.

Despotism was less subtle elsewhere in Italy. To prevent internal social conflict and foreign intrigue from paralyzing their cities, the dominant groups in
many cities cooperated to install a hired strongman, known as a *podesta*, to maintain law and order. Because these despots could not depend on the divided populace, they operated through mercenary armies.

Political turbulence and warfare gave birth to diplomacy, through which the
various city-states stayed abreast of foreign military developments and, if shrewd
enough, gained power and advantage without actually going to war. Most city-
states established resident embassies during the fifteenth century. Their ambassadors became their watchful eyes and ears at rival courts.

Renaissance culture was promoted as vigorously by despots as by republicans and by popes as enthusiastically as by the secularized ones.

HUMANISM

Humanism was the scholarly study of the Latin and Greek classics and the ancient
Church Fathers both for their own sake and to promote a rebirth of ancient norms
and values. Humanists advocated the *studia humanitatis*, a liberal arts program
that embraced grammar, rhetoric, poetry, history, politics, and moral philosophy.

The first humanists were orators and poets. They wrote original literature in both the classical and the **vernacular** languages, inspired by the newly discovered works of the ancients, and they taught rhetoric within the universities. Their talents were sought as secretaries, speech writers, and diplomats in princely and papal courts.

Classical and Christian antiquity had been studied before the Italian Renaissance—during the Carolingian renaissance of the ninth century, for example. However, the Italian Renaissance of the late Middle Ages was more secular and lay dominated, had broader interests, recovered more manuscripts, and possessed far superior technical skills than earlier rebirths of antiquity.

Unlike their Scholastic rivals, humanists were not content only to summarize and compare the views of recognized authorities on a question, but instead went directly to the original source and drew their own conclusions. Avidly searching out manuscript collections, Italian humanists made the full sources of Greek and Latin antiquity available to scholars during the fourteenth and fifteenth centuries. Mastery of Latin and Greek was their surgeon's tool. There is a kernel of truth—but only a kernel—in the arrogant boast of the humanists that the period between themselves and classical civilization was a "dark middle age."

Church and Empire

910	Monastary of Cluny founded
918	Henry I becomes King of Germany
951	Otto I invades Italy
955	Otto I defeats the Hungarians at Lechfeld
962	Otto I crowned emperor by Pope John XII
1077	Gregory VII pardons Henry IV at Canossa
1122	Concordat of Worms settles the investiture controversy
1152–1190	Reign of Frederick Barbarossa
1198–1215	Reign of Innocent III
1214	Collapse of the claims of Otto IV
1220	Frederick II crowned emperor
1232	Frederick II devolves authority to the German princes
1257	The German monarchy becomes elective

Petrarch, Dante, and Boccaccio   Francesco Petrarch (1304–1374) was the father of humanism. He left the legal profession to pursue his love of letters and poetry. Petrarch celebrated ancient Rome in his writings and tirelessly collected ancient manuscripts; among his finds were letters by Cicero. His critical textual studies, elitism, and contempt for the allegedly useless learning of the Scholastics were shared by many later humanists.

Petrarch was far more secular in orientation than Dante Alighieri (1265–1321), whose *Vita Nuova* and *Divine Comedy* form, with Petrarch's sonnets, the cornerstones of Italian vernacular literature. Petrarch's student and friend Giovanni Boccaccio (1313–1375), author of the *Decameron,* 100 bawdy tales told by three men and seven women in a country retreat from the plague that ravaged Florence in 1348, also pioneered humanist studies. An avid collector of manuscripts, Boccaccio assembled an encyclopedia of Greek and Roman mythology.

Educational Reforms and Goals   The classical ideal of a useful education that produces well-rounded people inspired far-reaching reforms in traditional education. The most influential Italian Renaissance tract on education, Pietro Paolo Vergerio's (1349–1420) *On the Morals That Befit a Free Man,* was written directly from classical models. Vittorino da Feltre (d. 1446) directed his students to a highly disciplined reading of ancient authors, together with vigorous physical exercise and games with intellectual pursuits.

Educated and cultured noblewomen also had a prominent place at Renaissance courts, among them Christine de Pisan (1363?–1434). She was an expert in classical, French, and Italian languages and literature and became a well-known woman of letters in the courts of Europe. Her most famous work, *The City of Ladies,* describes the accomplishments of the great women of history.

vernacular   The everyday language spoken by the people as opposed to Latin.

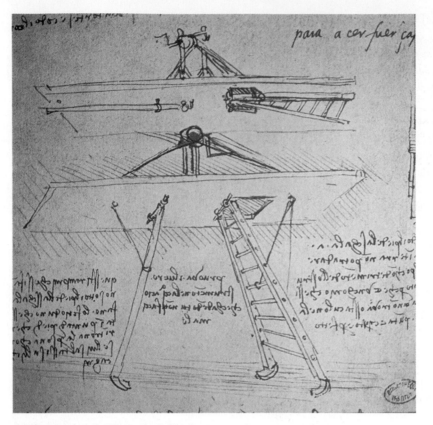

Aviation drawings by Leonardo da Vinci (1452–1519), who imagined a possible flying machine with a retractable ladder for boarding.

David Forbert/SuperStock, Inc.

RENAISSANCE ART

In Renaissance Italy, as later in Reformation Europe, the values and interests of the laity were less subordinated to those of the clergy. In education, culture, and religion, medieval Christian values were adjusting to a more this-worldly spirit. Men and women began again to appreciate and even to glorify the secular world, secular learning, and purely human pursuits as ends in themselves.

This perspective on life is especially prominent in the painting and sculpture of the High Renaissance (late fifteenth and early sixteenth centuries), when Renaissance art reached its full maturity. In imitation of Greek and Roman art, painters and sculptors attempted to create harmonious, symmetrical, and properly proportioned figures, portraying the human form with a glorified realism. Whereas Byzantine and Gothic art had been religious and idealized in the extreme, Renaissance art, especially in the fifteenth century, realistically reproduced nature and human beings as a part of nature.

Renaissance artists took advantage of new technical skills and materials developed during the fifteenth century: the use of oil paints, using shading to enhance realism (**chiaroscuro**), and adjusting the size of figures to give the viewer a feeling of continuity with the painting (linear perspective). Compared with their flat Byzantine and Gothic counterparts, Renaissance paintings seem filled with energy and life and stand out from the canvas in three dimensions. The great masters of the High Renaissance included Leonardo da Vinci (1452–1519), Raphael (1483–1520), and Michelangelo Buonarroti (1475–1564).

Leonardo da Vinci Leonardo personified the Renaissance ideal of the universal person, one who is not only a jack-of-all-trades but also a master of many. A military engineer and advocate of scientific experimentation, he dissected corpses to learn anatomy and was a self-taught botanist. He foresaw such modern machines as airplanes and submarines. The variety of his interests tended to shorten his attention span, so that he constantly moved from one activity to another. As a painter, his great skill lay in conveying inner moods through complex facial features, such as that seen in the most famous of his paintings, the *Mona Lisa.*

Raphael Raphael, who died young (37), is famous for his tender madonnas. Art historians also praise his fresco *The School of Athens*, which depicts Plato and Aristotle surrounded by philosophy and science, as one of the most perfect examples of Renaissance artistic theory and technique.

Michelangelo This melancholy genius also excelled in a variety of arts and crafts. His 18-foot godlike sculpture *David* is a perfect example of the Renaissance artist's devotion to harmony, symmetry, and proportion, as well as his extreme glorification of the human form. Four different popes commissioned works by Michelangelo, the best known of which are the frescoes for the Sistine Chapel, painted for Pope Julius II (r.1503–1513).

chiaroscuro The use of shading to enhance naturalness in painting and drawing.

Raphael's portrait (ca. 1515) of Baldassare Castiglione (1478–1529), now in the Louvre. Castiglione, author of the *Book of the Courtier*, was Raphael's close friend. The self-restraint and inner calm that he considered the chief qualities of the gentleman are also qualities of Raphael's art, reflected in the portrait's perfect balance and harmony. This painting greatly influenced Rembrandt, who later tried unsuccessfully to buy it.

Cliche des Musées Nationaux, Paris

His later works mark, artistically and philosophically, the passing of High Renaissance painting and the advent of a new, experimental style known as *mannerism*, which reached its peak in the late sixteenth and early seventeenth centuries. It derived its name from the fact that it permitted the artist to express his own individual perceptions and feelings, to paint, compose, or write in a "mannered" or "affected" way. Tintoretto (d. 1594) and especially El Greco (d. 1614) became its supreme representatives.

ITALY'S POLITICAL DECLINE:
THE FRENCH INVASIONS (1494–1527)

Autonomous city-states of Italy had always preserved their peace and safety from foreign invasion by cooperation with each other. However, in 1494 Naples, supported by Florence and the Borgia pope Alexander VI (1492–1503), prepared to attack

mannerism   A style of art in the mid to late sixteenth century that permitted artists to express their own "manner" or feelings in contrast to the symmetry and simplicity of the art of the High Renaissance.

Michelangelo's *Pietà* (made between 1498 and 1500), St. Peter's, Rome. This work of the artist's youth, sculpted between his twenty-third and twenty-fifth years, portrays a Mary who is younger than her son. Unsurpassed in delicacy, realism, and emotional impact, it exemplifies the creativity of the Italian Renaissance.

Scala/Art Resource, N.Y.

Milan. At this point, the Milanese despot Ludovico il Moro (r. 1476–1499) invited the French to revive their dynastic claim to Naples. But France also had dynastic claims to Milan, and the French appetite for new territory became insatiable once French armies had crossed the Alps and reestablished themselves in Italy.

The French king Charles VIII (r. 1483–1498) responded rapidly to Ludovico's call. Within five months, he had crossed the Alps (August 1495) and raced as conqueror through Florence and the Papal States into Naples.

Charles's lightning march through Italy alarmed Ferdinand of Aragon (r. 1479–1516), who was also king of Sicily and helped to create a counteralliance: the League of Venice, which was able to force Charles to retreat.

The French returned to Italy under Charles's successor, Louis XII (r. 1498–1515), this time assisted by the Borgia pope Alexander VI (1492–1503). Alexander, probably the most corrupt pope in history, sought to secure a political base in Romagna, officially part of the Papal States, for his son Cesare.

Seeing that a French alliance could allow him to reestablish control over the region, Alexander agreed to abandon the League of Venice, which made the league too weak to resist a French reconquest of Milan. Louis successfully invaded Milan in August 1499. In 1500 he and Ferdinand of Aragon divided Naples between themselves, while the pope and Cesare Borgia conquered the Romagna without opposition.

In 1503 Cardinal Giuliano della Rovere became Pope Julius II (1503–1513). He suppressed the Borgias and placed their newly conquered lands in Romagna under papal jurisdiction. After fully securing the Papal States with French aid, Julius changed sides and sought to rid Italy of his former ally, the French invaders. Julius, Ferdinand of Aragon, and Venice formed a Holy League in October 1511, and soon Emperor Maximilian I (r. 1493–1519) and the Swiss joined them. By 1512 the French were in full retreat.

The French invaded Italy again under Louis's successor, Francis I (r. 1515–1547). French armies massacred Swiss soldiers of the Holy League at Marignano in September 1515. That victory won from the Medici pope Leo X (r. 1513–1521) an agreement known as the Concordat of Bologna (August 1516), which gave the French king control over the French clergy and the right to collect taxes from them, in exchange for French recognition of the pope's superiority over church councils. This helped keep France Catholic after the outbreak of the Protestant Reformation. But the new French entry into Italy also led to the first of four major wars with Spain in the first half of the sixteenth century: the Habsburg-Valois wars, none of which France won.

NICCOLÒ MACHIAVELLI

The foreign invasions made a shambles of Italy. One who watched as French, Spanish, and German armies wreaked havoc on his country was Niccolò Machiavelli (1469–1527). The more he saw, the more convinced he became that Italian political unity and independence were ends that justified any means. Machiavelli admired the heroic acts of ancient Roman rulers, what Renaissance people called their *Virtu*. Romanticizing the old Roman citizenry, he lamented the absence of heroism among his compatriots. Such a perspective caused his interpretation of both ancient and contemporary history to be exaggerated.

The juxtaposition of what Machiavelli believed the ancient Romans had been with the failure of contemporary Romans to realize such high ideals made him the famous cynic we know in the popular epithet *Machiavellian*. Only an unscrupulous strongman, he concluded, using duplicity and terror, could impose order on so divided and selfish a people. Machiavelli seems to have been in earnest when he advised rulers to discover the advantages of fraud and brutality. (See "Machiavelli Discusses the Most Important Trait of a Ruler.") He apparently hoped to see a strong ruler emerge from the Medici family. The Medicis, however, were not destined to be Italy's deliverers. The second Medici pope, Clement VII (r. 1523–1534), watched helplessly as Rome was sacked by the army of Emperor Charles V (r. 1519–1556) in 1527, the year of Machiavelli's death.

REVIVAL OF MONARCHY: NATION BUILDING IN THE FIFTEENTH CENTURY

With the emergence of sovereign rulers after 1450, unified national monarchies progressively replaced fragmented and divisive feudal governance. The dynastic and chivalric ideals of feudalism did not however disappear. Minor territorial princes survived, and representative assemblies even grew in influence in some regions. But by the late fifteenth and early sixteenth centuries, the old problem of the one and the many was being decided clearly in favor of monarchy.

In the feudal monarchy of the High Middle Ages the basic powers of government were divided between the king and his semiautonomous vassals. The nobility and the towns acted with varying degrees of unity and success through such evolving representative bodies as the English Parliament, the French Estates General, and the Spanish Cortes to thwart the centralization of royal power. However, as a result of the Hundred Years' War and the schism in the church, the landed nobility and the clergy were in decline in the late Middle Ages. The increasingly important towns now began to ally with the king. Loyal, businesswise townspeople, not the nobility and the clergy, staffed the royal offices, becoming the king's lawyers, bookkeepers, military tacticians, and diplomats. This new alliance between king and town would slowly break the bonds of feudal society and make possible the rise of the modern sovereign state.

In a sovereign state, the powers of taxation, war making, and law enforcement are no longer the local right of semiautonomous vassals but are

Major Political Events of the Italian Renaissance (1375–1527)	
1378–1382	Ciompi revolt in Florence
1434	Medici rule in Florence established by Cosimo de' Medici
1454–1455	Treaty of Lodi allies Milan, Naples, and Florence (in effect until 1494)
1494	Charles VIII of France invades Italy
1495	League of Venice unites Venice, Milan, the Papal States, the Holy Roman Empire, and Spain against France
1499	Louis XII invades Milan (the second French invasion of Italy)
1500	The Borgias conquer Romagna
1512–1513	The Holy League (Pope Julius II, Ferdinand of Aragon, Emperor Maximilian I, and Venice) defeat the French
1513	Machiavelli writes *The Prince*
1515	Francis I leads the third French invasion of Italy
1516	Concordat of Bologna between France and the papacy
1527	Sack of Rome by imperial soldiers

WHAT WERE the bases for the rise of the modern sovereign state in the fifteenth century?

• HISTORY'S VOICES •

MACHIAVELLI DISCUSSES THE MOST IMPORTANT TRAIT FOR A RULER

ow would you characterize Machiavelli's view of humankind?

WHY IS the ability to inspire fear more important for a ruler than the ability to inspire love? Are there any limitations on a ruler?

Here the question arises; whether it is better to be loved than feared or feared than loved. The answer is that it would be desirable to be both but, since that is difficult, it is much safer to be feared than to be loved, if one must choose. For on men in general this observation may be made: they are ungrateful, fickle, and deceitful, eager to avoid dangers, and avid for gain, and while you are useful to them they are all with you, offering you their blood, their property, their lives, and their sons so long as danger is remote . . . but when it approaches they turn on you. Any prince, trusting only in their words and having no other preparations made, will fall to his ruin, for friendships that are bought at a price and not by greatness and nobility of soul are paid for indeed, but they are not owned and cannot be called upon in time of need. Men have less hesitation in offending a man who is loved than one who is feared, for love is held by a bond of obligation which, as men are wicked, is broken whenever personal advantage suggests it, but fear is accompanied by the dread of punishment which never relaxes.

From Niccolò Machiavelli, *The Prince* (1513), trans. and ed. by Thomas G. Bergin (New York: Appleton-Century-Crofts, 1947), p. 48.

concentrated in the monarch and exercised by his chosen agents. Taxes, wars, and laws become national rather than merely regional matters. Only as monarchs were able to act independently of the nobility and the representative assemblies could they overcome the decentralization that had been the basic obstacle to nation building.

Monarchies also began to create standing national armies in the fifteenth century. As the noble cavalry receded and the infantry and the artillery became the backbone of armies, mercenary soldiers were recruited from Switzerland and Germany to form the mainstay of the "king's army."

The growing cost of warfare increased the need to develop new national sources of royal income. The expansion of royal revenues was especially hampered by the stubborn belief among the highest classes that they were immune from government taxation. The nobility guarded their properties and traditional rights and despised taxation as an insult and a humiliation. Royal revenues accordingly grew at the expense of those least able to resist and least able to pay. Monarchs had several options. As feudal lords they could collect rents from their royal domain. They might also levy national taxes on basic food and clothing, such as the *gabelle* or salt tax in France and the *alcabala* or 10 percent sales tax on commercial transactions in Spain. Kings could also levy direct taxes on the peasantry and on commercial transactions in towns under royal protection. This they did through agreeable representative assemblies of the privileged classes in which the peasantry did not sit. The French *taille* was such a tax. Sale of public offices and the issuance of high-interest government bonds appeared in the fifteenth century as innovative fund-raising devices. But kings did not levy taxes on the powerful nobility. They turned to rich nobles, as they did to the great bankers of Italy and Germany, for loans, bargaining with the privileged classes, who often remained as much the kings' creditors and competitors as their subjects.

taille The direct tax on the French peasantry.

The Cathedral of St. Basil in Moscow. Built between 1544 and 1560 during the reign of Ivan the Terrible, it reflects the enduring Byzantine influence on Russian architecture.

Sovfoto/Eastfoto

MEDIEVAL RUSSIA

In the late tenth century, Prince Vladimir of Kiev (r. 972–1015), then Russia's dominant city, received delegations of Muslims, Roman Catholics, Jews, and Greek Orthodox Christians, each group hoping to win the Russians to its religion. Prince Vladimir chose Greek Orthodoxy, which became the religion of Russia, adding a new cultural bond to the long-standing commercial ties the Russians had with the Byzantine Empire.

Vladimir's successor, Yaroslav the Wise (r. 1016–1054), developed Kiev into a magnificent political and cultural center, but after his death, rivalry among princes challenged Kiev's dominance, and it became just one of several national centers.

Mongol Rule (1243–1480)   Mongol (or Tatar) armies (see Chapters 8 and 13) invaded Russia in 1223, and Kiev fell in 1240. Russian cities became tribute-paying principalities of the segment of the Mongol Empire called the *Golden Horde*, which had its capital at Sarai, on the lower Volga.

 11.8
Kuyuk Khan, Letter to Pope Innocent IV

Golden Horde   Name given to the Mongol rulers of Russia from 1240 to 1480.

Mongol rule further divided Russia from the West but left Russian political institutions and religion largely intact. Thanks to their far-flung trade, the Mongolians brought most Russians greater peace and prosperity than they had enjoyed before.

Russian Liberation The princes of Moscow cooperated with the Mongols and grew wealthy. They then gradually expanded the principality through land purchases, colonization, and conquest.

In 1380 Grand Duke Dimitri of Moscow (1350–1389) defeated Tatar forces at Kulikov Meadow in a victory that marked the beginning of the decline of Mongolian hegemony. Another century would pass before Ivan III, called Ivan the Great (d. 1505), would bring all of northern Russia under Moscow's control and end Mongol rule in 1480. By the last quarter of the fifteenth century, Moscow had replaced Kiev as the political and religious center of Russia. In Russian eyes it was destined to become the "third Rome" after the fall of Constantinople to the Turks in 1453.

FRANCE

There were two cornerstones of French nation building in the fifteenth century. The first was the collapse of the English holdings in France following the Hundred Years' War. The second was the defeat of Charles the Bold (r. 1467–1477) and the duchy of Burgundy. Perhaps Europe's strongest political power in the mid-fifteenth century, Burgundy aspired to lead a dominant middle kingdom between France and the Holy Roman Empire. It might have succeeded had not the Continental powers joined together in opposition. When Charles the Bold was killed at Nancy in 1477, the dream of Burgundian empire died with him.

The dissolution of Burgundy ended its constant intrigue against the French king and left Louis XI (r. 1461–1483) free to secure the monarchy. The newly acquired Burgundian lands and his own Angevin inheritance permitted the king to double the size of his kingdom. Louis harnessed the nobility and expanded trade and industry.

A strong nation is a two-edged sword. It was because Louis's successors inherited such a secure and efficient government that France was able to pursue Italian conquests in the 1490s and to fight a long series of losing wars with the Habsburgs in the first half of the sixteenth century. By the mid-sixteenth century France was again a defeated nation and almost as divided internally as it had been during the Hundred Years' War.

SPAIN

Spain, too, became a strong country in the late fifteenth century. Both Castile and Aragon had been poorly ruled, divided kingdoms in the mid-fifteenth century. The marriage of Isabella of Castile (r. 1474–1504) and Ferdinand of Aragon (r. 1479–1516) changed that situation. The two future sovereigns married in 1469, despite strong protests from neighboring Portugal and France, both of which foresaw the formidable European power such a union would create. Castile was by far the richer and more populous of the two, having an estimated five million inhabitants to Aragon's population of under one million. Castile was also distinguished by its lucrative sheep-farming industry, which was run by a government-backed organization called the *Mesta*, another example of developing centralized economic planning. Although the two kingdoms were dynastically united by the marriage of Ferdinand and Isabella in 1469, each retained its own government agencies—separate laws, armies, coinage, and taxation—and cultural traditions.

Ferdinand and Isabella could do together what neither was able to accomplish alone: subdue their realms, secure their borders, and venture abroad militarily. Townspeople allied themselves with the crown and progressively replaced the nobility within the royal administration. The crown also extended its authority over the wealthy chivalric orders, a further circumscription of the power of the nobility.

Spain had long been remarkable as a place where three religions—Islam, Judaism, and Christianity—coexisted with a certain degree of toleration. This toleration ended dramatically under Ferdinand and Isabella, who made Spain the prime example of state-controlled religion. Ferdinand and Isabella exercised almost total control over the Spanish church as they placed religion in the service of national unity. They appointed the higher clergy and the officers of the Inquisition. The Inquisition, run by Tomás de Torquemada (d. 1498), Isabella's confessor, was a key national agency established in 1479 to monitor the activity of converted Jews (*conversos*) and Muslims (*Moriscos*) in Spain. In 1492 the Jews were exiled and their properties were confiscated. In 1502 nonconverting Moors in Granada were driven into exile. Spanish spiritual life remained largely uniform and regimented, a major reason for Spain's remaining a loyal Catholic country throughout the sixteenth century and providing a base of operation for the European Counter-Reformation.

Ferdinand and Isabella had wide horizons. They contracted anti-French marriage alliances that came to determine much of European history in the sixteenth century. In 1496 their eldest daughter, Joanna, later known as "the Mad" (1479–1555), married Archduke Philip (1478–1506), the son of Emperor Maximilian I (r. 1493–1519). Their son, Charles I, the first ruler over a united Spain, came by his inheritance and election as Emperor Charles V in 1519 to rule over a European kingdom almost equal in size to that of Charlemagne. A second daughter, Catherine of Aragon (1485–1536), married King Henry VIII of England. The failure of this latter marriage became the key factor in the emergence of the Anglican Church and the English Reformation.

The new Spanish power was also evident in Ferdinand and Isabella's promotion of overseas exploration. Their patronage of the Genoese adventurer Christopher Columbus (1451–1506), who discovered the islands of the Caribbean while sailing west in search of a shorter route to the spice markets of the Far East, led to the creation of the Spanish Empire in Mexico and Peru, whose gold and silver mines helped to make Spain Europe's dominant power in the sixteenth century.

ENGLAND

The last half of the fifteenth century was a period of especially difficult political trial for the English. Following the Hundred Years' War, a defeated England was subjected to internal warfare between two rival branches of the royal family, the House of York and the House of Lancaster. This conflict, known to us today as the Wars of the Roses (as York's symbol, according to legend, was a white rose, and Lancaster's a red rose), kept England in turmoil from 1455 to 1485.

The Lancastrian monarchy of Henry VI (r. 1422–1461) was consistently challenged by the Duke of York and his supporters in the prosperous southern towns. In 1461 Edward IV (r. 1461–1483), son of the Duke of York, seized power and, assisted by loyal and able ministers, effectively bent Parliament to his will. His brother and successor was Richard III (r. 1483–1485), whose reign saw the growth of support for the exiled Lancastrian Henry Tudor. Henry returned to England to defeat Richard on Bosworth Field in August 1485.

Henry Tudor ruled as Henry VII (r. 1485–1509), the first of the new Tudor dynasty that would endure until 1603. To bring the rival royal families together and to make the hereditary claim of his offspring to the throne uncontestable, Henry married Edward IV's daughter, Elizabeth of York. He succeeded in disciplining the English nobility through a special and much-feared instrument of the royal will known as the Court of Star Chamber. Henry shrewdly construed legal precedents to the advantage of the crown, using English law to further his own ends. He confiscated so much noble land and fortunes that he governed without dependence on Parliament for royal funds, always a cornerstone of strong monarchy. Henry thus began to shape a monarchy that became one of early modern Europe's most exemplary governments during the reign of his granddaughter, Elizabeth I (r. 1558–1603).

SUMMARY

Medieval Society Medieval society was divided in theory into three main groups: clergy (those who prayed), nobility (those who fought as mounted warriors), and laborers (peasants and artisans). The rise of merchants, self-governing towns, and universities helped break down this division. By supporting rulers against the nobility, towns gave kings the resources—money and university-trained bureaucrats and lawyers—to build national governments. Much of medieval history involves the struggle by rulers to assert their authority over powerful local lords and the church.

Church and State The medieval papacy sought to extend its power over both church and state. In the tenth century, the Cluny reform movement increased popular respect for the church and strengthened the papacy. In the Investiture Struggle, the papacy secured the independence of the clergy by enlisting the support of the German princes against the Holy Roman Emperors, thus weakening imperial power in Germany. The First Crusade further strengthened papal prestige. But, by the end of the thirteenth century, kings had become more powerful than popes, and the French king, Philip the Fair, was able to defy the papacy. In the fourteenth century, the Great Schism further weakened papal prestige. Although it was able to fend off a movement to make church councils superior to popes, the papacy never recovered its authority over national rulers.

Nation Building By the fifteenth century, England, France, and Spain had developed into strong national monarchies with centralized bureaucracies and professional armies. Although medieval institutions, such as the English Parliament, in theory limited royal power, in practice monarchs in these countries held unchallenged authority. The Great Schism, the Hundred Years' War, and the Black Death had weakened the church and the nobility, while townspeople supported the kings. A similar process was beginning in Russia where the rulers of Moscow were extending their authority after throwing off Mongol rule. In the Empire, however, regional lords had defeated the emperors' attempts to build a strong central state.

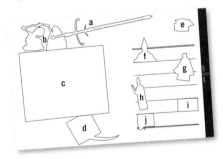

IMAGE KEY
for pages 296–297

a. Two-handed sword, circa 1600
b. "A Dance of Death" by Hartmann Schedel
c. Students attending a lecture, detail of the Tomb of Giovanni da Legnano
d. "Q" in a square on a page from Divina Proportione, by Luca Pacioli
e. Plan by Leonardo da Vinci for a flying machine
f. Pope Innocent III
g. Medieval monk's habit
h. Statue of Pope Boniface VIII
i. Cosimo de' Medici
j. Joan of Arc

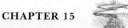

The Renaissance The Renaissance, which began in the Italian city-states in the late fourteenth century, marks the transition from the medieval to the modern world. Humanism, the scholarly study of the Greek and Latin classics and the ancient Church fathers, promoted a rebirth of ancient norms and values and the classical ideal of an educated, well rounded person. The growth of secular values led to a great burst of artistic activity by artists such as da Vinci, Raphael, and Michelangelo. The political weakness of the Italian states invited foreign intervention by France, Spain, and the Habsburgs. The sack of Rome by imperial forces in 1527 marks the end of the Renaissance.

REVIEW QUESTIONS

1. Why did the Cluny reform movement succeed?

2. Was the investiture controversy a political or a religious conflict?

3. Why did Germany remain divided while France and England began to unite into strong states during the High Middle Ages?

4. How did the responsibilities of the nobility differ from those of the clergy and the peasantry during the High Middle Ages?

5. What gave rise to towns, and how did they change traditional medieval society?

6. What was "reborn" in the Renaissance?

KEY TERMS

Black Death (p. 314)

chiaroscuro (p. 318)

Crusades (p. 300)

Curia (p. 315)

Golden Horde (p. 323)

Great Schism (p. 315)

guild (p. 302)

Holy Roman Empire (p. 315)

humanism (p. 316)

Magna Carta (p. 308)

mannerism (p. 319)

regular clergy (p. 305)

Renaissance (p. 316)

Scholasticism (p. 304)

secular clergy (p. 305)

studia humanitatis (p. 316)

taille (p. 322)

vernacular (p. 317)

  For additional study resources for this chapter, go to:
www.prenhall.com/craig/chapter15

PART 4 · THE WORLD IN TRANSITION

EUROPE

1517–1555	Protestant Reformation
1533–1584	Ivan the Terrible of Russia reigns
1540	Jesuit Order founded by Ignatius Loyola
1543–1727	Scientific Revolution
1556–1598	Philip II of Spain reigns
1558–1603	Elizabeth I of England reigns
1562–1598	French Wars of Religion
1581	The Netherlands declares its independence from the Spanish Habsburgs
1588	Defeat of the Spanish Armada
1589–1610	Henry IV, Navarre, founds Bourbon dynasty of France

▲ Queen Elizabeth I

NEAR EAST / INDIA

1500–1722	Safavid Shi'ite rule in Iran
1512–1520	Ottoman ruler Selim I
1520–1566	Ottoman ruler Suleiman the Magnificent
1525–1527	Babur founds Mughal dynasty in India
1540	Hungary under Ottoman rule
1556–1605	Akbar the Great of India reigns
1571	Battle of Lepanto; Ottomans defeated
ca. 1571–1640	Safavid philosopher-writer Mullah Sadra
1588–1629	Shah Abbas I of Iran reigns

Leaf from "Divan" ▶
by the poet, Hafiz

EAST ASIA

1500–1800	Commercial revolution in Ming-Ch'ing China; trade with Europe; flourishing of the novel
1543	Portuguese arrive in Japan
1568–1600	Era of unification follows end of Warring States Era in Japan
1587	Spanish arrive in Japan
1588	Hideyoshi's sword hunt in Japan
1592–1598	Ming troops battle Hideyoshi's army in Korea

Feluccas ▶
on the Nile

AFRICA

1506	East coast pf Africa under Portuguese domination
1507	Mozambique founded by Portuguese
1517	Spanish crown authorizes slave trade to its South American colonies; rapid increase in importation of slaves to the New World
1554–1659	Sa'did Sultanate in Morocco
1575	Union of Bornu and Kanem by Idris Alawma (r. 1575–1610); Kanem-Bornu state the most fully Islamic in West Africa
1591	Moroccan army defeats Songhai army; Songhai Empire collapses

THE AMERICAS

1519	Conquest of the Aztecs by Cortes; Aztec ruler, Montezuma (r. 1502–1519) killed; Tenochtitlán destroyed
1529	Mexico City becomes capital of the viceroyalty of New Spain
1533	Pizarro begins his conquest of the Incas
1536	Spanish under Mendoza arrive in Argentina
1544	Lima becomes capital of the viceroyalty of Peru
1584	Sir Walter Raleigh sends expedition to Roanoke Island (North Carolina)

◀ Algonquin village of Secotton

▲ Aztec drawing of Spanish conquest of Mexico

1618–1648	Thirty Years' War
1640–1688	Frederick William, the Great Elector, reigns in Brandenburg-Prussia
1642–1646	Puritan Revolution in England
1643–1715	Louis XIV of France reigns
1682–1725	Peter the Great of Russia reigns
1688	Glorious Revolution in England
1690	"Second Treatise of Civil Government," by John Locke

◄ Louis XIV of France

1701	Act of Settlement provides for Protestant succession to English throne
1702–1713	War of Spanish Succession
1740–1748	War of Austrian Succession
1756–1763	Seven Years' War
ca. 1750	Industrial Revolution begins in England
1772	First partition of Poland
1789	First French Revolution
1793 and 1795	Last two partitions of Poland

▲ "Evening" by Francis Wheatley

1628–1657	Shah Jahan reigns; builds Taj Mahal as mausoleum for his beloved wife
1646	Founding of Maratha Empire
1648	Delhi becomes the capital of Mughal Empire
1658–1707	Shah Aurangzeb, the "World Conqueror," reigns in India; end of religious toleration toward Hindus; beginning Mughal decline
1669–1683	Last military expansion by Ottomans: 1669, seize Crete; 1670s, the Ukraine; 1683, Vienna

▲ The Taj Mahal

1700	Sikhs and Marathas bring down Mughal Imperial Power
1708	British East India Company and New East India Company merge
1722	Last Safavid ruler forced to abdicate
1724	Rise in the Deccan of the Islamic state of Hyderabad
1725	Nadir Shah of Afganhistan becomes ruler of Persia
1739	Persian invasion of northern India, by Nadir Shah
1748–1761	Ahmad Shah Durrani of Afghanistan invades India
1757	British victory at Plassey, in Bengal

1600	Tokugawa Ieyasu wins battle of Sekigahara, completes unification of Japan
1600–1868	Tokugawa shogunate in Edo
1630s	Seclusion adopted as national policy in Japan
1644–1694	Bashō, Japanese poet
1644–1911	Ch'ing (Manchu) dynasty in China
1661-1722	K'ang Hsi reign in China
1673–1681	Revolt of southern generals in China
1699	British East India Company arrives in China

◄ "White Heron" castle in Jimeji

1701	Forty-seven ro-nin incident in Japan
1716–1733	Reforms of Tokugawa Yoshimune in Japan
1737–1795	Reign of Ch'ien Lung in China
1742	Christianity banned in China
1784	American traders arrive in China
1787–1793	Matsudaira Sadanobu's reforms in Japan
1798	White Lotus Rebellion in China

Manchu emperor ► Ch'ien Lung

1600s	English, Dutch, and French enter the slave trade; slaves imported to sugar plantations in the Caribbean
1619	First African slaves in North America land in Virginia
1652	First Cape Colony settlement of Dutch East India Company
1660–1856	Omani domination of East Africa; Omani state centered in Zanzibar; 1698, takes Mozambique from Portuguese

◄ Slave labor on sugar plantation in Brazil and the West Indies

1702	Asiento Guinea Trade Company founded for slave trade between Africa and the Americas
1700s	Transatlantic slave trade at its height
1741–1856	United Sultanate of Oman and Zanzibar
1754–1817	Usman Dan Fodio, founder of sultanate in northern and central Nigeria; the Fulani become the ruling class in the region
1762	End of Funj Sultanate in eastern Sudanic region

◄ The Friday Mosque at Shela

1607	The London Company establishes Jamestown Colony (Virginia)
1608	Champlain founds Quebec
1619	Slave labor introduced at Jamestown (Virginia)

1733	Georgia founded as last English colony in North America
1739–1763	Era of trade wars in Americas between Great Britain and the French and Spanish
1763	Peace of Paris establishes British government in Canada
1776–1781	American Revolution
1783–1830	Simón Bolívar, Latin American soldier, statesman
1789	U.S. Constitution
1791	Negro slave revolt in French Santo Domingo
1791	Canada Constitution Act divides the country into Upper and Lower Canada

A Catholic portrayal of Martin Luther tempting Jesus (1547). Reformation propaganda often portrayed the pope as the Antichrist or the devil. Here Catholic propaganda turns the tables on the Protestant reformers by portraying a figure of Martin Luther as the devil (note the monstrous feet and tail under his academic robes). Versuchung Christi 1547, Gemälde, Bonn, Rheinisches Landesmuseum, Inv. Nr. 58.3

16

THE AGE OF REFORMATION AND RELIGIOUS WARS

WHAT WERE the motives for the European voyages of discovery in the late fifteenth and sixteenth centuries?

WHY DID Martin Luther break with the Roman Catholic Church?

HOW DID the Reformation change religious and social life?

WHAT WAS the final result of the wars of religion in France, the Netherlands, and Germany?

WHY DID witch hunts and panics erupt across Western Europe between 1400 and 1700?

IMAGE KEY
Image Key for pages 330–331
is on page 367.

In the second decade of the sixteenth century, a powerful religious movement began in Saxony in Germany and rapidly spread throughout northern Europe, deeply affecting society and politics as well as the spiritual lives of men and women. Attacking what they believed to be burdensome superstitions that robbed people of both their money and their peace of mind, Protestant reformers led a revolt against the medieval church. In a short time, hundreds of thousands of people from all social classes set aside the beliefs of centuries and adopted a more simplified religious practice.

The Protestant Reformation challenged aspects of the Renaissance, especially its tendency to follow classical sources in glorifying human nature and its loyalty to traditional religion. Protestants were more impressed by the human potential for evil than by the inclination to do good; they encouraged parents, teachers, and magistrates to be firm disciplinarians. On the other hand, Protestants also embraced many Renaissance values, especially in educational reform and in learning ancient languages, for here they found the tools to master Scripture and challenge the papacy.

Protestantism was not the only reform movement to grow out of the religious grievances and reforms of the late Middle Ages. Within the church itself a reform was emerging that would give birth to new religious orders, rebut Protestantism, and win back a great many of its converts.

As different groups identified their political and social goals with either Protestantism or Catholicism, a hundred years of bloody opposition between Protestants and Catholics darkened the second half of the sixteenth century and the first half of the seventeenth. In the second half of the sixteenth century the political conflict that had previously been confined to central Europe and a struggle for Lutheran rights and freedoms shifted to western Europe—to France, the Netherlands, England, and Scotland—and became a struggle for Calvinist recognition. In France Calvinists fought Catholic rulers for the right to form their own communities, to practice their chosen religion openly, and to exclude from their lands those they deemed heretical. During the Thirty Years' War (1618–1648), international armies of varying religious persuasions clashed in central and northern Europe. By 1649 English Puritans had overthrown the Stuart monarchy and the Anglican Church.

For Europe the late fifteenth and the sixteenth centuries were also a period of unprecedented territorial expansion. Permanent colonies were established within the Americas, and the exploitation of the New World's human and mineral resources began. Imported American gold and silver spurred scientific invention and a new weapons industry. The new bullion also helped create an international traffic in African slaves as rival tribes sold their captives to the Portuguese. These slaves were brought in ever-increasing numbers to work the mines and the plantations of the New World as replacements for faltering American natives.

ON THE EVE OF THE REFORMATION

THE DISCOVERY OF A NEW WORLD

WHAT WERE the motives for the European voyages of discovery in the late fifteenth and sixteenth centuries?

The discovery of the Americas dramatically expanded the geographical and intellectual horizons of Europeans. Knowledge of the New World's inhabitants and exploitation of its vast wealth set new cultural and economic forces in motion throughout western Europe. Beginning with the successful voyages of Christopher Columbus (1451–1506) in the late fifteenth century, commercial supremacy started to shift from the Mediterranean and the Baltic to the Atlantic seaboard, and western Europe's global expansion began in earnest (see Map 16–1).

Gold and Spices   Mercenary motives, reinforced by traditional missionary ideals, had earlier inspired Prince Henry the Navigator (1394–1460) to sponsor Portuguese exploration of the African coast. His main object was the gold trade, which

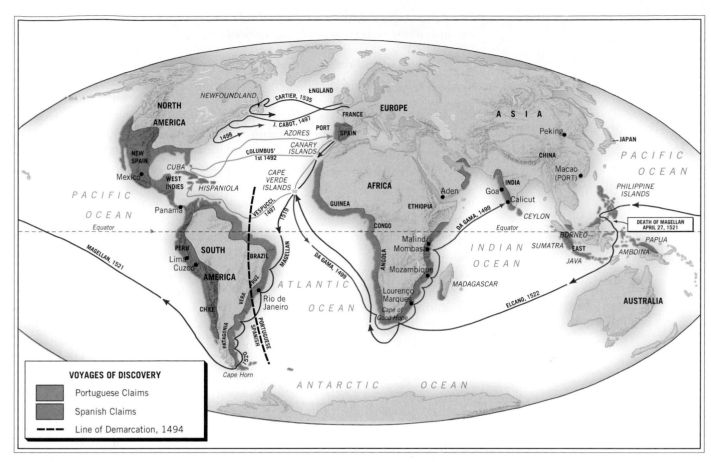

MAP 16–1
European voyages of discovery and the colonial claims of Spain and Portugal in the fifteenth and sixteenth centuries.
The map dramatizes Europe's global expansion in the fifteenth and sixteenth centuries.

WHY DID Europeans want to find a sea route to Asia?

Muslims had monopolized for centuries. By the late fifteenth century, gold from Guinea was entering Europe on Portuguese ships calling at the port cities of Lisbon and Antwerp, rather than via the traditional Arab overland routes. Antwerp became the financial center of Europe, a commercial crossroads where enterprise and daring could find capital funds.

The rush for gold quickly expanded into a rush for the spice markets of India as well. In the fifteenth century most Europeans ate a dull combination of bread and gruel, cabbage, turnips, peas, lentils, and onions, together with what meat became available during seasonal periods of slaughter. Spices, especially pepper and cloves, were in great demand both as preservatives and to enhance the taste of food.

Bartholomew Dias (d. 1500) opened the Portuguese Empire in the East when he rounded the Cape of Good Hope at the tip of Africa in 1487. A decade later, in 1498, Vasco da Gama (d. 1524) stood on the shores of India. When he returned to Portugal, his cargo was worth sixty times the cost of the voyage. Later, the Portuguese established themselves firmly on the Malabar coast with colonies in Goa and Calcutta and successfully challenged the Arabs and the Venetians for control of the European spice trade.

While the Portuguese concentrated on the Indian Ocean, the Spanish set sail across the Atlantic, hoping to establish a shorter route to the rich spice markets

of the East Indies. Rather than beat the Portuguese at their own game, however, Columbus discovered the Americas instead.

The Voyages of Columbus On October 12, 1492, after a 33-day voyage from the Canary Islands, Columbus landed in San Salvador (Watlings Island) in the eastern Bahamas. Having undertaken his journey in the belief that Japan would be the first landmass he would reach as he sailed west, he thought San Salvador was an outer island of Japan. That belief was based on Marco Polo's account of his years in China during the thirteenth century and the global map of Martin Behaim, which showed only ocean between the west coast of Europe and the east coast of Asia.

14.5
Christopher Columbus

Naked and extremely friendly natives met Columbus and his crew on the beaches of the New World. They were Taino Indians, who spoke a variant of a language known as Arawak. Mistaking the island for the East Indies, Columbus called the native people Indians, a name that stuck even after it became known that he had discovered a new continent. The natives' generosity amazed Columbus. They freely gave his men all the corn and yams they desired, along with many sexual favors as well. "They never say no," Columbus marveled. At the same time he observed how easily they could be enslaved.

On the heels of Columbus, Amerigo Vespucci (1451–1512), after whom America is named, and Ferdinand Magellan (1480–1521) carefully explored the coastline of South America. Their travels documented that the new lands discovered by Columbus were not the outermost territory of the Far East, but a new continent that opened on the still greater Pacific Ocean. Magellan, in search of a westward route to the East Indies, sailed to the Philippines, where he died.

Impact on Europe and America Columbus's voyage of 1492 marked, unknowingly to those who undertook and financed it, the beginning of more than three centuries of Spanish conquest, exploitation, and administration of a vast American empire. What had begun as voyages of discovery soon became expeditions of conquest that resembled the warfare of Christian Aragon and Castile against the Islamic Moors. Those wars had just ended in 1492, and they imbued the early Spanish explorers with a zeal for conquering and converting non-Christian peoples.

The voyages to the New World had important consequences for the cultures of both Europe and America. For Spain the venture created the largest and longest-surviving European trading bloc, while spurring other European countries to undertake their own colonial ventures. The great wealth from its American possessions financed Spain's commanding role in the age's religious and political conflicts. It also ignited a gradual, Europe-wide inflation during the sixteenth century.

For the native peoples of America, the voyages triggered a long period of conquest that virtually destroyed their civilizations, as warfare, new diseases, and exploitation of labor and resources devastated their populations. In both South and North America, Spanish rule set an imprint of Roman Catholicism, economic dependency, and hierarchical social structure that is still highly visible today.

RELIGION AND SOCIETY

The Reformation broke out first in the free imperial cities of Germany and Switzerland. There were about 65 such cities, and each was in a sense a little kingdom unto itself. Most had Protestant movements, but with mixed success and duration. Some quickly turned Protestant and remained so. Some were Protestant only for a short time. Others developed mixed confessions, frowning on sectarianism and aggressive proselytizing, and letting Catholics and Protestants coexist.

What seemed a life-and-death struggle with higher princely or royal authority was not the only conflict cities were experiencing. They also suffered deep internal social and political divisions. Certain groups favored the Reformation more than others. In many places, guilds like that of the printers, whose members were prospering both socially and economically, and who had a history of conflict with local authority, were in the forefront of the Reformation. Evidence suggests that people who felt pushed around and bullied by either local or distant authority—a guild by an autocratic local government; a city or region by a prince or king—perceived in the Protestant movement an ally, at least initially.

Social and political experience thus coalesced with the larger religious issues in both town and countryside. When Martin Luther and his comrades wrote, preached, and sang about a priesthood of all believers, scorned the authority of ecclesiastical landlords, and ridiculed papal laws as arbitrary human inventions, they touched political as well as religious nerves in German and Swiss cities. This was also true in the villages, for the peasants on the land also heard in the Protestant sermon and pamphlet a promise of political liberation and even a degree of social betterment.

The printing press made possible the diffusion of Renaissance learning. But no book stimulated throught more at this time than did the Bible. With Gutemberg's publication of a printed Bible in 1454, scholars gained access to a dependable, standardized text, so that Scripture could be discussed and debated as never before.

Huntigton Library

Popular Movements and Criticism of the Church   The Protestant Reformation could also not have occurred without the monumental crises of the late medieval church and the Renaissance papacy. For many people, the church had ceased to provide a viable foundation for religious piety. Laity and clerics alike began to seek a more heartfelt, idealistic, and often—in the eyes of the pope—increasingly heretical religious piety. The late Middle Ages were marked by independent lay and clerical efforts to reform local religious practice and by widespread experimentation with new religious forms that shared a common goal of religious simplicity in imitation of Christ.

A variety of factors contributed to the growth of lay criticism of the church. The laity in the cities were becoming increasingly knowledgeable about the world and those who controlled their lives. They traveled widely—as soldiers, pilgrims, explorers, and traders. New postal systems and the printing press increased the information at their disposal. The new age of books and libraries raised literacy and heightened curiosity. Laypersons were increasingly able to take the initiative in shaping the cultural life of their communities.

Secular Control over Religious Life   On the eve of the Reformation, Rome's international network of church offices began to fall apart in many areas, hurried along by a growing sense of regional identity—incipient nationalism—and local secular administrative competence. The late medieval church had permitted important ecclesiastical posts ("benefices") to be sold to the highest bidders and had not enforced residency requirements in parishes. Rare was the late medieval German town that did not have complaints about the maladministration, concubinage, or fiscalism of its clergy, especially the higher clergy (bishops, abbots, and prelates).

City governments also sought to restrict the growth of ecclesiastical properties and clerical privileges and to improve local religious life by bringing the clergy under the local tax code and by endowing new clerical positions for well-trained and conscientious preachers.

THE NORTHERN RENAISSANCE

The scholarly works of northern humanists created a climate favorable to religious and educational reforms. Northern humanism was initially stimulated by the importation of Italian learning through such varied intermediaries as students who had studied in Italy, merchants, and the Brothers of the Common Life. The northern humanists tended to come from more diverse social backgrounds and to be more devoted to religious reforms than were their Italian counterparts. They were also more willing to write for lay audiences.

The growth of schools and lay education combined with the invention of cheap paper to create a mass audience for printed books. In response, Johann Gutenberg (d. 1468) invented printing with movable type in the German city of Mainz around 1450. Thereafter, books were rapidly and handsomely produced on topics both profound and practical. By 1500, printing presses operated in at least 60 German cities and in more than 200 throughout Europe. A new medium now existed for politicians, humanists, and reformers alike.

The most famous of the northern humanists was Desiderius Erasmus (1466–1536), the "prince of the humanists." Idealistic and pacifistic, Erasmus gained fame as both an educational and a religious reformer. He aspired to unite the classical ideals of humanity and civic virtue with the Christian ideals of love and piety. He believed that disciplined study of the classics and the Bible, if begun early enough, was the best way to reform both individuals and society. He summarized his own beliefs with the phrase *philosophia Christi*, a simple, ethical piety in imitation of Christ. He set this ideal against what he believed to be the dogmatic, ceremonial, and factious religious practice of the late Middle Ages. To promote his own religious beliefs, Erasmus edited the works of the Church Fathers and made a Greek edition of the New Testament (1516), which became the basis for a new, more accurate Latin translation (1519). Martin Luther later used both these works as the basis for his famous German translation.

The best known of early English humanists was Sir Thomas More (1478–1535), a close friend of Erasmus. It was while visiting More that Erasmus wrote his most famous work, *The Praise of Folly* (1511), an amusing and profound exposé of human self-deception that was quickly translated from the original Latin into many vernacular languages. More's *Utopia* (1516), a criticism of contemporary society, depicts an imaginary society based on reason and tolerance that requires everyone to work and has rid itself of all social and political injustice. Although More would remain staunchly Catholic, humanism in England, as in Germany, paved the way for the English Reformation. A circle of English humanists, under the direction of Henry VIII's minister Thomas Cromwell, translated and disseminated late medieval criticisms of the papacy and many of Erasmus's satirical writings as well.

Whereas in Germany, England, and France humanism helped the Protestants, in Spain it entered the service of the Catholic Church. Here the key figure was Francisco Jiménez de Cisneros (1437–1517), a confessor to Queen Isabella, and after 1508 Grand Inquisitor—a position from which he was able to enforce the strictest religious orthodoxy. Jiménez was a conduit for humanist scholarship and learning. He founded the University of Alcalá near Madrid in 1509, printed a Greek edition of the New Testament, and translated many religious tracts that aided clerical reform and control of lay religious life. His greatest achievement, taking 15 years to complete, was the Complutensian Polyglot Bible, a six-volume work that placed the Hebrew, Greek, and Latin versions of the Bible in parallel columns. Such scholarly projects and internal church reforms joined with the repressive measures of Ferdinand and Isabella to keep Spain strictly Catholic.

THE REFORMATION

MARTIN LUTHER AND THE GERMAN REFORMATION TO 1525

Late medieval Germany lacked the political unity to enforce "national" religious reforms during the late Middle Ages. What happened on a unified national level in England and France occurred only locally and piecemeal in Germany. As popular resentment of clerical immunities and ecclesiastical abuses, especially regarding the selling of indulgences, spread among German cities and towns, an unorganized "national" opposition to Rome formed. German humanists had long given voice to such criticism, and by 1517 it provided a solid foundation for Martin Luther's reform.

Luther (1483–1546), the son of a successful Thuringian miner, attended the University of Erfurt, taking a master of arts degree in 1505. He registered with the Law Faculty, but he never began that course of study. To the shock and disappointment of his parents, he joined the Order of the Hermits of Saint Augustine in Erfurt on July 17, 1505. In 1511 he was transferred to the Augustinian monastery in Wittenberg, where he earned his doctorate in theology (1512), thereafter to become a leader within the monastery, the new university, and the spiritual life of the city.

The Attack on Indulgences   **Reformation** theology grew out of a problem common to many clergy and laity at this time: the failure of traditional medieval religion to provide full personal or intellectual satisfaction. Luther was especially plagued by the disproportion between his own sense of sinfulness and the perfect righteousness that medieval theology taught that God required for salvation. Traditional church teaching and the sacraments were no consolation. Luther wrote that he came to despise the phrase "righteousness of God," for it seemed to demand of him a perfection he knew neither he nor any other human being could ever achieve. His insight into the meaning of "justification by faith alone" was a gradual process that extended over several years, between 1513 and 1518. The righteousness God demands, he concluded, does not come from many religious works but is present in full measure in those who believe and trust in the redemptive life and death of Jesus Christ.

This new theology made **indulgences** unacceptable. An indulgence was a remission of the temporal penalty imposed by the priest on penitents as a "work of satisfaction" for their sins. According to medieval theology, after the priest had absolved penitents of guilt for their sins, God still imposed on them a temporal penalty, a manageable "work of satisfaction" that the penitent could perform here and now (for example, through prayers, fasting, almsgiving, retreats, and pilgrimages). Penitents who defaulted on such prescribed works of satisfaction could expect to suffer for their sins in purgatory.

At this point, indulgences became an aid to laity made genuinely anxious by their belief in a future suffering in purgatory for unrepented sins. Originally, indulgences had been given only for the true self-sacrifice of going on a crusade to the Holy Land. By Luther's time, they were regularly dispensed for small cash payments (modest sums that were regarded as almsgiving) and were presented to the laity as remitting not only their own future punishments, but also those of their dead relatives presumed to be suffering in purgatory.

In 1517 a Jubilee indulgence, proclaimed under Pope Julius II (r. 1503–1513) to raise funds for the rebuilding of Saint Peter's in Rome, was revived and preached

WHY DID Martin Luther break with the Roman Catholic Church?

 **13.4**
Martin Luther

Reformation   The sixteenth-century religious movement that sought to reform the Roman Catholic Church and led to the establishment of Protestantism.

indulgences   Remission of the temporal penalty of punishment in purgatory that remained after sins had been forgiven.

A Catholic portrayal of Martin Luther tempting Jesus (1547). Reformation propaganda often portrayed the pope as the Antichrist or the devil. Here Catholic propaganda turns the tables on the Protestant reformers by portraying a figure of Martin Luther as the devil (note the monstrous feet and tail under his academic robes)

Versuchung Christi, 1547, Gemälde, Bonn, Rheinisches Landesmuseum, Inv. Nr. 58.3

on the borders of Saxony in the territories of Archbishop Albrecht of Mainz, who had large debts. The selling of the indulgence was a joint venture by Albrecht, the Augsburg banking house of Fugger, and Pope Leo X (r. 1513–1521), half the proceeds going to the pope and half to Albrecht and his creditors. The famous indulgence preacher John Tetzel (d. 1519) exhorted the crowds:

> Don't you hear the voices of your dead parents and other relatives crying out, "Have mercy on us, for we suffer great punishment and pain. From this you could release us with a few alms. . . . We have created you, fed you, cared for you, and left you our temporal goods. Why do you treat us so cruelly and leave us to suffer in the flames, when it takes only a little to save us?"[1]

When on October 31, 1517, Luther posted his 95 theses against indulgences on the door of Castle Church in Wittenberg, he condemned the impression created by Tetzel that indulgences remitted sins and released the dead from punishment in purgatory.

Election of Charles V and the Diet of Worms   As sanctions were being prepared against Luther, Emperor Maximilian I died (January 12, 1519), diverting attention from heresy in Saxony to the contest for a new emperor. The pope backed the French king, Francis I. However, Charles I of Spain, then 19, succeeded his grandfather and became Emperor Charles V (r. 1519–1556). Charles was assisted by a long tradition of Habsburg imperial rule and massive Fugger loans, which secured the votes of the seven electors.

During the same month in which Charles was elected emperor, Luther debated (June 27, 1519) the Ingolstadt professor John Eck (1486–1543) in Leipzig. During this contest Luther challenged the infallibility of the pope and the inerrancy of church councils, appealing for the first time to the sovereign authority of Scripture alone. He burned all his bridges to the old church when he defended Jan Hus, a condemned heretic. In 1520 Luther signaled his new direction with three famous pamphlets: the *Address to the Christian Nobility of the German Nation*, which urged the German princes to force reforms on the Roman Church, especially to curtail its political and economic power in Germany; the *Babylonian Captivity of the Church*, which attacked the traditional seven sacraments, arguing that only two were proper, and which exalted the authority of Scripture, church councils, and secular princes over that of the pope; and the eloquent *Freedom of a Christian*, which summarized the new teaching of salvation by faith alone. On June 15, 1520, the papal bull *Exsurge Domine* condemned Luther for heresy and gave him 60 days to retract. The final bull of excommunication, *Decet Pontificem Romanum*, came on January 3, 1521.

In April 1521 Luther presented his views before a diet of the empire in Worms, over which Charles V presided. Ordered to recant, Luther refused. On May 26, 1521, he was placed under the imperial ban, thereafter an "outlaw" within the empire. Saxon Elector Frederick the Wise, who for largely political reasons became his protector, hid him in Wartburg Castle. There he spent almost a year in seclusion, from April 1521 to March 1522. During his stay he translated the New Testament into German, using Erasmus's new Greek text, and he attempted by correspondence to oversee the first stages of the Reformation in Wittenberg.

The Reformation was greatly assisted in these early years by the emperor's war with France and the advance of the Ottoman Turks into eastern Europe. Against

Diet of Worms The meeting of the representatives (diet) of the Holy Roman Empire presided over by the Emperor Charles V at the German city of Worms in 1521 at which Martin Luther was ordered to recant his ninety-five theses. Luther refused and was declared outlaw although he was protected by the Elector of Saxony and other German princes.

---

[1] *Die Reformation in Augenzeugen Berichten*, ed. by Helmar Junghans (Dusseldorf: Karl Rauch Verlag, 1967), p. 44.

The punishment of a peasant leader in a village near Heilbronn. After the defeat of rebellious peasants in and around the city of Heilbronn, Jacob Rorbach, a well-to-do peasant leader from a nearby village, was tied to a stake and slowly roasted to death.

© Badische Landesbibliothek

both adversaries Charles V, who also remained a Spanish king with dynastic responsibilities outside the empire, needed German troops; to that end, he promoted friendly relations with the German princes. Between 1521 and 1559, Spain (the Habsburg dynasty) and France (the Valois dynasty) fought four major wars. In 1526 the Turks overran Hungary at the Battle of Mohacs, while in western Europe the French-led League of Cognac formed against Charles for the second Habsburg-Valois war. Thus preoccupied, the emperor agreed through his representatives at the German Diet of Speyer in 1526 that each German territory was free to enforce the Edict of Worms (1521) against Luther "so as to be able to answer in good conscience to God and the emperor." That concession, in effect, gave the German princes territorial sovereignty in religious matters and the Reformation time to put down deep roots.

The Peasants' Revolt In its first decade, the Protestant movement suffered more from internal division than from imperial interference. By 1525 Luther had become as much an object of protest within Germany as was the pope.

Like the German humanists, the German peasantry had at first believed Luther to be an ally. Defiant of efforts by territorial princes to override their traditional laws and customs, peasant leaders saw in Luther's teaching of religious freedom and criticism of monastic landowners a point of view close to their own, and they openly solicited his support of their political and economic rights, including their revolutionary request for release from serfdom. Luther and his followers sympathized with the peasants, but the Lutherans were no social revolutionaries. When the peasants revolted in 1524–1525, Luther condemned them in the strongest possible terms as "unchristian" and urged the princes to crush their revolt without mercy. Tens of thousands of peasants (estimates run between 70,000 and 100,000) had died by the time the revolt was put down.

For Luther, the freedom of the Christian was an inner release from guilt and anxiety, not a right to restructure society by violent revolution. Had Luther supported the Peasants' Revolt, he would have also ended any chance of his reform surviving beyond the 1520s.

ZWINGLI AND THE SWISS REFORMATION

Although Luther's was the first, Switzerland and France had their own independent reform movements almost simultaneously with Germany's. Switzerland was a loose confederacy of 13 autonomous cantons or states and allied areas. Some became Protestant, some remained Catholic, and a few managed to effect a compromise. The two preconditions of the Swiss Reformation were the growth of national sentiment and a desire for church reform.

The Reformation in Zurich Ulrich Zwingli (1484–1531), the leader of the Swiss Reformation, was widely known for opposition to the sale of indulgences and religious superstition. The people's priest in Zurich, he made the city his base for reform. Zwingli's reform guideline was simple and effective: whatever lacked literal support in Scripture was to be neither believed nor practiced. After a public disputation in January 1523, based on his Scripture test, Zurich became, to all intents and purposes, a Protestant city and the center of the Swiss Reformation. Its harsh discipline in pursuit of its religious ideals made it one of the first examples of a "puritanical" Protestant city.

The Marburg Colloquy Landgrave Philip of Hesse (1504–1567) sought to unite Swiss and German Protestants in a mutual defense pact, a potentially significant political alliance. His efforts were spoiled, however, by theological disagreements between Luther and Zwingli over the nature of Christ's presence in the Eucharist. Zwingli maintained a symbolic interpretation of Christ's words, "This is my body"; Christ, he argued, was only spiritually, not bodily, present in the bread and wine of the Eucharist. Luther, to the contrary, insisted that Christ's human nature could share the properties of his divine nature; hence, where Christ was spiritually present, he could also be bodily present, for his was a special nature.

Philip of Hesse brought the two Protestant leaders together in his castle in Marburg in early October 1529, but they were unable to work out their differences on this issue. Luther left thinking Zwingli a dangerous fanatic. The disagreement splintered the Protestant movement theologically and politically.

ANABAPTISTS AND RADICAL PROTESTANTS

The moderate pace and seemingly small ethical results of the Lutheran and Zwinglian reformations discontented many people, among them some of the original co-workers of Luther and Zwingli. Many desired a more rapid and thorough implementation of primitive Christianity and accused the major reformers of going only halfway. The most important of these radical groups were the Anabaptists, the sixteenth-century ancestors of the modern Mennonites and Amish. The Anabaptists were especially distinguished by their rejection of infant baptism and their insistence on only adult baptism (*Anabaptism* derives from the Greek word meaning "to rebaptize"), believing that baptism as a consenting adult conformed to Scripture and was more respectful of human freedom.

Anabaptists physically separated from society to form a more perfect community in imitation of what they believed to be the example of the first Christians. Due to the close connection between religious and civic life in this period, the political authorities viewed such separatism as a threat to basic social bonds.

At first Anabaptism drew its adherents from all social classes. But as Lutherans and Zwinglians joined with Catholics in opposition to it, a more rural, agrarian class came to make up the great majority of Anabaptists. In 1529 rebaptism became a capital offense throughout the Holy Roman Empire. It has been estimated that between 1525 and 1618 at least 1,000 and perhaps as many as 5,000 men and women were executed for rebaptizing themselves as adults.

JOHN CALVIN AND THE GENEVAN REFORMATION

Calvinism was the religious ideology that inspired or accompanied massive political resistance in France, the Netherlands, and Scotland. Believing in both divine predestination and the individual's responsibility to create a godly society, Calvinists became zealous reformers. In a famous and controversial study, *The Protestant Ethic and the Spirit of Capitalism* (1904), the German sociologist Max Weber argued that this peculiar combination of religious confidence and self-disciplined activism produced an ethic congenial to emergent capitalism, bringing Calvinism and later Puritanism into close association with the development of modern capitalist societies.

Political Revolt and Religious Reform in Geneva   Whereas in Saxony religious reform paved the way for a political revolution against the emperor, in Geneva a political revolution against the local prince-bishop laid the foundation for religious change. In late 1533 the Protestant city of Bern sent Protestant reformers to Geneva and by the summer of 1535, after much internal turmoil, the Protestants triumphed. On May 21, 1536, the city voted officially to adopt the Reformation: "to live according to the Gospel and the Word of God . . . without . . . any more masses, statues, idols, or other papal abuses."

A portrait of the young John Calvin.
Bibliotheque Publique et Universitaire, Geneva

John Calvin (1509–1564), a reform-minded humanist and lawyer, arrived in Geneva after these events, in July 1536. The local Protestant reformer persuaded him to stay and assist the Reformation. Before a year had passed, Calvin had drawn up articles for the governance of the new church, as well as a catechism to guide and discipline the people. As a result of the strong measures proposed to govern Geneva's moral life, many suspected the reformers of trying to create a "new papacy." In February 1538 they were exiled from the city.

Calvin went to Strasbourg, a model Protestant city, where he became pastor to the French exiles. During his two years in Strasbourg he wrote biblical commentaries and a second edition of his masterful *Institutes of the Christian Religion*, which many consider the definitive theological statement of the Protestant faith. He also married and participated in the ecumenical discussions urged on Protestants and Catholics by Charles V. Most important, he learned from the Strasbourg reformer Martin Bucer (1491–1551) how to implement the Protestant Reformation successfully.

Calvin's Geneva In 1540 Geneva elected officials favorable to Calvin and he was invited to return. Within months of his arrival, new ecclesiastical ordinances were implemented that allowed the magistrates and the clergy to cooperate in matters of internal discipline.

Calvin and his followers were motivated above all by a desire to make society godly. The "elect," Calvin taught, should live a manifestly God-pleasing life, if they were truly God's elect. The majesty of God demanded nothing less. The consistory, a judicial body composed of clergy and laity, became his instrument of power. It enforced the strictest moral discipline, meting out punishments for a broad range of moral and religious transgressions, and became unpopular among many Genevans.

After 1555 the city's magistrates were all devout Calvinists, and Geneva became home to thousands of exiled Protestants who had been driven out of France, England, and Scotland. Refugees (more than 5,000), most of them utterly loyal to Calvin, came to make up over one third of the population of Geneva. From this time until his death in 1564, Calvin's position in the city was greatly strengthened and the magistrates were very cooperative.

POLITICAL CONSOLIDATION OF THE LUTHERAN REFORMATION

By 1530 the Reformation was in Europe to stay. It would, however, take several decades and major attempts to eradicate it before all would recognize this fact. With the political triumph of Lutheranism in the empire by the 1550s, Protestant movements elsewhere gained a new lease on life.

Expansion of the Reformation In the 1530s German Lutherans formed regional consistories, which oversaw and administered the new Protestant churches. These consistories replaced the old Catholic episcopates. Under the leadership of Philip Melanchthon (1497–1560), Luther's most admired colleague, educational reforms were enacted that provided for compulsory primary education, schools for girls, a humanist revision of the traditional curriculum, and catechetical instruction of the laity in the new religion.

The Reformation also dug in elsewhere. Introduced into Denmark by Christian II (r. 1513–1523), Lutheranism became the state religion under Christian III (r. 1536–1559). In Sweden, Gustavus Vasa (r. 1523–1560), supported by a nobility greedy for church lands, confiscated church property and subjected the clergy to royal authority at the Diet of Vesteras (1527). In politically splintered Poland, Lutherans, Calvinists, and others found room to practice their beliefs. The absence of a central political authority made Poland a model of religious pluralism and toleration in the second half of the sixteenth century.

Reaction Against Protestants: The "Interim"   Charles V made abortive efforts in 1540–1541 to enforce a compromise agreement between Protestants and Catholics. As these and other conciliar efforts failed, he turned to a military solution. In 1547 imperial armies crushed the Protestant Schmalkaldic League.

The emperor established puppet rulers in Saxony and Hesse and issued as imperial law the Augsburg Interim, a new order that Protestants everywhere must readopt Catholic beliefs and practices. But the Reformation was too entrenched by 1547 to be ended even by brute force. Confronted by fierce Protestant resistance and weary from three decades of war, the emperor was forced to relent.

The Peace of Augsburg in September 1555 made the division of Christendom permanent. This agreement recognized in law what had already been well established in practice: *cuius regio, eius religio*, meaning that the ruler of a land would determine the religion of the land. Lutherans were permitted to retain all church lands forcibly seized before 1552. Those discontented with the religion of their region were permitted to migrate to another.

Calvinism was not recognized as a legal form of Christian belief and practice by the Peace of Augsburg. Calvinists remained determined not only to secure the right to worship publicly as they pleased, but also to shape society according to their own religious convictions. They organized to lead national revolutions throughout northern Europe.

THE ENGLISH REFORMATION TO 1553

Late medieval England had a well-earned reputation for defending the rights of the crown against the pope. It was, however, the unhappy marriage of King Henry VIII (r. 1509–1547) that ensured the success of the English protest against the church.

The King's Affair   Henry had married Catherine of Aragon (d. 1536), a daughter of Ferdinand and Isabella of Spain, and the aunt of Emperor Charles V. By 1527 the union had produced only one surviving child, a daughter, Mary Tudor.

Progress of Protestant Reformation on the Continent

1517	Luther posts 95 theses against indulgences
1519	Charles I of Spain elected Holy Roman emperor (as Charles V)
1519	Luther challenges infallibility of pope and inerrancy of church councils at Leipzig Debate
1521	Papal bull excommunicates Luther for heresy
1521	Diet of Worms condemns Luther
1521–1522	Luther translates the New Testament into German
1524–1525	Peasants' Revolt in Germany
1529	Marburg Colloquy between Luther and Zwingli
1530	Diet of Augsburg fails to settle religious differences
1531	Formation of Protestant Schmalkaldic League
1536	Calvin arrives in Geneva
1540	Jesuits, founded by Ignatius of Loyola, recognized as order by pope
1546	Luther dies
1547	Armies of Charles V crush Schmalkaldic League
1555	Peace of Augsburg recognizes rights of Lutherans to worship as they please
1545–1563	Council of Trent institutes reforms and responds to the Reformation

Main Events of the English Reformation

1529	Reformation Parliament convenes
1532	Parliament passes the Submission of the Clergy, an act placing canon law and the English clergy under royal jurisdiction
1533	Henry VIII weds Anne Boleyn
1534	Act of Succession makes Anne Boleyn's children legitimate heirs to the English throne
1534	Act of Supremacy declares Henry VIII the only supreme head of the Church of England
1535	Thomas More executed for opposition to Acts of Succession and Supremacy
1535	Publication of Coverdale Bible
1539	Henry VIII imposes the Six Articles, condemning Protestantism and reasserting traditional doctrine
1547	Edward VI succeeds to the throne
1549	First Act of Uniformity imposes Book of Common Prayer on English churches
1553–1558	Mary Tudor restores Catholic doctrine
1558–1603	Elizabeth I fashions an Anglican religious settlement

Henry was justifiably concerned about the political consequences of leaving only a female heir. People in this period believed it unnatural for women to rule over men. At best, a woman ruler meant a contested reign; at worst, turmoil and revolution. Henry even came to believe that his union with Catherine, who had had numerous miscarriages and stillbirths, had been cursed by God, because before their marriage Catherine had briefly been the wife of his late brother, Arthur.

By 1527 Henry, thoroughly enamored of Anne Boleyn (ca. 1504–1536), one of Catherine's ladies in waiting, decided to put Catherine aside and marry Anne. This he could not do in Catholic England without papal annulment of the marriage to Catherine. And therein lay a problem. In 1527 the reigning pope, Clement VII (r. 1523–1534), was a prisoner of Charles V, Catherine's nephew. Even if this had not been the case, it would have been virtually impossible for the pope to grant an annulment of the marriage. Not only had it survived for eighteen years, but it had been made possible in the first place by a special papal dispensation required because Queen Catherine had previously been the wife of Henry's brother, Arthur.

After Cardinal Wolsey (1475–1530), Lord Chancellor of England since 1515, failed to secure the annulment, Thomas Cranmer (1489–1556) and Thomas Cromwell (1485–1540), both of whom harbored Lutheran sympathies, became the king's closest advisers. Finding the way to a papal annulment closed, Henry's new advisers struck a different course: Why not simply declare the king supreme in English spiritual affairs as he was in English temporal affairs? Then the king could settle his own affair.

Reformation Parliament   In 1529 Parliament convened for what would be a seven-year session that earned it the title of "Reformation Parliament." It passed a flood of legislation that harassed and finally placed royal reins on the clergy. In January 1531 the clergy publicly recognized Henry as head of the church in England "as far as the law of Christ allows." In 1533 Parliament passed the Submission of the Clergy, effectively placing canon law under royal control and thereby the clergy under royal jurisdiction.

In January 1533 Henry wed the pregnant Anne Boleyn, with Thomas Cranmer officiating. In 1534 Parliament ended all payments by the English clergy and laity to Rome and gave Henry sole jurisdiction over high ecclesiastical appointments. The Act of Succession in the same year made Anne Boleyn's children legitimate heirs to the throne, and the Act of Supremacy declared Henry "the only supreme head in earth of the church of England."

The Protestant Reformation Under Edward VI   Despite his political break with Rome, Henry remained decidedly conservative in his religious beliefs, and Catholic doctrine remained prominent in a country seething with Protestant sentiment. Henry forbade the English clergy to marry and threatened to execute clergy caught twice in concubinage. The Six Articles of 1539 reaffirmed **transubstantiation**, denied the Eucharistic cup to the laity, declared celibate vows inviolable, provided for private Masses, and ordered the continuation of auricular confession.

transubstantiation   The doctrine that the entire substances of the bread and wine are changed in the Eucharist into the body and blood of Christ.

Edward VI (r. 1547–1553), Henry's son by his third wife, Jane Seymour, became king at age 10. Under his regents, England enacted much of the Protestant Reformation. Henry's Six Articles and laws against heresy were repealed, and clerical marriage and Communion with the cup were sanctioned. An Act of Uniformity imposed Thomas Cranmer's Book of Common Prayer on all English churches, which were stripped of their images and altars. His 42-article confession of faith set forth a moderate Protestant doctrine.

These changes were short-lived because in 1553 Catherine of Aragon's daughter, Mary Tudor (d. 1558), succeeded to the throne and restored Catholic doctrine and practice with a single-mindedness that rivaled that of her father. It was not until the reign of Anne Boleyn's daughter, Elizabeth I (r. 1558–1603), that a lasting religious settlement was worked out in England.

CATHOLIC REFORM AND COUNTER-REFORMATION

The Protestant Reformation did not take the medieval church completely by surprise. There were many internal criticisms and efforts at reform before there was a **Counter-Reformation** in reaction to Protestant successes.

Sources of Catholic Reform   Before the Reformation began, ambitious proposals had been made for church reform. But sixteenth-century popes, mindful of how the Councils of Constance and Basel had stripped the pope of his traditional powers, quickly squelched such efforts to bring about basic changes in the laws and institutions of the church. Despite such papal foot-dragging, the church was not without its reformers. Many new religious orders sprang up in the sixteenth century to lead a broad revival of piety within the church.

The Ecstasy of Saint Teresa of Avila, by Gianlorenzo Bernini (1598–1680). Mystics like Saint Teresa and Saint John of the cross helped revive the traditional piety of medieval monasticism.
© Scala/Art Resource, N.Y.

Ignatius of Loyola and the Society of Jesus   Of the various reform groups, none was more instrumental in the success of the Counter-Reformation than the Society of Jesus, the new order of Jesuits. Organized by Ignatius of Loyola in the 1530s, it was officially recognized by the church in 1540. Within a century the society had more than 15,000 members scattered throughout the world, with thriving missions in India, Japan, and the Americas.

Ignatius of Loyola (1491–1556) was a heroic figure. A dashing courtier and caballero in his youth, he began his spiritual pilgrimage in 1521 after having been seriously wounded in the legs during a battle with the French. During a lengthy and painful convalescence, he read Christian classics. So impressed was he with the heroic self-sacrifice of the church's saints and their methods of overcoming mental anguish and pain that he underwent a profound religious conversion. Henceforth, he too would serve the church as a soldier of Christ.

After recuperating, Ignatius applied the lessons he had learned during his convalescence to a program of religious and moral self-discipline that came to be embodied in the *Spiritual Exercises*. This psychologically perceptive devotional

Counter-Reformation   The sixteenth-century reform movement in the Roman Catholic Church in reaction to the Protestant Reformation.

guide contained mental and emotional exercises designed to teach one absolute spiritual self-mastery. A person could shape his or her own behavior, even create a new religious self, through disciplined study and regular practice.

Whereas in Jesuit eyes Protestants had distinguished themselves by disobedience to church authority and by religious innovation, the exercises of Ignatius were intended to teach good Catholics to submit without question to higher church authority and spiritual direction. Perfect discipline and self-control were the essential conditions of such obedience. To these were added the enthusiasm of traditional spirituality and mysticism and uncompromising loyalty to the church's cause above all else. This potent combination helped counter the Reformation and win many Protestants back to the Catholic fold, especially in Austria and Germany.

The Council of Trent (1545–1563)   The broad success of the Reformation and the insistence of the emperor Charles V forced Pope Paul III (r. 1534–1549) to call a general council of the church to reassert church doctrine. The pope also appointed a reform commission, whose report, presented in February 1537, bluntly criticized the fiscality and simony[2] of the papal Curia (court) as the primary source of the church's loss of esteem. The report was so critical that Paul attempted unsuccessfully to suppress its publication, and Protestants reprinted and circulated it to justify their criticism.

The long-delayed council met in 1545 in the imperial city of Trent in northern Italy. There were three sessions, spread over eighteen years, with long interruptions due to war, plague, and politics. Unlike the general councils of the fifteenth century, Trent was strictly under the pope's control, with high Italian prelates prominent in the proceedings.

The council's most important reforms concerned internal church discipline. The selling of church offices and other religious goods was forbidden. Trent strengthened the authority of local bishops so they could effectively discipline popular religious practice. Bishops who resided in Rome were forced to move to their appointed seats of authority. They had to preach regularly and conduct annual visitations. Parish priests were required to be neatly dressed, better educated, strictly celibate, and active among their parishioners. To train better priests, Trent also called for the establishment of a seminary in every diocese.

The Council did not make a single doctrinal concession to the Protestants, however. In the face of Protestant criticism, the Council of Trent reaffirmed the traditional scholastic education of the clergy; the role of good works in salvation; the authority of tradition; the seven sacraments; transubstantiation; the withholding of the Eucharistic cup from the laity; clerical celibacy; the reality of purgatory; the veneration of saints, relics, and sacred images; and the granting of letters of indulgence.

Rulers initially resisted Trent's reform decrees, fearing a revival of papal political power within their lands. But in time the new legislation took hold, and parish life revived under the guidance of a devout and better-trained clergy.

THE REFORMATION'S ACHIEVEMENTS

THE REVOLUTION IN RELIGIOUS PRACTICES AND INSTITUTIONS

Although politically conservative, the Reformation brought about far-reaching changes in traditional religious practices and institutions in many lands. By the end of the sixteenth century, what had disappeared or was radically altered was often dramatic.

HOW DID the Reformation change religious and social life?

---

[2]The sin of selling of sacred or spiritual things, in this instance church offices.

Religion in Fifteenth-Century Life   In the fifteenth century, on the streets of the great cities of central Europe that later turned Protestant (for example, Zurich, Strasbourg, Nuremberg, or Geneva), the clergy and the religious were everywhere. They made up 6 to 8 percent of the total urban population, and they exercised considerable political as well as spiritual power. They legislated and taxed; they tried cases in special church courts; and they enforced their laws with threats of excommunication.

The church calendar regulated daily life. About one-third of the year was given over to some kind of religious observance or celebration. There were frequent periods of fasting. On almost a hundred days out of the year a pious Christian could not, without special dispensation, eat eggs, butter, fat, or meat.

Monasteries and especially nunneries were prominent and influential institutions. The children of society's most powerful citizens resided there. Local aristocrats were closely identified with particular churches and chapels, whose walls recorded their lineage and proclaimed their generosity. On the streets, friars from near and far begged alms from passersby. In the churches the Mass and liturgy were read entirely in Latin. Images of saints were regularly displayed, and on certain holidays their relics were paraded about and venerated.

There was a booming business at local religious shrines. Pilgrims gathered there by the hundreds, even thousands, many sick and dying, all in search of a cure or a miracle, but also for diversion and entertainment. Several times during the year special preachers arrived in the city to sell letters of indulgence.

Many clergy walked the streets with concubines and children, although they were sworn to celibacy and forbidden marriage. The church tolerated such relationships upon payment of penitential fines.

People everywhere could be heard complaining about the clergy's exemption from taxation and, in many instances, also from the civil criminal code. People also grumbled about having to support church offices whose occupants actually lived and worked elsewhere. Townspeople also expressed concern that the church had too much influence over education and culture.

Religion in Sixteenth-Century Life   In these same cities after the Reformation had firmly established itself, few changes in politics and society were evident. The same aristocratic families governed as before, and the rich generally got richer and the poor poorer. But overall numbers of clergy fell by two-thirds and religious holidays shrunk by one-third. Monasteries and nunneries were nearly absent. Many were transformed into hospices for the sick and poor or into educational institutions, their endowments also turned over to these new purposes. A few cloisters remained for very devout old monks and nuns, who could not be pensioned off or who lacked families and friends to care for them. But these remaining cloisters died out with their inhabitants.

In the churches, which had also been reduced in number by at least a third, worship was conducted almost completely in the vernacular. In some, particularly those in Zwinglian cities, the walls were stripped bare and white-washed to make sure the congregation meditated only on God's Word. The laity observed no obligatory fasts. Indulgence preachers no longer appeared. Local shrines were closed down, and anyone found openly venerating saints, relics, and images was subject to fine and punishment.

Copies of Luther's translation of the New Testament, or more often excerpts from it, could be found in private homes, and meditation on them was encouraged by the new clergy. The clergy could marry, and most did. They paid taxes and were punished for their crimes in civil courts. Domestic moral life was regulated

A young couple in love (ca. 1480)
by an anonymous artist.

Bildarchiv Preussicher Kulturbesitz

by committees composed of roughly equal numbers of laity and clergy, over whose decisions secular magistrates had the last word.

Not all Protestant clergy remained enthusiastic about this new lay authority in religion. And the laity themselves were also ambivalent about certain aspects of the Reformation. Over half of the original converts returned to the Catholic fold before the end of the sixteenth century. Whereas half of Europe could be counted in the Protestant camp in the mid-sixteenth century, only a fifth would be there by the mid-seventeenth century.[3]

THE REFORMATION AND THE CHANGING ROLE OF WOMEN

The Protestant reformers took a positive stand on clerical marriage and strongly opposed monasticism and the celibate life. From this position they challenged the medieval tendency alternately to degrade women as temptresses (following the model of Eve) and to exalt them as virgins (following the model of Mary). Protestants opposed the popular antiwoman and antimarriage literature of the Middle Ages. They praised woman in her own right, but especially in her biblical vocation as mother and housewife. Although from a modern perspective, women remained subject to men, new marriage laws gave them greater security and protection.

Relief of sexual frustration and a remedy of fornication were prominent in Protestant arguments for marriage. But the reformers also viewed their wives as indispensable companions in their work, and this not solely because they took domestic cares off their husbands' minds. Luther, who married in 1525 at the age of 42, wrote of women:

Imagine what it would be like without women. The home, cities, economic life, and government would virtually disappear. Men cannot do without women. Even if it were possible for men to beget and bear children, they still could not do without women.[4]

John Calvin wrote at the death of his wife:

I have been bereaved of the best companion of my life, of one who, had it been so ordered, would not only have been the willing sharer of my indigence, but even of my death. During her life she was the faithful helper of my ministry.[5]

Such tributes were intended in part to overcome Catholic criticism that marriage distracted the cleric from his ministry. They were primarily the expression of a new value placed on the estate of marriage and family life. In opposition to the celibate ideal of the Middle Ages, Protestants stressed as no religious movement before them the sacredness of home and family. This attitude contributed to a more respectful and sharing relationship between husbands and wives and between parents and children.

The ideal of the companionate marriage—that is, of husband and wife as coworkers in a special God-ordained community of the family, sharing authority equally within the household—led to an important expansion of the grounds for divorce in Protestant cities as early as the 1520s. Women now had an equal right with men to divorce and remarry in good conscience—unlike in Catholicism, where only a separation from bed and table, not divorce and remarriage, was permitted a couple in a failed marriage. The reformers were actually more willing to

[3]Geoffrey Parker, *Europe in Crisis, 1598–1648* (Ithaca, N.Y.: Cornell University Press, 1979), p. 50.

[4]*Luther's Works*, Vol. 54: *Table Talk*, ed. and trans. by Theodore G. Tappert (Philadelphia: Fortress Press, 1967), p. 161.

[5]*Letters of John Calvin*, Vol. 2, trans. by J. Bonnet (Edinburgh: T. Constable, 1858), p. 216.

• HISTORY'S VOICES •

A GERMAN MOTHER ADVISES HER 15-YEAR-OLD SON, WHO IS AWAY FROM HOME AT SCHOOL FOR THE FIRST TIME (1578)

Although only 14 miles away from his Nuremberg home, Friedrich Behaim was 15 and on his own for the first time at the Altdorf Academy, where he would spend the next three years of his life. As there was daily traffic back and forth, mother and son could correspond regularly and Frau Behaim could give her son needed advice and articles of clothing.

WHAT IS the mother most concerned about? What do her concerns suggest about life in the sixteenth century? Does she appear to be more strict and demanding of her son than a modern mother would be? Is the son clueless, or adroitly manipulating the mother?

Dear son Friederich . . . You write that you have been unable to get by on the money [I gave you]. I will let it pass this quarter, but see that you manage on it in the future. Enclosed is another gulden. As for your clothes, I do not have Martin [a servant] here with me now (we are quarreling), but he has begun to work on your clothes. He has made stockings for your leather holiday trousers, which I am sending you with this letter. Since your everyday trousers are so bad, wear these for now until a new pair of woolen ones can be made and sent to you, which I will do as soon as I can. Send me your old trousers in the sack I sent you the pitcher in. As for the smock that you think should be lined [for the winter], I worry that the skirt may be too short and will not keep you warm. You can certainly wear it for another summer if it is not too small for you then and the weather not too warm. Just keep it clean and brushed. I will have a new coat made for you at the earliest.

You also write about [unhappiness with] your food. You must be patient for a while. You may not at the outset lodge a complaint against [your master], and especially while you are sitting at his table. [Only] he may speak out who eats his food and is also an authority in the house. So it would be better if the Inspector, who is there for a reason, reports it to him.

Will you once tell me who your table companions are! Also, let me know by All Saints what you have spent on beer and what you owe the tailor, so I may know how much money to send you.

As for your [sore] throat, there is nothing you can take for it but warm mead. Gargle often with it and keep your head warm. Put a muffler or scarf around your neck and wear your night coat when you are in your room. Avoid cold drinks and sit perhaps for a while by the fire. And do not forget to be bled on time. [People then bled themselves once or twice a year as a health measure] . . . When you need paper, let me know . . .

I am sending some cleaning flakes for your leather pants. After you have worn them three times, put some on the knees . . . I will have your old coat patched and send it to you with the next carter [so that you can wear it] until the new one is made. Send me the two sacks with the next carter. You will find the [aforementioned] gulden in the trouser foot tied with a string.

Nothing more for now. God bless. 14 October, 1578.
—Mrs. Paul Behaim

From *Three Behaim Boys: Growing Up in Early Modern Germany—A Chronicle of Their Lives*, ed. and trans. by Steven Ozment, pp. 107–108. Copyright © 1990 Yale University Press. Reprinted by permission of Yale University Press.

permit divorce and remarriage on grounds of adultery and abandonment than were secular magistrates, who feared liberal divorce laws would lead to social upheaval.

Protestant doctrines were as attractive to women as they were to men. Renegade nuns wrote exposés of the nunnery in the name of Christian freedom and justification by faith, declaring that the nunnery was no special woman's place at all and that supervisory male clergy (who alone could hear the nuns' confessions and administer the Sacrament to them) made their lives as unpleasant and burdensome as any abusive husband. Women in the higher classes, who enjoyed new social and political freedoms during the Renaissance, found in Protestant theology a religious complement to their greater independence in other walks of life. Some cloistered noblewomen, however, protested the closing of nunneries. They believed the cloister provided them with a more interesting and independent way of life than they would have known in the secular world.

Because they wanted women to become pious housewives, Protestants also encouraged the education of girls to literacy in the vernacular, expecting them thereafter to model their lives on the Bible. During their studies, however, women found biblical passages that suggested they were equal to men in the presence of God. Education also gave some women a role as independent authors in the Reformation. From a modern perspective, these may seem like small advances, but they were significant, if indirect, steps in the direction of the emancipation of women. (See "A German Mother advises her 15-year-old Son.")

THE WARS OF RELIGION

WHAT WAS the final result of the wars of religion in France, the Netherlands, and Germany?

After the Council of Trent adjourned in 1563, Catholics began a Jesuit-led counteroffensive against Protestants. At the time of John Calvin's death in 1564, Geneva had become both a refuge for Europe's persecuted Protestants and an international school for Protestant resistance, producing leaders fully equal to the new Catholic challenge.

Genevan Calvinism and the reformed Catholicism of the Council of Trent were two equally dogmatic, aggressive, and irreconcilable church systems. Calvinists may have looked like "new papists" to critics when they dominated cities like Geneva, but when as minorities they found their civil and religious rights denied in the empire and elsewhere, they became true firebrands and revolutionaries.

Calvinism adopted a presbyterian organization that magnified regional and local religious authority. Boards of presbyters, or elders, representing the many individual Calvinist congregations, directly shaped the policy of the church at large. By contrast, the Counter-Reformation sponsored a centralized episcopal church system, hierarchically arranged from pope to parish priest and stressing absolute obedience to the person at the top. The high clergy—the pope and his bishops—not the synods of local churches, ruled supreme. Calvinism attracted proponents of political decentralization who opposed totalitarian rulers, whereas Catholicism remained congenial to proponents of absolute monarchy determined to maintain "one king, one church, one law."

The wars of religion were both internal national conflicts and truly international wars. Catholic and Protestant subjects struggled to control France, the Netherlands, and England. The Catholic governments of France and Spain conspired and finally sent armies against Protestant regimes in England and the Netherlands. The outbreak of the Thirty Years' War in 1618 made the international dimensions of the religious conflict especially clear; before it ended in 1648, the war drew every major European nation directly or indirectly into its deadly net.

FRENCH WARS OF RELIGION (1562–1598)

When Henry II (r. 1547–1559) died accidentally during a tournament in 1559, his sickly 15-year-old son, Francis II (d. 1560), came to the throne under the regency of the queen mother, Catherine de Médicis (1519–1589). With the monarchy so weakened, three powerful families began to compete to control France.

The St. Bartholemew's Day Massacre, as depicted by the contemporary Protestant painter François Dubois. In this notorious event, 3,000 Protestants were slaughtered in Paris and an estimated 20,000 others died throughout France. The massacre transformed the religious struggle in France from a contest for political power into an all-out war between Protestants and Catholics.

Musée Cantonal des Beaux Arts, Palais de Rumine, Lausanne

They were the Bourbons, whose power lay in the south and west; the Montmorency-Châtillons, who controlled the center of France; and the Guises, who were dominant in eastern France. The Guises were by far the strongest, and the name of *Guise* was interchangeable with militant, ultra-Catholicism. The Bourbon and Montmorency Châtillon families, in contrast, developed strong **Huguenot** sympathies, largely for political reasons. (French Protestants were called Huguenots after Besançon Hughes, the leader of Geneva's political revolt against the Savoyards in the late 1520s.) The Bourbon Louis I, prince of Condé (d. 1569), and the Montmorency-Châtillon admiral Gaspard de Coligny (1519–1572) became the political leaders of the French Protestant resistance.

Often for quite different reasons, ambitious aristocrats and discontented townspeople joined Calvinist churches in opposition to the Guise-dominated French monarchy. In 1561 over 2,000 Huguenot congregations existed throughout France. Although they made up only about a fifteenth of the population, Huguenots held important geographic areas and represented the more powerful segments of French society. Over two-fifths of the French aristocracy became Huguenots. Many apparently hoped to establish within France a principle of territorial sovereignty akin to that secured within the Holy Roman Empire by the Peace of Augsburg (1555). Calvinism thus indirectly served the forces of political decentralization.

Huguenots   French Calvinists.

Catherine de Médicis and the Guises   Following Francis II's death in 1560, Catherine de Médicis continued as regent for her second son, Charles IX (r. 1560–1574). Fearing the Guises, Catherine, whose first concern was always to preserve the monarchy, sought allies among the Protestants. Early in 1562 she granted Protestants freedom to worship publicly outside towns—although only privately within them—and to hold synods, or church assemblies. In March of the same year this royal toleration ended when the Duke of Guise surprised a Protestant congregation worshiping illegally at Vassy in Champagne and proceeded to massacre several score—an event that marked the beginning of the French wars of religion. Perpetually caught between fanatical Huguenot and Guise extremes, Queen Catherine always sought to play the one side against the other. She wanted a Catholic France but not a Guise-dominated monarchy.

On August 22, 1572, four days after the Huguenot Henry of Navarre had married Charles IX's sister—another sign of growing Protestant power in the queen mother's eye—the Huguenot leader Coligny, who increasingly had the king's ear, was wounded by an assassin's bullet. Catherine had apparently been a part of this Guise plot to eliminate Coligny. After its failure, she feared both the king's reaction to her complicity and the Huguenot response under a recovered Coligny. Catherine convinced Charles that a Huguenot coup was afoot, inspired by Coligny, and that only the swift execution of Protestant leaders could save the crown from a Protestant attack on Paris. On the eve of Saint Bartholomew's Day, August 24, 1572, Coligny and 3,000 fellow Huguenots were butchered in Paris. Within three days an estimated 20,000 Huguenots were executed in coordinated attacks throughout France.

This event changed the nature of the struggle between Protestants and Catholics both within and beyond the borders of France. It was thereafter no longer an internal contest between Guise and Bourbon factions for French political influence, nor was it simply a Huguenot campaign to win basic religious freedoms. Henceforth, in Protestant eyes, it became an international struggle to the death for sheer survival against an adversary whose cruelty justified any means of resistance.

The Rise to Power of Henry of Navarre   Henry III (r. 1574–1589), who was Henry II's third son and the last Valois king, found the monarchy wedged between a radical Catholic League, formed in 1576 by Henry of Guise, and vengeful Huguenots. Like the queen mother, Henry III sought to steer a middle course, and in this effort he received support from a growing body of neutral Catholics and Huguenots who put the political survival of France above its religious unity. Such *politiques*, as they were called, were prepared to compromise religious creeds to save the nation.

In the mid-1580s the Catholic League, supported by the Spanish, became completely dominant in Paris. Henry III failed to rout the league with a surprise attack in 1588 and had to flee Paris. Forced by his weakened position into guerrilla tactics, the king had both the Duke and the Cardinal of Guise assassinated. The Catholic League reacted with a fury that matched the earlier Huguenot response to the Massacre of Saint Bartholomew's Day. The king was now forced to strike an alliance with his Protestant cousin and heir, Henry of Navarre, in April 1589.

As the two Henrys prepared to attack Paris, however, a fanatical Dominican friar murdered Henry III. Thereupon the Bourbon Huguenot Henry of Navarre became Henry IV of France (r. 1589–1610).

Henry IV came to the throne as a *politique*, weary of religious strife and prepared to place political peace above absolute religious unity. He believed that a royal policy of tolerant Catholicism would be the best way to achieve such peace. On July 25, 1593, he publicly abjured the Protestant faith and embraced the traditional and majority religion of his country. "Paris is worth a Mass," he is reported to have said.

The Edict of Nantes   Five years later, on April 13, 1598, Henry IV's famous Edict of Nantes proclaimed a formal religious settlement. In 1591 he had already assured the Huguenots of at least qualified religious freedoms. The Edict of Nantes made good that promise. It recognized and sanctioned minority religious rights within what was to remain an officially Catholic country. This religious truce—and it was never more than that—granted the Huguenots, who by this time numbered well over a million, freedom of public worship, the right of assembly, admission to public offices and universities, and permission to maintain fortified towns. Most of the new freedoms, however, were to be exercised within their own localities. Concession of the right to fortify towns reveals the continuing distrust between French Protestants and Catholics. The edict only transformed a long hot war between irreconcilable enemies into a long cold war. To its critics, it created a state within a state.

A Catholic fanatic assassinated Henry IV in May 1610. Although Henry is best remembered for the Edict of Nantes, the political and economic policies he put in place were equally important. They laid the foundations for the transformation of France into the absolutist state it would become in the seventeenth century. Ironically, in pursuit of the political and religious unity that had escaped Henry IV, his grandson Louis XIV (r. 1643–1715), calling for "one king, one church, one law," would later revoke the Edict of Nantes in 1685 (see Chapter 20). This action would force France and Europe to learn again by bitter experience the hard lessons of the wars of religion. Rare is the politician who learns from the lessons of history rather than repeat its mistakes.

The Milch Cow, a sixteenth-century satirical painting depicting the Netherlands as a land all the great powers of Europe wish to exploit. Elizabeth of England is feeding her (England had long-standing commerical ties with Flanders); Philip II of Spain is attempting to ride her (Spain was trying to reassert its control over the entire region); William of Orange is trying to milk her (he was the leader of the anti-Spanish rebellion); and the king of France holds her by the tail (France hoped to profit from the rebellion at Spain's expense).

Rijksmuseum, Amsterdam

IMPERIAL SPAIN AND THE REIGN OF PHILIP II (1556–1598)

Until the English defeated his mighty Armada in 1588, no one person stood larger in the second half of the sixteenth century than Philip II of Spain. During the first half of his reign, attention focused on the Mediterranean and Turkish expansion. On October 7, 1571, a Holy League of Spain, Venice, and the pope defeated the Turks at Lepanto in the largest naval battle of the sixteenth century. Before the engagement ended, 30,000 Turks had died and over one-third of the Turkish fleet was sunk or captured.

Revolt in the Netherlands   The spectacular Spanish military success in southern Europe was not repeated in northern Europe when Philip attempted to impose his will within the Netherlands and on England and France. The resistance of the Netherlands especially proved the undoing of Spanish dreams of world empire.

The Netherlands were the richest area in Europe. The merchant towns of the Netherlands were however, Europe's most independent; many, like magnificent Antwerp, were also Calvinist strongholds. A stubborn opposition to the Spanish overlords formed under William of Nassau, the Prince of Orange (r. 1533–1584). Like other successful rulers in this period, William of Orange was a *politique* who placed the Netherlands' political autonomy and well-being above religious creeds. He personally passed through successive Catholic, Lutheran, and Calvinist stages.

The year 1564 saw the first fusion of political and religious opposition to Spanish rule, the result of Philip II's unwise insistence that the decrees of the Council of Trent be enforced throughout the Netherlands. A national covenant was drawn up called the Compromise, a solemn pledge to resist the decrees of Trent and the Inquisition.

Philip dispatched the Duke of Alba (1508–1582) to suppress the revolt. His army of 10,000 men marched northward from Milan in 1567 in a show of combined Spanish and papal might. A special tribunal, known to the Spanish as the Council of Troubles and among the Netherlanders as the Council of Blood, reigned over the land. Several thousand suspected heretics were publicly executed before Alba's reign of terror ended.

William of Orange had been an exile in Germany during these turbulent years. He now emerged as the leader of a broad movement for the Netherlands' independence from Spain.

After a decade of persecution and warfare, the 10 largely Catholic southern provinces (what is roughly modern Belgium) came together in 1576 with the seven largely Protestant northern provinces (what is roughly the modern Netherlands) in unified opposition to Spain. This union, known as the Pacification of Ghent, declared internal regional sovereignty in matters of religion. It was a Netherlands version of the Peace of Augsburg.

After more fighting, in January 1579 the southern provinces formed the Union of Arras and made peace with Spain. The northern provinces responded with the formation of the Union of Utrecht and continued the struggle. Spanish preoccupation with France and England in the 1580s permitted the northern provinces to drive out all Spanish soldiers by 1593. In 1596 France and England formally recognized the independence of these provinces. However, the northern provinces did not formally conclude peace with Spain until 1609, when the Twelve Years' Truce concluded their virtual independence. But Spain did not fully recognize that independence until the Peace of Westphalia in 1648.

ENGLAND AND SPAIN (1558–1603)

Elizabeth I   Elizabeth I (r. 1558–1603), the daughter of Henry VIII and Anne Boleyn, was perhaps the most astute politician of the sixteenth century in both domestic and foreign policy. She repealed the anti-Protestant legislation of her predecessor Mary Tudor and guided a religious settlement through Parliament that prevented England from being torn asunder by religious differences in the sixteenth century, as the Continent was.

Catholic extremists hoped to replace Elizabeth with the Catholic Mary Stuart, Queen of Scots. But Elizabeth acted swiftly against Catholic assassination plots and rarely let emotion override her political instincts.

Elizabeth dealt cautiously with the Puritans, Protestants who sought to "purify" the national church of every vestige of "popery" and to make its Protestant doctrine more precise. The Puritans had two special grievances: (1) the retention

Elizabeth I (1558–1603) standing on a map of England in 1592. An astute, if sometimes erratic, politician in foreign and domestic policy, Elizabeth was one of most successful rulers of the sixteenth century.

National Portrait Gallery, London

MAP EXPLORATION

Interactive map: To explore this map further, go to **http://www.prenhall.com/craig2/map16.2**

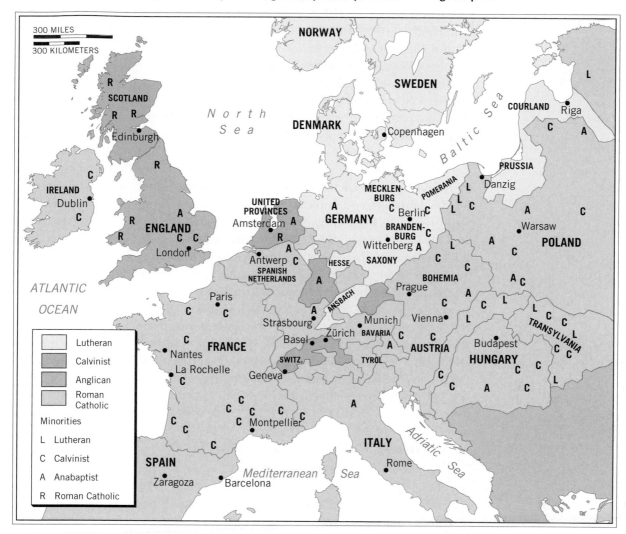

MAP 16–2

Religious division ca. 1600.   By 1600 few could expect Christians to return to a uniform religious allegiance. In Spain and southern Italy Catholicism remained relatively unchallenged, but note the existence elsewhere of large religious minorities, both Catholic and Protestant.

WHY DID the Wars of Religion fail to reestablish religious uniformity in the Holy Roman Empire?

of Catholic ceremony and vestments within the Church of England, and (2) the continuation of the episcopal system of church governance.

Sixteenth-century Puritans were not separatists, however. They worked through Parliament to create an alternative national church of semi-autonomous congregations governed by representative presbyteries (hence, Presbyterians), following the model of Calvin and Geneva. The more extreme Puritans wanted every congregation to be autonomous, a law unto itself, with no higher control. They came to be known as Congregationalists. Elizabeth refused to tolerate this group, whose views she considered subversive.

Deterioration of Relations with Spain A series of events led inexorably to war between England and Spain, despite the sincere desires of both Philip II and Elizabeth to avoid it. Following Spain's victory at Lepanto in 1571, England signed a mutual defense pact with France. Also in the 1570s, Elizabeth's famous seamen, John Hawkins (1532–1595) and Sir Francis Drake (?1545–1596), began to prey regularly on Spanish shipping in the Americas. Drake's circumnavigation of the globe between 1577 and 1580 was one in a series of dramatic demonstrations of English ascendancy on the high seas. In 1585 Elizabeth signed a treaty that committed English soldiers to the Netherlands. These events made a tinderbox of English-Spanish relations. The spark that finally touched it off was Elizabeth's reluctant execution of Mary, Queen of Scots (1542–1587) on February 18, 1587, for complicity in a plot to assassinate Elizabeth. Philip II ordered his Armada to make ready.

On May 30, 1588, a mighty fleet of 130 ships bearing 25,000 sailors and soldiers under the command of the Duke of Medina-Sidonia set sail for England. But the day belonged completely to the English. The barges that were to transport Spanish soldiers from the galleons onto English shores were prevented from leaving Calais and Dunkirk. The swifter English and Netherlands ships, assisted by an "English wind," dispersed the waiting Spanish fleet, over a third of which never returned to Spain. The Armada's defeat gave heart to Protestant resistance everywhere. Spain never fully recovered from it. By the time of Philip's death on September 13, 1598, his forces had been rebuffed by the French and the Dutch. His seventeenth-century successors were all inferior leaders who never knew responsibilities equal to Philip's; nor did Spain ever again know such imperial grandeur. The French soon dominated the Continent, while the Dutch and the English whittled away Spain's overseas empire.

Elizabeth died on March 23, 1603, leaving behind her a strong nation poised to expand into a global empire.

THE THIRTY YEARS' WAR (1618–1648)

The Thirty Years' War in the Holy Roman Empire was the last and most destructive of the wars of religion. Religious and political differences had long set Catholics against Protestants and Calvinists against Lutherans. What made the Thirty Years' War so devastating was the now entrenched hatred of the various sides and their seeming determination to sacrifice all for their territorial sovereignty and religious beliefs. As the conflicts multiplied, virtually every major European land became involved either directly or indirectly. When the hostilities ended in 1648, the peace terms shaped much of the map of northern Europe as we know it today.

Fragmented Germany During the second half of the sixteenth century, Germany was an almost ungovernable land of 360 autonomous political entities. The Peace of Augsburg (1555) had given each a significant degree of sovereignty within its own borders. Each levied its own tolls and tariffs and coined its own money, practices that made land travel and trade between the various regions difficult, where not impossible. Many of these little "states" also had great power pretensions. Political decentralization and fragmentation characterized Germany as the seventeenth century opened; it was not a unified nation like Spain, England, or even strife-torn France.

Religious Division Religious conflict accentuated the international and internal political divisions. The Holy Roman Empire was about equally divided between Catholics and Protestants, the latter having perhaps a slight numerical edge by 1600. The terms of the Peace of Augsburg (1555) had attempted to freeze the

MAP 16–3

The Holy Roman Empire ca. 1618.   On the eve of the Thirty Years' War the empire was politically and religiously fragmented, as this somewhat simplified map reveals. Lutherans dominated the north and Catholics the south, while Calvinists controlled the United Provinces and the Palatinate and also had an important presence in Switzerland and Brandenburg.

DID THE Holy Roman Empire emerge from the Wars of Religion stronger or weaker?

territorial holdings of the Lutherans and the Catholics. In the intervening years, however, the Lutherans had gained political control in many Catholic areas, as had the Catholics in a few previously Lutheran areas. There was also religious strife between liberal and conservative Lutherans and between Lutherans and the growing numbers of Calvinists.

As elsewhere in Europe, Calvinism was the political and religious leaven within the Holy Roman Empire. Unrecognized as a legal religion by the Peace of Augsburg, Calvinism established a strong foothold within the empire when Elector

OVERVIEW

THE RELIGIOUS DIVISIONS OF EUROPE

The Reformation permanently shattered the religious unity of Western Europe that had existed since the fifth century C.E. It also gave rise to more than a century of warfare, in which Catholics fought Protestants, and Protestants fought each other all in the name of faith. By 1648 when the Treaty of Westphalia ended the Thirty Years' War, Europe remained divided into mostly Catholic regions, mostly Protestant regions, and those areas with large religious minorities. Most of these divisions have persisted to the present day.

Country	Religion
Scotland	Calvinist
England	Protestant (Anglicans, Calvinists, and Anabaptists); a declining Catholic minority
Ireland	Mostly Catholic but with a Protestant minority (Anglicans and Calvinists) mainly in the north
France	Catholic but with substantial numbers of Calvinists
Belgium	Catholic
Netherlands	A Calvinist majority, but with a large Catholic minority
Spain	Catholic
Portugal	Catholic
Sandinavia	Lutheran
Switzerland	Almost evenly divided between Catholics and Protestants (both Calvinists and Lutherans)
Italy	Catholic
Austria	Catholic
Germany	The north was predominately Protestant (Lutheran, Calvinist, Anabaptist); the south and the Rhineland were mostly Catholic; but each area had religious minorities
Hungary	Mostly Catholic, but with a large Calvinist minority
Poland	Catholic
Lithuania	Catholic
Latvia	Lutheran
Estonia	Lutheran
Croatia	Catholic
Slovenia	Catholic
Bohemia (modern Czech Republic)	Catholic
Slovakia	Catholic

Frederick III (r. 1559–1576), a devout convert to Calvinism, made it the official religion within the Palatinate in 1559. By 1609 Palatine Calvinists headed a Protestant defensive alliance supported by Spain's sixteenth-century enemies: England, France, and the Netherlands.

If the Calvinists were active within the Holy Roman Empire, so also were their Catholic counterparts, the Jesuits. Staunchly Catholic Bavaria, supported by Spain, became militarily and ideologically for the Counter-Reformation what the Palatinate was for Protestantism. From Bavaria, the Jesuits launched successful missions throughout the empire. In 1609 Maximilian, Duke of Bavaria (1573–1651), organized a Catholic League to counter a new Protestant alliance that had been formed by the Calvinist Elector Palatine, Frederick IV (r. 1583–1610). When the league fielded a great army under the command of Jean't Senclaes, Count of Tilly (1559–1632), the stage was set, internally and internationally, for the Thirty Years' War, the worst European catastrophe since the Black Death of the fourteenth century.

The Treaty of Westphalia   In 1648 all hostilities within the Holy Roman Empire were brought to an end by the Treaty of Westphalia. It firmly reasserted the major feature of the religious settlement of the Peace of Augsburg (1555), as rulers were again permitted to determine the religion of their lands. The treaty also gave the Calvinists their long-sought legal recognition while still denying it to sectarians. The independence of the Swiss Confederacy and the United Provinces of Holland, long recognized in fact, now became law.

By confirming the territorial sovereignty of Germany's many political entities, the Treaty of Westphalia perpetuated German division and political weakness into the modern period. However, two German states attained international significance during the seventeenth century: Austria and Brandenburg-Prussia. The petty regionalism within the empire also reflected on a small scale the drift of larger European politics. During the seventeenth century distinctive nation-states, each with its own political, cultural, and religious identity, reached maturity and firmly established the competitive nationalism of the modern world.

SUPERSTITION AND ENLIGHTENMENT: THE BATTLE WITHIN

Religious reform and warfare permanently changed religious institutions in major European lands. They also moved intellectuals to rethink human nature and society. One side of that reconsideration was dark and cynical, perhaps because the peak years of religious warfare had also been those of the great European witch hunts. Another side, however, was brilliantly skeptical and constructive, reflecting the growing scientific movement of the years between 1500 and 1700.

WHY DID witch hunts and panics erupt across Western Europe between 1400 and 1700?

WITCH HUNTS AND PANIC

Nowhere is the dark side of the period better seen than in the witch hunts and panics that erupted in almost every western land. Between 1400 and 1700, courts sentenced an estimated 70,000 to 100,000 people to death for harmful magic (*maleficium*) and diabolical witchcraft. In addition to inflicting harm on their neighbors, these witches were said to attend mass meetings known as sabbats, to which they were believed to fly. They were also accused of indulging in sexual orgies with the devil, who appeared in animal form, most often as a he-goat. Still other charges against them were cannibalism (they were alleged to be especially fond of small Christian children) and a variety of ritual acts and practices designed to insult every Christian belief and value.

Where did such beliefs come from, and how could seemingly enlightened people believe them? Their roots were in society at large, in both popular and elite cultures, especially the clergy.

Village Origins   In village societies, so-called cunning folk played a positive role in helping people cope with calamity. People turned to them for help in the face of natural disasters or physical disabilities. The cunning folk provided consolation and gave people hope that such calamities might be averted or reversed by magical means. They thus provided an important service and kept village life moving forward.

Possession of magical powers, for good or ill, made one an important person within village society. Not surprisingly, claims to such powers most often were made by the people most in need of security and influence—namely, the old and the impoverished, especially single or widowed women. Witch beliefs in village society may also have been a way of defying urban Christian society's attempts to impose its laws and institutions on the countryside. From this perspective, village Satanism became a fanciful substitute for an impossible social revolt, a way of spurning the values of one's new masters. It is also possible, although unlikely, that witch beliefs in rural society had a foundation in local fertility cults, whose semipagan practices, designed to ensure good harvests, may have acquired the features of diabolical witchcraft under church persecution.

Influence of the Clergy   Popular belief in magic was the essential foundation of the great witch hunts of the sixteenth and seventeenth centuries. Yet the contribution of learned society was equally great. The Christian clergy also practiced magic, that of the holy sacraments, and the exorcism of demons was one of their traditional functions within society. Fear of demons and the devil, which the clergy actively encouraged, allowed them to assert their moral authority and enforce religious conformity.

In the late thirteenth century the church declared that only its priests possessed legitimate magical power. Since such power was not human, theologians reasoned, it had to come either from God or from the devil. If it came from God, then it was properly confined to and exercised only by the church. Those who practiced magic outside the church evidently derived their power from the devil. From such reasoning grew accusations of "pacts" between non-Christian magicians and Satan.

The church based its intolerance of magic outside its walls on sincere belief in and fear of the devil. But attacking witches was also a way for established Christian society to extend its power and influence into new areas. To accuse, try, and execute witches was also a declaration of moral and political authority over a village or territory. As the cunning folk were local spiritual authorities, revered and feared by people, their removal became a major step in establishing a Christian beachhead in village society.

Why Women?   A good 80 percent of the victims of witch hunts were women, most single and between 45 and 60 years of age. This has suggested to some that misogyny fueled the witch hunts. Based on male hatred and sexual fear of women, and occurring at a time when women threatened to break out from under male control, witch hunts, it has been argued, were simply woman hunts. Older single women may, however, have been vulnerable for more basic social reasons. They were a largely dependent social group in need of public assistance and natural targets for the "social engineering" of the witch hunts. Some accused witches were women who sought to protect and empower themselves within their communities by claiming supernatural powers.

However, gender may have played a largely circumstantial role. Because of their economic straits, more women than men laid claim to the supernatural powers that made them influential in village society. They thus found themselves on the front lines in disproportionate numbers when the church declared war against all who practiced magic without its blessing. Also, the involvement of many of these women in midwifery associated them with the deaths of beloved wives and infants and thus made them targets of local resentment and accusations. Both the church and their neighbors were prepared to think and say the worst about these women. It was a deadly combination.

Witch Panics   Political self-aggrandizement also played a role. As governments expanded and attempted to control their realms, they, like the church, wanted to eliminate all competition for the loyalty of their subjects. Secular rulers as well as the pope could pronounce their competitors "devilish."

Some also argue that the Reformation was responsible for the witch panics. Having weakened the traditional religious protections against demons and the devil, while still portraying them as powerful, the Reformation is said to have forced people to protect themselves by executing perceived witches.

End of the Witch Hunts   Many factors helped end the witch hunts. The emergence of a new, more scientific worldview made it difficult to believe in the powers of witches. When, in the seventeenth century, mind and matter came to be viewed as two independent realities, words and thoughts lost the ability to affect things. A witch's curse was merely words. With advances in medicine and the beginning of insurance companies, people learned to rely on themselves when faced with natural calamity and physical affliction; they no longer searched for supernatural causes and solutions. Witch hunts also tended to get out of hand. Accused witches sometimes alleged that important townspeople had also attended sabbats; even the judges could be so accused. At this point the trials ceased to serve the purposes of those who were conducting them. They not only became dysfunctional but threatened anarchy as well.

Although Protestants, like Catholics, hunted witches, the Reformation may also have contributed to an attitude of mind that put the devil in a more manageable perspective. Protestants ridiculed the sacramental magic of the old church as superstition and directed their faith to a sovereign God absolutely supreme over time and eternity. Even the devil was believed to serve God's purposes and acted only with his permission. Ultimately God was the only significant spiritual force in the universe. This belief made the devil a less fearsome creature. "One little word can slay him," Luther wrote of the devil in "A Mighty Fortress Is Our God," the great hymn of the Reformation.

WRITERS AND PHILOSOPHERS

By the end of the sixteenth century, many could no longer embrace either old Catholic or new Protestant absolutes. Intellectually as well as politically, the seventeenth century would be a period of transition, one already well prepared by the humanists and scientists of the Renaissance and post-Renaissance (see Chapter 24), who reacted strongly against medieval intellectual traditions.

The writers and philosophers of the late sixteenth and the seventeenth centuries were aware that they lived in a period of transition. Some embraced the emerging new science wholeheartedly (Hobbes and Locke), some tried to straddle the two ages (Cervantes and Shakespeare), and still others ignored or opposed the new developments that seemed mortally to threaten traditional values (Pascal).

Miguel de Cervantes Saavedra   Spanish literature of the sixteenth and seventeenth centuries was influenced by the peculiar religious and political history of Spain in this period. Spain was dominated by the Catholic Church, whose piety was strongly promoted by the state. The intertwining of Catholic piety and Spanish political power underlay literary preoccupation with medieval chivalric virtues—in particular, honor and loyalty.

Generally acknowledged to be the greatest Spanish writer of all time, Cervantes (1547–1616) was preoccupied in his work with the strengths and weaknesses of religious idealism. He was the son of a nomadic physician. Having received only a smattering of formal education, he educated himself by insatiable reading in vernacular literature and immersion in the school of life. As a young man, he worked in Rome for a Spanish cardinal. In 1570 he became a soldier and was decorated for gallantry at Lepanto (1571). He conceived and began to write his most famous work, *Don Quixote*, in 1603, while languishing in prison after conviction for theft.

The first part of *Don Quixote* appeared in 1605, and a second part in 1615. If, as many argue, the intent of this work was to satirize the chivalric romances so popular in Spain, Cervantes failed to conceal his deep affection for the character he had created as an object of ridicule, Don Quixote. Don Quixote, a none-too-stable middle-aged man, is driven mad by reading too many chivalric romances. He comes to believe that he is an aspirant to knighthood and must prove his worthiness. To this end, he acquires a rusty suit of armor, mounts an aged horse, and chooses for his inspiration a quite unworthy peasant girl whom he fancies to be a noble lady to whom he can, with honor, dedicate his life.

Don Quixote's foil in the story—Sancho Panza, a clever, worldly wise peasant who serves as his squire—watches with bemused skepticism, but also with genuine sympathy, as his lord does battle with a windmill (which he mistakes for a dragon) and repeatedly makes a fool of himself as he gallops across the countryside. The story ends tragically with Don Quixote's humiliating defeat by a well-meaning friend, who, disguised as a knight, bests Don Quixote in combat and forces him to renounce his quest for knighthood. The humiliated Don Quixote does not, however, come to his senses as a result. He returns sadly to his village to die a shamed and broken-hearted old man.

Throughout *Don Quixote*, Cervantes juxtaposed the down-to-earth realism of Sancho Panza with the old-fashioned religious idealism of Don Quixote. Cervantes admired the one as much as the other. He wanted his readers to remember that to be truly happy, men and women need dreams, even impossible ones, just as much as a sense of reality.

William Shakespeare   There is much less factual knowledge about William Shakespeare (1564–1616), the greatest playwright in the English language, than one would expect of such an important figure. He apparently worked as a school-

Miguel de Cervantes Saavedra (1547–1616), the author of *Don Quixote*, considered by many to be Spain's greatest writer.

Art Resource, N.Y.

teacher for a time and in this capacity acquired his broad knowledge of Renaissance learning and literature. His work shows none of the Puritan distress over worldliness. He took the new commercialism and the bawdy pleasures of the Elizabethan Age in stride and with amusement. In politics and religion, he was a man of his time and not inclined to offend his queen.

That Shakespeare was interested in politics is apparent from his history plays and the references to contemporary political events that fill all his plays. He seems to have viewed government simply, however, through the character of the individual ruler, whether Richard III or Elizabeth Tudor, not in terms of ideal systems or social goals. By modern standards he was a political conservative, accepting the social rankings and the power structure of his day and demonstrating unquestioned patriotism.

Shakespeare knew the theater as one who participated in every phase of its life. A member and principal dramatist of a famous company of actors known as the King's Men, he was a playwright, actor, and part owner of a theater. His work brought together in an original synthesis the best past and current achievements in the dramatic arts. He particularly mastered the psychology of human motivation and passion and had a unique talent for psychological penetration.

Shakespeare wrote histories, comedies, and tragedies. The tragedies are considered his unique achievement. Four of these were written within a three-year period: *Hamlet* (1603), *Othello* (1604), *King Lear* (1605), and *Macbeth* (1606). The most original of the tragedies, *Romeo and Juliet* (1597), transformed an old popular story into a moving drama of "star-cross'd lovers."

In his lifetime and ever since, Shakespeare has been immensely popular with both audiences and readers. As Ben Jonson (1572–1637), a contemporary classical dramatist who created his own school of poets, put it in a tribute affixed to the *First Folio* edition of Shakespeare's plays (1623): "He was not of an age, but for all time."

Blaise Pascal   Blaise Pascal (1623–1662) was a French mathematician and a physical scientist widely acclaimed by his contemporaries. Torn between the continuing dogmatism and the new skepticism of the seventeenth century, he aspired to write a work that would refute both the Jesuits, whose casuistry (i.e., confessional tactics designed to minimize and even excuse sinful acts) he considered a distortion of Christian teaching, and the skeptics, who either denied religion altogether (atheists) or accepted it only as it conformed to reason (deists). Pascal never realized such a definitive work, and his views on these matters exist only in piecemeal form. He wrote against the Jesuits in his *Provincial Letters* (1656–1657), and he left behind a provocative collection of reflections on humankind and religion that was published posthumously under the title *Pensées*.

Pascal was early influenced by the Jansenists, seventeenth-century Catholic opponents of the Jesuits. Although good Catholics, the Jansenists shared with the Calvinists Saint Augustine's belief in the total sinfulness of human beings, their eternal predestination by God, and their complete dependence on faith and grace for knowledge of God and salvation.

Pascal believed that reason and science, although attesting to human dignity, remained of no avail in religion. Here only the reasons of the heart and a "leap of faith" could prevail. Pascal saw two essential truths in the Christian religion: that a loving God, worthy of human attainment, exists; and that human beings, because they are corrupted in nature, are utterly unworthy of God. Pascal believed that the atheists and deists of the age had spurned the lesson of reason. For him, rational analysis of the human condition attested to humankind's utter mortality and corruption and exposed the weakness of reason itself in resolving the problems of human nature and destiny. Reason should rather drive those who truly heed it to faith and dependence on divine grace.

Pascal made a famous wager with the skeptics. It is a better bet, he argued, to believe that God exists and to stake everything on his promised mercy than not to do so; if God does exist, everything will be gained by the believer, whereas the loss incurred by having believed in God should he prove not to exist is, by comparison, very slight.

Pascal was convinced that belief in God measurably improved earthly life psychologically and disciplined it morally, regardless of whether God proved in the end to exist. He thought that great danger lay in the surrender of traditional religious values. Pascal urged his contemporaries to seek self-understanding by "learned ignorance" and to discover humankind's greatness by recognizing its misery. Thereby he hoped to counter what he believed to be the false optimism of the new rationalism and science.

Baruch Spinoza   The most controversial thinker of the seventeenth century was Baruch Spinoza (1632–1677), the son of a Jewish merchant of Amsterdam. Spinoza's philosophy caused his excommunication by his own synagogue in 1656. In 1670 he published his *Treatise on Religious and Political Philosophy*, a work that criticized the dogmatism of Dutch Calvinists and championed freedom of thought. During his lifetime, both Jews and Protestants attacked him as an atheist.

Spinoza's most influential writing, *Ethics*, appeared after his death in 1677. Religious leaders universally condemned it for its apparent espousal of pantheism. God and nature were so closely identified by Spinoza that little room seemed left either for divine revelation in Scripture or for the personal immortality of the soul, denials equally repugnant to Jews and to Christians.

The most controversial part of *Ethics* deals with the nature of substance and of God. According to Spinoza there is only one substance, which is self-caused, free, and infinite, and God is that substance. From this definition, it follows that everything that exists is in God and cannot even be conceived of apart from him. Such a doctrine is not literally pantheistic, because God is still seen to be more than the created world that he, as primal substance, embraces. Nonetheless, in Spinoza's view, statements about the natural world are also statements about divine nature. Mind and matter are seen to be extensions of the infinite substance of God; what transpires in the world of humankind and nature is a necessary outpouring of the Divine.

Such teaching clearly ran the danger of portraying the world as eternal and human actions as unfree and inevitable, the expression of a divine fatalism. Such points of view had been considered heresies by Jews and Christians because these views deny the creation of the world by God and destroy any voluntary basis for personal reward and punishment.

Thomas Hobbes   Thomas Hobbes (1588–1679) was the most original political philosopher of the seventeenth century. Although he never broke with the Church of England, he came to share basic Calvinist beliefs, especially the low view of human nature and the ideal of a commonwealth based on a covenant, both of which find eloquent expression in his political philosophy.

Hobbes was an urbane and much-traveled man and one of the most enthusiastic supporters of the new scientific movement. During the 1630s he visited Paris, where he came to know Descartes; after the outbreak of the Puritan Revolution (see Chapter 20) in 1640, he lived as an exile in Paris until 1651. Hobbes also spent time with Galileo (see Chapter 23) in Italy and took a special interest in the works of William Harvey. Harvey was a physiologist famed for the discovery of how blood circulated through the body; his scientific writings influenced Hobbes's own tracts on bodily motions.

Hobbes was driven to the vocation of political philosophy by the English Civil War (see Chapter 21). In 1651 his *Leviathan* appeared. Its subject was the political consequences of human passions, and its originality lay in (1) its making natural law, rather than common law (i.e., custom or precedent), the basis of all positive law; and (2) its defense of a representative theory of absolute authority against the theory of the divine right of kings. Hobbes maintained that statute law found its justification only as an expression of the law of nature and that rulers derived their authority from the consent of the people.

18.1
"The Mortal God":
Leviathan (1651)

Hobbes viewed humankind and society in a thoroughly materialistic and mechanical way. Human beings are defined as a collection of material particles in motion. All their psychological processes begin with and are derived from bare sensation, and all their motivations are egotistical, intended to increase pleasure and minimize pain.

Despite this seemingly low estimate of human beings, Hobbes believed much could be accomplished by the reasoned use of science. All was contingent, however, on the correct use of that greatest of all human powers, one compounded of the powers of most people: the commonwealth, in which people are united by their consent in one all-powerful person.

The key to Hobbes's political philosophy is a brilliant myth of the original state of humankind. According to this myth, human beings in the natural state are generally inclined to a "perpetual and restless desire of power after power that ceases only in death."[6] As all people desire—and in the state of nature have a natural right to—everything, their equality breeds enmity, competition, and diffidence, and the desire for glory begets perpetual quarreling—"a war of every man against every man."[7]

Whereas earlier and later philosophers saw the original human state as a paradise from which humankind had fallen, Hobbes saw it as a corruption from which only society had delivered people. Contrary to the views of Aristotle and of Christian thinkers like Thomas Aquinas, Hobbes saw human beings not as sociable, political animals, but as self-centered beasts, laws unto themselves, utterly without a master unless one is imposed by force.

According to Hobbes, people escape the impossible state of nature only by entering a social contract that creates a commonwealth tightly ruled by law and order. The social contract obliges every person, for the sake of peace and self-defense, to agree to set aside personal rights to all things. We should impose restrictions on the liberty of others only to the degree that we would allow others to restrict our own.

Because words and promises are insufficient to guarantee this state, the social contract also establishes the coercive force necessary to compel compliance with the covenant. Hobbes believed that the dangers of anarchy were far greater than those of tyranny, and he conceived of the ruler's power as absolute and unlimited. There is no room in Hobbes's political philosophy for political protest in the name of individual conscience, nor for resistance to legitimate authority by private individuals—features of *Leviathan* criticized by his contemporary Catholics and Puritans alike.

[6] *Leviathan Parts I and II*, ed. by H. W. Schneider (Indianapolis: Bobbs-Merrill, 1958), p. 86.
[7] Ibid., p. 106.

John Locke   John Locke (1632–1704) has proved to be the most influential political thinker of the seventeenth century.[8] His political philosophy came to be embodied in the so-called Glorious Revolution of 1688–1689 (Chapter 20). Although he was not as original as Hobbes, his political writings were a major source of the later Enlightenment criticism of absolutism, and they gave inspiration to both the American and French Revolutions.

Locke's two most famous works are the *Essay Concerning Human Understanding* (1690) (discussed in Chapter 23) and *Two Treatises of Government* (1690). Locke wrote *Two Treatises of Government* against the argument that rulers were absolute in their power. Rulers, Locke argued, remain bound to the law of nature, which is the voice of reason, teaching that "all mankind [are] equal and independent, [and] no one ought to harm another in his life, health, liberty, or possessions,"[9] inasmuch as all human beings are the images and property of God. According to Locke, people enter social contracts, empowering legislatures and monarchs to "umpire" their disputes, precisely to preserve their natural rights, and not to give rulers an absolute power over them.

"Whenever that end [namely, the preservation of life, liberty, and property for which power is given to rulers by a commonwealth] is manifestly neglected or opposed, the trust must necessarily be forfeited and the power devolved into the hands of those that gave it, who may place it anew where they think best for their safety and security."[10] From Locke's point of view, absolute monarchy was "inconsistent" with civil society and could be "no form of civil government at all."[11]

SUMMARY

Voyages of Discovery   In the late fifteenth century, Europe began to expand around the globe. Driven by both mercenary and religious motives, the Portuguese pioneered a sea route around Africa to India and the Far East, and the Spanish discovered the Americas. The consequences were immense for Europeans, native Americans, Africans, and Asians. In time, a truly global society would emerge.

The Reformation   The Reformation began in Germany with Martin Luther's attack on indulgences in 1517. Despite the opposition to the Reformation of Emperor Charles V, Luther had the support of many German princes. The Reformation shattered the religious unity of Europe. In Switzerland, Zwingli and Calvin launched their own versions of Protestantism. In England, Henry VIII repudiated papal authority when the pope refused to grant him a divorce. The different protestant sects were often as hostile to each other as they were to Catholicism. The Reformation also led to far-reaching changes in religious practices and social attitudes, including steps toward the advancement of women.

The Roman Catholic Church also acted to reform itself. The Council of Trent tightened church discipline and reaffirmed traditional doctrine. The Jesuits converted many Protestants back to Catholicism.

The Wars of Religion   The religious divisions of Europe led to more than a century of warfare from the 1520s to 1648. The chief battlegrounds were in France,

---

[8]Locke's scientific writings are discussed in Chapter 24.

[9]*The Second Treatise of Government*, ed. by T. P. Peardon (Indianapolis: Bobbs-Merrill, 1952), chap. 2, sects. 4–6, pp. 4–6.

[10]Ibid., chap. 13, sect. 149, p. 84.

[11]Ibid.

the Netherlands, and Germany. When the Thirty Years' War ended in 1648, Europe was permanently divided into Catholic and Protestant areas.

Superstition and Enlightenment The Reformation led to both dark and constructive views of human nature. Perhaps the darkest view was the witch crazes that erupted across Europe. Thousands of innocent people, mostly women, were persecuted and executed as witches between 1400 and 1700 by both Catholic and Protestant authorities.

In literature and philosophy, however, these years witnessed an outpouring of creative thinking. Among the greatest writers of the age were Cervantes, Shakespeare, Pascal, Spinoza, Hobbes, and Locke.

REVIEW QUESTIONS

1. What were the main problems of the church that contributed to the Protestant Reformation? Why was the church unable to suppress dissent as it had earlier?

2. Why did the Reformation begin in Germany?

3. What was the Catholic Reformation?

4. Why did Henry VIII break with the Catholic Church? Was the "new" religion he established really Protestant?

5. Were the wars of religion really over religion?

KEY TERMS

Counter-Reformation   (p. 345)   **indulgences**   (p. 337)

Diet of Worms   (p. 399)   **Reformation**   (p. 337)

Huguenot   (p. 351)   **transubstantiation**   (p. 344)

 For additional study resources for this chapter, go to:
www.prenhall.com/craig/chapter16

IMAGE KEY
for pages 330–331

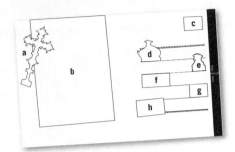

a. Fifteenth century Italian silver cross

b. Versuchung Christi (1547), a Catholic portrayal of Martin Luther tempting Jesus

c. Martin Luther and Katharina von Bora

d. Vasco da Gama

e. Martin Luther

f. Worshippers gathering at the Temple de Lyon

g. Le Massacre de la St-Barthelemy, entre 1572 et 1584

h. Public burning of three witches at Derneburg in October, 1555.

A bronze plaque showing three warriors from Benin, West Africa. Note that the two small figures in the background apparently depict Portuguese or other European soldiers. Benin Plaque, Brass. Lost wax W. Africa 16th–17th c. A.D. Hillel Burger/Peabody Museum, Harvard University.

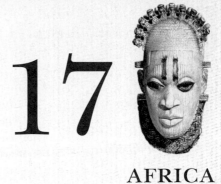

17

AFRICA
ca. 1000–1800

HOW DID Islam spread
south of the Sahara?

WHAT WERE the four most important states
in the Sahel between 1000 and 1600?

WHY DID Christianity
gradually disappear
in Nubia?

HOW DID the arrival of Europeans affect
the peoples of Coastal West and Central Africa?

HOW DID Swahili
language and culture develop?

HOW DID slavery affect race relations in the Cape Colony?

IMAGE KEY
Image Key for pages 368–369
is on page 386.

In this chapter we explore, region by region, some salient developments in Africa from 1000 to 1800. While the Atlantic slave trade is treated in Chapter 19, its importance must be kept in mind as we review the period's other developments. We begin with Africa above the equator, where the influence of Islam increased and where substantial empires and kingdoms developed and flourished. Then we discuss west, east, central, and southern Africa and the effects of first Arab-Islamic and then European influence in both regions.

NORTH AFRICA AND EGYPT

WHY WAS no single power able
to control North Africa for long?

In politics, this period witnessed the influential dynasties of the Fatimids (909–969 in Tunisia; 969–1171 in Egypt), the Almoravids (1056–1147 in Senegal and the western Sudan; 1062–1118 in Marrakesh and western North Africa; 1086–1147 in Spain), the Almohads (1130–1269 in western North Africa; 1145–1212 in Spain), the Ayyubids (1169–1250 in Egypt), the Mamluks (1250–1517 in Egypt and the eastern Mediterranean); and the Ottomans (from the fourteenth century) across most of mediterranean Africa. In general, a feisty regionalism characterized states, city-states, and tribal groups north of the Sahara and along the lower Nile, especially vis-à-vis external power centers, such as Baghdad and Spain. No single power controlled them for long. Regionalism persisted even after 1500, when most of North Africa came under the influence—and often direct control—of the Ottoman Empire.

By 1800, the nominally Ottoman domains from Egypt to Algeria were effectively independent principalities. In Egypt, the Ottomans had established direct rule after their defeat of the Mamluks in 1517, but by the seventeenth and eighteenth centuries, power had already passed to Egyptian governors descended from the former ruling Mamluks. The Mediterranean coastlands between Egypt and Morocco were officially Ottoman provinces, or regencies, whether under local governors or Ottoman deputies. By the eighteenth century, however, Algiers, Tripoli (in modern Libya), and Tunisia were virtually independent of the Ottomans.

Morocco was the only North African sultanate to remain fully independent after 1700. Its most important dynasty was that of the Sa'dis (1554–1659).

THE SPREAD OF ISLAM SOUTH OF THE SAHARA

HOW DID Islam spread south
of the Sahara?

By 1800, Islamic influence in sub-Saharan Africa affected most of the Sudanic belt and the coast of East Africa as far south as modern Zimbabwe. Typically, Islam never penetrated beyond the ruling or commercial classes of a region and tended to co-exist or blend with indigenous ideas. Nevertheless, Islam and its carriers brought commercial and political changes as well as the Qur'an, new religious practices, and literate culture on which innovations, from architecture and technology to intellectual life and administrative practice depended.

In East Africa, Islamic city-states along the coast from Mogadishu to Kilwa became a major factor. By contrast, in the western and central parts of the continent, Islam penetrated south of the Sahara into the Sudan by overland routes, primarily from North Africa and the Nile valley. Its agents were sometimes traders, but primarily emigrants from the east seeking new land.

From the 1030s, zealous militants known as Almoravids began an overt conversion campaign that extended to the western Sahel and Sahara. This movement eventually swept into Ghana, and finally Kumbi in 1076. Farther west, the Fulbe rulers of Takrur along the Senegal became Muslim in the 1030s and propagated their new faith among their subjects.

Sahelian Empires of the Western and Central Sudan

Urbanization and state formation in sub-Saharan Africa did not occur only in response to trans-Saharan trade with the Islamic world, which dates largely from the end of the first millennium. Substantial states had risen in the first millennium C.E. in the Sahel regions just south of the Sahara proper. From about 1000 to 1600, four of these developed into notable and relatively long-lived empires: Ghana, Mali, and Songhai in the western Sudan, and Kanem-Bornu in the central Sudan.

WHAT WERE the four most important states in the Sahel between 1000 and 1600?

Ghana

Ghana was located north of modern Ghana between and north of the inland Niger delta and the upper Senegal. It emerged as a regional power near the end of the first millennium and flourished for about two centuries. Its capital, Kumbi (or Kumbi Saleh), on the desert's edge, was well sited for the Saharan and Sahelian trade networks. Ghana's major population group were the Soninke. (*Ghana* is the Soninke term for "ruler.")

The Ghanaian rulers were matrilineally descended. The king was supreme judge and held court regularly to hear grievances. The royal ceremonies were embellished with the full trappings of regal wealth and power appropriate to a king held to be divinely blessed if not semi-divine himself.

Tribute from the empire's many chieftaincies and taxes on royal lands and crops supplemented the duties levied on all incoming and outgoing trade. This trade involved a variety of goods—notably imported salt, cloth, and metal goods such as copper—probably in exchange for gold and perhaps kola nuts from the south. The regime apparently also controlled the gold (and, presumably, the slave) trade that originated in the savannah to the south and west.

Although the king and court of Ghana did not convert to Islam, they made elaborate arrangements to accommodate Muslim traders and government servants in their own settlement a few miles from the royal preserve in Kumbi Saleh. Muslim traders were prominent in the court, literate Muslims administered the government, and Muslim legists advised the ruler. In Ghana's hierarchical society, slaves were at the bottom; farmers and draftsmen above them; merchants above them; and the king, his court, and the nobility on top.

A huge, well-trained army secured royal control and enabled the kings to extend their sway in the late tenth century to the Atlantic shore and to the south as well (see Map 17–1). Ghanaian troops captured Awdaghast, the important southern terminus of the trans-Saharan trade route to Morocco, from the Berbers in 992. The empire was, however, vulnerable to

The Djinguereber mosque in Timbuktu. This mud and wood building is typical of western Sudanese mosques. The distinctive tower of the mosque was a symbol of the presence of Islam, which came to places like Timbuktu in central and West Africa by way of overland trade routes.

Photograph by Eliot Elisofon, National Museum of African Art, Eliot Elisofon Archives, Smithsonian Institution, Washington, D.C.

MAP EXPLORATION

Interactive map: To explore this map further, go to **http://www.prenhall.com/craig2/map17.1**

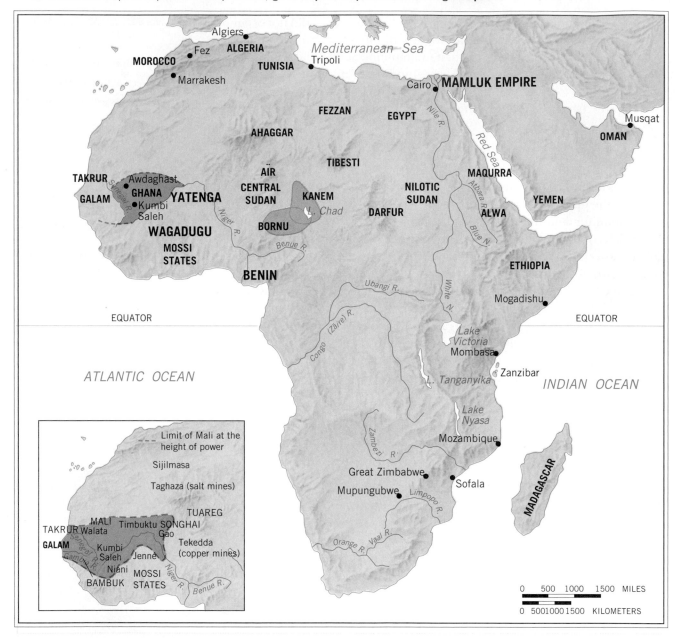

MAP 17–1

Africa circa 900–1500.   Shown are major cities and states referred to in the text. The main map shows the region of West Africa occupied by the empire of Ghana from circa 990 to circa 1180. The inset shows the region occupied by Mali between 1230 and 1450.

WHY WAS Ghana's location important for its prosperity?

attack from the desert fringe, as Almoravid Berber forces proved in 1054 when they took Awdaghast in a single raid.

Ghana's rulers may have converted to Islam soon after 1100. Ghana's empire was probably destroyed in the late twelfth century by the actively anti-Muslim Soso people from the mountains southeast of Kumbi Saleh.

MALI

After the Almoravids brought their reform movement to the western Sahel at the end of the eleventh century, their proselytizing zeal led to conversion of many of the region's ruling classes. It was, however, over a half-century after the breakup of Ghana's empire before anyone in the western Sahel, Muslim or non-Muslim, could reestablish an empire of comparable extent. With Ghana's collapse and the Almoravids' failure to build a new empire below the Sahara (largely because of their focus on North Africa), the western Sudan broke up into smaller kingdoms. The former Ghanaian provinces of Mande and Takrur were already independent before 1076, and in the early twelfth century Takrur's control of the Senegal valley and the gold-producing region of Galam made it briefly the strongest state in the western Sudan. Like Ghana, however, it was soon eclipsed by developments to the east, along the upper Niger—first the brief Soso ascendancy and then the rise of Mali.

In the mid-thirteenth century, the Keita ruling clan of a Ghanaian successor kingdom, Mali, forged a new and lasting empire. The Keita kings dominated enough of the Sahel to control the flow of West African gold from the Senegal regions and the forestlands south of the Niger to the trans-Saharan trade routes, and the influx of copper and especially salt in exchange. Because they were farther south, in the fertile land along the Niger, than their Ghanaian predecessors had been, they were better placed to control all trade on the upper Niger and to add to it the Gambia and Senegal trade to the west. They were also able to use war captives for plantation labor in the Niger inland delta to produce surplus food for trade.

Agriculture and cattle farming were the primary occupations of Mali's population and, together with the gold trade, the mainstays of the economy. Rice was grown in the river valleys and millet in the drier parts of the Sahel. Together with beans, yams, and other agricultural products, this made for a plentiful food supply. Fishing flourished along the Niger and elsewhere. Animal husbandry was strongest among pastoralists of the Sahel, such as the Fulani (or Fulbe), but cattle, sheep, and goats were also plentiful in the Niger valley by the fourteenth century. Many of the Fulani seem to have been attracted by excellent pasturages to the riverine regions. The chief craft specialties were metalworking (iron and gold) and weaving of cotton grown within the empire.

The Malinke, a southern Mande-speaking people of the upper Niger region, formed the core population of the new state. They apparently lived in walled

QUICK REVIEW

Mali

♦ Keita clan forged Mali in mid-thirteenth century

♦ Keiti kings controlled the flow of West African gold

♦ Agriculture and cattle farming were primary occupations of Mali's people

The great mosque at Jenne, one of the important commercial centers controlled by the empire of Mali in the 13th and 14th centuries.

Ann Stalcup

✦ HISTORY'S VOICES ✦

MUSLIM REFORM IN SONGHAI

 round 1500 Askia Muhammad al-Turi, the first Muslim among the rulers of Songhai, wrote to the North African Muslim theologian Muhammad al-Maghili (d. 1504) with a series of questions about proper Muslim practices. These excerpts are from the seventh question of al-Turi and the answers given by al-Maghili. Here one sees something of the zeal of the new convert to conform to traditional religious norms, as well as the rather strict and puritanical "official line" of the conservative Maliki ulama *on "pagan" mores. Also evident is the king's desire for bettering social order and his concern for justice in the market and elsewhere. However, also manifest is that many of the more strongly Shari'a-minded* ulama *did not want to compromise at all, let alone allow syncretism to emerge among formerly pagan, newly converted groups.*

WHAT ARE the problems and corresponding solutions listed in the letter? Which problem did al-Maghili find most serious? Why? Which do you think would have been most serious? Why?

From Al-Turi's Seventh Question

Among the people [of the Songhay Empire said Askia Muhammad], there are some who claim knowledge of the supernatural through sand divining and the like, or through the disposition of the stars . . . [while] some assert that they can write (talismans) to bring good fortune . . . or to ward off bad fortune. . . . Some defraud in weights and measures. . . .

One of their evil practices [continued Askia Muhammad] is the free mixing of men and women in the markets and streets and the failure of women to veil themselves . . . [while] among the people of Djenné [Jenne] it is an established custom for a girl not to cover any part of her body as long as she remains a virgin . . . and all the most beautiful girls walk about naked among people. . .

So give us legal ruling concerning these people and their ilk, and may God Most High reward you!

From Al-Maghili's Answer

The answer—and God it is who directs to the right course—is that everything you have mentioned concerning people's behavior in some parts of this country is gross error. It is the bounden duty of the commander of the Muslims and all other believers who have the power [replied al-Maghili] to change every one of these evil practices.

As for any who claims knowledge of the supernatural in the ways you have mentioned . . . he is a liar and an unbeliever. . . . Such people must be forced to renounce it by the sword. Then whoever renounces such deeds should be left in peace, but whoever persists should be killed with the sword as an unbeliever; his body should not be washed or shrouded, and he should not be buried in a Muslim graveyard. . . .

As for defrauding in weights and measures [continued al-Maghili] it is forbidden (*haram*) according to the Qur'an, the Sunna and the consensus of opinion of the learned men of the Muslim community. It is the bounden duty of the commander of the Muslims to appoint a trustworthy man in charge of the markets, and to safeguard people's means of subsistence. He should standardize all the scales in each province. . . . Similarly, all measures both large and small must be rectified so that they conform to a uniform standard. . . .

Now, what you mentioned about the free mixing of men and women and leaving the pudenda uncovered is one of the greatest abominations. The commander of the Muslims must exert himself to prevent all these things. . . . He should appoint trustworthy men to watch over this by day and night, in secret and in the open. This is not to be considered as spying on the Muslims; it is only a way of caring for them and curbing evildoers, especially when corruption becomes widespread in the land as it has done in Timbuktu and Djenné [Jenne] and so on.

From *The African Past*, trans. by J. O. Hunwick, reprinted in Basil Davidson (Grosset and Dunlap, The Universal Library), pp. 86–88. Reprinted by permission of Curtis Brown Ltd. Copyright © 1964 by Basil Davidson.

urban settlements typical of the western savannah region. Each walled town was surrounded by its own agricultural land, and held perhaps 1,000 to 15,000 people.

The Keita dynasty had converted early to Islam (ca. 1100). During Mali's heyday in the thirteenth and fourteenth centuries, its kings often made the pilgrimage to Mecca. From their travel in the central Islamic lands, they brought back new ideas about political and military organization. Through Muslim traders' networks, Islam also connected Mali to other areas of Africa.

Mali's imperial power was built largely by one leader, the Keita King Sundiata (or Sunjaata; r. 1230–1255). Sundiata and his successors, aided by significant population growth in the western savannah, exploited their agricultural resources and Malinke commercial skills to build an empire even more powerful than its Ghanaian predecessor. Sundiata extended his control well beyond the former domains of Ghana, west to the Atlantic coast and east beyond Timbuktu. By controlling the commercial entrepôts of Gao, Walata, and Jenne, he was able to dominate the Saharan as well as the Niger trade. He built his capital, Niani, into a major city. Niani was located on a tributary of the Niger in the savannah at the edge of the forest in a gold- and iron-rich region, well away from the lands of the Sahel nomads and well south of Ghana's capital, Kumbi. It had access to the forest trade products of gold, kola nuts, and palm oil; it was easily defended by virtue of its surrounding small hills; and it was easily reached by river. (See Sundiata)

The empire that Sundiata and his successors built ultimately encompassed three major regions and language groups of Sudanic West Africa: (1) the Senegal region (including Takrur), occupied by speakers of the West Atlantic Niger-Kongo language group (including Fulbe, Tukulor, Wolof, Serer); (2) the central Mande states between Senegal and Niger, occupied by the Niger-Kongo-speaking Soninke and Mandinke peoples; and (3) the peoples of the Niger in the Gao region who spoke Songhai, the only Nilo-Saharan language west of the Lake Chad basin.

Mali was less a centralized bureaucratic state than the center of a vast sphere of influence that included provinces and tribute-paying kingdoms. Many chieftaincies retained much of their independence but recognized the sovereignty of the supreme, sacred *mansa*, or "emperor," of the Malian realms.

The greatest Keita king proved to be Mansa Musa (r. 1312–1337), whose pilgrimage through Mamluk Cairo to Mecca in 1324 became famous. At home, he consolidated Mali's power, securing peace for most of his reign throughout his vast dominions. Musa's devoutness as a Muslim fostered the further spread of Islam in the empire and beyond. Under his rule, Timbuktu became known far and wide for its *madrasas* and libraries, and for its poets, scientists, and architects, making the city the leading intellectual center of sub-Saharan Islam as well as a major trading city of the Sahel.

Mali's dominance waned in the fifteenth century as the result of rivalries for succession to the throne. As time went on, subject dependencies became independent, and the empire withered. After 1450, a new Songhai power in Gao to the east ended Mali's imperial authority.

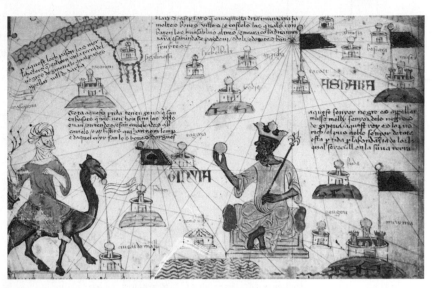

Mansa Musa early medieval painting
Cliche Bibliotheque Nationale de France, Paris

 **11.3**
Ibn Battuta in Mali

QUICK REVIEW

King Sundiata (r. 1230–1255)
- Built Mali's imperial power
- Mali's empire more powerful than Ghanaian predecessor
- Empire encompassed three major regions: Senegal, the central Mande states, and the peoples of the Niger in the Gao region

 11.1
Mansa Musa: The "King Who Sits on a Mountain of Gold"

MAP EXPLORATION

Interactive map: To explore this map further, go to **http://www.prenhall.com/craig2/map17.2**

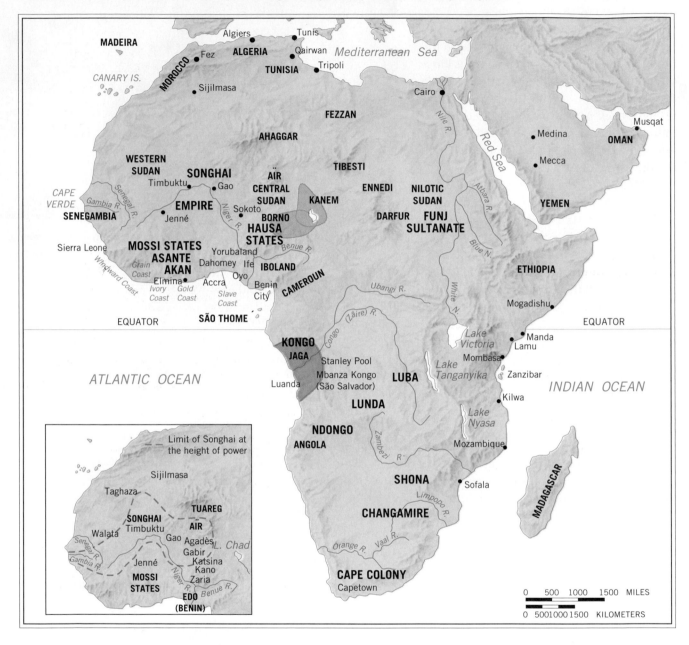

MAP 17–2

Africa ca. 1500–1800.   Important towns, regions, peoples, and states. The inset shows the empire of Songhai at its greatest extent in the early 16th century.

WHAT WAS Songhai's major source of wealth?

SONGHAI

Gao became an imperial power in the reign of Sonni Ali (1464–1492). Sonni Ali made the Songhai Empire so powerful that it dominated the political history of the western Sudan for more than a century and was arguably the most powerful state in Africa (see Map 17–2).

Askia Muhammad al-Turi (r. 1493–1528) continued Sonni Ali's expansionist policies. Between them, Sonni Ali and Askia Muhammad built an empire that stretched from near the Atlantic into the Sahara and the central Sudan. The ancient caravan trade across the Sahara to the North African coasts provided their major source of wealth.

Muhammad al-Turi was an enthusiastic Muslim. He built up the Songhai state after the model of the Islamic empire of Mali. In his reign, Muslim scholars made Timbuktu a major intellectual and legal training center for the whole Sudan. Nevertheless, his reforms failed to Islamize the empire or to ensure a strong central state under his less able successors.

The last powerful Askia leader was Askia Dawud (r. 1549–1583), under whom Songhai economic prosperity and intellectual life peaked. Still, difficulties mounted. Civil war broke out over succession to the throne in 1586, and the empire was divided. The once-great state became only one among many regional competitors in the western Sudan.

KANEM AND KANEM-BORNU

A fourth sizable Sahelian empire, Kanem, in the central Sudan, arose after 1100. Roughly contemporaneous with the Malian Empire to the west, Kanem began as a southern Saharan confederation of the black nomadic tribes known as Zaghawah. Their key leader, Mai Dunama Dibbalemi (r. ca. 1221–1259), was probably the first Kanuri leader to embrace Islam, which appears to have entrenched itself among the Kanuri ruling class during his reign. Dibbalemi used Islam to sanction his rule and provide a rationale for expansion through *jihad,* or holy "struggle" against polytheists.

Dibbalemi and his successors expanded Kanuri power to control important trade routes to Libya and Egypt.

Civil strife, largely over the royal succession, weakened the Kanuri state from the later fourteenth century, and after 1400, the locus of power shifted from Kanem proper westward, to the land of Bornu, southwest of Lake Chad. Near the end of the sixteenth century, firearms and Turkish military instructors enabled the Kanuri leader Idris Alawma (r. ca. 1575–1610) to unify Kanem and Bornu. He set up an avowedly Islamic state and extended his rule even into Hausaland, between Bornu and the Niger River. The center of trading activity as well as political power and security now shifted from the Niger Bend east to the territory under Kanuri control.

Deriving its prosperity from the trans-Saharan trade, Idris Alawma's regional empire survived for nearly a century, but by 1700, its power had been reduced by the Hausa states to the west (see Chapter 31).

Sahelian Empires of the Western Sudan

ca. 990–ca. 1180?	Empire of Ghana
1076	Ghana loses Awdaghast to Almoravids
1180–1230	Soso clan briefly controls the old Ghanaian territories
ca. 1230–1450	Empire of Mali, founded by Sundiata
1230–1255	Reign of Sundiata
1312–1337	Reign of Mansa Musa
1374	Independent Songhai state emerges in Gao after throwing off Malian rule
ca. 1450–1600	Songhai empire at Gao
1464–1591	Askia dynasty
1464–1492	Reign of Sonni Ali
1493–1528	Reign of Askia Muhammad al-Turi
1549–1583	Reign of Askia Dawud
1590s	Collapse of the Songhai Empire

THE EASTERN SUDAN

The Christian states of Maqurra and Alwa in the Nilotic Sudan, or Nubia, lasted for more than 600 years from their early seventh-century beginnings. Often thought of as isolated, Christian Nubia in fact maintained political, religious, and commercial contact with Egypt, the Red Sea world, and the east-central and even central Sudan. From late Fatimid times onward, both

WHY DID Christianity gradually disappear in Nubia?

Central Sudanic Empires	
ca. 1100–1500	Kanuri Empire of Kanem
ca. 1220s–1400	Height of Empire of Kanem
1221–1259	Reign of Mai Dunama Dibbalemi
1575–1846	Kanuri Empire of Kanem-Bornu
1575–1610	Reign of Idris Alawma, major architect of the state

Maqurra and Alwa were subject to growing Muslim minorities. The result was a long-term intermingling of Arabic and Nubian cultures and the creation of a new Nilotic Sudanese people and culture.

Islam spread slowly with Arab immigration into the upper Nile region. A significant factor in the gradual disappearance of Christianity in Nubia was the apparently elite character of Christianity there and its association with foreign Egyptian Coptic Christianity. Maqurra became officially Muslim at the beginning of the fourteenth century. The Islamization of Alwa came somewhat later, under the Funj sultanate that replaced the Alwa state.

The Funj state flourished from just after 1500 until 1762. The Funj developed an Islamic society whose Arabized character was unique in sub-Saharan Africa. A much-reduced Funj state held out until an Ottoman-Egyptian invasion in 1821.

THE FORESTLANDS—COASTAL WEST AND CENTRAL AFRICA

WEST AFRICAN FOREST KINGDOMS: THE EXAMPLE OF BENIN

Many states had developed in West Africa centuries before the first Portuguese reports in 1485. Benin, the best known of these kingdoms, reflects, especially in its art, the sophistication of West African culture before 1500.

HOW DID the arrival of Europeans affect the peoples of Coastal West and Central Africa?

Benin State and Society   Some kind of distinct kingdom of Benin likely existed as early as the twelfth century, and the power of the king, or **oba**, at this time was sharply limited by the **uzama**, an order of hereditary indigenous chiefs. Only in the fifteenth century, with King Ewuare, did Benin become a royal autocracy and a large state of major regional importance.

Ewuare apparently established a government in which he had sweeping authority, although he exercised it in light of the deliberations of a royal council formed from the palace *uzama* and the townspeople. He gave each chief specific administrative responsibilities and rank in the government hierarchy. Ewuare and his successors engaged in major wars of expansion and claimed for the office of *oba* and increasing ritual authority.

In the seventeenth century, the *oba* was transformed from a military leader into a religious figure with supernatural powers. Human sacrifice, specifically of slaves, seems to have accompanied the cult of deceased kings. Succession by primogeniture was discontinued, and new *obas* were chosen by the *uzama* from any branch of the royal family.

Benin Art   The lasting significance of Benin lies in its court art, especially its famous brass sculptures. The splendid terra-cotta, ivory, and brass statuary sculpture of Ife-Benin are among the glories of human creativity. These magnificent sculptures, initially realistic or naturalistic and later sometimes highly stylized, seem to be wholly indigenous African products.

oba   Title of the king of Benin.

uzama   An order of hereditary chiefs in Benin.

The best sculptures are cast bronze plaques depicting legendary and historical scenes. These were mounted on the walls and columns of the royal palace in Benin City. There are also brass heads, apparently of royalty. Similar sculptures have been found both well to the north and in the Niger delta. Recent excavations east of the Niger at Igbo-Ukwu have unearthed stunning terra-cottas and bronzes that belong to the same general artistic culture, which is dated as early as the ninth century. These artifacts testify to the high cultural level attained in traditional African societies that had little or no contact with the extra-African world.

Benin	
ca. 1100–1897	Benin state
ca. 1300	First Ife king of Benin state
1440–1475	Reign of Ewuare

EUROPEAN ARRIVALS ON THE COASTLANDS

Along the coasts of West and central Africa, many changes occurred between 1500 and 1800, including those connected with trade in West African gold and other commodities and the effects associated with the importation and spread in West and central Africa of food crops, such as maize, peanuts, squash, sweet potatoes, cocoa, and cassava (manioc) from the Americas. The gradual involvement of Africa in the emerging global economic system paved the way for eventual colonial domination of the continent, especially its coastal regions, by the Europeans. The European names for segments of the coastline—the Grain (or Pepper) Coast, the Ivory Coast, the Gold Coast, and the Slave Coast—identify the main exports that could be extracted by ship and vividly indicate the nature of the emerging relationship.

Senegambia   In West Africa, Senegambia—which takes its name from the Senegal and Gambia Rivers—was one of the earliest regions affected by European trade. Its maritime trade with European powers, like the older overland trade, was primarily in gold and products such as salt, cotton goods, hides, and copper. Senegambian states also provided perhaps a third of all African slaves exported during the sixteenth century. Thereafter, the focus of the slave trade shifted south and east along the coast. Over time, Portuguese-African mulattos and the British came to control the Gambia River trade, while the French won the Senegal River markets.

The Gold Coast   The Gold Coast derives its name from its importance after 1500 as the outlet for West Africa's gold fields. Here, beginning with the Portuguese at Elmina in 1481, European states and companies built coastal forts to protect their trade. The trade encouraged the growth of larger states—like the Akan forest states near the coast and the Gonja state just north of the forest—perhaps because they could better control commerce.

The intensive contact of the Gold Coast with Europeans also led to the spread of American crops, notably maize and cassava, into the region, which contributed to substantial population growth. Slaves became big business here in the late seventeenth century, especially in the Accra region. The economy was so disrupted by the slave trade that gold mining declined. Eventually more gold came into the Gold Coast from the sale of slaves than went out from its mines.

This naturalistic brass head (29 cm high), which dates to the thirteenth century, conveys the remarkable power of the art of Benin.
© Frank Willet

Central Africa

1300s	Kongo kingdom founded
1483	Portuguese come to central African coast
ca. 1506–1543	Reign of Affonso I as king of Kongo
1571	Angola becomes Portuguese proprietary colony

CENTRAL AFRICA

The vast center of the subcontinent is bounded by swamps in the north, coastal rain forests to the west, highlands to the east, and deserts in the south. Before 1500, these natural barriers impeded international contact and trade with the interior.

The coming of the Portuguese broke down this isolation, albeit slowly. The Portuguese came looking for gold and silver but found none. Instead, they exported such goods as ivory and palm cloth. Ultimately, their main export was slaves, first to the Portuguese sugar plantations on Sao Thomé island in the Gulf of Guinea, then to Brazil.

The Kongo Kingdom   Kongo was the major state with which the Portuguese dealt after coming to central Africa in 1483. Dating from probably the fourteenth century, the Kongo kingdom was located on a fertile, well-watered plateau south of the lower Zaïre River valley, between the coast and the Kwango River in the east. Here, astride the border between forest and grassland, the Kongo kings had built a central government based on a pyramid structure of tax or tribute collec-

This Benin bronze plaque came from the palace of the Obas of Benin and dates to the Edo period of Benin culture, 1575–1625. It depicts two Portuguese males, perhaps a father and son, holding hands. It is likely that they represent the traders or government officials who came to the African coasts in increasing numbers from the end of the fifteenth century on. On the West African coast and in Central Africa they trafficked in a variety of things ranging from ivory to human slaves, the latter gradually displacing everything else.

Art Resource, N.Y.

tion balanced by rewards for those faithful in paying their taxes. Kongo society was dominated by the king, whose authority was tied to acceptance of him as a kind of spiritual spokesman of the gods or ancestors. By 1600, Kongo was half the size of England and alongside farming boasted a high state of specialization in weaving and pottery, salt production, fishing, and metalworking.

The Portuguese brought Mediterranean goods, preeminently luxury textiles from North Africa, to trade for African goods. Such luxuries augmented the prestige and wealth of the ruler and his elites. However, slaves became the primary export that could be used to obtain foreign luxury goods. Imports such as fine clothing, tobacco, and alcohol did nothing to replace the labor pool lost to slavery.

At first the Portuguese put time and effort into education and Christian proselytizing, but the need for more slaves brought a focus on exploiting the human resources of central Africa. Regional rulers sought to procure slaves from neighboring kingdoms, as did Portuguese traders who went inland themselves. As the demand grew, local rulers increasingly attacked neighbors to garner slaves for Portuguese traders (see Chapter 19).

The Kongo ruler Affonso I (r. ca. 1506–1543), a Christian convert, began by welcoming Jesuit missionaries and supporting conversion. But in time he broke with the Jesuits and encouraged traditional practices, even though he himself remained a Christian. Affonso had constant difficulty curbing slaving practices and provincial governors who often dealt directly with the Portuguese, undermining royal authority. Affonso's successor restricted Portuguese activity to Mpinda harbor and the Kongo capital of Mbanza Kongo (São Salvador). A few years later, Portuguese attempts to name the Kongo royal successor caused a bloody uprising against them that led in turn to a Portuguese boycott on trade with the kingdom.

Thereafter, disastrous internal wars shattered the Kongo state. Kongo, however, enjoyed renewed vigor in the seventeenth century. Its kings ruled as divine-right monarchs at the apex of a complex sociopolitical pyramid that rose from district headmen through provincial governors to the court nobility and king. Royal power came to depend on a guard of musket-armed hired soldiers. The financial base of the kingdom rested on tribute from officials holding positions at the king's pleasure and on taxes and tolls on commerce. Christianity, the state religion, was accommodated to traditional beliefs. Kongo sculpture, iron and copper technology, and dance and music flourished.

Angola To the south, in Portuguese Angola, the experience was even worse than in Kongo. By 1600, Angola was exporting thousands of slaves yearly through the port of Luanda. In less than a century, the hinterland had been plundered. The Portuguese arrival had brought economic and social catastrophe.

EAST AFRICA

SWAHILI CULTURE AND COMMERCE

The participation of East African port towns in the lucrative southern-seas trade was ancient. Arabs, Indonesians, and even Indians had trafficked there for centuries. From the eighth century onward, Islam traveled with Arab and Persian sailors and merchants to these southerly trading centers. In the thirteenth century, Muslim

East and Southeast Africa	
900–1500	"Great Zimbabwe" civilization
ca. 1200–1400	Development of Bantu Kiswahili language
ca. 1300–1600	Height of Swahili culture
1698	Omani forces take Mombasa, oust Portuguese from East Africa north of the port of Mozambique
1741–1856	United sultanate of Oman and Zanzibar

HOW DID Swahili language and culture develop?

Fort Jesus, Mombasa, Kenia.

Robert Harding World Imagery

Swahili A language and culture that developed from the interaction of native Africans and Arabs along the East African coast.

traders from Arabia and Iran began to come in increased numbers and to dominate the coastal cities. Henceforward, Islamic faith and culture were often predominant along the seacoast, from Mogadishu to Kilwa.

By this time, a common language had developed from the interaction of Bantu and Arabic speakers along the coast. This tongue is called **Swahili**, or *Kiswahili*, from the Arabic *sawahil*, "coastlands."

Swahili language and culture probably developed first in the northern towns of Manda, Lamu, and Mombasa, then farther south along the coast to Kilwa. Likewise, the spread of Islam was largely limited to the coastal civilization and did not reach inland. This contrasts with lands farther north, in the Horn of Africa, where Islamic kingdoms developed in the Somali hinterland as well as on the coast.

Swahili civilization reached its apogee in the fourteenth and fifteenth centuries. The harbor trading towns were the administrative centers of the local Swahili states, and most of them were sited on coastal islands or easily defended peninsulas. To these ports came merchants from abroad and from the African hinterlands, some to settle and stay. These towns had impressive

QUICK REVIEW

East African Port Towns

- Part of trade with Middle East, Asia, and India
- Tied together by common language, *Swahili*
- Swahili civilization reached its peak in the fourteenth and fifteenth centuries

OVERVIEW

MAJOR AFRICAN STATES, 1000–1800

North Africa	Sahel	Eastern Sudan	West and Central Africa	East Africa	Southern Africa
Morocco	Ghana	Maqurra	Benin	Zanzibar	"Great Zimbabwe"
Algiers	Mali	Alwa	Kongo		
Tunis	Snghai	Funj			
Tripoli	Kanem				
Egypt					

mosques, fortress-palaces, harbor fortifications, fancy residences, and commercial buildings.

Today, historians are recognizing that the Swahili states' ruling dynasties were probably African in origin, with an admixture of Arab or Persian immigrant blood. Swahili coastal centers boasted an advanced, cosmopolitan level of culture; by comparison, most of the populace in the small villages lived in mud houses and sometimes stone houses and earned their living by farming or fishing, the two basic coastal occupations besides trade. Society seems to have consisted of three principal groups: the local nobility, the commoners, and resident foreigners engaged in local commerce. Slaves constituted a fourth class of people, although their local extent (as opposed to their sale) is disputed.

"Great Zimbabwe," so called because it is the most impressive of 300 such stone ruins in modern Zimbabwe and neighboring countries. These sites give clear evidence of the advanced Iron Age mining and cattle-raising culture that flourished in this region between about 1000 and 1500 C.E. The people, thought to have been of Bantu origins, apparently had a highly developed trade in gold and copper with outsiders, including Arabs on the east coast. As yet, all too little is known about this impressive society.

Robert Aberman and Barbara Heller/Art Resource, N.Y.

Southern Africa

1652 First Cape Colony settlement of Dutch East India Company

1795 British replace Dutch as masters of Cape Colony

The flourishing trade of the coastal centers was fed mainly by export of inland ivory. Other exports included gold, slaves, turtle shells, ambergris, leopard skins, pearls, fish, sandalwood, ebony, and local cotton cloth. The chief imports were cloth, porcelain, glassware, china, glass beads, and glazed pottery. Certain exports tended to dominate particular ports: cloth, sandalwood, ebony, and ivory at Mogadishu; ivory at Manda; and gold at Kilwa. Cowrie shells were a common currency in inland trade, but coins were used in the major trading centers. The gold trade itself apparently became important only in the fifteenth century.

THE PORTUGUESE AND THE OMANIS OF ZANZIBAR

The decline of the original Swahili civilization in the sixteenth century can be attributed primarily to the arrival of the Portuguese and their destruction of the old oceanic trade (in particular, the Islamic commercial monopoly) and the main Islamic city-states along the eastern coast.

In Africa, as everywhere, the Portuguese saw the "**Moors**" as implacable enemies. Many Portuguese viewed the struggle to wrest the commerce and seaports of Africa and Asia from Islamic control as a Christian crusade.

The initial Portuguese victories along the African coast led to the submission of many small Islamic coastal ports and states. Still, there was no concerted effort to spread Christianity. Thus, the long-term cultural and religious consequences of the Portuguese presence were slight. After 1660, the eastern Arabian state of Oman ejected the Portuguese everywhere north of Mozambique.

The Omanis soon shifted their home base to Zanzibar, which became a major power in East Africa. Their control of the coastal ivory and slave trade seems to have fueled a substantial recovery of prosperity by the later eighteenth century. The domination of the east coast by Omani African sultans, descendants of the earlier invaders, continued until 1856. Thereafter, Zanzibar and its coastal holdings became independent, and then passed to the British. Still, the Islamic impact on the whole coast survives today.

Moors The Spanish and Portuguese term for Muslims.

SOUTHERN AFRICA

SOUTHEASTERN AFRICA: "GREAT ZIMBABWE"

At about the same time that the east-coast trading centers were beginning to flourish, a purely African civilization was enjoying its heyday inland in modern southern Zimbabwe. It was founded in the tenth or eleventh century by Bantu-speaking Shona people, who still inhabit the same general area today. It seems to have become a large and prosperous state between the late thirteenth and the late fifteenth centuries. We know it only through the archaeological remains of an estimated 150 settlements in the Zambezi-Limpopo region.

The most impressive of these ruins is known today as "Great Zimbabwe"—a huge, 60-odd-acre site encompassing two major building complexes. One—the so-called acropolis—is a series of stone enclosures on a high hill. It overlooks another, much larger enclosure that contains many ruins and a circular tower, all surrounded by a massive wall some 32 feet high and up to 17 feet thick. The acropolis complex may have contained a shrine, whereas the larger enclosure was apparently the royal palace and fort. The stonework reflects a wealthy and sophisticated society. Artifacts from the site include gold

HOW DID slavery affect race relations in the Cape Colony?

14.1
Kilwa, Mombasa, and the Portuguese: Realities of Empire

and copper ornaments, soapstone carvings, and imported beads, as well as china, glass, and porcelain of Chinese, Syrian, and Persian origins.

The state itself seems to have had partial control of the increasing gold trade between inland areas and the east coast. We can speculate that this large settlement was the capital city of a prosperous empire and the residence of a ruling elite. Its wider domain was made up mostly of smaller settlements whose inhabitants lived by subsistence agriculture and cattle raising and whose culture was considerably different from that of the capital.

Without written or new archaeological sources, we shall likely never know exactly what allowed this impressive civilization to develop and to dominate its region for nearly 200 years.

THE PORTUGUESE IN SOUTHEASTERN AFRICA

The Portuguese destroyed Swahili control of both the inland gold trade and the overseas trade. Their chief objective was to obtain gold from the interior, though they derived little lasting profit from the enterprise.

All along the Zambezi, however, a lasting and destabilizing consequence of Portuguese intrusion was the creation of quasi-tribal chiefdoms led by mixed-blood Portuguese landholders, who were descended from the first Portuguese estate holders along the Zambezi. By the late eighteenth century, they were too strong for either the Portuguese or the regional African rulers to control. They remind us of how diverse the peoples of modern Africa are.

SOUTH AFRICA: THE CAPE COLONY

In South Africa, the Dutch planted the first European colonials almost inadvertently, yet the consequences of their action were to be ultimately as grave and far-reaching as any European incursion onto African soil. The first Cape settlement was built in 1652 by the Dutch East India Company as a resupply point and way station for Dutch vessels on their way back and forth between the Netherlands and the East Indies. The support station gradually became a settler community, the forebears of the Afrikaners of modern South Africa.

The local Khoikhoi (see Chapter 6) had neither a strong political organization nor an economic base beyond their herds. They bartered livestock freely to Dutch ships. As Company employees established farms to supply the Cape station, they began to displace the Khoikhoi. Conflicts led to the consolidation of European landholdings and a breakdown of Khoikhoi society. Military success led to even greater Dutch control of the Khoikhoi by the 1670s. The Khoikhoi became the chief source of colonial wage labor.

Artifacts from Great Zimbabwe include this carving (steatite, 40.5 cm high). It is thought that it represents a mythical eagle that carries messages from man to the gods. It dates to ca. 1200–1400 C.E.

Werner Forman Archive/Art Resource, N.Y.

The colony also imported slaves. Slavery set the tone for relations between the emergent, and ostensibly "white," Afrikaner population and the "coloreds" of other races. Free or not, the latter were eventually identified with slave peoples.

After the first settlers spread out around the Company station, nomadic white livestock farmers, or **Trekboers**, moved more widely afield, leaving the richer, but limited, farming lands of the coast for the drier interior tableland. There they contested still wider groups of Khoikhoi cattle herders for the best grazing lands. Again the Khoikhoi lost. By 1700, their way of life was destroyed.

The Cape society in this period was thus a diverse one. The Dutch Company officials (including Dutch Reformed ministers), the emerging Afrikaners (both settled colonists and Trekboers), the Khoikhoi, and the slaves of diverse nationality played differing roles. Intermarriage and cohabitation of masters and slaves added to the complexity. The emergence of *Afrikaans*, a new vernacular language of the colonials, shows that the Dutch immigrants themselves were also subject to acculturation processes. By the time of English domination after 1795, the sociopolitical foundations—and the bases of the *Apartheid* doctrine—of modern South Africa were firmly laid.

Trekboers White livestock farmers in Cape Colony.

Afrikaans The new language, derived from Dutch, that evolved in the seventeenth- and eighteenth-century Cape Colony.

apartheid "Apartness," the term referring to racist policies enforced by the white-dominated regime that existed in South Africa from 1948 to 1992.

SUMMARY

North Africa Developments in African history from 1000 to 1800 varied from region to region. In North Africa, the key new factor was the imperial expansion of the Ottoman Empire as far west as Morocco. But regionalism soon rendered Ottoman authority in North Africa purely nominal.

Empires of the Sudan Several substantial states arose south of the Sahara: Ghana, Mali, Songhai, and Kanem. The ruling elites of these states converted to or were heavily influenced by Islam, although most of their populations clung to their older traditions. Much of the wealth of these states was tied to their control of the trans-Saharan trade routes. Farther south, in the coastal forestlands of Central Africa, another substantial kingdom arose in Benin, famous for its brass sculptures.

East Africa On the east coast, Islam influenced the development of the distinctive Swahili culture and language, and Islamic traders linked the region to India and East Asia.

The Coming of the Europeans The key development of the fifteenth century was the arrival of European traders, missionaries, and warships. The Portuguese and later Europeans came in search of commerce, converts to Christianity, and spheres of influence. Their arrival disrupted indigenous African culture and political relations and presaged Africa's involvement in and exploitation by a new, expanding global trading system dominated by Europeans.

IMAGE KEY
for pages 368–369

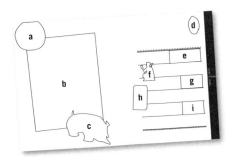

a. Moroccan Coin dating from Songhai Empire
b. Benin plaque
c. Golden rhino found at Mapungubwe
d. Ivory mask of a Benin king
e. Mosque in Mali
f. Mansa Musa early medieval painting
g. Coptic church
h. Benin plaque
i. Fort Jesus, Mombasa, Kenya, Africa

REVIEW QUESTIONS

1. Why did Islam succeed in sub-Saharan and East Africa? How did warfare and trade affect its success?

2. What was the importance of the empires of Ghana, Mali, and Songhai to world history? Why was the control of the trans-Saharan trade so

important to these kingdoms? What was the importance of Islamic culture to them? Why did each of these empires break up?

3. How did the Portuguese affect East and central Africa? How did European coastal activities affect the African interior?

4. How did the Portuguese and Dutch differ from or resemble the Arabs, Persians, and other Muslims who came as outsiders to sub-Saharan Africa?

5. Who were the Trekboers and what was their conflict with the Khoikhoi? How was the basis for Apartheid formed in this period?

KEY TERMS

Afrikaans   (p. 386)
apartheid   (p. 386)
Moors   (p. 384)

oba   (p. 378)
Swahili   (p. 382)

Trekboers   (p. 386)
uzama   (p. 378)

   For additional study resources for this chapter, go to:
www.prenhall.com/craig/chapter17

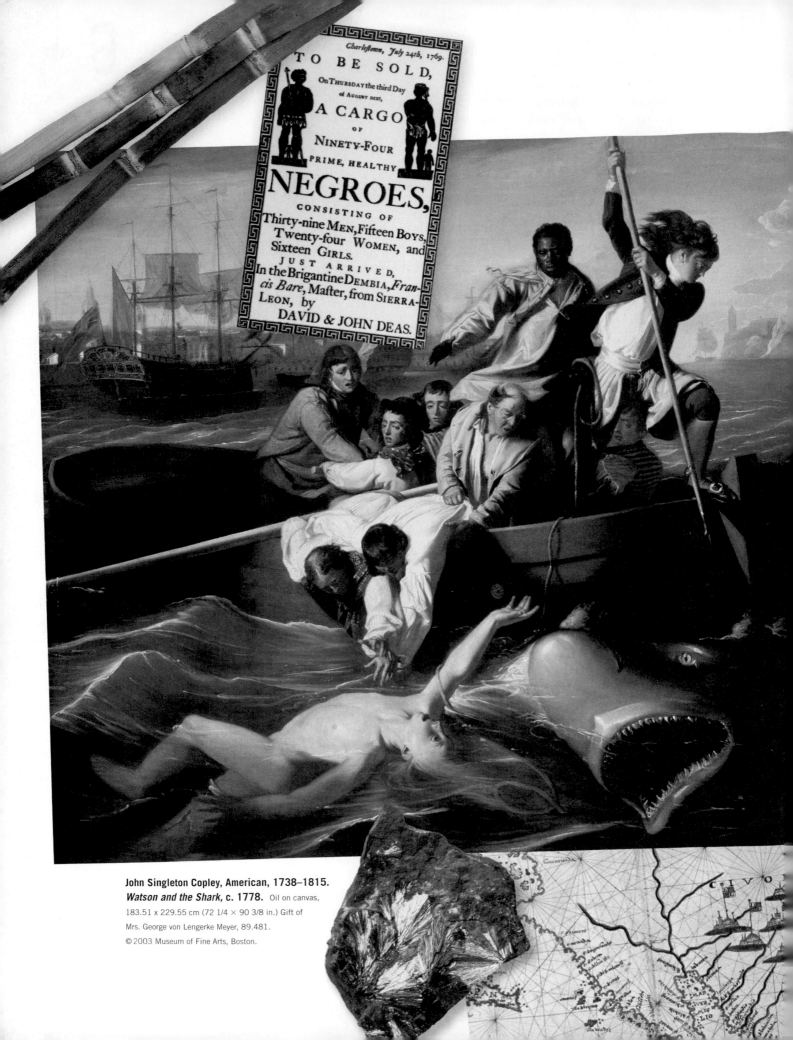

John Singleton Copley, American, 1738–1815.
Watson and the Shark, c. 1778. Oil on canvas,
183.51 x 229.55 cm (72 1/4 × 90 3/8 in.) Gift of
Mrs. George von Lengerke Meyer, 89.481.
© 2003 Museum of Fine Arts, Boston.

18

CONQUEST AND EXPLOITATION
The Development of the Transatlantic Economy

WHAT WAS
mercantilism?

WHAT ROLES did
the Roman Catholic Church
play in Spanish America?

HOW WERE

sugar production and slavery
intertwined in colonial Brazil?

HOW WERE the economies of the
French and British North American colonies
integrated into the transatlantic economy?

WHY WAS the transatlantic
slave trade so economically important?

IMAGE KEY

Image Key for pages 388–389 is on page 406.

The late fifteenth-century European encounter with the American continents made the region an area where European languages, legal and political institutions, trade, and religion prevail. These developments in the Americas gave Europe more influence over other world cultures than it would otherwise have achieved.

Within decades of the European voyages of discovery, native Americans, Europeans, and Africans began to interact in a manner unprecedented in human history. By the close of the sixteenth century, Europe, the Americas, and Africa had become linked in a vast transatlantic economy that extracted wealth from the American continents largely on the basis of the nonfree labor of impressed native Americans and imported African slaves in a plantation economy that eventually extended from Maryland to Brazil. The slave trade connected the economy of sections of Africa to the transatlantic economy and devastated the African people and cultures involved in it, but it also enriched the Americas with African culture.

MERCANTILIST THEORY OF ECONOMIC EXPLOITATION

WHAT WAS mercantilism?

The European empires of the sixteenth through the eighteenth centuries—empires based on commerce—existed primarily to enrich trade. Extensive trade rivalries sprang up around the world. The protection of these empires required naval power, and they depended largely on slave labor. Indeed, the Atlantic slave trade was a major way in which European merchants enriched themselves. That trade in turn forcibly brought the peoples of Africa into the life and culture of the New World.

If any formal economic theory lay behind these empires, it was **mercantilism**, a system in which governments heavily regulate trade and commerce to increase national wealth. Economic writers of the time believed that a nation had to gain more gold and silver bullion than its rivals.

From beginning to end, the economic well-being of the home country was the primary concern of mercantilist writers. Colonies existed to provide markets and natural resources for the home country, which furnished military security and political administration for the colonies. For decades, both sides assumed that the colonies were the inferior partner in the relationship. The mercantilist statesmen and traders regarded the world as an arena of scarce resources in which one national economy could grow only at the expense of others. The home country and its colonies were to trade exclusively with each other. National monopoly was the ruling principle.

Mercantilist ideas were always neater on paper than in practice. By the early eighteenth century, mercantilist assumptions were far removed from the realities of the colonies. The colonial and home markets did not mesh. Spain could not produce enough goods for South America. Economic production in the British North American colonies challenged English manufacturing.

Colonists of different countries wished to trade with each other. The governments could not control all their subjects. Clashes among colonists could lead to war between governments. The problems associated with the mercantile empires led to conflicts around the world.

mercantilism   Term used to describe close government control of the economy that sought to maximize exports and accumulate as much precious metals as possible to enable the state to defend its economic and political interests.

The Dutch established a major trading base at Batavia in the East Indies. The city they called Batavia is now Djakarta, Indonesia.

Bildarchiv Preussicher Kulturbesitz

ESTABLISHMENT
OF THE SPANISH EMPIRE IN AMERICA

CONQUEST OF THE AZTECS AND THE INCAS

Within 20 years of the arrival of Columbus (1451–1506), Spanish explorers in search of gold had claimed the major islands of the Caribbean and suppressed the native peoples. These actions presaged what was to occur on the continent.

In 1519, Hernan Cortés (1485–1547) landed in Mexico with about 500 men and a few horses. He opened communication with Moctezuma II (1466–1520), the Aztec emperor. Moctezuma hesitated to confront Cortés, attempting at first to appease him with gifts of gold. Cortés forged alliances with subject peoples of the Aztecs. His forces then marched on the Aztec capital of Tenochtitlán (modern Mexico City), where Moctezuma welcomed him. Cortés soon made Moctezuma a prisoner in his own capital. Moctezuma died in unexplained circumstances, and the Spaniards were driven from Tenochtitlán. But they returned, and the Aztecs were defeated in late 1521, Cortés proclaimed the Aztec Empire to be New Spain. (See The Conquest of Mexico.)

In 1532, Francisco Pizarro (c. 1478–1541) landed on the western coast of South America to take on the Inca Empire. His force included about 200 men armed with guns, swords, and horses, the military power of which the Incas did not understand. Pizarro lured the Inca ruler Atahualpa (c. 1500–1533) into a conference, then seized him and had him garroted in 1533. The Spaniards then captured Cuzco, the Inca capital, ending the Inca Empire.

WHAT ROLES did the Roman Catholic Church play in Spanish America?

QUICK REVIEW

Francisco Pizarro (c. 1478–1541)

◆ Invasion force landed in South America in 1532

◆ Forces included 200 men, horses, guns, and swords

◆ 1533: executed the Inca ruler and captured Cuzco

THE COLUMBIAN EXCHANGE

The same ships that that carried Europeans and Africans to the Americas also transported animals, plants, and diseases that had never before appeared in the New World. There was a similar transport back to Europe and Africa. Historians call this cross-continental flow "the Columbian exchange." The overall result was an ecological transformation that continues to shape the world.

To the Americas

Animals:	pigs, cattle, horses, goats, sheep, chickens
Plants:	apples, peaches, pears, apricots, plums, oranges, mangos, lemons, olives, melons, almonds, grapes, bananas, cherries, sugar cane, rice, wheat, oats, barley, onions, radishes, okra, dandelions, cabbage, and other green vegetables
Diseases:	smallpox, influenza, bubonic plague, typhoid, typhus, measles, chicken pox, malaria, and diphtheria

From the Americas

Animals:	turkeys
Plants:	maize, tomatoes, sweet peppers, chilis, potatoes, sweet potatoes, squash, pumpkins, manioc (tapioca), beans, cocoa, peanuts, pecans, pineapples, guavas, avocados, blueberries, and tobacco
Diseases:	syphilis

The conquests of Mexico and Peru are among the most dramatic and brutal events in modern world history. Small military forces armed with advanced weapons subdued, in a brief time, two advanced, powerful peoples. European diseases, especially smallpox, also aided the conquest. The native populations had long lived in isolation, and many succumbed to the new diseases. But beyond the drama and bloodshed, these conquests marked a turning point. Whole civilizations with long histories and enormous social, architectural, and technological achievements were destroyed. Native American cultures endured, but European culture had the upper hand.

THE ROMAN CATHOLIC CHURCH IN SPANISH AMERICA

The Spanish conquest of the West Indies, Mexico, and South America opened that region to the Roman Catholic faith. As it had in the Castilian reconquest of the Iberian peninsula from the Moors, religion played a central role in the conquest of the New World. In both cases, conversion justified military conquest and the extension of political control and dominance. As a consequence of this policy, the Roman Catholic Church in the New World was always a conservative force working to protect the interests of the Spanish authorities.

The relationship between political authority and the propagation of religious doctrine was even closer in the New World than on the Iberian peninsula. The papacy recognized that it could not from its own resources support so extensive a missionary effort and turned over much of the control of the church in the New World to the Spanish monarchy. There was thus always a close relationship between the monarchy and the church. The zeal of both increased in the sixteenth century as the papacy and the Habsburg monarchy determined that

A sixteenth-century Aztec drawing depicts a battle in the Spanish conquest of Mexico.

Corbis-Bettmann

Protestantism should have no foothold in America. As a consequence, the Roman Catholicism that spread throughout Spanish America took the form of the zealous faith of the Counter-Reformation.

The Roman Catholic Church, often represented by the Franciscans and Dominicans, and later by the Jesuits, sought to convert the native Americans and eradicate Indian religious practices. Thus, religious conversion represented, among other things, an attempt to destroy still another part of the native American culture. Furthermore, conversion did not bring acceptance; even until late in the eighteenth century, there were few native American Christian priests.

Tension, however, existed between the early Spanish conquerors and the friars. Without conquest, the church could not convert the Native Americans, but the priests often deplored the harsh conditions imposed on the native peoples. The most outspoken clerical critic of the Spanish conquerors was Bartolomé de Las Casas (1474–1566), a Dominican. He contended that conquest was not necessary for conversion. One result of his campaign was new royal regulations after 1550. Another was the "**Black Legend**," according to which all Spanish treatment of the Native Americans was inhumane. Those who created this view of Spanish behavior drew heavily on Las Casas's writings. Although substantially true, the "Black Legend" exaggerated the case against Spain. Certainly the rulers of the native empires—as the Aztec demands for sacrificial victims attest—had often themselves been cruel to their subject peoples.

15.1
The "Black Legend" of Spain:
Bartolomé de las Casas

Black Legend   The argument that Spanish treatment of native Americans was uniquely inhumane.

By the end of the sixteenth century, the church in Spanish America had become largely an institution upholding the colonial status quo. Although priests did defend the communal rights of Indian tribes, the colonial church prospered through its exploitation of the resources of the New World. Those who spoke for the church did not challenge Spanish domination, and the church only modestly moderated the forces exploiting human labor and material wealth. By the late eighteenth century, the Roman Catholic Church had become one of the most conservative forces in Latin America.

ECONOMIES OF EXPLOITATION IN THE SPANISH EMPIRE

Colonial Spanish America had an economy of exploitation in two senses. First, its organization of labor involved dependent servitude or slavery. Second, resources were exploited for the economic advantage of Spain.

VARIETIES OF ECONOMIC ACTIVITY

The early *conquistadores* ("conquerors") had been interested primarily in gold, but by the middle of the sixteenth century, silver mining provided the chief source of metallic wealth. The great silver mining centers were in Bolivia and northern Mexico. The Spanish crown received one-fifth of all mining revenues. Silver mining for the benefit of Spaniards and the Spanish crown epitomized the extractive economy on which Latin American colonial life was based.

This extractive economy required labor, but there were too few Spanish colonists to provide it, and most of the colonists who came to the Americas were unwilling to provide wage labor. So, the Spaniards looked first to the native population and then to African slaves. Indian labor dominated on the continent and African labor in the Caribbean.

Encomienda The Spanish devised a series of institutions to exploit native American labor. The first was the *encomienda*, a formal grant by the crown of the right to the labor of a specific number of native Americans for a particular time. *Encomienda* as an institution declined by the middle of the sixteenth century. The Spanish crown disliked the *encomienda* system. The monarchy was distressed by reports from clergy that the native Americans were being mistreated and feared that *encomienda* holders were becoming a powerful nobility in the New World.

Repartimiento The passing of the *encomienda* led to the **repartimiento**, largely copied from the draft labor practices of the Incas. *Repartimiento* required adult male native Americans to devote a set number of days of labor annually to Spanish economic enterprises. The time limitation on *repartimiento* led some Spanish managers to use their workers harshly, and native Americans sometimes did not survive their days of labor rotation.

The Hacienda The *hacienda*, which dominated rural and agricultural life in Spanish colonies on the continent, developed when the crown made grants of land. These grants led to large landed estates owned by *peninsulares*, whites born in Spain, or creoles, whites born in America. The crown thus continued to use the resources of the New World for patronage without directly impinging on the native Americans because the grazing that occurred on the *haciendas* required less labor than did the mines. *Haciendas* would become one of the most important

---

HOW WERE sugar production and slavery intertwined in colonial Brazil?

---

conquistadores Meaning "conquerors." The Spanish conquerors of the New World.

encomienda The grant by the Spanish crown to a colonist of the labor of a specific number of Indians for a set period of time.

repartimiento A labor tax in Spanish America that required adult male native Americans devote a set number of days a year to Spanish economic enterprises.

hacienda Large landed estates in Spanish America.

peninsulares Persons born in Spain who settled in the Spanish colonies.

features of Latin American life. Laborers on the *hacienda* were usually in formal servitude to the owner and had to buy goods for everyday living on credit from him. They were rarely able to repay the resulting debts and thus could not leave. This system was known as **debt peonage**. The *hacienda* economy produced foodstuffs for mining areas and urban centers.

THE DECLINE OF THE NATIVE AMERICAN POPULATION

The conquest, the exploitation, and the forced labor (and European diseases) decimated the Indian population. From the sixteenth century, native Americans began to die off in huge numbers. In New Spain (Mexico) alone, the population probably declined from approximately 25 million to fewer than two million within the first century after the conquest. Thereafter, the Indian population began to expand slowly, but the precipitous drop eliminated the easy supply of exploitable labor.

COMMERCIAL REGULATION

Because Queen Isabella of Castile (r. 1474–1504) had commissioned Columbus, the legal link between the New World and Spain was the crown of Castile. Government of America was assigned to the Council of the Indies, which nominated the viceroys of New Spain and Peru, the chief executives in the New World. Each of the viceroyalties included subordinate judicial councils known as *audiencias*. A variety of local officers presided over municipal councils. Virtually all political power flowed from the top of this political structure downward; there was little local initiative or self-government (see Map 18–1).

The colonial political structures existed largely to support the commercial goals of Spain. But the system of monopolistic trade regulation was often breached. The Casa de Contratación (House of Trade) in Seville regulated all trade with the New World and was the most influential institution of the Spanish Empire. The entire organization was geared to benefit the Spanish monarchy and privileged merchant groups.

A complicated system of trade and bullion fleets administered from Seville maintained the trade monopoly. Each year a fleet of commercial vessels controlled by Seville merchants, escorted by warships, carried merchandise from Spain to specified ports in America. These included Portobello, Veracruz, and Cartagena. There were no authorized ports on the Pacific Coast. Areas such as Buenos Aires received goods only after the shipments had been unloaded at one of the authorized ports. After selling their wares, the ships were loaded with silver and gold bullion, usually wintered in fortified Caribbean ports, and then sailed back to Spain. Regulations prohibited the Spanish colonists from trading directly with each other and from building their own shipping and commercial industry. Foreign merchants were also forbidden to breach the Spanish monopoly.

COLONIAL BRAZIL AND SLAVERY

In 1494, by the Treaty of Tordesillas, the pope divided the seaborne empires of Spain and Portugal by drawing a line west of the Cape Verde Islands. In 1500, a Portuguese explorer landed in present-day Brazil, which extended east of the papal line, and thus Portugal gained a major hold in South America.

Portugal had fewer resources to devote to its New World empire than did Spain. The crown permitted private persons to exploit the region. The native

debt peonage The requirement that laborers remain and continue to work on a hacienda until they had paid their debts to the owner for goods bought from him on credit.

DISPUTED BY
ENGLAND,
RUSSIA,
AND SPAIN

VICEROYALTY
OF
NEW SPAIN

Rio Grande

A T L A N T I C

EFFECTIVE FRONTIER OF *O C E A N*
SPANISH SETTLEMENT

Gulf of Mexico

Mexico
City
Veracruz

Santo Domingo
Caribbean Sea

Portobelo Cartagena Caracas

**VICEROYALTY OF
NEW GRANADA**
Separated From
Viceroyalty of
Peru,
1717, 1739

Bogotá

Quito

GUIANA

Amazon R.

P A C I F I C

**VICEROYALTY
OF
PERU**
Lima

**VICEROYALTY
OF
BRAZIL**

Pernambuco

Bahia

O C E A N

Portosi

São Paulo

Rio de Janeiro

**VICEROYALTY
OF
LA PLATA**
Separated From the
Viceroyalty of Peru,
1776

Santiago

Buenos
Aires

**AUDIENCIA
OF CHILE**

Claimed but not
settled by Spain

MAP 18–1

Viceroyalties in Latin America in 1780.   Spain organized its vast holdings in the New World into viceroyalties, each of which had its own governor and other administrative officials.

HOW EFFECTIVE was Spain's control over its New World colonies?

The sugar plantations of Brazil and the West Indies were a major source of the demand for slave labor. Slaves are here shown grinding sugar cane and refining sugar, which was then exported to the consumer markets in Europe.

Hulton/Corbis-Bettmann

people in the lands that Portugal governed lived in small, nomadic groups. As a result, in contrast to the Spanish, the Portuguese imported Africans as slaves rather than using the native Indian population.

By the mid-sixteenth century, sugar production had gained preeminence in the Brazilian economy. The dominance of sugar meant the dominance of slavery. Slavery became even more important when in the early eighteenth century, gold was discovered in southern Brazil. Nowhere, except perhaps in the West Indies, was slavery so important as it was in Brazil, where it persisted until 1888.

The taxation and administration associated with gold mining brought new wealth to the Portuguese monarchy, allowing it to rule without recourse to the Cortés or traditional parliament for taxation. Through transatlantic trade, the new wealth generated from Brazilian gold also filtered into all the major trading nations.

FRENCH AND BRITISH NORTH AMERICA

French explorers had pressed down the St. Lawrence River valley in Canada during the seventeenth century. French fur traders and missionaries had followed, with the French government supporting the missionary effort. By the end of the seventeenth century, a sparsely populated French presence existed in Canada. The largest settlement was Quebec, founded in 1608. It was primarily through the fur trade that French Canada functioned as part of the early transatlantic economy.

Beginning with the first successful settlement in Jamestown, Virginia, in 1607, the eastern seaboard of the United States became populated by English

HOW WERE the economies of the French and British North American colonies integrated into the transatlantic economy?

Fur traders and Indians: engraving, 1777.

©The Granger Collection, New York

colonies. With the exception of Maryland, these colonies were Protestant. The Church of England dominated the southern colonies. In New England, varieties of Protestantism associated with or derived from Calvinism were in the ascendancy. In their religious affiliations, the English-speaking colonies manifested two important traits derived from the English experience. First, much of their religious life was organized around self-governing congregations. Second, their religious outlook derived from those forms of Protestantism that were suspicious of central political authority. In this regard, their cultural and political outlook differed sharply from the cultural and political outlook associated with the Roman Catholicism of the Spanish empire. In a sense, the values of the extreme Reformation and Counter-Reformation confronted each other in the Americas.

The English colonists had complex interactions with the native American populations. They had only modest interest in missionary enterprise. As in South America, new diseases imported from Europe took a high toll of the native population. Unlike Mexico and Peru, however, North America had no large native American cities. The native American populations were dispersed, and intertribal animosity was intense. The English often used one tribe against another, and the native Americans also tried to use the English or the French in their own conflicts. From the late seventeenth century through the American Revoution, however, the native Americans of North America were drawn into the Anglo-French Wars that were fought there as well as Europe. (See Chapter 21.)

The largest economic activity throughout the English-speaking colonies was agriculture. From New England through the Middle Atlantic states, there were mostly small farms tilled by free white labor; from Virginia southward it was the plantation economy, dependent on slavery. The principal ports—Boston, Newport, New York, Philadelphia, Baltimore, and Charleston—were primarily trading centers through which goods moved back and forth between the colonies and England and the West Indies. The commercial economies of these cities were all related to the transatlantic slave trade.

Until the 1760s, the political values of the Americans resembled those of their English counterparts. They were monarchists but suspicious of monarchical power. Their politics involved patronage and individual favors. Their society was hierarchical, with an elite that functioned like a colonial aristocracy and many ordinary people who were dependent on that aristocracy. Throughout the colonies during the eighteenth century, the Anglican church grew in influence and membership. The prosperity of the colonies might eventually have led them to separate from England, but in 1750 few people thought that would occur.

Both England and France had important sugar islands in the Caribbean with plantations worked by African slaves. The trade and commerce of the northern British colonies were closely related to meeting the needs of these islands.

SLAVERY IN THE AMERICAS

Black slavery was the final mode of forced or subservient labor in the New World. It extended throughout the Americas.

ESTABLISHMENT OF SLAVERY

As the numbers of native Americans in South America declined, the Spanish and Portuguese turned to African slaves. By the late 1500s, in the West Indies and the cities of South America, black slaves surpassed the white population.

On much of the South American continent dominated by Spain, slavery declined during the late seventeenth century. It continued to prosper, however, in Brazil and in the Caribbean. Later, starting with the importation of slaves to Jamestown in 1619, slavery became a fundamental institution in British North America.

One of the forces that led to the spread of slavery in Brazil and the West Indies was the cultivation of sugar. Only slave labor could provide enough workers for the sugar plantations. As the production of sugar expanded, so did the demand for slaves.

By 1700, the Caribbean Islands were the world center for sugar production. As the European appetite for sugar grew, the slave population expanded. By 1725, black slaves may have constituted almost 90 percent of the population throughout the West Indies. There and in Brazil and the southern British colonies, prosperity and slavery went hand in hand. The wealthiest colonies were those that raised consumer staples, such as sugar, rice, tobacco, or cotton, by slave labor.

THE PLANTATION ECONOMY AND TRANSATLANTIC TRADE

The plantations that stretched from Maryland through the West Indies and into Brazil formed a vast corridor of slave societies. This kind of society, in its total dependence on slave labor and racial differences, had not existed before the European discovery and exploitation of the Americas. The social and economic influence of plantation slavery also touched West Africa, Europe, and New England. It persisted from the sixteenth century through the second half of the nineteenth century. Every society in which it existed still contends with its effects.

Captured by Mandingo enemies and sold to a Maryland tobacco planter, Job Ben Solomon accomplished the nearly impossible feat of returning to Africa as a freeman. By demonstrating his talents as a Muslim scholar, including his ability to write the entire Qur'an from memory, he astonished his owners and eventually convinced them to let him go home.

"The Fortunate Slave," An Illustration of African Slavery in the early 18th century by Douglas Grant (1968). From "Some Memoirs of the Life of Job," by Thomas Bluett 1734. Photo by Robert D. Rubic/Precision Chromes, Inc. The New York Public Library, Research Libraries

WHICH economic factors led to the spread of slavery in the New World?

plantation economy   The economic system stretching between Chesapeake Bay and Brazil that produced crops, especially sugar, cotton, and tobacco, using slave labor on large estates.

Africans who survived the voyage across the Atlantic were immediately sold into slavery in the Americas. This slave-auction notice relates to a group of slaves whose ship had stopped at Charleston, South Carolina, and then landed elsewhere in the region to auction its human cargo. Notice the concern to assure potential buyers that the slaves were healthy.

Corbis-Bettmann

The slave trade was part of the larger system of transatlantic trade that linked Europe, Africa, and the European colonies in the Americas. In this system, the Americas supplied labor-intensive raw materials like tobacco, sugar, coffee, precious metals, cotton, and indigo. Europe supplied manufactured goods like textiles, liquor, guns, metal wares, and beads, not to mention cash. And Africa supplied gold, ivory, wood, palm oil, gum, and other products, as well as the slaves who provided the labor to create the American products. By the eighteenth century, slaves were the predominant African export.

SLAVERY ON THE PLANTATIONS

The plantations in the Americas to which the African slaves arrived produced for an overseas market that was part of a larger integrated transatlantic economy. In turn, plantation owners imported virtually all the finished or manufactured goods they consumed.

The conditions of plantation slaves differed from colony to colony. Vast slave holdings were the exception. Black slaves living in Portuguese areas had the fewest legal protections. In the Spanish colonies, the church provided some protection, but devoted more effort protecting native Americans. Slave codes in the British and the French colonies provided only the most limited protection. Regulations were intended to prevent slave revolt and favored the master rather than the slave. Masters were permitted to punish slaves by harsh corporal punishment. Slaves were forbidden to gather in large groups lest they plan a revolt. In most slave-owning societies, slave marriages were not recognized by law. The children of slaves were owned by the owner of the parents. Slave families could be separated by sale or inheritance.

The death rate among slaves was high. Their lives were sacrificed to the ongoing expansion of the plantations that made their owners wealthy and that produced goods for consumers in Europe.

The African slaves who were transported to the Americas were converted to Christianity: in the Spanish domains to Roman Catholicism, and in the English colonies to Protestantism. In both cases, they became largely separated from African religious outlooks. Although slaves did manage to mix Christianity with African religion, the conversion of Africans to Christianity represented another example of the crushing of non-European cultural values in the New World.

Europeans were also prejudiced against black Africans. Many Europeans thought Africans were savages or looked down on them because they were slaves. These attitudes had been shared by both Christians and Muslims in the Mediterranean world, where slavery had long existed. Furthermore, many European cultures attached negative connotations to blackness. Although racial thinking in regard to slavery became more important in the nineteenth century, the fact that slaves were differentiated from the rest of the population by race as well as by their status as chattel property was fundamental to the system.

AFRICA AND THE TRANSATLANTIC SLAVE TRADE

It was the establishment of plantations demanding slave labor that drew Africa into the heart of the transatlantic economy. As native Americans were decimated by conquest and disease or proved unsatisfactory as plantation laborers, colonial entrepreneurs began to look elsewhere for plantation labor. First the Portuguese, and then the Spanish, Dutch, French, and English turned to Africa for slaves. The Atlantic slave trade was not overtly the result of racist principles but of the economic needs of the colonial powers and their willingness to exploit weaker peoples to satisfy them. However, this willingness was based on the tacit racist assumption that non-European, nonwhite tribal peoples could be enslaved for European purposes.

The Portuguese were the principal carriers throughout most of the history of the trade. During the eighteenth century, which saw the greatest shipments, the French and English carried almost half the total traffic. Americans were avid slavers who managed to make considerable profits even after Britain and the United States outlawed slaving in 1807.

Slaving was an important part of the massive new overseas trade that financed much European and American economic development that so changed the west during the nineteenth century. This trade, bought at the price of immense human suffering, helped propel Europe and some of its colonial offshoots in the Americas into world dominance.

THE BACKGROUND OF SLAVERY

Slavery seems to have been a tragic fact of human societies as far back as we can trace it. Although linked to warfare, it cannot be explained by military or economic necessity.

Virtually every premodern state around the globe depended on slavery. The Mediterranean and African worlds were no exception. Slave institutions in sub-Saharan Africa were ancient. The Islamic states of southwestern Asia and North Africa increased this traffic, although they took fewer slaves from Africa than from Eastern Europe and central Asia. (Hence it is not surprising that the word *slave* is derived ultimately from *Slav.*) Both Mediterranean-Christian and Islamic peoples were using slaves—mostly Greeks, Bulgarians, Turkish prisoners of war, and Black Sea Tartars, but also Africans—before the voyages of discovery opened sub-Saharan sources of slaves for the new European colonies.

Not all forms of slavery were as dehumanizing as the chattel slavery in the Americas. Islamic law, for example, ameliorated slavery. All slavery, however, involved the forceful exploitation and degradation of human beings, the denial of basic freedoms, and the sundering of family ties.

Africa suffered immense social devastation when it was the chief supplier of slaves to the world. The societies that were built on the exploitation of African slavery also suffered enduring consequences, not the least of which is racism.

SLAVERY AND SLAVING IN AFRICA

The trade that supplied African slaves to the Islamic lands and Asia has been termed the "oriental" slave trade. The Sudan and the Horn of Africa were the two prime sources of slaves for

15.3
Olaudah Equiano, The Life of Olaudah Equiano, on Gustavus Vassa, The African

15.2
"Our Kingdom is Being Lost:" Nzinga Mbemba (Affonso I)

This 18th-century print shows bound African captives being forced to a slaving port. It was largely African middlemen who captured slaves in the interior and marched them to the coast.

North Wind Picture Archives

Estimated Slave Imports into the Americas and Old World by Region, 1451–1870

British North America	523,000
Spanish America	1,687,000
British Caribbean	2,443,000
French Caribbean	1,655,000
Dutch Caribbean	500,000
Danish Caribbean	50,000
Brazil (Portuguese)	4,190,000
Old World	297,000
Total	**11,345,000**

Figures as calculated by James A. Rawley, *The Transatlantic Slave Trade: A History* (New York: W. W. Norton, 1981), p. 428, based on his and other more recent revisions of the careful but older estimates of Philip D. Curtin, *The Atlantic Slave Trade: A Census* (Madison: University of Wisconsin Press, 1969), especially pp. 266, 268.

Conquest of the Americas and the Transatlantic Slave Trade

1494	The Treaty of Tordesillas divides the seaborne empires of Spain and Portugal
1500	The Portuguese arrive in Brazil
1519–1521	Hernan Cortés conquers the Aztec Empire
1531–1533	Francisco Pizarro conquers the Inca Empire
1607	Jamestown, Virginia, first permanent English settlement in North America founded
1608	The French found Quebec
1619	First African slaves brought to British North America
1650	Transatlantic slave trade becomes bigger than the older oriental slave trade
1700s	Over six million slaves imported from Africa to the Americas
1807	Slavery abolished in British domains
1808	The importation of slaves abolished in the United States
1874–1928	Indigenous African slavery abolished
1888	Slavery abolished in Brazil

this trade. The trade managed by Europeans is called the "occidental" slave trade. Voyages beginning in the fifteenth century by first the Portuguese and then other Europeans made the western coasts of Africa as far south as Angola the prime slaving areas.

Before the full development of the transatlantic slave trade by about 1650, slavery and slave trading had been no more significant in Africa than anywhere else.[1] Indigenous African slavery resembled that of other premodern societies. Estimates suggest that about 10,000 slaves per year, most of them female, were taken from sub-Saharan Africa through the oriental trade.

By about 1650, the newer occidental slave trade of the Europeans had become as large as the oriental trade and for the ensuing two centuries far surpassed it. It affected all of Africa, disrupting especially western and central African society. As a result of the demand for young male slaves on the plantations of the Americas, West Africa experienced a sharp drain on its productive male population. Between 1640 and 1690, the number of slaves sold to European carriers doubled, indicating the increasing participation of Africans in the trade. The demand for slaves increased internal warfare in western and central Africa. Moreover, as the external trade destroyed the male-female population balance, an internal market for female slaves arose.

These developments accelerated during the eighteenth century, when African states and slave traders were most heavily involved in the trade. The population declined sharply in the coastal and inland areas hardest hit by the ravages of the trade.

As European and American nations began to outlaw slaving and slavery in the nineteenth century, the oriental and internal trades increased. Slave exports from East Africa and the Sudan and Horn increased after about 1780, and indigenous African slavery also expanded. This traffic was dominated by the same figures—merchants, warlords, and rulers—who had profited from external trade.

Indigenous African slavery began a real decline only at the end of the nineteenth century because of the dominance of European colonial regimes and internal changes. The formal end of African indigenous slavery occurred only in 1928 in Sierra Leone.

THE AFRICAN SIDE OF THE TRANSATLANTIC TRADE

Africans were actively involved in the transatlantic slave trade. European slave traders generally obtained their human cargoes from private or government-sponsored African middlemen along the coast. This situation was the result of both the ability of Africans to control inland trade and the vulnerability of Europeans to tropical disease. Thus, it was largely African middlemen who undertook the capture or procurement of slaves and the

[1]The summary follows closely that of P. Manning, *Slavery and African Life: Occidental, Oriental, and African Slave Trades* (Cambridge: Cambridge University Press, 1990), pp. 127–140.

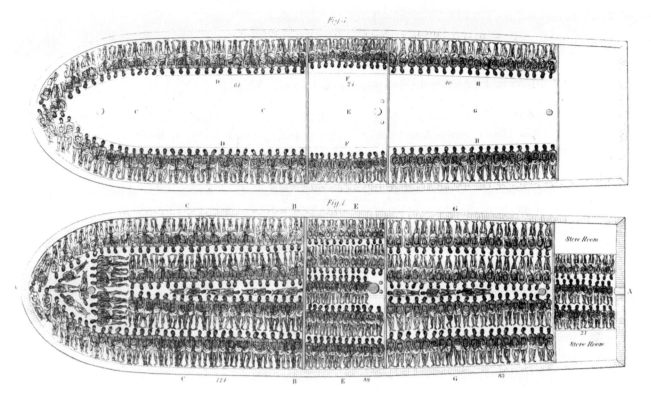

Loading plan for the main decks of the 320-ton slave ship Brookes. The Brookes was only 25 feet wide and 100 feet long, but as many as 609 slaves were crammed on board for the night-marish passage to the Americas. The average space allowed each person was only about 78 inches by 16 inches.

Photographs and Prints Division, Schomburg Center for Research in Black Culture, The New York Public Library, Astor, Lenox, and Tilder Foundations

difficult task of marching them to the coast. These middlemen were generally either wealthy merchants or the agents of African chieftaincies or kingdoms.

The media of exchange varied. At first they usually involved barter for goods from gold dust or firearms to alcohol. In time, they increasingly involved monetary payments. This exchange drained productive resources (human beings) in return for nonproductive wealth.

The chief West and central African slaving regions provided different numbers of slaves at different times, and the total number of exported slaves varied between periods. When one area could not meet demand, the European traders shifted to other points. Traders went where population density and African merchant or state suppliers promised the best numbers and prices.

THE EXTENT OF THE SLAVE TRADE

The slave trade varied sharply in extent from period to period. The period of greatest activity, 1701–1810, accounted for over 60 percent of the total, and even the final half-century of slaving until 1870 accounted for over 20 percent of the total. The Portuguese transported more than a million slaves to Brazil between 1811 and 1870. We would do well to remember how long it took the "modern" occidental world to abolish the trade in African slaves.

The overall number of African slaves exported during the occidental trade—effectively, between 1451 and 1870—is still debated and must be seen in the larger context of all types of slaving in Africa in the same period. A major unknown is the number of slaves who died under the brutal conditions to which they were subjected when captured and transported overland and by sea. The most reliable estimates pertain only to those slaves who actually landed abroad. As the accompanying table shows, just those who actually reached an American or Old World destination in the occidental trade totaled more than 11 million.

·HISTORY'S VOICES·

A SLAVE TRADER DESCRIBES THE ATLANTIC PASSAGE

During 1693 and 1694, Captain Thomas Phillips carried slaves from Africa to Barbados on the ship Hannibal. The financial backer of the voyage was the Royal African Company of London, which held an English crown monopoly on slave trading. Phillips sailed to the west coast of Africa, where he purchased the Africans who were sold into slavery by an African king. Then he set sail westward.

WHO ARE the various people described in this document who in one way or another were involved in or profited from the slave trade? What dangers did the Africans face on the voyage? What contemporary attitudes could have led this ship captain to treat and think of his human cargo simply as goods to be transported? What are the grounds of his self-pity for the difficulties he met?

Having bought my complement of 700 slaves, 480 men and 220 women, and finish'd all my business at Whidaw [on the Gold Coast of Africa], I took my leave of the old king and his cappasheirs [attendants], and parted, with many affectionate expressions on both sides, being forced to promise him that I would return again the next year, with several things he desired me to bring from England. . . . I set sail the 27th of July in the morning, accompany'd with the East-India Merchant, who had bought 650 slaves, for the Island of St. Thomas . . . from which we took our departure on August 25th and set sail for Barbadoes.

We spent in our passage from St. Thomas to Barbadoes two months eleven days, from the 25th of August to the 4th of November following: in which time there happened such sickness and mortality among my poor men and Negroes. Of the first we buried 14, and of the last 320, which was a great detriment to our voyage, the Royal African Company losing ten pounds by every slave that died, and the owners of the ship ten pounds ten

shillings, being the freight agreed on to be paid by the charter-party for every Negro delivered alive ashore to the African Company's agents at Barbadoes. . . . The loss in all amounted to near 6500 pounds sterling.

The distemper which my men as well as the blacks mostly died of was the white flux, which was so violent and inveterate that no medicine would in the least check it, so that when any of our men were seized with it, we esteemed him a dead man, as he generally proved. . . .

The Negroes are so incident to the small-pox that few ships that carry them escape without it, and sometimes it makes vast havock and destruction among them. But tho' we had 100 at a time sick of it, and that it went thro' the ship, yet we lost not above a dozen by it. All the assistance we gave the diseased was only as much water as they desir'd to drink, and some palm-oil to annoint their sores, and they would generally recover without any other helps but what kind nature gave them. . . .

But what the small pox spar'd, the flux swept off, to our great regret, after all our pains and care to give them their messes in due order and season, keeping their lodgings as clean and sweet as possible, and enduring so much misery and stench so long among a parcel of creatures nastier than swine, and after all our expectations to be defeated by their mortality. . . .

No gold-finders can endure so much noisome slavery as they do who carry Negroes; for those have some respite and satisfaction, but we endure twice the misery; and yet by their mortality our voyages are ruin'd, and we pine and fret ourselves to death, and take so much pains to so little purpose.

From Thomas Phillips, *"Journal," A Collection of Voyages and Travels*, Vol. VI, ed. by Awnsham and John Churchill (London, 1746), as quoted in Thomas Howard, ed., *Black Voyage: Eyewitness Accounts of the Atlantic Slave Trade* (Boston: Little, Brown and Company, 1971), pp. 85–87.

At a minimum, Africa lost some 13 million people to the Atlantic trade alone. Another five million or more were lost to the oriental trade. Finally, according to the estimate of one expert, an additional 15 million people were enslaved within African societies themselves.[2] (See "A Slave Trader Describes the Atlantic Passage".)

[2]Manning, pp. 37, 170–171.

CONSEQUENCES OF THE SLAVE TRADE FOR AFRICA

These statistics hint at the massive impact slave trading had on African life. Still, the actual effects remain disputed. We do not know for certain if the Atlantic trade brought net population loss or gain to specific areas of West Africa. The rapid spread of maize and cassava cultivation in forest regions after these plants had been imported from the Americas may have fueled African population increases that offset regional human loss through slaving. We know, however, that slaving took away many of the strongest young men and, in the oriental-trade zones, most of the young women.

Similarly, we do not know if more slaves were captured as byproducts of local wars or from pure slave raiding, but we do know they were captured and removed from their societies.

Nor do we know if slaving always inhibited trade or stimulated it because commerce in African products from ivory to wood and hides often accompanied that in slaves. Still, we do know that the exchange of productive human beings for money or goods that were not used to build a productive economy was a loss for African society.

Finally, because we do not yet have accurate estimates of the total population of Africa at different times over the four centuries of the Atlantic slave trade, we cannot determine with certainty its demographic impact. We can, however, make educated guesses. If, for example, tropical Africa had 50 million inhabitants in 1600, it would then have had 30 percent of the combined population of the Americas, the Middle East, Europe, and Africa. If in 1900, after the depredations of the slave trade, it had 70 million inhabitants, its population would have dropped to about 10 percent of the combined population of the same world regions. Current estimates indicate that overall African population growth suffered significantly as a result of the slave trade. Figures like these also give some idea of slavery's probable impact on Africa's ability to keep up with the modern industrializing world.[3]

Even in West and central Africa, which bore the brunt of the Atlantic trade, its impact and the response to it were varied. In a few cases, kingdoms such as Dahomey (the present Republic of Benin) seem to have derived immense economic profit by making slaving a state monopoly. Other kingdoms derived no gain from it. In many instances, including the rise of Asante power or the fall of the Yoruba Oyo Empire, increased slaving was a result as well as a cause of regional change. Increased warfare meant increased prisoners to be sold off; however, whether slaving gave good cause for war is still unclear.

Similarly, if one can establish, as seems evident, a major increase in indigenous slavery as a result of the external trade to occident and orient, we have to assume major social consequences for African society, but the specific consequences would differ according to regional situations. For example, in West

In the American South, the islands of the Caribbean, and in Brazil, the slaves labored on sugar plantations under the authority of overseers.

The Granger Collection

---

[3]On all of the preceding points regarding probable impact of the trade, see Manning, pp. 126–148, 168–176.

QUICK REVIEW

Difficulties in Determining Consequences of the Slave Trade

◆ Do not know how slave trade affected specific West African regions

◆ Cannot determine number of slaves captured during wars and captured during pure slave raiding

◆ Do not know how slave trading affected commerce in African products

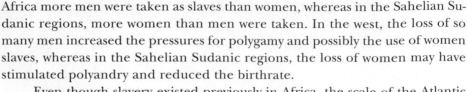

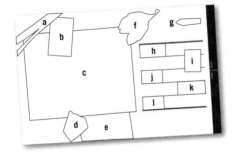

IMAGE KEY

for pages 388–389

a. Sugarcane stems
b. A poster for a slave auction in Charleston
c. John Singleton Copley, "Watson and the Shark", ca. 1778
d. A chunk of silver metal and rock
e. Spanish map showing the seven cities of Cibola and Baja California, 16th Century
f. Dried tobacco leaves
g. Slave ship, ca. 1790
h. Samuel Scott, "Old Custom House Quay"
i. Bartoleme de Las Casas
j. Slaves grinding sugar cane and refining sugar
k. Fur traders and Indians
l. Slaves harvest sugar cane on a plantation

Africa more men were taken as slaves than women, whereas in the Sahelian Sudanic regions, more women than men were taken. In the west, the loss of so many men increased the pressures for polygamy and possibly the use of women slaves, whereas in the Sahelian Sudanic regions, the loss of women may have stimulated polyandry and reduced the birthrate.

Even though slavery existed previously in Africa, the scale of the Atlantic trade was unprecedented and hence had an unprecedented impact. In general, the slave trade changed patterns of life and balances of power in the main affected areas, whether by stimulating trade or warfare, by disrupting market and political structures, by increasing slavery inside Africa, or by disturbing the male-female ratio (and hence the work-force balance and birthrate patterns) and consequently the basic social institution of monogamous marriage.

The overseas slave trade at the least siphoned indigenous energy into counterproductive or destructive directions. This, in turn, inhibited true economic development. The Atlantic slave trade was one of the most tragic aspects of European involvement in Africa.

SUMMARY

European Conquest of the New World The contact between the native peoples of the American continents and the European explorers of the fifteenth and sixteenth centuries transformed world history. In the Americas, the native peoples had established a wide variety of civilizations. Some of their most remarkable architectural monuments and cities were constructed during the centuries when European civilizations were reeling from the collapse of Roman power. Until the European explorations, the civilizations of the Americas and Eurasia and Africa had had no significant contact with each other.

Within half a century of the landing of Columbus, millions of America's native peoples had encountered Europeans intent on conquest, exploitation, and religious conversion. Because of their advanced weapons, navies, and the new diseases they brought with them, as well as internal divisions among the native Americans, the Europeans achieved a rapid conquest.

The Transatlantic Economy In both North and South America, economies of exploitation were established. In Latin America, various institutions were developed to extract native labor. From the mid-Atlantic English colonies through the Caribbean and into Brazil, slave-labor plantation systems were established. The slaves were forcibly imported from Africa and sold in America to plantation owners. The economies and peoples of Europe, Africa, and the Americas were thus drawn into a vast worldwide web of production based on slave labor.

Slavery The impact of slavery in the Americas was not limited to the life of the black slaves. Whites in the New World numbered about 12 million in 1820, compared to some six million blacks. However, only about two million whites had migrated there, compared to some 11 million or more Africans forcibly imported as slaves. Such numbers reveal the effects of brutal slave conditions and the high mortality and low birthrates of slave populations.

None of these statistics, however, enables us to asses the role that slavery has played in the Americas or, in particular, the United States. The United States actually received only a bit more than a quarter as many slaves as did Brazil alone or the British and French Caribbean regions together, yet the consequences of the forced migration of just over a half-million Africans remain massive. Consider just the American Civil War and the endurance of racism and inequality or, more positively, the African contribution to American industrial development, language, music, literature, and artistic culture. The Atlantic slave trade's impact continues to be felt at both ends of the original "trade."

REVIEW QUESTIONS

1. How were small groups of Spaniards able to conquer the Aztec and Inca Empires?

2. What was the basis of the mercantilist theory of economics? What was the relationship between the colonial economies and those of the homelands?

3. Why did forced labor and slavery develop in tropical colonies? How was slavery in the Americas different from slavery in earlier societies?

4. What was the effect of the transatlantic slave trade on African societies? What role did Africans themselves play in the slave trade?

KEY TERMS

Black Legend (p. 393)

conquistadores (p. 394)

debt peonage (p. 395)

encomienda (p. 394)

hacienda (p. 394)

mercantilism (p. 390)

peninsulares (p. 394)

plantation economy (p. 399)

repartimiento (p. 394)

 For additional study resources for this chapter, go to:
www.prenhall.com/craig/chapter18

Mother Bathing her Son. Woodblock print by Kitagawa Utamaro (1753–1806). Note the cooper's craft seen in the tub, the wooden clog, the simple yet elegant kimono design, and a second kimono hanging to dry in the upper right corner. Kitagawa Utamaro (1753–1806), "Mother Bathing Her Son." Print. Color woodblock print, oban, tate-e, nishiki-e, mica 14 7/8" × 10 1/8" (37.8 × 25.7 cm.). The Nelson-Atkins Museum of Art, Kansas City, Missouri (Purchase: Nelson Trust). ©The Nelson Gallery Foundation. All reproduction rights reserved.

19

EAST ASIA IN THE LATE TRADITIONAL ERA

WHY DID the Chinese accept Manchu rule?

WHAT WAS the "Warring States Era" in Japan?

HOW DID the Tokugawa control Japan?

HOW DID Chinese culture influence Korea and Vietnam?

IMAGE KEY
Image Key for pages 408–409 is on page 432.

This chapter underlines the dynamism of both China and Japan during the centuries between the "medieval" and the "modern" eras. "Late traditional society" does not mean "late static society." In both countries the society became more integrated and the apparatus of government became more sophisticated. These advances shaped Chinese and Japanese responses to the West during the nineteenth century. Even Korea and Vietnam did not lack dynamism. But during these centuries the West was transformed. As we view East Asia from the perspective of Europe, it appears to have been caught in a tar pit of slow motion, but it was actually the West that had accelerated.

LATE IMPERIAL CHINA

MING (1368–1644) AND QING (1644–1911) DYNASTIES

WHY DID the Chinese accept Manchu rule?

The Ming and the Qing were China's last dynasties. The first was Chinese, the second a dynasty of conquest (Manchus). They were nevertheless remarkably similar in their institutions and pattern of rule.

LAND AND PEOPLE

China's population reached about 410 million people in the mid-nineteenth century. This population density stimulated commerce and gave new prominence to the scholar-gentry. Population growth was paralleled by an increase in the food supply.

There are many unanswered questions regarding the population growth during these six centuries. Was there a decline in the death rate and, if so, why? Or did the development of new lands and technology enable more mouths to be fed? Certainly the Ming-Qing era was the longest continuous period of good government in Chinese history. But by the early nineteenth century, the Chinese standard of living may have begun to decline. An ever-increasing population was no blessing.

CHINA'S THIRD COMMERCIAL REVOLUTION

Early Ming emperors, isolationist and agrarian in orientation, operated government monopolies that stifled enterprise and depressed the southeastern coastal region with their restrictions on maritime trade and shipping. In the mid-sixteenth century, commerce started to grow again, buoyed by the surge of population and agriculture and a relaxation of government controls. If the growth during the Han and Song dynasties may be called China's first and second commercial revolutions, then the expansion between 1500 and 1800 was the third. By the early nineteenth century, China was the most highly commercialized nonindustrial society in the world.

One stimulus to commerce was imported silver. The Chinese balance of trade was favorable. Beginning in the mid-sixteenth century, silver from Japan entered China, and from the 1570s, Spanish galleons brought in Mexican and Peruvian silver. In the eighteenth century, private **Shaanxi banks** opened branches throughout China to facilitate the transfer of funds and extend credit for trade. Eventually they opened offices in Singapore, Japan, and Russia. As in Europe, so in China, the influx of silver and the overall increase in liquidity led to inflation and commercial growth.

Urban growth between 1500 and 1800 was mainly at the level of market towns. These towns provided the link between the local markets and the larger provincial capitals and cities. The commercial integration of local, intermediate, and large cities spread over all of China. Interregional trade also gained. But

Shaanxi banks Private commercial banks in China under the Manchus.

China did not develop a national economy. Seven or eight regional economies, each the size of a large European nation, were the focus for most economic activity. But a new level of trade developed among them, especially where water transport made such trade economical.

Women and the Commercial Revolution   The Confucian family ideal changed little during the Ming and Qing dynasties. A woman was expected first to obey her parents, then her husband, and finally her son—when he became the new family head. Physically, women became more restricted as footbinding spread through the upper classes and to some commoners. One exception to the rule was the Manchus. One Manchu (Qing) emperor even issued an edict banning footbinding, but it was ignored by the Chinese.

As population grew and the size of the average landholding shrunk, more women worked at home, making products for commercial markets. And as their contribution to the household income grew, their voice in household decisions often became larger than Confucian doctrines would suggest.

Political System   One might expect these massive demographic and economic changes to have produced a profound change in the political superstructure of China. They did not. Government during the Ming and Qing was much like that of the Sung or Yuan, only stronger. The sources of strength of the Ming-Qing system were the spread of education, the use of Confucianism as an ideology, stronger emperors, better government finances, more competent officials, and a larger gentry class with an expanded role in local society.

Role of Confucianism   Confucian teachings were more widespread in late imperial China than ever before. There were more schools. Academies preparing candidates for the civil service examinations multiplied. Literacy outpaced population growth. The Confucian view of society was patriarchal. The family, headed by the father, was the basic unit. The emperor, the son of Heaven and the ruler-father of the empire, stood at its apex. In between were the district magistrates, the "father-mother officials." The idea of the state as the family writ large carried with it duties and obligations at every level.

In comparison to Europe, where religious philosophies were less involved with the state and where a revolution in science was reshaping religious and political doctrines, the greater unity and integration of the Chinese worldview cannot be denied.

Emperor   Ming-Qing emperors were more powerful than ever and made all important and many unimportant decisions. They wielded despotic powers at their courts. They had secret police and prisons where those who gave even minor offense might be tortured. Even high officials might suffer humiliating and fatal punishment. The dedication and loyalty even of officials who were cruelly mistreated attest to the depth of their Confucian ethical formation.

During the Qing, the life-and-death authority of emperors did not diminish, but officials were generally better treated. As foreign rulers, the Manchu emperors took care not to alienate Chinese officials.

The Forbidden Palace in Peking was an icon of the emperor's majesty. The entire palace complex focused on the ruler. Its massive walls and vast courtyards progress to the audience hall where the emperor sat on an elevated dais above the officials, who knelt before him. Behind the audience hall were the emperor's private chambers and his harem. By the seventeenth century, there were 9,000 palace

QUICK REVIEW

Women Under the Qing and Ming
◆ Confucian family ideal changed little during the Ming and Qing eras
◆ Footbinding spread among the upper classes and some commoners
◆ As population grew, more women worked at home

The great Manchu emperor Qianlong
(r. 1736–1795).

© Metropolitan Museum of Art, Rogers Fund, 1942
(42.141.8)

Gentry In China, a largely urban,
landowning class that represented
local interests and functioned as quasi-
bureaucrats under the magistrates.

ladies and perhaps as many as 70,000 eunuchs. The glory of
the emperor extended to his family, whose members were
awarded vast estates in North China.

Bureaucracy A second component of the Ming-Qing system was the government itself. At the top were the military, the
censorate, and the administrative branch; beneath the administration were the six ministries and the web of provincial,
prefectural, and district offices. But government was better financed than during earlier dynasties. As late as the 1580s,
huge surpluses were accumulated at both the central and the
provincial levels. Only during the last 50 years of the Ming
did soaring military expenses bankrupt government finances.
Then, in the second half of the seventeenth century, the
Manchus reestablished a strong central government and restored the flow of taxes to levels close to those of the Ming.

The good government the Ming-Qing system brought
to China was largely a product of the ethical commitment and
ability of its officials. No officials in the world today approach
in power or prestige those of the Ming and the Qing. When
the Portuguese arrived early in the sixteenth century, they
called these officials "mandarins." The rewards of an official
career were so great that the competition to enter it was intense. As population grew and schools increased, entrance
became ever more competitive.

After being screened at the district office, a candidate
took the county examination. If he passed, he became a member of the gentry and was exempted from state labor service.
Even this examination required years of study. About half a million passed each year. The second hurdle was the provincial
examination held every third year. Only one in a hundred was
successful. The final hurdle was the metropolitan examination, also held triennially. Fewer than 90 passed each year.

Gentry A final component in the Ming-Qing system was the
gentry class. It was an intermediate layer between the elite bureaucracy above and the village below. The lowest level of
bureaucratic government was the district magistrate. Although the
population increased sixfold during the Ming and the Qing, the
number of district magistrates increased only from 1,171 to 1,470.
To prevent conflicts of interest, an outsider was appointed as district magistrate. His office compound had a large staff of secretaries and advisers, but
to govern effectively, he had to obtain the cooperation of the local literati or gentry.

By *gentry* we do not mean a rural elite, like English squires. The Chinese
gentry was largely urban, living in market towns or district seats. Socially and
educationally, its members were of the same class as the magistrate—a world
apart from clerks or village headmen. They usually owned land, which enabled
them to avoid manual labor and to send their children to private academies. As
absentee landlords whose lands were worked by sharecroppers, they were often
exploitative. But they also acted as local leaders. They represented community
interests vis-à-vis the bureaucracy. They also performed quasi-official functions
on behalf of their communities: maintaining schools and Confucian temples;

repairing roads, bridges, canals, and dikes. The gentry class was the matrix from which officials arose; it was the local upholder of Confucian values.

Pattern of Manchu Rule   The collapse of the Ming dynasty in 1644 and the establishment of Manchu rule was less of a break than might be imagined. First, the transition was short. Second, the Manchus, unlike the Mongols, were already partially Sinicized. Even before entering China, they had ruled over Chinese who had settled in Manchuria.

In the late sixteenth century, an able leader unified the Manchurian tribes, proclaimed a new dynasty, and established a Confucian government. When the Ming collapsed, the Manchus presented themselves as the conservative upholders of the Confucian order. The Chinese gentry preferred the Manchus to Chinese rebel leaders, whom they regarded as bandits. After the Manchu conquest, most officials served the new dynasty. The Qing as a Chinese dynasty dates from 1644.

As a tiny fraction of the Chinese population, the Manchus adopted institutions to maintain themselves as an ethnically separate elite group. One was their military organization. Manchu garrison forces were segregated and not put under the jurisdiction of Chinese officials. They were given stipends and lands to cultivate. They were forbidden to marry Chinese, their children had to study Manchu, and they were not permitted to bind the feet of their daughters. In 1668, northern and central Manchuria were closed to Chinese immigrants.

The second institutional feature was the appointment of one Chinese and one Manchu to each key post in the central government. At the provincial level, Chinese governors were overseen by Manchu governor-generals. Most officials and all district magistrates beneath the governors were Chinese.

A particular strength of the Manchu dynasty was the long reigns of two extremely able emperors, Kangxi (1661–1722) and Qianlong (1736–1795). Kangxi was a man of great vigor. He rose at dawn to read official documents before meeting with officials. He presided over palace examinations. Well versed in the Confucian classics, he won the support of scholars.

Kangxi also displayed an interest in European science, a subject he studied with Jesuit court astronomers. He opened four ports to foreign trade and carried out public works, improving the dikes on the Huai and Yellow Rivers and dredging the Grand Canal. During his reign, he made six tours of China's southern provinces. Kangxi, in short, was a model emperor.

Qianlong began his reign in 1736. During his reign the Qing dynasty attained its highest level of prosperity and power. Like Kangxi, he was vigorous, wise, conscientious, careful, and hard-working. He visited South China on inspection tours and patronized scholars on a grand scale.

Only in his last years did Qianlong lose his grip and permit a court favorite to practice corruption on an almost unprecedented scale. In 1796, the White Lotus Rebellion broke out. Qianlong's successor put down the rebellion, but the ample financial reserves that had existed throughout the eighteenth century were never reestablished. China nevertheless entered the nineteenth century with its government intact and with a peaceful and stable society. There were few signs of what was to come.

Late Imperial China

Ming Dynasty 1368–1644

1368–1398	Reign of first Ming emperor; Chinese armies invade Manchuria, Mongolia, and eastern Central Asia
1402–1424	Reign of third Ming emperor; Chinese armies invade Vietnam and Mongolia
1405–1433	Voyage of Zheng Hi to India and Africa
1415	Grand Canal reopened
1472–1529	Wang Yang-min, philosopher
1592–1598	Chinese army battles Japanese army in Korea

Ch'ing (Manchu) Dynasty 1644–1911

1668	Manchuria closed to Chinese immigrants (by Willow Palisade)
1661–1722	Reign of Kangxi
1681	Suppression of revolts by Chinese generals
1683	Taiwan captured
1689	China and Russia sign Treaty of Nerchinsk
1736–1795	Reign of Qianlong
1793	Macartney mission

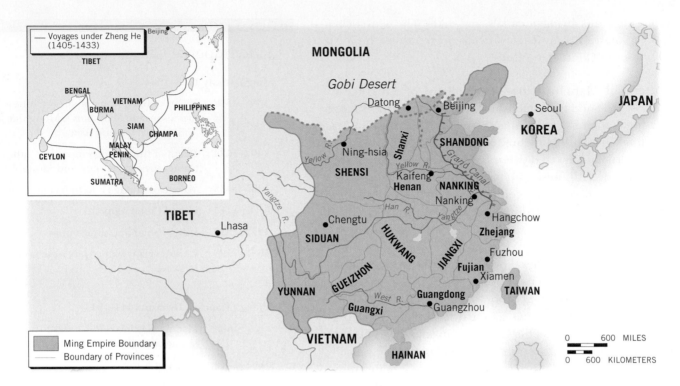

MAP 19–1

Ming Empire and the voyages of Zheng HE.   The ships of Cheng Ho, venturing beyond Southeast Asia and India, reached the coast of East Africa.

WHAT WAS the purpose of Zheng He's voyages?

MING–QING FOREIGN RELATIONS

Ming   The first Ming emperor (r. 1368–1398) oversaw the expansion of China's borders. At his death, China controlled the northern steppe and had regained control of the southern tier of Chinese provinces (see Map 19–1). During the reign of the third Ming emperor (1402–1424), northern Vietnam became a Chinese province for two decades.

The Ming emperors "managed" China's frontiers with the tribute system. In this system, the ambassadors of vassal kings acted out their subordination to the universal ruler of the celestial kingdom. An ambassador approached the emperor, performed the kowtow (kneeling three times and each time bowing his head to the floor three times), and presented his gifts. In return, the vassal kings were sent seals confirming their status, given permission to use the Chinese calendar and year-period names, and appointed to the Ming nobility.

The most far-ranging ventures of the third Ming emperor were the maritime expeditions that sailed to Southeast Asia, India, the Arabian Gulf, and East Africa between 1405 and 1433. They were commanded by the eunuch Zheng He, a Muslim from Yunnan (see Map 19–1). The first of these armadas had 62 major ships and carried 28,000 sailors, soldiers, and merchants. Trade was not the primary purpose. The expeditions were intended to make China's glory known to distant kingdoms and to enroll them in the tribute system.

The expeditions ended as abruptly as they had begun. They were costly at a time when the dynasty was fighting in Mongolia and building Beijing. What was remarkable about these expeditions was not that they came a half-century earlier than the Portuguese voyages of discovery, but that China had the necessary maritime technology and yet decided not to use it. China lacked the combination of restlessness, greed, faith, and curiosity that would motivate the Portuguese.

The chief threat to the Ming dynasty was the Mongols. In the 1430s they captured the emperor, and in 1550 they overran Peking, but were defeated by a Chinese army in the 1560s and signed a peace treaty in 1571.

A second threat came from Japan. Pirates raided the Chinese coast in the fifteenth and sixteenth centuries, and Hideyoshi, after unifying Japan, invaded and occupied Korea in 1592 and 1597–1598. Eventually China sent troops. The Japanese withdrew after the death of Hideyoshi. But the strain on Ming finances had weakened the dynasty.

16.2
Dynastic Change in China
Tears a Family Apart

Qing   The final and successful foreign threat to the Ming was the Manchus. After coming to power in 1644, the Manchu court spent decades consolidating its rule within China. Chinese generals who had helped the Manchus revolted and were supported by a pirate state on Taiwan. The emperor Kangxi suppressed the revolts; in 1683 he took Taiwan, which became a part of China for the first time.

As always, the principal foreign threats to China came from the north and northwest. By the 1660s, Russian traders, trappers, and adventurers had reached northern Manchuria, where they built forts and traded with the eastern Mongols. During the 1680s, Kangxi drove the Russians from the lower Amur River. This victory led to the 1689 Treaty of Nerchinsk, which excluded Russia from northern Manchuria.

In the west, the situation was more complex, with a three-corner relationship among Russia, the western Mongols, and Tibet. Kangxi, and then Qianlong, campaigned against the Mongols, invaded Tibet, and in 1727 signed a new treaty with Russia. During the campaigns, the Chinese temporarily came to control millions of square miles of new territories. It is a telling comment on the Chinese concept of empire that ever since that time, even after China's borders contracted during the nineteenth century, the Chinese have insisted that the Manchu conquests of non-Chinese peoples define their legitimate borders. The roots of the present-day contention over borders between China and the countries of the former Soviet Union go back to these events during the eighteenth century, as does the Chinese claim to Tibet.

Contacts with the West   Europeans had made their way to China during the Tang and the Yuan dynasties. But only with Europe's oceanic expansion in the sixteenth century did they arrive in large numbers. Some came as missionaries, of whom the most successful were the Jesuits. They studied Chinese and the Confucian classics and conversed with scholars. They used their knowledge of astronomy, geography, engraving, and firearms to win entry to the court at Beijing and appointments in the bureau of astronomy.

When the Manchus came to power in 1644, the Jesuits kept their position. They appealed to the curiosity of the court with instruments such as telescopes, clocks, and clavichords. They tried to propagate Christianity. They attacked Daoism and Buddhism, but argued that Confucianism as a rational philosophy complemented Christianity, just as Aristotle's teaching complemented Christian theology in Europe. They interpreted the Confucian rites of ancestor worship as secular and nonantagonistic to Christianity. A few high court officials were converted.

Meanwhile, their Franciscan and Dominican rivals had reported to Rome that the Jesuits condoned the Confucian rites. Papal bulls in 1715 and 1742 forbade Chinese Christians to participate in the family rites of ancestor worship. Thereupon the emperor banned Christianity in China.

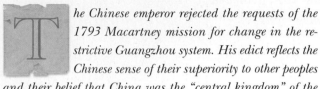

QIANLONG'S EDICT TO KING GEORGE III OF ENGLAND

he Chinese emperor rejected the requests of the 1793 Macartney mission for change in the restrictive Guangzhou system. His edict reflects the Chinese sense of their superiority to other peoples and their belief that China was the "central kingdom" of the world.

WHAT PHILOSOPHICAL principles underlie the emperor's sense of superiority?

You, O King, are so inclined toward our civilization that you have sent a special envoy across the seas to bring to our Court your memorial of congratulations on the occasion of my birthday and to present your native products as an expression of your thoughtfulness. On perusing your memorial, so simply worded and sincerely conceived, I am impressed by your genuine respectfulness and friendliness and greatly pleased. . . .

The Celestial Court has pacified and possessed the territory within the four seas. Its sole aim is to do its utmost to achieve good government and to manage political affairs, attaching no value to strange jewels and precious objects. The various articles presented by you, O King, this time are accepted by my special order to the office in charge of such functions in consideration of the offerings having come from a long distance with sincere good wishes. As a matter of fact, the virtue and prestige of the Celestial Dynasty having spread far and wide, the kings of the myriad nations come by land and sea with all sorts of precious things. Consequently there is nothing we lack, as your principal envoy and others have themselves observed. We have never set much store on strange or ingenious objects, nor do we need any more of your country's manufactures. . . .

Reprinted by permission of the publisher from *China's Response to the West: A Documentary Survey*, 1839–1923, by Ssu-yu Teng and John K. Fairbank, Cambridge, MA: Harvard University Press. Copyright © 1954, 1979 by the President and Fellows of Harvard College, Copyright renewed 1982 by Ssy-yu Teng and John King Fairbank.

16.5
Letter to King George: China and Great Britain

QUICK REVIEW

Chinese Contacts with the West
- Europeans arrived in China in number after the sixteenth century
- The most successful missionaries were the Jesuits
- By the eighteenth century, Europeans could only trade at Guangzhou

Other Europeans came to China to trade. The Portuguese came first in the early sixteenth century and were permitted to trade on a tiny peninsula at Macao. They were followed by Dutch from the East Indies (Indonesia), by the British East India Company in 1699, and by Americans in 1784.

By the early eighteenth century, westerners could trade only at Guangzhou, outside its walls along the river. They could not bring their wives to China. They were subject to Chinese law and were under the control of official merchant guilds. Nevertheless, the trade was profitable to both sides.

The British East India Company developed a triangular commerce among China, India, and Britain. For China, this trade produced an influx of specie, and the Chinese officials in charge grew immensely wealthy. Chafing under the restrictions, the British government in 1793 sent the Macartney mission to China to negotiate the opening of other ports, fixed tariffs, representation at Peking, and so on. The emperor Qianlong permitted Lord Macartney (1736–1806) to present his gifts, which the Chinese described as tribute, but he turned down Macartney's requests. Western trade remained encapsulated at Guangzhou. (See Qianlong's Edict to King George III of England.")

MING-QING CULTURE

Chinese culture had begun to turn inward during the Song in reaction to Buddhism. This tendency continued into the Ming and Qing, when Chinese culture became virtually impervious to outside influences. This reflected a tradition and a social order that had stood the test of time, but it also indicated a closed system of ideas with weaknesses that would become apparent in the nineteenth century.

Ming and Qing Chinese esteemed most highly the traditional categories of high culture: painting, calligraphy, poetry, and philosophy. Porcelains of great beauty were also produced. The pottery industry of Europe was begun during the sixteenth century to imitate these wares, and Chinese and Japanese influences have dominated Western ceramics down to the present. Chinese today, however, see the novel as the characteristic cultural achievement of the Ming and Qing.

The novel in China grew out of plot-books used by earlier storytellers. Like the stories, Chinese novels consisted of episodes strung together. As most novels were written in colloquial Chinese, which was not quite respectable in the society of scholars, their authors wrote under pseudonyms.

JAPAN

The two segments of late traditional Japan could not be more different. The Warring States era (1467–1600), the last phase of Japan's medieval history, saw the unleashing of internal wars and anarchy. Within a century, all vestiges of the old manorial or estate system had been scrapped and almost all of the Ashikaga lords had been overthrown. The Tokugawa era (1600–1868) that followed saw Japan with a stronger government than ever. During the Tokugawa era, Japanese culture was transformed, preparing it for the challenge it would face during the mid-nineteenth century.

WARRING STATES ERA (1467–1600)

In 1467, a dispute arose over who would be the next Ashikaga shôgun. The dispute led to wars throughout Japan for eleven years. Most of Kyoto was destroyed in the fighting, and the authority of the Ashikaga *bakufu* came to an end. This first war ended in 1477, but the fighting resumed and continued for more than a century.

WAR OF ALL AGAINST ALL

Even before 1467, the Ashikaga equilibrium had been precarious. The regional **daimyo** lords had relied on their relationship to the *bakufu* to hold their stronger vassals in check, while relying on these vassals to preserve their independence against strong neighbors. The collapse of *bakufu* authority after 1467 left the regional lords standing alone, removing the last barrier to internecine wars. The regional lords, however, were too weak to stand alone. They became prey to the stronger among their vassals as well as to powerful neighboring states.

By the end of the sixteenth century, hundreds of little "Warring States daimyo" had emerged, each with his own warrior band. The constant wars among these men were not unlike those of the early feudal era in Europe. The most efficient in revamping their domain for military ends survived. The less ruthless, who clung to old ways, were defeated and absorbed.

As fighting continued, local states gave way to regional states until in the late sixteenth century, all of Japan was brought under the hegemony of a single

Ming dynasty ink painting by Wudi (1479–1508). The seated human figure is a part of the tranquility of nature. Nature, densely concentrated at the left and lower portions of the painting, stretches off into space in the middle and upper right portion.

WHAT WAS the "Warring States Era" in Japan?

daimyo   Japanese territorial lord.

Warring States Era in Japan

1543	Portuguese arrive in Japan
1575	Battle of Nagashino
1582	Oda Nobunaga is assassinated
1587	Spanish arrive in Japan
1588	Hideyoshi's sword hunt
1590	Hideyoshi unifies Japan
1592, 1597–1598	Hideyoshi sends armies to Korea; battles fought against Chinese troops
1597	Hideyoshi bans Christianity
1598	Hideyoshi dies
1600	Tokugawa victory in Battle of Sekigahara

16.7
The Laws for Military House
(Buke Shohatto), 1615

"The Arrival of the Portuguese in Japan."
Portuguese merchants arrived in Japan
in 1543 from India and the East Indies.
Their crews were multiethnic and they
brought Jesuit priests as well.

Giraudon/Art Resource, N.Y.

lord, Toyotomi Hideyoshi (1536–1598). But it was only with the victory of Tokugawa Ieyasu (1542–1616) at the Battle of Sekigahara in 1600 that true unification was finally achieved. Ieyasu's unification was based on a sweeping transformation of Japan's society.

How should one characterize the society that emerged from the Warring States? Does the word *feudal* apply? In some respects, it does: By the late sixteenth century all warriors in Japan were part of a pyramid of vassals and lords headed by a single overlord; warriors of rank held fiefs and vassals of their own.

In other respects, Japan was more like postfeudal Europe. First, most of the military class were soldiers, not aristocrats. Even though they were called samurai and were vassals, they were not given fiefs but were paid with stipends of rice. Second, unlike, say, feudal England, where the military class was about one-quarter of 1 percent of the population, in mid-sixteenth-century Japan it may have reached 7 or 8 percent. It was more of a size with the mercenary armies of Europe during the fifteenth or sixteenth centuries. Third, the recruitment of village warriors gave rise to problems as well. Taxes became harder to collect. Local samurai were often involved in uprisings that sometimes involved whole provinces. Again, the parallels with postfeudal Europe seem closer. Fourth, even in a feudal society, not everything is feudal. Commercial growth continued in the Warring States era.

FOREIGN RELATIONS AND TRADE

Japanese pirate-traders plied the seas of East Asia during the fifteenth and sixteenth centuries. To halt their depredations, the Ming emperor invited the third Ashikaga shōgun to trade with China. An agreement was reached in 1404. However, piracy stopped only after Japan was reunified at the close of the sixteenth century.

The content of the trade reflected the progress of Japanese crafts. Early Japanese exports to China were raw materials, but by the sixteenth century, manufactured goods were rising in importance. In exchange, Japan received copper cash, porcelains, paintings, books, and medicines. Then, in 1635, the imposition of seclusion ended Japan's foreign trade: No Japanese could leave Japan, and the construction of large ships was prohibited.

Overlapping Japan's maritime expansion in the seas of East Asia was the arrival of European ships. Portuguese pirate-traders arrived in Japan in 1543. Spanish galleons came in 1587. They were followed by the Dutch and the English after the turn of the century.

The Portuguese became important as shippers. They carried Southeast Asian goods and Japanese silver to China and Chinese silk to Japan, and they used their profits to buy spices for the European market.

Traders brought with them Jesuit missionaries. They directed their efforts toward the samurai. Christian converts numbered about 300,000 in 1600. That is to say, in the late sixteenth century, a higher percentage of Japanese were Christian than today.

It is difficult to explain why Christianity met with greater success in Japan than in other Asian lands. When introduced, it was seen as a new Buddhist sect. There seemed little difference to the Japanese between the cosmic Buddha of Shingon and the Christian God, between the paradise of Amida and the Christian Heaven, or between prayers to Kannon—the female *bodhisattva* of mercy—and to the Virgin Mary. The Japanese also noted the theological similarity between the pietism of the Pure Land sect and that of Christianity. The personal example of the Jesuits was also important.

The fortunes of Christianity began to decline in 1597, when six Spanish Franciscans and 20 Japanese converts were crucified in Nagasaki. It was said that Spanish merchants and priests represented the first step toward the conquest of Japan. Sporadic persecutions continued until 1614, when Tokugawa Ieyasu formally banned the foreign religion. Some Christians recanted. More than 3,000 others were martyred.

The last resistance was an uprising in 1637 and 1638 in which 37,000 Christians died. After that, Christianity survived in Japan only as a hidden religion. A few of these "hidden Christians" reemerged in the later nineteenth century.

TOKUGAWA ERA (1600–1868)

POLITICAL ENGINEERING AND ECONOMIC GROWTH DURING THE SEVENTEENTH CENTURY

After the unifications of 1590 and 1600, Japan's leaders sought to create a peaceful, stable, orderly society. By the middle or late seventeenth century, Japan's society and political system had been radically reengineered. Vigorous economic and demographic growth had also occurred. This combination of political and economic change made the seventeenth century a period of great dynamism.

HOW DID the Tokugawa control Japan?

Hideyoshi's Rule   In the summer of 1588, Hideyoshi ordered a "sword hunt" to disarm the peasants. Once the hunt was completed, the 5 percent of the population who remained samurai used their monopoly on weapons to control the other 95 percent.

Hideyoshi next moved to freeze the social classes. Samurai were prohibited from quitting the service of their lord. Peasants were barred from abandoning their fields to become townspeople. This policy succeeded. Samurai, farmers, and townspeople tended to marry within their respective classes, and each class developed a unique cultural character.

Having disarmed the peasantry, Hideyoshi ordered surveys to define each parcel of land by location, size, soil quality, product, and cultivator's name. Hideyoshi's survey laid the foundations for a systematic land tax. Domains and fiefs were henceforth ranked in terms of their assessed yield.

Establishment of Tokugawa Rule   Hideyoshi assumed that his vassals would honor their oaths of loyalty to his heir. He was especially trustful of his great ally Tokugawa Ieyasu. His trust was misplaced. After his death in 1598, Hideyoshi's former vassals broke into two opposing camps and fought a great battle in 1600 from which Tokugawa Ieyasu emerged victorious. Ieyasu established his headquarters in Edo (today's Tokyo), in the center of his military holdings in eastern Japan (see Map 19–2). He took the title of shôgun in 1603 and called his government the *bakufu*. Ieyasu then used his military power to reorganize Japan.

MAP EXPLORATION

Interactive map: To explore this map further, go to **http://www.prenhall.com/craig2/map19.2**

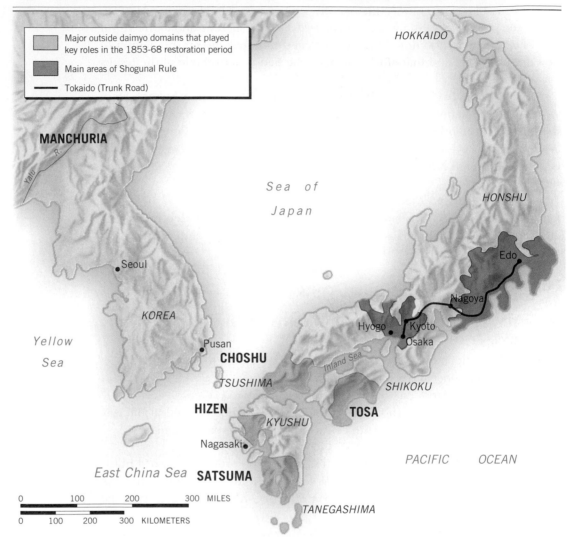

MAP 19–2

Tokugawa Japan and the Korean peninsula.   The area between Edo and Osaka in central Honshu was both the political base of the Tokugawa *bakufu* and its rice basket. The domains that would overthrow the Tokugawa *bakufu* in the late nineteenth century were mostly in outlying areas of southwestern Japan.

WHAT CONTROLS did the Tokugawa impose to control the daimyo?

Ieyasu's first move was to confiscate the lands of his defeated enemies and to reward his vassals and allies. During the first quarter of the seventeenth century, the *bakufu* confiscated the domains of 150 daimyo and transferred 229 daimyo from one domain to another. The transfers severed long-standing ties between daimyo and their disarmed former village retainers. When a daimyo was transferred to a new fief, he took his samurai retainers with him. The entire arrangement constituted a defensive system, with the staunchest Tokugawa supporters nearest to the center of power.

The Tokugawa also established other controls. Legal codes regulated the imperial court, the temples and shrines, and the daimyo. Military houses were enjoined to use men of ability and to practice frugality. Only with *bakufu* consent could daimyo marry or repair their castles.

A second control was a hostage system that required the wives and children of daimyo to reside permanently in Edo and the daimyo themselves to spend every second year in Edo. This transformed feudal lords into courtiers.

A third key control was the national policy of seclusion. Seclusion was no barrier to cultural imports from China and Korea. But except for small Chinese and Dutch trading contingents at Nagasaki, no foreigners were permitted to enter Japan, and on pain of death, no Japanese were allowed to go abroad. Nor could oceangoing ships be built. This policy was strictly enforced until 1854. Seclusion enclosed the system of Tokugawa rule. Cut off from outside political contacts, for Japanese, Japan became the world.

The Seventeenth-Century Economy   The political dynamism of the period from Hideyoshi through the first century of Tokugawa rule was matched by economic growth. Resources no longer needed for war were allocated to land reclamation and agriculture. The result was a doubling of agricultural production, as well as a doubling of population from about 12 million in 1600 to 24 million in 1700.

Peace also sustained growth in commerce. The medieval guilds were abolished and Japan's central markets freed from monopolistic restrictions. The result was a burgeoning of trade and the formation of a national market network. As this network expanded, economic functions became more differentiated and efficient.

Economic growth and the national integration of the economy led to a richness and diversity in urban life. Townsmen governed their districts. Samurai city managers watched over the city as a whole. Official services were provided by schools, police, and firefighters. But there were also servants, cooks, messengers, restaurant owners, priests, doctors, teachers, sword sharpeners, book lenders, instructors in the martial arts, prostitutes, and bathhouse attendants. In the world of popular arts, there were woodblock printers and artists, book publishers, puppeteers, acrobatic troupes, storytellers, and **Kabuki** and **Nō** actors. Merchant establishments included money changers, pawnbrokers, peddlers, small shops, single-price retail establishments like the House of Mitsui, and great wholesale merchants.

EIGHTEENTH AND EARLY NINETEENTH CENTURIES

By the late seventeenth century, the political engineering of the Tokugawa state was complete. After that, few important changes were made in governing institutions. In the economy, too, dynamic growth gave way to slower growth within a high-level equilibrium. Yet changes of a different kind were under way.

Cycles of Reform   Most political history of late Tokugawa Japan is written in terms of alternating cycles of laxity and reform. Even during the mid-seventeenth century, the expenses of the *bakufu* and daimyo states were often greater than their income. In part, the reason was structural: Taxes were based on agriculture in an economy that was becoming commercial. In part, it was simple mathematics: After the samurai were paid their stipends, not enough was left for the expenses of domain government and the costs of the Edo establishments. In part, it was the toll of extraordinary costs, such as a *bakufu* levy, the wedding of a daimyo's daughter, or the rebuilding of a castle after a fire. And finally, in part, it was a taste for luxury among daimyo and retainers of rank.

Over the years a familiar pattern emerged. To make ends meet, domains would borrow from merchants. Then, as finances became even more difficult, a reformist clique of officials would return the domain to a more frugal and austere

Kabuki   A realistic form of Japanese theater similar to English Elizabethan drama.

Nō play   A highly stylized form of Japanese drama in which the chorus provides the narrative line as in classical Greek plays.

The commercial district of Osaka, the "kitchen" of Tokugawa Japan. Warehouses bear the crests of their merchant houses. Ships (upper right) loaded with rice, cotton goods, sake, and other goods are about to depart for Edo (Tokyo). Their captains vied with one another to arrive first and get the best price.

Courtesy A. Craig

way of life. But since no one likes to practice frugality forever, a new round of spending would begin. The *bakufu* carried out three great reforms:

1716–1733	Tokugawa Yoshimune	17 years
1787–1793	Matsudaira Sadanobu	6 years
1841–1843	Mizuno Tadakuni	2 years

The first two were long and successful; the third was not. Its failure set the stage for the ineffective response of the *bakufu* to the West in the mid-nineteenth century.

Bureaucratization The balance between centralization and decentralization lasted, until the end of the Tokugawa era. Not a single domain ever tried to overthrow the *bakufu* hegemony. Nor did the *bakufu* ever try to extend its control over the domains. But bureaucracy grew steadily both within the *bakufu* and domains. By 1850, all but the largest samurai fiefs were administered by district officials who collected the standard domain taxes and forwarded to the samurai their income. Along with the growth in bureaucracy was the proliferation of administrative codes and paperwork: records of births, adoptions, name changes, samurai ranks, fief registers, stipend registers, land and tax registers, court proceedings, and so on.

Of course, there were limits to bureaucratization. Only samurai could aspire to official posts. They came to the office wearing their two swords. Decision-making posts were limited to upper-ranking samurai. But in periods of financial crises a demand arose for men of ability, and middle- or lower-middle-ranking samurai became staff assistants to bureaucrats of rank.

The Later Tokugawa Economy By 1700, the economy approached the limit of expansion within the available technology. The population reached 26 million early in the eighteenth century and was at the same figure in the mid-nineteenth century, a period during which the population of China more than doubled.

After 1700, taxes became stabilized and land surveys were few. Evidence suggests little increase in grain production and only slow growth in agricultural byproducts.

Some families made conscious efforts to limit their size to raise their standard of living. Contraception and abortion were common place, and infanticide was practiced in hard times. But periodic disease, shortages of food, and late marriages among the poor were more important factors.

Some farmers remained independent cultivators, but about a quarter of all cultivated lands were worked by tenants by the mid-nineteenth century. Most landlords were small, and often were village leaders. They were not at all like the Chinese gentry. The misery of the lower stratum of rural society contributed to an increase in peasant uprisings during the late eighteenth and early nineteenth centuries. Authorities had no difficulty quelling them, and no uprising in Japan approached those of late Manchu China.

Commerce grew slowly during the late Tokugawa. In the early eighteenth century, it was reencased within guilds. Merchants paid set fees in return for monopoly privileges in central marketplaces. Guilds were also reestablished in the domains, and some domains established domain-run monopolies on products such as wax, paper, indigo, or sugar. The problem facing domain leaders was how to share in the profits without injuring the competitive standing of domain exports. Most late Tokugawa commercial growth was in countryside industries—*sake*, soy sauce, dyes, silks, or cotton. Some were organized and financed by city merchants. Others competed with city merchants, shipping directly to the end markets to circumvent monopoly controls. The expansion of labor in such rural industries may explain the population shrinkage in late Tokugawa cities.

The largest question about the Tokugawa economy concerns its relation to Japan's rapid industrialization in the late nineteenth century. Some scholars have suggested that Japan had a "running start." Others have stressed Japanese backwardness in comparison with European late developers. The question is still unresolved.

Tokugawa Era (1600–1868)	
1600	Tokugawa Ieyasu reunifies Japan
1615	"Laws of Military Houses" issued
1639	Seclusion policy adopted
1642	Edo hostage system in place
1644–1694	Bashō, poet
1653–1724	Chikamatsu Monzaemon, dramatist
1701	The forty-seven rōnin avenge their lord
1853, 1854	Commodore Matthew Perry visits Japan

TOKUGAWA CULTURE

Two hundred fifty years of peace and prosperity provided a base for an ever more complex culture and a broader popular participation in cultural life. In the villages, Buddhism became more deeply rooted; new folk religions proliferated; by the early nineteenth century most well-to-do farmers could read and write. The aristocratic culture of the ranking samurai houses also remained vigorous. Nō plays continued to be staged. The medieval tradition of black ink paintings was continued by the Kanō school and other artists.

The Ashikaga tradition of restraint, simplicity, and naturalness in architecture was extended. The imperial villa in Katsura outside of Kyoto has its roots in medieval architecture and to this day inspires Japanese architects. The gilded and colored screen paintings that had surged in popularity during Hideyoshi's rule developed further, culminating in the powerful works of Ogata Kōrin (1658–1716).

Zen Buddhism, having declined during the Warring States period, was revitalized by the monk Hakuin (1686–1769). One of the great cultural figures of the Tokugawa era, Hakuin was also a writer, a painter, a calligrapher, and a sculptor.

Some scholars have argued that Tokugawa urban culture had a double structure. On the one hand were the samurai, serious and high-minded, who produced a vast body of Chinese-style paintings, poetry, and philosophical treatises. On the other hand was the culture of the townspeople: low-brow, irreverent, secular, satirical, and often scatological. The samurai esteemed Sung-style paintings of mountains and waterfalls, often adorned with quotations from the Confucian classics or

Mother Bathing Her Son, Woodblock print (37.8 × 25.7 cm) by Kitagawa Utamaro (1753–1806). Note the tenderness with which the mother bathes her son.

T'ang poetry. The townspeople collected prints of local beauties, actors, courtesans, and scenes from everyday life. Samurai moralists saw money as the root of evil. Merchants saw it as their goal in life.

Literature and Drama   Is cultural creativity more likely during periods of economic growth and political change or during periods of stability? The greatest works of literature and philosophy of Tokugawa Japan were produced between 1650 and 1725, just as the initial political transformation was being completed, but the economy still growing and the society not yet set in its ways.

One of the major literary figures and certainly the most entertaining was Ihara Saikaku (1642–1693), who is generally credited with having recreated the Japanese novel. Saikaku was the heir to an Osaka merchant house. He was raised to be its master, but after his wife died he let the head clerk manage the business and devoted himself to poetry, the theater, and the pleasure quarters. At the age of forty he wrote and illustrated *The Life of an Amorous Man*, the story of a modern and bawdy Prince Genji who cuts a swath through bathhouse girls, shrine maidens, courtesans, and boy actors. The success of the work led to a sequel, *The Life of an Amorous Woman*, the tale of a woman undone by passion.

A second major figure of Osaka culture at the turn of the century was the dramatist Chikamatsu Monzaemon (1653–1724). Born a samurai, Chikamatsu wrote for both the Kabuki and the puppet theater. Kabuki had begun early in the seventeenth century as suggestive skits and erotic dances performed by actresses. In 1629, the *bakufu* forbade women to perform on the stage. By the 1660s, Kabuki had evolved into a more serious drama with male actors playing both male and female roles.

The three main types of Kabuki plays were dance pieces, which were influenced by the tradition of the Nō; domestic dramas; and historical pieces. Chikamatsu wrote all three. In contrast to Saikaku's protagonists, the men and women in Chikamatsu's dramas struggle to fulfill the duties and obligations of their stations in life. Only when their passions become uncontrollable do the plays end in tragedy. The emotional intensity of the ending is heightened by the restraint shown by the actors before they reach their breaking point.

It is interesting to compare Kabuki and the Nō drama. Nō is like early Greek drama in that the chorus provides the narrative line. In Nō, the stylization of action is extreme. In Kabuki, as in Elizabethan drama, the actors declaim their lines in the dramatic realism demanded by the commoner theatergoers of seventeenth-century Japan.

In the early eighteenth century, Kabuki was displaced in popularity by the puppet theater (Bunraku). Many of Chikamatsu's plays were written for this genre. In the late eighteenth century, the puppet theater, in turn, declined, and Kabuki again blossomed as Japan's premier form of drama.

Confucian Thought   The most important change in Tokugawa intellectual life was that the ruling elite abandoned the religious worldview of Buddhism in favor of the more secular Confucianism, opening many avenues for further changes.

The great figures of Tokugawa Confucianism lived in the late seventeenth and early eighteenth centuries. They succeeded in adapting Chinese Confucianism to fit Japanese society. One problem, for example, was that in Chinese Confucianism there was no place for a shōgun, whereas in the Japanese tradition of sun-line emperors, there was no room for the Mandate of Heaven. Most Tokugawa thinkers handled this discrepancy by saying that Heaven gave the emperor its mandate and that the emperor then entrusted political authority to the shōgun. One philosopher suggested that the divine emperor acted for Heaven and gave the mandate to the shōgun. Neither solution was very comfortable, for, in fact, the emperor was as much a puppet as those in the Osaka theater.

Another problem was the difference between China's centralized bureaucratic government and Japan's "feudal" system of lord-vassal relationships. Samurai loyalty was clearly not that of a scholar-official to the Chinese emperor. Some Japanese Confucianists solved this problem by saying that it was China that had deviated from the feudal society of the Chou sages, whereas in Japan, Tokugawa Ieyasu had recreated just such a society.

A third problem concerned the "central flowery kingdom" and the barbarians around it. No philosopher could bring himself to say that Japan was the real middle kingdom and China the barbarian, but some argued that centrality was relative, and still others suggested that China under barbarian Manchu rule had lost its claim to universality. These are just a few of a large range of problems related to Japanese political organization, Shinto, and Japanese family practices. By the early eighteenth century, these problems had been addressed, and a revised Confucianism acceptable for use in Japan had come into being.

Another point to note is the continuing intellectual vitality of Japanese thought into the mid-nineteenth century. This vitality is partly explained by the disputes among different schools of Confucianism and partly, perhaps, by Japan's lack of an examination system. The best energies of its samurai youth were not channeled into writing the conventional and sterile "eight-legged essay" that was required for the Chinese examination system. Official preferment—within the constraints of Japan's hereditary system—was more likely to be obtained by writing a proposal for domain reforms.

The intellectual vitality was also a result of the rapid expansion of schools from the early eighteenth century. By the early nineteenth century, every domain had its own official school. Commoner schools, in which reading, writing, and the rudiments of Confucianism were taught, grew apace. In the first half of the nineteenth century, private academies also appeared throughout the country. By the midnineteenth century, about 40 to 50 percent of the male population and 15 to 20 percent of the female population was literate—a far higher rate than in most of the world, and on a par with some European late developers.

Other Developments in Thought   For Tokugawa scholars, the emotional problem of how to deal with China was vexing. They praised China as the teacher country and respected its creative tradition. They studied its history, philosophy, and literature. But they also sought to retain a separate Japanese identity. Most scholars dealt with this problem by adapting Confucianism to fit Japan. But two schools, National Studies and Dutch Studies, criticized the Chinese influence on Japanese life and culture.

National Studies began as philological studies of ancient Japanese texts. One source of its inspiration was Shinto. Another was the Neo-Confucian School of Ancient Learning. Just as the School of Ancient Learning had sought to discover the original, true meanings of the Chinese classics before they were contaminated by Sung metaphysics, so the scholars in the National Studies tradition tried to find in the Japanese classics the original true character of Japan before it had been contaminated by Chinese ideas. On studying these works, they found that the early Japanese spirit was free, spontaneous, clean, lofty, and honest, in contrast to the Chinese spirit, which they characterized as rigid, cramped, and artificial. National Studies also reaffirmed Japan's emperor institution.

National Studies became influential during the late Tokugawa era and influenced the Meiji Restoration. Its doctrines continued thereafter as one strain of Japanese ultranationalism.

National Studies   A Japanese intellectual tradition that emphasized native Japanese culture and institutions and rejected the influence of Chinese Confucianism.

A second development was Dutch Studies. After Christianity had been proscribed and the policy of seclusion adopted, all Western books were banned in Japan. Some knowledge of Dutch was maintained among the official interpreters who dealt with the Dutch at Nagasaki. The ban on Western books (except for those propagating Christianity) was ended in 1720 by the shōgun Tokugawa Yoshimune (r. 1716–1745).

During the eighteenth century, a school of "Dutch medicine" became established in Japan. Japanese pioneers early recognized that Western anatomy texts were superior to Chinese. The first Japanese dissection of a corpse occurred in 1754. By the mid-nineteenth century, there were schools of Dutch Studies in the main cities of Japan, and instruction was available in some domains as well. Medicine was the primary occupation of those who studied Dutch. But some knowledge of Western astronomy, geography, botany, physics, chemistry, and arts also entered Japan.

From the late eighteenth century, the Japanese began to be aware of the West, and especially of Russia, as a threat to Japan. In 1791, a concerned scholar wrote *A Discussion of the Military Problems of a Maritime Nation*, advocating strong navy and coastal defenses. During the early nineteenth century, such concerns mounted. A sudden expansion in Dutch Studies occurred after Commodore Matthew Perry's visits to Japan in 1853 and 1854. During the 1860s, Dutch Studies became Western Studies, as English, French, German, and Russian were added to the languages studied at the *bakufu* Institute for the Investigation of Barbarian Books. In sum, Dutch Studies laid a foundation on which the Japanese built quickly when the need arose for knowledge of the West.

KOREA AND VIETNAM

HOW DID Chinese culture influence Korea and Vietnam?

A feature of world history, noted earlier, is the spread of heartland civilizations into their surrounding areas. In East Asia, the heartland civilization was that of China, the surrounding areas that were able to take in Chinese learning were Japan, Korea, and Vietnam. Like the Japanese, Koreans and Vietnamese devised a writing system using Chinese ideographs. They partially modeled their governments on those of China. They accepted Chinese Buddhism and Confucianism, and with them Chinese conceptions of the universe, state, and human relationships. The Confucian definitions of the relations between ruler and minister, father and son, and husband and wife were emphasized in Korea and Vietnam as they were in China. But at the same time, Koreans and Vietnamese, who spoke non-Chinese tongues, saw themselves as separate peoples, and gradually came to take pride in their independence. In Europe, Germany might be a parallel case: it became civilized by borrowing the heartland Greco-Christian culture of the Mediterranean area, but it kept its original tongue and elements from its earlier culture.

KOREA

A range of mountains along its northern rim divides the Korean peninsula from Manchuria, making it a distinct geographical unit. Mountains continue south through the eastern third of Korea, while in the west and south are coastal plains and broad river valleys. Two further geographical factors affected Korean history. One was that the northwestern corner of Korea was only 300 miles from the northeastern corner of historical China: close enough for Korea to be vulnerable to invasions by its powerful neighbor but far enough away so that most of the time China found it easier to treat Korea as a tributary than to control it directly. The other factor was that the southern rim of Korea was just 100 miles from Japan.

EARLY HISTORY

During the first millennium B.C.E., agriculture, bronze, and iron were introduced to Korea, transforming its primitive society. But Koreans were still ruled by tribal chiefdoms in 108 B.C.E. when the Han Emperor Wu Ti sent an army into north Korea to menace the flank of the Hunnish (Hsiung Nu) Empire that had spread across the steppe to the north of China. Wu Ti built a Chinese city which survived into the fourth century C.E., and established commanderies and prefectures to administer the land.

Between the fourth and seventh centuries, three archaic states emerged from earlier tribal confederations. Silla, one of the three, together with armies from T'ang China, conquered the other two in the seventh century. Silla was recognized by China in 675 as an autonomous tribute state. The period of Silla rule may be likened to Nara Japan: Korea borrowed Chinese writing, established some government offices on the Chinese model, sent annual embassies to the T'ang court, and took in Chinese Buddhism and Chinese arts and philosophies. Yet within the Silla government, birth mattered more than scholarship and rule by aristocrats continued, while in village Korea, the worship of nature deities was only lightly touched by the Buddhism that spread among the ruling elites.

Silla underwent a normal end-of-dynasty decline, and in 918, a warlord general founded a new dynasty, the Koryo. The English word "Korea" is derived from this dynastic name. This was a creative period. Korean scholars advanced in their mastery of Chinese principles of government. New genres of poetry and literature appeared. Korean potters made celadon vases rivaling those of China. Printing using moveable metallic type was invented during the thirteenth century. But most important was the growth of Buddhism. Temples, monasteries, and nunneries were built throughout the land, and Buddhist arts flourished.

Despite cultural advances, the Koryo state was weak. Its economy was undeveloped: trade was by barter, and Chinese missions commented on the extravagance of officials in the capital and the squalor of commoners and slaves in Korea's villages. The dynasty was aristocratic, and as centuries passed, private estates and armies arose, and civil officials were replaced by military men. Frequent incursions from across Korea's northern border weakened the state. The cost of wars with the Mongols was particularly high. The Koryo court survived as long as it did by becoming in succession the tributary of the Sung, Liao, Chin, and Mongol dynasties.

THE CHOSON ERA: LATE TRADITIONAL KOREA

In 1392, a Koryo general, Yi Songgye, founded a new dynasty. It lasted until 1910; its amazing longevity was directly related to the stability of Ming-Ch'ing China.

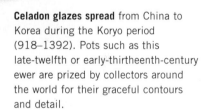

Celadon glazes spread from China to Korea during the Koryo period (918–1392). Pots such as this late-twelfth or early-thirteenth-century ewer are prized by collectors around the world for their graceful contours and detail.

Melon-shaped Ewer, Stoneware, Korio Dynasty, ca. 12th century H. 9" × Diam. 19-1/2". Korea. The Avery Brundage Collection, Asian Art Museum of San Francisco

Korea

108 B.C.E.– 4th century C.E.	Chinese rule in northern Korea
4th century C.E.–675	Three archaic states
675–918	Silla
918–1392	Koryo
1392–1910	Choson
1592, 1596	Japanese invasions of Korea
1627, 1637	Manchu invasions of Korea
1671	Famine

After seizing power, Yi carried out an extensive land reform and strengthened his government by absorbing into his officialdom members of the great Koryo families. During the Yi or Choson period, these elite families, known as *yangban*, monopolized education, official posts, and land. Beneath them were the commoners known as "good people," tax-paying free subjects of the king. Beneath the commoners and constituting perhaps one-third of the population were government and private slaves. Korean scholars argue that they were not like slaves in other lands, since there were no slave auctions, and, following Confucian teachings, husbands were not separated from their wives. But Korean slaves were nonetheless property. They were often attached to land, they could be given as gifts, and their children were slaves to be used as their owners willed.

Early Choson culture showed many signs of vigor. Lyrical poetry and then prose reached new heights. The most important intellectual trend was the gradual movement of the *yangban* away from Buddhism and their acceptance of Neo-Confucianism.

But at mid-dynasty, invasions dealt a severe blow to the well-being of Choson society. Hideyoshi, having brought all of Japan under his control, decided to conquer China through Korea. His samurai armies devastated Korea in 1592 and 1596. The invasions ended with his death in 1598. On both occasions the Ming court sent troops to aid its tributary, but the Chinese armies devastated the land almost as much as had the Japanese. A third disaster occurred in 1627 and 1637 when Manchu troops invaded pro-Ming Korea. The result of these multiple incursions was a drop in taxable land to about a quarter of its late-sixteenth-century level. Behind this statistic lay famine, death, and misery.

Had the late-sixteenth-century Choson government been stronger, it might have recovered. But cliques of officials had begun to fight among themselves over official positions. Many in the losing factions were executed or imprisoned. As the struggles became more fierce, the effectiveness of government declined. High officials in Seoul used their power to garner private agricultural estates, and established local academies to prepare their own kinsmen for the official examinations.

From the mid-seventeenth century on, Korea offers a mixed picture. Literacy rose and a new popular fiction of fables, romances, and novels appeared. Women writers became important for the first time. Among some *yangban* there was a philosophic reaction against what was perceived as the emptiness of Neo-Confucianism. Calling for "practical learning" to effect a renewal of Korean society, scholars criticized the Confucian classics and outlined plans for administrative reforms and the encouragement of commerce. Unfortunately, their recommendations were not adopted, and the society continued its decline. More Koreans died in the famine of 1671 than during Hideyoshi's invasions. Overtaxation, drought, floods, pestilence, and famine became commonplace. Robberies occurred in daytime Seoul, and bandits plagued the countryside. Disgruntled officials led peasants in revolts in 1811 and 1862. Because of the concentration of officials, wealth, and military power at Seoul and because of Manchu support for the ruling house, neither revolt toppled the dynasty, but the revolts left Korea unable to meet the challenges it would soon face.

yangban Elite Korean families of the Choson period.

VIETNAM

SOUTHEAST ASIA

The historical civilizations of Southeast Asia were shaped by three movements. One was the movement of peoples and languages from north to south. Ranges of mountains rising in Tibet and South China divide Southeast Asia into river valleys.

The Mon and Burmese peoples had moved from the southeast slopes of the Tibetan plateau into the Upper Irrawaddy by 500 B.C.E. and continued south, founding the kingdom of Pagan in 847 C.E. Thai tribes moved south from China down the valley of the Chao Phraya River somewhat later, founding the kingdoms of Sukhothai (1238–1419) and Ayutthaya (1350–1767). Even today Thai-speaking tribes are found in south China. The Vietnamese, too, arose in the north and moved into present-day central and south Vietnam only in recent historical times.

A second movement was the Indianization of Southeast Asia. Between the first and fifteenth centuries, Indian traders and missionaries established outposts throughout southeast Asia. As Hinduism and Buddhism spread through the region, Indian-type states with god-kings were established, and Indian scripts, legal codes, literature, drama, art, and music were adopted. Today, Burma, Thailand, and Cambodia retain an Indian-type of Buddhism.

A third movement was of Arab and Indian traders who sailed across the Indian Ocean to dominate trade with the Spice Islands (the Moluccas of present-day Indonesia) between the thirteenth and fifteenth centuries. They married into local ruling families and spread Islam. Local rulers who converted became sultans. Today Malaysia and Indonesia are predominantly Muslim.

EARLY VIETNAMESE HISTORY

Vietnam, however, was untouched by either Indian or Islamic culture. Most of its higher culture came from China.

To comprehend Vietnamese history, one must distinguish between the people and the land. Until the fifteenth century C.E., the Vietnamese people inhabited only a small portion of what is today Vietnam, the basin of the Red River. Central Vietnam and the southeastern coast were ruled by the state of Champa. Most of the Mekong River delta in the south was ruled by Cambodian empires. (See Map 19–3.)

The political history of the Vietnamese began in 208 B.C.E., when a renegade Han dynasty general formed the state of Nan Yueh. It ruled over southeastern China and the Red River basin from its capital, which was near present-day Canton. In Vietnamese, the Chinese ideograph "Yueh" is read "Viet." The name "Vietnam," literally "Viet to the south," is derived from the name of this early state. In 111 B.C.E., Han Wu Ti brought it under Chinese rule.

For more than a millennium after 111 B.C.E., Vietnam was ruled by China. The administrative center was a fort with a Chinese governor and Chinese troops. The governor ruled through Vietnamese who were the heads of powerful local families. Then in 39 C.E., the Truong sisters led a revolt against Chinese rule—the husband of one sister had been executed by the Chinese. Thereafter, more officials were sent from China and direct bureaucratic rule was instituted. Later Vietnamese historians made the two sisters into national heroes.

During these early centuries, change was slow. Buddhism was introduced into Vietnam from China. Chinese officials and immigrants married Vietnamese women, which led to the formation of a Sino-Vietnamese political elite. The influence of Chinese higher culture was largely confined to this elite.

The pace of change increased during the T'ang dynasty (618–907). Vietnam was still treated as a border region, but Chinese administration became stronger. Vietnam

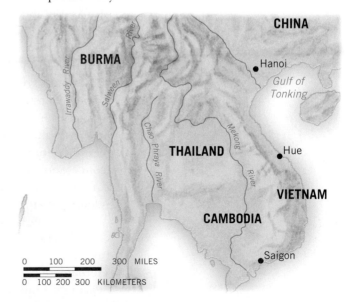

MAP 19–3
Vietnam and neighboring Southeast Asia.

WHICH RELIGIONS intermingled in Southeast Asia?

Annam The Chinese term for Vietnam.

was divided into provinces, which the Chinese referred to as *Annam*, the "pacified south." This name was never lost: when the French came to Vietnam in the nineteenth century, they called its people the *Annamese*.

Japan and Korea also reached out and took in Chinese learning during the Tang. Was Vietnam's experience a parallel case? In some respects it was. In all three societies, Buddhism entered, flourished in the capitals, and then percolated into local areas, where it absorbed earlier religious traditions. In all three, other aspects of China's higher culture affected mainly the elites. In villages, an older way of life continued. But the differences were also significant. Japanese and Korean rulers reached out for Chinese civilization, and used it for their own ends. In Vietnam, because the rulers were Chinese, no such transformation occurred.

LATE TRADITIONAL VIETNAM

Ten major revolts occurred during Chinese rule—a not unusual number for a Chinese border region with a non-Chinese population. The last revolt, in 939 when China was weak, led to an independent Vietnamese government. Vietnam never again became a part of China.

Several approaches have been used in writing the history of Vietnam's second millennium. One sees it in terms of dynasties:

Ly	1009–1225
Tran	1225–1400
Le	1428–1787
Nguyen	1802–1880s

As in China, dynasties began with strong military figures, who established courts, extended their control over the countryside, and collected taxes. Most founders of dynasties were members of the Sino-Vietnamese elite. Dynasties ended with the decentralization of power, the breakdown of taxation, and the rise of regional armies. But the idea of a "dynastic cycle" of slow administrative decline fits Vietnam less well than China. For one thing, even early in a dynasty, administrations were weaker than in China. Local magnates contested central control for longer periods. For another, each new Chinese dynasty invaded Vietnam, to regain control over an area that had once been ruled by China. These invasions often reshaped dynasties. The Tran dynasty, for example, was extended for 20 extra years by supporting Ming forces. For still another, the dynastic name was sometimes kept even after its ruling house had lost power. During the seventeenth and eighteenth centuries, for example, Vietnam was divided into two states, one ruling from Hanoi and the other from Hue. In short, though the "dynasty" may be a convenient unit for dividing the second millennium into large blocks of time, it is less useful for analysis.

Another approach is to see Vietnam in relation to the Chinese state and Chinese civilization. Although Chinese invasions of Vietnam were unsuccessful, Vietnamese rulers found it easier to "manage" China than to defy it. Every Vietnamese dynasty became a "tributary" of China. Missions were sent to China bearing tribute. The head of the mission professed the Vietnamese ruler's submission to the Chinese emperor and performed the kowtow. In correspondence with the Chinese "emperor," too, the Vietnamese rulers styled themselves as "kings," a title indicating their subordinate status. But this formal submission was little more than a ritual. Within Vietnam, Vietnamese rulers styled themselves as "emperors." They claimed their mandate to rule came directly

OVERVIEW

THE RELIGIONS OF SOUTHEAST ASIA

The countries of Southeast Asia, the area between India and China, have been influenced by Indian, Chinese, Muslim, and, since the sixteenth century, Western culture and religion. Hinduism, Buddhism, Islam, and Christianity were all brought to the area by invaders, merchants, and missionaries. Their presence is reflected in the religious makeup of the countries of Southeast Asia in the twenty-first century. While most of these countries are predominately Buddhist, Muslim, or Christian, most of them also include many adherents of other religions.

Predominately Buddhist	Burma Thailand, but with a significant Muslim minority Cambodia Laos Vietnam, but with a large Christian, primarily Roman Catholic, minority Singapore; includes Muslim, Christian, and Hindu minorities
Predominately Muslim	Indonesia; but the island of Bali is Hindu, and there is a large Christian minority Malaysia, but with Hindu, Buddhist, and Christian minorities Brunei
Predominately Christian	Philippines, but with a large Muslim minority

from Heaven, equal to the mandate received by the Chinese ruler. They denied the universaity of the Chinese imperium by referring to China not as the Middle Kingdom but as the Northern Court—their own government being the Southern Court. Yet over the centuries, the imprint of Chinese culture became more pronounced. One highpoint was the era of Le Thanh Tong (1442–1497), one of the strongest figures in Vietnamese history. Le used Chinese culture and institutions as an advanced technology to strengthen his government. He established schools, introduced Neo-Confucianism, institutionalized an examination system, and promulgated a legal code that remained in effect through the rest of the dynasty.

A third approach to Vietnamese history is to see it as a steady "march to the south" between the fifteenth and eighteenth centuries. Vietnam has been likened to two baskets on a carrying pole. One basket is the Red River delta centering on Hanoi in the north, the other the Mekong delta centering on Saigon in the south. The pole is the narrow mountainous strip of central Vietnam. Until the fifteenth century, Vietnamese inhabited only the north. Central and southeastern Vietnam was Champa, the kingdom of the Chams, a Malayan people who engaged in trade and piracy. The Chams converted to Islam. For centuries Vietnamese and Chams waged intermittent wars. In 1357 when Tran Rule was weak, a Cham army pillaged Hanoi. But under Le Thanh Tong, Vietnam destroyed Champa.

Settlers from the crowded Red River delta began to pour into the south. Political authority followed the settlers. During the seventeenth century, the Cambodian empire of Angkor was unable to resist. By 1700, a southern Vietnamese state with a capital at Hue had conquered Saigon, and by 1757 it had occupied present-day southern Vietnam. This chain of events made south Vietnam different from the north. It was less Confucian and, as a frontier society, less

IMAGE KEY

for pages 408–409

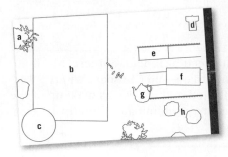

a. Long grain rice
b. Kitagawa Utamaro (1753–1806), "Mother Bathing Her Son"
c. Chinese carved lacquer box
d. Karaori kimono
e. Tai Chin, "Fisherman on an Autumn River", (1390–1460)
f. Woodblock print of the commercial disctrict of Osaka
g. Stoneware ewer from the the Koryo dynasty in Korea
h. A pile of table salt

educated. It included large minority populations of Muslim Chams and Cambodians, who practiced a Southeast Asian form of Buddhism. Massive emigrations of Chinese into southeast Asia also began during these centuries. Today about one million Chinese live in south Vietnam alone and play key roles in its economy. Such ethnic and religious diversity made the south far more difficult to govern than the more homogeneous north.

During the last half of the eighteenth century, Vietnam was wracked by further wars. In 1802, one warlord established Vietnam's last dynasty, the Nguyen. Its capital was at Hue. In coming to power, the new emperor had been aided by French advisors, several of whom were rewarded with high posts. The Nguyen dynasty, nonetheless, became more Chinese than any previous dynasty. It adopted the law codes of Manchu China and established institutions such as the Six Boards, Hanlin Academy, Censorate, and a hierarchy of civil and military officials recruited by examinations. The reasons for these initiatives were to placate Confucian scholars in the north, to strengthen the court, and to weaken the military figures who had helped the dynasty's rise. From the time of the second emperor, it also became anti-French and anti-Christian.

During the first half of the nineteenth century, Vietnam was probably governed better than any other Southeast Asian state. But it had weaknesses. There were tensions between the north, which was overpopulated, well schooled, and furnished most of the official class, and the south, which was ethnically diverse, educationally backward, and poorly represented in government. Trade and artisanal industries were less developed than in China and Japan, only small amounts of specie circulated, and periodic markets were more common than permanent market towns. The government rested on a society composed largely of self-sufficient villages. In sum, Vietnam entered the second half of the nineteenth century even less prepared than China or Japan for the challenges posed by the West.

SUMMARY

China China's last two imperial dynasties were the Ming (1368–1644) and the Qing or Manchus (1644–1911). Although China could not match the dynamism of the West during these years, its society became more integrated and its government more sophisticated. The population reached 410 million, cities grew, and commerce expanded. Chinese government depended on the Confucian bureaucracy and the gentry class. Under the Manchus, China expanded to the east and annexed Taiwan. There also was growing trade with the West, especially Britain, but it was conducted under highly restricted terms by Chinese officials.

Japan After more than a century of civil war among the warrior aristocracy (the Warring States Era, 1467–1600), the Tokugawa shoguns (1600–1868) restored order. Their government controlled the aristocracy and encouraged economic growth. Christianity, which had made many converts in Japan, was driven underground, and Japan was closed to the outside world except for a small Dutch presence at Nagasaki. Japanese drama, literature, and art flourished, as did commercial life.

Korea and Vietnam China considered both Korea and Vietnam to be tributary states, and both countries adopted Chinese Confucian culture and forms of government while preserving their political independence.

REVIEW QUESTIONS

1. Why did the economy grow in late traditional China?

2. Did Manchu rule resemble Mongol rule, or was it different? In what regards were Kangxi and Ch'ien Lung indistinguishable from Chinese emperors?

3. How did Ming-Qing foreign relations set the stage for China's nineteenth-century encounter with the West?

4. How did military technology in Japan change during the fifteenth and sixteenth centuries?

5. How was Chinese culture a "technology" used by Japan, Korea, and Vietnam for state building? Why were the results in each country so different?

KEY TERMS

Annam   (p. 430)

daimyo   (p. 417)

gentry   (p. 412)

Kabuki   (p. 421)

Nō play   (p. 421)

National Studies   (p. 425)

Shensi banks   (p. 410)

yangban   (p. 428)

 For additional study resources for this chapter, go to:
www.prenhall.com/craig/chapter19

Louis XIV of France (r. 1643–1715) was the dominant
European monarch in the second half of the 17th century.
The powerful centralized monarchy he created established
the prototype for the mode of government later termed
absolutism. Giraudon/Art Resource

20

EUROPEAN STATE BUILDING AND WORLDWIDE CONFLICT

HOW DID England and France develop differently in the seventeenth century?

WHY DID the Stuart kings quarrel with the English Parliament?

HOW DID Louis XIV consolidate his power?

WHAT DID Peter the Great hope to achieve with his reforms in Russia?

WHY DID Prussia become a rival to the Habsburgs?

WHAT WERE the results of the colonial struggles of the mid-eighteenth century?

IMAGE KEY
Image Key for pages 434–435
is on page 454.

Between the early seventeenth and mid-twentieth century no region so dominated other parts of the world as Europe. For three and a half centuries, northwestern Europe became the chief driving force in world historical development. This era of European dominance coincided with a shift in power within Europe itself from the Mediterranean to the states of the northwest and later north-central Europe.

By the mid-eighteenth century, five major states had come to dominate European politics and would continue to do so until at least World War I. They were Great Britain, France, Austria, Prussia, and Russia. Through their military strength, economic development, and in some cases colonial empires, they would affect virtually every other world civilization.

In the mid-eighteenth century, these five successful states entered upon three quarters of a century of warfare among themselves. These wars were fought both in Europe and in the European colonial empires, making them the first extensive world wars arising from conflict in Europe. These conflicts represented the most extensive European impact on the non-European world since the early sixteenth century, when the Spanish had conquered the civilizations of Mexico and Peru.

TWO MODELS OF EUROPEAN POLITICAL DEVELOPMENT

HOW DID England and France develop differently in the seventeenth century?

In the second half of the sixteenth century, changes in military organization, weapons, and tactics increased the cost of warfare. Because traditional sources of income could not finance these costs and those of government, monarchs sought new revenues. Only monarchies that built a secure financial base that was not dependent on noble estates, diets, or assemblies achieved absolute rule. The French monarchy succeeded in this effort; the English monarchy failed. That success and failure led to the two models of government—**absolutism** in France and parliamentary monarchy in England—that shaped subsequent political development in Europe.

In their pursuit of income, English monarchs of the seventeenth century threatened the local interests of the nobility and landed and commercial elite. These groups invoked traditional English liberties to resist the monarchs.

The experience of Louis XIV (r. 1643–1715), the French king, was different. After 1660 he made the French nobility dependent on his goodwill. In turn, he supported their place in a firm social hierarchy. But Louis accepted the authority of the noble-dominated ***Parlement*** of Paris to register royal decrees before they became law, and he permitted regional parlements to exercise authority over local administration and taxation.

Religious factors also affected the political destinies of England and France. In England, Puritanism overturned the Stuart monarchy. Louis XIV, in contrast, crushed the Protestant communities of France.

There were also major institutional differences between the two countries. The English Parliament had long bargained with the monarch. In the early seventeenth century, Parliament was not the strong institution it would become, nor was the transformation it underwent during the century inevitable. The institutional basis for it, however, was in place. Parliament expected to be consulted, and the English had a tradition of liberty to which members of Parliament could appeal against the monarchy.

France lacked similarly strong traditions. The Estates General played no role after 1614. It was not called again until the eve of the French Revolution in 1789. Opposition to the monarchy lacked both an institutional base and a forum in which political skills might have been developed.

Finally, personalities were important. During the first half of the century, France profited from the guidance of two able statesmen, Cardinals Richelieu and Mazarin.

absolutism   Term applied to strong centralized continental monarchies that attempted to make royal power dominant over aristocracies and other regional authorities.

parlement   A French regional court dominated by hereditary nobility. The most important was the Parlement of Paris, which claimed the right to register royal decrees before they could become law.

OVERVIEW

GREAT POWERS AND DECLINING POWERS IN EUROPE

In the seventeenth and eighteenth centuries, five European states—Britain, France, Austria, Prussia, and Russia—became European great powers and remained so until and, in every case except Austria, even after the end of World War I in 1918. At the same time, four other states that had been major European powers declined permanently into secondary status. The table below lists the main strengths of the rising powers and the main sources of weakness of the declining states.

Five Great Powers

State	Government	Strengths
Britain	Constitutional Monarchy	Commercial and financial resources; navy; colonial empire; overseas trade; intellectual liberty; growing industry; religious toleration
France	Semi-absolute Monarchy	Army; large population; cultural preeminence; colonial empire; intellectual vibrancy
Austria	Semi-absolute Monarchy	Imperial prestige; dynastic loyalty: army
Prussia	Absolute Monarchy	Army; efficient bureaucracy
Russia	Absolute Monarchy	Army; large population; extensive natural resources; imperial control over church and state

Four Declining Powers

State	Government	Weaknesses
Spain	Absolute Monarchy	Stagnant economy; inefficient government; weak military; enforced religious and intellectual conformity
Ottoman Empire	Absolute Monarchy	Backward economy; unstable government; resistance to change; outmoded military
Sweden	Constitutional Monarchy	Small population; weak economy
Netherlands	Republic	Divided government; small population; declining economy

Mazarin trained Louis XIV to be a hard-working monarch. Louis employed capable ministers. The first four Stuart monarchs of England (r. 1603–1689), on the other hand, were distrusted. Their judgment was faulty. They offended significant groups of their subjects. In a strongly Protestant nation, they were suspected of Catholic sympathies.

In both England and France, the nobility and large landowners stood at the top of the social hierarchy and sought to protect their interests. Important segments of the British nobility and landed classes came to believe that the Stuarts sought to undermine their local standing. Parliamentary government was the result of the efforts of these English landed classes to protect their interests and limit the power of the monarchy to interfere with life on the local level. The French nobility under Louis XIV, in contrast, concluded that the best way to secure their interests was to support the throne.

CONSTITUTIONAL CRISIS AND SETTLEMENT IN STUART ENGLAND

JAMES I

In 1603, James VI of Scotland (r. 1603–1625), the son of Mary Stuart, Queen of Scots, succeeded Elizabeth I as James I of England. He also inherited a royal debt and a divided church. Parliament met only when the monarch summoned it, which James hoped to do rarely. In place of parliamentarily approved revenues, James levied new custom duties known as impositions. Members of Parliament regarded this as an affront to their authority over the royal purse, but they did not seek a serious confrontation.

Puritans within the Church of England had hoped that James would further reform the English church. But he supported the Anglican episcopacy.

James's foreign policy also roused opposition. In 1604, he concluded peace with Spain, England's longtime adversary. His subjects considered this a sign of pro-Catholic sentiment. James's attempt to relax laws against Catholics increased their suspicions, as did his hesitancy in 1618 to rush English troops to the aid of German Protestants at the outbreak of the Thirty Years' War. His efforts to arrange a marriage between his son Charles and a Spanish princess and then Charles's marriage in 1625 to Henrietta Marie of France further increased religious suspicions. In 1624, England again went to war against Spain in response to parliamentary pressures.

CHARLES I

Parliament had favored the war with Spain but would not adequately finance it because its members distrusted the monarchy. Unable to gain adequate funds from Parliament, Charles I (r. 1625–1649) resorted to extraparliamentary measures. These included levying new tariffs and duties, attempting to collect discontinued taxes, and subjecting English property owners to a so-called forced loan and then imprisoning those who refused to pay. These actions, as well as quartering troops in private homes, challenged local control of nobles and landowners.

When Parliament met in 1628, its members would grant new funds only if Charles recognized the Petition of Right. This required that there should be no forced loans or taxation without the consent of Parliament, that no freeman should be imprisoned without due cause, and that troops should not be billeted in private homes. It thus expressed resentment and resistance to the monarchy on the local level. Charles agreed to the petition.

Years of Personal Rule   In 1629, Parliament declared that religious innovations leading to "popery" and the levying of taxes without parliamentary consent were treason. Charles promptly dissolved Parliament and did not recall it until 1640.

To allow Charles to rule without renegotiating financial arrangements with Parliament, his chief minister, Thomas Wentworth (1593–1641; after 1640, earl of Strafford), instituted a

---

puritans   English Protestants who sought to "purify" the Church of England of any vestiges of Catholicism.

England

1603	James VI of Scotland becomes James I of England
1625	Charles I becomes king of England
1628	Petition of Right
1629	Charles I dissolves Parliament and embarks on eleven years of personal rule
1640	April–May, Short Parliament; November, Long Parliament convenes
1641	Great Remonstrance
1642	Outbreak of the Civil War
1649	Charles I executed
1649–1660	Various attempts at a Puritan Commonwealth
1660	Charles II restored to the English throne
1670	Secret Treaty of Dover between France and England
1672	Parliament passes the Test Act
1685	James II becomes king of England
1688	Glorious Revolution
1689	William III and Mary II come to the throne of England
1701	Act of Settlement provides for Hanoverian Succession
1702–1714	Queen Anne, the last of the Stuarts
1714	George I of Hanover becomes king of England
1721–1742	Ascendancy of Sir Robert Walpole

policy known as *thorough*. This policy imposed strict efficiency and administrative centralization in government. Its goal was absolute royal control of England. Its success depended on the king's ability to operate independently of Parliament, which no law required him to summon.

Charles might have ruled indefinitely without Parliament had not his religious policies provoked war with Scotland, where Charles hoped to impose religious conformity. In 1637, Charles and Archbishop William Laud (1573–1645) tried to impose on Scotland the English episcopal system and prayer book. The Scots rebelled, and Charles, with insufficient resources for war, was forced to call Parliament. Parliament refused even to consider funds for war until the king agreed to redress a long list of political and religious grievances. The king, in response, immediately dissolved Parliament. When the Scots defeated an English army at Newburn in the summer of 1640, Charles reconvened Parliament for a long and fateful duration.

THE LONG PARLIAMENT AND CIVIL WAR

The landowners and the merchant classes represented in Parliament resented the king's financial measures and paternalistic rule. The Puritans in Parliament resented his religious policies. The Long Parliament (1640–1660) thus acted with widespread support when it convened in November 1640.

Charles I ruled for several years without calling Parliament, but once he began a war with Scotland, he needed revenues that only Parliament could supply.

Photographique de la Réunion des Musées Nationaux/Cliche des Musées Nationaux

The House of Commons impeached Strafford and Laud. Both were later executed. Parliament abolished the courts that had enforced royal policy and resolved that no more than three years should elapse between its meetings and that it could not be dissolved without its own consent.

Parliament, however, was divided over religion. Both moderate Puritans (the Presbyterians) and more extreme Puritans (the Independents) wanted to abolish the episcopacy and the *Book of Common Prayer*. The majority Presbyterians sought to reshape England religiously along Calvinist lines, with local congregations subject to higher representative governing bodies (presbyteries). Independents wanted every congregation to be its own final authority. But many conservatives in both houses of Parliament were determined to preserve the English church in its current form. These divisions intensified in October 1641, when Parliament was asked to fund an army to suppress a rebellion in Scotland.

Civil War   On December 1, 1641, Parliament presented the king with the "Grand Remonstrance," a summary of popular and parliamentary grievances against the crown. In January 1642, the king left London and began to raise an army. Shocked, the House of Commons passed the Militia Ordinance, which gave Parliament authority to raise an army of its own. For the next four years (1642–1646), civil war engulfed England. There were nobility, gentry, and townspeople on both sides. The chief factor distinguishing them was religion; the Puritans tended to favor Parliament.

Oliver Cromwell's New Model Army defeated the royalists in the English Civil War. After the execution of Charles 1 in 1699, Cromwell dominated the short-lived English republic, conquered Ireland and Scotland and ruled as Lord Protector from 1653 until his death in 1658.

Historical Pictures

QUICK REVIEW

Charles II (r. 1660–1685)

◆ England returned to the 1642 status quo when Charles assumed throne

◆ Charles favored religious toleration

◆ Issued Declaration of Indulgence in 1672 suspending all laws against non-Anglicans

---

OLIVER CROMWELL AND THE PURITAN REPUBLIC

Two factors led to Parliament's victory. The first was an alliance with Scotland in 1643 that committed Parliament to a Presbyterian church. The second was the reorganization of the parliamentary army under Oliver Cromwell (1599–1658). Cromwell and his "godly men" were willing to tolerate an established majority church, but only if it permitted Protestant dissenters to worship outside it.

Defeated by June 1645, Charles tried to take advantage of divisions within Parliament, but Cromwell and his army foiled him. In 1649, after a trial by a special court, Charles was executed. Parliament then abolished the monarchy, the House of Lords, and the Anglican Church.

From 1649 to 1660, England was dominated by Cromwell. His army conquered Ireland and Scotland. Cromwell, however, was no politician. In 1653, he disbanded Parliament and ruled thereafter as Lord Protector.

Cromwell's military dictatorship, however, was harsh and hated. When he died in 1658, the English were ready to restore both the Anglican Church and the monarchy.

THE RESTORATION OF THE MONARCHY

Charles II (r. 1660–1685) returned to England amid rejoicing. A man of charm and political skill, Charles set a refreshing new tone after 11 years of Puritanism. England returned to the status quo of 1642, with a hereditary monarch, a Parliament that met only when the king summoned it, and the Anglican Church, with its bishops and prayer book, supreme in religion.

The king, however, had secret Catholic sympathies and favored religious toleration. He wanted to allow loyal Catholics and Puritans to worship freely. But in Parliament, even the ultraroyalist Anglicans did not believe patriotism and religion could be separated. Between 1661 and 1665, through a series of laws known as the Clarendon Code, Parliament excluded Roman Catholics, Presbyterians, and Independents from the religious and political life of the nation.

In 1670, England and France allied against the Dutch, their chief commercial competitor. Charles secretly pledged to announce his conversion to Catholicism as soon as conditions in England permitted. In return for this announcement (which was never made), Louis XIV promised to pay Charles a subsidy. As a sign of good faith, Charles issued a Declaration of Indulgence in 1672 suspending all laws against Roman Catholics and non-Anglican Protestants. But Parliament passed the Test Act requiring all officials of the crown, civil and military, to swear an oath against the doctrine of transubstantiation—which no loyal Roman Catholic could honestly do. Parliament had aimed the Test Act at the king's brother, James, duke of York, heir to the throne and a convert to Catholicism.

JAMES II

When James II (r. 1685–1688) became king in 1685, he demanded the repeal of the Test Act. When Parliament balked, he dissolved it and appointed Catholics to high positions. In 1687, he issued another Declaration of Indulgence suspending all religious tests and permitting free worship. These actions represented a royal attack on the local authority of nobles, landowners, the church, and other corporate bodies whose members believed they possessed legal privileges.

The English had hoped that James would be succeeded by Mary (r. 1689–1694), his Protestant eldest daughter. She was the wife of William III of Orange (1650–1702), *stadtholder* of the Netherlands. But on June 20, 1688, James II's second wife gave birth to a son. There was now a Catholic male heir to the throne.

The parliamentary opposition invited William to invade England to preserve the Anglican Church and parliamentary government.

THE "GLORIOUS REVOLUTION"

William of Orange arrived with his army in November 1688, and James fled to France. Parliament in 1689 proclaimed William III and Mary II the new monarchs, thus completing the **"Glorious Revolution."** William and Mary recognized a Bill of Rights that limited the powers of the monarchy and guaranteed the civil liberties of the English privileged classes. Henceforth, England's monarchs would be subject to law and would rule by the consent of Parliament. The Bill of Rights also prohibited Roman Catholics from occupying the English throne. The Toleration Act of 1689 permitted worship by all Protestants and outlawed Roman Catholics.

The Act of Settlement in 1701 provided for the English crown to go to the Protestant House of Hanover in Germany if Anne (r. 1702–1714), the second daughter of James II and the heir to the childless William III, died without issue. At Anne's death, the Elector of Hanover became King George I of England (r. 1714–1727).

THE AGE OF WALPOLE

George I confronted a challenge to his title. The son of James II landed in Scotland in December 1715 but was soon defeated.

However, the political situation remained in flux until Robert Walpole (1676–1745) took over the government. George I gave Walpole his full confidence. For this reason, Walpole has often been regarded as the first prime minister of Great Britain—although he never bore the title—and the originator of the cabinet system of government.

The source of his power was the combination of the support of the king, Walpole's ability to handle the House of Commons, and his control of government patronage. Through the skillful use of patronage, Walpole bought support from people who wanted jobs, favors, and government contracts. Corruption cemented political loyalty.

The eighteenth-century British House of Commons was neither a democratic nor a representative body. Each county elected two members, but if the more powerful landed families agreed on the candidates, as often happened, there was no contest. Other members were elected from units called *boroughs*, most of which had few electors. Proper management could control the composition of the House of Commons. (See "Lady Mary Wortley Montague Advises Her Husband on Election to Parliament.")

The structure of Parliament resulted in the domination of the government of England by the owners of property and especially by wealthy nobles. They were suspicious of an administrative bureaucracy controlled by the crown or its ministers. For this reason, they or their agents served as local government administrators, judges, militia commanders, and tax collectors. In this sense, the British nobility and landowners governed the nation. Moreover, because they regarded

William and Mary became the monarchs of England in 1689. Their accession brought England's economic and military resources into the balance against the France of Louis XIV.

Robert Harding Picture Library, London

Glorious Revolution The largely peaceful replacement of James II by William and Mary as English monarchs in 1688. It marked the beginning of constitutional monarchy in Britain.

·HISTORY'S VOICES·

LADY MARY WORTLEY MONTAGUE ADVISES HER HUSBAND ON ELECTION TO PARLIAMENT

*I**n this letter of 1714, Lady Mary Wortley Montague discussed how her husband might be elected to the House of Commons. Note her emphasis on knowing the right people and on having large amounts of money to spend on voters. Eventually her husband was elected in a borough that was controlled through government patronage.*

WHAT ARE the various ways in which candidates and their supporters used money to campaign? What role did friendships play in the campaigning? How important do the political ideas or positions of the candidates seem to be? Women could not vote in eighteenth-century parliamentary elections, but what kind of influence do they seem to exert?

You seem not to have received my letters, or not to have understood them: you had been chose undoubtedly at York, if you had declared in time; but there is not any gentleman or tradesman disengaged at this time; they are treating every night. Lord Carlisle and the Thompsons have given their interest to Mr. Jenkins. I agree with you of the necessity of your standing this Parliament, which, perhaps, may be more considerable than any that are to follow it; but, as you proceed, 'tis my opinion, you will spend your money and not be chose. I believe there is hardly a borough unengaged. I expect every letter should tell me you are sure of some place; and, as far as I can perceive you are sure of none. As it has been managed, perhaps it will be the best way to deposit a certain sum in some friend's hands, and buy some little Cornish borough: it would, undoubtedly, look better to be chose for a considerable town; but I take it to be now too late. If you have any thoughts of Newark, it will be absolutely necessary for you to enquire after Lord Lexington's interest; and your best way to apply yourself to Lord Holdernesse, who is both a Whig and an honest man. He is now in town, and you may enquire of him if Brigadier Sutton stands there; and if not, try to engage him for you. Lord Lexington is so ill at the Bath, that it is a doubt if he will live 'till the elections; and if he dies, one of his heiresses, and the whole interest of his estate, will probably fall on Lord Holdernesse.

'Tis a surprize to me, that you cannot make sure of some borough, when a number of your friends bring in so many Parliament-men without trouble or expense. 'Tis too late to mention it now, but you might have applied to Lady Winchester, as Sir Joseph Jekyl did last year, and by her interest the Duke of Bolton brought him in for nothing; I am sure she would be more zealous to serve me, than Lady Jekyl.

From Lord Wharncliffe, ed., *Letters and Works of Lady Mary Wortley Montague*, 3rd ed., Vol. 1 (London, 1861), p. 211.

Parliament as the political sovereign, there was no absence of central political authority. The supremacy of Parliament provided Britain with the unity that elsewhere in Europe was achieved through absolutism.

British political life was freer than on the Continent. Walpole's power had limits. Parliament could not wholly ignore popular pressure. Many members of Parliament maintained independent views. Newspapers and debate flourished. Free speech could be exercised, as could freedom of association. There was no large standing army. Walpole's enemies could openly oppose his policies.

Walpole's ascendancy, which lasted from 1721 to 1742, brought the nation stability. He maintained peace abroad and promoted the status quo at home. All forms of economic enterprise seemed to prosper. The navy became stronger. As a result, Great Britain became not only a European power of the first order but eventually a world power. Its government and economy were models for progressive Europeans.

RISE OF ABSOLUTE MONARCHY IN FRANCE: THE WORLD OF LOUIS XIV

T he groundwork for Louis XIV's absolutism (r. 1643–1715) had been laid first by Cardinal Richelieu (1585–1642), the chief minister for Louis XIII (r. 1610–1643), and then by Cardinal Mazarin (1602–1661). Richelieu and Mazarin had tried to impose direct royal administration on France. These efforts aroused rebellions among French nobles between 1649 and 1652.

These rebellions convinced Louis XIV that heavy-handed policies could endanger the monarchy. Louis would concentrate unprecedented authority in the monarchy, but his genius was to make the monarchy the most powerful institution in France while also assuring the nobles and other wealthy groups of their influence on the local level. Rather than destroying existing institutions, Louis worked through them. Nevertheless, the king was clearly the senior partner in the relationship.

HOW DID Louis XIV consolidate his power?

YEARS OF PERSONAL RULE

On the death of Mazarin in 1661, Louis XIV assumed control of the government at the age of 23. He appointed no chief minister and ruled through councils that controlled foreign affairs, the army, domestic administration, and economic regulations. Each day he spent hours with the chief ministers of these councils, whom he chose from families long in royal service or from among people beginning to rise in the social structure. Unlike the more ancient noble families, they depended solely on the king.

Louis made sure, however, that the nobility and other major social groups would benefit from his authority. He never tried to abolish noble institutions or limit their local authority. Local *parlements* enjoyed considerable latitude. Louis did clash with the *Parlement* of Paris, which had the right to register royal laws. In 1673 he curtailed its power.

VERSAILLES

Louis and his advisors became masters of propaganda and political image. Louis never missed an opportunity to impress the grandeur of his crown on the French people. The central element of the image of the monarchy was the palace of Versailles. More than any other monarch, Louis XIV used the physical setting of his court to exert political control. Versailles, on the outskirts of Paris, became Louis's permanent residence after 1682. It was a temple to royalty, designed to proclaim the glory of the Sun King, as Louis was known. With magnificent fountains and gardens, it housed thousands of nobles, officials, and servants. Although it consumed over half Louis's annual revenues, Versailles paid political dividends.

Louis was the chief source of favors and patronage in France. To emphasize his prominence, he organized life at court around his daily routine. Elaborate etiquette governed life at Versailles. The king's rising and dressing were times of rare intimacy, when nobles could whisper in his ear. Fortunate nobles held his candle as they accompanied him to his bed.

Some nobles avoided Versailles. They managed their estates and cultivated their local influence. Others were too poor to cut a figure at court. The nobility understood, however, that Louis would not threaten their local social standing. Louis supported France's traditional social structure and the social privileges of the nobility.

QUICK REVIEW

Versailles
- Palace of Versailles: central element in the image of the French monarchy
- Nobles who wanted Louis's favor congregated at Versailles
- Life at Versailles governed by elaborate etiquette

Versailles, as painted in 1668 by Pierre Patel the Elder (1605–1676). The central building is the hunting lodge built for Louis XIII earlier in the century. The wings that appear here were some of Louis XIV's first expansions.

Giraudon/Art Resource, N.Y.

18.2
The Ideal Absolute State (1697): Jean Domat

divine right of kings The theory that monarchs are appointed by and answerable only to God.

KING BY DIVINE RIGHT

An important source for Louis' concept of royal authority was Bishop Jacques-Bénigne Bossuet (1627–1704). Bossuet defended what he called the "**divine right of kings**" and cited examples of Old Testament rulers appointed by and answerable only to God. Bossuet argued that only God could judge the king. Although kings might be duty bound to reflect God's will, as God's regents on Earth they were not bound to the dictates of mere nobles and parliaments. Such assumptions lay behind Louis XIV's alleged declaration: "*L'état, c'est moi*" ("I am the state").

Despite these claims, Louis's rule did not exert the oppressive control over the daily lives of his subjects that police states would do in the nineteenth and twentieth centuries. His absolutism functioned primarily in the classic areas of European state action—war and peace, religion, and economic oversight. Even at the height of his power, local institutions retained their administrative authority. The king and his ministers supported the social and financial privileges of these local elites. But Louis prevented them from interfering with his authority on the national level. This system would endure until the end of the eighteenth century.

LOUIS'S EARLY WARS

By the late 1660s, France was superior to any other European nation in administrative bureaucracy, armed forces, and national unity. Louis could afford to raise and maintain a powerful army and was in a position to dominate Europe. He spent most of his reign looking to extend the borders of his domain and displace the power of the Habsburgs.

The early wars of Louis XIV included conflicts with Spain and the United Netherlands. In 1667, Louis's armies invaded Flanders and the Franche-Comté. By the Treaty of Aix-la-Chapelle (1668) he gained control of certain towns bordering the Spanish Netherlands.[1]

Louis invaded the Netherlands in 1672. The war ended inconclusively, but France gained more territory.

REVOCATION OF THE EDICT OF NANTES

After the Edict of Nantes in 1598, relations between Catholics (nine tenths of the French population) and Protestants had remained hostile. The Catholic Church supported persecution as pious and patriotic.

Louis was determined to unify France religiously. He hounded the Huguenots out of public life and bribed them to convert to Catholicism. He bullied them by quartering troops in their towns. Finally, Louis revoked the Edict of Nantes in 1685. Protestant churches and schools were closed, ministers exiled, nonconverting laity forced to be galley slaves, and children baptized by Catholic priests.

The revocation was a blunder. Protestants considered Louis a fanatic to be resisted at all costs. The revocation prompted the emigration of more than a quarter million people, who joined the resistance to France in England, Germany, Holland, and the New World.

France	
1649–1652	The Fronde, a revolt of nobility and townspeople against the crown
1661	Louis assumes personal rule
1667–1668	War of Devolution fought over Louis' claims to the Spanish Netherlands
1672	France invades the United Provinces
1678–1679	Peace of Nimwegen
1682	Louis establishes his court at Versailles
1685	Edict of Nantes revoked
1689–1697	Nine Years' War between France and the League of Augsburg
1697	Peace of Ryswick
1702–1714	War of the Spanish Succession
1713	Treaty of Utrecht between England and France
1714	Treaty of Rastadt between the emperor and France
1726–1743	Ascendency of Cardinal Fleury

WAR OF THE SPANISH SUCCESSION

On November 1, 1700, Charles II of Spain (r. 1665–1700) died without direct heirs. He left his inheritance to Louis' grandson, who became Philip V of Spain (r. 1700–1746).

Spain and its American empire appeared to have fallen to France. In September 1701, England, Holland, and the Holy Roman Empire formed the Grand Alliance to preserve the balance of power. Louis increased the political stakes by recognizing the Stuart claim to the English throne.

In 1701, the War of the Spanish Succession (1701–1714) began. France went to war with inadequate finances, a poorly equipped army, and mediocre generals. The English, in contrast, had advanced weaponry and superior tactics. John Churchill, the duke of Marlborough (1650–1722), bested Louis' soldiers in every major engagement, although French arms triumphed in Spain.

France finally made peace with England at Utrecht in 1713 and with Holland and the emperor at Rastadt in 1714. Philip V remained king of Spain but England got Gibraltar, making it a Mediterranean power (see Map 20–1). Louis recognized the House of Hanover.

After Louis' death, the monarchy weakened. France was exhausted. Louis XV (r. 1715–1774) was only five years old at his accession, and the regency allowed the *Parlement* of Paris greater authority. By 1726, the political direction of the nation had come under Cardinal Fleury (1653–1743). Like Walpole in Britain, he pursued economic prosperity at home and peace abroad.

18.3
The Sighs of Enslaved France (1690): Pierre Jurieu

---

[1]The political divisions during the seventeenth and eighteenth centuries in what are today the Netherlands and Belgium were complex. The independence of the United Netherlands, a loosely federated union, was recognized at the Peace of Westphalia in 1648. Most of its population were Protestants. It was often referred to as "Holland." Present-day Belgium was governed by the Habsburgs, first Spanish, then Austrian—after 1714. Its population was Roman Catholic.

MAP 20–1
Europe in 1714. The War of the Spanish Succession ended a year before the death of Louis XIV. The Bourbons had secured the Spanish throne, but Spain had forfeited its possessions in Flanders and Italy.

WHICH COUNTRIES benefitted the most from the war?

RUSSIA ENTERS THE EUROPEAN POLITICAL ARENA

WHAT DID Peter the Great hope to achieve with his reforms in Russia?

The emergence of Russia as a European power was a new factor in European politics. Russia had been considered part of Europe only by courtesy. Hemmed in by Sweden and the Ottoman Empire, Russia had no warm-water ports. There was little trade. Russia did have vast, largely undeveloped natural and human resources.

YEARS OF TURMOIL

Ivan IV (r. 1533–1584), known as Ivan the Terrible, appointed able advisors, undertook sensible revisions of the law and local government, and reorganized the army.

Then about 1560, he began to distrust virtually everyone and imprisoned, tortured, and executed *boyars* (nobles) without cause or trial. He even killed his own son.

Ivan's reign was followed by a period of anarchy known as the Time of Troubles. In 1613, an assembly of nobles elected as tsar Michael Romanov (r. 1613–1645), whose dynasty ruled Russia until 1917.

Michael Romanov and his two successors brought stability to Russia. The country, however, remained weak. The *boyars* controlled the bureaucracy. The tsars faced the danger of mutiny from the *streltsy*, or Moscow garrison.

PETER THE GREAT

In 1682, a 10-year-old boy ascended the Russian throne as co-ruler with his half brother. His name was Peter (r. 1682–1725). He and his feeble half brother, Ivan V (d. 1696), had come to power on the shoulders of the *streltsy*. Violence had surrounded the succession. The turmoil of his youth convinced Peter that the power of the tsar must be made secure and that Russian military power had to be increased.

Peter I, who came to be known as Peter the Great, was an imitator of the first order. The products and workers from the West who had filtered into Russia impressed him. In 1697, he made a visit, supposedly in disguise, to western Europe. There he inspected shipyards, docks, and the manufacture of military hardware and returned to Moscow determined to copy what he had seen, for he knew that only warfare would make Russia a great power. The tsar's drive to modernize his nation had four areas of concern: taming the boyars and the *streltsy*, achieving secular control of the church, reorganizing the internal administration, and developing the economy.

Peter pursued each of these goals with ruthlessness. His successes allowed him to expand his military strength. By bringing the boyars, *streltsy*, and church under control, Peter curbed the groups that might have opposed his expansion of the army and navy. Developing Russia's economy enabled him to finance his military ventures.

He made a sustained attack on the *boyars* and demanded they serve his state. In 1722, Peter published a **Table of Ranks**, which henceforth equated a person's social position and privileges with his rank in the bureaucracy or the army rather than with his position in the nobility. However, the Russian nobility never became perfectly loyal to the state. It repeatedly sought to reassert its independence.

The *streltsy* fared less well than the boyars. In 1698, they had rebelled while Peter was on his European tour. When he returned, almost 1,200 of the rebels were put to death.

Peter dealt with the Russian Orthodox Church with similar ruthlessness. He wanted to prevent the clergy from opposing westernization and sought to prevent the church hierarchy from making religious reforms that might provoke popular discontent. In 1721, Peter replaced the position of patriarch of the Russian church with a synod headed by a layman.

In his reorganization of domestic administration, Peter looked to Swedish models, creating "colleges," or bureaus, composed of several officials. The colleges were to look after foreign affairs, war, and economic matters. In 1711, Peter

Rise of Russian Power

1533–1584	Reign of Ivan the Terrible
1584–1613	Time of Troubles
1613	Michael Romanov becomes tsar
1682	Peter the Great becomes tsar as a boy
1689	Peter assumes personal rule
1697	European tour of Peter the Great
1698	Peter suppresses the *streltsy*
1700	The Great Northern War opens between Russia and Sweden; Russia defeated at Narva by Charles XII
1703	Saint Petersburg founded
1709	Russia defeats Sweden at Poltava
1718	Death of Alexis, son of Peter the Great
1721	Peace of Nystad ends the Great Northern War
1721	Peter establishes control over the Russian church
1722	The Table of Ranks
1725	Peter dies, leaving an uncertain succession

boyars   The Russian nobility.

streltsy   Professional troops who made up the Moscow garrison. They were suppressed by Peter the Great.

Table of Ranks   An official hierarchy established by Peter the Great in imperial Russia that equated a person's social position and privileges with his rank in the state bureaucracy or army.

Peter the Great built St. Petersburg on the Gulf of Finland to provide Russia with better contact with western Europe. He moved Russia's capital there from Moscow in 1703. This is an eighteenth century view of the city.

The Granger Collection

created a senate of nine members to direct the central government when the tsar was away with the army. The purpose of these reforms was to establish a bureaucracy that could collect and spend tax revenues to support an efficient army.

Peter's economic policies were closely related to his military needs. He encouraged the establishment of an iron industry in the Ural Mountains. He sent prominent young Russians abroad to acquire technical and organizational skills. He attempted to lure western European craftsmen to Russia. However, these efforts had only marginal success.

Peter was determined to secure warm-water ports that would allow Russia to trade with the West and intervene in European affairs. This led to wars with the Ottoman Empire and Sweden. Peter's armies captured Azov on the Black Sea in 1696, but he had to return it in 1711.

Peter had more success against Sweden in the Great Northern War (1700–1721). In 1721, the Peace of Nystad confirmed the Russian conquest of Estonia, Livonia, and part of Finland. Henceforth, Russia possessed warm-water ports and a permanent influence on European affairs.

At one point, the domestic and foreign policies of Peter the Great intersected. This was at the spot on the Gulf of Finland where Peter founded his new capital of Saint Petersburg. There he built government structures and compelled his *boyars* to construct town houses. Saint Petersburg symbolized a new orientation for Russia toward western Europe.

Despite his success on the Baltic, Peter's reign ended with a great question mark. He had long quarreled with his only son, Alexis, who was imprisoned in 1718 and died mysteriously. When Peter died in 1725, Russia had no firmer policy on succession than it had had when he acceded to the throne. For more than thirty years after his death, soldiers and nobles would determine who ruled Russia. Peter had laid the foundations of a modern Russia, but he had failed to lay the foundations of a stable state.

CENTRAL AND EASTERN EUROPE

As Russia became a major European power, the political contours of central Europe also changed. The Habsburgs expanded their political base outside of Germany. Within Germany, the Hohenzollerns forged Prussia into a major state. Thereafter, the Habsburg Empire and Prussia would duel for Germany. By the middle of the century, that conflict would become united with the colonial conflict between Great Britain and France to create the first worldwide European war.

WHY DID Prussia become a rival to the Habsburgs?

THE HABSBURG EMPIRE AND THE PRAGMATIC SANCTION

The close of the Thirty Years' War marked a turning point for the Austrian Habsburgs. In alliance with their Spanish cousins, they had hoped to bring Germany under their control and back to the Catholic fold. In this they had failed, and the decline of Spanish power meant that the Austrian Habsburgs were on their own.

After 1648, the Habsburgs retained a firm hold on the title of Holy Roman Emperor, but the power of the emperor depended on the cooperation he could elicit from the various political bodies in the empire. These included large units (such as Saxony, Hanover, Bavaria, and Brandenburg) and scores of small German cities, bishoprics, and principalities. The Habsburgs also began to consolidate their power within their hereditary possessions outside the Holy Roman Empire, which included the Crown of Saint Wenceslas, encompassing the kingdom of Bohemia (in the modern Czech Republic) and the duchies of Moravia and Silesia; and the Crown of Saint Stephen, which ruled Hungary, Croatia, and Transylvania. Much of Hungary was only liberated from the Turks at the end of the seventeenth century (1699).

In 1714, the Habsburgs received the former Spanish (thereafter Austrian) Netherlands and Lombardy. Thereafter, Habsburgs power would be based primarily on their territories outside Germany.

In each of their many territories, the Habsburgs ruled by virtue of a different title and needed the cooperation of the local nobility. They repeatedly had to bargain with nobles in one part of Europe to maintain their position in another. Their domains and peoples were so diverse that almost no grounds existed on which to unify them politically. Even Roman Catholicism proved ineffective as a common bond, particularly in Hungary, the most recalcitrant province, where many Magyar nobles were Calvinist and seemed ever ready to rebel. Habsburg rulers established central councils to chart common policies for their far-flung domains. Virtually all of these bodies, however, dealt with only a portion of the Habsburg holdings.

Despite these internal difficulties, Leopold I (r. 1658–1705) managed to resist the advances of the Turks into central Europe, which included a siege of Vienna in 1683, and to thwart the aggression of Louis XIV. He also extended his territorial holdings over much of the Balkans. Strength in the east gave the Habsburgs greater political leverage in Germany.

Austria and Prussia

1640–1688	Reign of Frederick William, the Great Elector
1658–1705	Leopold I rules Austria and resists the Turks and Louis XIV
1683	Turkish siege of Vienna
1701	Frederick I becomes "King in Prussia"
1699	Peace between Turks and Habsburgs
1711–1740	Charles VI rules Austria and secures agreement to the Pragmatic Sanction
1713–1740	Frederick William I builds the military power of Prussia
1740	Maria Theresa succeeds to the Habsburg throne; Frederick II invades Silesia

Charles VI (r. 1711–1740) had no male heir and feared that on his death the Habsburg lands might fall prey to the surrounding powers. To prevent that disaster, he devoted most of his reign to seeking the approval of his family, the estates of his realms, and foreign powers for a document called the ***Pragmatic Sanction.***

This provided the legal basis for a single line of inheritance within the Habsburg dynasty through Charles VI's daughter Maria Theresa (1740–1780). Other members of the Habsburg family recognized her as the rightful heir. After extracting concessions from Charles, the nobles of the various Habsburg domains and the other European rulers did likewise. Charles VI believed that he had secured legal unity for the Habsburg Empire and a safe succession for his daughter. However, his failure to provide his daughter with a strong army or a full treasury left her inheritance open to foreign aggression. Less than two months after his death, in December 1740, Frederick II of Prussia invaded the Habsburg province of Silesia. Maria Theresa had to fight for her inheritance.

Maria Theresa of Austria provided the leadership that saved the Habsburg Empire from possible disintegration after the Prussian invasion of Silesia in 1740.

Kunsthistorisches Museum, Vienna

PRUSSIA AND THE HOHENZOLLERNS

The rise of Prussia occurred within the German power vacuum created by the Peace of Westphalia. It is the story of the extraordinary Hohenzollern family, which had ruled Brandenburg since 1417. Through inheritance, the family had acquired East Prussia and other territories that by the late seventeenth century represented a block of territory within the Holy Roman Empire, second in size only to that of the Habsburgs.

The person who began to forge these areas into a modern state was Frederick William (r. 1640–1688), who became known as the Great Elector. He established himself and his successors as the central uniting power by breaking the medieval parliaments or estates, organizing a royal bureaucracy, and building a strong army.

There was a political and social trade-off between the Elector and his nobles. These *Junkers*, or German noble landlords, in exchange for their obedience to the Hohenzollerns, received the right to demand obedience from their serfs. Frederick William also tended to choose as the local administrators of the tax structure men who would normally have been members of the noble branch of the old parliament. He thus coopted potential opponents into his service. The taxes fell most heavily on the peasants and the urban classes. As the years passed, *Junkers* dominated the army officer corps. Officials and army officers took an oath of loyalty to the Elector. The army and the Elector thus came to embody the otherwise absent unity of the state.

Yet even with the considerable accomplishments of the Great Elector, the house of Hohenzollern did not possess a crown. The achievement of a royal title

Pragmatic Sanction The legal basis negotiated by the Emperor Charles VI (r. 1711–1740) for the Habsburg succession through his daughter Maria Theresa (r. 1740–1780).

Junkers The noble landlords of Prussia.

was the accomplishment of Frederick I (r. 1688–1713). In the War of the Spanish Succession, he put his army at the disposal of the Habsburg Holy Roman Emperor Leopold I. In exchange, the emperor permitted Frederick to assume the title of "King in Prussia" in 1701.

His successor, Frederick William I (r. 1713–1740), organized the bureaucracy along military lines. The discipline that he applied to the army was fanatical. The Prussian military grew from about 39,000 in 1713 to over 80,000 in 1740, making it the third- or fourth-largest army in Europe. Prussia's population, in contrast, ranked thirteenth in size. Laws, customs, and royal attention made the officer corps the highest social class of the state. Military service thus attracted the sons of *Junkers*. In this fashion, the army, the *Junker* nobility, and the monarchy became forged into a single political entity. Military priorities and values dominated Prussian government, society, and daily life.

THE FIRST WORLDWIDE WARS

The War of the Spanish Succession had been fought mainly in Europe. The wars that Europe fought between 1739 and 1763 were worldwide in scope and impact. By the end of the conflicts, the French had been driven out of North America and the British had established a domination in India that would last until 1947.

WHAT WERE the results of the colonial struggles of the mid-eighteenth century?

THE COLONIAL ARENA

The Treaty of Utrecht established the boundaries of empire during the first half of the eighteenth century. Except for Portuguese Brazil, Spain controlled South America, as well as Florida, Mexico, California, Cuba, and half of Hispaniola. The British Empire consisted of the colonies along the North Atlantic seaboard, Nova Scotia, Newfoundland, Jamaica, and Barbados. Britain also possessed trading stations on the Indian subcontinent. The Dutch controlled Surinam, or Dutch Guiana, in South America; trading stations in Ceylon and Bengal; and the trade with Java in what is today Indonesia.

The French had also established an empire in America and southern Asia. It covered the Saint Lawrence River valley; the Ohio and Mississippi River valleys; Saint Domingue (Haiti), Guadeloupe, and Martinique in the West Indies; and stations in India and West Africa. The economy of their West Indian islands resembled those of the Spanish and the British. Their holdings in Canada were sparsely populated, and the economy was based on agriculture and the fur trade. French and English settlers in North America clashed throughout the eighteenth century.

The Treaty of Utrecht gave the British a 30-year *asiento*, or contract, to furnish slaves to the Spanish Empire and the right to send one ship each year to the trading fair at Portobello. Little but friction arose from these rights. Much to the chagrin of the British, the Spanish government under the Bourbons maintained coastal patrols that searched English vessels for contraband.

British commercial interests put great pressure on Parliament to do something about Spanish interference in their trade. Robert Walpole could not resist these pressures, and in late 1739, Great Britain went to war with Spain. This might have been a minor clash, but as a result of the Prussian invasion of Silesia, it became the opening encounter in a series of worldwide European wars that lasted off and on until 1815.

Mid-Eighteenth Century Conflicts

THE WAR OF THE AUSTRIAN SUCCESSION (1740–1748)

In December 1740, the new king of Prussia, Frederick II, (r. 1740–1786, Frederick the Great) seized the Austrian province of Silesia. The invasion shattered the Pragmatic Sanction and upset the continental balance of power. In response to the Prussian aggression, Maria Theresa of Austria recognized Hungary as the most important of her crowns and promised the Magyars local autonomy. She thus preserved the Habsburg state, but at great cost to the power of the central monarchy.

The war over the Austrian succession and the British-Spanish commercial conflict could have remained separate disputes. What united them was the role of France. A group of aggressive court aristocrats compelled the elderly Cardinal Fleury to support the Prussian aggression against Austria, the traditional enemy of France.

This proved to be one of the most fateful decisions in world history. French aid to Prussia helped to consolidate a powerful German state that later endangered France itself. The French move against Austria also brought Great Britain into the continental war against France and Prussia to assure that Belgium remained in the friendly hands of Austria. The British-French conflict expanded to the New World. The war ended in 1748 with the Treaty of Aix-la-Chapelle. Prussia retained Silesia, but the treaty was a truce rather than a permanent peace.

THE SEVEN YEARS' WAR (1756–1763)

Before the rivalries again erupted into war, a shift of alliances took place. In 1756, Prussia and Great Britain signed a defensive alliance aimed at preventing the entry of foreign troops into the Germanies. Great Britain, the ally of Austria since the wars of Louis XIV, had now joined forces with Austria's major enemy. Later in 1756, Austria achieved a defensive alliance with France.

Conflict between France and Great Britain had continued unofficially in the Ohio River valley and in upper New England. These skirmishes were the prelude to what is known in American history as the French and Indian War. Once again, however, the king of Prussia opened a general European war that extended into a colonial theater.

In August 1756, what would become the Seven Years' War opened when Frederick II invaded Saxony in a preemptive strike against a conspiracy by Saxony, Austria, and France to destroy Prussian power. In 1757, France and Austria were joined by Sweden, Russia, and the smaller German states. Two factors, in addition to Frederick's strong leadership, saved Prussia—British financial aid and the death in 1762 of Empress Elizabeth of Russia (r. 1741–1762). Her successor Tsar Peter III (d. 1762), a fervent admirer of Frederick, immediately made peace with Prussia, thus allowing Frederick to hold off Austria and France. The Treaty of Hubertusburg of 1763 closed the continental conflict with no significant changes in prewar borders.

More impressive than the survival of Prussia were the victories of Great Britain. The architect of victory was William Pitt the Elder (1708–1778). Pitt pumped huge subsidies to Frederick the Great. But North America was Pitt's real concern. He wanted all of North America east of the Mississippi for Great Britain, and he directed unprecedented resources into the overseas colonial conflict. The French government was unwilling and unable to direct similar resources against the English in America. In September 1759, the British took Quebec City. Montreal fell the next year. The French Empire in Canada was over.

Pitt's colonial vision, however, was global. The French West Indies fell to British fleets. On the Indian subcontinent, British forces under Robert Clive (1725–1774) defeated the French in 1757 at the Battle of Plassey. This victory opened the way for the eventual conquest of all India by the British East India Company. Never had any other European power experienced such a complete worldwide military victory. Never had a European military victory affected so many non-Europeans.

By the Treaty of Paris of 1763, Pitt was no longer in office. George III (r. 1760–1820) had replaced Pitt with the Earl of Bute (1713–1792) in 1762. The new minister was responsible for the peace settlement, in which Britain received Canada, the Ohio River valley, and the eastern half of the Mississippi River valley. France retained footholds in India and regained West Indies sugar islands.

The mid-century wars among European powers resulted in a new balance of power on the European continent and the high seas. Great Britain gained a world empire, and Prussia was recognized as a great continental power. With the surrender of Canada, France retreated from North America and thus opened the way for a continent dominated by the English language and Protestantism. By contrast, Latin America would be dominated by the Spanish and Portuguese languages and Roman Catholicism. For many years, West Africa would continue to furnish slaves to both Americas. On the subcontinent of Asia, the foundations were laid for almost two centuries of British dominance. By 1760, therefore, a true world economy had been established in which political and economic developments in one region could affect others.

SUMMARY

Models of European Political Development In the seventeenth and eighteenth centuries, five great powers emerged in Europe: France, Britain, Austria, Prussia, and Russia. Through their military strength, economic development, and in some cases colonial empires, they would affect virtually every other world civilization.

Britain In the seventeenth century conflict between the Stuart kings and Parliament arising out of political, religious, and economic issues led to civil war, the execution of Charles I, a short-lived English republic under Oliver Cromwell, and in 1688–1689 the "Glorious Revolution" that finally limited royal authority and established the supremacy of Parliament. Eighteenth-century was not a democracy, but its people had more rights and liberties than the subjects of the absolutist monarchs who ruled the other European great powers.

In a series of worldwide colonial struggles with France, Britain used its commercial resources and navy to profit from France's entanglements in Europe and emerge supreme in North America and India.

France Under Louis XIV (r. 1643–1715), France became the model of an absolute monarchy. Louis used his splendid court at Versailles to overawe the

IMAGE KEY

for pages 434–435

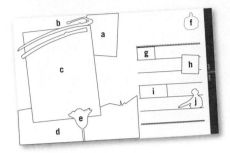

a. Charles II, King of England, wearing the royal crown

b. Sabre and scabbard

c. Louis XIV of France

d. St. Petersburg- Winter Palace 1754–1761

e. A yellow and purple flaming parrot tulip

f. Crown of Louis XV, 1722

g. Cardinal Richelieu

h. Oliver Cromwell

i. St Petersburg, Russia

j. Frederick II, King of Prussia, 1712–1786

French aristocracy and promote a glittering image of French culture that impressed all of Europe. While the king did much to centralize royal authority, he was not able completely to overcome opposition from the French elites who sought to reassert their influence under his successors. His revocation of the Edict of Nantes weakened France by driving thousands of French Protestants into exile.

Louis pursued an aggressive foreign policy that expanded France's borders but cost France dearly in wealth and resources and provoked strong opposition from the other European powers. In the war of the Spanish Succession, he succeeded in placing his grandson on the throne of Spain, but the war left France exhausted.

Russia Russia became a great power under Peter the Great (r. 1682–1725). Peter curbed the power of the Russian church and aristocracy and opened Russia to Western technology and military and commercial influences. His wars with Sweden gave Russia a coastline on the Baltic where Peter built his new capital, Saint Petersburg. He also built an efficient army and navy and established a centralized bureaucracy to collect revenue.

Central Europe The Habsburgs remained Holy Roman Emperors but their power rested on their hereditary domains–Austria, Hungary, Bohemia, and northern Italy. Although the Habsburgs reconquered Hungary from the Ottomans, the rise of Prussia under the Hohenzollerns challenged Habsburg dominance in Central Europe. The Hohenzollern rulers built Prussia from a collection of scattered German states into a great power by developing an efficient bureaucracy and a powerful army. Under Frederick II (r. 1740–1786), Prussia emerged from a series of wars with Austria, France, and Russia as one of the strongest European states and the rival to Habsburg power in Central Europe.

REVIEW QUESTIONS

1. By the end of the seventeenth century, England and France had different systems of government with different religious policies. What were the main differences? Why did each nation develop as it did?

2. Why did the English king and Parliament come into conflict in the 1640s? What was the Glorious Revolution?

3. How did Louis XIV consolidate his monarchy? What was Louis' religious policy?

4. How did the Hohenzollern family create the state of Prussia? Why was the military so important in Prussia?

5. How and why did Russia emerge as a great power? How were Peter the Great's domestic reforms related to his military ambitions?

6. What were the main points of conflict between Britain and France in the Americas and India? Which countries emerged stronger from the Seven Years' War?

KEY TERMS

absolutism   (p. 436)
boyars   (p. 447)
divine right of kings   (p. 444)
Glorious Revolution   (p. 441)
Junkers   (p. 450)

parlements   (p. 436)
Pragmatic Sanction   (p. 450)
Puritans   (p. 438)
streltsy   (p. 447)
Table of Ranks   (p. 447)

 For additional study resources for this chapter, go to:
www.prenhall.com/craig/chapter20

F. Boucher, *The Breakfast.* 1739. Francois Boucher (1703–1770),
"Breakfast." Louvre, Paris, France. Copyright Scala/Art Resource, NY.

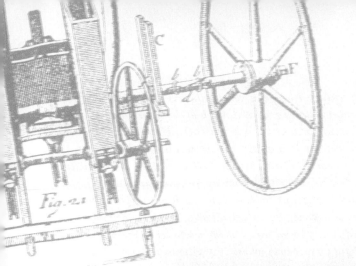

21

EUROPEAN SOCIETY UNDER THE OLD REGIME

WHAT WAS the Old Regime?

WHY WAS land the economic basis of 18th-century life?

WHAT WAS the *family economy*?

HOW DID Europe's growing industrialization affect its relations with the rest of the world?

WHAT KINDS of cities in Europe grew fastest between 1600 and 1750?

WHY WERE Jews discriminated against under the Old Regime?

IMAGE KEY

Image Key for pages 456–457 is on page 475.

WHAT WAS the Old Regime?

Old Regime Term applied to the pattern of social, political, and economic relationships and institutions that existed in Europe before the French Revolution.

At the opening of the eighteenth century, European merchants and traders dominated the transatlantic economy and European states governed much of the American continents. During the century, the peoples living primarily in northwestern Europe undertook a series of economic advances that laid the foundation for the social and economic transformation of the world. These developments, known collectively as the Industrial Revolution, gave Europe a productive capacity previously unknown in human history. That economic advance enabled Europeans to dominate much of the world both economically and militarily. At the same time, the industrial achievement of Europe became an example that less economically advanced areas of the world would seek to imitate. This potential for change emerged in a society whose institutions had been designed to inhibit social and economic change.

During the French Revolution and its aftermath, the patterns of social, political, and economic relationships that had existed in France before 1789 were referred to as the ancien régime, *or the "Old Regime." The term has come to be applied generally to the life and institutions of prerevolutionary continental Europe. Tradition, hierarchy, corporateness, and privilege were the chief social characteristics of the Old Regime. Yet change and innovation were fermenting in its midst.*

LIFE IN THE OLD REGIME

Socially, prerevolutionary Europe was based on (1) aristocratic elites with many inherited legal privileges; (2) established churches intimately related to the state and the aristocracy; (3) an urban labor force usually organized into guilds; and (4) a rural peasantry subject to high taxes and feudal dues.

Few outside the political, commercial, and intellectual elite wanted change. This was especially true of social relationships. Both nobles and peasants called for the restoration of traditional or customary rights. The nobles asserted what they considered their ancient rights against the expanding monarchical bureaucracies. The peasants, through petitions and revolts, called for their customary manorial rights.

Except for the early industrial development in Britain, the economy was also traditional. The grain harvest remained crucial for both the population and governments.

HIERARCHY AND PRIVILEGE

The medieval sense of hierarchy became more rigid during the century. It was enforced by the corporate nature of social relationships. Each state or society was considered a community composed of smaller communities. Eighteenth-century Europeans did not enjoy what Americans regard as individual rights. Instead, persons enjoyed such rights and privileges as were guaranteed to whatever communities or groups of which they were a part. The "community" might include the village, the municipality, the nobility, the church, the guild, a university, or the parish. In turn, each of these bodies enjoyed certain privileges, such as exemption from taxation or degrading punishment, the right to practice a trade or pursue a particular occupation, or, for the church, the right to collect the tithe.

ARISTOCRACY

The eighteenth century was the great age of the aristocracy. The nobility constituted 1 to 5 percent of the population of any given country. It was the single wealthiest sector of the population; possessed the most power; and dominated society.

Land provided the aristocracy with its largest source of income, but the influence of aristocrats was felt in every area of life. To be an aristocrat was a matter of birth and legal privilege; but aristocracies differed from country to country.

GREAT BRITAIN

The smallest, wealthiest, and most socially responsible aristocracy resided in Great Britain. It consisted of about 400 families, whose eldest male members sat in the House of Lords. These families also controlled most seats in the House of Commons and owned one-fourth of the arable land in Britain. Increasingly, they invested in commerce, canals, urban real estate, mines, and industrial ventures. Because only the eldest son inherited the title and the land, younger sons moved into commerce, the army, the professions, and the church. Most members of the House of Commons were also landowners. They paid taxes and had few legal privileges, but their control of local government gave them immense power. Socially and politically, the aristocracy dominated the English counties.

FRANCE

In France, the nobility was theoretically divided between nobles of the sword and those of the robe. The former families' nobility derived from military service; the latter had gained their titles either by serving in the bureaucracy or by purchasing them.

The nobility who held favor with the royal court at Versailles reaped the wealth that came from holding high office. By the late 1780s, appointments to the church, the army, and the bureaucracy tended to go to the court aristocracy. Other nobles, known as *hobereaux*, lived in the provinces and were sometimes no better off than well-to-do peasants.

Eighteenth-century France had some of the best roads in the world, but they were often built with forced labor. French peasants were required to work part of each year on such projects. This system, called the *corvée*, was not abolished until the French Revolution in 1789.

Claude Vernet "Construction of a Road." Louvre, Paris/Giraudon/Art Resource, N.Y.

18.5
"What Is the Third Estate?"
(January 1789): The Abbé
Sie yès

All French aristocrats enjoyed hereditary privileges. They were exempt from many taxes and were not subject to the royal *corvées*, or labor donations. Moreover, they could collect feudal dues from their tenants and enjoyed exclusive hunting and fishing rights.

EASTERN EUROPE

In Poland, thousands of nobles were entirely exempt from taxes. Until 1768 they could legally execute their serfs. A few rich nobles dominated the Polish state.

In Austria and Hungary, the nobility had broad judicial powers over the peasantry and enjoyed exemptions from taxation. In Prussia, after the accession of Frederick the Great in 1740, the position of the *Junkers* became stronger. Frederick's wars required their support. He drew his officers and bureaucrats almost wholly from the *Junker* class. Prussian nobles also enjoyed extensive authority over their serfs.

In Russia, a new, service nobility arose in the eighteenth century. Peter the Great linked noble status to state service through the Table of Ranks (1722). Resistance to state service created among Russian nobles a self-conscious class identity. In 1785, in the Charter of the Nobility, Catherine the Great granted a legal definition of noble rights and privileges in exchange for assurances of voluntary state service from the nobility. The noble privileges included the right of transmitting noble status to one's wife and children, the judicial protection of noble rights and property, power over the serfs, and exemption from personal taxes.

Throughout the century, in a European-wide ***aristocratic resurgence***, the various nobilities sought to protect their social position and privileges. First, all nobilities attempted to restrict entry into their ranks. Second, they attempted to monopolize appointments to the officer corps, the government, and the church. The nobles thus hoped to control the power of the monarchies. Third, they attempted to use institutions they already controlled—the British Parliament, the French *parlements*, local aristocratic estates, and provincial diets—against the monarchies. Fourth, the aristocracies pressed the peasantry for higher rents or forgotten feudal dues.

corvée A French labor tax requiring peasants to work on roads, bridges, and canals.

aristocratic resurgence Eighteenth-century aristocratic efforts to resist the expanding power of European monarchies.

THE LAND AND ITS TILLERS

Land was the economic basis of eighteenth-century life. Over three-fourths of Europeans lived on the land, and most never traveled more than a few miles from their birthplaces. Except for the nobility and the wealthier landowners, the dwellers on the land were poor and led hard lives.

WHY WAS land the economic basis of eighteenth-century life?

PEASANTS AND SERFS

The major forms of rural social dependency related to the land. Those who worked the land were subject to immense influence or direct control by the landowners who also controlled local government and the courts.

Landlord power increased as one moved from west to east. Most French peasants owned some land, but a few were serfs. However, nearly all peasants were subject to feudal dues and forced labor on the lord's estate for a number of days each year.

In Prussia and Austria, despite attempts by the monarchies to improve the lot of the serfs, the landlords continued to exercise almost complete control over them. Moreover, throughout continental Europe the burden of state taxation fell on the tillers of the soil. Many agricultural laborers were forced to undertake supplemental work to pay the tax collector. Through legal privileges and the ability to demand concessions from the monarchs, the landlords escaped numerous taxes. They also presided over the manorial courts.

The condition of the serfs was the worst in Russia. They were regarded merely as economic commodities. Their services were attached to an individual lord rather than to a particular plot of land. Russian landlords could demand as many as six days a week of labor, and like Prussian and Austrian landlords, they could punish their serfs. However, custom, tradition, and law did provide a few protections. For example, the marriages of serfs, unlike those of most slaves throughout the world, were legally recognized. The landlord could not disband the family of a serf.

The Russian monarchy contributed to the degradation of the serfs. Peter the Great (r. 1682–1725) gave whole villages to favored nobles. Catherine the Great (r. 1762–1796) confirmed the authority of the nobles over their serfs in exchange for the nobility's political cooperation. This situation led to unrest. There were over 50 peasant revolts between 1762 and 1769.

Western Europe was more tranquil, but England experienced numerous enclosure riots. Rural rebellions were violent, but the peasants and serfs normally directed their wrath against property rather than persons. The rebels usually sought to reassert traditional or customary rights against practices they perceived as innovations. In this respect, the peasant revolts were conservative in nature.

Emelyan Pugachev (1726–1775) led the largest peasant revolt in Russian history. In this contemporary propaganda picture he is shown in chains. An inscription in Russian and German was printed below the picture decrying the evils of revolution and insurrection.

Bildarchiv Preussischer Kulturbesitz

FAMILY STRUCTURES
AND THE FAMILY ECONOMY

In preindustrial Europe, the household was the basic unit of production and consumption. Other than in cities, few productive establishments employed more than a handful of people not belonging to the owner's family. This mode of economic organization is known as the *family economy*.

WHAT WAS the *family economy*?

HOUSEHOLDS

What was a household under the Old Regime? There were two basic models, one characterizing northwestern Europe and the other eastern Europe.

In northwestern Europe, the household usually consisted of a married couple, their children through their early teenage years, and servants. Except for the wealthy, households were small. High mortality and late marriage meant that grandparents rarely lived in the same household as their grandchildren. The family structure of north-western Europe was thus nuclear rather than extended; that is to say, these families consisted of parents and children rather than of several generations under the same roof.

Children lived with their parents only until their early teens. Then they normally left home to enter the workforce of young servants. A child of a skilled

family economy The basic structure of production and consumption in preindustrial Europe.

artisan might remain with his or her parents to acquire the skill, but only rarely would more than one child do so because their labor was more valuable elsewhere.

These young men and women who had left home would eventually marry and form independent households of their own. This practice of moving away from home is known as *neolocalism*. The effort to acquire the economic resources to establish a household meant the age of marriage would be relatively late: for men, over 26, and for women, over 23. The marriage often occurred at the end of a long courtship when the woman was pregnant. The new couple would soon employ a servant, and everyone, including the children, would help the household support itself.

In preindustrial Europe, a servant—either male or female—was hired, often under a contract, to work for the head of the household in exchange for room, board, and wages. The servant was usually young and not socially inferior to his or her employer. Normally, the servant was an integral part of the household and ate with the family. Young men and women became servants when their labor was no longer needed in their parents' household or when they could earn more money for their family outside it. Being a servant for several years allowed young people to acquire skills and save enough to begin their own households. This period of working as a servant between leaving home and beginning a new household largely explains the late age of marriage in north-western Europe.

As one moved east, the structure of the household and the pattern of marriage changed. In Russia and elsewhere in eastern Europe, marrying involved not starting a new household but continuing in and expanding one already established. Consequently, marriage occurred early, before the age of twenty for both men and women. Children were born to parents of a much younger age than in western Europe. Eastern European households tended to be larger than those in the west. The rural Russian household could have more than 20 members, with three or even four generations living together.

The landholding pattern in eastern Europe accounted, at least in part, for these patterns of marriage and the family. The lords of the manor who owned land wanted to ensure that it would be cultivated so that they could receive their rents. They discouraged single-generation family households because the death or serious illness of a person in such a household might mean that the land assigned to it would go out of cultivation.

THE FAMILY ECONOMY

Throughout Europe, the household was the fundamental unit of production and consumption. People thought and worked in terms of sustaining the economic life of the family, and family members saw themselves as working together in an interdependent rather than an independent or individualistic manner. The goal of the family household was to produce or secure through wages enough food to support its members. In the countryside, that effort virtually always involved farming. In cities and towns, artisan production or working for another person was the usual pattern. Almost everyone lived within a household because ordinary people could rarely support themselves independently. Indeed, except for members of religious orders, people living outside a household were viewed with suspicion.

Everyone in the household had to work. On a farm, much of the effort went into raising food or producing agricultural goods that could be exchanged for food. In western Europe, however, few people had enough land to support their households from farming alone, so one or more family members might work elsewhere and send wages home. Within this family economy, all of the goods and income produced went to the benefit of the household rather than to the individual family member. The need to survive poor harvests or economic slumps meant that no one could be idle.

The family economy also dominated the life of skilled urban artisans. The father was usually the chief craftsman with one or more servants in his employ. He would also expect his children to work in the enterprise. His eldest child was usually trained in the trade. His wife often sold the wares, or had a small shop. The wife of a merchant also often ran the husband's business, especially when he traveled to purchase new goods. In any case, everyone in the family was involved. If business was poor, family members would look for employment elsewhere, not to support themselves but to help the family unit survive.

In western Europe, the death of a father could destroy the economy of the household. The family's economic life usually depended on his land or skills. The widow might take on the farm or the business, or her children might do so. She usually sought to remarry quickly to have the labor and skills of a male in the household and to prevent herself from falling into dependence. The high mortality rate meant that many households were second family groups with stepchildren. But some households simply dissolved. In desperate situations, survivors resorted to crime or begging. The personal, emotional, and economic vulnerability of the family economy cannot be overemphasized.

In eastern Europe, the family economy existed in the context of serfdom and landlord domination. Peasants thought in terms of their families and of expanding the land available for cultivation. The village structure may have mitigated the pressures of the family economy, as did the multigenerational family. Dependence on the land was the chief fact of life, and there were fewer artisan and merchant households and far less mobility than in western Europe.

Painted by the English artist Francis Wheatley (1747–1801) near the close of the eighteenth century, this scene is part of a series illustrating a day in the life of an idealized farm family. Note the artist's assumptions about the division of labor by gender. Men work in the fields, women work in the home or look after the needs of men and children. As other illustrations in this chapter show, many eighteenth-century women in fact worked outside the home, but considerable social pressure was developing at this time to restrict them to domestic roles. This painting and the others in the series are thus more prescriptive than descriptive, intended in part to persuade their viewers that women belonged in their separate family sphere. Many, perhaps most, families living in the countryside could not maintain the closeness that these paintings extol. To survive, many had to send members to work on other farms or even to other regions.

Francis Wheatley (RA)(1747–1801), "Evening," signed and dated 1799, oil on canvas, 17 × 21 in. (44.5 × 54.5 cm), Yale Center for British Art, Paul Mellon Collection, B1977.14.118

WOMEN AND THE FAMILY ECONOMY

The family economy established the chief constraints on the lives and personal experiences of women in preindustrial society. In western Europe, a woman's life experience was largely the function of her capacity to establish and maintain a household. For women, marriage was an economic necessity. A woman outside a household was vulnerable. Unless she was an aristocrat or a member of a religious order, she probably could not support herself by her own efforts. Much of a woman's life was devoted first to aiding her parents' household and then to getting her own household as an adult. Bearing and rearing children were subordinate to these goals.

By the age of seven, a girl was expected to contribute to the household work. On a farm, she might look after chickens or water animals or carry food to adult workers. In an urban artisan's household, she would do light work. The girl would remain at home as long as she made a real contribution to the family enterprise or her labor elsewhere was not more valuable to the family. An artisan's daughter might not leave home until marriage because she could learn valuable skills from her parents.

On farms, most girls would leave home between the ages of 12 and 14. They might go to another farm, but were more likely to migrate to a town or city. They would rarely travel more than 30 miles from their parents' household and would then normally become servants.

The young woman's chief goal was to accumulate a dowry. Marriage within the family economy was a joint economic undertaking, and the wife was expected to make an immediate contribution of capital to establish the household. A young woman might work for ten years or more to accumulate a dowry.

Within the marriage, earning enough money or producing enough farm goods to ensure an adequate food supply was the dominant concern. Domestic duties, childbearing, and child rearing were subordinate to economic survival. Consequently, couples would often practice birth control, usually through *coitus interruptus*, or withdrawal of the male before ejaculation. Young children were often placed with wet nurses so the mother could continue to contribute to the household economy. The wet nurse, in turn, was contributing to her own household. The child would be reintegrated into its family when it was weaned.

A married woman's work was a function of her husband's occupation. If the peasant household possessed enough land to support itself, the wife literally carried things for her husband—water, food, seed, grain, and the like. But few peasants had such landholdings. If the husband had to do work other than farming, such as fishing or migrant labor, the wife might plow, plant, and harvest. In the city, the wife of an artisan or merchant often acted like a business manager. When her husband died, she might take over the business, perhaps hiring an artisan.

Finally, if economic disaster struck, often it was the wife who sent family members off to find work elsewhere or even to beg.

In all phases of life within the family economy, women led active, often decisive roles. Finding a functional place in the household was essential to their well-being, but their function was also essential to its ongoing well-being. (See "Priscilla Wakefield Demands More Occupations Be Opened to Women.")

CHILDREN AND THE WORLD OF THE FAMILY ECONOMY

Childbirth was a time of danger to both mother and infant. Puerperal fever and other infections from unsterilized medical instruments were common. Not all midwives were skillful. The poverty and wretched housing of most Europeans endangered the newborn child and the mother.

QUICK REVIEW

Women in Preindustrial Society

- By age of seven girls contributed to household work
- Most girls left home between ages of 12 and 14
- A young woman's chief goal was to accumulate a dowry

• HISTORY'S VOICES •

PRISCILLA WAKEFIELD DEMANDS MORE OCCUPATIONS BE OPENED TO WOMEN

*A**t the end of the eighteenth century, several English women writers began to demand a wider life for women. Priscilla Wakefield was among such authors. She was concerned that women found themselves able to pursue only occupations that paid poorly. Often they were excluded from work on the grounds of their alleged physical weakness. She also believed that women should receive equal wages for equal work. Many of the issues she raised have yet to be adequately addressed on behalf of women.*

FROM READING this passage, what do you understand to have been the arguments at the end of the eighteenth century to limit the kinds of employment that women might enter? Why did women receive lower wages for work similar to or the same as that done by men? What occupations traditionally filled by men does Wakefield believe women might also pursue?

Another heavy discouragement to the industry of women, is the inequality of the reward of their labor, compared with that of men; an injustice which pervades every species of employment performed by both sexes.

In employments which depend on bodily strength, the distinction is just; for it cannot be pretended that the generality of women can earn as much as men, when the produce of their labor is the result of corporeal exertion; but it is a subject of great regret, that this inequality should prevail even where an equal share of skill and application is exerted. Male stay-makers, mantua-makers, and hairdressers, are better paid than female artists of the same professions; but surely it will never be urged as an apology for this disproportion, that women are not as capable of making stays, gowns, dressing hair, and similar arts, as men; if they are not superior to them, it can only be accounted for upon this principle, that the prices they receive for their labor are not sufficient to repay them for the expense of qualifying themselves for their business; and that they sink under the mortification of being regarded as artisans of inferior estimation. . . .

Besides these employments which are commonly performed by women, and those already shown to be suitable for such persons as are above the condition of hard labor, there are some professions and trades customarily in the hands of men, which might be conveniently exercised by either sex.—Watchmaking requiring more ingenuity than strength, seems peculiarly adapted to women; as do many parts of the business of stationer, particularly, ruling account books or making pens. The compounding of medicines in an apothecary's shop, requires no other talents than care and exactness; and if opening a vein occasionally be a indispensable requisite, a woman may acquire the capacity of doing it, for those of her own sex at least, without any reasonable objection. . . . Pastry and confectionery appear particularly consonant to the habits of women, though generally performed by men; perhaps the heat of the ovens, and the strength requisite to fill and empty them, may render male assistants necessary; but certain women are most eligible to mix up the ingredients, and prepare the various kinds of cakes for baking.—Light turnery and toy-making depend more upon dexterity and invention than force, and are therefore suitable work for women and children. . . .

Farming, as far as respects the theory, is commensurate with the powers of the female mind: nor is the practice of inspecting agricultural processes incompatible with the delicacy of their frames if their constitution be good.

From Priscilla Wakefield, *Reflections on the Present Condition of the Female Sex* (1798), (London, 1817), pp. 125–127, as quoted in Bridget Hill, ed., *Eighteenth-Century Women: An Anthology.* Copyright © 1984 George Allen & Unwin, pp. 227–228.

However, the birth of a child was not always welcome. The child might be illegitimate or an economic burden. Through at least the end of the seventeenth century, infanticide was practiced, especially among the poor. Unwanted infants might be smothered or exposed to the elements. These practices were one result of the ignorance and prejudice surrounding contraception. Although many married couples seem to have succeeded in limiting their families, unmarried young people whose sexual relationships may have been the result of a fleeting acquaintance were less fortunate. Numerous young women, especially among servants, found themselves pregnant and without husbands. This situation and the consequent birth of illegitimate children seem to have become more frequent during the eighteenth century. It probably arose from the more frequent migration of young people from their homes and the disturbance of traditional village life through enclosures (to be discussed later), the commercialization of agriculture, wars, and the late-century revolutions.

In the late seventeenth and early eighteenth centuries, reflecting a new interest in preserving the lives of abandoned children, large foundling hospitals were established in the major nations. Sadness and tragedy were the lot of abandoned children. Most were illegitimate infants, but many seem to have been left with the foundling hospitals because their parents could not support them. Parents would sometimes leave personal tokens on the abandoned baby in the vain hope that they might reclaim the child. Few children were so reclaimed. Leaving a child at a foundling hospital did not guarantee its survival. In Paris, only about 10 percent of all abandoned children lived to the age of 10 years.

Despite these perils, children did grow up across Europe. The world of the child may not have received the kind of attention it does today, but during the eighteenth century the seeds of that modern sensibility were sown. Particularly among the upper classes, new interest arose in the education of children. However, most education remained in the hands of the churches. Most Europeans remained illiterate. Not until the late nineteenth century did childhood and education become inextricably linked. Then children would be reared to become members of a national citizenry. In the Old Regime, they were reared to contribute to the economy of their parents' family and then to set up their own households.

Growth of Agriculture and Population

Thus far, this chapter has examined those groups who sought stability and resisted change. Other groups, however, pursued new directions in social and economic life that would during the next century transform first Europe and then much of the rest of the world. These developments first appeared in agriculture.

The Revolution in Agriculture

The main goal of traditional European peasant society was to ensure the local food supply. That supply was never certain and became more uncertain the farther east one traveled. A failed harvest meant starvation. Food was often harder to find in the country than in cities because city governments usually stored reserves of grain.

Poor harvests also raised grain prices. Even small increases in the cost of food could squeeze peasant or artisan families. If prices increased sharply, many of those families fell back on poor relief from their local government or the church. Peasants felt helpless before the whims of nature and the marketplace, and resisted changes that they felt might endanger the sure supply of food, which they believed traditional cultivation practices ensured.

During the century, bread prices slowly but steadily rose, spurred largely by population growth. This put pressure on the poor. Prices rose faster than urban wages and brought no appreciable advantage to the small peasant producer. Instead, the rise in grain prices benefited landowners and those wealthier peasants who had surplus grain to sell.

The increasing price of grain allowed landlords to improve their income and lifestyle. They began a series of innovations in farm production that are known as the *agricultural revolution.*

New Crops and New Methods   This movement began during the sixteenth and seventeenth centuries in the Low Countries, where Dutch landlords and farmers devised better ways to drain land so that they could farm more areas. They also experimented with new crops, such as clover and turnips, that would increase the supply of animal fodder and replenish the soil.

In England during the early eighteenth century, new methods of farming, crops, and modes of landholding led to greater productivity. This advance in food production was necessary for an industrial society to develop. It ensured adequate food for the cities and freed surplus agricultural labor for industrial production. The changing modes of agriculture sponsored by the landlords undermined the assumptions of traditional peasant production. Farming now took place not only to provide the local food supply but to earn the landlord a profit.

Enclosure Replaces Open-Field Method   Many of the agricultural innovations, which were adopted only slowly, were incompatible with the existing organization of land in Britain. Small cultivators in village communities farmed most of the soil. Each farmer tilled an assortment of unconnected strips. The two- or three-field systems of rotation left much land unproductive each year. Animals grazed on the common land in the summer and on the stubble of the harvest in the winter. Until at least the middle of the eighteenth century, the decisions about what crops would be planted were made communally. The system discouraged improvement and favored the poorer farmers, who needed the common land and stubble fields for their animals. Traditional methods aimed to produce a steady but not a growing supply of food.

In the second half of the eighteenth century, the rising price of wheat encouraged landlords to consolidate or enclose their lands to increase production. The **enclosures** were intended to use land more rationally and raise profits. The process involved the fencing of common lands, the reclamation of untilled waste, and the transformation of strips into block fields. These procedures disrupted economic and social life. Riots often ensued. Because many British farmers either owned their strips or rented them in a manner that amounted to ownership, the landlords had to resort to parliamentary acts to legalize the enclosure of the land, which they owned but rented to the farmers. Because the large landowners controlled Parliament, such measures passed easily. In 1801, a general enclosure act streamlined the process.

The enclosures have remained controversial. They increased food production on larger agricultural units but also disrupted small traditional communities and forced many off the land. However, the enclosures did not depopulate the countryside. In some counties where the enclosures took place, the population increased. New soil had come into production, and services subsidiary to farming expanded.

Limited Improvements in Eastern Europe   In Prussia, Austria, Poland, and Russia, agricultural improvement was minimal. There, the chief method of increasing production was to farm previously untilled lands. By extending tillage, the great landlords sought to squeeze more labor from their serfs rather than greater productivity from the soil. As in the west, the goal was increased profits for the landlords. The only significant nutritional gain landlords achieved was the introduction of maize and the potato.

agricultural revolution   The innovations in farm production that began in the eighteenth century and led to a scientific and mechanized agriculture.

enclosures   The consolidation or fencing in of common lands by British landlords to increase production and achieve greater commercial profits. It also involved the reclamation of waste land and the consolidation of strips into block fields.

POPULATION EXPANSION

Agricultural improvement was both a cause and a result of an immense expansion in the population of Europe. Our current population explosion seems to have had its origins in the eighteenth century. In 1700, Europe's population, excluding the Ottoman Empire, was between 100 million and 120 million people. By 1800, the figure had risen to almost 190 million, and by 1850 to 260 million. Such extraordinary growth put new demands on resources and pressure on social organizations.

The population expansion occurred in both the country and the cities. Only a limited consensus exists about the causes of this growth. There was a decline in the death rate. There were fewer wars and epidemics in the eighteenth century. Hygiene and sanitation improved. But changes in the food supply may have been the chief reason for sustained population growth. One contributing factor was expanding grain production. Even more important was the widespread cultivation of the potato. An acre of potatoes could feed one peasant's family for an entire year. With this more certain food supply, more children could survive.

THE EIGHTEENTH-CENTURY INDUSTRIAL REVOLUTION

AN EVENT IN WORLD HISTORY

HOW DID Europe's growing industrialization affect its relations with the rest of the world?

In the late eighteenth century, the European economy began to industrialize. This development distinguished Europe and eventually North America from the rest of the world for the next two centuries. The consumer products of the industrializing businesses gave Europeans new goods to sell throughout the world and thus encouraged more international trade in which Western nations supplied the finished goods in exchange for raw materials. The prosperity of other areas of the globe became economically dependent on European and American demand. The wealth achieved through this uneven commerce allowed Europeans to dominate world markets for two centuries.

Furthermore, iron and steel production and the new technologies allowed European states and the United States to build more powerful military forces, especially navies, than those of Africa, Latin America, or Asia. The economic and military dominance of the West arose from the industrial achievement.

Much of the history of the non-Western world from the middle of the eighteenth century to the present can be understood in terms of how it reacted to its penetration by Europeans and Americans made wealthy and powerful through industrialized economies. Africa and Latin America became dependent economies. Japan successfully imitated the European pattern. China did not and became indirectly ruled by Europeans. The Chinese revolutions of the twentieth century are efforts to achieve self-direction. Southeast Asia and the Middle East became drawn into the network of resource supply to the West; they could move toward economic independence only through imitation or, like Arab nations in the early 1970s, by refusing to supply oil to the West. The industrialization that commenced in small factories in eighteenth-century Europe has changed the world more than any other single development in the last two centuries.

The European **Industrial Revolution** of the eighteenth century achieved sustained economic growth. Previously, production had been limited. The economy of a province or a country might grow, but soon reached a plateau. However, since the late eighteenth century, the economy of Europe has expanded

Industrial Revolution Mechanization of the European economy that began in Britain in the second half of the eighteenth century.

relatively uninterruptedly. Even during economic downturns the Western economy has continued to grow.

At considerable social cost and dislocation, industrialism produced more goods and services than ever before. Industrialism in Europe overcame the economy of scarcity. The new means of production demanded new skills and discipline in work and a large labor force. The produced goods met consumer demand and created new demands. In the long run, industrialism raised the standard of living; the poverty in which most Europeans had always lived was overcome. Industrialization provided human beings greater control over nature than they had ever known.

The wealth produced by industrialism upset the political and social structures of the Old Regime and led to reforms. The economic elite of the emerging industrial society would challenge the dominance of the aristocracy. Industrialization undermined communities and displaced many people. These processes repeated themselves wherever industrialization occurred during the next two centuries.

Grain production lay at the heart of eighteenth-century farming. In this engraving farm workers can be seen threshing wheat, winnowing the grain, and finally putting the grain in bags so it can be carried to a mill and ground into flour. In many cases the mill would be owned by the local landlord, who would charge peasants for its use.

Bildarchiv Preussischer Kulturbesitz

INDUSTRIAL LEADERSHIP OF GREAT BRITAIN

The Industrial Revolution began, in Britain. Britain was the largest free-trade area in Europe, with good roads and waterways without internal trade barriers. There were rich deposits of coal and iron ore. The political structure was stable, and property was secure. Sound banking and public credit created a good investment climate. Taxation was heavy, but it received legal approval from Parliament. Taxes were efficiently and fairly collected, largely from indirect taxes with all regions and persons from all classes paying the same taxes. Besides satisfying domestic consumer demand, the British economy also benefited from the demand for goods from British colonies.

Finally, British society was relatively mobile. Persons who had money could rise socially. The British aristocracy would accept people who had amassed large fortunes. The combination of these factors plus the progressive state of British agriculture provided the nation with a marginal advantage in the creation of a new mode of economic production. No less important, the wars and revolutions of the late eighteenth and early nineteenth centuries disrupted those parts of the Continent where an industrialized economy might also have begun to develop.

New Methods of Textile Production   Although eighteenth-century society was devoted primarily to agriculture, manufacturing permeated the countryside. Peasants often spun thread or wove textiles in winter. Under the ***domestic*** or ***putting-out*** system, urban textile merchants took wool or other unfinished fiber to peasants, who spun it into thread. The agent then transported the thread to other peasants, who wove it into the finished product. The merchant sold the wares. Sometimes the spinners or weavers owned their own equipment, but more often the merchant capitalist owned the machinery as well as the raw material.

Eighteenth-century industrial development took place within a rural setting. The peasant family living in a cottage, not the factory, was the basic unit of production. The family economy, not the industrial factory economy, characterized the century.

domestic or putting-out system of textile production   Method of producing textiles in which agents furnished raw materials to households whose members spun them into thread and then wove cloth, which the agents then sold as finished products.

OVERVIEW

WHY THE INDUSTRIAL REVOLUTION BEGAN IN BRITAIN

Great Britain was the home of the Industrial Revolution, and until the middle of the nineteenth century, it maintained the industrial leadership of Europe. Several factors contributed to the early industrialization of Britain.

Natural Resources	Britain had extensive deposits of coal and iron ore.
Infrastructure	Britain had an extensive network of roads and canals that facilitated the shipment of raw materials and goods.
Society	1. The predominance of London: London was the largest city in Europe and the social, commercial, financial, and political center of Britain. It was thus both an enormous market for consumer goods itself and created a demand for these goods in the rest of Britain, which sought to emulate London fashions. 2. The prevalence of newspapers: Newspapers thrived in Britain, and advertisements in them increased consumer demand for goods. 3. Wealth in Britain brought status: British society was relatively mobile. Wealthy merchants and entrepreneurs could rise socially, enter the aristocracy, and enjoy political influence.
Government, Financial Institutions, and Empire	1. The rule of law: Britain had a stable government that guaranteed property rights. 2. Britain was a free trade area. No internal tolls inhibited the shipment of goods and raw materials within Britain. 3. Britain had a sound system of banking and public credit that created a stable climate for investing in commerce and industry. 4. Taxes were collected efficiently and fairly. No class was exempt from paying taxes. 5. The colonial empire: British colonies were both a market for British goods and sources of raw materials for British manufacturers.

spinning jenny A machine invented in England by James Hargreaves around 1765 to mass-produce thread.

water frame A water-powered device invented by Richard Arkwright to produce a more durable cotton fabric. It led to the shift in the production of cotton textiles from households to factories.

However, by mid-century, demand for cotton textiles was growing more rapidly than production, particularly in Great Britain, whose growing population wanted cotton textiles, as did its colonies in North America. The most famous inventions of the Industrial Revolution were devised in response to consumer demand for cotton textiles.

Cotton textile weavers had the technical capacity to produce enough fabric to satisfy demand, but the spinners could not produce as much thread as the weavers needed. This imbalance had been created during the 1730s by James Kay's flying shuttle, which increased the productivity of the weavers. To eliminate this bottleneck, in about 1765 James Hargreaves (d. 1778) invented the **spinning jenny**, which by the close of the century allowed as many as 120 spindles of thread to be spun.

The spinning jenny was still used in the cottage. The invention that took cotton textile manufacture from the home to the factory was Richard Arkwright's (1732–1792) **water frame**, patented in 1769. It was a water-powered device to produce a purely cotton fabric rather than one containing linen for durability. Numerous factories sprang up in the countryside near the necessary water power. From the 1780s onward, the cotton industry could meet an ever-expanding demand. By 1815, cotton composed 40 percent of the value of British domestic exports.

The Steam Engine   The new technology in textile manufacture revolutionized a major consumer industry. But the invention that more than any other enabled industrialization to grow on itself and expand into one area of production after another was the steam engine. This machine provided for the first time in human history an unlimited source of inanimate power. Unlike engines powered by water or wind, the steam engine, driven by burning coal, was a portable source of industrial power that did not fail or falter as the seasons changed. Unlike human or animal power, the steam engine depended on mineral energy that never tired. Finally, the steam engine could be applied to many industrial and, eventually, transportation uses.

The first practical engine using steam power was invented by Thomas Newcomen (1663–1729) in the early eighteenth century. It was large, inefficient, and practically untransportable. Nonetheless, English mine operators used it to pump water out of coal and tin mines.

During the 1760s, James Watt (1736–1819) understood that if the condenser were separated from the piston and the cylinder, much greater efficiency would result. In 1769, he patented his new invention, and in 1776, the Watt steam engine found its first commercial application pumping water from mines. By the early nineteenth century, the steam engine had become the prime mover for industry. With its application to ships and then to wagons on iron rails, it also revolutionized transportation.

Iron Production   High-quality iron has been basic to industrial development. It constitutes the chief element of heavy industry and land or sea transport and is the material out of which most productive machinery has been manufactured. During the early eighteenth century, British ironmakers produced less than 25,000 tons annually. Three factors held back production. First, charcoal rather than coke was used to smelt the ore. Charcoal, which is derived from wood, was becoming scarce, and it did not burn at as high a temperature as coke, which is derived from coal. Second, until the perfection of the steam engine, insufficient blasts could be achieved in the furnaces. Finally, the demand for iron was limited. The elimination of the first two problems eliminated the third.

In the course of the century, British ironmakers began to use coke, and the steam engine provided new power for the blast furnaces. Coke was abundant because of Britain's large coal deposits. The steam engine improved iron production and increased the demand for iron.

In 1784, Henry Cort (1740–1800) introduced a new method for melting and stirring the molten ore. Cort's process produced a purer iron. He also developed a rolling mill that shaped the still-molten metal into bars, rails, or other forms. Previously, the metal had been pounded into these forms.

These innovations achieved a better, more versatile, and cheaper product. The demand for iron grew as its price fell. By the early nineteenth century, annual British iron production amounted to over a million tons. The lower cost of iron in turn lowered the cost of steam engines and allowed them to be used more widely.

Major Inventions in the Textile-Manufacturing Revolution

1733	James Kay's flying shuttle
1765	James Hargreaves's spinning jenny (patent 1770)
1769	James Watt's steam engine patent
1769	Richard Arkwright's water frame patent
1787	Edmund Cartwright's power loom

CITIES

PATTERNS OF PREINDUSTRIAL URBANIZATION

Remarkable changes occurred in city growth between 1500 and 1800. In 1500, 156 cities within Europe (excluding Hungary and Russia) had a population greater than 10,000. Only Paris, Milan, Venice, and Naples had more than 100,000 inhabitants.

WHAT KINDS of cities in Europe grew fastest between 1600 and 1750?

By 1800, 363 cities had 10,000 or more inhabitants, and 17 of those had populations larger than 100,000. The percentage of the European population living in urban areas had risen from over 5 percent to over 9 percent. The urban concentration had also shifted from Mediterranean Europe to the north.

These raw figures conceal changes that took place in how cities grew and how the population distributed itself. Urban development in the sixteenth century was followed in the seventeenth by leveling and decline. New growth began in the early eighteenth century and accelerated thereafter.

Growth of Capitals and Ports   Capitals and ports were the urban areas that displayed the most growth and vigor between 1600 and 1750. This reflects the success of monarchical state building and the burgeoning of groups related to the process of government who lived in the capitals. The growth of port cities reflects the expansion of European overseas trade and especially that of the Atlantic routes. With the exception of Lyons, France, significant growth did not take place in industrial cities. Furthermore, between 1600 and 1750, cities with populations of fewer than 40,000 inhabitants declined. These cities included older landlocked trading centers, medieval industrial cities, and ecclesiastical centers. They contributed less to the new political regimes, and since rural labor was cheaper than urban labor, cities with concentrations of labor declined as production sites were moved from urban workshops into the countryside.

New Cities and Growth of Small Towns   After 1750, large cities grew more slowly. New cities arose, and older smaller cities began to grow. Several factors were at work. First was the overall population increase. Second, the early stages of the Industrial Revolution, particularly in Britain, occurred in the countryside and aided the growth of smaller towns and cities near the factories. Factory organization itself fostered new concentrations of population. But cities also grew because of the new prosperity of European agriculture. Greater agricultural production aided the growth of nearby market towns and other urban centers. This new pattern of urban growth—new cities and the expansion of smaller existing cities—would continue into the nineteenth century.

URBAN CLASSES

Social divisions were as marked in the cities of the eighteenth century as they were in the industrial centers of the nineteenth.

The Upper Classes   At the top of the urban social structure stood a small group of nobles, large merchants, bankers, financiers, clergy, and government officials. These men (and they were always men) controlled the affairs of the town through its corporation or city council. These rights of self-government had generally been granted by a royal charter that gave the city corporation the power to select its own members.

The Middle Class   The prosperous merchants, tradesmen, bankers, and professional people were the most dynamic element of the urban population and constituted the middle class, or *bourgeoisie*. Middle-class people lived in the cities and towns, and their sources of income had little to do with the land. The middle class normally supported reform, change, and economic growth. Middle-class businessmen and professionals often found their pursuit of profit and prestige blocked by aristocratic privilege and social exclusiveness. The bourgeoisie (and some progressive aristocrats) also wanted more rational regulations for trade and commerce.

Consumption of all forms of consumer goods increased greatly in the eighteenth century. This engraving illustrates a shop, probably in Paris. Here women, working apparently for a woman manager, are making dresses and hats to meet the demands of the fashion trade.

Bildarchiv Preussischer Kulturbesitz

During the eighteenth century, the middle class and the aristocracy frequently collided. The former often imitated the lifestyle of the latter, and nobles increasingly embraced the commercial spirit of the middle class. Both were seeking to enhance their existing power and prestige. However, tradition and political connection gave the advantage to the nobility. Consequently, the middle class increasingly resented the aristocracy, especially as the bourgeoisie grew wealthier and more numerous and the aristocratic control of power tightened.

On the other hand, the middle class also tended to fear the lower urban classes. The lower orders constituted a potentially violent threat to property and, in their poverty, a drain on national resources. The lower orders, however, were much more varied than either the city aristocracy or the middle class cared to admit.

Artisans   Shopkeepers, artisans, and wage earners constituted the single largest group in any city. They had their own culture, values, and institutions. Like the peasants, they were conservative. Their economic position was vulnerable. If a poor harvest raised the price of food, their businesses suffered.

The life of these artisans and shopkeepers centered on their work. They usually lived near or at their place of employment. Most of them worked in shops with fewer than a half-dozen other craftsmen. Their primary institution had been the guild, but most guilds had lost influence.

Nevertheless, the guilds played a conservative role. They did not seek economic growth or innovation. They attempted to preserve the jobs and the skills of their members and to prevent too many people from learning a particular skill.

The guilds also provided a framework for social and economic advancement. A young boy might become an apprentice to learn a craft or trade. After several years he would be made a journeyman. Still later, he might become a master. The artisan could also receive social benefits from the guilds, including aid for his family during sickness or the promise of admission into the guild for his son. The guilds constituted the chief protection for artisans against the commercial market.

THE AGE OF THE GHETTO

Most European Jews lived in Eastern Europe. In the eighteenth century, three million Jews dwelled in Poland, Lithuania, and Ukraine. There were perhaps 150,000 in the Habsburg lands around 1760. Fewer than 100,000 lived in Germany and approximately 40,000 in France. England and Holland had Jewish populations of fewer than 10,000. Even fewer Jews lived in Italy.

Jews dwelled in most nations without enjoying the rights and privileges of other subjects, unless such rights were specifically granted to them. They were aliens whose status might be changed at the whim of rulers.

The Jews of Europe under the Old Regime lived apart from non-Jews. In cities they usually lived in distinct districts known as **ghettos**; in the countryside, in Jewish villages. Thus, this period in Jewish history is known as the age of the ghetto, or separate community. Jews were also treated as a distinct people religiously and legally. In Poland for much of the century they were virtually self-governing. Elsewhere they lived under the burden of discriminatory legislation. Except in England, Jews could not mix in the mainstream of the societies in which they dwelled.

During the seventeenth century, a few Jews helped finance the wars of rulers. These financiers came to be known as "court Jews." They tended to marry among themselves. Their position at court and their financial abilities may have brought them privilege and fame, but court Jews often failed to have their loans repaid.

However, most European Jews lived in poverty. They occupied the most undesirable sections of cities or poor rural villages. A few were money lenders, but most worked at the lowest occupations. Their religious beliefs, rituals, and community set them apart. A wall of laws and social institutions—as well as the physical walls of the ghetto—kept them in positions of social inferiority.

Under the Old Regime, this discrimination was based on religious separateness. Jews who converted to Christianity were welcomed into the major political and social institutions of European society. But until the late eighteenth century, those Jews who remained loyal to their faith were not free to pursue the professions or often change residence and stood outside the political structures of the nations in which they lived. Jews could be expelled from the cities where they dwelled and their property confiscated. They were regarded as socially and religiously inferior. Their children could be taken away from them and given Christian instruction. And their non-Jewish neighbors might turn violently against them.

ghettos Separate communities in which Jews were required by law to live.

SUMMARY

The European Old Regime Eighteenth-century European society was traditional, hierarchical, corporate, and privileged. These features had characterized Europe and the world for centuries. All societies also confronted the scarce food supplies. For the eighteenth century, however, an improved food supply helped support a larger population, New agricultural techniques and the expanding population created pressures on social structures.

Commerce also grew during the eighteenth century. Agriculture became more commercialized, with more money payments. Cities expanded.

Changes in European Society European society stood on the brink of a new era in which the social, economic, and political relationships of centuries would be destroyed. The commercial spirit and the values of the marketplace clashed with the traditions of peasants and guilds. That commercial spirit brought social change; by the early nineteenth century it led to a conception of human beings as individuals rather than as members of communities.

The expansion of the European population further stimulated change and challenge to tradition, hierarchy, and corporateness. The traditional economic and social organization (the family economy) had presupposed a stable or declining population. A larger population meant that new ways had to be devised to solve old problems. The social hierarchy had to accommodate itself to more people. Corporate groups, such as the guilds, had to confront an expanded labor force. New wealth, created by committee and industry's meant that birth would cease to determine social relationships.

Industrialization would also affect Europe's relations with much of the non-European world. For the first time in history, major changes in one region of Europe left virtually no corner of the globe untouched. By the close of the eighteenth century, a movement toward world interconnectedness and interdependence had begun.

IMAGE KEY
for pages 456–457

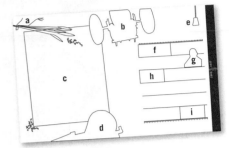

a. Grains of wild einkorn
b. Jethro Tull's wheat drill, ca. 1701
c. Francois Boucher (1703–1770), *Breakfast*
d. Hargreaves' spinning jenny
e. Long handled churn
f. Claude Joseph Vernet, *Construction of a Road*
g. Emelyan Pugachev
h. Francis Wheatley *Evening*
i. The Jewish quarter Kazimlesz in Kracow, Poland

REVIEW QUESTIONS

1. What was the economic basis of the life of the nobility? What authority did they have over other groups in their societies?

2. What was the *family economy*? How did the family economy constrain the lives of women?

3. What caused the Agricultural Revolution? How did technological innovations help change European agriculture?

4. Why did Europe's population increase in the eighteenth century? What were the effects of the population explosion?

5. What caused the Industrial Revolution of the eighteenth century? Why did Great Britain take the lead in the Industrial Revolution?

6. During the eighteenth century, what changes took place in the distribution of population in cities and towns?

KEY TERMS

agricultural revolution (p. 467)
aristocratic resurgence (p. 460)
corvée (p. 460)
domestic or putting-out system
  of textile production (p. 469)

enclosures (p. 467)
family economy (p. 461)
ghettos (p. 474)
Industrial Revolution (p. 468)
Old Regime (p. 458)

spinning jenny (p. 470)
water frame (p. 470)

 For additional study resources for this chapter, go to:
www.prenhall.com/craig/chapter21

Jahangir showing preference to the Chishti Sufi shaykh and saint Husain over three temporal rulers: the Ottoman emperor, the King of England, and a Hindu prince. The Timurid emperor presents a book to Shaykh Husain, the descendant of the great Chishti saint Mu'inuddin, while ignoring the temporal rulers in the lower left corner. The artist copied the likeness of King James I from an English portrait given to Jahangir by Sirr Thomas Roe, the British ambassador from 1615–1619. The magnificent floral borders to the miniature (ca. 1615–1618) were added in 1727 by Muhammad Sadiq. Bichitr, "Jahangir Preferring a Sufi Shaikh to Kings", ca. 1660–70. Album page. Opaque watercolor, gold and ink on paper. 25.3 cm H ×18.1 cm W (10" × 7 1/8"). Courtesy of the Freer Gallery of Art, Smithsonian Institution, Washington, D.C.

22

THE LAST GREAT ISLAMIC EMPIRES
1500–1800

WHY WAS the Ottoman Empire increasingly unable to compete with the European powers?

WHAT ROLE did Shi'ite ideology play in the Safavid Empire?

WHAT ROLE did religious intolerance play in the decline of the Mughal Empire?

WHAT WERE the most important Islamic states in central and southern Asia?

HOW DID the arrival of Europeans affect the control of the commerce in southeast Asia?

IMAGE KEY

Image Key for pages 476–477 is on page 489.

Between 1450 and 1650, Islamic culture and statecraft blossomed. The creation of the Ottoman, Safavid, and Mughal Empires marked the global apogee of Islamic culture and power (see Map 22–1).

In 1600, Islamic civilization seemed as strong and vital as that of western Europe, China, or Japan. Yet by the late seventeenth century, Islamic power was in retreat before the rising tide of western European military and economic imperialism, even though Islamic cultural life and Muslim religion flourished.

MAP EXPLORATION

Interactive map: To explore this map further, go to **http://www.prenhall.com/craig2/map22.1**

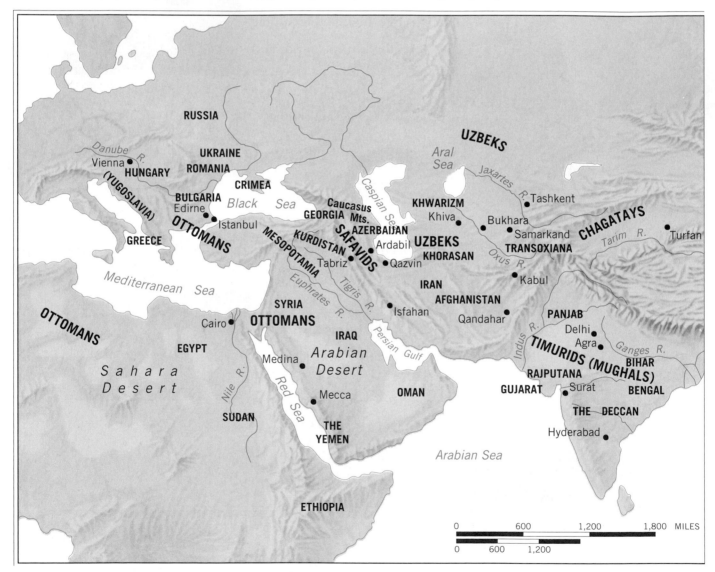

MAP 22–1

Sixteenth-century Islamic empires.   Major Islamic dynasties in the central Islamic lands, ca. 1600. Note that the Sharifian state of Morocco does not show on the far left of this map.

IN 1600, what were the most important Islamic empires?

ISLAMIC EMPIRES

THE OTTOMAN EMPIRE

ORIGINS AND DEVELOPMENT OF THE OTTOMAN STATE BEFORE 1600

The Ottomans were a Turkish dynasty that reached Anatolia (Asia Minor) in the time of the Seljuks of Rum (1098–1308). In the fourteenth century, the Ottomans expanded into central Anatolia and west across the Dardanelles (in 1356) onto European soil. The Ottomans built a formidable fighting force.

By 1402, Ottoman control extended as far as the Danube. Constantinople fell in 1453 to Sultan Mehmed II, "the Conqueror" (r. 1451–1481). It became the Ottoman capital and was renamed "Istanbul." After hundreds of years, Byzantium, the center of eastern Christendom, was no more.

By 1512, Ottoman rule was secure in southeastern Europe. Under Selim I (r. 1512–1520) and Süleyman, "the Lawgiver" ("Süleyman the Magnificent"; r. 1520–1566), this sovereignty was greatly expanded. Selim subjugated Egypt (1517), Syria-Palestine, and most of North Africa. The Yemen and western Arabia, including Mecca and Medina, also were brought under Ottoman rule. Süleyman extended Ottoman control in the Caucasus and Mesopotamia. He also brought most of Hungary under Ottoman rule.

The Ottoman ruler could now claim to be the caliph for all Muslims. This claim was symbolized by the title "Protector of the Sacred Places [Mecca and Medina]" and emperor (*padishah*).

THE "CLASSICAL" OTTOMAN ORDER

The entire Ottoman state was organized as one vast military institution. It was supported by the productivity of its Muslim and non-Muslim subjects. The ruling class were Muslims and had to give utter allegiance to the sultan. The state organization included the palace and the administrative, military, and religious or learned institutions.

Several measures helped ensure the strength of the sultan. Young Ottoman princes were given leadership training in the provinces, which gave them experience of life outside the capital. Stability of succession was guaranteed by fratricide in the ruling family, which continued until the late sixteenth century. The succession was theoretically left to God, the strongest aspirant to the sultanate having to seize power, after which he was expected to execute his brothers to eliminate claims to the throne.

By institutionalizing the religious institution, the Ottomans made the religious scholars, or *ulama*, an arm of the government under a single religious authority, the **Grand Mufti** or "Shaykh of Islam." This branch of the state was open only to Muslim men and included the entire system of courts and judges.

Although the religious establishment upheld the ***Shari'a*** and the sultan recognized its authority, the functional law of the land was the state administrative law, or ***Qanun***, established by the ruler. This had been a de facto characteristic of most Islamic states, but under the Ottomans, administrative law was highly organized.

As for the military institution, the Ottoman rulers kept its loyalty by checks on the power of the old landed aristocracy and by the use of slave soldiers with allegiance only to the sultan. To sustain the quality of these slave troops, the Ottomans developed the provincial slave levy, or ***devshirme***. This selected Christian boys from the peasantry to be raised as Muslims. They were trained to serve in both army and bureaucracy. The most famous slave corps was the **Janissaries**, the elite infantry of the empire.

WHY WAS the Ottoman Empire increasingly unable to compete with the European powers?

 12.2
Süleyman "The Lawgiver" and the Advantages of Islam: Oigier de Busbecq

 12.4
The Ottomans: Empire-builders at the Crossroads of Three Continents

Ottoman Empire   The imperial Turkish state centered in Constantinople that ruled large parts of the Balkans, North Africa, and the Middle East until 1918.

padishah   Meaning "emperor." One of the titles of the Ottoman monarchs.

Grand Mufti   The chief religious authority of the Ottoman Empire. Also called "the Shaykh of Islam."

Shari'a   Islamic religious law.

Qanun   Ottoman administrative law.

devshirme   The system under the Ottoman Empire that required each province to furnish a levy of Christian boys who were raised as Muslims and became soldiers in the Ottoman army.

Janissaries   Elite Ottoman troops who were recruited through the *devshirme*.

Süleyman the Lawgiver (r. 1520–1566), giving advice to the Crown Prince, Mehmed Khan. From a contemporaneous Ottoman miniature.

Folio 79a of the *Talikizade Shenamesi*, Library of the Topkapi Palace Museum, A3592/Photograph courtesy of Talat Halman

QUICK REVIEW

Ottoman Culture

- Katib Chelebi (d. 1657): most illustrious figure in Ottoman literature
- Distinctly Ottoman artistic forms emerged in the late sixteenth century
- Sinan (d. 1578) was the leading Ottoman architect of his day

AFTER SÜLEYMAN: CHALLENGES AND CHANGE

The reign of Süleyman marked the peak of Ottoman prestige and power. Beginning with his weak son, Selim II (1566–1574), the empire was plagued by corruption, decentralization, and maritime setbacks. Agricultural failures, commercial imbalances, and inflation were hard to check. Yet culturally, the seventeenth and eighteenth centuries were impressive. Overall, the two centuries seesawed between decline and vitality.

Political and Military Developments   The post–Süleyman era began with the loss of territory in the east to the Persian Safavids (1603). By this time the Ottoman military apparatus was weakened, partly from fighting two-front wars with the Safavids and the Habsburgs and partly because of European advances in technology. The Janissaries, once the backbone of Ottoman power, became disruptive and tried to influence decision making and even dynastic succession. Finally, the increasing employment of mercenaries resulted in peacetime in the release of masses of unemployed armed men into the countryside, which led to the sacking of provincial towns, banditry, and revolts.

Economic Developments   Financing the Ottoman state grew ever more difficult. The increase in the Janissary corps from 12,000 to 36,000 men by 1600 drained state coffers. Fluctuations in silver caused inflation. The Ottomans encouraged imports, since too many exports would have raised domestic prices. This damaged the Ottoman economy in the long run. The population doubled in the sixteenth century, which led to increased unemployment. Decentralization paved the way for the rise of provincial notables (*ayan*), who became virtually independent in the eighteenth century.

Culture and Society   The seventeenth and eighteenth centuries were an era of vitality in culture, but the *ulama* became an aristocratic social elite. Major religious posts were controlled by a handful of families and became hereditary sinecures that were often sold or leased.

In literature, Katib Chelebi (d. 1657) was only the most illustrious of many polymaths who wrote histories, social commentary, geographies, and encyclopedic works. Ottoman art in the latter sixteenth century produced distinctively Ottoman artistic and architectural forms. The greatest name here is that of the imperial master architect Sinan (d. 1578). The first half of the eighteenth century was the golden age of Ottoman poetry and art; it also saw the first Ottoman printing press.

Socially, the period saw the consolidation of Ottoman society as a multi-ethnic and multi-religious state. Considerable Jewish immigration into Ottoman societies following their expulsion from Spain (1492) had brought new craftsmen, physicians, bankers, scholars, and entertainers. The large Christian population of the empire was well treated, but in the seventeenth century they began to suffer increasing discrimination. As a result, the Christians looked to Europe and Russia for liberation.

Overall, in the eighteenth century strained relations between Muslims and non-Muslims increased, in part because of the rise in the economic and social status of non-Muslims—in particular the rich mercantile middle class. Non-Muslims monopolized foreign trade, and in the eighteenth century, European countries gave many of them citizenship, which allowed them the trade privileges granted to foreign governments by the sultan.

ayan   Ottoman notables.

One of the major social institutions of later Ottoman society, the coffeehouse, flourished from the mid-sixteenth century on. The Ottoman coffeehouse rapidly became a major common space for socializing. Here people gathered to drink coffee, play games, read, and discuss public affairs. The coffeehouse stimulated the development of a common Ottoman urban culture among lower and middle classes.

THE DECLINE OF OTTOMAN MILITARY AND POLITICAL POWER

After the failure in 1683 of a second siege of Vienna, the Ottomans were driven out of Hungary and Belgrade and never again threatened Europe. The treaty of Karlowitz sealed the loss of Hungary to Austria (1699). Defeat by Russia cost the Ottomans the Crimea, which made the tsar the protector of the Orthodox Christians of the Islamic empire (1774). Henceforth, the Ottomans were prey to the West, never regaining their earlier power and influence before their final demise in 1918.

Outflanked by Russia to their north and by European sea power to the south and west, the Ottomans found themselves blocked in the east by their Shi'ite foes in Iran. They could not support their expensive wars. Ultimately, their dependence on an agrarian economy proved insufficient to face the commercial and industrial powers of Europe.

THE SAFAVID SHI'ITE EMPIRE

ORIGINS

As noted in Chapter 14, Iranian history changed under the Safavid dynasty after 1500. The Safavids had begun in the fourteenth century as hereditary Turkish spiritual leaders of a Sunni Sufi order in the northwestern Iranian province of Azerbaijan. In the fifteenth century, the Safavid order evolved a new and militant Shi'ite ideology. The Safavid spiritual masters (*shaykhs*, or **pirs**) of the order claimed descent from the seventh imam of the Twelver Shia (see Chapter 14), which made them (the *pirs*) the focus of Shi'ite religious allegiance.

The growing strength of the Safavids brought about conflict with the dominant Sunni groups around Tabriz. The Safavids emerged victorious in 1501 under the leadership of the young Safavid master-designate Isma'il, who extended his sovereignty over the southern Caucasus, Azerbaijan, the Tigris-Euphrates valley, and western Iran by 1506. In the east, by 1512 the Safavids had taken eastern Iran from the Uzbek Turks. The Uzbeks, however, became implacable foes of the Safavids and throughout the ensuing century often forced them to fight a debilitating two-front war, with Uzbeks in the east, and Ottomans in the west.

Strong central rule now united Iran for the first time since the Abbasid caliphate. It was a regime based on the existing Persian bureaucratic institutions. Shah Isma'il enforced Shi'ite conformity on the Sunni majority, and Shi'ite conformity slowly took root across the realm—perhaps bolstered by Persian self-consciousness in the face of the Sunni Ottomans, Arabs, Uzbeks, and Mughals who surrounded Iran.

In the west, however, the better-armed army of Selim I defeated the Safavids in 1514, marking the beginning of a series of Ottoman-Safavid conflicts over the next two centuries. This defeat gave the Ottomans control of the Fertile Crescent and forced the Safavids to move their capital and their focus eastward to Isfahan.

The Ottoman Empire

ca. 1280	Foundation of early Ottoman principality in Anatolia
1356	Ottomans Cross Dardanelles into Europe
1451–1481	Rule of Sultan Mehmed II, "the Conqueror"
1453	Fall of Constantinople to Mehmed the Conqueror
1512–1520	Rule of Selim I
1517	Ottoman conquest of Egypt, assumption of claim to Abbasid caliphal succession from Mamluks
1520–1566	Rule of Süleyman. "the Lawgiver"
1578	Death of Ottoman master architect, Sinan
1683	Ottoman siege of Vienna
1699	Treaty of Karlowitz, loss of Hungarian and other European territory
1774	Loss of Crimea to Russia; tsar becomes formal protector of Ottoman Orthodox Christians
1918	End of empire

WHAT ROLE did Shi'ite ideology play in the Safavid Empire?

pirs Shi'ite holy men.

The Safavid Empire

ca. 1500	Rise of Safavids under Shah Isma'il
1501–1512	Safavid conquest of greater Iran; Shi'ite state founded
1588–1629	Rule of Shah Abbas I
1722	Forced abdication of last Safavid ruler
1736–1747	Rule of the Sunni Afghan leader, Nadir Shah; revival of Sunni monarchy in Iran
1739	Nadir Shah sacks Delhi

12.5
The Safavid Shi'ite Empire of Persia

Shah Abbas I receiving a diplomatic embassy from the Turks in 1609.

Staatliche Museen zu Berlin/Bildarchiv Preussischer Kulturbesitz-Museum für Islamic Kunst

SHAH ABBAS I

Tahmasp I (r. 1524–1576) managed to survive attacks by both Ottomans and Uzbeks. In part, the strength of Shi'ite religious feeling and the allegiance of the bureaucracy enabled the regime to survive. A few years later, the greatest Safavid ruler, Shah Abbas I (r. 1588–1629), brought able leadership to the Safavid domains. He pushed the Ottomans out of Azerbaijan and Iraq and turned back Uzbek invasions in Khorasan. He also sought alliances with the Ottomans' European enemies. This latter tactic, used by several Safavid rulers, reflects the division the new militant Persian Shi'ism had brought to the Islamic world. Abbas also opened trade with the English and Dutch. His reign brought prosperity to Iran, symbolized by the magnificent capital he built at Isfahan.

SAFAVID DECLINE

After Shah Abbas, with the exception of Abbas II (1642–1666) and Husayn I (1694–1722), the empire never again enjoyed able leadership. This led finally to its decline and collapse, the chief causes of which were (1) continued pressure from Ottoman and Uzbek armies; (2) the concentration of wealth at the center of, and the corresponding economic decline in, the empire; and (3) the power and bigotry of the Shi'ite *ulama*. The conservative *ulama* introduced a Shi'ite legalism and emphasized their own authority over that of the Safavid monarch. They also persecuted religious minorities and encouraged hatred of Sunni Muslims.

One result of Shi'ite exclusivism was tribal revolts among the Sunni Afghans. An Afghan leader took Qandahar (in modern Afghanistan) and then captured Isfahan and forced the abdication of Husayn I in 1722. Safavid princes managed to retake western Iran, but the empire's greatness was past. A revived, but officially Sunni, monarchy under Nadir Shah (r. 1736–1747) restored much of Iran's lost territories. However, his military ventures, which included the conquest of Delhi, sapped the empire's finances. After his despotic reign, Iran could not regain stability for another half-century.

CULTURE AND LEARNING

The most impressive aspect of Safavid times, besides the conversion of Iran to Shi'ism, was the cultural renaissance of the sixteenth and seventeenth centuries. The traditions of painting, with their origins in the powerful miniatures of the preceding century, were cultivated and modified in Safavid times. Portraiture and scenes from everyday life became popular. Among the most developed crafts were ceramic tiles, porcelain, and carpets. In architecture, the magnificent public squares, parks, palaces, hospitals, caravanserais, mosques, and other buildings of Isfahan constructed in Shah Abbas's time give evidence of Safavid taste.

The Safavid age also saw a distinctively Shi'ite piety develop. It focused on commemorating the suffering of the imams and loyalty to the Shi'ite *ulama*, who (through their knowledge of the Qur'an and the traditions from Muhammad and the Imams) alone provided guidance in the absence of the hidden imam (see Chapter 11).

THE EMPIRE OF THE INDIAN TIMURIDS, OR "MUGHALS"

Invaders from the northwest in the early sixteenth century ended the political fragmentation that had reduced the Delhi sultanate to only one among many Indian states. These invaders were descended from Timur (Tamerlane) and known, not entirely correctly, as the **Mughals** (a Persianate form of *Mongol*). In 1525–1527, the founder of the Mughal dynasty, Babur, marched on India. Before his death in 1530, he ruled an empire stretching from the Himalaya to the Deccan. Akbar "the Great" (r. 1556–1605), however, was the real founder of the Mughal Empire, and the greatest Indian ruler since Ashoka (ca. 264–223 B.C.E.).

AKBAR'S REIGN

Akbar added North India and the northern Deccan to the Mughal dominions. Even more significant, however, were his governmental reforms, cultural patronage, and religious toleration. He reorganized government and rationalized the tax system. His marriages with Rajput princesses and his appointment of Hindus to power eased Muslim-Hindu tensions. So did his cancellation of the poll tax on non-Muslims (1564). Under his leadership, the Mughal Empire became a truly Indian empire.

Akbar showed unusual interest in different religious traditions. He frequently brought together representatives of all faiths to discuss religion. Akbar tried to promulgate among his intimates a new monotheistic creed that subsumed Muslim, Hindu, and other viewpoints. However, his ideas died with him. (See "Some Reforms of Akbar.")

THE LAST GREAT MUGHALS

Akbar's three immediate successors were Jahangir (r. 1605–1627), Shah Jahan (r. 1628–1658), and Awrangzeb (r. 1658–1707). Although each left behind significant achievements, none matched Akbar. The problems of sustaining an Indian empire took their toll on Mughal power. The reigns of Jahangir and Shah Jahan were the golden age of Mughal culture. But the burdens imposed by military campaigns and the erosion of Akbar's administrative and tax reforms led to economic decline. Jahangir set a fateful precedent in permitting English merchants to establish a trading post at Surat on the western coast in Gujarat. No less a burden on the treasury were Shah Jahan's elaborate building projects, the most magnificent of which was the Taj Mahal (built 1632–1653), the unparalleled tomb that he built for his beloved consort, Mumtaz.

With Shah Jahan, religious toleration retreated; under Awrangzeb, religious fanaticism reversed Akbar's earlier policies. The resulting disorder hastened the decline of Mughal power. Awrangzeb persecuted non-Muslims, destroying Hindu temples, reimposing the poll tax (1679), and alienating the Rajput leaders, whose forebears Akbar had cultivated. His intransigent policies coincided with the spread of the militant Sikh movement and the rise of Hindu Maratha nationalism.

SIKHS AND MARATHAS

In the late sixteenth and early seventeenth centuries, the Sikhs, who trace their origins to the irenic teachings of Guru Nanak (d. 1538), developed into a distinctive religious movement. Neither Muslim nor Hindu, they had their own scripture, ritual, and ideals. Angered by their rejection of Islam, Awrangzeb earned their lasting enmity by persecution. Thereafter, the Sikhs developed into a formidable military force. Awrangzeb and his successors had to contend with repeated Sikh uprisings.

The Hindu Marathas, led by Shivaji (d. 1680), rose in religious and nationalistic fervor to found their own empire about 1646. On Shivaji's death, the Maratha army was the most disciplined force in India. After Awrangzeb's death, the Marathas brought

---

WHAT ROLE did religious intolerance play in the decline of the Mughal Empire?

QUICK REVIEW

Akbar (r. 1556-1605)
- Added North India and the northern Deccan to Mughal Empire
- Carried out extensive governmental reforms
- Interested in a variety of religious faiths

QUICK REVIEW

Awrangzeb (r. 1658-1707)
- Reversed policy of religious toleration
- Persecuted non-Muslims
- Policies coincided with spread of militant Sikh movement and rise of Hindu Maratha nationalism

---

Mughals   Descendants of the Mongols who established an Islamic empire in India in the sixteenth century with its capital at Delhi.

·HISTORY'S VOICES·

SOME REFORMS OF AKBAR

kbar (r. 1556–1605) was certainly one of history's great rulers, but some of his fame is surely due to the laudatory quality of the voluminous Persian chronicle of his reign written by Abu'l-Fazl (d. 1602). The often exaggerated praise was, however, a convention of such Persian works. It would not have hidden from its readers Abu'l-Fazl's message about the statecraft and significant achievements of his ruler.

WHAT DOES this excerpt suggest might have been some practical reasons for Akbar's reforms? How does this document compare to others concerned with law, leadership, and government? See for example: "Hammurabi's Code on Women, Marriage, and Divorce in Babylonia" (Chapter 1), "Athenian Democracy: An Unfriendly View" (Chapter 3), and "The Edicts of Ashoka" (Chapter 4).

One of the glorious boons by His Majesty the Shahinshah which shone forth in this auspicious year was the abolition of enslavement. The victorious troops which came into the wide territories of India used in their tyranny to make prisoners of the wives and children and other relatives of the people of India, and used to enjoy them or sell them. His Majesty the Shahinshah, out of his thorough recognition of and worship of God, and from his abundant foresight and right thinking gave orders that no soldier of the victorious armies should in any part of his dominions act in this manner. Although a number of savage natures who were ignorant of the world should make their fastnesses a subject of pride and come forth to do battle, and then be defeated by virtue of the emperor's daily increasing empire, still their families must be protected from the onset of the world-conquering armies. No soldier, high or low, was to

enslave them, but was to permit them to go freely to their homes and relations. It was for excellent reasons that His Majesty gave his attention to this subject, for although the binding, killing or striking the haughty and the chastising the stiff-necked are part of the struggle for empire—and this is a point about which both sound jurists and innovators are agreed—yet it is outside of the canons of justice to regard the chastisement of women and innocent children as the chastisement of the contumacious. If the husbands have taken the path of insolence, how is it the fault of the wives, and if the fathers have chosen the road of opposition what fault have the children committed? Moreover the wives and innocent children of such factions are not munitions of war! In addition to these sound reasons there was the fact that many covetous and blindhearted persons from vain imaginings or unjust thoughts, or merely out of cupidity attacked villages and estates and plundered them, and when questioned about it said a thousand things and behaved with neglect and indifference. But when final orders were passed for the abolition of this practice, no tribe was afterwards oppressed by wicked persons on suspicion of sedition. As the purposes of the Shahinshah were entirely right and just, the blissful result ensued that the wild and rebellious inhabitants of portions of India placed the ring of devotion in the ear of obedience, and became the materials of world-empire. Both was religion set in order, for its essence is the distribution of justice, and things temporal were regulated, for their perfection lies in the obedience of mankind.

"Some Reforms of Akbar" from *The Islamic world*, 1973, M. R. Waldman and W. H. McNeill, (from *The Akbarnama* trans. by H. Beveridge–The Asiatic Society, 1905–1939).

about a confederation of the Deccan States under their leadership. While acknowledging Mughal sovereignty, the Marathas controlled far more of India after 1740 than did the Mughals.

POLITICAL DECLINE

In addition to these wars, other factors sealed the fate of the Mughal Empire after Awrangzeb's death in 1707: the rise in the Deccan of the powerful Islamic state of Hyderabad in 1724; the Persian invasion of North India by Nadir Shah in 1739; the invasions (1748–1761) by the Afghan tribal leader Ahmad Shah Durrani

(r. 1747–1773); and the British victories over Bengali forces at Plassey in Bengal (1757) and over the French on the southeastern coast (1740–1763). By 1819, the dominance of the British East India Company had eclipsed Indian power, even though the Mughal line came to an official end only in 1858.

RELIGIOUS DEVELOPMENTS

The period from about 1500 to 1650 was of major importance for Indian religious life. In the sixteenth century, a number of religious figures preached a piety that transcended the legalism of both the *ulama* and the Brahmans and rejected caste distinctions. In these ideas, we can see both Muslim Sufi and Hindu *bhakti* influences at work. Guru Nanak, the spiritual father of the Sikh movement, preached faith and devotion to one loving and merciful God. He opposed narrow allegiance to particular creeds or rites and excessive pride in external religious observance. Dadu (d. 1603) preached a similar message. He was born a Muslim but strove to get people to go beyond Muslim or Hindu allegiance.

There was also a Hindu revival epitomized by Chaitanya (d. ca. 1533), who stressed total devotion to Lord Krishna. The forebears of present-day Hare Krishna devotees, his followers spread his ecstatic public praise of God and his message of the equality of all in God's sight. Tulasidas's (d. 1623) retelling of the *Ramayana* remains among the most popular works of Indian literature. Tulasidas used the story of Rama's adventures to present *bhakti* ideas that remain alive in Hindu life.

Muslim eclectic tendencies came primarily from the Sufis. By 1500, the Chishtiya Sufi order especially had won many converts to Islam. Such Sufis were, however, often opposed by the *ulama*, many of whom were royal advisers and judges responsible for upholding the religious law. The more intolerant side of the spirit of Awrangzeb's time eventually won the day. The possibilities for Hindu-Muslim rapprochement waned, presaging the communal strife that has so marred southern Asian history in our own century.

ISLAMIC ASIA

ISLAMIZATION AND ISOLATION

The solid footing of Islam in Central Asia can be traced to the fifteenth century. Even in the preceding century, as the peoples of western Central Asia had begun to shift to a settled existence, the familiar pattern of Islamic diffusion from trading and urban centers had set in. Islamization was slowed only in the late sixteenth century by the conversion of Mongolia proper to Buddhism. In the region between the Aral and Caspian Seas, the most important states were founded by Uzbek and Chaghatay Turks.

UZBEKS AND CHAGHATAYS

During the fifteenth century, a new steppe khanate had been formed by the unification in 1428 of assorted clans of Turks and Mongols known as the Uzbeks. In time, an Uzbek leader who was descended from Genghis Khan, Muhammad Shaybani (d. 1510), invaded Transoxiana (1495–1500) and founded an Uzbek Islamic empire. Muhammad's line

Worldly and Spiritual Drunkenness.
This painting (opaque water color, ink and gold on paper, 28.9 × 21.6 cm) by the great 16th-century Safavid Iranian court painter Sultan Muhammad is from an illustrated copy of the *Diwan*, or collected works of the lyric and mystical poet Hafiz (1319–1389?). Hafiz appears himself as a drunken figure in the upper window. The entire picture plays the worldly drunkenness and debauchery of the characters in the center against the spiritual inebriation of the dancing Sufis in the garden and the angels on the roof. The angels, too, are shown drinking, a visual reference to the line of Hafiz at the top: "The angel of mercy took the cup of revelry."

WHAT WERE the most important Islamic states in central and southern Asia?

The great central square of the Registan, in Samarkand, with the 17th-century Shir Dar Madrasa on the right and the 15th-century Ulugh Beg Madrasa on the left. Samarkand and other major Central Asian cities were centers of Islamic culture and learning as well as political power.

Michael Gotin

continued Uzbek rule in Transoxiana at Bukhara into the eighteenth century, while another Uzbek line ruled the khanate of Khiva in western Turkestan from 1512 to 1872.

Of the other Central Asian Islamic states after 1500, the most significant was that of the Chaghatay Turks. From about 1514, a revived Chaghatay state in eastern Turkestan lasted until 1678.

CONSEQUENCES OF THE SHI'ITE RIFT

On the face of it, the Ottoman, Mughal, Safavid, and Central Asian were Islamic states that had much in common. Yet the deep religious division between the Shi'ite Safavids and their Sunni neighbors proved stronger than their common bonds. The result was a geographic division that isolated Central Asian Muslims.

Shi'ite-Sunni political competition was sharpened by Safavid militancy, to which the Sunni states responded in kind. Attempts to form alliances with non-Muslim states became a commonplace of Shi'ite and Sunni tactics. Although trade went on, the international flow of Islamic commerce was hurt by a militant Shi'ite state astride the overland trade routes of the larger Islamic world. The Safavid Shi'ite schism also ruptured the cultural traditions of the "abode of Islam." The militant Shi'ism of Iran isolated Central Asia from the rest of the Muslim world after 1500. However healthy Islam remained in this region, its contact with the Islamic heartlands shrank. Contact came primarily through pilgrims, Sufis, *ulama*, and students. Central Asian Islam mostly developed in isolation, peripheral to the Islamic mainstream.

POWER SHIFTS IN THE SOUTHERN SEAS

HOW DID the arrival of Europeans affect the control of the commerce in southeast Asia?

Along the southern rim of Asia, from the Red Sea and East Africa to the South China Sea, the first half of the second millennium witnessed the spread of Islamic religion and culture. In port cities, Islamic traders established thriving communities that often became the dominant presence. Typically this first stage of conversion was followed by Islam's transmission to

OVERVIEW

MAJOR ISLAMIC STATES, CA. 1600

The fifteenth to the eighteenth centuries were the age of the last great Islamic empires. These states dominated the Islamic world, which stretched from Morocco on the Atlantic coast of North Africa across the Near East and along the eastern coast of Africa to the southeast Asian islands that today make up the Republic of Indonesia. Despite these political divisions and the religious divide between Sunni and Shi'ite Muslims, in many respects the Islamic world formed a single cultural unit.

State	Location	Islamic Tradition
Ottoman Empire	Balkans, Anatolia, North Africa, Syria, Iraq, Arabia	Sunni
Safavid Empire	Iran, Afghanistan Caucasus	Shi'ite
Mughal Empire	India	Sunni
Uzbeks	Central Asia: Kiva, Bokhara	Sunni
Chaghatays	Central Asia: Tukistan	Sunni
Acheh	Sumatra	Sunni

surrounding areas and inland centers of Hindu, Buddhist, or pagan culture. In this transmission, Sufi orders played the main role. However, conquest by Muslim coastal states quickened the process in Indonesia and East Africa.

Hindus were the chief religious group the Muslims displaced. Islam never ousted the Indian Buddhist cultures of Burma, Thailand, and Indochina. Islam did, however, win most of Malaysia, Sumatra, Java, and the "Spice Islands" of the Moluccas. By the end of the fifteenth century, Islam had also spread along the East African coast.

CONTROL OF THE SOUTHERN SEAS

The Portuguese reached the East African coast in 1498. In the following three centuries, the history of the lands along the trade routes of the southern Asian seas was bound not only with Islamic networks but with the rising power of Christian western Europe. The key attractions of these diverse lands were their commercial and strategic possibilities.

In the sixteenth century, the Europeans began to displace by force the Muslims who dominated the maritime southern rim of Asia. European success was based on national support systems and superior warships. The effectiveness of this combination was evident along the west coast of India, where the Portuguese carved out a power base in the early sixteenth century at the expense of Muslim traders. They did so through superior naval power, exploitation of indigenous rivalries, and terror.

However, Islamization continued apace, even in the face of Christian proselytizing and European power. The Muslims

India: The Mughals and Contemporary Indian Powers

1525–1527	Rule of Babur, founder of Indian Timurid state
1538	Death of Guru Nanak, founder of Siteh religious tradition
1556–1605	Rule of Akbar "the Great"
1605–1627	Rule of Jahangir
1628–1658	Rule of Shah Jahan, builder of the Taj Mahal
1646	Founding of Maratha Empire
1658–1707	Rule of Awrangzeb
1680	Death of Maratha leader, Shivaji
1708	Death of tenth and last Sikh guru, Gobind Singh
1724	Rise of Hyderabad state
1739	Iranian invasion of North India under Nadir Shah
1757	British East India Company victory over Bengali forces at Plassey

The Taj Mahal. Probably the most beautiful tomb in the world, the Taj was built from 1631 to 1653 by Shah Jahan for his beloved wife, Mumtaz Mahal. Located on the south bank of the Yamuna River at Agra, the Mughal capital, the Taj Mahal remains the jewel of Mughal architecture.

Michael Gotin

rarely abandoned their faith, which proved generally attractive to new peoples they encountered. The result was usually an Islamicized and racially mixed population.

The upshot of these developments was that while European imperialism had considerable military and economic success, European culture and Christian missionary work made little headway against Islam. Only in the Philippines did a substantial population become Christian.

THE INDIES: ACHEH

In Indonesian archipelago, substantial Islamic sultanates arose in the sixteenth and seventeenth centuries, of which the most powerful was Acheh, in northwestern Sumatra (ca. 1524–1910).

Acheh provided the only counterweight to the Portuguese presence across the straits in Malacca (Malaysia). The Portuguese subdued it, and Acheh thrived until the end of the sixteenth century. In the first half of the seventeenth century, the sultanate controlled both coasts of Sumatra and parts of the Malay peninsula. Meanwhile, also in the seventeenth century, the Dutch replaced the Portuguese. In the early twentieth century, the Dutch finally won full control after nearly 40 years of war with Acheh (1873–1910).

SUMMARY

The Last Islamic Empires   The period from 1500 to 1800, marks the cultural and political blossoming of the last Islamic empires and their sharp decline. The Islamic vitality in the first half of this period was exemplified in the Ottoman, Safavid, and Mughal Empires. All three built vast bureaucracies and arguably the greatest cities in the world of their time. They patronized the arts. Yet they were conservative societies. Economically they remained tied to agricultural production and taxation based on land. They did not undergo the social or religio-political revolutions that rocked the West after 1500 or the sort of generative changes in material and intellectual life that the Western world experienced during the same period. There was no compelling challenge to traditional Islamic ideals, even though numerous Islamic movements of the eighteenth century did call for reform.

Decline   By the latter half of this period, all these empires were in economic, political, and military decline, even if intellectual and artistic vigor held on.

Thus, it is not surprising that European expansionism impinged in these three centuries upon Africa, India, Indonesia, and the Islamic heartland, rather than the reverse. None of the Islamic states, fared well in their encounters with Europeans during this age. Their growing domination of the world's seas allowed Europeans to contain or to bypass the major Islamic lands in their quest for commercial empires.

Industrial development joined economic wealth and political stability by the late 1700s to give the West global military supremacy for the first time. Before 1800,

The Southern Seas: Arrival of the Portuguese

1498	The Portuguese come to the East African coast and to the west coast of India
1500–1512	The Portuguese establish bases on west Indian coast, replace Muslims as Indian Ocean power
early 1500s	Muslim sultanates replace Hindu states in Java, Sumatra
1524–1910	State of Acheh in northwestern Sumatra
1600s	Major increase in Islamization and connected spread of Malay language in the archipelago
1641	Dutch conquest of Malacca
ca. 1800	Dutch replace Muslim states as main archipelago power
1873–1910	War between Holland and Acheh

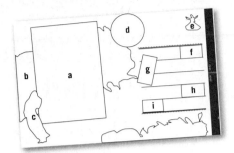

IMAGE KEY
for pages 476–477

a. Emperor Jahangir seated on an hourglass conversing with a Muslim mystic
b. Lion, Ch'ilin and Dragon set in floral sprays mid 16th Century, Turkey
c. Riaz Abbasi, *Woman with a veil* ca. 1590–95
d. Ottoman Sultan Mehmed II
e. Whirling dervishes
f. Ottoman Sultan Suleyman I
g. Ardabil carpet from Safavid dynasty in Iran
h. Samarcande, Place du Reghistan
i. The Christ Church in Dutch Square, Melaka, Malaysia

the Europeans were able to bring only minor Islamic states under colonial administrations. However, the footholds they gained in Africa, India, and Southeast Asia laid the groundwork for rapid colonial expansion after 1800. The age of the last great Muslim empires was the beginning of the first great modern European empires.

REVIEW QUESTIONS

1. Why did the Ottoman Empire expand into Europe? Why did the empire fail to hold certain areas in Europe?

2. What were the most important reasons for the success of the Safavid Empire in Iran? Who were its major foes?

3. What were the most important elements that united all Islamic states? Why was there a lack of unity between these states from 1500 to 1800?

4. What were Akbar's main policies toward the Hindu population? How did the Sikhs develop into a formidable military power?

5. Why were outside powers attracted to the South Seas lands?

KEY TERMS

ayan (p. 480)
devshirme (p. 479)
Grand Mufti (p. 479)
Janissaries (p. 479)

Mughals (p. 483)
Ottoman Empire (p. 479)
padishah (p. 479)
pirs (p. 481)

Qanun (p. 479)
Shari'a (p. 479)

For additional study resources for this chapter, go to:
www.prenhall.com/craig/chapter22

The "Other" in the Early Modern Period

THE EARLY modern era (c. 1350–1750 C.E.) experienced increased trade and movements of peoples throughout the world. How did artists depict the strangers whom they often found in their midst, and their experiences of people from other cultures?

In the West, the early modern period coincides with what is often called the "Age of Discovery," when Europeans "discovered" the New World, and sailed for the first time to sub-Saharan Africa and Asia. Other cultures too increased their encounters with peoples from other parts of the world. Artists depicted the foreigners according to their people's experiences with them. They drew, painted, or sculpted them in the style of art most familiar to them, but emphasized those aspects of the foreigners they found most remarkable, strange, attractive, or repulsive.

◀ **This superb painting** of an Indian of African origin demonstrates that Africans were voyagers to other lands and that not all Africans who went elsewhere went as slaves. The man in this image is a merchant, probably a member of the Janjeera people, originally from Ethiopia. Janjeera merchants went to India in the Middle Ages. Some remained and during the fifteenth century they and their descendants obtained positions of power and authority in local governments. The sumptuous dress and dignified bearing of this man suggests wealth and influence.

K. L. Kamat

◀ **In the fifteenth** and sixteenth centuries the Portuguese explored the coast of West Africa, where they established trading outposts and forts, and the beginnings of the Atlantic slave trade. One of Africa's most important products was ivory, which African artisans carved into exquisite objects for the luxury trade. Saltcellars like the one depicted here, carved in Nigeria at the court of Benin in the fifteenth or sixteenth century, were popular in Portugal. African artists carving for a Portuguese audience often depicted Portuguese merchants, emphasizing those aspects of the Europeans which most impressed them, the heavy beards, symbol of the European's different features and style of dress, and the cross, heavy armor, and sword.

African, Nigeria, Edo peoples, court of Benin, Saltcellar: Portuguese Figure, 15th–16th century, Ivory; H. 7-1/8 in. (18.1 cm). The Metropolitan Museum of Art, Louis V. Bell and Rogers Funds, 1972.(972.63ab) Phoytograph by Stan Reis. Photograph © 1984 The Metropolitan Museum of Art

In Asia and Africa, early modern Europeans went as traders rather than as conquerors. In the New World, disease, superior weaponry, horses, and political disunity of the native peoples permitted Europeans to engage in conquest. This image from the Florentine codex depicts the fall of the Aztec capital Tenochtitlán.

Note the Spanish mounted on horses on the left. The Aztec had never seen horses before and they were greatly terrified. The codex, produced in the sixteenth century by natives under the supervision of a Spaniard, Fray Bernardino de Sahagún, is the product of a blending of Spanish and Aztec culture and art styles.

Courtesy of the Library of Congress

▲ **This image shows** a portion of a Namban screen from the Momoyama period in late sixteenth-century Japan. Europeans, beginning with the Portuguese, began arriving in Japan at the end of the sixteenth century. The Japanese found the strangely dressed Portuguese merchants, and the African slaves, Indian pilots, and Catholic clerics who accompanied them fascinating.

De Young Memorial Museum/San Francisco/USA

EUROPE

1756–1763	Seven Years' War
1762–1796	Catherine II, "the Great" reigns in Russia
1763	Peace of Paris Seven Years' War
1772	First partition of Poland
1783	Peace of Paris
1789	French Revolution begins
1793 and 1795	Last partitions of Poland

◄ July 14, 1789, Bastille
prison, Paris

Sir Isaac
Newton ►

NEAR EAST / INDIA

1757	British victory at Plassey, in Bengal
1761	English oust French from India
1772–1784	Warren Hastings' administration in India
1772–1833	Ram Mohan Roy, Hindu reformer in India
1794–1925	Qajar shahs in Iran
1805–1849	Muhammad Ali in Egypt

▲ Muhammad Ali

EAST ASIA

1753–1806	Kitagawa Utamaro, Tokugawa era artist
1787–1793	Matsudaira Sadanobu's reforms in Japan
1789	White Lotus Rebellion in China
1823–1901	Li Hung-chang, powerful Chinese governor-general

◄ Utamaro
woodblock print

AFRICA

1754–1817	Usman Dan Fodio, founder of Sultanate in northern and central Nigeria
1762	End of Funj sultanate in eastern Sudanic region

THE AMERICAS

1759–1788	Spain reorganizes government of its American Empire
1776	American Declaration of Independence
1791	First ten amendments to U.S. Constitution (Bill of Rights) ratified
1791	Negro slave revolt in French Santo Domingo
1794	Canada Constitutional Act divides the country into Upper and Lower Canada

The "Boston Massacre" of ►
March 5, 1770 by Paul Revere

1804–1814 Napoleon's empire
1814–1815 Congress of Vienna
1830–1848 Louis Philippe reigns in France
1832 First British Reform Act
1837–1901 Queen Victoria of England
1848 Revolutions across Europe

1835 Introduction of English education in India
ca. 1839–1880 Tanzimat reforms, Ottoman Empire
1839–1897 Muslim intellectual Jamal al-Din Al-Afghani
1845–1905 Muhammad Abduh

◄ *British colonial rule in India (1880)*

1835–1908 Empress Dowager Tz'u-hsi
1839–1842 Opium War; 1842, Treaty of Nanking grants Hong Kong to the British and allows them to trade in China
1844 Similar treaties made between China and France and the United States

Armed Chinese junk ► *during the Opium War*

1804 Fulani Jihad into Hausa lands
1806 British take Cape Colony from the Dutch
1817–1828 Zulu chief Shaka reigns
1830–1847 French invasion of Algeria
1830s Dutch settlers, the Boers, expand northward from Cape Colony
1848–1885 Sudanese Madhi, Muhammad Ahmad

1804 Haitian independence
1808–1824 Wars of independence in Latin America
1822 Brazilian independence
1847 Mexican War

Simón Bolívar ►

Commencing in the 16th century with new theory and observations in astronomy, a new age of European science opened. It was upon the confidence inspired by the new science that European thinkers of the 17th and 18th centuries established a framework of reformist thought that became known as the Enlightenment. This illustration from the Danish observatory of Tycho Brahe indicates the sense of wonder evoked by the new astronomy. Royal Geographical Society, London

23

THE AGE OF
EUROPEAN ENLIGHTENMENT

WHAT WAS the Scientific Revolution?

WHY WAS the Encyclopedia so important?

WHY DID the philosophes regard
the church as the chief enemy
of reform and human happiness?

HOW DID the Philosophes hope
that reason would change society?

WHAT WAS

enlightened absolutism?

IMAGE KEY
Image Key for pages 494–495
is on page 509.

Scientific Revolution The sweeping change in the scientific view of the universe that occurred in the West in the sixteenth and seventeenth centuries.

Enlightenment The eighteenth-century movement led by the *philosophes* that held that change and reform were both desirable through the application of reason and science.

WHAT WAS the Scientific Revolution?

17.1
The Heliocentric Statement (ca. 1520) Nicolaus Copernicus

Ptolemaic system The pre-Copernican explanation of the universe, which placed the Earth at the center of the universe.

No intellectual force during the past three centuries has so transformed the world as western science and technology. Today, the impact of science on human life remains dominant and scientific knowledge, for military advantage as well as medical and economic advance, is a goal of modern states. The emergence of science as this culturally transforming force began in Europe during the sixteenth century in a process known as the **Scientific Revolution**, *which gained momentum during the next two centuries.*

The impact of science could make itself felt only when the conviction spread that change and reform were possible and desirable. This attitude came into its own in Europe only after 1700. The movement that fostered such thinking is called the **Enlightenment**. *It combined confidence in the human mind inspired by the Scientific Revolution and faith in the power of rational criticism to challenge tradition and revealed religion. The rationality of the physical universe became a standard against which the traditions of society could be measured and criticized. As a result, the spirit of innovation and improvement came to characterize modern Western society. This outlook would become perhaps the most important European cultural export to the rest of the world.*

THE SCIENTIFIC REVOLUTION

The sixteenth and seventeenth centuries witnessed a sweeping change in the scientific view of the universe. From being the center of the universe, the Earth was seen as only a planet orbiting the sun, which itself became one of millions of stars. This transformation led to a rethinking of moral and religious matters as well as of scientific theory. Science and the scientific method set a new standard for evaluating knowledge in the West.

The process by which this new view of scientific knowledge came to be established is termed the Scientific Revolution. It was a long, complex movement that never involved more than a few hundred people. However, it ultimately revolutionized how Europeans thought about nature and themselves. This new outlook would be exported to the world.

NICOLAUS COPERNICUS

Copernicus (1473–1543), a Polish astronomer, published *On the Revolutions of the Heavenly Spheres*. Before Copernicus, the standard explanation of the Earth and the heavens was that associated with Ptolemy's (ca. 90–168) *Almagest* (150 C.E.). The **Ptolemaic system** assumed that the Earth was the center of the universe. Above the Earth lay a series of crystalline spheres, containing the moon, the sun, the planers, and the stars. Aristotelian physics underpinned the Ptolemaic systems. The Earth had to be the center because of its heaviness. The other heavenly bodies had to be enclosed in the crystalline spheres to move. Nothing could move unless something was moving it. The state of rest was natural; motion required explanation.

However, the planets could be seen moving in noncircular patterns around the Earth. At times they appeared to be going backward. The Ptolemaic systems explained that these strange motions occurred primarily through *epicycles*: The planets made a second revolution in an orbit tangent to their primary orbit around the Earth. The Ptolemaic explanations were effective as long as one assumed Aristotelian physics and the Christian belief that the Earth rested at the center of the created universe.

Copernicus challenged this picture in the most conservative manner possible. He suggested that if the Earth were assumed to move about the sun in a circle, the difficulties with the Ptolemaic systems would become simpler. His motive was to construct a more mathematically elegant basis for astronomy: With the sun at the center of the universe, mathematical astronomy would make more sense. It meant that the planets were actually moving in circular orbits and only seemed to be doing otherwise as a result of the position of observers on Earth.

Except for the modification in the position of the Earth, most of Copernicus's book was Ptolemaic, but it allowed others who were discontented with the Ptolemaic systems to think in new directions.

Copernicus's fusion of mathematical astronomy with empirical data and observation became the model for the new scientific thought.

TYCHO BRAHE AND JOHANNES KEPLER

The Danish astronomer Tycho Brahe (1546–1601) advocated a different kind of Earth-centered system in which the moon and the sun revolved around the Earth, and the other planets revolved around the sun. His major weapon against Copernican astronomy was accurate tables of astronomical observations, made with the naked eye.

When Brahe died, these tables came into the possession of Johannes Kepler (1571–1630), a German astronomer. Kepler was a convinced Copernican, but after much work, he discovered that to keep the sun at the center of things, he must abandon Copernicus's circular orbits. The mathematical relationships that emerged from Brahe's observations suggested that the orbits of the planets were elliptical. Kepler published his findings in 1609. He had solved the problems of planetary orbits by using Copernicus's sun-centered universe and Brahe's empirical data, but the available theories could not explain why the planetary orbits were elliptical. That solution awaited the work of Sir Isaac Newton.

Tycho Brahe in the Uranienburg observatory on the Danish island of Hven (1587). Brahe made the most important observations of the stars since antiquity. Kepler used his data to solve the problem of planetary motion in a way that supported Copernicus's sun-centered view of the universe. Ironically, Brahe himself had opposed Copernicus's view.

Bildarchiv Preussischer Kulturbesitz

GALILEO GALILEI

In 1609, the Italian scientist Galileo Galilei (1564–1642) first turned a telescope on the heavens. He saw stars where none had been known to exist, mountains on the moon, spots moving across the sun, and moons orbiting Jupiter. The heavens were far more complex than anyone had suspected, and the Ptolemaic system could not accommodate these new phenomena.

Galileo publicized his findings and arguments for the Copernican system in his *Dialogues on the Two Chief Systems of the World* (1632). He was condemned by the Roman Catholic Church and compelled to recant his opinions. However, he is reputed to have muttered, "It [the Earth] still moves."

Galileo articulated the concept of a universe totally subject to mathematical laws. He believed that the smallest atom behaved with the same mathematical precision as the largest heavenly sphere.

Galileo championed the application of mathematics to scientific investigation and the goal of reducing phenomena to mathematical formulas. However, the English philosopher Francis Bacon advocated a method based solely on **empiricism**. Both empirical induction and mathematical analysis proved fundamental to scientific investigation.

empiricism The use of experiment and observation derived from sensory evidence to construct scientific theory or philosophy of knowledge.

FRANCIS BACON

Bacon (1561–1626) attacked the scholastic belief that most truth had already been discovered and the scholastic reverence for tradition and the work of the ancients. He urged contemporaries to strike out on their own in search of a new understanding of nature.

Bacon was one of the first major European writers to champion innovation and change. Most people in Bacon's day thought that the best era of human history lay in antiquity. Bacon dissented from that view. He looked to a future of material improvement achieved through the empirical examination of nature. His great achievement was persuading thinkers that scientific thought must conform to empirical experience.

17.4
Isaac Newton

Sir Isaac Newton discovered the mathematical and physical laws governing the force of gravity. Newton believed that religion and science were compatible and mutually supportive, and that the study of nature gave one a better understanding of the Creator. This portrait of Newton is by Sir Godfrey Kneller.

Sir Godfrey Kneller. Sir Isaac Newton. Bildarchiv Preussischer Kulturbesitz

RENÉ DESCARTES

René Descartes (1596–1650) was a gifted French mathematician who invented analytic geometry. He popularized a scientific method that relied more on deduction than empirical observation. Descartes's *Discourse on Method* (1637) tried to put all human thought on a mathematical footing. To arrive at truth, Descartes said that it was necessary to question all ideas except those that were clear and distinct. The only idea worthy of trust was one that persuaded one's own reason of its truth.

Descartes divided existing things into two basic categories: things thought and things occupying space. Thinking was characteristic of the mind, and extension (things occupying space), of the body. Since space was measurable by mathematical means, mathematical laws governed the world of extension. These can be grasped by reason, for mathematical truths have the capacity to form a coherent system in which each part is deduced from some other part. Spirits, divinities, or immaterial things have no place in the world of extension. It belongs to the scientist who uses mathematical reason to comprehend the mechanical properties of matter.

In the natural sciences, Descartes's deductive methodology eventually lost favor to induction, the process by which a scientist arrives at a hypothesis by generalizing from discrete bits of empirical data. But his approach remained popular with people who pondered subjects for which little empirical data was available—political theory, psychology, ethics, and theology.

ISAAC NEWTON

Isaac Newton (1642–1727) solved the major remaining problem of planetary motion and established a basis for physics that endured for more than two centuries. In 1687, he published *The Mathematical Principles of Natural Philosophy*, better known by its Latin title, *Principia Mathematica*. Newton was indebted to Galileo's view that inertia could exist in either a state of motion or a state of rest, and Galileo's mathematical bias permeated Newton's thought. Newton reasoned that all physical objects moved through mutual attraction. Every object in the universe affected every other object through gravity, which explained why the planets moved in an orderly manner. Newton demonstrated the effect of gravity mathematically, but did not explain gravity itself.

Newton was a mathematical genius, but he also upheld the importance of empirical data and observation. The final test of any theory for him was whether it described what could actually be observed.

With the work of Newton, the natural universe became a realm of law and regularity. Spirits and divinities were no longer necessary to explain it, a point of view that contributed to skepticism about witchcraft. Thus, the Scientific Revolution liberated human beings from the fear of a chaotic universe. Most of the scientists were devout. For them, God, the Creator of a rational, lawful nature, must also be rational. To study nature was to better understand that Creator. Science and faith were mutually supporting.

This reconciliation of faith and science allowed the new physics and astronomy to spread rapidly. Faith in a rational God encouraged faith in the rationality of human beings and in their capacity to improve their lot. The Scientific Revolution provided the model for the desirability of change and for criticizing inherited views.

JOHN LOCKE

John Locke (1632–1704) attempted to achieve a lawful picture of the human mind similar to that which Newton had presented of nature. In the *Essay Concerning Human Understanding* (1690), Locke envisioned the human mind as being blank at the time of birth. People were born with no innate ideas; all knowledge is derived from sense experience. Each individual mind grows through experience as it confronts sensation. What people know is not the external world in itself but the results of the interaction of their minds with the outside world. Human nature can be molded by modifying the environment. Locke also rejected the Christian view that human beings were flawed by original sin. Human beings do not need to wait for divine aid. They can take charge of their own destiny.

THE ENLIGHTENMENT

The movement known as the Enlightenment included writers living at different times in various countries. Its early exponents, known as the *philosophes*, popularized the rationalism and scientific ideas of the seventeenth century. They exposed contemporary social and political abuses and argued that reform was necessary and possible. They confronted oppression and religious condemnation. Yet by the mid-century they had convinced Europeans that change was a good idea.

VOLTAIRE

The most influential of the *philosophes* was François Marie Arouet, known as Voltaire (1694–1778). During the 1720s, Voltaire had offended the French authorities and been briefly imprisoned. In 1733, after visiting England, he published *Letters on the English*, which praised English intellectual and political freedom and indirectly criticized French society. In 1738, he published *Elements of the Philosophy of Newton*, which popularized the thought of the great scientist. Both works enhanced his reputation.

Thereafter, Voltaire lived either in France or near Geneva, just across the French border, where the royal authorities could not bother him. His essays, history, plays, stories, and letters made him the literary dictator of Europe. He turned the venom of his satire against one evil after another in French and European life. In *Candide* (1759), he attacked war, religious persecution, and unwarranted optimism about the human condition. Like most *philosophes*, Voltaire believed that

---

Major Publication Dates of the Enlightenment

1687	Newton's *Principia Mathematica*
1690	Locke's *Essay Concerning Human Understanding*
1733	Voltaire's *Letters on the English*
1738	Voltaire's *Elements of the Philosophy of Newton*
1748	Montesquieu's *Spirit of the Laws*
1750	Rousseau's *Discourse on the Moral Effects of the Arts and Sciences*
1751	First volume of the *Encyclopedia* edited by Diderot and d'Alembert
1755	Rousseau's *Discourse on the Origin of Inequality*
1762	Rousseau's *Social Contract*
1763	Voltaire's *Treatise on Toleration*
1776	Smith's *Wealth of Nations*
1779	Lessing's *Nathan the Wise*
1792	Wollstonecraft's *A Vindication of the Rights of Woman*

WHY WAS the *Encyclopedia* so important?

---

philosophes The eighteenth-century writers and critics who forged the new attitudes favorable to change. They sought to apply reason and common sense to the institutions and societies of their day.

MAJOR FIGURES IN THE SCIENTIFIC REVOLUTION

The Scientific Revolution was a major turning point in Western culture. Although the Scientific Revolution never involved more than a few hundred people, the ideas they formulated and publicized gradually overturned the theological and religious modes of thought that were central to the medieval worldview. Humankind and life on Earth became the focus of Western thinking, and Western intellectuals developed more selfconfidence in their capacity to shape the world and their own lives. Below is a list of the major scientific thinkers of the sixteenth and seventeenth centuries and their most important accomplishments.

Nicolaus Copernicus (1473–1543)	Argued that the Earth moved around the sun. His combination of mathematical astronomy with empirical observation and data became the model of scientific thought.
Tycho Brahe (1546–1601)	Compiled accurate tables of astronomical observations.
Johannes Kepler (1571–1601)	Used Brahe's data to argue that the orbits of the planets were elliptical.
Galileo Galilei (1564–1642)	First astronomer to use a telescope. Argued that mathematical laws governed the universe.
Francis Bacon (1561–1626)	Argued that scientific thought must conform to empirical evidence. Championed innovation and change.
René Descartes (1596–1650)	Invented analytical geometry. Argued that the world was governed by mathematical laws that could be deduced by reason.
Isaac Newton (1642–1727)	Explained the effect of gravity mathematically and established a theoretical basis for physics that endured until the late nineteenth century.
John Locke (1632–1704)	Argued that human nature was a blank slate that could be molded by modifying the environment. Human beings could thus take charge of their own destiny without divine aid.

human society could and should be improved. But he was never certain that reform, if achieved, would be permanent. Enlightenment optimism constituted a tempered hopefulness rather than a glib certainty. Pessimism was an undercurrent in most Enlightenment works.

THE ENCYCLOPEDIA

The mid-century witnessed the publication of the *Encyclopedia*, one of the greatest monuments of the Enlightenment. Under the leadership of Denis Diderot (1713–1784) and Jean le Rond d'Alembert (1717–1783), the first volume appeared in 1751. When completed in 1772, it numbered 17 volumes of text and 11 of plates. The *Encyclopedia* was the product of more than 100 authors, and its editors had solicited articles from the major French *philosophes*. The project reached fruition only after attempts to censor it and halt its publication. The *Encyclopedia* set forth the most advanced critical ideas in religion, government, and philosophy. The articles represented a plea for freedom of expression but also provided information on manufacturing, canal building, and agriculture.

The *Encyclopedia* had been designed to secularize learning, and the articles concentrated on humanity and its well-being. The encyclopedists looked to antiquity rather than to the Christian centuries for their intellectual and ethical models. The welfare of humankind lay in the application of reason to human relationships. The *Encyclopedia* diffused enlightened thought over the Continent, drawing in German and Russian thinkers.

THE ENLIGHTENMENT AND RELIGION

In the eyes of the *philosophes*, the chief enemy of the improvement and happiness of humankind was the church. Roman Catholicism especially invited their criticism. But all the churches perpetuated a religious view of humankind and nature and taught that human beings were sinful and required divine grace. Religion turned human interest away from this world to the world to come. For the *philosophes*, the churches fostered intolerance and bigotry.

DEISM

The *philosophes* believed that religion should be reasonable and lead to moral behavior. The Newtonian worldview had convinced many that nature was rational. Therefore, the God who had created nature must also be rational, and the religion through which that God was worshiped should be rational. Lockean philosophy, which limited human knowledge to empirical experience, cast doubt on divine revelation. These considerations gave rise to a movement for enlightened religion known as *deism.*

There were two major points in the deists' creed. The first was a belief in a rational God, which they thought could be empirically deduced from nature. Because a rational God must also favor rational morality, the second point was a belief in life after death, when rewards and punishments would be meted out according to the virtue of the life a person had led.

Deism was empirical, tolerant, reasonable, and capable of encouraging virtuous living. It was the major positive religious component of the Enlightenment.

TOLERATION

Such a life required religious toleration. Voltaire championed this cause. In 1762, the French authorities ordered the execution of a Huguenot named Jean Calas (1698–1762) for having allegedly murdered his son to prevent him from converting to Roman Catholicism. Calas had been tortured and publicly strangled without confessing his guilt.

Voltaire made the dead man's cause his own. In 1763 he published a *Treatise on Toleration* and hounded the authorities until in 1765 the decision against Calas was reversed. For Voltaire, the case illustrated religious fanaticism and the need for rational judicial reform. In 1779, the German writer Gotthold Lessing (1729–1781) wrote *Nathan the Wise* as a plea for toleration of all religious faiths. All of these calls for toleration argued that secular values were more important than religious ones. (See "Maria Theresa and Joseph II of Austria Debate Toleration.")

WHY DID the *philosophes* regard the church as the chief enemy of reform and human happiness?

17.6
On Universal Toleration: Voltaire

deism   A belief in a rational God who had created the universe, but then allowed it to function without his interference according to the mechanisms of nature and a belief in rewards and punishments after death for human action.

Charles de Secondat, Baron de Montesquieu (1689–1755) was the author of *The Spirit of the Laws*, possibly the most influential work of political thought of the eighteenth century.
Hulton/UPI/Corbis

· HISTORY'S VOICES ·

MARIA THERESA AND JOSEPH II OF AUSTRIA DEBATE TOLERATION

*I*n 1765, Joseph, the eldest son of the Empress Maria Theresa, had become co-regent with his mother. He began to believe that some measures of religious toleration should be introduced into the Habsburg realms. Maria Theresa, whose opinions on many political issues were quite advanced, adamantly refused to consider adopting a policy of toleration. This exchange of letters sets forth their sharply differing positions. The toleration of Protestants in dispute related only to Lutherans and Calvinists. Maria Theresa died in 1780; the next year Joseph issued an edict of toleration.

HOW DOES Joseph define toleration, and why does Maria Theresa believe it is the same as religious indifference? Why does Maria Theresa fear that toleration will bring about political as well as religious turmoil? Why does Maria Theresa think the belief in toleration has come from Joseph's acquaintance with wicked books? Compare the positions for and against religious toleration expressed in this correspondence to the actions of previous European rulers.

Joseph to Maria Theresa, July 20, 1777

. . . [I]t is only the word "toleration" which has caused the misunderstanding. You have taken it in quite a different meaning [from mine expressed in an earlier letter]. God preserve me from thinking it a matter of indifference whether the citizens turn Protestant or remain Catholic, still less, whether they cleave to, or at least observe, the cult which they have inherited from their fathers! I would give all I possess if all the Protestants of your states would go over to Catholicism.

The word "toleration," as I understand it, means only that I would employ any persons, without distinction of religion, in purely temporal matters, allow them to own property, practice trades, be citizens, if they were qualified and if this would be of advantage to the State and its industry. Those who, unfortunately, adhere to a false faith, are far further from being converted if they remain in their own country than if they migrate into another, in which they can hear and see the convincing truths of the Catholic faith. Similarly, the undisturbed practice of their religion makes them far better subjects and causes them to avoid irreligion, which is a far greater danger to our Catholics than if one lets them see others practice their religion unimpeded. . . .

Maria Theresa to Joseph, Late July, 1777

Without a dominant religion? Toleration, indifference are precisely the true means of undermining everything, taking away every foundation; we others will then be the greatest losers. . . . He is no friend of humanity, as the popular phrase is, who allows everyone his own thoughts. I am speaking only in the political sense, not as a Christian; nothing is so necessary and salutary as religion. Will you allow everyone to fashion his own religion as he pleases? No fixed cult, no subordination to the Church—what will then become of us? The result will not be quiet and contentment; its outcome will be the rule of the stronger and more unhappy times like those which we have already seen. A manifesto by you to this effect can produce the utmost distress and make you responsible for many thousands of souls. And what are my own sufferings, when I see you entangled in opinions so erroneous? What is at stake is not only the welfare of the State but your own salvation. . . . Turning your eyes and ears everywhere, mingling your spirit of contradiction with the simultaneous desire to create something, you are ruining yourself and dragging the Monarchy down with you into the abyss. . . . I only wish to live so long as I can hope to descend to my ancestors with the consolation that my son will be as great, as religious as his forebears, that he will return from his erroneous views, from those wicked books whose authors parade their cleverness at the expense of all that is most holy and most worthy of respect in the world, who want to introduce an imaginary freedom which can never exist and which degenerates into license and into complete revolution.

From *The Habsburg and Hohenzollern Dynasties in the Seventeenth and Eighteenth Centuries*, C. A. Macartney, ed., Copyright © 1980, Walker and Company, pp. 151–153. Reprinted by permission.

THE ENLIGHTENMENT AND SOCIETY

The *philosophes* believed that the application of human reason to society would reveal laws in human relationships similar to those found in physical nature. The discovery of social laws would remove the inhumanity that existed through ignorance of them.

ADAM SMITH

The most important Enlightenment exposition of economics was Adam Smith's (1723–1790) *An Inquiry into the Nature and Causes of the Wealth of Nations* (1776). Smith urged that the mercantile system of England be abolished. These modes of economic regulation by the state were intended to preserve the wealth of the nation and capture wealth from other nations. But Smith believed that they constricted wealth and production. He wanted to unleash individuals to pursue their own economic interest. The free pursuit of economic self-interest would ensure economic expansion as each person sought enrichment by meeting the demands of the marketplace.

Smith saw nature as a boundless expanse of physical resources to be exploited for the benefit of humankind. This idea, which dominated western life until recent years, stemmed from the Enlightenment. When Smith wrote, the population of the world was smaller, its people were poorer, and the quantity of undeveloped resources per capita was much greater. For people of the eighteenth century, the improvement of the human condition seemed to lie in the uninhibited exploitation of natural resources.

Smith is usually regarded as the founder of *laissez-faire* economics, which has argued for a limited role for government in economic life. However, Smith was not opposed to all government activity in the economy. The state should provide schools, armies, navies, and roads and undertake commercial ventures that were desirable but too risky for private enterprise. Indeed, most of the *philosophes* were less doctrinaire than any brief summary of their thought may suggest. They recognized human passions as well as reason. They adopted reason and nature as tools to create a climate of opinion that would allow humanity to flourish.

MONTESQUIEU AND *THE SPIRIT OF THE LAWS*

Charles Louis de Secondat, Baron de Montesquieu (1689–1755), was a French noble magistrate. His work *The Spirit of the Laws* (1748) was perhaps the most influential book of the century. Montesquieu pursued an empirical method, taking examples from both ancient and modern nations. He concluded that no single set of political laws could apply to all peoples at all times and in all places. Only a careful examination and evaluation of many variables could reveal what mode of government would prove most beneficial to a particular people. A century later, such speculations would have been classified as sociology.

For France, Montesquieu believed in a monarchy whose power was tempered and limited by intermediary institutions, including the aristocracy, the towns, the *parlements*, and other corporate bodies that enjoyed liberties that the monarch must respect. Their role was to limit the power of the monarchy and thus to preserve the liberty of the subjects. Montesquieu was a political conservative, but he hoped to achieve reform, for he considered the oppressive and inefficient absolutism of the monarchy responsible for degrading French life.

One of Montesquieu's most influential ideas was the division of power. He took Great Britain for his model: executive power resided in the king, legislative power in the Parliament, and judicial power in the courts. Any two branches could

---

HOW DID the *philosophes* hope that reason would change human society?

QUICK REVIEW

Adam Smith (1723-1790)

- Advocated abolition of mercantile system
- Smith saw nature as set of physical resources to be exploited by human beings
- Smith was in favor of limited government activity in the economy

---

laissez-faire   French phrase meaning "allow to do." In economics, the doctrine of minimal government interference in the working of the economy.

The writings of Jean-Jacques Rousseau
(1712–1778) raised some of the most profound social and ethical questions of the Enlightenment. This portrait by Maurice Quentin was made ca. 1740

Bildarchiv Preussischer Kulturbesitz

check and balance the power of the other. His perception of the eighteenth-century British constitution was incorrect, but the analysis illustrated his sense of the need to limit power through a constitution, and for legislatures, not monarchs, to make laws. Montesquieu's ideas had an enduring effect on the liberal democracies of the next two centuries.

ROUSSEAU

Jean-Jacques Rousseau (1712–1778) had a deep antipathy toward the society in which he lived. In 1750, in his *Discourse on the Moral Effects of the Arts and Sciences*, he contended that civilization and enlightenment had corrupted human nature. In 1755, in a *Discourse on the Origin of Inequality*, Rousseau blamed much of the evil in the world on maldistribution of property. Rousseau felt that the real purpose of society should be to nurture better people. His vision of reform was much more radical than that of other philosophers.

The Social Contract (1762) outlines the kind of political structure that Rousseau believed would overcome the evils of contemporary society. Most eighteenth-century political thinkers regarded society as a collection of independent individuals pursuing selfish goals. They wished to liberate these individuals from the undue bonds of government. Rousseau suggested that society is more important than its individual members, because they are what they are only as a result of their relationship to the larger community. Independent human beings living alone can achieve little. Through their relationship to the larger community, they become moral creatures capable of significant action. Rousseau drew on Plato and Calvin to define freedom as obedience to law. In his case, the law to be obeyed was that created by the general will. This concept normally indicated the will of the majority of voting citizens who acted with adequate information and under the influence of virtuous customs and morals. Rousseau believed that the general will must always be right and that to obey it was to be free. This argument led him to conclude that some people must be forced to be free. He thus justified radical direct democracy and collective action against individual citizens.

WOMEN IN THE THOUGHT AND PRACTICE OF THE ENLIGHTENMENT

Women, especially in France, helped to promote the careers of the *philosophes*. In Paris, the salons of women such as Marie-Thérèse Geoffrin (1699–1777), Julie de Lespinasse (1733–1776), and Claudine de Tencin (1689–1749) gave the *philosophes* a receptive environment for their ideas. These women were well connected to political figures who could help protect the *philosophes*. The Marquise de Pompadour (1721–1764), the mistress of Louis XV, for example, helped overcome efforts to censor the *Encyclopedia*.

Nonetheless, the *philosophes* advocated no radical changes in the social condition of women. Montesquieu, for example, believed women were not naturally inferior to men and should have a wider role in society. Yet he expected men to dominate marriage and family. Furthermore, although he supported the right of women to divorce and opposed laws that oppressed them, he upheld the ideal of female chastity.

In the *Encyclopedia*, the articles that dealt with women emphasized their physical inferiority, usually attributed to menstruation or childbearing, and conveyed the sense that women were reared to be frivolous. The encyclopedists discussed women primarily as daughters, wives, and mothers, and considered motherhood their most important occupation. The encyclopedists also upheld a double standard of sexual behavior. However, illustrations in the *Encyclopedia* showed women, many of them lower- and working-class, deeply involved in economic activity.

The salon of Mme. Marie-Thérèse Geoffrin (1699–1777) was one of the most important gathering spots for Enlightenment writers during the middle of the 18th century. Well-connected women such as Mme. Geoffrin were instrumental in helping the *philosophes* they patronized to bring their ideas to the attention of influential people in French society and politics.

Giraudon/Art Resource, N.Y.

Rousseau urged a traditional role for women. In his novel *Émile* (1762) he declared that women should be educated to be subordinate to men, emphasizing their function in bearing and rearing children. He portrayed them as weaker and inferior to men, except perhaps for their capacity for feeling and giving love, and excluded them from political life. Women were assigned the domestic sphere alone.

Despite these views and his own ill treatment of the women who bore his many children, Rousseau achieved a vast following among women in the eighteenth century, perhaps because his writings stressed women's emotions and subjective feelings. He portrayed the domestic life and the role of wife and mother as a noble vocation, giving middle- and upper-class women a sense that their lives had purpose.

In 1792, in *A Vindication of the Rights of Woman*, Mary Wollstonecraft (1759–1797) brought Rousseau before the judgment of the rational Enlightenment ideal of progressive knowledge. Wollstonecraft accused Rousseau and others who upheld traditional roles for women of attempting to narrow women's vision and limit their experience. She argued that to confine women to the separate domestic sphere because of their supposed physiological limitations was to make them the sensual slaves of men and prevent them from achieving their own moral or intellectual identity. Denying good education to women would impede human progress. Wollstonecraft was demanding for women the kind of intellectual liberty that male writers of the Enlightenment were championing for men.

ENLIGHTENED ABSOLUTISM

During the last third of the century, several European rulers embraced many of the *philosophes*' reforms. *Enlightened absolutism* is the term used to describe this phenomenon. The phrase indicates monarchical government dedicated to the rational strengthening of the central absolutist administration at the cost of lesser centers of power. The monarchs most closely associated with it—Frederick II of Prussia, Joseph II of Austria, and Catherine II of Russia—often found that the political and social realities of their realms caused them to moderate both their enlightenment and their absolutism. They corresponded with *philosophes*, invited them

WHAT WAS enlightened absolutism?

Russia from Peter the Great through Catherine the Great

1725	Death of Peter the Great
1741–1762	Elizabeth
1762	Peter III
1762	Catherine II (the Great) becomes empress
1767	Legislative Commission summoned
1768	War with Turkey
1771–1774	Pugachev's Rebellion
1772	First Partition of Poland
1774	Treaty of Kuchuk-Kainardji ends war with Turkey
1775	Reorganization of local government
1783	Russia annexes the Crimea
1785	Catherine issues the Charter of the Nobility
1793	Second Partition of Poland
1795	Third Partition of Poland
1796	Death of Catherine the Great

to court, and imposed reforms that contemporaries believed derived from suggestions of the *philosophes*.

However, the relationship between these rulers and the writers of the Enlightenment was more complicated. The rulers sought the rational economic and social integration of their realms to achieve military strength. They and their advisers used "enlightened" reforms to pursue many goals admired by the *philosophes* but also to further what the *philosophes* considered irrational militarism.

JOSEPH II OF AUSTRIA

No eighteenth-century ruler so embodied rational, impersonal force as the emperor Joseph II of Austria, the son of Maria Theresa (r. 1740–1780). He prided himself on a narrow, passionless rationality, which he sought to impose on the Habsburg domains. Joseph II genuinely wished to improve the lot of his peoples. His well-intentioned efforts led to aristocratic and peasant rebellions from Hungary to the Austrian Netherlands.

Austria was the most diverse state of the eighteenth century. The Habsburgs never succeeded in creating a unified administrative structure or strong aristocratic loyalty. The price of preserving the monarchy during the War of the Austrian Succession (1740–1748) had been guarantees of aristocratic independence, especially in Hungary.

During and after the conflict, however, Maria Theresa had strengthened her powers in Austria and Bohemia. She imposed a more efficient system of tax collection that extracted funds even from the clergy and the nobles, and she established central councils to deal with governmental problems. She tried to bring all educational institutions into the service of the crown so that she could have enough educated officials, and she expanded primary education.

Maria Theresa was also concerned about the peasants and serfs and limited the services that landowners could demand from them. This concern arose from her desire to assure a good military recruitment pool. In her desire to stimulate prosperity and military strength by royal initiative, Maria Theresa anticipated the policies of her son.

However, his reforms were more wide ranging than his mother's. His greatest ambition was to overcome the pluralism of the Habsburg holdings by increasing the power of the central monarchy that Maria Theresa had wisely not disturbed. In particular, Joseph sought to lessen Hungarian autonomy. He refused to have himself crowned king of Hungary and thus avoided having to guarantee Hungarian privileges in a coronation oath. He reorganized local government in Hungary to increase the authority of his own officials, and he required the use of German in government. But the Magyar nobility resisted, and in 1790 Joseph had to rescind most of his centralizing measures.

In religion, Joseph extended freedom of worship to Lutherans, Calvinists, and the Greek Orthodox, and relieved the Jews of signs of personal degradation and gave them the right of private worship. Joseph also sought to control the Roman Catholic Church. He forbade direct communication between bishops and the pope. He dissolved over 600 monasteries and confiscated their lands, and replaced the traditional Roman Catholic seminaries with eight general seminaries that emphasized parish duties. Joseph's policies made Roman Catholic priests the employees of

QUICK REVIEW

Joseph II of Austria (r. 1765-1790)

- ✦ Attempted widespread reforms based on Enlightenment principles
- ✦ Resistance forced Joseph to rescind most of his centralizing efforts
- ✦ Abolished serfdom and gave peasants more personal freedom

the state and ended the independent influence of the church. These ecclesiastical policies, known as *Josephinism*, prefigured those of the French Revolution.

Joseph believed that reducing traditional burdens would make the peasants more productive and industrious. He abolished the servile status of serfdom and gave peasants more personal freedom. They could marry, engage in skilled work, or have their children trained in skills without permission of the landlord. The manorial courts were reformed, and peasants could appeal to royal officials. Joseph also encouraged landlords to change land leases, so that it would be easier for peasants to inherit them or to transfer them to another peasant.

In 1789, Joseph proposed a new system of land taxation. All proprietors were to be taxed, regardless of social status. But in 1790 Joseph died, and the system never went into effect. However, his measures had stirred up turmoil. Peasants revolted over disagreements about their newly granted rights. The nobles protested the taxation scheme. His brother Leopold II (r. 1790–1792), although sympathetic to Joseph's goals, had to repeal many of the most controversial decrees.

CATHERINE THE GREAT OF RUSSIA

Joseph II never grasped the necessity of cultivating support for his policies. Catherine II (r. 1762–1796) understood the fragility of the Romanov dynasty's power.

After the death of Peter the Great in 1725, the court nobles and the army had determined the Russian succession. Peter's daughter Elizabeth (r. 1741–1762) was succeeded by Peter III, one of her nephews. He was a weak and possibly insane ruler who had been married in 1745 to a young German princess, the future Catherine the Great. After a few months, Peter III was deposed and murdered with Catherine's approval, and she was proclaimed empress.

Catherine's familiarity with the Enlightenment and western Europe convinced her that Russia must make reforms to remain a great power. Since she had come to the throne through a palace coup, she understood that any major reform must enjoy wide support.

Consequently, in 1767 Catherine summoned a Legislative Commission to advise her on revising the government of Russia. There were over 500 delegates from all sectors of Russian life. Catherine wrote a set of *Instructions*, containing ideas drawn from the *philosophes*. Catherine dismissed the commission before several of its key committees reported, but it had gathered a vast amount of information about conditions in Russia, and its debates suggested that most Russians saw no alternative to an autocratic monarchy. Catherine herself had no intention of departing from absolutism.

Catherine carried out limited reforms on her own authority. In 1775, she reorganized local government to solve problems brought to light by the Legislative Commission. She put most local offices into the hands of nobles rather than creating a royal bureaucracy. In 1785, Catherine issued the Charter of the Nobility, which guaranteed noble rights and privileges. She issued a similar charter to the towns of her realms. The empress had to favor the nobles. She had too few educated subjects to

MAP EXPLORATION
Interactive map: To explore this map further, go to
http://www.prenhall.com/craig2/map23.1

MAP 23–1

Expansion of Russia, 1689–1796. The overriding territorial aim of the two most powerful Russian monarchs of the 18th century, Peter the Great (in the first quarter of the century) and Catherine the Great (in the last half of the century) was to secure navigable outlets to the sea in both the north and the south for Russia's vast empire; hence Peter's push to the Baltic Sea and Catherine's to the Black Sea. Catherine also managed to acquire much of Poland through the partitions of that country.

WHICH EMPIRE came into direct conflict with Russian expansion?

Catherine the Great, here portrayed as a young princess, ascended to the Russian throne after the murder of her husband. She tried initially to enact major reforms but she never intended to abandon absolutism. She assured the nobility of their rights and by the end of her reign had imposed press censorship.

Corbis-Bettmann

establish an independent bureaucracy, and the treasury could not afford an army strictly loyal to the crown. So Catherine strengthened her crown by a convenient alliance with her nobles and urban leaders.

Catherine continued the Russian drive for warm-water ports. This led to warfare with the Turks between 1768 and 1774, when the Treaty of Kuchuk-Kainardji gave Russia a direct outlet on the Black Sea. Catherine annexed the Crimea in 1783.

THE PARTITION OF POLAND

These Russian military successes made the other states of eastern Europe uneasy. Their anxieties were allayed by the First Partition of Poland (see Map 23-1). Frederick the Great made a proposal to Russia and Austria that would give each something it wanted, prevent conflict among them, and save appearances. After complicated, secret negotiations among the three powers, the Polish state lost approximately one-third of its territory. Two additional partitions of Poland in 1793 and 1795 removed it from the map of Europe until 1919. Without a strong central government, Poland's political weakness made the country and its resources ripe for plunderous aggression by the strong states that surround it.

MAP 23–2
Partitions of Poland, 1772, 1793, and 1795. The eradication of Poland from the map displayed eighteenth-century power politics at its most extreme.

WHY WAS Poland so easily destroyed in the eighteenth century?

SUMMARY

The Scientific Revolution The scientific ideas of the sixteenth and seventeenth centuries changed the way Western intellectuals thought about the world and humankind. Instead of a view of nature and humanity based on Scripture and divine revelation, Western thinkers came to rely on mathematical laws, empirical data, and experimentation. Copernicus, Kepler, and Galileo overturned the ancient idea, sanctioned by the Bible, that the Earth was the center of the universe and that the sun and the planets revolved around it. Galileo and Descartes maintained that the world was governed by mathematical laws. Francis Bacon urged the necessity for observation and experimentation. Newton showed the effects of gravity and established an enduring basis for physics. Locke argued that human beings were masters of their own destiny.

The Enlightenment The Enlightenment *philosophes* used reason as a basis for reform and to advocate progressive social, economic, and political movements. Voltaire attacked religious intolerance and advocated strong central government to impose rational solutions to social and political problems. Montesquieu and other *philosophes* argued for limited, constitutional government. Rousseau wished to reform society in the name of virtue rather than material happiness. He maintained that in the pursuit of virtue the needs of society were more important than those of the individual. The spirit of the Enlightenment continues to pervade Western society.

Enlightened Absolutism Enlightened absolutism was a form of monarchical government dedicated to the rational strengthening of the central government. Many of the reforms enlightened monarchs imposed were influenced by the ideas of the *philosophes*, but the chief goal of these rulers was to increase their own authority and military strength, as witnessed by the partitions of Poland among Russia, Prussia, and Austria at the end of the eighteenth century. The most important enlightened monarchs were Frederick II of Prussia, Joseph II of Austria, and Catherine the Great of Russia.

IMAGE KEY
for pages 494–495

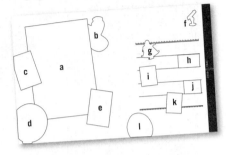

a. Astronomer Tycho Brahe from the *Atlas Major* by Joan Blaeu
b. Jean-Jacques Rousseau
c. Embroidery tools and techniques from *Encyclopedia* by Denis Diderot
d. Engraving of John Locke
e. A slaughterhouse and butchering tools from *Encyclopedia* by Denis Diderot
f. Newton's first telescope
g. One of Galileo's early telescopes.
h. The composing room of a print shop
i. Voltaire (Francois-Marie Arouet)
j. The salon of Mme. Marie-Therese Geoffrin
k. Russian empress Catherine II
l. Author Mary Wollstonecraft

REVIEW QUESTIONS

1. What did Copernicus, Galileo, and Newton contribute to the Scientific Revolution? In what ways was the Scientific Revolution truly revolutionary?

2. How did the Enlightenment change Western attitudes toward reform, faith, and reason? How important were Voltaire and the *Encyclopedia* in the success of the Enlightenment?

3. Why did the *philosophes* consider organized religion to be their greatest enemy?

4. What were the separate spheres Rousseau imagined men and women occupying? Did Rousseau value the individual or society more?

5. What motivated the enlightened monarchs' reforms?

KEY TERMS

deism (p. 501)
empiricism (p. 497)
Enlightenment (p. 496)
laissez-faire (p. 503)
philosophes (p. 499)
Ptolemaic system (p. 496)
Scientific Revolution (p. 496)

 For additional study resources for this chapter, go to:
www.prenhall.com/craig/chapter23

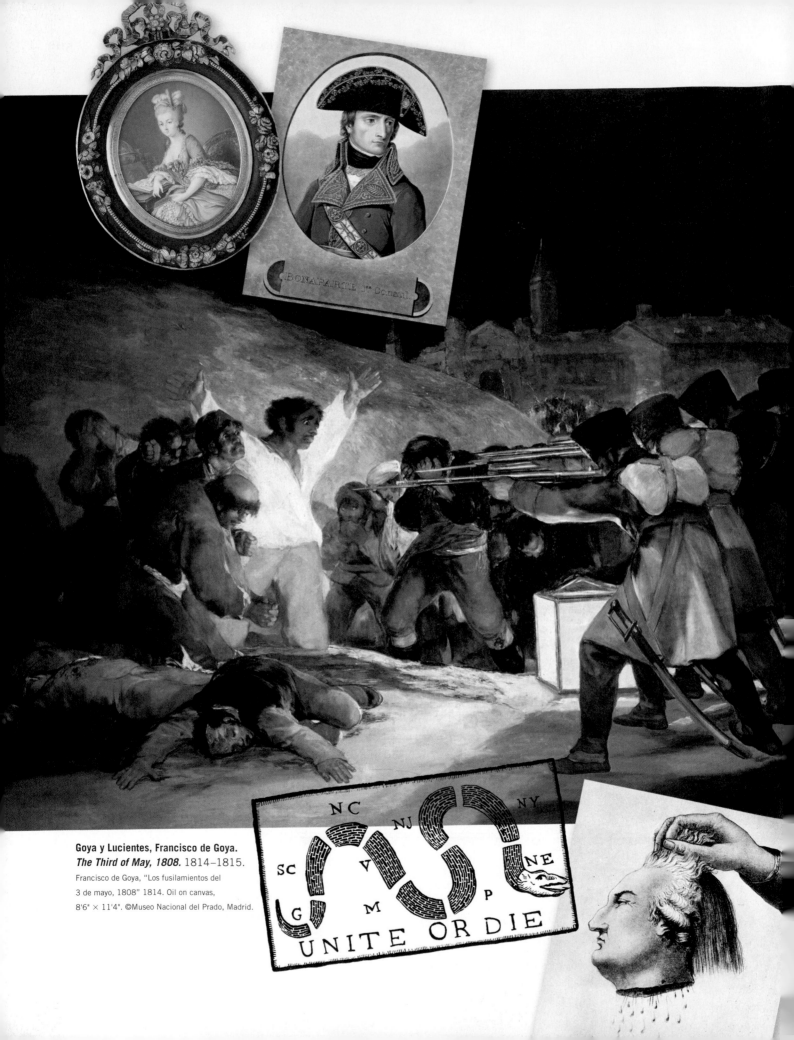

Goya y Lucientes, Francisco de Goya.
The Third of May, 1808. 1814–1815.

Francisco de Goya, "Los fusilamientos del
3 de mayo, 1808" 1814. Oil on canvas,
8'6" × 11'4". ©Museo Nacional del Prado, Madrid.

UNITE OR DIE

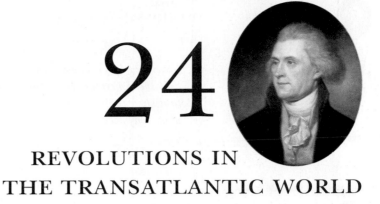

24

REVOLUTIONS IN THE TRANSATLANTIC WORLD

WHAT WAS the new sense of liberty that arose from the American Revolution?

HOW DID the French Revolution and Napoleon transform France's government and society?

WHY DID Latin America throw off Spanish and Portuguese rule?

WHY DID slavery become unacceptable in Western society?

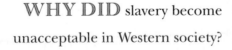

IMAGE KEY
Image Key for pages 510–511
is on page 532.

Between 1776 and 1824, a world-transforming series of revolutions occurred in France and the Americas. In a half century, the peoples of the two American continents established their independence of European political control. In Europe, the French monarchy collapsed. All the revolutionary leaders sought to establish new governments based largely on Enlightenment principles. The era also witnessed the commencement of an international crusade to abolish first the slave trade and then slavery in the transatlantic world.

WHAT WAS the new sense of liberty that arose from the American Revolution?

MAP EXPLORATION

Interactive map: To explore this map further, go to
http://www.prenhall.com/craig2/map24.1

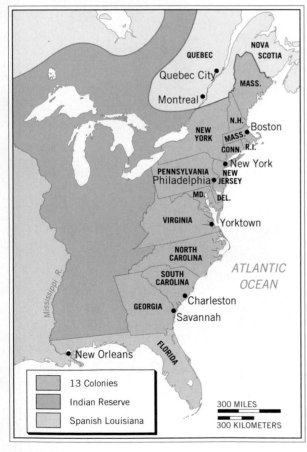

MAP 24–1

North America in 1763.   In the year of the victory over France, the English colonies lay along the Atlantic seaboard. The difficulties of organizing authority over the previous French territory in Canada and west of the Appalachian Mountains would contribute to the coming of the American Revolution.

HOW WOULD westward expansion affect Native Americans?

REVOLUTION IN THE BRITISH COLONIES IN NORTH AMERICA

RESISTANCE TO THE IMPERIAL SEARCH FOR REVENUE

After the Treaty of Paris in 1763 ended the Seven Years' War, the British government faced two imperial problems. The first was the cost of empire, which the British felt they could no longer carry alone. The second was the need to organize a vast new territory: all of North America east of the Mississippi.

The British drive for revenue began in 1764 with the Sugar Act, which attempted to produce more revenue from imports into the colonies by the rigorous collection of what was actually a reduced tax on sugar. Smugglers were to be tried in admiralty courts without juries. The next year, Parliament passed the Stamp Act, which put a tax on legal documents and other items. The British considered these taxes just because they had been approved by Parliament and because the revenue was to be spent in the colonies. The Americans responded that they alone had the right to tax themselves and that they were not represented in Parliament.

In the face of protest and disorder in America, Parliament repealed the Stamp Act in 1766 but claimed the power to legislate for the colonies.

AMERICAN POLITICAL IDEAS

The American colonists believed that the English Revolution of 1688 had established their own fundamental liberties. They claimed that George III (r. 1760–1820) and the British Parliament were attacking those liberties and dissolving the bonds of allegiance that had united the two peoples. The colonists thus employed a theory that had been developed to justify an aristocratic rebellion in England to support their own popular revolution.

In addition to these Whig political ideas, largely derived from John Locke (1632–1704), the Americans had also become familiar with British political writers called the *Commonwealthmen*, who held republican political ideas that had their roots in the radical thought of the Puritan revolution. They regarded much parliamentary taxation as a means of financing political corruption and attacked standing armies as instruments of tyranny. The policy of Great Britain toward America after the Treaty of Paris made many colonists believe that the worst fears of the Commonwealthmen were coming true.

CRISIS AND INDEPENDENCE

In May 1773, Parliament allowed the East India Company to import tea directly into the American colonies. Although the law lowered the price of tea, it retained a tax on it without the colonists' consent. In Boston, a shipload of tea was thrown into the harbor, known since as the Boston Tea Party.

The British ministry of Lord North (1732–1792) was determined to assert the authority of Parliament over the colonies. In 1774, Parliament closed the port of Boston, reorganized the government of Massachusetts, allowed troops to be quartered in private homes, and removed the trials of royal customs officials to England. Parliament also extended the boundaries of Quebec to include the Ohio River valley which the Americans regarded as an attempt to prevent the extension of their mode of self-government westward beyond the Appalachian Mountains.

During these years, committees of correspondence, composed of citizens critical of Britain, had been established throughout the colonies. In September 1774, these committees organized the First Continental Congress in Philadelphia. This body failed to persuade Parliament to abandon its attempt at direct supervision of colonial affairs. In 1775, the battles of Lexington, Concord, and Bunker Hill were fought, and the Second Continental Congress undertook the government of the colonies. In August 1775, George III declared the colonies in rebellion. During the winter, Thomas Paine's (1737–1809) pamphlet *Common Sense* galvanized public opinion in favor of separation from Great Britain. A colonial army and navy were organized. Finally, on July 4, 1776, the Continental Congress adopted the Declaration of Independence. The War of the American Revolution continued until 1781, when the forces of George Washington (1732–1799) defeated those of Lord Cornwallis (1738–1805) at Yorktown. In 1778, however, the war had widened into a European conflict when the French government supported the rebellion. In 1779, Spain also came to the aid of the colonies. The 1783 Treaty of Paris concluded the conflict, and the thirteen American colonies had established their independence.

As the crisis with Britain unfolded, the American colonists came to see themselves as first preserving traditional English liberties and then as developing a new sense of liberty. By the mid-1770s, the colonists had embraced republican political ideals. After the Constitution was adopted in 1788, Americans insisted on a bill of rights to protect civil liberties. The Americans would reject the aristocratic social hierarchy that had existed in the colonies. They would embrace democratic ideals, even if the franchise remained limited. They would assert the equality of white male citizens before the law and in social relations. They would reject social status based on birth and inheritance and assert the necessity of liberty for all citizens to improve their social standing and economic lot by engaging in free commercial activity. They did not free their slaves, nor did they address the rights of women or Native Americans, but the American Revolution produced a society freer than any the world had seen, one that would expand political and social liberty. The American Revolution was a radical movement, the influence of which would increase as Americans moved across the continent and as other peoples began to question traditional European government. The American Revolution would inspire the Wars of Independence in Latin America and liberal and radical political movements in Europe.

The American Revolution

1760	George III becomes king
1763	Treaty of Paris concludes the Seven Years' War
1764	Sugar Act
1765	Stamp Act
1766	Stamp Act repealed and Declaratory Act passed
1770	Lord North becomes George III's chief minister
1773	Boston Tea Party
1774	First Continental Congress
1775	Second Continental Congress
1776	Declaration of Independence
1778	France enters the war on the side of America
1781	British forces surrender at Yorktown
1783	Treaty of Paris concludes War of the American Revolution

18.4
Declaration of Independence:
Revolutionary Declarations

REVOLUTION IN FRANCE

T he French monarchy emerged from the Seven Years' War defeated and deeply in debt. Support for the American Revolution exacerbated its financial difficulties. Given the economic vitality of France, the government debt was not overly large, but the government could not collect sufficient taxes to service and repay the debt.

Between 1786 and 1788, Louis XVI's (r. 1774–1792) ministers failed to persuade the aristocracy and the church to pay more taxes. As these negotiations dragged on, the *parlement* of Paris declared that only the Estates General could institute new taxes. The Estates General had not met since 1614. In July 1788, Louis agreed to convene the Estates General.

REVOLUTIONS OF 1789

The Estates General Becomes the National Assembly The Estates General had three divisions: the First Estate of the clergy, the Second Estate of the nobility, and the **Third Estate**, representing everyone else. The Estates General met at Versailles in May 1789. On June 1, the Third Estate, composed largely of local officials, professional men, and lawyers, invited the clergy and nobles to join it in organizing a new legislative body. A few of the lower clergy did so. On June 17, that body declared itself the National Assembly.

Three days later, finding themselves accidentally locked out of their usual meeting place, the National Assembly moved to a nearby tennis court, where its members took the famous Tennis Court Oath to sit until they had given France a constitution. Louis XVI ordered the National Assembly to desist, but most of the clergy and many nobles joined the assembly. On June 27, the king capitulated and the National Assembly became the National Constituent Assembly.

Fall of the Bastille Two new factors soon intruded. First, Louis XVI attempted to regain the initiative by mustering troops near Versailles and Paris. This was the beginning of a poorly executed, royal attempt to halt the revolution. Most of the National Constituent Assembly wished to create a constitutional monarchy, but Louis's refusal to cooperate thwarted that effort.

The second new factor was the populace of Paris. The mustering of royal troops created anxiety in the city, where there had been several bread riots. By June, the Parisians were organizing a citizen militia and collecting arms.

On July 14, a crowd marched to the Bastille in search of weapons for the militia. This great fortress had once held political prisoners. The troops in the Bastille fired into the crowd which then stormed the fortress, released its seven prisoners, none of whom was there for political reasons, and killed the governor. They found no weapons.

This was the first of many *journées*, or days when the populace of Paris would redirect the course of the revolution. Similar disturbances took place in the provincial cities. Louis XVI came to Paris and recognized the new elected government of the city and its National Guard.

The Great Fear and Surrender of Feudal Privileges As disturbances erupted in various cities, the *Great Fear* swept across the French countryside. Peasants were reclaiming rights and property that they had lost through the aristocratic resurgence of the last quarter century, as well as venting their anger against the injustices of rural life. The Great Fear witnessed the burning of châteaux, the destruction of documents, and the refusal by peasants to pay feudal dues.

HOW DID the French Revolution and Napoleon transform France's government and society?

QUICK REVIEW

National Assembly

♦ June 17, 1789: Third Estate declares itself National Assembly

♦ Tennis Court Oath: pledge to sit until France had a constitution

♦ June 27, 1789: king capitulates to National Assembly

18.8
Edmund Burke: Reflections on the Revolution in France

Third Estate The branch of the French Estates General representing all of the kingdom outside the nobility and the clergy.

On July 14, 1789, crowds stormed the Bastille, a prison in Paris. This event, whose only practical effect was to free a few prisoners, marked the first time the populace of Paris redirected the course of the revolution.

Musee de la Ville de Paris, Musee Carnavalet/ Giraudon/Art Resource, NY

On the night of August 4, 1789, aristocrats in the assembly attempted to halt the disorder. By prearrangement, liberal nobles and churchmen surrendered hunting and fishing rights, judicial authority, tithes, and special exemptions. These nobles gave up what they had already lost and what they could not have regained without civil war. Later, many would also be compensated for their losses. Nonetheless, after August 4 all French citizens were subject to the same laws.

Declaration of the Rights of Man and Citizen   On August 27, 1789, the assembly issued the *Declaration of the Rights of Man and Citizen*. It proclaimed that all men were born free and equal with natural rights to liberty, property, and personal safety. Governments existed to protect those rights. All political sovereignty resided in the nation and its representatives. All citizens were to be equal before the law and to be equally admissible to public offices according to their natural abilities and character. There were to be due process of law and presumption of innocence until proof of guilt. Freedom of religion was affirmed. Taxation was to be apportioned equally according to capacity to pay. Property was a sacred right.

 18.7
Declaration of the Rights of Man and Citizen

Louis XVI stalled before ratifying the declaration and the aristocratic renunciation of feudalism. His hesitations fanned suspicions that he might try to resort to force. Moreover, bread shortages continued. On October 5, several thousand Parisian women marched to Versailles, demanding more bread. This was one of several occasions when women played a major role in the Parisian crowd. The king agreed to sanction the decrees of the assembly, but the Parisians demanded that Louis and his family return to Paris. The monarch had no choice.

On October 6, 1789, he and his family followed the crowd and settled in the palace of the Tuileries. The assembly went too. Thereafter, both Paris and France remained relatively stable until the summer of 1792.

RECONSTRUCTION OF FRANCE

The National Constituent Assembly set about reorganizing France. The assembly was determined to protect property and limit the impact on national life of small-property owners as well as of the unpropertied elements of the nation. While championing equality before the law, the assembly spurned social equality and extensive democracy. It thus charted a course that nineteenth-century liberals across Europe and in other areas of the world would follow.

Political Reorganization   The Constitution of 1791 established a constitutional monarchy. There was a unicameral Legislative Assembly. The monarch could delay but not halt legislation. Voting was restricted to about 50,000 citizens of the French nation of 26 million.

The exclusion of women from both voting and holding office did not pass unnoticed. In 1791, Olympe de Gouges (d. 1793), a butcher's daughter who became a radical in Paris, composed a *Declaration of the Rights of Woman*, which she ironically addressed to Queen Marie Antoinette (1755–1793). Much of the document added the word *woman* to the *Declaration of the Rights of Man and Citizen*. That strategy demanded that women be regarded as citizens and not merely as daughters, sisters, wives, and mothers of citizens. Olympe de Gouges further outlined rights that would permit women to own property and require men to recognize the paternity of their children. She called for equality of the sexes in marriage and improved education for women. Her demands illustrated how the public listing of rights in the *Declaration of the Rights of Man and Citizen* created expectations even among those it did not cover. (See "French Women Petition to Bear Arms")

The National Constituent Assembly replaced the ancient French Provinces with 83 departments *(départements)*. The ancient judicial courts, including the *parlements*, were replaced by uniform courts with elected judges and prosecutors. Legal procedures were simplified, and the most degrading punishments abolished.

Economic Policy   The National Constituent Assembly suppressed the guilds, liberated the grain trade, and established the metric system of uniform weights and measures. In 1790, the assembly placed the burden of proof on the peasants to rid themselves of the residual feudal dues for which compensation was to be paid. In 1791, it enacted the Chapelier Law forbidding worker associations, thereby crushing the attempts of urban workers to protect their wages. Peasants and workers were to be left to the mercy of the free marketplace.

The assembly decided to pay the troublesome royal debt by confiscating and selling the lands of the Roman Catholic Church. The assembly authorized the issuance of ***assignats***, or government bonds, the value of which was guaranteed by the revenue generated from the sale of church property. When the *assignats* began to circulate as currency, the assembly issued even larger quantities of them to liquidate the national debt. However, the value of *assignats* soon began to fall. Inflation increased and put new stress on the urban poor.

Civil Constitution of the Clergy   In July 1790, the assembly issued the Civil Constitution of the Clergy, which transformed the Roman Catholic Church into a branch of the state. This measure reduced the number of bishoprics, made borders of dioceses conform to those of the new departments, and provided for the

assignats   Government bonds based on the value of confiscated church lands issued during the early French Revolution.

A VARENNE · LE 22   JUIN 1791 ·

A CORDÉE A M.
50 MILLE LIVRE
20 MILLE LIVRE

Gardes nationaux qui ont bravé les menaces d'un détachement de hussards, qui avoit été commandé par le traître Bouillé! M. Sauce, Procureur de la Commune, a invité le Roi d'entrer chez lui, & de s'y reposer lui & sa famille. Le généreux citoyen de Varennes n'a point accepté les offres du Roi, disant qu'il devoit tout à sa patrie.

election of priests and bishops, who became salaried employees of the state. The assembly consulted neither the pope nor the French clergy about these changes. The king approved the measure reluctantly.

The Civil Constitution of the Clergy roused immense opposition within the French church. The assembly ruled that all clergy must take an oath to support the Civil Constitution. Only about half the clergy did so. In reprisal, the assembly designated the clergy who had not taken the oath as "refractory" and removed them from their clerical functions. Refractory priests immediately attempted to celebrate mass.

In February 1791, the pope condemned not only the Civil Constitution of the Clergy but also the *Declaration of the Rights of Man and Citizen.* That condemnation marked the opening of a Roman Catholic offensive against liberalism and revolution that continued for over a century. Within France itself, the pope's action meant that religious devotion and revolutionary loyalty became incompatible for many people. French citizens divided between supporters of the constitutional priests and of the refractory clergy. Louis XVI favored the latter.

Counterrevolutionary Activity   In the summer of 1791, the queen and some nobles persuaded Louis XVI to flee. The escape failed. Thereafter, the leaders of the National Constituent Assembly knew that the chief counterrevolutionary sat on the French throne.

On August 27, 1791, Leopold II of Austria (r. 1790–1792), who was the brother of Marie Antoinette, and Frederick William II (r. 1786–1797) of Prussia issued the Declaration of Pillnitz. They promised to intervene in France to protect the royal family if the other major European powers agreed. The latter provision rendered the statement meaningless because Great Britain would not consent. However, the revolutionaries felt surrounded by aristocratic and monarchical foes.

In September 1791, the National Constituent Assembly forbade its members to sit in the Legislative Assembly then being elected. This new body met on October 1.

One of the key events of the French Revolution was the unsuccessful attempt by Louis XVI and his family to escape the country in June 1791. They were recognized and captured in the French city of Varennes and then returned to Paris under armed escort.

Corbis-Bettmann

· HISTORY'S VOICES ·

FRENCH WOMEN PETITION TO BEAR ARMS

The issue of women serving in the revolutionary French military appeared early in the revolution. In March 1791, Pauline Léon presented a petition to the National Assembly on behalf of more than 300 Parisian women asking the right to bear arms and train for military service for the revolution. Similar requests were made during the next two years. Some women did serve in the military, but in 1793, legislation specifically forbade it on the grounds that women belonged in the domestic sphere and that military service would lead them to abandon family duties.

CITOYENNE IS the feminine form of the French word for citizen. How does this petition seek to challenge the concept of citizenship in the *French Declaration of the Rights of Man and Citizen?* How do these petitioners relate their demand to bear arms to their role as women in French society? How do the petitioners relate their demands to the use of all national resources against the enemies of the revolution?

Patriotic women come before you to claim the right which any individual has to defend his life and liberty.

. . . We are *citoyennes* [female citizens], and we cannot be indifferent to the fate of the fatherland.

. . . Yes, Gentlemen, we need arms, and we come to ask your permission to procure them. May our weakness be no obstacle; courage and intrepidity will supplant it, and the love of the fatherland and hatred of tyrants will allow us to brave all dangers with ease. . . .

No, Gentlemen, We will [use arms] only to defend ourselves the same as you; you cannot refuse us, and society cannot deny the right nature gives us, unless you pretend the *Declaration of Rights* does not apply to women and that they should let their throats be cut like lambs, without the right to defend themselves. For can you believe the tyrants would spare us? . . . Why then not terrorize aristocracy and tyranny with all the resources of civic effort and the pure zeal, zeal which cold men can well call fanaticism and exaggeration, but which is only the natural result of a heart burning with love for the public weal? . . .

. . . If, for reasons we cannot guess, you refuse our just demands, these women you have raised to the ranks of *citoyennes* by granting that title to their husbands, these women who have sampled the promises of liberty, who have conceived the hope of placing free men in the world, and who have sworn to live free or die—such women, I say, will never consent to concede the day to slaves; they will die first. They will uphold their oath, and a dagger aimed at their breasts will deliver them from the misfortunes of slavery! They will die, regretting not life, but the uselessness of their death; regretting moreover, not having been able to drench their hands in the impure blood of the enemies of the fatherland and to avenge some of their own!

But, Gentlemen, let us cast our eyes away from these cruel extremes. Whatever the rages and plots of aristocrats, they will not succeed in vanquishing a whole people of united brothers armed to defend their rights. We also demand only the honor of sharing their exhaustion and glorious labors and of making tyrants see that women also have blood to shed for the service of the fatherland in danger.

Gentlemen, here is what we hope to obtain from your justice and equity:

1. Permission to procure pikes, pistols, and sabres (even muskets for those who are strong enough to use them), within police regulations.

2. Permission to assemble on festival days and Sundays on the Champ de la Fédération, or in other suitable places, to practice maneuvers with these arms.

3. Permission to name the former French Guards to command us, always in conformity with the rules which the mayor's wisdom prescribes for good order and public calm.

From "French Women Petition to Bear Arms" in *Women in Revolutionary Paris 1789–1795*, trans. by Darline Gay Levy, Harriet Branson Applewhite, and Mary Durham Johnson. © 1979 by the Board of Trustees of the University of Illinois. Used with permission of the authors and the University of Illinois Press.

A Second Revolution

Since the earliest days of the revolution, clubs of politically like-minded persons had organized themselves in Paris. The best organized were the *Jacobins*, who were linked to clubs in the provinces. In the Legislative Assembly, a group of Jacobins known as the *Girondists* (because many came from the department of the Gironde) led it on April 20, 1792, to declare war on Austria.

End of the Monarchy   The war radicalized the revolution and led to the *second revolution*, which established a republic. The war went poorly, and the revolution seemed in danger. Late in July, under radical working-class pressure, the government of Paris passed to a committee, or commune, of representatives from the municipal wards. On August 10, 1792, a large crowd invaded the Tuileries and forced Louis XVI and Marie Antoinette to take refuge in the Legislative Assembly. During the disturbance, royal guards and many Parisians died. Thereafter, the royal family was imprisoned, and the king suspended from his political functions.

The Convention and the Role of Sans-Culottes   In early September, the Paris Commune killed about 1,200 people in the city jails. Most were common criminals whom the crowd had assumed were counterrevolutionaries. The Commune then compelled the Legislative Assembly to call for the election, by universal manhood suffrage, of a new assembly to write a democratic constitution. That body, called the **Convention**, met on September 21, 1792.

The Convention declared France a republic. The second revolution had been the work of radical Jacobins and of the people of Paris known as the *sans-culottes*, meaning "without breeches," from the long trousers that, as working people, they wore instead of aristocratic knee breeches. The *sans-culottes* were shopkeepers, artisans, wage earners, and a few factory workers. The politics of the Old Regime had ignored them, and the National Constituent Assembly had left them victims of unregulated economic liberty.

The *sans-culottes* sought price controls for food. They resented most forms of social inequality and were hostile to the aristocracy and the original leaders of the revolution. They advocated a community of small property owners. They were antimonarchical, republican, and suspicious of government.

In contrast, the Jacobins were republicans who favored representative government and an unregulated economy. However, once the Convention began its deliberations, the more extreme Jacobins, known as the Mountain, worked with the *sans-culottes* to carry the revolution forward and win the war.

In December 1792, Louis XVI was put on trial and convicted of conspiring against the state. He was beheaded on January 21, 1793.

France was now at war with virtually all Europe. Civil war soon followed. In March 1793, aristocratic officers and priests commenced a royalist revolt in western France with local popular support.

The Reign of Terror and Its Aftermath

The **Reign of Terror** is the name given to the months of quasi-judicial executions and murders from autumn 1793 to mid-summer 1794. The Terror can be understood only in the context of the internal and external wars on the one hand, and the revolutionary expectations of the Convention and the *sans-culottes* on the other.

Committee of Public Safety   In April 1793, the Convention established a Committee of Public Safety that eventually enjoyed almost dictatorial power to save the revolution from enemies at home and abroad. It generally enjoyed a working political relationship with the *sans-culottes* of Paris.

Jacobins   The radical republican party during the French Revolution that displaced the Girondins.

Convention   French radical legislative body from 1792 to 1794.

sans-culottes   Meaning "without breeches." The lower-middle classes and artisans of Paris during the French Revolution.

Reign of Terror   The period between the summer of 1793 and the end of July 1794 when the French revolutionary state used extensive executions and violence to defend the Revolution and suppress its alleged internal enemies.

Louis XVI was executed on January 21, 1793.

Execution of Louis XVI. Aquatint. French, 18th century. Musée de la Ville de Paris, Musée Carnavalet, Paris, France. Giraudon/Art Resource, NY

In June 1793, the Parisian *sans-culottes* invaded the Convention and secured the expulsion of the Girondists. That gave the Mountain complete control. August 23 saw a **levée en masse**, or general military requisition of population, which conscripted males into the army and directed economic production for military purposes. On September 29, a maximum on prices was established in accord with *sans-culottes'* demands. During these same months, the armies of the revolution crushed many of the counterrevolutionary disturbances in the provinces.

The Society of Revolutionary Republican Women   In May 1793, Pauline Léon and Claire Lacombe founded the Society of Revolutionary Republican Women, which became increasingly radical. Its members sought stricter price controls, worked to ferret out food hoarders, and brawled with market women thought to be insufficiently revolutionary. The women of the Society also demanded the right to wear the revolutionary cap worn only by male citizens. By October 1793, the Jacobins in the Convention had begun to fear the turmoil the Society was causing and banned all women's clubs and societies.

There were other examples of repression of women in 1793. Olympe de Gouges opposed the Terror. She was tried and guillotined in November 1793. Women were excluded from the French army and from attending the galleries of the Convention.

Dechristianization   In October 1793, the Convention proclaimed a new calendar dating from the first day of the French Republic. There were 12 months of 30 days with names associated with the seasons and climate. In November 1793, the Convention decreed the Cathedral of Notre Dame to be a Temple of Reason. The legislature then sent trusted members, known as deputies-on-mission, into the

levée en masse   The French revolutionary conscription (1792) of all males into the army and the harnessing of the economy for war production.

provinces to enforce dechristianization by closing churches and persecuting clergy and believers. This religious policy roused much opposition and separated the provinces from the revolutionary government in Paris.

Progress of the Terror   During late 1793 and early 1794, Maximilien Robespierre (1758–1794) emerged as the chief figure on the Committee of Public Safety. The Jacobin Club provided his base of power. A shrewd politician, he depended on the support of the *sans-culottes* of Paris and opposed dechristianization as a political blunder.

The Reign of Terror manifested itself through a series of revolutionary tribunals established by the Convention during the summer of 1793. The tribunals were to try the enemies of the republic, but the definition of enemy shifted as the months passed. Marie Antoinette, other members of the royal family, and aristocrats were executed in October 1793. They were followed by Girondist politicians.

By early 1794, the Terror had moved to the provinces, where the deputies-on-mission presided over the execution of thousands of people. In Paris during the winter of 1794, Robespierre turned the Terror against republican political figures of the left and right and exterminated the leaders who might have threatened his own position. On June 10, he secured a law that permitted the revolutionary tribunal to convict suspects without evidence.

In May 1794, at the height of his power, Robespierre, considering the worship of reason too abstract for most citizens, abolished it and established the Cult of the Supreme Being. He did not long preside over this new religion. On July 27 (the Ninth of Thermidor), members of the Convention, by prearrangement, shouted him down when he rose to speak. Robespierre was executed the next day.

The Reign of Terror had claimed 40,000 victims. Most were peasants and *sans-culottes* who had rebelled against the revolutionary government. By the late summer of 1794, provincial uprisings had been crushed and the war against foreign enemies was going well. Those factors and the feeling that the revolution had consumed enough of its own children brought the Terror to an end.

The Thermidorian Reaction: End of the Terror and Establishment of the Directory   The tempering of the revolution, called the **Thermidorian Reaction**, began in July 1794. It set up a new constitutional regime. The influence of wealthy middle-class and professional people replaced that of the *sans-culottes*. Many of the people responsible for the Terror were removed from public life. The Jacobin Club was closed.

The Thermidorian Constitution of the Year III was a conservative document that provided for a bicameral legislative government favoring property owners. The executive body, consisting of a five-person Directory, was elected by the upper legislative house.

True to their belief in an unregulated economy, the Thermidorians repealed the ceiling on prices. When food riots resulted during the winter of 1794–1795, the Convention put them down to prove that the era of the *sans-culottes journées* had ended. On October 5, 1795, Paris rebelled. A general named Napoleon Bonaparte (1769–1821) dispersed the crowd with artillery. Other enemies of the Directory would be more difficult to disperse.

THE NAPOLEONIC ERA

Napoleon Bonaparte was born in 1769 to a poor noble family in Corsica. France had annexed Corsica in 1768, and he obtained a commission as a French artillery officer. He was a fiery Jacobin. In 1793, he played a leading role in recovering the port of Toulon from the British. As a reward, the government appointed him a brigadier general. His defense of the new regime in 1794 won him a command in Italy. By

On the way to her execution in 1793, Marie Antoinette was sketched from life by Jacques-Louis Daxid as she passed his window.

Bibliotheque Nationale. Paris. France/Giraudon/Art Resource. N.Y.

QUICK REVIEW

The Terror
- Began with creation of revolutionary tribunals in summer of 1793
- Executions spread from Paris to the provinces
- Reign of Terror claimed about 40,000 victims

Thermidorean Reaction   The reaction against the radicalism of the French Revolution that began in July 1794. Associated with the end of terror and establishment of the Directory.

The French Revolution

1789

May 5	Estates General opens at Versailles
June 17	Third Estate declares itself the National Assembly
June 20	National Assembly takes the Tennis Court Oath
July 14	Fall of the Bastille
July	Great Fear spreads in the countryside
August 4	Nobles surrender their feudal rights in a meeting of the National Constituent Assembly
August 27	*Declaration of the Rights of Man and Citizen*
October 5–6	Parisian women march to Versailles and force Louis XVI and his family to return to Paris

1790

July 12	Civil Constitution of the Clergy adopted
July 14	New constitution accepted by the king

1791

June 20–24	Louis XVI and his family attempt to flee France
August 27	Declaration of Pillnitz
October 1	Legislative Assembly meets

1792

April 20	France declares war on Austria
August 10	Tuileries palace stormed, and Louis XVI takes refuge with the Legislative Assembly
September 2–7	September Massacres
September 21	Convention meets, and monarchy abolished

1793

January 21	Louis XVI executed
February 1	France declares war on Great Britain
March	Counterrevolution breaks out
April 6	Committee of Public Safety formed
July	Robespierre enters Committee of Public Safety
August 23	*Levée en masse* proclaimed
September 29	Maximum prices set on food and other commodities
October 16	Queen Marie Antoinette executed
November 10	Cult of Reason proclaimed; revolutionary calendar

1794

May 7	Cult of the Supreme Being proclaimed
July 27	Ninth of Thermidor and fall of Robespierre
July 28	Robespierre executed

1795

August 22	Constitution of the Year III adopted, establishing the Directory

October 1797, he had crushed the Austrians and concluded the Treaty of Campo Formio, which took Austria out of the war. Italy and Switzerland lay under French domination.

In November 1797, the triumphant Bonaparte returned to Paris to confront France's only remaining enemy, Britain. Judging it impossible to invade England at that time, he chose to capture Egypt from the Ottoman Empire and cut off British communication with India. But the invasion of Egypt was a failure. Admiral Horatio Nelson (1758–1805) destroyed the French fleet, and the French army was stranded. The Russians, Austrians, and Ottomans joined Britain to form the Second Coalition. In 1799, the Russian and Austrian armies defeated the French in Italy and Switzerland and threatened to invade France.

Napoleon returned to France in October 1799. On November 10, 1799 (19 Brumaire) he overthrew the Directory. Bonaparte issued the Constitution of the Year VII in December 1799, establishing himself as the First Consul. The constitution received approval from the electorate in a rigged plebiscite. The **Consulate** closed the revolution in France.

The Consulate in France (1799–1804) Bonaparte quickly achieved peace. Russia had already left the Second Coalition. A victory over Austria at Marengo in Italy in 1800 took Austria out of the war. In 1802, Britain concluded the Treaty of Amiens, which temporarily brought peace to Europe.

Consulate French government dominated by Napoleon from 1799 to 1804.

Bonaparte also restored peace and order at home. Although he used generosity, flattery, and bribery to win over some of his enemies, issued a general amnesty, and employed persons from all political factions, Bonaparte suppressed political opposition. He established centralized administration in which all departments were managed by prefects appointed by the central government in Paris. He employed secret police. He stamped out royalist rebellions and plots.

Napoleon also alleviated the hostility of French Catholics. In 1801, he concluded a concordat with Pope Pius VII (r. 1800–1823). Both refractory and constitutional clergy were forced to resign. Their replacements received their spiritual investiture from the pope, but the state named the bishops and paid their salaries and the salary of one priest in each parish. In return, the church gave up its claims to its confiscated property. The clergy had to swear an oath of loyalty to the state, and the Organic Articles of 1802 established the supremacy of state over church. Similar laws applied to the Protestant and Jewish communities.

In 1802, another plebiscite appointed Napoleon consul for life. He transformed the basic laws and institutions of France on the basis of both liberal principles derived from the Enlightenment and the revolution and conservative principles going back to the Old Regime, on the one hand, and the spirit that had triumphed at Thermidor, on the other. This was especially true of the Civil Code of 1804, usually called the Napoleonic Code. However, these laws stopped far short of the full equality advocated by liberal rationalists. Fathers were granted extensive control over their children and men over their wives. Labor unions were forbidden, and the rights of workers were inferior to those of employers.

In 1804, Bonaparte seized on a bomb attack on his life to make himself emperor. Another new constitution, ratified by a plebiscite, designated Napoleon Emperor of the French. Napoleon summoned the pope to Notre Dame to take part in the coronation, but Napoleon crowned himself.

Napoleon's Empire (1804–1814)   Between his coronation as emperor and his final defeat at Waterloo (1815), Napoleon conquered most of Europe. France's victories ended the Old Regime and its feudal trappings in western Europe, and forced the eastern European states to reorganize themselves. Everywhere, Napoleon's advance unleashed nationalism.

The Treaty of Amiens with Britain (1802) could not last, and Britain declared war again in May 1803. William Pitt the Younger (1759–1806) returned to office as prime minister in 1804 and persuaded Russia and Austria to move again against French aggression. On October 21, 1805, Lord Nelson destroyed the French and Spanish fleets at the Battle of Trafalgar just off the Spanish coast. Nelson was killed, but Trafalgar guaranteed British control of the sea.

On land, however, between October 1805 and July 1807, Napoleon defeated the armies of Austria, Prussia, and Russia. He forced Austria to withdraw from northern Italy, where Napoleon became king. He replaced the Holy Roman Empire with the Confederation of the Rhine. Prussia and Russia became his allies.

Napoleon could not be secure until he had defeated Britain. Unable to compete with the British navy, he adopted economic warfare to cut off British trade with Europe. He hoped to cripple British commercial and financial power and drive the British from the war. Nonetheless, the British economy survived because of its access to the Americas and the eastern Mediterranean. Known as the Continental System, Napoleon's policies harmed the European economies and roused resentment.

The Wars of Liberation   In 1807, a French army invaded the Iberian Peninsula to force Portugal to abandon its alliance with Britain. When a revolt broke out in Madrid in 1808, Napoleon deposed the Spanish Bourbons and placed

In this early 19th century cartoon England, personified by a caricature of William Pitt, and France, personified by a caricature of Napoleon, are carving out their areas of interest around the globe.

Cartoon by Gillray/Corbis-Bettmann

his brother Joseph (1768–1844) on the Spanish throne. Attacks on the church increased public outrage.

In Spain, Napoleon faced guerrilla warfare, and the British landed an army under Sir Arthur Wellesley (1769–1852), later the duke of Wellington, to support the Spanish. Thus began the long peninsular campaign that would play a critical role in Napoleon's defeat.

The Austrians renewed the war in 1809, but the French won the battle of Wagram. The resulting peace deprived Austria of 3.5 million subjects. Another spoil of victory was the Archduchess Marie Louise (1791–1847), Francis I's (r. 1792–1835) 18-year-old daughter, whom Napoleon married for dynastic purposes after divorcing Josephine de Beauharnais (1763–1814), who had borne him no children.

The Franco-Russian alliance was faltering. The Continental System had harmed the Russian economy, and Napoleon's organization of a Polish state, the Grand Duchy of Warsaw, on the Russian doorstep angered Tsar Alexander I (r. 1800–1825). In 1810, Russia withdrew from the Continental System and began to prepare for war.

To stifle the Russian military threat, Napoleon amassed an army of over 600,000 men, but the Russians retreated before his advance and destroyed all food and supplies as well. The so-called Grand Army of Napoleon could not live off the country, and Russia was too vast for supply lines.

In September 1812, Russian public opinion forced the army to fight. At Borodino, the French had 30,000 casualties and the Russians almost twice as many. Yet the Russian army was not destroyed. By October, after occupying Moscow, the Grand Army was forced to retreat. Perhaps only 100,000 lived to tell the tale.

In 1813, patriotic pressure and national ambition brought together the last and most powerful coalition against Napoleon. Financed by the British, the Russians drove westward to be joined by Prussia and Austria. From the west, Wellington marched his peninsular army into France. Napoleon waged a skillful campaign but met decisive defeat in October at Leipzig. At the end of March 1814, the allied army marched into Paris. Napoleon abdicated and went into exile on the island of Elba off the coast of Italy.

THE CONGRESS OF VIENNA AND THE EUROPEAN SETTLEMENT

Once Napoleon was removed, the allies began to pursue their own separate ambitions. The key person among the allies was Viscount Castlereagh (1769–1822), the British foreign secretary. Even before the victorious armies had entered Paris, he achieved the Treaty of Chaumont on March 9, 1814, providing for the restoration of the Bourbons to the French throne and the contraction of France to its 1792 frontiers. Remaining problems were left for a conference at Vienna.

The Congress of Vienna met from September 1814 until November 1815. The victors agreed that no single state should be allowed to dominate Europe. They constructed a series of states to prevent French expansion (see Map 24–1). Thus, they established the kingdom of the Netherlands in the north and added Genoa to Piedmont in the south. Prussia was given new territories in the west to deter French aggression along the Rhine River. Austria was given full control of northern Italy to prevent a repetition of Napoleon's conquests there. Most of Napoleon's arrangements in the rest of Germany were left untouched. The Holy Roman Empire was not revived. The Congress established the rule of legitimate monarchs and rejected any hint of the republican and democratic politics that had flowed from the French Revolution.

However, eastern Europe divided the victors. Alexander I wanted Russia to govern all of Poland. Prussia wanted all of Saxony. Austria, however, refused to see Prussian power grow and Russia penetrate deeper into Europe. The Polish-Saxon question enabled France to rejoin the great powers. The French Foreign Minister Talleyrand (1754–1838) negotiated a secret treaty with Britain and Austria. When the news leaked out, the tsar agreed to become ruler of a smaller Poland, and Prussia settled for part of Saxony. Thereafter, France was included as a fifth great power in all deliberations.

Napoleon's escape from Elba on March 1, 1815, further restored unity among the victors. The allies sent their armies to crush him. Wellington and the Prussians defeated Napoleon at Waterloo in Belgium on June 18, 1815. Napoleon was exiled to Saint Helena, a tiny island off the coast of Africa, where he died in 1821.

The main outlines of the Vienna Settlement remained in place. The alliance between England, Austria, Prussia, and Russia was renewed on November 20, 1815. Henceforth, it was a coalition for the maintenance of peace. Its existence and later operation represented an important departure in European affairs. The statesmen at Vienna, unlike their eighteenth-century counterparts, had seen the armies of the French Revolution change borders and overturn the political and social order of the continent. They were determined to prevent a recurrence of those upheavals. Their purpose was to establish a framework for stability, not to punish defeated France. The great powers through the Vienna Settlement framed international relations so that the

Napoleonic Europe

1797	Napoleon concludes Treaty of Campo Formio
1799	Consulate established
1801	Concordat between France and papacy
1802	Treaty of Amiens
1803	War renewed between France and Britain
1804	Napoleonic Civil Code issued; Napoleon crowned emperor
1805	Nelson defeats French fleet at Trafalgar
1806	Continental System
1808	Beginning of Spanish resistance to Napoleonic domination
1809	Wagram; Napoleon marries Archduchess Marie Louise of Austria
1812	Invasion of Russia
1813	Leipzig
1814	Congress of Vienna convenes (September)
1815	Waterloo (June 18); Holy Alliance formed (September 26)
1821	Napoleon dies on Saint Helena

MAP EXPLORATION

Interactive map: To explore this map further, go to **http://www.prenhall.com/craig2/map24.2**

MAP 24–2

Europe 1815, after the Congress of Vienna.   The Congress of Vienna achieved the post-Napoleonic territorial adjustments shown on the map. The most notable arrangements dealt with areas along France's borders (the Netherlands, Prussia, Switzerland, and Piedmont) and in Poland and northern Italy.

WHY DID the statesmen at the Congress of Vienna seek to place strong states on the borders of France?

major powers would respect that settlement and not, as in the eighteenth century, use military force to change it.

The Congress of Vienna arranged an acceptable settlement for Europe that produced a long-lasting peace. Its work has been criticized for failing to recognize and provide for the great forces that would stir the nineteenth century—

OVERVIEW

THE VIENNA SETTLEMENT

The Congress of Vienna met from September 1814 to November 1815 to redraw the map of Europe after the defeat of Napoleon. With few exceptions, the borders the Congress agreed on remained in place until the 1850s. The statesmen at Vienna wanted to prevent another outbreak of the wars that had followed the French Revolution. The main principles behind their deliberations were a determination to confine France, which they saw as the home of revolution, within its traditional boundaries: legitimacy, by which they meant the restoration of Europe's traditional monarchs to their thrones; and compensation—the idea that the states that had defeated Napoleon deserved to be "compensated" for their expenditure of lives and treasure with new territory. Below is a summary of what the statesmen at Vienna achieved.

France	was reduced to its 1792 frontiers and ringed along its borders with a series of strengthened states to discourage French aggression. Thus, Prussia was given the Rhineland along France's eastern frontier; the Kingdom of the Netherlands was created to the north of France by combining Belgium and Holland; and the Kingdom of Sardinia on France's southern border was strengthened by the addition of the great port of Genoa.
Italy	Austria was compensated by becoming the dominant power in Italy and by being given Lombardy and Venetia. The Papal States were reconstituted, and the legitimate Italian rulers were restored to their thrones: the House of Savoy in Piedmont-Sardinia, the Bourbons in the Two Sicilies and Lucca; the Habsburgs in Tuscany, Modena, and Parma. Most of these rulers depended on Austrian support. The old republics of Venice and Genoa, which Napoleon had abolished, were not restored.
Germany	The Holy Roman Empire was not revived. Instead, it was replaced by a loose Germanic Confederation of mostly monarchical states under the presidency of Austria. Prussia was compensated by receiving two-thirds of Saxony, which had been an ally of Napoleon.
Scandinavia	Denmark, another ally of Napoleon, had to cede Norway as compensation to Sweden, which had lost Finland to Russia.
Poland	Poland was not restored as an independent state. It remained divided among Prussia, Austria, and Russia. Russia was compensated by being given the largest share of Poland.
Britain	was compensated with a number of former French and Dutch colonies. It also became the dominant naval power in the Mediterranean by annexing Malta in the central Mediterranean and the Ionian Islands at the mouth of the Adriatic.

nationalism and democracy—but such criticism is inappropriate. The settlement, like all such agreements, was aimed at solving past ills, and in that it succeeded. The Vienna settlement spared Europe a general war until 1914.

WARS OF INDEPENDENCE IN LATIN AMERICA

The wars of the French Revolution and Napoleon sparked movements for independence throughout Latin America. Between 1804 and 1824, France was driven from Haiti, Portugal lost control of Brazil, and Spain was forced to withdraw from all of its American empire except for Cuba and Puerto Rico. Three centuries of Iberian colonial government over the South American continent ended.

WHY DID Latin America throw off Spanish and Portuguese rule?

EIGHTEENTH-CENTURY DEVELOPMENTS

Spain was one of the defeated powers in 1763. Charles III (r. 1759–1788) was convinced that the American colonial system had to be changed. After 1765, the monarch abolished the monopolies of Seville and Cádiz, and opened more South

Toussaint L'Ouverture (1744-1803) began the revolt that led to Haitian, independence in 1804.

Historical Pictures Collection/Stock Montage. Inc.

American and Caribbean ports to trade, and authorized commerce between American ports. In 1776 he organized a fourth viceroyalty that included much of present-day Argentina, Uruguay, Paraguay, and Bolivia. Charles III also attempted to make tax collection more efficient and to eliminate bureaucratic corruption. To achieve those ends, he introduced into the empire *intendents*, who were royal bureaucrats loyal only to the crown.

These reforms returned the empire to direct Spanish control. Many *peninsulares*, whites born in Spain, went to the New World to fill new posts at the expense of **Creoles**, whites born in America. Expanding trade brought more Spanish merchants to Latin America. Economic life continued to be organized for the benefit of Spain.

FIRST MOVEMENTS TOWARD INDEPENDENCE

Haiti achieved independence from France in 1804, following a slave revolt that commenced in 1794 led by Toussaint L'Ouverture (1746–1803). Haiti's revolution involved the popular uprising of a repressed social group, which proved the great exception in the Latin American drive for liberty from European masters. On the South American continent it was the Creole elite who led the movements against Spain and Portugal. Few Indians, blacks, mestizos, mulattos, or slaves became involved or benefited from the end of Iberian rule. The Creoles were determined that political independence from Spain and Portugal should not cause social disruption or the loss of their privileges. In this respect they were not unlike American revolutionaries in the southern colonies who wanted to reject British rule but keep their slaves, or French revolutionaries who did not want to extend liberty to the French working class.

Creole complaints resembled those of the American colonists against Great Britain. Merchants wanted to trade more freely within the region and with North America and Europe. They wanted commercial regulations that would benefit them rather than Spain. Creoles also feared that Spanish imperial regulations would harm their interests, and they resented Spanish policies favoring *peninsulares* for political patronage.

From the 1790s onward, Spain suffered reverses in the wars associated with the French Revolution and Napoleon, and the commercial situation turned against the inhabitants of the Spanish Empire. The military pressures led the Spanish monarchy into a desperate search for new revenues, including increased taxation and the confiscation of property in the American Empire. The policies harmed the economic life of the Creole elite.

Creole leaders had read the Enlightenment *philosophes* and regarded their reforms as potentially beneficial to the region. They were also well aware of the political philosophy of the American Revolution. The event that transformed Creole discontent into revolt against the Spanish government occurred when Napoleon toppled the Portuguese monarchy in 1807 and the Spanish government in 1808, and then placed his own brother on the throne of Spain. The Portuguese royal family fled to Brazil, but the Bourbon monarchy of Spain seemed vanquished.

The Creole elite feared that a liberal Napoleonic monarchy in Spain would harm their economic and social interests and would drain the region of resources for Napoleon's wars. To protect their interests, Creole juntas, or political committees, between 1808 and 1810 claimed the right to govern regions of Latin America. The Spanish would not again directly govern the continent and after 10 years of warfare had to recognize Latin American independence.

peninsulares   Native-born Spaniards who immigrated from Spain to settle in the Spanish colonies.

Creoles   Persons of European descent who were born in the Spanish colonies.

SAN MARTÍN IN RÍO DE LA PLATA

The first region to assert its independence was the Río de la Plata, or modern Argentina. In 1810, the junta in Buenos Aires thrust off Spanish authority and sent liberation forces against Paraguay and Uruguay. The armies were defeated, but Paraguay asserted its own independence, and Uruguay was absorbed by Brazil.

The Buenos Aires government then determined to liberate Peru, the greatest stronghold of royalist power and loyalty on the continent. By 1814, José de San Martín (1778–1850) had led an army over the Andes Mountains. By early 1817, he had occupied Santiago in Chile, and established Bernardo O'Higgins (1778–1842) as supreme dictator. In 1821, he drove royalist forces from Lima and assumed the title of Protector of Peru.

SIMÓN BOLÍVAR'S LIBERATION OF VENEZUELA

In 1810, as a firm advocate of both independence and republicanism, Simón Bolívar (1783–1830) had helped organize a liberating junta in Caracas, Venezuela. Between 1811 and 1814, civil war broke out as royalists, slaves, and cowboys challenged the authority of the republican government. Bolívar had to go into exile. In 1819, with help from Haiti, he captured Bogotá, capital of New Granada (including modern Colombia, Bolivia, and Ecuador), as a base for attacking Venezuela. In 1821, his forces captured Caracas, and he was named president.

Simón Bolívar was the liberator of much of Latin America. He inclined toward a policy of political liberalism.

Hulton/Corbis-Bettmann

In July 1822, the armies of Bolívar and San Martín liberated Quito. The two leaders disagreed about the future political structure of Latin America. San Martín believed that monarchies were required; Bolívar maintained his republicanism. Not long thereafter San Martín went into exile in Europe. In 1823, Bolívar sent troops to Peru. On December 9, 1824, at the battle of Ayacucho, the Spanish royalist forces were defeated. The battle marked the end of Spain's effort to retain its American empire.

INDEPENDENCE IN NEW SPAIN

The drive for independence in New Spain, which included present-day Mexico as well as Texas, California, and the rest of the southwestern United States, illustrates the socially conservative outcome of the Latin American colonial revolutions. As elsewhere, a local governing junta was organized. But before it had undertaken any significant measures, a Creole priest, Miguel Hidalgo y Costilla (1753–1811), issued a call for rebellion to the Indians in his parish. They and other repressed groups responded. Father Hidalgo set forth a program of social change. Soon he had 80,000 followers, but in July 1811 he was captured and executed. Leadership of his movement then fell to José María Morelos y Pavón (1765–1815), a more radical mestizo priest. He was executed in 1815.

In 1820, however, a revolution in Spain forced Ferdinand VII (r. 1813–1833) to accept a liberal constitution. Conservative Mexicans feared that the new liberal monarchy would attempt to impose liberal reforms on Mexico. Therefore, for the most conservative of reasons, they created an independent Mexico governed by persons determined to resist social reform.

The Wars of Latin American Independence

1759–1788	Charles III of Spain carries out imperial reforms
1794	Toussaint L'Ouverture leads slave revolt in Haiti
1804	Independence of Haiti
1807	Portuguese royal family flees to Brazil
1808	Spanish monarchy falls to Napoleon
1808–1810	Creole Committees organized to govern much of Latin America
1810	Buenos Aires junta sends forces to liberate Paraguay and Uruguay
1811	Miguel Hidalgo y Costilla leads rebellion in New Spain and is executed
1811–1815	José María Morelos y Pavón leads rebellion in New Spain and is executed
1814	San Martín organizes army
1815	Brazil declared a kingdom
1817	San Martín occupies Santiago, Chile
1820	Revolution in Spain
1821 February 24	New Spain declares independence
June 29	Bolívar captures Caracas, Venezuela
July 28	San Martín liberates Peru
1822 July 26–27	San Martín goes into exile
September 7	Dom Pedro declares Brazilian independence
1824	Battle of Ayacucho—final Spanish defeat

WHY DID slavery become unacceptable in Western society?

Great Britain was sympathetic to the independence movements in Latin America. Independence opened the markets of the continent to British trade. In 1823, Britain supported the American Monroe Doctrine that prohibited further intervention by European powers in America. Britain soon recognized the Spanish colonies as independent states. Through the rest of the century, British commercial interests dominated Latin America.

BRAZILIAN INDEPENDENCE

Brazilian independence came relatively peacefully. As already noted, the Portuguese royal family and several thousand officials took refuge in Brazil in 1807. Their arrival transformed Rio de Janeiro into a court city. The prince regent Joao (r. 1816–1826) in 1815 made Brazil a kingdom; it was no longer merely a colony of Portugal. Then in 1820 a revolution occurred in Portugal, and its leaders demanded Joao's return to Lisbon and the return of Brazil to colonial status. Joao, who had become Joao VI in 1816, returned to Portugal but left his son Pedro (r. 1822–1831) as regent in Brazil. In 1822, Pedro embraced Brazilian independence and became emperor of Brazil, which remained a monarchy until 1889.

TOWARD THE ABOLITION OF SLAVERY IN THE TRANSATLANTIC ECONOMY

In 1750, few questioned the institution of slavery; by 1888, slavery no longer existed in the transatlantic economy. This transformation of economic and social life occurred as the result of an international effort, first to abolish the slave trade and then to abolish slavery itself. No previous society had attempted to abolish slavery. Its abolition in the transatlantic world is one of the most permanent achievements of the eighteenth-century Enlightenment and revolutions.

The eighteenth-century crusade against slavery originated among writers of the Enlightenment and religious critics. The general Enlightenment rhetoric of equality stood in sharp contrast to the radical inequality of slavery. Adam Smith's emphasis in *The Wealth of Nations* on free labor and free markets undermined economic defenses of slavery. Some Europeans also looked on African slaves as having been robbed of an original innocence. In such a climate, slavery grew to be regarded as unacceptable.

Just as the slave system was a transatlantic affair, so was the crusade against it. The initial religious protest against slavery originated among eighteenth-century English Quakers. But Quaker communities in America soon also wrote and organized against the institution. By the earliest stages of the American Revolution, small groups of reformers, usually spearheaded by Quakers, had established an antislavery network. Emancipation gradually spread among the northern states. In 1787, the Continental Congress forbade slavery in the Northwest Territory north of the Ohio River.

However, Great Britain became the center for the antislavery movement. During the early 1780s, the antislavery reformers in Britain decided to work toward ending the slave trade rather than slavery itself. To many, the slave trade appeared a more obvious crime than the holding of slaves. Furthermore, attacking slavery itself involved serious issues of property rights. The antislavery groups also believed that if the trade were ended, planters would have to treat their remaining slaves more humanely.

While the British reformers worked for the abolition of the slave trade, some slaves took matters into their own hands. The slave revolt in Haiti was a warning to slave owners throughout the West Indies. Other slave revolts occurred in Virginia, South Carolina, and British-controlled Demarra. Each of these was suppressed.

For economic reasons, some British West Indies planters began to consider abolition of the slave trade useful to their interests. The planters were experiencing soil exhaustion and increased competition. There was a glut of sugar on the market, and the price was falling. Without new slaves, competing French planters would lack the labor they needed to exploit their islands.

By 1807, abolition sentiment was strong enough for Parliament to prohibit slave trading from any British port. Thereafter, the suppression of this trade became a pillar of nineteenth-century British foreign policy. The British navy maintained a squadron off West Africa to halt slave traders.

Sentiment to abolish slavery itself increased. In 1833, following the passage of the Reform Bill in Great Britain, Parliament abolished the right of British subjects to hold slaves. In the British West Indies, 750,000 slaves were freed within a few years.

Leaders of the Latin American wars of independence, disposed by Enlightenment ideas to disapprove of slavery, had sought the support of slaves by promises of emancipation. The newly independent nations slowly freed their slaves to maintain good relations with Britain, from whom they needed economic support. Slavery disappeared from Latin America by the middle of the century, with the important exception of Brazil.

The other old colonial powers in the New World were slower to abolish slavery. Portugal did nothing about slavery in Brazil, and its independent government continued slavery. Portugal ended slavery elsewhere in its American possessions in 1836; the Swedes, in 1847; the Danes, in 1848, but the Dutch not until 1863. France had a significant antislavery movement, but did not abolish slavery in its West Indian possessions until 1848.

Despite all of these achievements, during the first 30 years of the nineteenth century slavery achieved new footholds in the transatlantic world. These areas included the lower south of the United States for the cultivation of cotton, Brazil for the cultivation of coffee, and Cuba for the cultivation of sugar. World demand for those products made the slave system economically viable in those regions. Slavery would end in the United States only after the Civil War. In Cuba it would persist until 1886, and full emancipation would occur in Brazil only in 1888. (See Chapters 26, 27, and 30.)

The emancipation crusade, like slave trading itself, drew Europeans into African affairs. In 1787, the British established a colony for free blacks from Britain in Sierra Leone. The French established a smaller experiment at Libreville in Gabon. The most famous and lasting attempt to settle former black slaves in Africa was the establishment of Liberia through the efforts of the American Colonization Society after 1817. Liberia became an independent republic in 1847. These efforts to move former slaves back to Africa had only modest success, but they did affect the future of West Africa itself.

Other antislavery reformers were less interested in establishing outposts for settlement of former slaves than in transforming the African economy itself. These reformers attempted to spread both Christianity and free trade to Africa, hoping to exchange British manufactured goods for tropical goods produced by Africans. These commercial efforts of the antislavery movement marked the first serious intrusions of European powers into the heart of Africa.

After the American Civil War finally halted any large-scale demand for slaves from Africa, the antislavery reformers began to focus on ending the slave trade in East Africa and the Indian Ocean. This new drive against slavery and the slave trade in Africa itself became one of the rationales for the establishment of the late-nineteenth century colonial empires.

SUMMARY

The Transatlantic Revolutions The revolutions and the crusade against slavery that occurred throughout the transatlantic world between 1776 and the 1830s transformed three continents. In North America, in France and other parts of Europe, and in South America, political experiments challenged government by both monarchy and aristocracy. The foundations of modern liberal democracy were laid. The largest republic since ancient times had been established in North America. In France, written constitutions and elected legislatures remained essential parts of the government. In Latin America, republicanism triumphed everywhere except Brazil. Never again could government be undertaken in these regions without some form of participation by the governed.

Economic and Social Liberalization The expanding forms of political liberty found their counterparts in an economic life freed from the constraints of the old colonial empires and the slavery that marked their plantations. The new American republic constituted a vast free trade zone. Its commerce was open to the world. And for the first time since the encounter with Europe, Latin America could trade freely among its own peoples and those of the rest of the world. In France and Europe, where the Napoleonic armies had carried the doctrines of the rights of man, economic life had been rationalized and freed from the domination of local authorities and local weights and measures. National law formed the framework for economic activity. The movement to abolish slavery fostered a wage economy of free laborers. That kind of economy would generate its own set of problems and social dislocation, but it was nonetheless an economy of free human beings.

Nationalism Finally, the age of transatlantic revolutions saw the emergence of nationalism as a political force. All of the revolutions, because of their popular political base, had given power to the idea of nations defined by their own character and historical past rather than by dynastic rulers. The Americans saw themselves as forming a new kind of nation. The French had demonstrated the power of a nation mobilized for military purposes. In turn, the aggression of France had aroused national sentiment, especially in Great Britain, Spain, and Germany. The new nations of Latin America also sought to define themselves by their heritage and historical experience rather than by their past in the Spanish and Portuguese Empires.

These various revolutions, their political doctrines, and their social and economic departures provided examples to peoples elsewhere in the world. But even more important, the transatlantic revolutions and eventual abolition of slavery meant that new political classes and independent nations would become actors on the world scene. Europeans would have to deal with a score of new nations in the

IMAGE KEY
for pages 510–511

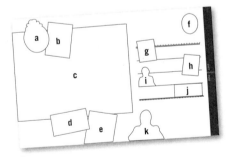

a. Marie Antoinette
b. Napoleon
c. Francisco de Goya, *Los fusilamientos del 3 de mayo,* 1808
d. Engraving printed by Benjamin Franklin
e. Severed head of Louis XVI
f. Thomas Jefferson
g. The Bostonians paying the excise man, or tarring & feathering
h. French Revolution: Liberte, Egalite: poster
i. Simón Bolívar
j. Slave quarters of a Spanish slave ship
k. Francois Dominique Toussaint L'Ouverture

Americas. The rest of the world confronted new nations freed from the direction and authority of European powers. The political changes in Europe meant that those nations and their relationships with the rest of the world would be directed by a broader range of groups than in the past.

REVIEW QUESTIONS

1. To what extent were the American colonists influenced by their position in the transatlantic economy and by European ideas and political developments?

2. How was the Estates General transformed into the National Assembly? How were France and its government reorganized in the early years of the revolution? Why was the Civil Constitution of the Clergy a blunder?

3. Why did the revolution of 1792 occur? What were the causes of the Reign of Terror?

4. How did Napoleon rise to power? What were his major domestic achievements? Why did he decide to invade Russia? What were the major outlines of the peace settlement achieved by the Congress of Vienna?

5. What political changes took place in Latin America between 1804 and 1824? What were the main reasons for Creole discontent with Spanish rule?

6. What intellectual and religious factors contributed to the rise of the antislavery movement? Why did slavery receive a new lease on life during the same years that the antislavery movement emerged?

KEY TERMS

assignats   (p. 516)
Consulate   (p. 522)
Convention   (p. 519)
Creoles   (p. 528)

Jacobins   (p. 519)
levée en masse   (p. 520)
peninsulares   (p. 528)
Reign of Terror   (p. 519)

sans-culottes   (p. 519)
Thermidorean Reaction   (p. 521)
Third Estate   (p. 514)

 For additional study resources for this chapter, go to:
www.prenhall.com/craig/chapter24

Liberty Leading the People
by Eugene Delacroix is a famous
evocation of the Revolution of 1830.

Giraudin/Art Resource, N.Y.

25

POLITICAL CONSOLIDATION IN NINETEENTH-CENTURY EUROPE AND NORTH AMERICA

1815 – 1880

WHAT IS nationalism?

WHY WERE efforts to achieve political liberalism more successful in France and Britain than in Russia between 1815 and 1830s?

WHAT WERE the causes of the American Civil War?

HOW DID Canada achieve united self-government?

WHAT WERE the steps that led to a united Italy?

HOW DID nationalism affect the Habsburg Empire?

IMAGE KEY

Image Key for pages 534–535 is on page 562.

During the nineteenth century, two fundamental long-term developments occurred in the northern transatlantic world that would have a profound impact over the decades in every culture on the face of the Earth. First, in both Europe and North America there took place a process of political consolidation that made the nation-states of that region the strongest of the period. Second, and directly contributing to that political strength, there emerged in Europe and North America powerful, new industrial economies with a new kind of society no longer based primarily on the land. As a direct result of this political consolidation and industrialization, the nations of the northern transatlantic became the world's major military powers. By the close of the nineteenth century and well into the twentieth this political and military power allowed the nations of Europe and the United States to exert unprecedented political, military, and economic influence around the globe. It was on the basis of that power that many people in Europe and North America came to claim superiority to people dwelling in other cultures and other regions. Moreover, the manner in which Europeans and to a lesser extent Americans developed sets of ideas to explain what was happening politically and economically in their region would later be used by peoples elsewhere in the world as they responded to the worldwide power that the northern transatlantic powers exerted.

The present chapter will examine the process of political consolidation in the northern transatlantic world, while Chapter 26 will explore the social changes that occurred there in the nineteenth century. Although we will consider the two processes separately, each contributed to the other.

NATIONALISM

WHAT IS nationalism?

Nationalism is based on the relatively modern concept that a nation is composed of people who are joined together by the bonds of common language, customs, culture, and history, and who, because of those bonds, should share the same government. That is to say, political and ethnic boundaries should coincide. This idea came into its own during the late eighteenth and early nineteenth centuries.

Nationalism and Opposition to the Vienna Settlement   Nationalists opposed the principle upheld at the Congress of Vienna that legitimate monarchies or dynasties should provide the basis for political unity. Nationalists protested multinational states such as the Austrian or Russian Empires. They also objected to peoples of the same ethnic group, such as Germans and Italians, dwelling in political units smaller than that of the ethnic nation.

Creating Nations   Nationalists created nations in the nineteenth century. During the first half of the century, writers spread *nationalistic* concepts. Many were historians who chronicled a people's past or literary scholars who established a national literature by collecting and publishing earlier writings in the people's language. In effect, they gave a people a sense of their past and a literature of their own, which schoolteachers spread.

The language to be used in schools and government was a point of contention for nationalists. In France and Italy, official versions of the national language were imposed in the schools. In eastern Europe, nationalists attempted to resurrect the national language. Often these resurrected languages were virtually invented by scholars. This process led to far more linguistic uniformity within European nations than had existed before the nineteenth century. Proficiency in the official language became a path to advancement. A uniform language helped to persuade people who had not thought of themselves as constituting a nation that they were a nation.

nationalism   The belief that one is part of a nation, defined as a community with its own language, traditions, customs, and history that distinguish it from other nations and make it the primary focus of a person's loyalty and sense of identity.

Meaning of Nationhood   Nationalists used a variety of arguments to express what they meant by nationhood. Some argued that gathering, for example, Italians into a unified Italy would promote economic and administrative efficiency. Others claimed that nations, like biological species, were distinct creations of God.

A significant difficulty for nationalism was, and is, determining which ethnic groups could be considered nations, with claims to territory and political autonomy. In theory, any of them could, but nationhood came to be associated with groups that were large enough to support an economy, that had a history of significant cultural association, that possessed a cultural elite that could nourish the national language, and that could conquer other peoples to protect their own independence. Many smaller ethnic groups claimed to fulfill these criteria but could not achieve either independence or recognition. They could and did, however, create unrest within the political units they inhabited. Such was the situation in Europe.

Regions of Nationalistic Pressure in Europe   During the nineteenth century, nationalists challenged the political status quo in six major areas of Europe. Irish nationalists wanted independence or at least self-government from Britain. German nationalists sought political unity for all German-speaking peoples, challenging the multinational Austrian Empire and pitting Prussia and Austria against each other. Italian nationalists sought to unify the peninsula and drive out the Austrians. Polish nationalists struggled, primarily against Russia, to restore Poland as an independent nation. In eastern Europe, Hungarians, Czechs, Slovenes, and others sought either autonomy or formal recognition within the Austrian Empire. Finally, in the Balkans, national groups sought independence from Ottoman and Russian control. In each area, nationalist activity ebbed and flowed. The dominant governments often thought they needed only to repress the activity or ride it out. During the century, however, nationalists changed the map and political culture of Europe.

EARLY-NINETEENTH-CENTURY LIBERALISM

European liberals derived their political ideas from the Enlightenment, the example of English liberties, and the French *Declaration of the Rights of Man and Citizen*. Liberals sought to establish a framework of legal equality, religious toleration, and freedom of the press, and to limit the arbitrary power of the government. They believed that the legitimacy of government emanated from the freely given consent of the governed expressed through elected parliaments. Most important, free government required that state or crown ministers be responsible to the representatives of the nation rather than to the monarch.

These goals were limited. The people who espoused them tended to be those who were excluded from the existing political processes but whose wealth and education made them believe such exclusion was unjustified. Liberals were often academics, members of the learned professions, and people involved in commerce and manufacturing. They were products of the career open to talent. The existing monarchical and aristocratic regimes often failed to recognize their status and interests.

European liberals were not democrats. They despised the lower classes. Liberals transformed the eighteenth-century concept of aristocratic liberty into a new concept of privilege based on wealth and property. By the mid-century, this meant that throughout Europe, liberals had separated themselves from the working class.

20.3
Fustel de Coulanges, "What Is a Nation?" A Reply to Mr. Mommsen, Professor in Berlin

liberalism   In the nineteenth century, support for representative government dominated by the propertied classes and minimal government interference in the economy.

In the first half of the nineteenth century, political liberals generally did not support political rights for women, but liberal political principles provided women with strong arguments to do so.

Economics   The economic goals of the liberals also furthered their separation from the working class. Here, the Enlightenment and the economic thought deriving from Adam Smith set the pattern. The landed and commercial middle class wanted to be able to manufacture and sell goods freely. They thus favored the removal of barriers to trade and, from the 1830s onward, the construction of railways as well.

European economic liberals opposed the old paternalistic legislation that established wages and labor practices by governments or guilds. Labor was simply a commodity to be bought and sold freely. Liberals sought an economic structure in which people were free to use their talents and property to enrich themselves. The liberals contended that this would lead to more goods and services for everyone at lower prices.

The economic goals of European liberals found many followers outside Europe among groups who favored the expansion of free trade, new transport systems, and a free market in labor. In the United States, people of this outlook often attacked slavery as inefficient and paternalistic. In Latin America, political liberals sought to remove paternalistic legislation that had protected Native Americans under Spanish rule.

The idea of the career open to talent could be applied to suppressed national groups who were not permitted to realize their cultural or political potential. The efficient government and administration required by commerce and industry would mean replacing the small German and Italian states with larger political units. Moreover, nationalist groups could gain the sympathy of liberals by espousing representative government and political liberty.

LIBERALISM AND NATIONALISM IN MODERN WORLD HISTORY

WHAT POLITICAL and economic goals did nineteenth-century liberals wish to achieve?

The wars of the French Revolution in Europe had demonstrated by the early nineteenth century that the ideals of political liberalism could easily spread across dynastic borders. In time those liberal ideals as well as those of nationalism would spread around the globe. Thus, what began as a European development is also important for global history. The concept of the rights of man and citizen could be used during the Wars of Independence in Latin America to challenge Spanish government. By the close of the nineteenth century those same ideals could be turned against the colonial government that Europeans imposed on Africa and Asia. Furthermore, the belief that people should have the right to govern themselves would inspire the settlers who spread across both the United States and Canada as well as those who came to live in Australia and New Zealand. Similarly, the belief that individual ethnic groups should constitute independent nations became a major political idea whereby peoples living under European colonial government during the late nineteenth and even more importantly the twentieth centuries would challenge the right of Europeans and later Americans to govern them or to dominate their lives informally through economic power. Political developments in Europe during the early nineteenth century would produce a profound impact around the globe during the next century.

EFFORTS TO LIBERALIZE EARLY-NINETEENTH-CENTURY EUROPEAN POLITICAL STRUCTURES

E uropean nations certainly did not move toward liberal political structures rapidly or without considerable conflict. Indeed after the Congress of Vienna most conservatives had hoped that they had established walls against liberal advances. Three examples will indicate the different experiences that different European liberals confronted early in the nineteenth century.

WHY WERE efforts to achieve political liberalism more successful in France and Britain than in Russia between 1815 and the 1830s?

RUSSIA: THE DECEMBRIST REVOLT OF 1825 AND THE AUTOCRACY OF NICHOLAS I

In the process of driving Napoleon's army across Europe, and then occupying defeated France, many officers in the Russian army were introduced to the ideas of the French Revolution and the Enlightenment. They realized how economically backward and politically stifled Russia was. Under these conditions, groups within the officer corps formed secret societies. These societies were small and divided in their goals; they agreed only that the government of Russia must change. Sometime during 1825 they seem to have decided to carry out a coup d'état in 1826.

Other events intervened. In late November 1825 Tsar Alexander I suddenly and unexpectedly died. His death created two crises. The first was a dynastic one: Alexander had no direct heir. His brother Constantine stood next in line to the throne. However, Constantine, who was the commander of Russian forces in Poland, had renounced any claim to be tsar. Through a series of secret instructions made public only after his death, Alexander had named his younger brother, Nicholas (r. 1825–1855), as the new tsar. Once Alexander was dead, the legality of these instructions became uncertain. Constantine acknowledged Nicholas as tsar, and Nicholas acknowledged Constantine. This family muddle continued for about three weeks, during which Russia actually had no ruler, to the astonishment of Europe. Then, in early December, the army command reported to Nicholas the existence of a conspiracy among certain officers. Able to wait no longer, Nicholas had himself declared tsar.

The second crisis now unfolded—a plot by junior officers to rally the troops under their command to the cause of reform. On December 26, 1825, the army was to take the oath of allegiance to Nicholas, who was less popular than Constantine and was regarded as more conservative. Nearly all of the regiments did so. But the Moscow regiment, whose chief officers, surprisingly, were not secret society members, marched into the Senate Square in Saint Petersburg and refused to swear allegiance. Rather, they called for Constantine and a constitution. Attempts to settle the situation peacefully failed. Late in the afternoon Nicholas ordered cavalry and artillery to attack the insurgents. Five of the plotters were executed, and over 100 other officers were exiled to Siberia.

The immediate result of the revolt was the crushing of liberalism as even a moderate political influence in Russia. Nicholas I also manifested extreme conservatism in foreign affairs. Russia under Nicholas became the policeman of Europe, ever ready to provide troops to suppress liberal and nationalist movements. Except for a modest experiment early in the twentieth century, tsarist Russia would never know genuinely liberal political structures.

Liberty Leading the People by Eugene Delacroix is a famous evocation of the Revolution of 1830

Giraudon/Art Resource, N.Y.

REVOLUTION IN FRANCE (1830)

In 1824 Louis XVIII (r. 1814–1824), the Bourbon restored to the throne of France by the Congress of Vienna, died. He was succeeded by his brother, Charles X (r. 1824–1830). The new king considered himself a monarch by divine right and he also moved to restore lands that the French aristocrats had lost during the revolution. He also pressed other conservative measures through the Chamber of Deputies. Opposition soon developed. After elections in 1827 Charles began to govern somewhat less conservatively, but French liberals wanted a genuinely constitutional regime. Matters came to a head in 1829 when Charles abandoned efforts to accommodate liberals and appointed an ultra-royalist ministry, but his efforts backfired.

In 1830 Charles X called for new elections, in which the liberals scored a stunning victory. Instead of attempting to accommodate the new Chamber of Deputies, the king and his ministers decided to undertake a royalist seizure of power. In June and July 1830 the ministry had sent a naval expedition against Algeria. On July 9 reports of its victory, and the consequent foundation of a French empire in North Africa, reached Paris. On July 25, 1830, under the euphoria of this foreign diversion, Charles X issued the Four Ordinances, which restricted freedom of the press, dissolved the recently elected Chamber of Deputies, and called for new elections under a franchise restricted to the wealthiest people in the country.

Liberal newspapers immediately called on the nation to reject the monarch's actions. The laboring populace of Paris, burdened since 1827 by an economic downturn, took to the streets and erected barricades. The king called out troops, and over 1,800 people died during the ensuing battles in the city. On August 2 Charles X abdicated and left France for exile in England. The liberals in the Chamber of Deputies named a new ministry composed of constitutional monarchists. They proclaimed Louis Philippe (r. 1830–1848), the Duke of Orléans, the head of the liberal branch of the royal family, the new monarch. Under what became known as the **July Monarchy**, Louis Philippe was called the king of the French rather than of France. The king had to cooperate with the Chamber of Deputies; he could not dispense with laws on his own authority. The revolutionary tricolor replaced the white flag of the Bourbons. The Charter, or constitution, was regarded as embodying the rights of the people rather than a concession granted by the monarch. Catholicism was recognized only as the religion of the majority of the people, not the official religion. Censorship was abolished. The franchise, though still restricted, was extended. Socially, however, the Revolution of 1830 proved quite conservative. The landed oligarchy retained its economic, political, and social influence. Money became the path to power and influence in the government. There was much corruption. Most important, the liberal monarchy displayed scant sympathy for the lower and working classes.

July Monarchy The French regime set up after the overthrow of the Bourbons in July 1830.

Britain: From The Great Reform Bill (1832) to Home Rule for Ireland

The passage of the **Great Reform Bill**, which became law in 1832, was the result of events different from those that occurred on the Continent. In Britain the forces of conservatism and reform compromised with each other. As a result, during the century Great Britain became for most people the exemplary liberal state not only of Europe but of the world.

English determination to maintain the union with Ireland caused the first step in the reform process. England's relationship to Ireland was not unlike that of Russia's to Poland or Austria's to Hungary. The Act of Union in 1800 between England and Ireland suppressed the separate Irish parliament. The Irish now sent representatives to the British parliament at Westminster, but only Protestant Irishmen could be elected to represent overwhelmingly Catholic Ireland.

During the 1820s, under the leadership of Daniel O'Connell (1775–1847), Irish nationalists organized the Catholic Association to agitate for Catholic emancipation, as the movement for legal rights for Roman Catholics was known. In 1828 O'Connell was elected to Parliament but could not legally take his seat. The British ministry of the Duke of Wellington (1769–1852) realized that henceforth Ireland might elect a predominantly Catholic delegation to Parliament. If they were not seated, civil war might erupt. Consequently, in 1829 Wellington and Robert Peel (1788–1850) steered the **Catholic Emancipation** Act through Parliament. Roman Catholics could now become members of Parliament. This measure, together with the repeal in 1828 of restrictions against Protestant nonconformists, ended the monopoly held by members of the Church of England on British political life.

Catholic emancipation alienated many of Wellington's Tory supporters. In the election of 1830 many supporters of parliamentary reform were returned to Parliament. Even some Tories believed that parliamentary reform was necessary because they had concluded that Catholic emancipation could have been passed only by a corrupt House of Commons. The Wellington ministry soon fell. The Tories were badly divided, and King William IV (r. 1830–1837) turned to the Whigs under the leadership of Earl Grey (1764–1845) to form a government.

The Whig ministry soon presented the House of Commons with a major reform bill that had two broad goals. The first was to replace "rotten" boroughs, which had few voters, with representatives for the previously unrepresented manufacturing districts and cities. The second was to increase the number of voters in England and Wales. In 1831 the House of Commons narrowly defeated the bill. Grey called for a new election, in which a majority in favor of the bill was returned to the Commons. The House of Commons passed the reform bill, but the House of Lords rejected it. Mass meetings were held throughout the country, and riots broke out in several cities. Finally, William IV agreed to create enough new peers to give a third reform bill a majority in the House of Lords. Under this pressure, the measure became law in 1832.

The Great Reform Act expanded the size of the English electorate, but it was not a democratic measure. The electorate was increased by over 200,000 persons, or by almost 50 percent. The basis of voting, however, remained a property qualification. Some working-class voters actually lost the vote when their old franchise rights were abolished. New urban boroughs gave the growing cities a voice in the House of Commons. Yet the passage of the Reform Act did not, as it was once thought, constitute the triumph of the middle-class interest in England. For every new urban electoral district, a new rural district was also drawn. It was expected that the aristocracy would dominate the rural elections.

Great Reform Bill (1832)   A limited reform of the British House of Commons and an expansion of the electorate to include a wider variety of the propertied classes. It laid the groundwork for further orderly reforms within the British constitutional system.

Catholic Emancipation   The grant of full political rights to Roman Catholics in Britain in 1829.

Although passed with much turmoil and conflict the Great Reform Act established the foundations for long-term political stability in Britain. During the 1840s a major working-class political movement known as **Chartism** would bring the demands of industrial workers into the political process. Despite the tensions created by Chartism, British political structures maintained themselves. Throughout the second half of the nineteenth century, Great Britain continued to symbolize the confident liberal state. A large body of ideas emphasizing competition and individualism was accepted by the members of all classes. Even the leaders of trade unions during these years asked only to receive some of the fruits of prosperity and to prove their own social respectability. Parliament itself continued to provide an institution that permitted the absorption of new groups and interests into the existing political processes.

The most important example of the opening of parliamentary processes was the Second Reform Act passed by a Conservative government in 1867. It increased the number of voters from approximately 1,430,000 to 2,470,000. Britain had taken a major step toward democracy. Benjamin Disraeli (1804–1881), who led the Conservatives in the House of Commons, thought significant portions of the working class would eventually support Conservative candidates who were responsive to social issues. He also thought the growing suburban middle class would become more conservative.

Gladstone and Disraeli   The election of 1868, however, which followed the Second Reform Act, dashed Disraeli's hopes. William Gladstone (1809–1898) became the new prime minister. His ministry of 1868–1874 witnessed the culmination of classical British liberalism. Gladstone introduced competitive examinations into the civil service, abolished the purchase of army officers' commissions, and introduced the secret ballot. He opened Oxford and Cambridge universities to students of all religious denominations and, by the Education Act of 1870, made the British government responsible for establishing and running elementary schools, which had been supported by the various churches.

The liberal policy of creating popular support for the nation by extending political liberty and reforming abuses had its conservative counterpart in concern about social reform. Disraeli succeeded Gladstone as prime minister in 1874. Whereas Gladstone looked to individualism, free trade, and competition to solve social problems, Disraeli believed the state should protect weaker citizens. In his view, paternalistic legislation would alleviate class antagonism. His most important measures were the Public Health Act of 1875, which consolidated and extended previous sanitary legislation, and the Artisans Dwelling Act of 1875, through which the government became actively involved in providing housing for the working class.

The Irish Question   Ireland remained a major issue for the British government. From the late 1860s onward, Irish nationalists had sought to achieve home rule for Ireland, by which they meant more Irish control of local government. Their demands of the British government very much resembled the demands that first the Hungarians and then the Czechs made toward the Habsburg government, which will be considered later in this chapter. The Irish, like the Hungarians and Czechs in the Habsburg Empire, proved a profoundly disruptive force in British politics.

The leader of the Irish movement for **home rule** was Charles Stewart Parnell (1846–1891). By 1885 Parnell had organized 85 Irish members of the House of Commons into a tightly disciplined party that often voted as a bloc. In the elec-

---

QUICK REVIEW

William Gladstone (1809–1898)

◆ Became prime minister in election of 1868

◆ His ministry witnessed the culmination of classical British liberalism

◆ Carried out reforms of governmental abuses and extended political liberty

---

Chartism   The first large-scale European working-class political movement. It sought political reforms that would favor the interests of skilled British workers in the 1830s and 1840s.

home rule   The advocacy of a large measure of administrative autonomy for Ireland within the British Empire between the 1880s and 1914.

tion of 1885 the Irish Party emerged holding the balance of power between the English Liberals and Conservatives. The Irish could decide which party would take office. In December 1885 Gladstone announced support for home rule for Ireland, and Parnell gave his votes to the formation of a Liberal ministry. However, the issue split the Liberal Party. In 1886 a group known as the Liberal Unionists joined with the Conservatives to defeat Gladstone's Home Rule Bill. Gladstone called for a new election, which the Liberals lost. They remained permanently divided. The new Conservative ministry of Lord Salisbury (1830–1903) attempted to reconcile the Irish to the English government through public works and administrative reform. The policy had only marginal success.

In 1892 Gladstone returned to power and sponsored a second Home Rule Bill that passed the House of Commons but was defeated in the House of Lords. With the failure of this bill, further action on the Irish question was suspended until a Liberal ministry passed the third Home Rule Bill in the summer of 1914. However, the implementation of home rule was suspended for the duration of World War I.

As already noted, the Irish question affected British politics much the way that the nationalities problem affected Austria. Normal British domestic issues could not be adequately addressed because of the political divisions created by Ireland. The split of the Liberal Party hurt the cause of further social and political reform. The people who could agree about reforms could not agree on Ireland, and Ireland seemed more important. Because the two traditional parties failed to deal with the social questions, by the turn of the century a newly organized Labour Party began to fill the vacuum.

1848: YEAR OF REVOLUTIONS IN EUROPE

In 1848 a series of liberal and nationalistic revolutions and revolts spread across Europe. No single factor caused this general revolutionary groundswell; rather, similar conditions existed in several countries. Severe food shortages had prevailed since 1846 due to poor harvests. The commercial and industrial economy was in recession, with widespread unemployment. However, the dynamic for change in 1848 originated not with the working classes but with the political liberals, who were generally drawn from the middle classes. Throughout the Continent liberals were pushing for more representative governments, civil liberty, and unregulated economic life.

To put additional pressure on their governments, the liberals began to appeal for the support of the urban working classes, even though the goals of the two groups were different. The working classes sought improved employment and better working conditions rather than political reform for its own sake. The liberals refused to follow political revolution with social reform and thus isolated themselves from their temporary working-class allies. Once separated from potential mass support, the liberal revolutions became an easy prey to the armies of reactionary governments. As a result, the revolutions of 1848 failed to establish genuinely liberal or national states.

What are known in European history as the Revolutions of 1848 were confined to the Continent, where the results were important for the individual nation-states. In France the monarchy of Louis Philippe was overthrown and briefly replaced by a republic. In 1851 the republic was in turn overthrown in a military coup led by Louis Napoleon, a nephew of the first Napoleon. Thereafter Louis Napoleon created the Second Empire and took the title of Napoleon III. In Prussia and the Austrian Empire short-lived revolutions brought political liberals and nationalists to the fore, but in each case those revolutions were suppressed by the military. The same was true of efforts by Italian nationalists to thrust off Austrian rule of Italy.

20.2
Irish National Identity
and Destiny: Three Views

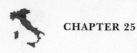

From the standpoint of world history, however, the chief importance of the failed liberal and national Revolutions of 1848 was the emergence on the European continent of strongly conservative governments that would dominate the scene for the next quarter century. The turmoil of 1848 through 1850 ended the era of liberal revolution that had begun in 1789. Liberals and nationalists had discovered that rational argument and local insurrections would not help them to achieve their goals. The working class also adopted new tactics and organization. The era of the riot and urban insurrection was ending. In the future, workers would turn to trade unions and political parties to achieve their political and social goals. Finally, after the Revolutions of 1848, the political initiative in Europe passed for a time to the conservative political groups.

The defeat of liberal political forces in 1848 and the triumph of conservative powers also influenced the modernization of Japan. Within a few years Japan would emerge from its long self-imposed isolation. After the Meiji Restoration the new leaders of Japan looked to European examples of successful modern nations. The nation they would most clearly copy was the conservative, militaristic Germany that emerged after the defeat of the liberals of 1848.

TESTING THE NEW AMERICAN REPUBLIC

WHAT WERE the causes of the American Civil War?

While the nations of Western Europe very slowly embraced political liberalism, the United States of America was continuing its bold republican political experiment. By the first quarter of the century, however, serious sectional tensions had arisen, the most important of which related to the presence of black slavery in the Southern states.

TOWARD SECTIONAL CONFLICT

The Constitutional Convention of 1788 had debated the sectional difference in a dispute over what proportion of the slave population, if any, would be counted in determining how many seats the Southern states were allotted in the House of Representatives. A compromise allowed the slave-holding states to count three fifths of their slaves when calculating their population for representation in Congress. The Constitution also forbade any federal attempt to prevent the importation of slaves before 1808. Between 1788 and 1808 thousands of slaves were imported into the United States.

The westward movement, however, meant that slavery could not be permanently ignored. The Ordinance of 1787, passed by Congress under the Articles of Confederation, had prohibited slavery in the Northwest Territory, which embraced the future states of Ohio, Indiana, Illinois, Michigan, and Wisconsin. Territory south of the Ohio River and beyond the Mississippi River was, however, open to slavery, and there it spread. By 1820 the number of slave and free states was evenly divided; this meant an equal number of senators from slave and free states. That year, Missouri was admitted as a slave state and Maine as a free one. It was also decided that in the future no slave states would be carved out of land north of the southern border of Missouri. For the time being, this Missouri Compromise ended congressional debate over slavery. Nonetheless, the economies of the North and the South were rapidly diverging.

Northern Economic Development   Family farms, free labor, commerce, and early industrialization in textiles characterized the economy of the Northern states. Northern farmers tended primarily to produce foodstuffs for their local communities. The farms were relatively small and worked by families. Farm laborers were free. Similarly, free laborers worked in the towns, on the ships, and in the factories of the North. The political spokesmen for the North tended to favor tariffs to protect their young industries from cheaper foreign competition. In this favoring of tariffs, many Americans whose political views otherwise often resembled European liberals differed from their European counterparts.

The North was the site of the earliest textile factories in the United States. Samuel Slater had established the first textile mill in Rhode Island in 1790. He had learned how to manufacture textiles in the new mills of industrializing Great Britain. His transfer of that technology to America illustrates how important British and European advances were transported to the United States. Much of the early industrialization of the United States depended on such technological transfers. By the second decade of the nineteenth century the North had hundreds of cotton factories. These mills used cotton that was produced in the South, but most Southern cotton was sold overseas, mainly to the growing British textile industry.

During the second quarter of the century innovations in transportation led to the fuller integration of different parts of the Northern economy. Canals were built to link the major rivers with manufacturing and agricultural markets. The most famous was the Erie Canal, which connected the Hudson River to the Great Lakes. Other canals linked the Great Lakes to the Ohio River. Major efforts were undertaken to make the Ohio, Mississippi, and Missouri Rivers navigable, which allowed steamboats to transport goods. But by the late 1840s, in America as in Europe, the major transportation innovation was the railroad. Most of the railways linked the Northeast and the West and fostered the commercial agriculture of the Midwest. Its products were sold in the Northeast and exported from Northern ports. Hence, the development of east–west railways undermined the older river-based trade routes along the Ohio and down the Mississippi. Few major lines ran north and south, so former ties between the sections based on the rivers weakened. The building of the early railways also aided the development of the Northern coal and iron industries. The further expansion of railways at midcentury caused new sectional tensions, as it became clear the railways could open for settlement vast territories, and thus could also open a national debate over the future of slavery. That prospect sharpened the sectional debate and led to civil war.

Rivers, canals, and railways allowed the upper Midwest to develop into a rich area for agriculture. In this sense much of the Northern economy was as rural and agricultural as the Southern. What most distinguished the two regions was free versus slave labor. The Southern economy depended on slavery and could expand only if slavery were allowed to expand as well.

The Southern Economy   The overwhelmingly rural economy of the American South was dependent on cotton and slavery. In those respects, the Southern economy resembled the economies of many Latin American countries, which were based on exporting a single crop or natural resource and on slave labor. The South had to export goods, primarily raw cotton, either to the North or to Europe, primarily to Great Britain, to maintain its standard of living.

Cotton was king. The invention of the cotton gin by Eli Whitney (1765–1825) in 1793 made cotton cultivation much more profitable because the seed no longer had to be laboriously picked out of the new cotton by hand. The industrial revolution in textiles kept cotton prices high, and the expansion in world population kept the demand for cotton cloth steady. The South profited from growing the cotton, New England from shipping it, and other parts of the North from supplying the manufactured goods the South needed. The South had virtually no incentive to diversify its agriculture.

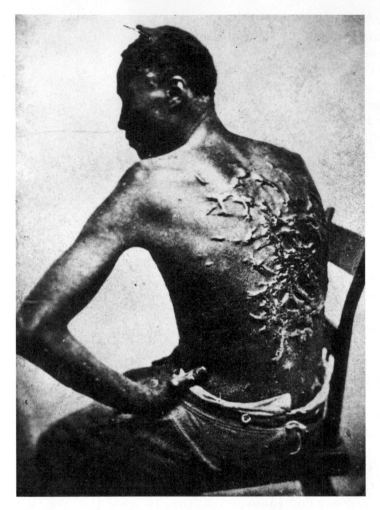

This Louisiana slave named Gordon was photographed in 1863 after he had escaped to Union lines during the Civil War. He bears the permanent scars of the violence that lay at the heart of the slave system. Few slaves were so brutally marked, but all lived with the threat of beatings if they failed to obey.

Slavery in the American South   Slavery was abolished in the North by the early nineteenth century largely in response to the egalitarian values of the American Revolution. In any case, slavery had never been fundamental to the Northern economy. But in the South, the expansion of the cotton empire in the Mississippi Delta in the early nineteenth century gave slavery a new lease on life. Although most Southern families never owned slaves and relatively few slave owners had possessed more than a few slaves, the institution of slavery survived for many reasons. For one, it was economically viable, and no one could devise a way politically or socially acceptable to white Southerners to abolish it. No less important was the strong commitment to the protection of private property, which included slaves, throughout American society in both the North and the South. Perhaps the most basic reason for the endurance of slavery after the early nineteenth century, however, was racist thinking that saw blacks as fundamentally inferior to whites. Such thinking was not peculiar to the South, but it functioned there as one more argument against abolishing slavery.

What was the life of an American slave like? All American slaves were nonwhite, the descendants of Africans who had been forcibly captured and shipped in the most wretched of conditions to the United States (see Chapter 17). Despite much miscegenation among Africans and their white slave owners and Native Americans, the various slave codes defined as black virtually anyone who had African antecedents. Slaves were regarded as chattel property; that is, they could be sold, given away, or even gambled away like any other piece of property. They had no recourse to law or constitutional protections and could be, and often were, treated badly by their masters. Whipping and beating were permitted. State laws protected slaves from extreme violence, but were laxly enforced; slaves lived with no serious protection from the law or legal authorities. Their standard of living was generally poor. Although owners wanted to see their slave investments reproduce themselves, slaves suffered from overwork and from diseases associated with poor nutrition, sanitation, and housing.

Slaves worked primarily in the fields, where they plowed, hoed, and harvested cotton, rice, sugar, tobacco, or corn. They were usually organized into work gangs supervised by white overseers. This work was, like all farming, seasonal; but during planting or harvest seasons, labor would persist from sunrise to sunset. Children would work in the fields as helpers. Older or more privileged slaves might work in the house, cleaning, cooking, or taking care of children.

Recent scholarship has emphasized how the slave communities helped to preserve the family life and inner personalities of the slaves. Some elements of African culture persisted in the slave communities. African legends were passed on orally. Religion proved extraordinarily important. Slaves also adopted for their own cultural needs the Old Testament stories of the Jews' liberation from Egypt. They also often combined elements of African religion with evangelical Protestantism. Yet despite these efforts to preserve a sense of community and even of family, marriages and family lives of slaves had no legal recognition. The integrity of the slave family could be violated at the master's whim or changing economic circumstances. White masters and their sons often sexually exploited black slave women. Because slaves were property, they could be sold for profit or transported when the owner moved to a different region. Consequently, families could be, and were, separated by sale or perhaps after an owner's death. Many young children were reared and cared for by other slaves to whom they were not related. In a world of white dominance, the institutions, customs, and religions of the slave community were the only means black slaves had to protect the autonomy of their own personalities.

THE ABOLITIONIST MOVEMENT

During the 1830s a militant antislavery movement emerged in the North. Its leaders and followers refused to accept what they regarded as the moral compromise of living in a nation that tolerated slavery. Abolitionists such as William Lloyd Garrison, editor of *The Liberator*, condemned the Union and the Constitution as structures that perpetuated slavery. Former slaves who had escaped slavery, such as Frederick Douglass and Sojourner Truth, and freeborn black Americans, such as Daniel A. Payne, also joined the cause. (See "Daniel A. Payne Denounces American Slavery.") The antislavery movement, which was initially only one of many American reform movements, gained new adherents during the 1840s as the question of extending slavery into the new territories came to the fore in 1847 toward the end of the Mexican War (1846–1848). That military victory added significant new territory in the Southwest and California, in addition to Texas, which had been annexed in 1845. Through negotiations with Britain the United States also acquired the vast Oregon Territory in the Northwest in 1846 (see Map 25–1).

Victory in the Mexican War opened debate on the extension of slavery into the huge new territory it created. Southerners feared that the changing climate of national debate and the opening of territories where slavery might be prohibited would give the South a minority status and thus eventually overturn its political and social culture. Northerners came to believe that a slave-power conspiracy controlled the federal government. The Compromise of 1850 temporarily restored political calm and stability, and reassured the South. But many Northerners came to believe that the compromise only demonstrated the strength of the slave-power conspiracy in Washington.

In 1854 the introduction of the Kansas-Nebraska Bill renewed the formal national political debate over slavery and galvanized the antislavery forces. The principle of the bill, introduced by Stephen A. Douglas (1813–1861), was that of popular sovereignty. The people of each new territory would decide whether slavery was to be permitted within its borders. Douglas was thus willing to repeal the Missouri Compromise, which had prohibited slavery in most of the Louisiana Territory. Popular sovereignty meant that every newly organized territory had to debate slavery. In 1854 the new Republican Party was organized largely in opposition to the Kansas-Nebraska Bill. Not everyone, however, was willing just to argue. For example, John Brown went to Kansas, where armed conflict had already broken out, and carried out virtual guerrilla warfare against slaveholding settlers. During 1854 "Bleeding Kansas" was in a state of civil war.

In 1857, in the Dred Scott decision, the Supreme Court effectively repealed the Missouri Compromise by declaring that Congress could not prohibit slavery in the territories. The decision further declared that slaves did not become free by living in free states and that slaves did not have rights that others were bound to respect. For radical antislavery Northerners, the decision raised the most serious questions about the morality of the Union itself, and it demonstrated again a Southern conspiracy to protect slavery. Thereafter, slavery dominated national political debate.

MAP EXPLORATION

Interactive map: To explore this map further, go to **http://www.prenhall.com/craig2/map25.1**

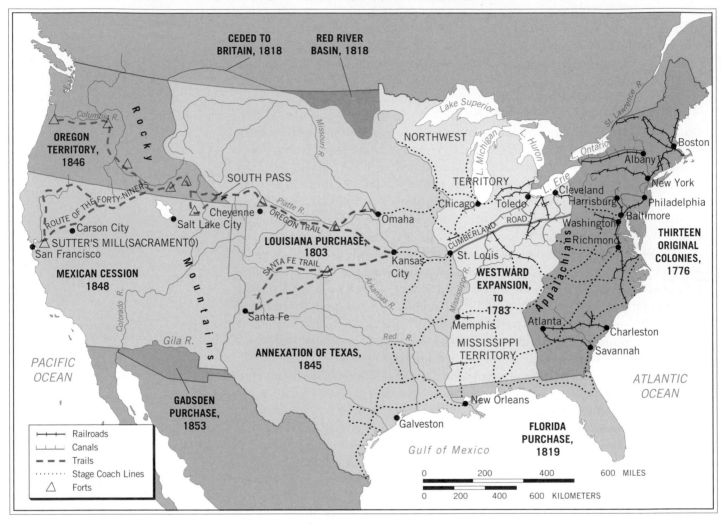

MAP 25–1

Nineteenth-century North America.   During the nineteenth century the United States expanded across the entire North American continent. The revolutionary settlement had provided most of the land east of the Mississippi. The single largest addition thereafter was the Louisiana Purchase of 1803. The annexation of Texas, and later the Mexican Cession following the Mexican War, added the major Southwestern territories. The borders of the Oregon Territory were settled through long, difficult negotiations with Great Britain.

HOW DID the westward expansion of the United States help cause the Civil War?

In 1859 John Brown seized the federal arsenal at Harpers Ferry, Virginia, as part of an effort to foment a possible slave rebellion. He was captured, tried, and hanged, further increasing sectional polarization. Radical Southerners feared more than ever a Northern conspiracy to attack the institution of slavery, while Northern radicals feared that the South would use the federal government to protect slavery. Thus the politics of both sections became radicalized.

· HISTORY'S VOICES ·

DANIEL A. PAYNE DENOUNCES AMERICAN SLAVERY

*D*aniel A. Payne was an African American who became an ordained Lutheran minister. He delivered this speech in June 1839, at his ordination. Though born in Charleston, South Carolina, he was the son of free African Americans. As a young man he had opened a school in that state to educate African American children. He had to abandon this effort after the legislature prohibited teaching free or enslaved African Americans to read and write. Later he became president of Wilberforce University in Xenia, Ohio, which was dedicated to the education of African Americans.

ON WHAT grounds does Payne condemn slavery? What examples of moral brutalization does Payne associate with slavery? How does he bring religious arguments against the evils of slavery?

. . . I am opposed to slavery, not because it enslaves the black man, but because it enslaves *man*. And were all the slaveholders in this land men of color, and the slaves white men, I would be as thorough and uncompromising an abolitionist as I now am; for whatever and whenever I may see a being in the form of a man, enslaved by his fellow man, without respect to his complexion, I shall lift up my voice to plead his cause, against all the claims of his proud oppressor; and I shall do it not merely from the sympathy which man feels towards suffering man, but because *God, the living God*, whom I dare not disobey, has commanded me to open my mouth for the dumb, and to plead the cause of the oppressed.

Slavery brutalizes man. . . . This being God created but a little lower than the angels, and crowned him with glory and honor; but slavery hurls him down from his elevated position, to the level of brutes, strikes this crown of glory from his head and fastens upon his neck the galling yoke, and compels him to labor like an ox, through summer's sun and winter's snow, without remuneration. Does a man take the calf from the cow and sell it to the butcher? So slavery tears the child from the arms of the reluctant mother, and barters it to the soul trader for a young colt, or some other commodity! Does

the bird catcher tear away the dove from his mate? So slavery separates the groaning husband from the embraces of his distracted and weeping wife! . . . The very moment that a man conceives the diabolic design of enslaving his brother's body, that very moment does he also conceive the still more heinous design of fettering his will, for well does he know that in order to make his dominion supreme over the body, he must fetter the living spring of all its motions. Hence, the first lesson the slave is taught is to yield his will unreservedly and exclusively to the dictates of his master. And if a slave desires to educate himself or his children, in obedience to the dictates of reason or the laws of God, he does not, he cannot do it without the consent of his master. . . .

In view of the moral agency of man, God hath most wisely and graciously given him a code of laws, and certain positive percepts, to control and regulate moral actions. This code of laws, and these positive percepts, with the divine influence which they are naturally calculated to exert on the mind of man, constitutes his moral government. . . .

Now, slavery nullifies these laws and percepts—weakens and destroys their influence over the human mind, and hinders men from yielding universal and entire obedience to them; therefore slavery subverts the moral government of God. This is the climax of the sin of slavery. . . .

. . . Slavery never legislates for the religious instruction of slaves, but, on the contrary, legislates to perpetuate their ignorance; and there are laws this very moment in the statute books of South Carolina and other states, prohibiting the religious instruction of slaves. . . .

In a word, slavery tramples the laws of the living God under its unhallowed feet—weakens and destroys the influence which those laws are calculated to exert over the mind of man, and constrains the oppressed to blaspheme the name of the Almighty.

Speech originally printed in the *Lutheran Herald and Journal of the Fort Plain, N. Y., Franckean Synod*, Vol. 1, No 15 (August 1, 1839) as reprinted in Philip S. Foner, ed., *The Voice of Black America: Major Speeches by Negroes in the United States, 1797–1971*. Copyright © 1972, New York: Simon & Schuster, pp. 67–71.

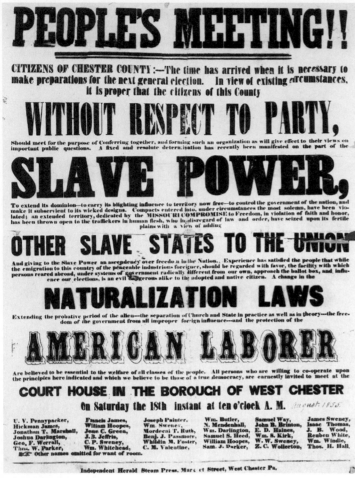

PEOPLE'S MEETING!!

CITIZENS OF CHESTER COUNTY:—The time has arrived when it is necessary to make preparations for the next general election. In view of existing circumstances, it is proper that the citizens of this County

WITHOUT RESPECT TO PARTY,

Should meet for the purpose of Conferring together, and forming such an organization as will give effect to their views on important public questions. A fixed and resolute determination has recently been manifested on the part of the

SLAVE POWER,

To extend its dominion—to carry its blighting influence to territory now free—to control the government of the nation, and make it subservient to its wicked designs. Compacts entered into, under circumstances the most solemn, have been violated; an extended territory, dedicated by the MISSOURI COMPROMISE to Freedom, in violation of faith and honor, has been thrown open to the traffickers in human flesh, who in disregard of law and order, have seized upon its fertile plains with a view of adding

OTHER SLAVE STATES TO THE UNION

And giving to the Slave Power an ascendency over freedom in the Nation. Experience has satisfied the people that while the emigration to this country of the peaceable industrious foreigner, should be regarded with favor, the facility with which persons reared abroad, under systems of government radically different from our own, approach the ballot box, and influence our elections, is an evil dangerous alike to the adopted and native citizen. A change in the

NATURALIZATION LAWS

Extending the probative period of the alien—the separation of Church and State in practice as well as in theory—the freedom of the government from all improper foreign influence—and the protection of the

AMERICAN LABORER

Are believed to be essential to the welfare of all classes of the people. All persons who are willing to co-operate upon the principles here indicated and which we believe to be those of a true democracy, are earnestly invited to meet at the

COURT HOUSE IN THE BOROUGH OF WEST CHESTER

On Saturday the 18th instant at ten o'clock A. M. August 1855.

U. V. Pennypacker, Francis James, Joseph Painter. Wm. Butler, Samuel Way, James Sweney,
Hickman James, William Hoopes, Wm. Sweney, N. Mendenhall, John B. Brinton, Isaac Thomas,
Jonathan T. Marshall, Jesse C. Green, Mordecai T. Ruth, Wm. Darlington, E. D. Haines, J. B. Wood,
Joshua Darlington, J.B. Jeffris, Benj. J. Passmore, Samuel S. Reed, Wm. S. Kirk, Reuben White,
Geo. F. Werrall, C. P. Sweney, Whildin M. Foster, William Hoopes, W. W. Sweney, Wm. Windle,
Thos. W. Parker, Wm. Whitehead, C. M. Valentine, Sam. J. Parker, Z. C. Wollerton, Thos. H. Hall.
Other names omitted for want of room.

Independent Herald Steam Press, Market Street, West Chester Pa.

This strident poster warns that "the Slave Power" aims "to control the government of the nation, and make it subservient to its wicked designs."

The Republican Party had become the party that opposed slavery, although most Republicans did not favor outright abolition. In 1858 Abraham Lincoln (1809–1865) ran against Stephen Douglas for the U.S. Senate in Illinois. Lincoln lost, but made a national reputation for himself in the debates leading up to the election. In 1860 Lincoln, the Republican candidate, was elected president. Neither he nor the Republican Party had campaigned for the abolition of slavery. Nonetheless, Southerners perceived his election as the victory of a party and a president dedicated to the eradication of slavery. In December 1860 Southern states began to secede and formed the Confederate States of America. Attempts at political compromise to maintain the Union failed, and when Confederate forces fired on Fort Sumter in Charleston harbor in April 1861, the most destructive war in U.S. history began.

The Civil War lasted almost exactly four years, and a different nation emerged from the violence. In 1863 Lincoln emancipated the slaves in the rebelling states. The Emancipation Proclamation transformed the Northern cause from that of suppressing a Southern rebellion into that of extending liberty. By the time the Confederacy was defeated in 1865, the South was occupied by Northern armies, its farms were often fallow, its transportation network disrupted, and many of its cities in ruins. Southern political leaders had virtually no impact on the immediate postwar decisions. The Thirteenth, Fourteenth, and Fifteenth Amendments to the Constitution largely recast the character of the Union. The Thirteenth abolished slavery, the Fourteenth granted citizenship to the former slaves, and the Fifteenth allowed them to vote. The Fourteenth Amendment also prohibited much political activity by people who had taken up arms against the Union. These amendments resolved the issues of slavery and the relative roles of the state and federal governments.

The Civil War and the Reconstruction era that followed it overturned the antebellum social and political structures of the South. The slaves were freed and for a time participated broadly and actively in the politics of the Southern states. For more than ten years federal troops occupied parts of the South. Many of the antebellum Southern leaders left political life. Economically, the South remained generally rural and still dependent on cotton. For the first time since the earliest colonial days, it became an area of free labor. Many of the freed slaves and poor whites who tilled the land remained hopelessly in debt to wealthier landowners. Attempts to bring manufacturing into the South met with limited success. Rampant racism also blocked free economic development. For the rest of the century the South remained in a semicolonial relationship to the North. More than ever, in order to pay for the goods and services it needed, the South had to export raw materials or partially finished goods to the North, according to the economic rules set by Northern manufacturers and financiers. Throughout the rural South, poverty was the norm.

Within the context of world history, the American Civil War is important for several reasons. With the exception of the Taiping Rebellion in China from 1851 to 1864, it was the greatest war that occurred anywhere in the world between the defeat of Napoleon in 1815 and the onset of World War I in 1914. It resulted in the establishment of a continent-wide free labor market, even though freed blacks lived in great poverty, and an economic dependence not unlike that of the rural classes of Latin America. The free labor market, purged of slavery, helped to open the entire North American continent to economic development. The war also allowed American political and economic interests to develop without the distraction of the debates over states' rights and the morality of slavery. Thereafter, free labor would become the American norm, and the debates over the role of industrial labor in the United States resembled those in Europe to be discussed in the next chapter.

THE CANADIAN EXPERIENCE

Under the Treaty of Paris of 1763, all of Canada came under the control of Great Britain. Canada then, as now, included both an English-speaking and a French-speaking population. The latter was concentrated primarily in Quebec. The Quebec Act of 1774, which had so disturbed the English colonists along the Atlantic seaboard, made the Roman Catholic Church the established church in Quebec. During the American Revolution approximately 30,000 English loyalists fled the colonies and settled in Canada. They thus established a larger English presence and were strongly loyal to the British Crown.

> HOW DID Canada achieve united self-government?

The tension between the French and English populations led, in part, to the Constitutional Act of 1791, which divided the colony into Upper Canada (primarily English in ethnic composition) and Lower Canada (primarily French). Each section had its own legislature, and a governor-general presided over the two provinces on behalf of the British Crown. Newfoundland, Nova Scotia, New Brunswick, Cape Breton Island, and Prince Edward Island remained separate colonies.

In the early nineteenth century relations with the United States were often tense. There were local disputes over the fur trade and fear that the United States would dominate Canada. That apprehension, along with the Anglo-French ethnic divisions, came to constitute two of the major themes of Canadian history.

By the late 1830s the political situation in Canada was beginning to generate considerable internal pressure. Tension arose between long-established families with powerful economic interests in both Upper and Lower Canada and new settlers who hoped to achieve prosperity for themselves. There were quarrels over the influence of the British Crown in local affairs. In 1837 rebellions occurred in both Upper and Lower Canada. Although there were relatively few casualties, the British realized that some action had to be taken.

ROAD TO SELF-GOVERNMENT

The British government, operating in the more liberal political climate following the first Reform Act (1832), was determined to avoid another North American revolution. Consequently, it sent the Earl of Durham (1792–1840) to Canada with extensive powers to make reforms. In 1839 his *Report on the Affairs of British North America* advocated responsible government for Canada. Durham contended that both Canadian provinces should be united into one political unit. He thought that such political unification would eventually lead to a thoroughly English culture throughout Canada which would overwhelm the French influence in Quebec. He also believed that most Canadian affairs should be in the hands of a Canadian legislature and that only foreign policy and defense should remain under British control. In effect, Durham wanted Canadians generally to govern themselves, so that English culture would dominate. His policy was carried out in the Canada Act of 1840, which gave the nation a single legislature composed of two houses.

The Durham *Report* established the political pattern that the British government would, to a greater or lesser extent, follow with its other English-speaking colonies during the nineteenth century. Britain sought to foster responsible self-government in Australia, New Zealand, and South Africa. The Canadian experience thus had a considerable impact throughout the world. But, until well into the twentieth century, the British government, like other Western imperial powers, also generally believed that nonwhite peoples, such as those of India, required direct British colonial administration.

KEEPING A DISTINCTIVE CULTURE

Canadians did learn to exercise self-government, but distinct English and French cultures continued to exist. Within the legislature there were almost always trade-offs between the eastern and western sections of the nation. Furthermore, during the American Civil War, fears arose that the American republic might seek to invade or dominate Canada. One response to this fear was an attempt to unite the Maritime Provinces in 1862. Those discussions led to broader considerations of the desirability for a stronger federation among all the parts of Canada.

The result of those debates and discussions was the British North America Act of 1867, which created a Canadian federation. Canadians hoped to avoid what they regarded as flaws in the constitution of the United States. The Canadian system of government was to be federal, but with much less emphasis on states' rights than in the United States. Canadians established a parliamentary mode of government, but also chose to retain the presence of the British monarchy in the person of the governor-general as head of state. The person who was most responsible for establishing this new government and who led it for most of the period between 1867 and 1891 was John A. MacDonald (1815–1891).

MIDCENTURY POLITICAL CONSOLIDATION IN EUROPE

WHAT WERE the steps that led to a united Italy?

During the same period that the United States and Canada established themselves as strong unified political entities in North America, major political consolidation occurred in Europe that would have an enormous impact on the rest of the world. As has so often been true in modern European history, war made change possible. In this case a conflict disrupted the international balance that had prevailed since 1815 and quickly unleashed forces that upset the political situation in several of the involved states. The war itself was in some respects less important than the political consequences that flowed from it during the next decade.

THE CRIMEAN WAR (1854–1856) AND ITALIAN UNIFICATION (1859–1870)

The Crimean War (1854–1856), named after the Black Sea peninsula on which it was largely fought, originated from a long-standing rivalry between Russia and the Ottoman Empire. Russia wanted to extend its influence over the Ottoman provinces of Moldavia and Walachia (now in Romania). In 1853 Russia went to war against the Ottomans on the pretext that the Ottomans had given Roman Catholic France, instead of Orthodox Russia, the right to protect Christians and Christian shrines in the Holy Land. The next year France and Great Britain supported the Ottoman Empire to protect their interests in the eastern Mediterranean, while

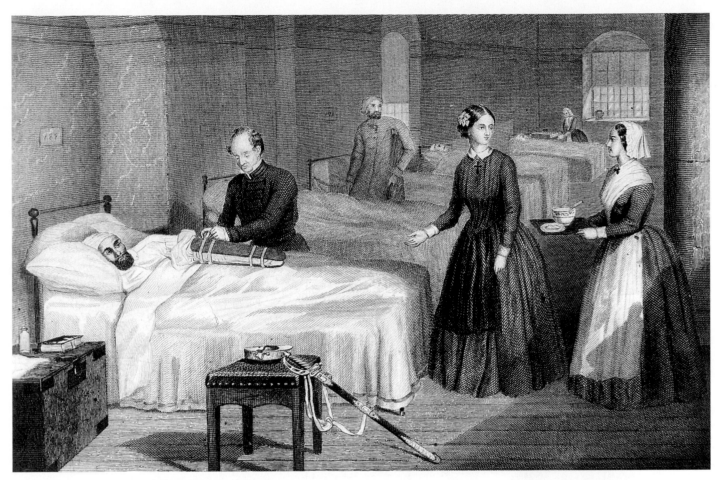

During the Crimean War, Florence Nightingale of Great Britain organized nursing care for the wounded.

Corbis-Bettmann Archive

Austria and Prussia remained neutral. The war quickly bogged down after the French and the British invaded the Crimea. In March 1856 a peace conference in Paris concluded a treaty highly unfavorable to Russia.

The Crimean War shattered the image of an invincible Russia that had prevailed since the close of the Napoleonic Wars. It also shattered the power of the Concert of Europe to settle international disputes on the Continent. The major European powers were no longer willing to cooperate to maintain the existing borders between themselves and their neighbors. For the next 25 years instability prevailed in European affairs, allowing a largely unchecked adventurism in foreign policy.

ITALIAN UNIFICATION

Italian nationalists had long wanted to unite the small absolutist principalities of the peninsula into a single state, but could not agree on how to do it. Romantic republicans such as Giuseppe Mazzini (1805–1872) and Giuseppe Garibaldi (1807–1882), sought to drive out the Austrians by popular military force and then to establish a republic. They not only failed but also frightened more moderate Italians. The person who eventually achieved unification was Count Camillo Cavour (1810–1861) the prime minister of Piedmont.

Piedmont (officially styled the "Kingdom of Sardinia"), in northwestern Italy, was the most independent state on the peninsula (see Map 25–2). It had unsuccessfully fought against Austria in 1848 and 1849. Following the second defeat, King Charles Albert (r. 1831–1849) abdicated in favor of his son, Victor Emmanuel II (r. 1849–1878). In 1852 the new monarch chose Cavour—a moderate liberal in economics and a strong monarchist who rejected republicanism—as his prime minister.

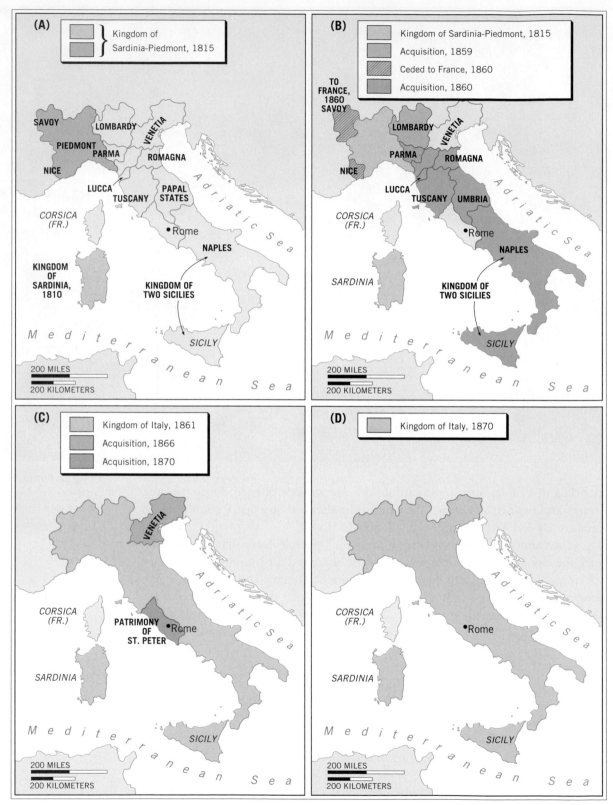

MAP 25–2

The unification of Italy. Beginning with the association of Sardinia and Piedmont by the Congress of Vienna in 1815, unification was achieved through the expansion of Piedmont between 1859 and 1870. Both Cavour's statesmanship and the campaigns of ardent nationalists played large roles.

WHAT WERE the stages of Italian unification between 1815 and 1870?

Cavour believed that if Italians proved themselves to be efficient and economically progressive, the great powers might decide that Italy could govern itself. He worked for free trade, railway construction, credit expansion, and agricultural improvement. He also fostered the Nationalist Society, which established chapters in other Italian states to press for unification under the leadership of Piedmont. Cavour furthermore believed that Italy could be unified only with the aid of France.

Cavour joined the French and British side in the Crimean War to be able to raise the question of Italian unification at the peace conference. There he gained no specific rewards, but did achieve the sympathy of Napoleon III (r. 1852–1870) of France. In 1858 Cavour and the French emperor met and plotted to start a war with Austria.

During the winter and spring of 1859 tension grew between Austria and Piedmont as the latter mobilized its army. In late April war erupted, and France came to Piedmont's aid. On June 4 the Austrians were defeated at Magenta, and on June 24, at Solferino in Lombardy. Fearing too extensive a Piedmontese victory, Napoleon III concluded a separate peace with Austria on July 11 at Villafranca. Piedmont received Lombardy, but the Veneto remained under Austrian control. Cavour felt betrayed by France, but nonetheless the war had driven Austria from most of northern Italy. Later that summer Parma, Modena, Tuscany, and the Romagna voted to unite with Piedmont.

At this point the forces of romantic republican nationalism compelled Cavour to pursue the complete unification of northern and southern Italy. In May 1860 Garibaldi landed in Sicily with more than 1,000 troops. He captured Palermo and prepared to attack the mainland. By September the city and kingdom of Naples, probably the most corrupt example of Italian absolutism, lay under his control. To forestall a republican victory Cavour rushed troops south to confront Garibaldi. On the way Cavour's troops conquered the Papal States except for the area around Rome, which remained under the direct control of the pope.

Garibaldi's nationalism won out over his republicanism, and he unhappily accepted the Piedmontese domination. In late 1860 Naples and Sicily voted to join the northern union forged by Piedmont. In March 1861 Victor Emmanuel II was proclaimed king of Italy. Three months later Cavour died. The new state was governed by the conservative constitution promulgated in 1848 by Charles Albert. Italy gained the Veneto in 1866 as a result of the war between Austria and Prussia, and Rome in 1870 as a result of the Franco-Prussian War.

GERMAN UNIFICATION

A united German nation was the single most important political development in Europe between 1848 and 1914. Germany was united by the conservative army and monarchy of Prussia and by Prussia's conservative prime minister, who sought to outflank the Prussian liberals.

HOW DID Bismarck succeed in unifying Germany?

William I (r. 1861–1888) regarded the Prussian army as his first concern. In 1860 his war minister and chief of staff proposed to enlarge the army and to increase the period of conscription from two to three years. The Prussian parliament, created by the constitution of 1850, refused to approve the necessary taxes. A deadlock continued for two years between the monarch and the Parliament dominated by liberals.

BISMARCK

In September 1862 William I turned for help to the person who, more than any other single individual, shaped the next thirty years of European history: Otto von Bismarck (1815–1898). Bismarck came from Junker stock, and his outlook was deeply informed by the most traditional Prussian values, including admiration for the monarchy, the nobility, and the army. After being appointed prime minister and foreign minister in 1862, Bismarck immediately moved against the liberal parliament. He contended that the Prussian constitution permitted the government to function on the basis of previously granted taxes. Therefore, taxes could be collected and spent, despite the parliamentary refusal to vote them. The army and most of the bureaucracy supported this interpretation of the constitution. However, in 1863 new elections sustained the liberal majority in the parliament. Bismarck had to find some way to attract popular support away from the liberals and toward the monarchy and the army. To that end, he set about uniting Germany through the conservative institutions of Prussia. The tactic amounted to diverting public attention from domestic matters to foreign affairs. It also meant that Prussia now assumed a position of leadership in the effort to unify Germany.

Bismarck pursued what was known as the *kleindeutsch*, or small German, solution to unification. Austria was to be excluded from German affairs when an opportunity presented itself. To achieve that end, Bismarck undertook two brief wars.

In 1864 he went to war with Denmark over the question of the duchies of Schleswig and Holstein, German-speaking areas that had long been administered by the Danish monarchy (see Map 25–3). The Austrians helped defeat

kleindeutsch Meaning "small German." The argument that the German-speaking portions of the Habsburg Empire should be excluded from a united Germany.

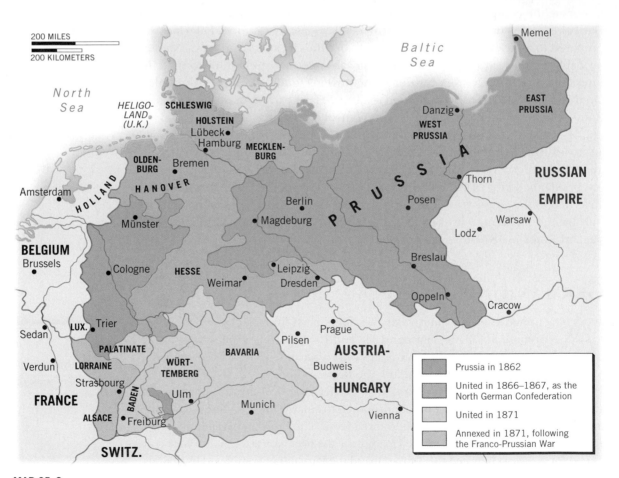

MAP 25–3

The unification of Germany. Under Bismarck's leadership, and with the strong support of its royal house, Prussia used diplomatic and military means, on both the German and international stages, to forcibly unify the German states into a strong national entity.

HOW DID Bismarck use military victories to unify Germany under Prussian leadership?

OVERVIEW

ITALIAN AND GERMAN UNIFICATION

The unifications of Italy and Germany, which took place between 1859 and 1871, were the two most important political developments that occurred in Europe between the end of the Napoleonic Wars in 1815 and the outbreak of World War I in 1914. The creations of the Kingdom of Italy in 1860 and of the German Empire in 1871 were the most significant nationalist triumphs of the nineteenth century. Moreover, the formation of these two states permanently changed the balance of power in Europe. Austria lost its historic role as the dominant power in Italian and German affairs, and Germany replaced France as continental Europe's most powerful nation. Below are the steps by which Italy and Germany achieved unification.

Italy	1855	Piedmont enters the Crimean War on the side of France and Britain.
	1858	Napoleon III of France and Count Cavour of Piedmont secretly discuss a war against Austria in Italy.
	1859	France and Piedmont defeat Austria. Austria cedes Lombardy to Piedmont. Tuscany, Parma, Modena and the Romagna revolt against their pro-Austrian rulers and vote to join Piedmont.
	1860	Garibaldi conquers Sicily and Naples. Cavour sends troops to occupy southern Italy and the Papal States except for Rome.
	1861	Proclamation of the Kingdom of Italy.
	1866	Italy receives Venetia in return for siding with Prussia against Austria in the Austro-Prussian War.
	1870	Italy occupies Rome when the French garrison is withdrawn to fight in the Franco-Prussian War.
Germany	1862	Otto von Bismarck becomes prime minister of Prussia.
	1863	Prussia and Austria defeat Denmark and occupy Schleswig-Holstein.
	1866	Prussia defeats Austria and forms the North German Confederation. Prussia annexes Hanover, Hesse, Nassau, and Frankfurt. The Habsburgs are excluded from German affairs.
	1870	Prussia defeats France in the Franco-Prussian War. The south German states of Bavaria, Wurtemberg, Baden, and Hesse Darmstadt fight alongside Prussia.
	1871	Proclamation of the German Empire. France cedes Alsace-Lorraine to Germany.

Denmark and then with Prussia undertook the joint administration of the two duchies. Thereafter, Bismarck concluded various alliances with France and Italy to gain their support against Austria. War between Prussia and Austria broke out in the summer of 1866. This Seven Weeks' War led to the decisive defeat of Austria at Koniggratz. The Prussian victory and the consequent Treaty of Prague excluded the Habsburgs from German affairs. Prussia became the only major power among the German states.

In 1867 Hanover, Hesse, Nassau, and the city of Frankfurt, all of which had supported Austria during the war, were annexed by Prussia, and their rulers deposed. Prussia and these newly incorporated territories, plus Schleswig and Holstein and the rest of the German states north of the Main River, constituted the North German Confederation. Prussia was its undisputed leader.

THE FRANCO-PRUSSIAN WAR AND THE GERMAN EMPIRE

Bismarck now awaited an opportunity to complete unification by bringing the states of southern Germany into the confederation. The occasion arose as a result of complex diplomacy surrounding the possibility of a cousin of William I of Prussia becoming king of Spain. France was, of course, opposed to the idea of a second state on its borders ruled by a Hohenzollern. Bismarck personally edited a press dispatch surrounding these negotiations to make it appear that

William I had insulted the French ambassador, even though the king had not done so. Bismarck intended to goad France into war, and he succeeded. On July 19 France declared war. Napoleon III hoped that victory would give his regime a new and stronger popular base. Once the war began, the states of southern Germany supported Prussia. On September 1, at Sedan, the Germans not only defeated the French army but also captured Napoleon III. By late September, Paris was besieged. It finally capitulated on January 28, 1871. Ten days earlier, in the Hall of Mirrors at the Palace of Versailles, the German Empire had been proclaimed. The rulers of the states of south Germany had requested William I to accept the imperial title. They, in turn, retained their thrones.

The unification of Germany established a strong, coherent state in the middle of Europe. It had been forged by the Prussian army and would be dominated by Prussian institutions. Its center of power rested on the monarchy and the military. It possessed enormous economic resources and nationalistic ambitions. For the next 80 years Europe would have to come to grips with this new political reality both on the Continent and abroad. The unification of Italy and Germany proved to many people that nationalistic goals could only be achieved by armed force. After its defeat at the hands of Prussia, France would within five years become a republic— the Third Republic—governed by a chamber of deputies, a senate, and a president.

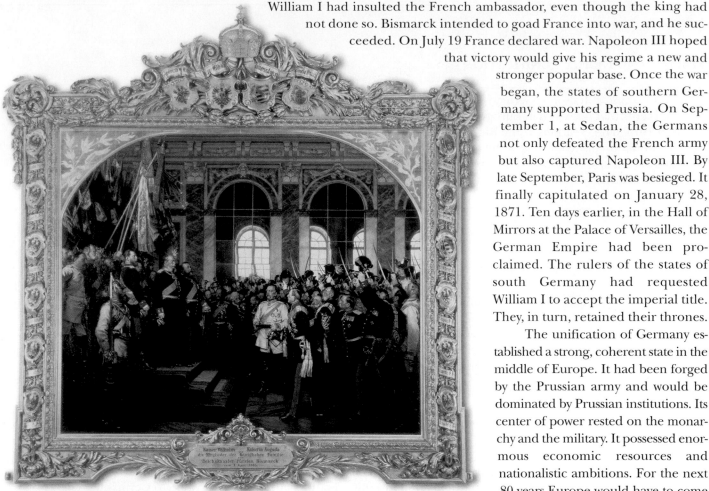

The proclamation of the German Empire in the Hall of Mirrors at Versailles, January 18, 1871, after the defeat of France in the Franco-Prussian War. Kaiser Wilhelm I is standing at the top of the steps under the flags; Bismarck is in the center in a white uniform.

Bildarchiv Preussicher Kulturbesitz/Original: Friedrich-sruher Fassung, Bismarck-Museum

UNREST OF NATIONALITIES IN EASTERN EUROPE

HOW DID nationalism affect the Habsburg Empire?

In the age of national states, liberal institutions, and industrialism, the Habsburg domains remained primarily dynastic, absolutist, and agrarian. Following the Revolutions of 1848 Emperor Francis Joseph (r. 1848–1916) and his ministers attempted to impose a centralized administration on the multinational empire. The system amounted to a military and bureaucratic government dominated by German-speaking Austrians. This situation was especially annoying to the Hungarians. The defeats in 1859 and 1866 and the exclusion of Austria from Italy and from German affairs compelled Francis Joseph to come to terms with the Hungarian nobility. The subsequent **Ausgleich**, or Compromise, of 1867 transformed the Habsburg Empire into a dual monarchy. Francis Joseph was crowned king of Hungary in Budapest. Except for the common monarch, foreign policy, and army, Austria and Hungary became almost separate states (see Map 25–4).

Ausgleich Meaning "compromise." The agreement between the Habsburg Emperor and the Hungarians to give Hungary considerable administrative autonomy in 1867. It created the Dual Monarchy, or Austria-Hungary.

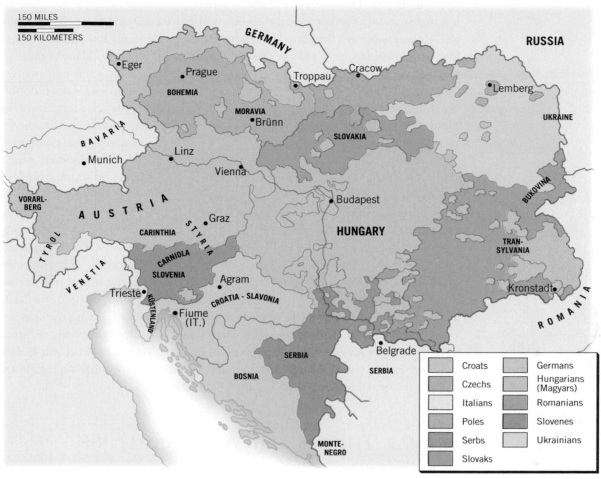

MAP 25–4

Nationalities within the Habsburg Empire.   The patchwork appearance reflects the unusual problem of the numerous ethnic groups that the Habsburgs could not, of course, meld into a modern national state. Only the Magyars were recognized in 1867, leaving nationalist Czechs, Slovaks, and the others chronically dissatisfied.

HOW DID the Compromise of 1867 affect the Habsburg Empire?

Many of the other national groups within the empire—including the Czechs, the Ruthenians, the Romanians, and the Serbo-Croatians—opposed the Compromise because it permitted the German-speaking Austrians and the Hungarian Magyars to dominate all other nationalities in their respective states. The Czechs of Bohemia were the most vocal group. For over twenty years they were conciliated by generous Austrian patronage and posts in the bureaucracy. By the turn of the century the Czechs had become more vocal. They and German-speaking groups in the Austrian Reichsrat disrupted Parliament rather than permit a compromise on language issues. The emperor ruled thereafter by imperial decree with the support of the bureaucracy. Constitutionalism was dead in Austria. It flourished in Hungary only because the Magyars used it to dominate competing national groups.

Nationalist unrest within the Habsburg Empire not only caused internal political difficulties, but also constituted one of the major sources of political instability for all of central and eastern Europe. Virtually all the nationality problems had a foreign policy as well as a domestic political dimension. Both the Serbo- Croatians and

20.1
Program of the Serb Society of National Defense [Narodna Odbrana]

the Poles believed they deserved a wholly independent state in union with their fellow nationals who lived outside the empire. Other national groups, such as Ukrainians, Romanians, and Bosnians, saw themselves as potentially linked to Russia, to Romania, to Serbia, or to a larger yet-to-be-established Slavic state. Many of these nationalities looked to Russia for protection. Out of these nationalistic tensions emerged much of the turmoil that would spark World War I. The dominant German population of Austria proper was generally loyal to the emperor. However, a significant segment of the Austrian German population was strongly nationalistic and yearned to be part of the united German state being established by Bismarck. These nationalistic Germans in the Austrian Empire often hated the non-German national groups, particularly the Jews. Such attitudes would influence the youth and young adulthood of Adolf Hitler (1889–1945) and shape many of his political opinions.

Nationality problems touched each of the three great central and eastern European empires—the German, the Russian, and the Austrian. All had Polish populations. Each shared at least two other major national groups. Each nationality regarded its own aspirations and discontents as more important than the larger good or even survival of the empire they inhabited. The stirrings of nationalism affected the fate of all three empires from the 1860s through the outbreak of World War I. The government of each would be overturned during the war, and the Austrian Empire would disappear. These same unresolved problems of central and eastern European nationalism would then lead directly to World War II. During more recent years they have led to civil war in what was formerly Yugoslavia and to the breakup of what used to be called Czechoslovakia.

RACIAL THEORY AND ANTI-SEMITISM

Articulated racial theory constituted a new component of late-century nationalistic unrest. Racial thinking or **racism** had long existed in Europe. Renaissance explorers had displayed considerable prejudice against nonwhites. Since at least the eighteenth century, biologists and anthropologists had classified human beings according to the color of their skin, their language, and their stage of civilization. Late-eighteenth-century linguistic scholars had observed similarities between many of the European languages and Sanskrit. They then postulated the existence of an ancient race called the Aryans, who had spoken the original language from which the rest derived. During the Romantic period, writers had called the different cultures of Europe *races*. The debates over slavery in the European colonies and the United States had given further opportunity for the development of racial theory. However, in the late nineteenth century the concept of race emerged as a single dominant explanation of the history and the character of large groups of people.

Arthur de Gobineau (1816–1882), a reactionary French diplomat, enunciated the first important theory of race as the major determinant of human history. In his four-volume *Essay on the Inequality of the Human Races* (1853–1854) Gobineau portrayed the troubles of Western civilization as being the result of the long degeneration of the original white Aryan race. It had unwisely intermarried with the inferior yellow and black races, thus diluting the greatness and ability that originally existed in its blood. Gobineau saw no way to reverse this degeneration.

Gobineau's essay remained relatively obscure for years. Houston Stewart Chamberlain (1855–1927), an Englishman who settled in Germany, put racial theory on an alleged scientific basis in his widely read two-volume work entitled *Foundations of the Nineteenth Century* (1899). He championed the concept of bio-

WHY DID anti-Semitism arise in the late nineteenth century?

racism The pseudoscientific theory that biological features of race determine human character and worth.

logical determinism through race. Through the use of contemporary genetic theory, Chamberlain argued in opposition to Gobineau that the human race could be improved and even that a superior race could be developed. Chamberlain then added another element. He pointed to the Jews as the major enemy of European racial regeneration. Chamberlain's book and the lesser works on which it drew thus aided the spread of **anti-Semitism**. Other writings in Germany emphasized the supposed racial and cultural dangers posed by the Jews to traditional German national life.

ANTI-SEMITISM AND THE BIRTH OF ZIONISM

Political and racial anti-Semitism, which cast such dark shadows across the twentieth century, emerged in part from this atmosphere of racial thought. Religious anti-Semitism dated from at least the Middle Ages. Since the French Revolution western European Jews had gradually gained entry into the civil life of Britain, France, Austria, and Germany (see Chapter 26). Popular anti-Semitism, which identified the Jewish community with money and banking interests, persisted. During the last third of the century, as finance capitalism changed the economic structure of Europe, people pressured by the changes became hostile toward the Jewish community. In Austria, Germany, and France various political leaders and parties used such anti-Semitism for their own considerable political advantage.

To this already ugly atmosphere, racial thought contributed the belief that no matter to what extent Jews assimilated themselves and their families into the culture and even the religion of their country, their Jewishness—and thus their alleged danger to the society—would remain. The problem of race was not in the character but in the blood of the Jew. An important Jewish response to this new, rabid outbreak of anti-Semitism was the launching in 1896 of the Zionist movement to found a separate Jewish state in Palestine. Its founder was the Austro-Hungarian Theodor Herzl (1860–1904). The advance of political anti-Semitism, especially in Austria and France, as well as Herzl's personal experiences of discrimination, convinced him that liberal politics and the institutions of the liberal state could not protect the Jews in Europe or ensure that they would be treated justly. In 1896 Herzl published *The Jewish State*, in which he called for a separate state in which the Jews of the world might be assured of those rights and liberties that they should be enjoying in the liberal states of Europe. Furthermore, Herzl followed the tactics of late-century mass democratic politics by directing his appeal in particular to the economically poor Jews who lived in the ghettos of eastern Europe and the slums of western Europe. The original call to **Zionism** thus combined a rejection of the anti-Semitism of Europe with a desire to establish some of the ideals of both liberalism and socialism in a state outside Europe.

Racial thinking and revived anti-Semitism were part of a wider late-century aggressive nationalism. Previously, nationalism had been a literary and liberal movement. From the 1870s onward, however, nationalism became a movement with mass support, well-financed organizations, and political parties. Nationalists tended to redefine nationality in terms of race and blood. The new nationalism opposed the internationalism of both liberalism and socialism. The ideal of nationality was used to overcome the pluralism of class, religion, and geography. The nation and

Theodor Herzl's visions of a Jewish state would eventually lead to the creation of Israel in 1948.

BBC Hulton/Corbis-Bettmann

anti-Semitism Prejudice, hostility, or legal discrimination against Jews.

Zionism The movement to create a Jewish state in Palestine (the Biblical Zion).

its duties replaced religion for many secularized people. It sometimes became a secular religion in the hands of state schoolteachers, who were replacing the clergy as the instructors of youth. This aggressive, racist nationalism would prove to be the most powerful ideology of the early twentieth century.

SUMMARY

Nationalism Nationalism is the modern concept that people who share the same customs, culture, language, and history should also share the same government. It became the most powerful European political ideology of the nineteenth and early twentieth centuries. Nationalists challenged both the domestic and the international order of the Vienna settlement in the decades after 1815.

Liberalism Politically, nineteenth-century liberals sought to establish constitutional governments that recognized civil liberties and made the executive responsible to a legislature elected by men of wealth and property. Economically, liberals wanted a laissez-faire economy with minimal government involvement. People should be free to use their talents and property to enrich themselves without the state intervening to protect the working classes or the poor. Liberals often supported nationalists' efforts to create a single national state that could function as a more efficient economic unit. Although efforts to liberalize tsarist Russia failed, liberalism largely triumphed in France after the Revolution of 1830 and in Britain after the passage of the Great Reform Bill. The British were, however, unable to resolve the problem of Irish nationalism in the nineteenth century.

Italian and German Unification With French assistance, Piedmont and its premier Count Camillo Cavour managed to unite most of the Italian peninsula by 1860. The new Kingdom of Italy was formed from the northern Italian duchies, Austrian Lombardy, the Papal States, and the Kingdom of the Two Sicilies. Austrian Venetia was added in 1866, and Italy occupied Papal Rome in 1870.

German unification was achieved by Prussia under the leadership of Otto von Bismarck between 1864 and 1871. In three victorious wars against Denmark, Austria, and France, Bismarck forged the German states into a German Empire dominated by Prussia. Germany was henceforth the dominant power on the European continent.

North America In the United States, westward expansion and war against Mexico brought vast new territories under the republic from the Mississippi River to the Pacific, but sectional conflict between North and South over economic issues and slavery led to the outbreak of the Civil War in 1861. Northern victory led to the abolition of slavery, the creation of a continent-wide free labor market, and enormous economic development that would make the United States the world's leading industrial power in the twentieth century.

Canada in these years achieved self-government from Britain and created a united Canadian federation in 1867. However, Canada remained part of the British Empire and retained its connection with the British monarchy.

Eastern Europe Nationalism created problems for the three eastern European empires: Germany, Russia, and Austria, but Habsburg Austria faced the greatest challenge from nationalism because it was a dynastic, not a national, state. Eleven different nationalities made up the Habsburg Monarchy, each with its own national

IMAGE KEY
for pages 534–535

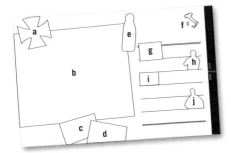

a. Portrait heads of Prussian leaders
b. Eugene Delacroix, Liberty Leading the People
c. Federal flag that flew over Ft. Sumter
d. Battle flag of the Second Battalion Hilliard's Alabama Legion
e. Susan B. Anthony medal
f. Relief Map of Italy
g. The leaders of Europe in debate during the Congress of Vienna
h. Gladstone
i. John Brown and his men were trapped by the fire of the U.S. Marines
j. Italian Nationalist General Garibaldi

aspirations. In 1867 the Habsburgs worked out the *Ausgleich*, or Compromise, with the Magyars, by which Hungary became an autonomous kingdom under the Habsburg emperor. Thereafter the Habsburg Monarchy became known as Austria-Hungary. However, Czechs, Croats, and other Slavs in the Monarchy became increasingly dissatisfied.

Racism and Anti-Semitism In the late nineteenth century, biological determinism, the concept that some peoples or races were inherently superior to others, took root in Western thought. In Germany, Austria, and France, some nationalists used the concept of race to blame the Jews for their countries' economic and political problems. Part of the Jewish response was the launching of the Zionist movement to found a separate Jewish state.

REVIEW QUESTIONS

1. What is nationalism? What areas saw significant nationalist movements between 1815 and 1830? Which were successful and which unsuccessful?

2. Who were the liberals and how did liberalism affect the political developments of the early nineteenth century? What relationship does liberalism have to nationalism?

3. What economic differences between the American North and the South gave rise to sectional conflict? Why was slavery the core issue in that conflict? How did the westward movement contribute to making slavery so important an issue?

4. Why was it so difficult to unify Italy?

5. Who was Otto von Bismarck and why did he try to unify Germany? What was Bismarck's method of unification and why did he succeed? What effect did the unification of Germany have on the rest of Europe?

6. What were the origins of the modern idea of racial theory? Who were its major proponents? How did the rise of such a theory change European anti-Semitism?

KEY TERMS

anti-Semitism (p. 561)

Ausgleich (p. 558)

Catholic Emancipation (p. 541)

Chartism (p. 542)

Great Reform Bill (1832) (p. 541)

home rule (p. 542)

July Monarchy (p. 540)

kleindeutsch (p. 556)

liberalism (p. 537)

nationalism (p. 536)

racism (p. 560)

Zionism (p. 561)

 For additional study resources for this chapter, go to:
www.prenhall.com/craig/chapter25

EUROPE

◄ Karl Marx

1852–1870	The Second French Empire, under Napoleon III
1854–1856	The Crimean War
1861	Italy unified
1861	Emancipation of Russian serfs
1866	Austro-Prussian War; creation of Dual Monarchy of Austria-Hungary in 1867
1870–1871	Franco-Prussian War; German Empire proclaimed in 1871
1873	Three Emperors League

▲ German Empire proclaimed

NEAR EAST/ INDIA

1857–1858	Sepoy Rebellion: India placed directly under the authority of the British government in 1858
1869	Suez Canal completed; 1875, British purchase controlling interest
1869–1948	Mohandas (Mahatma) Gandhi
1876–1949	Muhammad Ali Jinnah, "founder of Pakistan"

"Mahatma" Gandhi ►

EAST ASIA

1850–1873	Taiping and other rebellions
1853–1854	Commodore Perry "opens" Japan to the West, ending seclusion policy
1859	French seize Saigon
1860s	Establishment of treaty ports in China
1864	French protectorate over Cambodia
1868	Meiji Restoration in Japan
1870s	Civilization and Enlightenment movement in Japan
1870s–1890s	Self-Strengthening movement in China

The empress ► dowager Tz'u-hsi

AFRICA

1856–1884	King Mutasa of Buganda reigns
1870	British protectorate in Zanzibar
1879–1880	Henry M. Stanley gains the Congo for Belgium
1880s	Mahdist revival and uprising in Sudan
1880	French protectorate in Tunisia and the Ivory Coast

THE AMERICAS

1854	Kansas-Nebraska Act
1856	Dred Scott Decision
1859	Raid on Harper's Ferry
1860	Abraham Lincoln elected U.S. president
1861–1865	U.S. Civil War
1862–1867	French invasion of Mexico
1863	Emancipation Proclamation in United States
1865–1877	Reconstruction
1865–1870	Paraguayan War
1879–1880	Argentinian conquest of the desert

◄ Abraham Lincoln

PART 6 · INTO THE MODERN WORLD

1882 Triple Alliance
1890 Bismarck dismissed by Kaiser Wilhelm II
1902 Entente Cordiale
1905 January 22, "Bloody Sunday"
1905 Revolution in Russia
1914 War begins in Europe

◄ *Bloody Sunday*

1882 English occupation of Egypt
1886 India National Congress formed
1889–1964 Jawaharlal Nehru
1899 Ottoman sultan Abdulhamid II grants concession to Kaiser Wilhelm II to extend railway to Baghdad ("Berlin-to-Badhdad" Railway)
1908 "Young Turk" Revolt

1889 Meiji Constitution in Japan
1894–1895 Sino-Japanese War; Japan gets Taiwan as colony
1898–1900 Boxer Rebellion in China
1904–1905 Russo-Japanese War
1910 Japan annexes Korea
1911 Republican Revolution begins in China; Ch'ing dynasty overthrown

Promulgation ▶
of the
Meiji Constitution

1884–1885 International Conference in Berlin to prepare rules for further acquisition of African territory; the Congo Free State declared
1884 German Southwest Africa
1885 British control Nigeria and British East Africa
1894 French annex Dahomey
1899 German East Africa; British in Sudan
1899–1902 Boer War
1900 Nigeria a British Crown colony
1907 Orange Free State and the Transvaal join with Natal and Cape Colony to form the Union of South Africa
1911 Liberia becomes a virtual U.S. protectorate
1914 Ethiopia the only independent state in Africa

◄ *European exploitation of Africa*

1880s Slavery eliminated in Cuba and Brazil
1898 Spanish-American War
1901 Theodore Roosevelt elected U.S. president
1910–1917 Mexican Revolution
1912 Woodrow Wilson elected U.S. president

◄ *Slavery in Brazil*

Georges Seurat, (French, 1859–1891),
A Sunday on La Grande Jatte–1884.

Oil on canvas, 207.6 × 308 cm. Helen Birch

Bartlett Memorial Collection, 1926.224.

26

NORTHERN TRANSATLANTIC ECONOMY AND SOCIETY

1815 – 1914

WHAT DOES the term *proletarianization* mean?

WHY DID Europe become more urbanized after 1850?

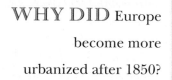

WHAT SOCIAL AND LEGAL disabilities did European women confront in the nineteenth century?

HOW DID emancipation affect Jewish participation in European social and political life outside of Russia?

WHY DID Marxism become so influential among European socialists?

HOW DID industrialization in the United States differ from industrialization in Europe?

IMAGE KEY
Image Key for pages 566–567
is on page 597.

During the nineteenth century, north-western Europe and the United States developed major industrial economies. These economies produced more goods and services than ever before in world history. This economic achievement undergirded the enormous international political power exerted by the industrial nations of the West from that time to the present.

The first half of the nineteenth century witnessed in Europe and to a lesser extent in the United States the emergence of a new kind of industrial labor force. These laborers worked in factories rather than in their homes or in small artisan workshops. More often than not the new industrial working class dwelled in cities. The presence and growth of this new labor force were the most important social developments of the century and would produce a vast influence on European and American political life. It was out of the social and political experience of this workforce that the political movement known as socialism arose.

In the second half of the nineteenth century European and American political, economic, and social life assumed many characteristics of our present-day world. In Europe nation-states with large electorates, political parties, centralized bureaucracies, and universal military service emerged. In the United States the politics associated with the Progressive movement brought the presidency to the center of American political life. On both sides of the North Atlantic, business adopted large-scale corporate structures, and the labor force organized itself into trade unions. The number of white-collar laborers grew as urban life became predominant throughout western Europe. But even as new vast cities arose in the United States, farming continued to spread across the central Midwest and upper Southwest. During this period, too, women began to assert new political awareness and to become politically active in both Europe and America.

During these same years Europe quietly became dependent on the resources and markets of the rest of the world. Farms in the United States, Canada, Latin America, Australia, and New Zealand supplied food to much of the world. Consequently climate changes in Kansas, Argentina, or New Zealand might now affect the European economy. However, before World War I the dependence was concealed by Europe's industrial, military, and financial supremacy. At the time Europeans assumed their supremacy to be natural, but the twentieth century would reveal it to have been temporary. Nevertheless, while it prevailed, Europeans dominated most of the other peoples of the earth and displayed extreme self-confidence. Toward the close of the nineteenth century the United States, having achieved the status of a major industrial power as well as an agricultural supplier, now entered the world stage as a military power, defeating Spain in the Spanish American War in 1898. With that victory, the United States also acquired its first colonial territories.

EUROPEAN FACTORY WORKERS AND URBAN ARTISANS

Although the seeds of industrial production had been sown in the eighteenth century, it was only in the nineteenth century that much of Europe headed toward a more fully industrial society. By 1830 only Great Britain had already attained that status, but new factories and railways were beginning to be constructed elsewhere in Europe. However, what characterized the second quarter of the century was less the triumph of industrialism than the final gasps of those economic groups that opposed it and were displaced by it. Intellectually, the period saw the formulation of the major creeds supporting and criticizing the new society.

In much of northern Europe both artisans and factory workers underwent a process of ***proletarianization***. This term indicates the entry of workers into a wage economy and their gradual loss of significant ownership of the means of production, such as tools and equipment, and of control over the conduct of their own

---

WHAT DOES the term
proletarianization mean?

19.1
Sybil (1845) Benjamin Disraeli

proletarianization The process whereby independent artisans and factory workers lose control of the means of production and of the conduct of their own trades to the owners of capital.

trades. The process occurred rapidly wherever the factory system arose. The factory owner provided the financial capital to construct the factory, purchase the machinery, and secure the raw materials. The factory workers contributed their labor for a wage. Those workers also submitted to factory discipline, which meant that work conditions became largely determined by the demands for smooth operation of the machines. Closing of factory gates to late workers, fines for lateness, dismissal for drunkenness, and public scolding of faulty laborers constituted attempts to enforce regularity on humans that would match the regularity of cables, wheels, and pistons. The factory workers had no direct say over the quality of the product or its price. It should be noted that for all their difficulties, factory conditions were often better than those of textile workers who resisted the factory mode of production. In particular, English hand-loom weavers, who continued to work in their homes, experienced decades of declining trade and growing poverty in their unsuccessful competition with power looms.

Urban artisans in the nineteenth century experienced proletarianization more slowly than factory workers, and machinery had little to do with the process. The emergence of factories in itself did not harm urban artisans. Many even prospered from the development. For example, the construction and maintenance of the new machines generated demand for metal workers, who consequently did well. The actual erection of factories and the expansion of cities benefited all craftsmen in the building trades, such as carpenters, roofers, joiners, and masons. The lower prices for machine-made textiles aided artisans involved in the making of clothing, such as tailors and hatters, by reducing the costs of their raw materials. Where the urban artisans encountered difficulty, and found their skills and livelihood threatened, was in the organization of production.

In the eighteenth century a European town or city workplace had usually consisted of a few artisans laboring for a master, first as apprentices and then as journeymen, according to established guild regulations and practices. The master owned the workshop and the larger equipment, and the apprentices and journeymen owned their tools. The journeyman could expect to become a master. This guild system had allowed considerable worker control over labor recruitment and training, production pace, product quality, and price.

In the nineteenth century the situation of the urban artisan changed. It became increasingly difficult for artisans to continue to exercise corporate or guild direction and control over their trades. The French Revolution had outlawed such organizations in France. Across Europe, political and economic liberals disapproved of labor and guild organizations and attempted to make them illegal.

Other destructive forces were also at work. The masters often found themselves under increased competitive pressure from larger, more heavily capitalized establishments or from the possibility of the introduction of machine production into a previously craft-dominated industry. In many workshops masters began to follow a practice, known in France as *confection*, whereby goods such as shoes, clothing, and furniture were produced in standard sizes and styles rather than by special orders for individual customers. This practice increased the division of labor in the workshop. Each artisan produced a smaller part of the uniform final product. Consequently, less skill was required of each artisan, and the particular skills possessed by a worker became less valuable. Masters also attempted to increase production and reduce their costs for piecework. Those attempts often led to work stoppages or strikes. Migrants from the countryside or small towns into the cities created, in some cases, a surplus of relatively unskilled workers who were willing to work for lower wages or under less favorable and protected conditions than traditional artisans. The dilution of skills and lower wages, caused not by

machinery but by changes in the organization of artisan production, made it much more difficult for urban journeymen ever to hope to become masters with their own workshops where they would be in charge. Increasingly, these artisans became lifetime wage laborers whose skills were simply bought and sold in the marketplace.

In the United States defenders of slavery frequently compared what they claimed to be the protected situation of slaves living on plantations with the plight of factory workers in both Europe and the northern United States. They argued that a free market in wage labor left workers worse off than slaves. But the situation in the European labor market as in the American North was much more complicated than the defenders of slavery contended.

NINETEENTH-CENTURY URBAN LIFE IN EUROPE

After 1850 the Continent and Great Britain became more urbanized than ever before. The rural migrants to the cities were largely uprooted from traditional social ties. They often confronted poor housing, social anonymity, and potential unemployment because they rarely possessed skills that would make them easily employable. The difficulties that people from different ethnic backgrounds had in mixing socially and the competition for too few jobs generated new varieties of political and social discontent, such as those experienced by the thousands of Russian Jews who migrated to western Europe. Much of the political anti-Semitism of the latter part of the century had its social roots in these problems of urban migration.

REDESIGN OF CITIES

The inward urban migration placed new social and economic demands on already strained city resources and gradually transformed the patterns of urban living. The centers of many major European cities were redesigned during the second half of the century. Previously, the central areas of cities had been places where many people from all social classes both lived and worked. From the middle of the century onward they became transformed into districts where relatively few people resided and where businesses, government offices, large retail stores, and theaters were located. Commerce, trade, government, and leisure activities now dominated central cities.

Development of Suburbs The commercial development of the central portions of cities, the clearing of slums, and the extension of railways into cities displaced many people who had previously lived in city centers. These developments also raised the price of centrally located urban land and raised the rents charged on buildings located in the centers of cities. Consequently, both the middle classes and the working class began to seek housing elsewhere. The middle classes sought to avoid urban congestion, the working class to find affordable housing. As a result, outside the urban cen-

WHY DID Europe become more urbanized after 1850?

The condition of European industrial workers entered the political debates on both sides of the Atlantic. This 1841 proslavery cartoon from the United States contrasts allegedly healthy, well-caredfor African American slaves with unemployed British factory workers living in poverty. American pro-slavery advocates also frequently made the comparison between supposed contented Southern slaves and miserable Northern "wages slaves."

Library of Congress

OVERVIEW

MAJOR EUROPEAN CITIES IN 1914

Between 1850 and the outbreak of World War I, European cities from Britain to Russia grew rapidly as rural populations moved to the cities in search of jobs, stimulation, and social opportunities. The tables below show the growth of seven major European cities between 1850 and 1910 and list 14 other European cities whose populations had grown to exceed 500,000 by 1914.

The Growth of Major Cities	1850	1880	1914
Berlin	419,000	1,122,000	2,071,000
Birmingham	233,000	437,000	840,000
Frankfurt	65,000	137,000	415,000
London	2,685,000	4,470,000	7,256,000
Madrid	281,000	398,000	600,000
Paris	1,053,000	2,269,000	2,888,000
Vienna	444,000	1,104,000	2,031,000

Cities with More than 500,000 People, 1914

Amsterdam	Hamburg	Munich
Barcelona	Istanbul	Naples
Brussels	Liverpool	St. Petersburg
Budapest	Manchester	Warsaw
Glasgow	Moscow	

ter proper, suburbs arose in virtually all countries to house the families whose bread-winner worked in the central city or in factories within the city limits and traveled back and forth by train or later by buses or bicycles.

URBAN SANITATION

Impact of Cholera   Broad concern for public health first manifested itself as a result of the great cholera epidemics of the 1830s and 1840s, during which thousands of Europeans, especially those in cities, had died. This disease of Asian origin, previously unknown in Europe, was unlike many other common deadly diseases of the day that touched only the poor; cholera struck persons from all classes and thus generated middle-class demand for a solution. Before the development of the bacterial theory of disease late in the century, physicians and sanitary reformers believed that cholera and other diseases were spread through infection from miasmas in the air. The miasmas, the presence of which was noted by their foul odors, were believed to arise from filth. The way to get rid of the dangerous, foul-smelling air was to clean up the cities.

New Water and Sewer Systems   The proposed solution to the health hazard was cleanliness, to be achieved through new water and sewer systems. Construction of these new facilities proceeded slowly. They were usually first begun

· HISTORY'S VOICES ·

A FRENCH PHYSICIAN DESCRIBES A WORKING-CLASS SLUM IN LILLE

It is difficult to conceive of the world before the sanitation movement. The work of medical doctors frequently carried them into working-class areas of industrial cities rarely visited by the middle class. Louis Villermé was such a French physician. He described the slums and living conditions of industrial workers. The passage here, published in 1840, describes a particularly notorious section of Lille, a major cotton-manufacturing town in northern France.

WHAT DOES this physician find most disturbing about the scene he describes? How is his description designed to evoke concern from a middle-class reader? How might the conditions described have led the poor of France toward socialism or radical politics? How would addressing the problems described have increased the role of government?

The poorest live in the cellars and attics. These cellars . . . open onto the streets or courtyards, and one enters them by a stairway which is very often at once the door and the window. . . . Commonly the height of the ceiling is six or six and a half feet at the highest point, and they are only ten to fourteen or fifteen feet wide.

It is in these somber and sad dwellings that a large number of workers eat, sleep, and even work. The light of day comes an hour later for them than for others, and the night an hour earlier.

Their furnishings normally consist, along with the tools of their profession, of a sort of cupboard or a plank on which to deposit food, a stove . . . a few pots, a little table, two or three poor chairs, and a dirty pallet of which the only pieces are a straw mattress and scraps of a blanket. . . .

In their obscure cellars, in their rooms, which one would take for cellars, the air is never renewed, it is infected; the walls are plastered with garbage. . . . If a bed exists, it is a few dirty, greasy planks; it is damp and putrescent straw; it is a coarse cloth whose color and fabric are hidden by a layer of grime; it is a blanket that resembles a sieve. . . . The furniture is dislocated, worm-eaten, covered with fifth. Utensils are thrown in disorder all over the dwelling. The windows, always closed, are covered by paper and glass, but so black, so smoke-encrusted, that the light is unable to penetrate . . . everywhere are piles of garbage, of ashes, of debris from vegetables picked up from the streets, of rotten straw; of animal nests of all sorts; thus, the air is unbreathable. One is exhausted, in these hovels, by a stale, nauseating, somewhat piquante odor, odor of filth, odor of garbage. . . .

And the poor themselves, what are they like in the middle of such a slum? Their clothing is in shreds, without substance, consumed, covered, no less than their hair, which knows no comb, with dust from the workshops. And their skin? . . . It is painted, it is hidden, if you wish, by indistinguishable deposits of diverse exudations.

From Louis René Villermé, *Tableau de l'état et de soie* (Paris, 1840), as quoted and trans. in William H. Sewell, Jr., *Work and Revolution in France: The Language of Labor from the Old Regime to 1848*. Copyright © 1980 Cambridge University Press, p. 224.

in capital cities and then much later in provincial cities. Some major urban areas lacked good water systems until after 1900. Nonetheless, the building of these systems constituted one of the major health and engineering achievements of the second half of the nineteenth century. Wherever these sanitary reforms were undertaken, the mortality rate decreased.

When the bacterial theory of disease had become fully accepted at the close of the century, the necessity of cleanliness assumed an ever greater role in public life. The discoveries of Louis Pasteur (1822–1895) in France, Robert Koch (1843–1910) in Germany, and Joseph Lister (1827–1912) in Britain paved the way for the slow acceptance of the use of antiseptics in medicine and public health policy. Thereafter, throughout Europe, the maintenance of public health and the physical well-being of national populations repeatedly opened the way for government intervention in the lives of citizens and vastly expanded the social role of medical and scientific experts and governmental bureaucracies.

HOUSING REFORM AND MIDDLE-CLASS VALUES

The information about working-class living conditions brought to light by the sanitary reformers also led to heated debates over the housing problem. The wretched dwellings of the poor were themselves a cause of poor sanitation and thus became one of the newly perceived health hazards. Furthermore, middle-class reformers and bureaucrats were shocked by the domestic arrangements of the poor, whose large families might live in a single room with no personal privacy. A single toilet facility might serve a whole block of tenements. These same reformers believed such terrible living conditions would cause political unrest. (See "A French Physician Describes a Working-Class Slum in Lille.")

Middle-class reformers thus turned to housing reform to solve the medical, moral, and political dangers posed by slums. They praised the home, as it was understood by the middle class, as a remedy for these dangers. Proper, decent housing would foster a good home life, which would in turn lead to a healthy, moral, and politically stable population. Later advocates of housing reform saw good housing as leading to good family life and then to strong national patriotism on the part of the well-housed family. It was also believed that the personal saving and investment required for owning a home would lead the working class to adopt the thrifty habits of the middle classes.

By the mid-1880s, as a result of mass migration into the cities, the housing issue had become a major political question. Governmental action seemed inescapable. The actual policies differed markedly in each country, but all were hesitant. In England an 1885 act lowered interest rates for the construction of cheap housing. A few years later town councils, especially that of London, began to construct public housing. In Germany action came later in the century, primarily through the initiative of municipalities. In 1894 France made credit more available for housing the poor, and this legislation was expanded after 1900. By 1914 the necessity for planning and action was fully recognized if not adequately addressed in much of Europe. The middle-class housing reformers had, moreover, defined the debate. The values and the character of the middle-class family house and home had become the ideal. The goal of housing reform across western Europe came to be that of a dwelling—whether a detached house or an affordable city apartment with several rooms.

NINETEENTH-CENTURY EUROPEAN WOMEN

The industrial economy ultimately produced an immense impact on the home and the family life of women. First, it took virtually all productive work out of the home and allowed many families to live on the wages of the male spouse alone. That transformation prepared the way for a new concept of gender-determined roles in the home and in general domestic life. Women came to be associated with domestic duties such as housekeeping, food preparation, child rearing and nurturing, and household management. The man came to be associated almost exclusively with breadwinning. Children were reared to match these gender patterns. Previously, this domestic division of labor had prevailed only among the relatively small middle and gentry class. During the nineteenth century it came to characterize the working class as well. Second,

WHAT SOCIAL and legal disabilities did European women confront in the nineteenth century?

19.3
Sadler Report: Child Labor

industrialization created new modes of employment that allowed many young women to earn enough money to marry or, if necessary, to support themselves independently. Third, industrialism, although fostering more employment for women, lowered the skills required of them.

WOMEN IN THE EARLY INDUSTRIAL REVOLUTION

Because the early Industrial Revolution had begun in textile production, women and their labor were deeply involved from the start. While both spinning and weaving were still domestic industries, women usually worked in all stages of production. Hand spinning was virtually always a woman's task. When spinning was moved into factories and involved large machines, however, men displaced women. The higher wages commanded by male cotton-factory workers allowed many women to stop working or to work only to supplement their husbands' wages.

With the next generation of machines in the 1820s unmarried women rapidly became employed in the factories. However, their jobs tended to require less skill than most work done by men and than women had previously exercised in the home production of textiles. There was thus a certain paradox in the impact of the factory on women. Many new jobs opened to them, but those jobs were less skilled than what had been available to them before. Moreover, the women in the factories were almost always young and single or widows. At marriage or perhaps at the birth of the first child, a woman usually found that her husband earned enough money for her to leave the factory. Factory owners also disliked employing married women because of the likelihood of pregnancy, the influence of husbands, and the duties of child rearing.

In Britain and elsewhere by midcentury, industrial factory work accounted for less than half of all employment for women. The largest group of employed women in France continued to work on the land. In England they were domestic servants. Domestic industries, such as lace glove and garment making and other kinds of needlework, employed many women. Their conditions of labor were almost always harsh, whether they worked in their homes or in sweated workshops. Generally all work done by women commanded low wages and involved low skills. They had virtually no way to protect themselves from exploitation. The charwoman was a common sight across the Continent and symbolized the plight of working women.

One of the most serious problems facing working women was the uncertainty of employment. Because they virtually always found themselves in the least skilled jobs and trades, their employment was never secure. Much of their work was seasonal. This was one reason so many working-class women feared they might be compelled to turn to prostitution. On the other hand, cities and the more complex economy did allow a greater variety of jobs. Movement to cities and entrance into the wage economy also gave women wider opportunities for marriage. Cohabitation before marriage seems to have been common. Parents did not arrange marriages as frequently as in the past. Marriage also generally meant that a woman would leave the workforce to live on her husband's earnings. If all went well, that arrangement might improve her situation, but if the husband became ill or died, or deserted her, she would have to reenter the market for unskilled labor at a much advanced age.

Nonetheless, many of the traditional practices associated with the family economy survived into the industrial era. As a young woman came of age, both family needs and her desire to marry still directed what she would do with her life. The most likely early occupation for a young woman was domestic service. A girl born in the country normally migrated to a nearby town or city for such employment, often living initially with a relative. As in the past, she would attempt to earn enough in wages to give herself a dowry so that she might marry and establish her own household. If she became a factory worker she would probably live in a supervised dormitory. Such dormitories were one of the ways factory owners attracted young women workers, by convincing parents that their daughters would be safe. The life of young women in the cities seems to have been more precarious than it had been earlier. There seem to have been fewer family and community ties. There were also perhaps more available young men. These men, who worked for wages rather than in the older apprenticeship structures, were more mobile, so relationships between men and women were often more fleeting. In any case, illegitimate births increased. That is to say, fewer women who became pregnant before marriage found the father willing to marry them.

Marriage in the wage industrial economy was also different. It still involved the starting of a separate household, but the structure of gender relationships within the household was different. Marriage was less an economic partnership: The husband might be able to support the entire family. The wage economy and the industrialization that separated workplace and home made it difficult for women to combine domestic duties with work. When married women worked, it was usually in the nonindustrial sector of the economy. More often than not children rather than the wife were sent to work, which may help explain the increase of fertility within marriages, since children in the wage economy tended to be an economic asset. Married women worked outside the home only when family needs or illness or the death of a spouse really required them to do so.

Within the home, the domestic duties of working-class women were an essential factor in the family wage economy. Homemaking came to the fore when a life at home had to be organized that was separate from the place of work. Wives were primarily concerned with food and cooking, but they often also were in charge of the family's finances. The role of the mother expanded when the children still living at home became wage earners. She was then providing home support for her entire wage-earning family. She created the environment to which the family members returned after work. The longer period of home life of working children may also have strengthened the affection between those children and their hardworking, homebound mothers.

WOMEN'S SOCIAL DISABILITIES

During the early nineteenth century virtually all European women faced social and legal disabilities in property rights, family law, and education. By the close of the century each area had shown improvement. In this period European women, like European men, led lives that reflected their social rank. Yet within each rank, the experience of women was distinct from that of men. Women remained, generally speaking, economically dependent and legally inferior, whatever their social class. Their position thus resembled that of women around the world in that all women found their lives circumscribed by traditional social customs and expectations.

Women and Property   Until the last quarter of the century in most European countries no married women, whatever their social class, could own property in their own names. In effect, upon marriage women lost to their husbands' control any property they owned or that they might inherit or earn by their own labor. Their legal identities were subsumed into their husbands' and they had no independent standing before the law. The courts saw the theft of a woman's purse as a theft of her husband's property. Because European society was based on private property and wage earning, these disabilities put married women at a great disadvantage, limiting their freedom to work, save, and relocate.

Reform of women's property rights came slowly. By 1882 Great Britain allowed married women to own property in their own right. In France, however, a married woman could not even open a savings account in her own name until 1895, and not until 1907 were married women granted possession of their own wages. In 1900 Germany allowed women to take jobs without their husbands' permission, but a German husband retained control of most of his wife's property except for her wages. Similar laws prevailed elsewhere in Europe.

Family Law   European family law also worked to the disadvantage of women. Legal codes required wives to obey their husbands. The Napoleonic Code and the remnants of Roman law made women legal minors throughout Europe. Divorce was difficult for most of the century. In England until 1857 divorce required an act of Parliament. Most nations did not permit divorce by mutual consent. French law forbade divorce between 1816 and 1884. Thereafter the chief recognized legal cause for divorce was cruelty and injury, which had to be proven in court. In Great Britain adultery was the usual cause for divorce, but a woman had to prove her husband's adultery plus other offenses, whereas a man only had to prove his wife's adultery. In Germany only adultery or serious maltreatment was recognized as grounds for divorce. Across Europe extramarital sexual relations of husbands were more tolerated than those of wives. Everywhere, divorce required legal hearings and proof, making the process expensive and all the more difficult for women who did not control their own property.

The authority of husbands also extended to children. A husband could take children away from their mother and give them to someone else to rear. Only the husband, in most countries, could permit his daughter to marry. In some countries he could virtually force his daughter to marry the man of his choice. In cases of divorce and separation, the husband normally assumed authority over children no matter how he had treated them previously.

The sexual and reproductive rights of women, which have been so widely debated recently, could hardly be discussed in the nineteenth century. Both contraception and abortion were illegal. The law on rape normally worked against women. Wherever they turned—whether to physicians or lawyers—women confronted an official or legal world populated and controlled by men.

Educational Barriers   Throughout the nineteenth century women had less access to education than men, and what was available to them was inferior. Not surprisingly, the percentage of illiterate women exceeded that of men. Most women were educated only enough for the domestic careers they were expected to follow.

University and professional education remained reserved for men until at least the third quarter of the century. The University of Zurich opened its doors to women in the 1860s. The University of London admitted women for degrees in 1878. Women were not awarded degrees at Oxford until 1920 or at Cambridge until 1921. They could not attend Sorbonne lectures until 1880. Just before the turn of the century universities and medical schools in the Austrian Empire allowed women to matriculate, but Prussian universities did not until after 1900. Russian women did not attend universities before 1914, but other institutions that awarded degrees were open to them. Italian universities were more open to both women students and women instructors than similar institutions elsewhere in Europe.

The absence of a system of private or public secondary education for women prevented most of them from gaining the qualifications they needed to enter a university whether or not the university prohibited them. Considerable evidence suggests that educated, professional men feared the competition of women. Women who attended universities and medical schools were sometimes labeled political radicals.

By 1900 men in the educated elites also feared the challenge educated women posed to traditional gender roles in the home and workplace. Restricting their access to secondary and university education helped bar women from social and economic advancement. Women would benefit only marginally from the expansion of professional employment that occurred during the late nineteenth and early twentieth centuries. Although a few women did enter the professions, especially medicine, most nations prevented women from becoming lawyers until after World War I.

Schoolteaching at the elementary level, which was seen as a female job because of its association with the nurturing of children, became a professional haven for women. Trained at institutions that were equivalent to normal schools, women schoolteachers were regarded as educated, but not as university educated. Secondary education remained largely the province of men.

The few women who pioneered in the professions and on government commissions and school boards or who dispersed birth control information faced grave social obstacles, personal humiliation, and often outright bigotry. These women and their male supporters were challenging that clear separation of life into male and female spheres that had emerged in middle-class European society during the nineteenth century. Women themselves often hesitated to support feminist causes or expanded opportunities for themselves because they had been so thoroughly acculturated into the recently stereotyped roles. Many women saw a real conflict between family responsibilities and feminism.

Major Dates in Late-Nineteenth-Century and Early-Twentieth-Century Women's History

1857	Revised English divorce law
1865	University of Zurich admits women for degrees
1869	John Stuart Mill's *The Subjection of Women*
1878	University of London admits women as candidates for degrees
1882	English Married Woman's Property Act
1894	Union of German Women's Organizations founded
1901	National Council of French Women founded
1903	British Women's Social and Political Union founded
1907	Norway permits women to vote on national issues
1910	British suffragettes adopt radical tactics
1918	Vote extended to some British women
1918	Weimar constitution allows German women to vote
1920–1921	Oxford and Cambridge Universities award degrees to women
1922	French Senate defeats bill extending vote to women
1928	Britain extends vote to women on same basis as men

NEW EMPLOYMENT PATTERNS FOR WOMEN

During the late nineteenth century two major developments affected the economic lives of women. The first was an expansion in the variety of jobs available outside the better-paying learned professions. The second was a withdrawal of married women from the workforce. These two seemingly contradictory developments require explanation.

Availability of New Jobs The expansion of governmental bureaucracies, the emergence of corporations and other large-scale businesses, and the expansion of retail stores opened many new employment opportunities for women. The need for elementary schoolteachers, usually women, grew with compulsory education laws. Technological inventions and innovations, such as the typewriter and eventually the telephone exchange, also fostered female employment. Women by the thousands became secretaries and clerks for governments and private businesses. More thousands became shop assistants.

Although these jobs did open new and often better employment opportunities for women, they nonetheless required low-level skills and involved minimal training. They were occupied primarily by unmarried women or widows. Few women had prominent positions.

Employers continued to pay women low wages because they assumed, often knowing better, that a woman did not need to support herself independently but could expect additional financial support from her father or husband. Consequently, a woman who did need to support herself independently could rarely find a job paying an adequate income or a position that paid as well as one held by a man who was supporting himself independently.

Withdrawal from the Labor Force   Most of the women filling these new service positions were young and unmarried. After marriage, or certainly after the birth of her first child, a woman normally withdrew from the labor force. She either did not work or she worked at home. This pattern was not new, but it had become more common by the end of the nineteenth century. The industrial occupations that women had filled in the mid–nineteenth century, especially textile and garment making, were shrinking. Those industries thus offered fewer jobs for either married or unmarried women. Employers in offices and retail stores preferred young, unmarried women whose family responsibilities would not interfere with their work. The decline in the number of births also meant that fewer married women were needed to look after other women's children.

The real wages paid to male workers increased during this period, thus reducing families' need for a second income. Also, thanks to improving health conditions, men lived longer than before, and so wives were less likely to be thrust into the workforce by an emergency. Smaller families also lowered the need for supplementary wages. Working children stayed longer at home and continued to contribute to the family's wage pool.

Finally, the cultural dominance of the middle class, with its generally idle wives, established a pattern of social expectations. The more prosperous a working-class family became, the less involved in employment its women were supposed to be. Indeed, the less income-producing work a wife did, the more prosperous and stable the family was considered.

Yet behind these generalities stands the enormous variety of social and economic experience late-nineteenth-century women actually encountered. As might be expected, social class largely determined these individual experiences.

LATE-NINETEENTH-CENTURY WORKING-CLASS WOMEN

Although less dominant than earlier in the century, the textile industry and garment making continued to employ many women. The German clothing-making trades illustrate the kind of vulnerable economic situation that women could encounter as a result of their limited skills and the organization of the trade. The manufacture of massmade clothes in Germany was designed to require minimal capital investment by manufacturers and to protect them from significant risk. A major manufacturer would arrange to produce clothing through a putting-out system. He would purchase the material and then put it out for tailoring. The clothing was made not in a factory but usually in independently owned, small sweatshops or by workers in their homes.

In Berlin in 1896 there were more than 80,000 garment workers, mostly women. When business was good, employment for these women was high. If business became poor, however, less and less work was put out, idling many of them. In effect, the workers who actually sewed the clothing carried much of the risk of the enterprise. Some women did work in factories, but they too were subject to layoffs. Furthermore, women in the clothing trade were nearly always in positions less skilled than those of the male tailors or the male middlemen who owned the workshops.

Although new opportunities opened to them in the late nineteenth century, many working-class women, like these women ironing in a laundry, remained in traditional occupations. As the wine bottle suggests, alcoholism was a problem for women as well as men engaged in tedious work. The painting is by Edgar Degas.

Photo R.M.N./Senice Photographique des Muses Nationaux, Paris

Women working at a telephone exchange. The invention of the telephone opened new employment opportunities for women.

Mary Evans Picture Library

The expectation of separate social and economic spheres for men and women and the definition of women's chief work as pertaining to the home contributed mightily to the exploitation of women workers outside the home. Because their wages were regarded merely as supplementing their husbands', they became particularly vulnerable to the economic exploitation that characterized the German putting-out system for clothing production. Women were nearly always treated as casual workers in Europe.

POVERTY AND PROSTITUTION

A major but little-recognized social fact of most nineteenth-century cities was the presence of a surplus of working women who did not fit the stereotype of wife or daughter supplementing a family's income. There were almost always many more women seeking employment than there were jobs. The economic vulnerability of women and the consequent poverty many of them faced were among the chief causes of prostitution. Any large late-nineteenth-century European city had thousands of prostitutes.

Prostitution was, of course, not new. It had always been one way for poor women to earn money. In the late nineteenth century, however, it was closely related to the difficulty encountered by poor women who were trying to make their way in an overcrowded female labor force. On the Continent prostitution was generally subject to governmental and municipal regulations. Those regulations were, it should be noted, passed and enforced by male legislatures and councils and were enforced by male police and physicians. In Great Britain prostitution received only minimal regulation.

Many myths and misunderstandings have surrounded the subject of prostitution. The most recent studies of the subject in England emphasize that most prostitutes were active on the streets for only a few years, generally from their late teens to about age 25. Certain cities—those with large army garrisons or naval ports or those, like London, with large transient populations—attracted many prostitutes. There were far fewer prostitutes in manufacturing towns, where there were more opportunities for steady employment and where community life was more stable.

Women who became prostitutes usually came from families of unskilled workers and had minimal skills and education themselves. Many had been servants. They also often were from broken homes or were orphaned. Contrary to many sensational late-century newspaper accounts, child prostitutes were rare. Furthermore, women were seldom seduced into prostitution by middle-class employers or middle-class clients, although working-class women were always potentially subject to such pressure. The customers of poor working-class prostitutes were primarily working-class men.

WOMEN OF THE MIDDLE CLASS

A vast social gap separated poor working-class women from their middle-class counterparts. Their fathers' and husbands' incomes permitted middle-class women to participate in the vast expansion of consumerism and domestic comfort that marked the late nineteenth and early twentieth centuries. They filled their homes with manufactured items. They enjoyed all the improvements of sanitation and electricity. They could command the services of numerous domestic servants. They moved into the fashionable new houses being constructed in the suburbs.

The Cult of Domesticity   For the middle classes the distinction between work and family, defined by gender, had become complete and constituted the model for all other social groups. Middle-class women, if at all possible, did not work. More than any other women, they became limited to the roles of wife and mother. As a result, they might enjoy great domestic luxury and comfort, but their lives were markedly circumscribed. Middle-class women largely became the product of a particular understanding of social life. The home was to be a private place of refuge from the life of business and the marketplace, a view set forth in women's journals across Europe.

As studies of the lives of middle-class women in northern France have suggested, this image of the middle-class home and of the role of women in the home is different from the one that had existed earlier in the nineteenth century. During the first half of the century, the spouse of a middle-class husband might contribute directly to the business, handling accounts or correspondence. These women also frequently left child rearing to nurses and governesses. The reasons for the change during the century are not certain, but it appears that men began to insist on doing business with other men. Magazines and books directed toward women began to praise motherhood, domesticity, religion, and charity as the proper work of women in accordance with the concept of separate spheres.

For middle-class French women, as well as for middle-class women elsewhere, the home came to be seen as the center of virtue, children, and the proper life. Marriages were usually arranged for some kind of family economic benefit. Romantic marriage was viewed as a danger to social stability. Most middle-class women in northern France married by the age of 21. Children were expected to follow soon after marriage, and the first child was often born within the first year. The rearing and nurturing of her children were a woman's chief task. She would receive no experience or training for any role other than that of dutiful daughter, wife, and mother.

Within the home a middle-class woman performed major roles. She was largely in charge of the household. She oversaw virtually all domestic management and child care. She was in charge of the home as a unit of consumption, which is why so much advertising was directed toward women. All this domestic activity, however, occurred within the limits of the approved middle-class lifestyle that strictly limited a woman's initiative. In her conspicuous idleness, a woman symbolized first her father's and then her husband's success.

POLITICAL FEMINISM

As can be seen from the previous discussion, liberal society and its values neither automatically nor inevitably improved the lot of women. In particular, it did not give them the vote or access to political activity. Male liberals feared that granting the vote to women would benefit political conservatives, because women were thought to be unduly controlled by the clergy. Consequently, anticlerical liberals often had difficulty working with feminists.

Obstacles to Achieving Equality   But women also were often reluctant to support feminist causes. Political issues relating to gender were only one of several priorities for many women. Some were sensitive to their class and economic interests. Others subordinated feminist political issues to national unity and nationalistic patriotism. Still others would not support particular feminist organizations because of differences over tactics. The various social and tactical differences among women often led to sharp divisions within the feminists' own ranks. Except in England, it was often difficult for working-class and middle-class women to cooperate. Roman Catholic feminists were uncomfortable with radical secularist feminists.

Although liberal society and law presented women with many obstacles, they also provided feminists with many of their intellectual and political tools. As early as 1792 in Britain, Mary Wollstonecraft (1759–1797), in *The Vindication of the Rights of Women*, had applied the revolutionary doctrines of the rights of man to the predicament of the members of her own sex (see Chapter 23). John Stuart Mill (1806–1873), with his wife Harriet Taylor (1804–1858), had applied the logic of liberal freedom to the position of women in *The Subjection of Women* (1869). The arguments for utility and efficiency so dear to middle-class liberals could be used to expose the human and social waste implicit in the inferior role assigned to women.

Furthermore, the socialist criticism of capitalist society often, though by no means always, included a harsh indictment of the social and economic position to which women had been relegated. The earliest statements of feminism arose from critics of the existing order and were often associated with people who had unorthodox opinions about sexuality, family life, and property. This hardened resistance to the feminist message, especially on the Continent.

These difficulties prevented Continental feminists from raising the kind of massive public support or mounting the large demonstrations that feminists in Great Britain and the United States could. Everywhere in Europe, however, including Britain, the feminist cause was badly divided over both goals and tactics.

Votes for Women in Britain   Europe's most advanced women's movement was in Great Britain. There Millicent Fawcett (1847–1929) led the moderate National Union of Women's Suffrage Societies. She believed Parliament would grant women the vote only when convinced that women would be respectable and responsible in their political activity. In 1908 this organization could rally almost half a million women in London. Fawcett was the wife of a former Liberal Party cabinet minister and economist. Her tactics were those of English liberals.

Emmeline Pankhurst (1858–1928) led a different and much more radical branch of British feminists. Pankhurst's husband had been active in both labor and

The creator of this poster cleverly reveals the hypocrisy and foolishness of denying the vote to women.

The Bridgeman Art Library International

Irish nationalist politics. Irish nationalists had developed numerous disruptive political tactics. Early labor politicians had also sometimes had confrontations with police over the right to hold meetings. In 1903 Pankhurst and her daughters founded the Women's Social and Political Union. For several years they and their followers, known derisively as **suffragettes**, lobbied publicly and privately for women's suffrage. By 1910, having failed to move the government, they turned to the violent tactics of arson, window breaking, and sabotage of postal boxes. They marched en masse on Parliament. The Liberal government of Herbert Asquith (1852–1928), prime minister from 1908 to 1916, imprisoned many of the demonstrators and force-fed those who went on hunger strikes in jail. The government refused to extend the franchise. Only in 1918, and then as a result of their contribution to the war effort, did some British women receive the vote.

Political Feminism on the Continent   The contrast of France and Germany shows how advanced the British women's movement was. In France, when Hubertine Auclert (1848–1914) began campaigning for the vote in the 1880s, she stood virtually alone. During the 1890s several women's organizations emerged. In 1901 the National Council of French Women (CNFF) was organized among upper-middle-class women, but it did not support the vote for women for several years. French Roman Catholic feminists, such as Marie Mauguet (1844–1928), supported the franchise. Almost all French feminists, however, rejected violence: They also were never able to organize mass rallies. The leaders of French feminism believed that the vote could be achieved through careful legalism. In 1919 the French Chamber of Deputies granted the vote to women, but in 1922 the French Senate defeated the bill. French women did not receive the right to vote until 1944 at the end of World War II.

In Germany feminist awareness and action were even more underdeveloped. German law actually forbade German women from political activity. Because no group in the German Empire enjoyed extensive political rights, women were not certain that they would benefit from demanding them. Any such demand would be regarded as subversive of both the state and society.

In 1894 the Union of German Women's Organizations (BDFK) was founded. By 1902 it was calling for the right to vote. But it was largely concerned with improving women's social conditions, their access to education, and their right to other protections. The group also worked to see women admitted to political or civic activity on the municipal level. Their work usually included education, child welfare, charity, and public health. The German Social Democratic Party supported women's suffrage, but that Socialist party was so disdained by the German authorities and German Roman Catholics that this support only made suffrage more suspect in their eyes. Women received the vote in Germany only in 1918 under the constitution of the Weimar Republic. Before World War I, only in Norway (1907) could women vote on national issues.

suffragettes   British women who lobbied and agitated for the right to vote in the early twentieth century.

JEWISH EMANCIPATION

One of the most important social changes to occur throughout Europe during the nineteenth century was the emancipation of European Jews from the narrow life of the ghetto into a world of equal or nearly equal citizenship and social status. This transformation represented one of the major social impacts of political liberalism on European life.

EARLY STEPS TO EQUAL CITIZENSHIP

Emancipation, slow and never fully completed, began in the late eighteenth century and continued throughout the nineteenth. It moved at different paces in different countries. In 1782 Joseph II (r. 1765–1790), the Habsburg emperor, issued a decree that placed the Jews of his empire under more or less the same laws as Christians. In France the National Assembly recognized Jews as French citizens in 1789. During the Napoleonic Wars Jewish communities in Italy and Germany were allowed to mix on a generally equal footing with the Christian population.

These various steps toward political emancipation were frequently limited or partially repealed with changes in rulers or governments. Even in countries that granted them political rights, Jews could not own land and could be subject to discriminatory taxes. Nonetheless, by the first half of the nineteenth century Jews in western Europe and to a much lesser extent in central and eastern Europe had begun to acquire equal or nearly equal citizenship.

In Russia, however, the traditional modes of prejudice and discrimination continued unabated until World War I. Jews were treated as aliens under Russian rule. The government undermined Jewish community life, limited publication of Jewish books, restricted areas where Jews might live, required internal passports from Jews, banned them from many forms of state service and from many institutions of higher education. The police and others were allowed to conduct **pogroms**—organized riots—against Jewish neighborhoods and villages.

BROADENED OPPORTUNITIES

After the Revolutions of 1848, and especially in western Europe, the situation of European Jews improved for several decades. Throughout Germany, Italy, the Low Countries, and Scandinavia, Jews were allowed full rights of citizenship. After 1858 Jews in Great Britain could sit in Parliament. In Austria-Hungary full legal rights were extended to Jews in 1867. From approximately 1850 to 1880 there was relatively little organized or overt prejudice toward Jews. They entered the professions and other occupations once closed to them. They participated fully in the literary and cultural life of their nations. They were active in the arts and music. They became leaders in science and education. Jews intermarried freely with non-Jews as legal prohibitions against such marriages were repealed during the last quarter of the century.

Outside of Russia, Jewish political figures served in the highest offices of the state. Politically they tended to be aligned with liberal parties because such groups had championed equal rights. Later in the century, especially in eastern Europe, many Jews became associated with the Socialist parties.

The prejudice that had been associated with religious attitudes toward Jews seemed to have dissipated, although it still appeared in rural Russia and eastern Europe. From these regions hundreds of thousands of European Jews immigrated to the United States. Almost anywhere in Europe Jews might encounter prejudice on a personal level. But in western Europe, including England, France,

HOW DID emancipation affect Jewish participation in European social and political life outside of Russia?

pogroms   Organized riots against Jews in the Russian Empire.

Italy, Germany, and the Low Countries, the Jewish populations seem to have felt relatively secure from the old dangers of legalized persecution and discrimination.

That began to change during the last two decades of the nineteenth century. In the 1870s anti-Semitic sentiments attributing the economic stagnation of that decade to Jewish bankers and financial interests began to be voiced. In the 1880s organized anti-Semitism erupted in Germany as it did in France in the 1890s. As we saw in the last chapter, those developments gave birth to Zionism, the movement to establish a Jewish state in Palestine. However, Zionism was initially a minority movement within the Jewish community. Most Jewish leaders believed the attacks on Jewish life to be temporary recurrences of older prejudice; they felt that their communities would remain safe under the legal protections that had been extended during the century. That analysis would be proved disastrously wrong during the 1930s and 1940s.

EUROPEAN LABOR, SOCIALISM, AND POLITICS TO WORLD WAR I

L ate-nineteenth-century industrialization and the rapid growth of a mass urban proletariat brought profound economic, social, and political changes to all the industrializing countries of Europe.

THE WORKING CLASSES

The late-century industrial expansion wrought further changes in the life of the labor force. There were many fewer artisans and highly skilled workers. For the first time, factory wage earners predominated. The increasingly mechanized factories often required less highly technical skills from their operatives. The unskilled work associated with shipping, transportation, and building also expanded. Work became more impersonal. Factories were located in cities, and most links between factory or day-labor employment and home life dissolved. Large corporate enterprise meant less personal contact between employers and their workers. During the late nineteenth century a few big businesses attempted to provide some security for their employees through company housing and pension plans. Although these efforts were sometimes pioneering, they were not adequate for the mass of the labor force.

Trade Unionism Workers still had to look to themselves to improve their situation. However, after 1848 European workers ceased taking to the streets to voice their grievances in the form of riots. They also stopped trying to revive the old paternalistic guilds. After midcentury the labor force accepted the fact of modern industrial production and its general downgrading of skills and attempted to receive more benefits from that system. Workers turned to new institutions and ideologies. Chief among them were trade unions, democratic political parties, and socialism.

Trade unionism came of age as legal protections were extended to unions throughout the second half of the century. Unions became fully legal in Great Britain in 1871 and were allowed to picket in 1875. In France the Third Republic fully legalized unions in 1884. After 1890 they could function in Germany with little disturbance. Initially, most trade unions were slow to enter the political process directly. As long as the traditional governing classes looked after labor interests, members of the working class rarely sought office themselves.

The midcentury organizational efforts of the unions aimed to improve the wages and working conditions of skilled workers. By the close of the century large

WHY DID Marxism become so influential among European socialists?

industrial unions for unskilled workers were also being organized. They confronted extensive opposition from employers, and were often recognized only after long strikes. In the decade before 1914 strikes were common throughout Europe as the unions attempted to raise wages to keep up with inflation. However, despite the advances of unions and the growth of their membership in 1910 to approximately three million in Britain, two million in Germany, and 977,000 in France, they never included a majority of the industrial labor force. The unions did represent a new collective fashion in which workers could associate to confront the economic difficulties of their lives and attain better security.

Democracy and Political Parties   The democratic franchise gave workers direct political influence, which meant they could no longer be ignored. Except for Russia, all the major European states adopted broad-based, if not perfectly democratic, electoral systems. Democracy brought new modes of popular pressure to bear on all governments. It meant that discontented groups could now voice their grievances and advocate their programs within government rather than from outside it.

The advent of democracy witnessed the formation for the first time in Europe of organized mass political parties, such as had existed throughout the nineteenth century in the United States. In the liberal European states with narrow electoral bases, most voters had been men of property who understood what they had at stake in politics. Organization had been minimal. The expansion of the electorate brought into the political processes many people whose level of political consciousness and interest was low. This electorate had to be organized and taught the nature of power and influence in the liberal democratic state. The organized political party—with its workers, newspapers, offices, social life, and discipline—was the vehicle that mobilized the new voters. The largest single group in these mass electorates was the working class. The democratization of politics presented the Socialists with opportunities and required the traditional ruling class to vie with them for the support of the new voters.

MARXIST CRITIQUE OF THE INDUSTRIAL ORDER

During the 1840s Karl Marx (1818–1883) produced the most influential of all critiques of the newly emerged industrial order. His analysis became so important because later in the century it was adopted by the leading Socialist political party in Germany, which in turn influenced most other European Socialist parties including a small group of exiled Russian Socialists led by V. I. Lenin. Marx was born in the Rhineland. His Jewish middle-class parents sent him to the University of Berlin, where he became deeply involved in radical politics. During 1842 and 1843 he edited the radical *Rhineland Gazette*. Soon the German authorities drove him into exile—first in Paris; then in Brussels; and finally, after 1849, in London.

In 1844 Marx met Friedrich Engels (1820–1895), another young middle-class German, whose father owned a textile factory in Manchester, England. The next year, Engels published *The Condition of the Working Class in England*, which presented a devastating picture of industrial life. The two men became fast friends. Late in 1847 they were asked to write a pamphlet for a newly organized and ultimately

---

Major Dates in the Development of Socialism

1864	International Working Men's Association (the First International) founded
1875	German Social Democratic Party founded
1876	First International dissolved
1878	German antisocialist laws passed
1884	British Fabian Society founded
1889	Second International founded
1891	German antisocialist laws permitted to expire
1891	German Social Democratic Party's Erfurt Program
1895	French *Confédération Générale du Travail* founded
1899	Eduard Bemstein's *Evolutionary Socialism*
1902	Formation of the British Labour party
1902	Lenin's *What Is to Be Done?*
1903	Bolshevik-Menshevik split
1904	"Opportunism" debated at the Amsterdam Congress of the Second International

short-lived secret Communist league. *The Communist Manifesto*, published in German, appeared early in 1848. Marx, Engels, and the league had adopted the name *Communist* because the term was more self-consciously radical than *Socialist*. *Communism* implied the outright abolition of private property rather than some less extensive rearrangement of society. The *Manifesto* itself was a work of fewer than 50 pages. It would become the most influential political document of modern European history, but that development lay in the future. At the time it was simply one more political tract. Moreover, neither Marx nor his thought had any effect on the revolutionary events of 1848.

19.8
Karl Marx and Friedrich Engels

In *The Communist Manifesto*, Marx and Engels contended that human history must be understood rationally and as a whole. According to their analysis, history is the record of humankind's coming to grips with physical nature to produce the goods necessary for survival. That basic productive process determines the structures, values, and ideas of a society. Historically, the organization of the means of production has always involved conflict between the classes who owned and controlled the means of production and those classes who worked for them. That necessary conflict has provided the engine for historical development; it is not an accidental by-product of mismanagement or bad intentions. Consequently, only a radical social transformation, not piecemeal reforms, can eliminate the social and economic evils inherent in the very structures of production. Such a revolution will occur as the inevitable outcome of the development of capitalism.

In Marx's and Engels's eyes, during the nineteenth century the class conflict that had characterized previous Western history had become a struggle between the bourgeoisie and the proletariat, or between the middle class and the workers. The character of capitalism ensured the sharpening of the struggle. Capitalist production and competition would steadily increase the size of the unpropertied proletariat. Large-scale mechanical production crushed both traditional and smaller industrial producers into the ranks of the proletariat. As the business structures grew larger and larger, smaller middle-class units would be squeezed out by the competitive pressures. Competition among the few remaining gigantic concerns would lead to more intense suffering by the proletariat. As the workers suffered increasingly from the competition among the ever-enlarging firms, they would foment revolution and finally overthrow the few remaining owners of the means of production. For a time the workers would organize the means of production through a dictatorship of the proletariat, which would eventually give way to a propertyless and classless communist society.

This proletarian revolution was inevitable, according to Marx and Engels. The structure of capitalism required competition and consolidation of enterprise. Although the class conflict involved in the contemporary process resembled that of the past, it differed in one major respect. The struggle between the capitalistic bourgeoisie and the industrial proletariat would culminate in a wholly new society that would be free of class conflict. The victorious proletariat, by its very nature, they contended, could not be a new oppressor class: "The proletarian movement is the self-conscious, independent movement of the immense majority, in the interest of the immense majority.[1] The result of the proletarian victory would be "an association, in which the free development of each is the condition for the free development of all.[2] The victory of the proletariat over the bourgeoisie represented the culmination of human history. For the first time, one group of people would not be oppressing another. Marx's analysis was conditioned by his own eco-

[1]Robert C. Tucker, ed., *The Marx-Engels Reader* (New York: W. W. Norton, 1972), p. 353
[2]Ibid.

nomic environment. The 1840s had seen much unemployment and deprivation. Capitalism, however, did not collapse as he predicted, nor did the middle class during the rest of the century or later become proletarianized. Rather, more and more people came to benefit from the industrial system. Nonetheless, within a generation Marxism had captured the imagination of many Socialists and large segments of the working class. Its doctrines were allegedly based on the empirical evidence of hard economic fact. This much proclaimed scientific aspect of **Marxism** helped the ideology, as science became more influential during the second half of the century. Marx had made the ultimate victory of socialism seem certain. His works also suggested that the path to socialism lay with revolution rather than reform. As Marxist thought permeated the international Socialist movement during the next 75 years, it would provide the ideological basis for some of the most momentous and ultimately repressive political movements in the history of virtually the entire modern world.

GERMANY: SOCIAL DEMOCRATS AND REVISIONISM

That the thought of Karl Marx ultimately came to exercise such vast influence was the result of his ideas becoming adopted by the German Social Democratic Party (SPD). Founded in 1875, the SPD suffered 12 years of persecution by Otto von Bismarck (1815–1898), who believed socialism would undermine German politics and society. In 1878 there was an attempt to assassinate Emperor William I (r. 1861–1888). Bismarck unfairly blamed the Socialists and steered antisocialist laws through the Reichstag, the German Parliament. These measures suppressed the organization, meetings, newspapers, and other public activities of the SPD. Nonetheless, the SPD steadily polled more votes in elections to the Reichstag.

Repression having failed, Bismarck enacted social welfare legislation to wean German workers from socialist loyalties. These measures provided health insurance, accident insurance, and old age and disability pensions. The German state itself thus organized a system of social security that did not change the system of property holding or politics.

In 1891, after forcing Bismarck's resignation, Emperor William II (r. 1888–1918) allowed the antisocialist legislation to expire. The SPD then had to decide how to operate as a legalized party. Their new direction was announced in the Erfurt Program of 1891. In good Marxist fashion, the program declared the imminent doom of capitalism and the necessity of socialist ownership of the means of production. However, these goals were to be achieved by legal political participation rather than by revolutionary activity. Since the revolution was inevitable, it was argued, the immediate task of Socialists was to improve workers' lives. In theory, the SPD was vehemently hostile to the German empire, but in practice the party functioned within its institutions.

This situation of the SPD, however, generated the most important internal socialist challenge to the orthodox Marxist analysis of capitalism and the socialist revolution. Eduard Bernstein (1850–1932) wrote what was regarded as his socialist heresy. Bernstein, who was familiar with the British **Fabians**, questioned whether

Karl Marx's Socialist philosophy eventually triumphed over most alternative versions of socialism in Europe, but his monumental work has been subject to varying interpretations, criticisms, and revisions that continue to this day.

Bildarchiv Preussischer Kulturbesitz

Marxism The theory of Karl Marx (1818–1883) and Friedrich Engels (FREE-drick ENG-ulz) (1820–1895) that history is the result of class conflict, which will end in the inevitable triumph of the industrial proletariat over the bourgeoisie and the abolition of private property and social class.

Fabians British socialists in the late nineteenth and early twentieth century who sought to achieve socialism through gradual, peaceful, and democratic means.

Marx and his later orthodox followers had been correct in their pessimistic appraisal of capitalism and the necessity of revolution. In *Evolutionary Socialism* (1899), Bernstein pointed to the rising standard of living in Europe, the ongoing power of the middle class, and the opening of the franchise to the working class. He argued that a humane socialist society required not revolution but more democracy and social reform. Bernstein's doctrines, known as *revisionism*, were widely debated among German Socialists and were finally condemned as theory, although the party actually pursued a peaceful, reformist program. His critics argued that evolution toward social democracy might be possible in liberal, parliamentary Britain but not in authoritarian, militaristic Germany with its basically powerless Reichstag. Therefore, the German SPD continued to advocate revolution.

The German debate over revisionism became important for the later history of Marxist socialism. The German SPD was, as noted, the most successful prewar Socialist party. Its rejection of an ideology of reform socialism in favor of revolutionary socialism influenced all Socialists who looked to the German example. Most significant, Lenin adopted this position, as did the other leaders of the Russian Revolution. Thereafter, wherever Soviet Marxism was influential, the goal of its efforts would be revolution rather than reform.

France: "Opportunism" Rejected

The major problem for French Socialists was their own internal division rather than government opposition. There were no fewer than five separate parties, plus other independent Socialists. They managed to elect approximately forty members to the Chamber of Deputies by the early 1890s.

At the turn of the century the two major factions of French socialism were led by Jean Jaurès (1859–1914) and Jules Guesde (1845–1922). Jaurès believed, like the revisionists in Germany, that Socialists should cooperate with radical middle-class ministries to enact social legislation. Guesde argued that Socialists could not support a bourgeois cabinet that they were theoretically dedicated to overthrowing. The quarrel came to a head in 1899, when Prime Minister René Waldeck-Rousseau (1846–1904) appointed the Socialist Alexander Millerand (1859–1943) to the Cabinet.

By 1904 "opportunism," the term applied to such Cabinet participation by Socialists, was debated at the Amsterdam Congress of the Second International. This organization had been founded in 1889 to unify the various national Socialist parties and trade unions. The Congress condemned "opportunism" in France and ordered the French Socialists to form a single party. Jaurès accepted the decision. French Socialists began to work together, and by 1914 the recently united Socialist Party was the second largest group in the Chamber of Deputies. But Socialist Party members would not again serve in a French Cabinet until 1936.

Great Britain: The Labour Party and Fabianism

No form of socialism made significant progress in Great Britain, the most advanced industrial society of the day. The members of the growing trade unions normally supported Liberal Party candidates. The "new unionism" of the late 1880s and the 1890s organized the dock workers, the gas workers, and similar unskilled groups. Employer resistance to unions heightened class antagonism. In 1892 Keir Hardie (1856–1915) became the first independent worker elected to Parliament. In 1893 the Socialist Independent Labour Party was founded, but it remained ineffective.

In 1901, however, a decision by the House of Lords (Britain's supreme court) removed the legal protection previously accorded union funds. The Trades Union

revisionism   The advocacy among nineteenth-century German socialists of achieving a humane socialist society through the evolution of democratic institutions, not revolution.

Congress responded by launching the Labour Party, which sent 29 members to Parliament in the election of 1906. Their goals did not yet encompass socialism. The British labor movement also became more militant. In scores of strikes, workers fought for wages to meet the rising cost of living. The government intervened to mediate these strikes, which in 1911 and 1912 involved the railways, the docks, and the mines.

British socialism itself remained primarily the preserve of intellectuals. The Socialists who exerted the most influence were from the Fabian Society, founded in 1884. The society took its name from Q. Fabius Maximus (d. 203 B.C.E.), the Roman general who defeated Hannibal by waiting before attacking. Its name thus indicated a gradualist approach to social reform. Its leading members were Sydney Webb (1859–1947) and Beatrice Webb (1858–1943), H. G. Wells (1866–1946), and George Bernard Shaw (1856–1950). Many of the Fabians were civil servants who believed that the problems of industry, the expansion of ownership, and the state direction of production could be solved and achieved gradually, peacefully, and democratically. They sought to educate the country to the rational wisdom of socialism. They were particularly interested in collective ownership on the municipal level, or so-called gas-and-water socialism.

RUSSIA: INDUSTRIAL DEVELOPMENT AND THE BIRTH OF BOLSHEVISM

Following its defeat in the Crimean War, the tsarist government in Russia had undertaken a series of major internal reforms. The most important of these was the emancipation of the serfs in 1861. That measure was extremely complicated and in effect required serfs to pay for their land. The poverty of the emancipated serfs became a political cause for groups of urban revolutionaries in Russia who succeeded in assassinating Tsar Alexander II (r. 1855–1881) in 1881. Thereafter, the government pursued a policy of general political repression.

At the same time in the late nineteenth century the tsarist government was determined to make Russia an industrial power. It favored the growth of heavy industries, such as railways, iron, and steel. A small but significant industrial proletariat arose. By 1900 Russia had approximately three million factory workers. Their working and living conditions were bad by any standard.

New political departures accompanied this economic development. In 1901 the Social Revolutionary Party was founded. It opposed industrialism and looked to the communal life of rural Russia as a model for the economic future. In 1903 the Constitutional Democratic Party, or Cadets, was formed. Liberal in outlook, the Cadets were drawn from people who participated in the *zemstvos* (local governments). They wanted a parliamentary regime with responsible ministries, civil liberties, and economic progress. The Cadets hoped to model themselves on the Liberal parties of western Europe.

Lenin's Early Thought and Career   The situation for Russian Socialists differed radically from that in other major European countries. Russia had no representative political institutions and only a small working class. The compromises and accommodations achieved elsewhere were meaningless in Russia, where socialism in both theory and practice had to be revolutionary. The Russian Social Democratic Party had been established in 1898. It was Marxist, and its members greatly admired the German SPD, but tsarist repression meant that it had to function in exile.

The leading late-nineteenth-century Russian Marxist was Georgii Plekhanov (1857–1918), based in Switzerland. His chief disciple was Vladimir Illich Ulyanov

Marxist revolutionary Vladimir Ilyich Lenin sits alone at a desk littered with papers and books.

Corbis/Bettman

Major Dates in Turn-of-the-Century Russian History

1895	Lenin arrested and sent to Siberia
1897	Eleven-and-a-half-hour workday established
1898	Russian Social Democratic Party founded
1900	Lenin leaves Russia for western Europe
1901	Social Revolutionary Party founded
1903	Constitutional Democratic Party (Cadets) founded
1903	Bolshevik-Menshevik split
1904	Russo-Japanese War begins
1905 (January)	Japan defeats Russia
1905 (January 22)	Revolution breaks out in Saint Petersburg after Bloody Sunday massacre
1905 (October 20)	General strike
1905 (October 26)	*October Manifesto* establishes constitutional government
1906 (May 10)	Meeting of first *Duma*
1906 (June)	Stolypin appointed prime minister
1906 (July 21)	Dissolution of first *Duma*
1906 (November)	Land redemption payments canceled for peasants
1907 (March 5–June 16)	Second *Duma* seated and dismissed
1907	Franchise changed and a third *Duma* elected, which sits until 1912
1911	Stolypin assassinated by a social revolutionary
1912	Fourth *Duma* elected
1914	World War I breaks out

(1870–1924), who took the name of Lenin. The future leader of the communist revolution was the son of a high bureaucrat. His older brother had been executed in 1887 for participating in a plot against Alexander III (r. 1881–1894). In 1893 Lenin moved to Saint Petersburg, where he briefly practiced law. Soon he, too, was drawn to the revolutionary groups among the factory workers. In 1895 he was exiled to Siberia. After his release in 1900, Lenin spent most of the next 17 years in Switzerland.

In Switzerland Lenin became deeply involved in the organizational and policy disputes of the exiled Russian Social Democrats. They all considered themselves Marxists, but quarreled about the proper nature of a Marxist revolution in primarily rural Russia and the structure of their own party. The Social Democrats were modernizers who favored further industrial development. Most believed that Russia must develop a large proletariat before the revolution could come. This same majority hoped to mold a mass political party like the German SPD.

Lenin dissented from both positions. In *What Is to Be Done?* (1902), he condemned any accommodations. He also criticized a trade unionism that settled for short-term gains rather than true revolutionary change for the working class. Lenin further rejected the concept of a mass party composed of workers. Revolutionary consciousness would not arise spontaneously from the working class. It must be carried to them by a small, elite party, "people who make revolutionary activity their profession."[3] The guiding principle of that party should be "the strictest secrecy, the strictest selection of members, and the training of professional revolutionaries."[4]

Establishment of the Bolsheviks In 1903, at the London Congress of the Russian Social Democratic Party, Lenin split the party ranks. Although it lost most of the votes during the congress, Lenin's group mustered a slim majority near the close. Thereafter, his faction assumed the name *Bolsheviks*, meaning "majority," and the other, more moderate, democratic revolutionary faction became known as the *Mensheviks*, or "minority." There was, of course, a considerable public relations advantage to the name *Bolshevik*. (In 1912 the Bolsheviks organized separately from other Social Democrats.) In 1905 Lenin complemented his organizational theory with a program for revolution in Russia. His *Two Tactics of Social Democracy in the Bourgeois-Democratic Revolution* urged that the socialist revolution unite the proletariat and the peasants. He grasped better than any other revolutionary the profound discontent in the Russian countryside. He knew that an alliance of workers and peasants in rebellion probably could not be suppressed. Lenin's two principles of an elite party and a dual social revolution allowed the Bolsheviks, in late 1917, to capture the leadership of the Russian Revolution and to transform the political face of the modern world.

Bolsheviks Meaning the "majority." Term Lenin applied to his faction of the Russian Social Democratic Party. It became the Communist Party of the Soviet Union after the Russian Revolution.

[3]Quoted in Albert Fried and Ronald Sanders, eds., *Socialist Thought: A Documentary History* (Garden City, NY: Anchor Doubleday, 1964), p. 459.

[4]Ibid., p. 468

The Revolution of 1905 and Its Aftermath   The quarrels among the Russian Socialists had no immediate influence within Russia itself. In 1904 Russia went to war with Japan, but the result was defeat and political crisis. The Japanese captured Port Arthur, Russia's base on the eastern coast of China, early in 1905. A few days later, on January 22, a priest named Father Gapon (1870–1906) led thousands of workers to petition the tsar for improvements in industrial conditions. As the petitioners approached the Winter Palace in Saint Petersburg, troops opened fire. About 100 people were killed, and many more were wounded.

Revolutionary disturbances spread throughout Russia: Sailors mutinied, peasants revolted, and property was attacked. An uncle of the tsar was assassinated. Liberal Constitutional Democratic leaders from the *zemstvos* demanded political reform. University students went on strike. In early October 1905 strikes broke out in Saint Petersburg, and worker groups, called *soviets*, virtually controlled the city. Tsar Nicholas II (r. 1894–1917) promised Russia constitutional government.

Early in 1906 the tsar announced the election of a parliament, the **Duma**, with two chambers. However, he reserved for himself ministerial appointments, financial policy, and military and foreign affairs. Nicholas named as his chief minister P. A. Stolypin (1862–1911). Neither the tsar nor his minister was sympathetic to the Duma. It would meet, disagreements would occur, and it would be dismissed. In 1906, however, the government canceled any redemptive payments the peasants still owed from the emancipation of the serfs in 1861. Thereafter Stolypin repressed rural discontent.

After Stolypin's assassination in 1911 by a social revolutionary, the tsarist government simply muddled along. But the imperial family became surrounded by scandal over the influence of Grigori Rasputin (1871?–1916), who seemed able to heal the tsar's hemophilic son, the heir to the throne. The undue influence of this strange and uncouth man, the continued social discontent, and the conservative resistance to liberal reforms rendered the position and policy of the tsar uncertain after 1911.

EUROPEAN SOCIALISM IN WORLD HISTORY

The debates among late-nineteenth- and early-twentieth-century European Socialists were complicated and in some respects obscure. They proved, however, significant not only for European politics but for political developments around the world and that is the reason why we have discussed them in some detail. The impact arose for two reasons. First, Europeans who immigrated to North and South America carried many of these socialist ideas and quarrels with them. They continued to debate the issues they debated in Europe in their new homelands. Second, by the end of the nineteenth century numerous students from different parts of the European empires in Africa and Asia traveled to Europe for education. There they confronted these debates among European Socialists. Many of those students later returned home to become leaders of anticolonial political movements and carried with them again the ideas and quarrels about methods, theory, and tactics they had encountered among European Socialists.

NORTH AMERICA
AND THE NEW INDUSTRIAL ECONOMY

The full industrialization of the United States followed a pattern not unlike that of nineteenth-century Europe. The first industry to become thoroughly mechanized was textile manufacture, followed by growth in the iron and steel industries. There were certain significant differences, however. The United States industrialized considerably later than Great Britain. Its major expansion in iron and steel took place after the Civil War and was thus approximately

Mensheviks   Meaning the "minority." Term Lenin applied to the majority moderate faction of the Russian Social Democratic Party opposed to him and the Bolsheviks.

soviets   Workers' and soldiers' councils formed in Russia during the Revolution.

Duma   The Russian parliament, after the revolution of 1905.

HOW DID industrialization in the United States differ from industrialization in Europe?

contemporary to the economic rise of the newly united Germany. In the United States there had always been enormous social respect for entrepreneurial enterprise. American manufacturers and commercial developers thus encountered little of the prejudice against trade and commerce that existed among the European aristocracy. Wealthy American businessmen had considerable political influence. The United States possessed an immense internal market that functioned without trade restraints for the shipment of unprocessed goods to factories or of finished products to their markets. Much of the capital for American industrial expansion came from British bankers who saw the United States as an area of secure investment. Finally, the United States had a relative shortage of labor and consequently relatively high wages, the factors that attracted so many immigrants to the industrial sector during the second half of the century.

In America as in Europe, however, the railways spurred the most intense industrial growth. The number of railway miles increased from approximately 50,000 in the mid-1860s to almost 200,000 by 1900. Much of the construction was made possible by vast European investments in the United States. The railways created enormous demand for iron, steel, coal, and lumber. They also stimulated settlement, vastly expanded markets, and helped to knit the country together.

EUROPEAN IMMIGRATION TO THE UNITED STATES

The same conditions that made American life so difficult for blacks and native Americans (see Chapter 24) turned the United States into a land of vast opportunity for white European immigrants. These immigrants faced religious and ethnic discrimination as well as frequent poverty in the United States; however, for many of them and their children, the social and economic structures of the United States allowed for assimilation and remarkable upward social mobility. This was especially true of those immigrants, mostly from northern and western Europe, who arrived between approximately 1840 and 1890—the great period of German, English, Welsh, Scottish, and Irish immigration. Among this group, the Irish undoubtedly encountered the most difficulties and resistance.

Toward the end of the century and well into the next—in what is sometimes known as the New Immigration—millions of people arrived from the Mediterranean, eastern Europe, and the Balkans. Most of these peoples left economically depressed areas, and financed their immigration themselves. However, some American companies did send ships to Italy for immigrants to work in American factories and mines.

These new immigrants, who generally came to work in the growing industrial cities, were perceived as fundamentally different from those who had come before them. They were seen and treated as of a lower class and inherently more difficult to assimilate than the earlier immigrants. Predominately Roman Catholic, Orthodox, and Jewish, they encountered much intolerance. The same kind of racial theory that spread through Europe during these years was present in the United States. These new immigrants were often regarded as being from less desirable racial stocks. As a result, turn-of-the-century immigrants often encountered serious prejudice and endured lives of enormous poverty. They also often settled into communities of people from their own ethnic background. What ultimately held them together were various private organizations, such as churches and synagogues, clubs, newspapers in their own languages, and social agencies they organized for themselves.

Although none of these immigrants faced the same legal discrimination as did American blacks, the Jews encountered restricted covenants on real estate, obstacles to joining private clubs, and quotas for admission to many schools and universities. Asian immigrants to the West Coast of the United States faced harsher prejudice.

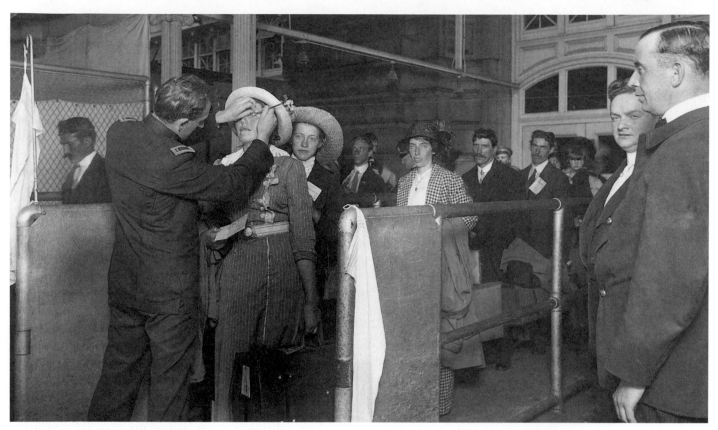

UNIONS: ORGANIZATION OF LABOR

The expansion of industrialism led to various attempts to organize labor unions. In America as in Europe, workers faced great resistance from employers and those who feared that labor unions might lead to socialism. Another difficulty arose from the social situation of the labor force itself. White laborers would not organize alongside blacks. Different ethnic minorities would not cooperate. The ongoing flood of immigration ensured a supply of workers willing to work for low wages. The owners of businesses more often than not could divide and conquer the sprawling, ethnically mixed labor force.

The first effort at labor organization occurred in the 1870s with the National Labor Union and railroad unions. In 1881 the American Federation of Labor (AFL) was founded. In contrast to earlier organizations and the advanced European socialist movement, such as that in Germany, it did not seek to transform the life of workers in a radical fashion but rather focused on higher wages and better working conditions. The AFL concentrated on organizing skilled workers; it did not seek to organize whole industries. Among its most effective leaders was Samuel Gompers (1850–1924). Other unions, such as the United Mine Workers and the Railway Brotherhoods, organized workers by industry.

The industrialization of the United States—again, like that of Europe—saw major periods of business crisis or downturn. Serious depressions occurred in both the 1870s and the 1890s. There was no government relief. What little relief there was came from local authorities and private charities. This pattern would continue until the Great Depression of the 1930s. The economic turmoil of the 1880s and 1890s spawned violent strikes. Perhaps the most famous of these incidents was the breaking of the Pullman strike in Chicago in 1894 by federal troops. The major goal of labor thereafter was to achieve the full legal right to organize. Although the Clayton Act of 1914 moved in that direction, the clear right to organize with the protection of the

In 1892 the federal government opened the immigration station on Ellis Island, located in New York City's harbor, where about 80 percent of the immigrants to the United States landed. As many as 5,000 passengers per day reported to federal immigration officers for questions about their background and for physical examinations, such as this eye exam. Only about 1 percent were quarantined or turned away for health problems.

Brown Brothers

federal government was achieved only through the legislation of Franklin Roosevelt's (1882–1945) New Deal in the 1930s.

Socialism was a path not taken by American labor and one not allowed to be taken. The leaders of the conservative unions worked against the Socialists, and spokesmen for business did everything possible to block their influence. The federal and state governments actively sought to repress socialist activities wherever they appeared. After the Bolshevik Revolution of 1917 virtually all American Socialists were persecuted as Bolshevists during the 1920s and beyond. The United States thus became the land where many social issues tended to be addressed by trade unions rather than by Socialist parties. Furthermore, although many conservative American political and business leaders disliked them, unions were not legally attacked here as they were in Britain, which led to the founding of the British Labour Party after the turn of the century.

In many European countries, Socialist parties, or ministers like Bismarck who attempted to outflank the Socialists, had pressed their governments to pass legislation providing social security and other social services. As with so many other policies favorable to labor, no significant legislation of this kind was passed in the United States, at either the federal or state level, until the New Deal.

THE PROGRESSIVES

Much of the power in American politics in the decades after the Civil War, especially in cities, often lay in the hands of political bosses. This system depended on patronage at every level of government. In return for jobs, contracts, licenses, favors, and sometimes actual services, the boss expected and received political support. Government was a vehicle for distributing spoils. The point of boss politics was not merely venality; it was also a way, however crude and unattractive, of organizing the disorderly social and economic forces of the great cities. It was a way of managing cities that were growing as never before with highly diverse populations.

Toward the close of the century, reform-minded political figures began to emerge on the city and state levels. These reformers feared that people such as themselves from the white upper-middle classes might soon lose political and social influence. Deeply disturbed by the corruption of much of political life, these reformers found the urban environment with its slums an unacceptable picture of disorder. They wanted to see more efficient and less corrupt government. They also wanted the government to become a direct agent of change and reform. Pursuing these goals, they ushered in what has been called the *progressive era*, which lasted from approximately 1890 through 1914. Although the Progressives were reformers, they were not always liberal by later standards. For example, Progressives in the South often disenfranchised blacks and poor whites by imposing literacy tests and similar devices.

The Progressives began their reform work on the local level, especially in the cities, before they launched into national politics. The disorder and extreme disparity of wealth and poverty in the cities disturbed them. Urban reformers believed that the politics of bosses and patronage robbed cities of the money needed to make them livable places. In place of patronage, they demanded social and municipal services to clean up the cities. They repeatedly attacked special interests who blocked reform. Progressive mayors called for lower utility rates and streetcar fares and also attacked police corruption.

SOCIAL REFORM

Not only politicians joined the progressive crusade. Churches began to address the question of social reform. It was in this era that the "Social Gospel" was first preached, with its message that Christianity involved civic action. Young men and women began to work in settlement houses in the slums. The most famous was Chicago's Hull House, led by Jane Addams (1860–1935). Other young persons from the middle class became active in housing and health reform, education, and charities. They conducted extensive surveys of the poorest parts of the great cities. These people believed that the urban environment could be cleaned up and social order made to prevail. Their vision of such social order was that of the white middle class.

Beginning in the midnineties, progressivism began to affect state governments. There the impulse toward reform involved various attempts to protect whole classes of persons who were perceived as unable to protect themselves against exploitation, especially children and women working under unwholesome conditions for low wages. Other aspects of progressivism at the state level involved the civil-service requirements and the regulation of railways. Virtually all of these reformers partook of the cult of science that was so influential in the late nineteenth century. They believed that the problems of society were susceptible to scientific, rational management. The general public interest should replace special interests.

THE PROGRESSIVE PRESIDENCY

Roosevelt   Theodore Roosevelt became president in 1901 after the assassination of William McKinley (1843–1901). He had been police commissioner of New York City and later a reforming governor of New York State. Roosevelt, in effect, created the modern American presidency. By force of personality and intelligence, he began to make the presidency the most important and powerful branch of government. As president, he began to set the agenda for national affairs and to define the problems that the federal government was to address. He surrounded himself with strong advisers and Cabinet members. He used his own knowledge of party patronage to beat the bosses at their own game.

In domestic policy, Roosevelt was determined to control the powerful business trusts. No centers of economic power should, through their organization, be stronger than the federal government. He successfully moved against some of the most powerful financiers in the country, such as J. P. Morgan and John D. Rockefeller. Through legislation associated with the term "Square Deal," Roosevelt attempted to assert the public interest over that of the various powerful special interests. He was not opposed to big business in itself, but he wanted it to operate according to rules established by the government for the public good.

In 1902 Roosevelt brought the moral power of the presidency to the aid of mine workers who were on strike. He appointed a commission to arbitrate the dispute. This was a major intrusion of the federal government into the economic system. It reversed the policies that had prevailed a decade earlier, when the government had used federal troops to break strikes. Roosevelt sought to make the presidency and the federal government the guarantor of fairness in economic relations. Thus he fostered the passage of the Pure Food and Drug Act and the Meat Packing Act in 1906, which protected the public against adulterated foodstuffs. Here again, the regulatory principle came to the fore. His conservation policies ensured that millions of acres of national forests came under the care of the federal government.

Roosevelt was associated with a vigorous, imperialistic foreign policy that had roots in the 1890s. In 1898 McKinley had led the nation into the Spanish-American War, and the United States had emerged as an imperial power with control of Cuba, Puerto Rico, Guam, and the Philippines. Roosevelt believed that the United States should be a major world power, and he sent a war fleet around the world. In Latin America naval intervention assured the success of the Panamanian revolt of 1903 against Colombia. A treaty with the new Panamanian government allowed the United States to construct and control a canal across the Isthmus of Panama. The United States was thus following the model of the European great powers, which had been intervening in Africa and Asia. Like the other great powers, the imperialist policies of the United States were built on a conviction of racial superiority.

Roosevelt was succeeded in 1909 by William Howard Taft (1857–1930), his hand-picked successor. Taft disappointed Roosevelt, and in 1912 the election was a three-way contest among Taft, Roosevelt (running as a third-party candidate), and Woodrow Wilson. The Democrat Wilson won and brought a different concept of progressivism to the White House.

Wilson Woodrow Wilson (1856–1924) was a former president of Princeton University and a reforming governor of New Jersey, where he had battled the bosses. While still an academic, he had criticized the weak presidency of the late nineteenth century. Wilson, like Roosevelt, accepted a modern industrialized nation. However, unlike Roosevelt, Wilson disliked big business almost in and of itself. He believed in economic competition in which the weak would receive protection from the government. Wilson termed his attitude and policy the New Freedom. Although he had pressed this idea during the campaign, in office he followed a policy of moderate regulation of business.

Wilson also had a different view of the presidency. He saw the office as responsible for leading Congress to legislative decisions. Wilson was the first American president since 1800 to deliver the State of the Union address to Congress in person. He presented Congress with a vast agenda of legislation and then worked carefully with the Democratic leadership to see that it was passed. Although Wilson appeared to be an advanced reformer, he retained many beliefs that have disappointed his later admirers. For example, he reinstated racial segregation in the federal civil service and opposed female suffrage.

Wilson had long seen his real goals in terms of domestic reform. But war broke out in Europe in August 1914. Although Wilson was reelected in 1916 on the slogan "He Kept Us Out of War!" in April 1917 he led the nation into the European conflict. The expertise that he and other Progressives had brought to the task of efficient domestic government was then turned to making the nation an effective military force. These two impulses—the first toward domestic reform, the second toward a strong international role—had long marked the progressive movement and would shape American history in the years after the war.

The American Progressives resembled political leaders of their generation in Great Britain. The Conservative Benjamin Disraeli (1804–1881) and Liberals William Gladstone (1809–1898) and David Lloyd-George (1863–1945) had supported various measures of social reforms. Elsewhere in Europe political leaders in France and Germany had undertaken reforms in housing and urban life to forestall the advance of socialism and to address the problems of industrialization and urbanization. These leaders had favored unprecedented use of central government authority and the establishment of stronger governments.

SUMMARY

Workers After 1850, European workers underwent a process of proletarianization as the process of industrialization spread across the continent. To protect their interests, European workers joined trade unions and socialist parties, such as the Labour Party in Britain. The Marxist critique of modern capitalism strongly influenced European socialism when the German Social Democratic Party adopted the thought of Karl Marx. In Russia, Lenin founded the Bolsheviks as an elite Marxist party that advocated the overthrow of the tsarist regime through a revolution of workers and peasants.

Urban Reform European cities grew rapidly after 1850. The growth of industry and the influx of new workers led to slums and a host of urban health and social problems. In response, middle-class reformers redesigned cities and improved sanitation, housing, and water and sewer systems.

Women Nineteenth-century women were divided along class lines. Unlike working-class women, most women of the upper and middle classes adopted a cult of domesticity and did not work outside the home. Most jobs available to women were low paying and insecure. Women of all classes faced social, political, and legal disabilities that were only gradually improved in the late nineteenth and early twentieth centuries. Before World War I, only Norway allowed women to vote, and few women could earn university degrees or enter the professions.

Jewish Emancipation With the exception of Russia, European countries had abolished their legal restrictions on Jews by the mid-nineteenth century. Jews became more fully integrated into European political and economic life. After 1880, however, anti-Semitism increased as Jews were blamed for economic and social problems.

The United States By 1914, the United States had become the world's leading industrial power. However, despite the creation of a mass industrial work force, socialism did not take root in the United States. Under presidents Theodore Roosevelt and Woodrow Wilson, the Progressive Movement enacted a number of social and political reforms. The United States also embarked on a more aggressive foreign policy with the Spanish-American War, the acquisition of a colonial empire, interventions in Latin America, and, under Wilson, participation in World War I.

IMAGE KEY

for pages 566–567

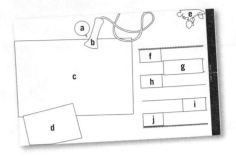

a. Bull Moose party campaign button
b. Old-fashioned telephone.
c. Georges Seurat, *A Sunday on La Grande Jatte-1884*
d. London workmen repairing a sewer
e. Potato plant
f. Giuseppe Pellizza da Volpedo, *Il Quarto Stato*, 1901, depicts a crowd of Italian socialists
g. Factories spewing smoke over the English landscape
h. Textile production
i. Jean Juares
j. Great Railroad Strike of 1877

REVIEW QUESTIONS

1. What accounts for the proletarianization of the European labor force?

2. How would you describe living conditions in European cities during the late nineteenth century? What factors contributed to those conditions? How did urban reform emerge?

3. What social factors limited the opportunities of women regardless of their class? Why did women grow discontented with their lot? What factors led to change?

4. What were the major characteristics of Jewish emancipation in the nineteenth century? How did late-century economic developments contribute to increasing prejudice against Jews?

5. How did the ideas of Karl Marx come to dominate late-nineteenth-century European socialism? What was the status of the working-class groups in the United States and Europe in 1860? What improvements if any had been achieved by 1914?

6. Were the tsars wise in attempting to modernize their country or would they have been better off leaving it as it was? How did Lenin's view of socialism differ from that of Socialists in western Europe? Why did socialism not emerge as a major political force in the United States?

KEY TERMS

Bolsheviks (p. 590)
Duma (p. 591)
Fabians (p. 587)
Marxism (p. 587)

Mensheviks (p. 590)
pogroms (p. 583)
proletarianization (p. 568)
revisionism (p. 588)

soviets (p. 591)
suffragettes (p. 582)

 For additional study resources for this chapter, go to:
www.prenhall.com/craig/chapter26

LEAL INTERPRETE
DE LOS "DESCAMISADOS"

Orgy—the Night of the Rich, **a mural by the Mexican artist Diego Rivera (1886–1957),** casts a scornful eye on the Europeanized decadence of Mexico's elite in the early 20th century. Diego Rivera, "Orgy—Night of the Rich" (La Orgia— La noche de los ricos), 1926. Mural, 2.05 x 1.54 m. Court of Fiestas, Level 3, North Wall. Secretaria de Education Publica, Mexico City, Mexico. Schalkwijk/Art Resource, NY. ©Banco de Mexico Diego Rivera.

27

LATIN AMERICA
From Independence to the 1940s

HOW DID the absence
of a social revolution affect
Latin America after independence?

WHAT WAS the economy
of dependence?

WHO WERE the *caudillos*?

WHY WAS the history of Brazil
after independence different from
that of Argentina and Mexico?

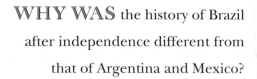

IMAGE KEY
Image Key for pages 598–599
is on page 615.

By the mid-1820s, Latin Americans had driven out their colonial rulers and broken the colonial trade monopolies (see Map 27–1). Although rich in natural resources, the region did not achieve widespread prosperity and political stability for more than a century after independence.

The explanations for why Latin America has been less stable and prosperous than Europe and North America appear to lie in the role it played in the integrated global economic system that began to develop when it achieved political independence. This system prevented Latin Americans from achieving economic independence. The region's leaders thought their nations could prosper by providing raw materials to the world economy. Most Latin American nations developed export economies devoted to raw materials or semi-finished goods. This decision made their export products vulnerable to worldwide fluctuations in demand. They were also susceptible to influence from foreign business interests and interference by the governments of the United States and Europe.

Latin America had much in common with Africa and Asia during the nineteenth and early twentieth centuries. In all three regions, nations or areas would specialize by filling a niche by supplying a particular raw product to the increasingly integrated world economy. This might bring initial prosperity but provided too narrow a base for sustained economic well-being. In contrast, the economic advance of the United States and Europe was largely due to their ability to dominate and exploit niche economies around the globe.

INDEPENDENCE WITHOUT REVOLUTION

T he Wars of Independence liberated Latin America from direct European control but left it economically exhausted and politically unstable. Only Brazil tended to prosper immediately after independence. In contrast, the new republics of the former Spanish Empire felt themselves vulnerable. Because the Wars of Independence had been civil wars, the new governments knew that many of their populations might welcome their collapse. Economic life contracted: In 1830 overall production was lower than in 1800. Difficult terrain over vast distances made interregional trade difficult. The old patterns of overseas trade had been disrupted. There was an absence of funds for investment. Many wealthy *peninsulares* departed. Consequently, Latin American governments and businesses looked to Britain for protection, markets, and investment.

Independence also created new sources of discontent. There was much disagreement about the character of the future government. Institutions, such as the Roman Catholic Church, sought to maintain their privileges. Indian communities found themselves subject to new exploitation. Quarrels arose between the Creole elites of different regions of the new nations. The agricultural hinterlands resented the predominance of the port cities. Investors or merchants from one Latin American nation found themselves in conflict with those of others over tariffs or mining regulations. Civilians became rivals of the military.

HOW DID the absence of a social revolution affect Latin America after independence?

ABSENCE OF SOCIAL CHANGE

Yet all the elites opposed social reform. The Creole victors in the Wars of Independence granted equal rights to all persons and, except for Brazil, had abolished slavery by 1855. However, the right to vote depended on a property qualification, and peasants remained subservient to their landlords. Colonial racial codes disappeared, but not racial prejudice. Persons of white or nearly white complexion tended to constitute the elite of Latin America. Most important, there were no major changes in landholding; the ruling classes protected the interests of landholders.

Except for Mexico in 1910, no Latin American nation until the 1950s experienced a revolution that overthrew the social and economic structures dating

MAP EXPLORATION

Interactive map: To explore this map further, go to **http://www.prenhall.com/craig2/map27.1**

MAP 27–1

Latin America In 1830.   By 1830 Latin America had been liberated from European government. This map shows the initial borders of the states of the region with the dates of their independence. The United Provinces of La Plata formed the nucleus of what later became Argentina.

HOW DID Brazil become a monarchy after independence?

from the colonial period. The absence of such social revolution is perhaps the most important factor in Latin American history during the first century of independence. The rise and fall of political regimes represented quarrels among the elite. Everyday life for most of the population did not change. Throughout the social structure, there was no mutual trust or allegiance to the political system.

CONTROL OF THE LAND

Most Latin Americans during the nineteenth century lived in the countryside. Agriculture was dominated by large *haciendas,* or plantations. The landowners ruled these estates as small domains. The *latifundia* (the large rural estates) grew larger during the nineteenth century from confiscated church lands and conquered Indian territories. Work was labor intensive because little machinery was available. For some products—salted meats, for example—there was a limited manufacturing stage in Latin America. Most crops, including grains, tobacco, sugar, coffee, and cacao, were exported.

Landowners constituted a society of their own. They sometimes formed family alliances with the wealthy urban classes who were involved in export commerce or the law. Younger sons might enter the army or the church. The landowners served in the national parliaments. Their wealth, literacy, and social connections made them the rulers of the countryside, and the army would protect them from any social uprising.

The rural work force was socially and economically dependent on the landowners. In Brazil, slavery persisted until 1888. In other rural areas, many people lived as virtual slaves. **Debt peonage** was widespread and often tied a peasant to the land like a serf. Later in the nineteenth century, the new lands that were opened were generally organized as large holdings with tenants rather than as small land holdings with independent farmers. This was different from both the United States and Canada. Poor transportation made internal travel difficult and kept many people on the land. Little effort was made to provide education, leaving Latin American peasants ignorant, lacking technological skills, and incapable of improving their condition.

The second half of the nineteenth century witnessed a remarkable growth in Latin American urban life. There was some movement from the countryside to the city and an influx of European and even Asian immigrants. Throughout this period there arose a political and social trade-off between the urban and rural elites. Each permitted the other to pursue its economic self-interest and repress discontent. Nonetheless, the growth of the urban centers shifted political influence to the cities and gave rise to an urban working class and the social discontents associated with many poor people working in difficult situations. Urban growth in Latin America created difficulties not unlike those that arose in Europe and the United States at about the same time.

SUBMISSIVE POLITICAL PHILOSOPHIES

The political philosophies embraced by the Creole elites also discouraged challenges to the social order. The political ideas associated with European liberalism, which flourished in Latin America after independence, supported republican government but limited the franchise to property holders. Thus in Latin America, as in Europe, liberalism protected property and tended to ignore the social problems of the poor. The Creole elite also exhibited racial prejudice toward nonwhites.

Economic liberalism and the need for British investment led to free trade. After independence, Latin America exported less than it had under colonial

debt peonage   A system that forces agricultural laborers (peons) to work and live on large estates until they have repaid their debts to the estate's owner.

rule and achieved a trade balance only by exporting precious metals. The general economic view was that Latin America would produce raw materials for export in exchange for manufactured goods imported from Europe, especially from Britain.

For most of the nineteenth century, the landed sector of the economy dominated because cheap imports and a shortage of local capital discouraged indigenous industrialism. Latin American liberals championed the great landed estates and the social dependence associated with them. The produce of the new land could contribute export goods to pay for the import of finished goods. Liberals thus favored confiscating land owned by the church and the Indians, because they did not exploit their lands in a progressive manner, according to the liberals.

During the second half of the century, **positivism**, the ideas of the French philosopher Auguste Comte (1798–1857), swept across Latin America. Comte and his followers had advocated the cult of technological progress. This undemocratic outlook suggested that either technocrats or authoritarians could best achieve modernization. It was popular among military officers and influenced the ongoing Latin American struggle between civilian and military elites. The great slogan of Latin American positivism, emblazoned on the flag of the Brazilian republic, was "Order and Progress." Groups that challenged the existing social order were unprogressive.

Toward the close of the century, the officer corps was often the most important educated elite in a country. Their education and attachment to the army gave them influence, generally conservative.

Finally, European theories of "scientific" racism were used to preserve the Latin American social status quo. Racial theory could attribute the economic backwardness of the region to its vast nonwhite or mixed blood population. This explanation shifted responsibility for the economic difficulties of Latin America away from the mostly white governing elites toward Indians, blacks, **mestizos**, and **mulattos**, who had long been exploited or repressed.

This conservative intellectual heritage affected twentieth-century political thought. First, it can be seen in the tendency of military groups in Latin America to view themselves as the guarantors of order. They were ready to seize control from civilians to thwart social change. Second, it can be seen in the way the political elites of Latin America opposed communism after the Russian Revolution. Governments used the fear of communism to resist political movements—communist or not—that advocated social reform or questioned property arrangements. Communism would become an even more powerful issue after the Cuban Revolution of 1957 installed a communist state in Latin America.

positivism The philosophy of Auguste Comte that science is the final, or positive, stage of human intellectual development because it involves exact descriptions of phenomena, without recourse to unobservable operative principles, such as gods or spirits.

mestizos Persons of mixed Native American and European descent.

mulattos Persons of mixed African and European descent.

ECONOMY OF DEPENDENCE

The Wars of Independence destroyed the colonial trade monopolies. But Latin America remained dependent on non-Latin American economies. Trade was free and the nations were independent, but other nations continued to shape Latin American economic life.

One of the chief reasons for this dependence was the absence of large internal markets. Trade after independence flowed in the same direction that it had flowed before independence because Europe remained the source of imports of finished goods. Furthermore, then as now, geographical barriers hindered internal trade, and European and American investments in railways facilitated exports.

WHAT WAS the economy of dependence?

Brazilian coffee being loaded onto a British ship. Most Latin American countries developed an export economy based on the exchange of agricultural products, raw materials, and semifinished goods for finished goods and services from abroad. From the 1890s onward, the coffee industry dominated both the political and economic life of Brazil.

Corbis-Bettmann

NEW EXPLOITATION OF RESOURCES

The Wars of Independence disrupted the Latin American economy. Mines were flooded; machinery was in disrepair; labor was dispersed. Agricultural production was also disrupted. To restore old industries such as mining, and gain access to steamships and railroads, Latin Americans had to turn to Europe and North America. For decades, Britain economically dominated Latin America. The desire to pour manufactured goods into Latin America led Britain and other nations to discourage the development of manufacturing industries there.

To pay for foreign imports, Latin American nations produced agricultural commodities. Production for the export market led governments to expand into unsettled territory and to confiscate the lands of the church.

After 1850, the Latin American republics became relatively more prosperous. Chile exported copper and nitrates as well as wheat. Peru exported guano for fertilizer. Coffee was becoming king in Venezuela, Brazil, Colombia, and Central America. Sugar continued to be produced in the West Indies and Cuba, which remained under Spanish control. Argentina supplied hides and tallow. But this limited prosperity was based on the export of agricultural commodities or raw materials and the importation of finished goods. Yet the export economy seemed to foster genuine economic growth.

Both the trading patterns for these goods and internal improvements in Latin American production linked the economy of the region to Europe and, after 1900, to the United States. Europeans and North Americans provided capital and the technological skills to build bridges, roads, railroads, steam lines, and mines. But whenever the economy of Europe or the United States floundered, Latin America was hurt. The region could not control its own economic destiny.

INCREASED FOREIGN INFLUENCE

During the late nineteenth century, the relative prosperity of the export sector increased the degree of dependence. The growing European demand gave Latin Americans a false sense of security. The vast profits to be made through mining and agricultural exports discouraged investment in local industry. Foreigners saw no reason to capitalize local industry that might replace imported goods. By late in the century, the wealthy in Latin America had, in effect, lost control of valuable sectors of their economy. For example, in 1901 British and other foreign investors owned approximately 80 percent of the Chilean nitrate industry.

Foreign powers also used their political and military influence to protect their economic interests. Britain, as the dominant power until the turn of the century, was frequently involved in the political affairs of the Latin American nations. From the Spanish-American War of 1898 onward, the United States began to exercise more direct influence in the region. In 1903, to facilitate its plans to build a canal across Panama, the United States participated in the rebellion that allowed Panama to separate from Colombia. The U.S. military intervened in the Caribbean and Central America. By the 1920s, the United States had replaced Britain as the dominant trading partner of Latin America.

United States interventions were one cost to Latin America of being a dependent economy. More significant costs, however, arose from fundamental shifts in world trade that were brought on by World War I and continued through the 1920s. First, the amount of trade carried on by European countries decreased. Second, during the 1920s world prices of agricultural commodities dropped. Latin American nations had to produce more goods to pay for their imports. Third, synthetic products manufactured in Europe or North America replaced the natural products supplied by Latin America. Finally, petroleum began to replace other natural products as an absolute percentage of world trade. This shift meant that petroleum-exporting countries, such as Mexico, gained a greater share of export income.

20.7
Francisco Garcia Calderón,
"The North American Peril"

ECONOMIC CRISES AND NEW DIRECTIONS

The Great Depression produced a crisis in this ***neocolonial economy***. Commodity prices collapsed. The republics of Latin America could not repay their debts to foreign banks. The Depression led to the beginning of a new economic era in Latin America after the conclusion of World War II. It was marked by economic nationalism and a determination to create national economies that were not wholly dependent on foreign events and wealth.

With the Depression, it became necessary to substitute domestic manufactured goods for those imported from abroad. Various nations pursued policies called ***import substitution***, and by the mid-1940s there were three varieties of manufacturing in Latin America. First, there were industries that, as in the past, transformed raw materials for export, such as food processing, mining, and petroleum refining. Second, there were industries addressing local demands, such as power plants and machine shops. Third, there were industries, basically assembly plants, that transformed imported materials to take advantage of cheap labor. None of this manufacturing involved heavy industry.

neocolonial economy   An economic relationship between a former colonial state and countries with more developed economies in which the former colony exports raw materials to and imports manufactured goods from the more developed nations.

import substitution   The replacement of imported goods with those manufactured domestically.

SEARCH FOR POLITICAL STABILITY

The new states of independent Latin America had no experience in self-government. The Spanish Empire had been ruled directly by the monarchy and by Spanish-born bureaucrats. This monarchical or paternalistic heritage survived in the proclivity of the Latin American political elites to tolerate or support strong executives. The early republic constitutions were frequently suspended or rewritten, so that a strong leader could consolidate his power. Such figures were called ***caudillos***. They usually came from the officer corps or enjoyed strong ties to the army. The real basis of their rule was force. *Caudillos* might support conservative causes, such as protection of the church or strong central government, or they might pursue liberal policies, such as the confiscation of church land, the extension of landed estates, and the development of education.

Even when *caudillos* were forced from office and parliamentary government was restored, the regimes that replaced them were neither genuinely liberal nor democratic. Parliamentary governments usually ruled by courtesy of the military and in the interest of the elites. No matter who ruled, the lives of most of the population changed little. Except for the Mexican Revolution of 1910, Latin American politics was run by and for the elite.

WHO WERE the *caudillos*?

caudillo   Latin American strongman, or dictator, usually with strong ties to the military.

THREE NATIONAL HISTORIES

WHY WAS the history of Brazil after independence different from that of Argentina and Mexico?

Argentina, Mexico, and Brazil possess over 50 percent of the land, people, and wealth of the region. Their histories illustrate the general themes of Latin American history.

ARGENTINA

Argentine history from independence to World War II can be divided into three eras. From the rebellion against Spain in 1810 until mid-century, the question of which region of the nation would be dominant was foremost. From 1853 until 1916, Argentina experienced economic expansion and large-scale immigration from Europe, which transformed its society and its world position. From 1916 to 1943, Argentines failed to establish a democratic state and struggled with an economy they did not control.

Buenos Aires versus the Provinces   In 1810, the junta in Buenos Aires overturned Spanish government. However, the other regions of the viceroyalty of Río de la Plata refused to accept its leadership. Paraguay, Uruguay, and Bolivia went their separate ways. Conflicts between Buenos Aires and the remaining provinces dominated the first seventy years of Argentine history. Eventually Buenos Aires established its primacy because it dominated trade on the Río de la Plata.

A commercial treaty in 1823 established Great Britain as a dominant trading partner. Thus began a deep intermeshing of trade and finance between the two nations that would continue for over a century. In 1831, the *caudillo* of the province of Buenos Aires, Juan Manuel de Rosas (1793–1877), negotiated the Pact of the Littoral, whereby Buenos Aires was put in charge of foreign relations and trade while the other provinces ran their own internal affairs. Within Buenos Aires, Rosas set up dictatorial rule. His major policies were expansion of trade and agriculture, suppression of the Indians, and nationalism.

Expansion and Growth of the Republic   Rosas's success in strengthening Buenos Aires bred resentment in other provinces. In 1852, Rosas was overthrown. The next year a federal constitution was promulgated for the Argentine Republic, but Buenos Aires remained economically and politically dominant.

The Argentine economy was agricultural, the chief exports at mid-century being animal products. Internal transportation was poor and the country was sparsely populated. Technological advances changed this situation during the last quarter of the century. In 1876, the first refrigerator ship steamed into Buenos Aires. Henceforth, it would be possible to transport Argentine beef to Europe. Furthermore, it became clear that wheat could be farmed throughout the pampas. In 1879 and 1880, the army carried out a major campaign against the Indian population. The British soon began to construct and manage railways to carry wheat to the coast, where it would be loaded on British and other foreign steamships. Government policy made the purchase of land by wealthy Argentines simple and cheap. The owners, in turn, rented the land to tenants. The predominance both of large landowners and of foreign business interests thus continued throughout the most significant economic transformation in Argentine history.

The vastly increased production of beef and wheat made Argentina one of the wealthiest nations of Latin America and an agricultural rival of the United States. The opening of land, even if only for tenant farming and not ownership, encouraged many

Chronology of Argentina

1810	Junta in Buenos Aires overthrows Spanish government
1827–1852	Era of Rosas's dictatorial government
1876	Ship refrigeration makes possible export of beef around the world
1879–1880	Conquest of the Desert against the Indian population
1914–1918	Argentina remains neutral in World War I
1930s	Period of strong influence of nationalist military
1943–1956	Era of Juan and Eva Perón

Europeans, particularly from Spain and Italy, to emigrate to Argentina. The immigrants also provided workers for the food-processing, service, and transportation industries in Buenos Aires. By 1900, Argentina had become much more urbanized and industrialized. More people had reason to be politically discontent. Moreover, the children of the immigrants often became the strongest Argentine nationalists during the twentieth century.

Prosperity quieted political opposition for a time. The conservative landed oligarchy governed under presidents who perpetuated a strong export economy. Like similar groups elsewhere, they ignored the social questions raised by urbanization and industrialization.

However, the urban middle and professional classes wanted a greater share in political life and an end to corruption. In 1890, these groups founded the Radical Party. Its leader, Hipólito Irigoyen (1850–1933), was elected president in 1916. Without significant support in the legislature, his presidency brought few changes. In World War I, Argentina traded with both sides. Nonetheless, the war put pressure on the economy, and labor agitation resulted. Irigoyen used troops against strikers. Thereafter, the Radical Party pursued policies that benefited landowners and urban business interests. This was possible because of the close relationship between agricultural producers and processors and because both the landed and the middle classes resisted concessions to the working classes.

Eva Perón was as influential as her husband, Juan Perón, during his years in power in the late 1940s and early 1950s. She was especially effective in attracting popular support for his government. They are shown here in a reception line in 1951.

Corbis-Bettmann

The Military in Ascendence   By the end of the 1920s, the Radical Party had become corrupt and directionless. The worldwide commodity depression hurt exports. In 1930, the military staged a coup. The officers returned power to conservative civilians, and Argentina remained dependent on the British export market.

In the 1930s, a right-wing nationalistic movement, *nacionalismo*, arose among writers, journalists, and a few politicians. It resembled the fascist political movements then active in Europe. Its supporters equated British and American domination of the economy with imperialism. They rejected liberalism, detested communism, were anti-Semitic, and supported the Roman Catholic Church. *Nacionalismo* advocated social reforms that recognized the needs of workers and the poor, but that also sought to promote social harmony rather than communist revolution or socialist reconstruction of the economy. In effect, these groups were anti-imperialistic, socially concerned, authoritarian, and sympathetic to the rule of a modern *caudillo*. World War II gave these attitudes and their supporters new influence.

The war closed most of Europe to Argentine exports, creating an economic crisis. In 1943, the military again seized control. Many of the officers were fiercely nationalistic children of immigrants. Some had become impressed by the fascist and Nazi movements and were hostile to Britain. They contended that the government must address social questions, industrialize the country, and liberate it from foreign economic control. In these respects, they echoed the *nacionalistas*.

Between 1943 and 1946, Juan Perón (1895–1974), one of the colonels involved in the 1943 coup, forged this social discontent and authoritarianism into a political movement known as **Perónism**. It was authoritarian, anti-communist, and

nacionalismo   A right-wing Argentine nationalist movement that arose in the 1930s and resembled European fascism.

Perónism   An authoritarian, nationalist movement founded in Argentina in the 1940s by the dictator Juan Perón.

·HISTORY'S VOICES·

EVA PERÓN EXPLAINS THE SOURCES OF HER POPULARITY

The Perónist movement in Argentina drew broad support from workers and the poor. The movement involved a cult of personality around both Perón and his wife Eva. In 1951, Eva Perón published a book entitled My Mission in Life (La razón de mi vida). *Here she explains how she sought to relate to her husband's political supporters.*

WHY WAS Eva Perón's accepting the name "Evita" a political act? How did her use of this name separate her from the ruling elites of Argentina? What is the role she projects for herself in her relationship to various social groups in Argentina? Do you believe her discussion of herself to be sincere or politically opportunistic?

When I chose to be "Evita," I chose the path of my people. . . .

Only the people call me "Evita." Only the *descamisados* [the "unshirted," as Perón's working-class followers were termed] learned to call me so. . . .

I appeared to them thus the day I went to meet the humble of my land, telling them that I preferred being "Evita" to being the wife of the president, if that "Evita" could help to mitigate some grief, or dry a tear.

If a man of the government, a leader, a politician, an ambassador, who normally calls me "Señora," should call me "Evita," it would sound as strange and out of place to me as if a street-urchin, a workingman, or a humble person of the people should call me "Señora." . . .

Now, if you ask me which I prefer, my reply would be immediately that I prefer the name by which I am known to the people.

When a street-urchin calls me "Evita," I feel as though I were the mother of all urchins, and of all the weak and the humble of my land.

When a working man calls me "Evita," I feel glad to be the companion of all the workingmen of my country and even of the whole world.

When a woman of my country calls me "Evita," I imagine myself her sister, and that of all the women of humanity,

And so, almost without noticing it, I have classified in these three examples the principal activities of "Evita" relating to the humble, the workers, and women.

The truth is that, without any artificial effort, at no personal cost, as though I had been born for all this, I feel myself responsible for the humble as though I were the mother of all of them; I fight shoulder to shoulder with the workers as though I were another of their companions from the workshop or factory; in front of the women who trust in me, I consider myself something like an elder sister, responsible to a certain degree for the destiny of all of them who have placed their hopes in me.

And certainly I do not deem this an honor but a responsibility. . . .

Yes. I confess that I have an ambition, one single, great personal ambition: I would like the name of "Evita" to figure somewhere in the history of my country.

From Lourdes Arizpe, "Peasant Women and Silence," translated by Laura Beard Milroy in *Women's Writing in Latin America: An Anthology* by Sara Castro-Klarén, Sylvia Malloy, and Beatriz Sarlo. Copyright © 1992 by Westview Press. Reprinted by permission of the author.

socially progressive. Perón understood that political power could be exerted by appeals to the Argentine working class. He gained the support of the trade unions that were opposed to communism. In 1946, he made himself the voice of working-class democracy, even though he created an authoritarian regime that only marginally addressed industrial problems. He was aided by his wife, the former actress Eva Duarte (1919–1952), who enjoyed charismatic support among the working class. (See "Eva Perón Explains the Sources of Her Popularity.")

Perón was the supreme twentieth-century embodiment of the *caudillo*. His power and appeal were rooted in the antiliberal attitudes that had been fostered by the corruption and aimlessness of Argentine politics during the Depression. He was ousted in 1956, but stability would continue to elude Argentine politics.

MEXICO

For the first century of Mexican independence, conservative forces held sway, but in 1910, the Mexican people launched the most far-reaching revolution in Latin American history.

Turmoil Follows Independence   The years from 1820 to 1876 were a time of turmoil, economic floundering, and humiliation. Independent Mexico attempted no liberal political experiments. Its first ruler was Agustín de Iturbide (1783–1824), who ruled until 1823 as an emperor. Thereafter, Mexico was governed by a succession of *caudillo* presidents, who depended on the army for support. The strongest of these figures was Antonio López de Santa Anna (1795–1863), a general and political opportunist who was finally exiled in 1855.

The mid-century movement against Santa Anna's autocracy was called **La Reforma**. In theory, its supporters were liberal, but Mexican liberalism was associated with anticlericalism, confiscation of church lands, and opposition to military influence on national life and politics. *La Reforma* aimed to produce political stability and civilian rule and attract foreign capital and immigrants. Its attack on the church led to further civil war. In January 1861, Benito Juárez (1806–1872) entered Mexico City as the temporary victor.

Political instability was matched by economic stagnation. The mines that had produced Mexico's colonial wealth were in poor condition, and the country could not repair them. The *hacienda* system left farming in a backward condition. Cheap imports of manufactured goods stifled domestic industries. Transportation was primitive. The government's remedy was massive foreign borrowing; as a result, interest payments ate up the national budget.

This 20th-century portrait of Benito Juárez (oil on canvas, 1948, from Presidential Collection of Portraits of Mexican Presidents) emphasizes his major accomplishments. The foreground shows him drafting the Constitution of 1857. In the background to the left is the execution of Maximilian; to the right are scenes of road construction and farmers (who, thanks to Juárez's reforms, were given clear title to their lands) working their fields.

Corbis-Bettmann

Foreign Intervention   Political weakness and economic disarray invited foreign intervention. The territorial ambitions of the United States led to war with Mexico in 1846 and the U. S. army occupied Mexico City. Mexico lost a vast portion of its territory, including what is now New Mexico, Arizona, and California.

Further foreign intervention occurred as a result of Juárez's liberal victory in 1861. Mexican conservatives and clerics invited the Austrian Archduke Maximilian (1832–1867) to become the emperor of Mexico. Napoleon III (r. 1852–1870) of France, who portrayed himself as a defender of the Roman Catholic Church, provided support for this venture. In May 1862, French troops invaded Mexico. Maximilian became emperor, but was unable to gain support from much of the population. In 1867, Juárez captured the unhappy emperor and executed him.

Díaz and Dictatorship   The liberal leaders continued their measures against the church but also failed to rally popular support. In 1876, Porfirio Díaz (1830–1915), a liberal general, seized power and retained it until 1911. He maintained one of the most successful dictatorships in Latin American history by giving almost every political sector something it wanted. He allowed landowners to purchase public land cheaply; he cultivated the army; and he made peace with the church. He used repression against opponents and bribery to cement the loyalty of his supporters. Wealthy Mexicans grew even richer, and Mexico became a respectable member of the international financial community. Foreign capital, especially from the United States, flooded the nation.

La Reforma   The nineteenth-century Mexican liberal reform movement that opposed Santa Ana's dictatorship and sought to foster economic progress, civilian rule, and political stability. It was strongly anti-clerical.

Chronology of Mexico

1820–1823	Agustín de Iturbide rules as emperor
1833–1855	Santa Anna dominates Mexican political scene
1846–1848	Mexico defeated by United States and loses considerable territory
1861	Victory of liberal forces under Juárez
1862–1867	French troops led by Archduke Maximilian of Austria invade Mexico
1876–1911	Era of Porfirio Díaz
1911	Beginning of Mexican Revolution Zapata proclaims Plan of Ayala
1917	Forces of Carranza proclaim constitution
1929	Institutional Revolutionary Party organized

Yet problems remained. The peasants wanted land. Many Mexicans were malnourished. Labor unrest afflicted the textile and mining industries. Real wages for the working class declined. The Panic of 1907 in the United States disrupted the Mexican economy. By 1910, the *Pax Porfiriana* was unravelling.

Revolution In 1911, Francisco Madero (d. 1913), a wealthy landowner and moderate liberal, led an insurrection that drove Díaz into exile. Shortly thereafter, Madero was elected president. He recognized the right of unions to strike, but was unwilling to undertake agrarian reform that might have changed the pattern of landholding. More radical leaders called for social change. Pancho Villa (1874–1923) in the north and Emiliano Zapata (1879–1919) in the south rallied mass followings of peasants who demanded fundamental changes in rural landholding. In late 1911, Zapata proclaimed his Plan of Ayala, which set forth a program of large-scale peasant confiscation of land. Much of the struggle during the next ten years would be between supporters and opponents of such agrarian reform.

Madero was squeezed between conservatives and the radical peasant revolutionaries. No one trusted him. In early 1913, he was overthrown by General Victoriano Huerta (1854–1916), who had help from the United States. In the meantime, Venustiano Carranza (1859–1920), a wealthy landowner, put himself at the head of a large army that initially received the support of both Zapata and Villa. On August 15, 1914, Carranza's forces entered Mexico City. Thereafter, disputes between Carranza, Villa, and Zapata arose both from political rivalry and from Carranza's refusal to embrace radical agrarian reform. Carranza eventually won out.

Carranza's political skills helped him build a broad base and edge out Villa and Zapata as the chief leader of the revolution. He separated the concerns of urban industrial workers from the land hunger of rural peasants, and thus doomed the effort to implement an agrarian revolution.

In early 1915, Carranza's army attacked Villa and Zapata. The peasant leaders still commanded regional support but could not win control of the nation. During 1916, Carranza confronted U. S. military intervention along the border that continued until early 1917, when the United States became involved in World War I in Europe. Throughout the turmoil in Mexico, the government of the United States attempted to protect American interests through diplomacy and military intervention.

By 1917, after years of civil war, Carranza's forces wrote a constitution. The Constitution of 1917 set forth a program for ongoing social revolution—never pursued with vigor—and political reform. Years would pass before all the provisions of the constitution could be enforced, but it provided the goals and ideals toward which Mexican governments were expected to strive.

Carranza and his subordinates recognized the agrarian problem but were cautious about addressing it. They admired the economic development they had seen in California and were determined to modernize Mexican political life and attract capital investment; Mexican leaders would share these goals from that time onward. Thus, despite the radical rhetoric and the upheaval among peasants that the revolution involved, the Mexican revolution saw the victory of a middle-class elite who would attempt to govern through enlightened paternalism.

The decade after 1917 witnessed both confusion and consolidation. In 1919, Zapata was killed. Carranza was assassinated in 1920, Villa in 1923. In this turmoil, Carranza's generals provided stability. During the 1920s, they served as presidents. They moved cau-

The forces of Emiliano Zapata march on Xochimilco in 1914. Women fought alongside men and played other prominent roles during the Mexican Revolution.

UPI/Corbis-Bettmann

tiously and hesitated to press land redistribution but were opposed by the Roman Catholic Church. In 1929, Plutarco Elías Calles (1877–1945) organized the **PRI**, the Institutional Revolutionary Party, which remained in power for the rest of the century.

In 1934, Lázaro Cárdenas (1895–1970) was elected president and moved to fulfill the promises of 1917. He turned tens of millions of acres of land over to peasant villages and nationalized the oil industry.

With the election of Manuel Ávila Camacho (1897–1955) in 1940, the era of revolutionary politics ended. Thereafter, the major issues in Mexico were those associated with postwar economic development. But unlike other Latin American nations, Mexico, because of its revolution, could confront those issues with a democratic perspective and a sense of social responsibility.

BRAZIL

Postcolonial Brazil differed from other newly independent nations in the region. Its language and heritage were Portuguese, not Spanish. For the first 67 years of its independence, it had a stable monarchical government. And it retained slavery until 1888.

Brazil became an independent empire in 1822. The first emperor, Pedro I (r. 1822–1831), while serving as regent for his father, the king of Portugal, had put himself at the head of the independence movement. Although he granted Brazil a constitution in 1823, Pedro's high-handed rule led to his abdication in 1831. Brazilians then took hold of their own destinies.

His 15-year-old son, Pedro II (r. 1831–1889), assumed power in 1840 and governed Brazil until 1889. Pedro II established a reputation as a constitutional monarch by asking leaders of both the conservative and the liberal political parties to form ministries. Consequently, Brazil enjoyed political stability.

PRI   The Institutional Revolutionary Party, which emerged from the Mexican revolution of 1911 and governed Mexico until the end of the twentieth century.

The Slavery Issue   The great divisive issue in Brazil was slavery. Sugar production remained the mainstay of the economy until the 1850s, when coffee cultivation began to dominate Brazilian agriculture. Like sugar planters, coffee producers also used

Slavery lasted longer in Brazil than in any other nation in North or South America. Antislavery groups circulated prints such as this one published in France to illustrate the brutality of slave life in Brazil.

The Granger Collection, N.Y.

slave labor, but their profits were much larger than those of the sugar producers, so a transition to free labor would have been easier for them. Coffee planters also tended to see themselves as economic progressives. Hence, people investing in coffee were more open to emancipation than those who had invested in sugar, which depended on slave labor to be profitable.

By 1850, Brazil had virtually ceased importing slaves. The end of slave imports doomed the institution of slavery because the slave population could not reproduce itself. It was nonetheless one thing to face this inevitability and another to abolish slavery.

The Paraguayan War of 1865–1870 postponed consideration of the slave question. This conflict pitted Brazil, Argentina, and Uruguay against Paraguay. The dictator of Paraguay, Francisco Solano López (1827–1870), fought a war of attrition. His death in battle ended the war, but only after more than half of the adult male population of Paraguay had been killed.

The end of the war returned slavery to the forefront of Brazilian politics. Brazil and the Spanish colonies of Puerto Rico and Cuba were now the only slave-holding countries in the hemisphere. The emperor favored gradual emancipation. A law of 1871 freed slaves owned by the crown and decreed legal freedom for future children of slaves, but it required them to work on plantations until the age of 21. However, throughout the 1870s and 1880s, the abolition movement grew in Brazil. In 1888, Pedro II was in Europe and his daughter was regent. She favored abolition and signed a law abolishing slavery without compensation to the slave owners. Thus ended slavery in Brazil.

A Republic Replaces Monarchy   It also brought to a head other issues that in 1889 ended the monarchy. Planters who received no financial compensation for their slaves were resentful. Roman Catholic clerics were disaffected by disputes with the emperor over education. Pedro II was unwell; his daughter, the heir to the throne, was unpopular. The officer corps of the army wanted more political influence. In November 1889, the army sent Pedro II into exile.

The Brazilian republic lasted from 1891 to 1930. Like the monarchy, it was dominated by a small group of wealthy persons. The political arrangement that allowed the republic to function smoothly was an agreement among the state governors. The president was to be chosen alternately from the states of São Paulo and Minas Gerais. In turn, the other eighteen governors had local political control. Fixed elections and patronage kept the system going. Literacy tests left few people qualified to vote. There was little organized opposition.

From the 1890s onward, the coffee industry dominated the nation. Around 1900, Brazil was producing over three-fourths of the world's coffee. The crop's success led to overproduction. To meet this problem, the government subsidized prices with loans from foreign banks and taxes on the rest of the economy, which felt exploited by the coffee interests. Throughout the life of the republic, Brazil produced essentially a single product for export and few goods for internal consumption.

Economic Problems and Military Coups   The end of slavery, the expansion of coffee production, and the beginning of urban industry attracted foreign immigrants. They tended to settle in the cities and constituted the core of the early industrial labor force. In Brazil, as elsewhere, World War I caused major economic disruption. Urban labor discontent appeared. The failure to address urban and industrial social problems and the political corruption led to attempted military coups. The revolts demonstrated that segments of the military wanted a modern nation that was not dependent on a single exportable product and a political system that recognized interests besides those of the coffee planters.

Coffee had ruled as the economic "king" of the Brazilian republic, and its collapse brought the republic down with it. In 1929, coffee prices hit record lows, and the economic structure of the republic lay in shambles. In October 1930, a military coup installed Getulio Vargas (1883–1954) in the presidency. Vargas governed Brazil until 1945.

The Vargas years represent a major turning point in Brazilian history. Vargas was initially supported by the reform elements in the military, middle-class groups, and urban workers. In office, he was a pragmatist who wanted to hold on to power and modernize Brazil. Vargas recognized the new social and economic groups shaping Brazilian political life. First with constitutionalism and then with dictatorship, he attempted to allow the government to act on behalf of those groups without allowing them to influence or direct the government in a democratic manner. However, he did not form his own political party or movement as Perón would later do in Argentina. Vargas rather attempted to function like a ringmaster directing the various forces in Brazilian life. His failure to establish a genuinely stable institutional political framework for a Brazil that included many interest groups besides the coffee planters still influences Brazil.

Vargas and his supporters sought to lessen dependence on coffee by fostering industries that would produce domestically goods that had previously been imported from abroad. The policy succeeded, and by the mid-1930s, domestic manufacturing was increasing. Vargas also established a legal framework for labor relations that included an eight-hour day and a minimum wage.

In the Brazilian context, these measures appeared reformist, if not necessarily liberal. However, in the late 1930s, Vargas confronted major political opposition and assumed dictatorial power in 1937. His regime thereafter was repressive. He claimed to have established an ***Estado Novo*** ("new state"). He presented himself as the protector of national stability against factions that would foster instability and of the national interest against international opponents.

Like the European dictators of the same era, Vargas used censorship, secret police, and torture. He also diversified and modernized the economy. In 1940, a five-year plan provided more state direction for the economy. His government favored the production of goods from heavy industry that would be used in Brazil itself. To maintain the support of trade unions, the state issued a progressive labor code. Siding with the Allies in World War II, Brazil built up large reserves of foreign currency through the export of foodstuffs. This economic activity and imposed political stability allowed the government to secure foreign loans for further economic development. By the end of the war, Brazil was becoming the major Latin American industrial power.

Participation in World War II on the side of the Allies had led many in Brazil to believe that they should not remain under a dictatorship. This attitude was widespread in the military, which had fought in Europe and established close contact with the United States. In 1945, the military carried out a coup, and Vargas retired temporarily from political life.

The new regime, which was democratic, continued the policy of economic development through foreign-financed industrialization. When in 1950 Vargas was

---

Chronology of Brazil

1822	Brazil becomes an independent empire
1840	Pedro II assumes personal rule
1840s and 1850s	Spread of coffee cultivation
1865–1870	Paraguayan War
1871	First law curbing slavery
1888	Slavery abolished
1889	Fall of the monarchy
1929	Collapse of coffee prices
1930–1945	Vargas Era
1957	Construction of Brasília begins
1964	Military takes control of the government

QUICK REVIEW

Getulio Vargas (1883–1954)

◆ October 1930: Vargas comes to power in military coup

◆ Vargas sought to represent a wider spectrum of Brazilian society without giving up personal power

◆ Assumed dictatorial power in 1937

Estado Novo The "new state" based on political stability and economic and social progress supposedly established by the dictator Getulio Vargas after 1937.

OVERVIEW

LATIN AMERICA'S DEPENDENT ECONOMY

After independence, most Latin American nations relied on export economies that sold raw materials or semi-finished goods, such as animal hides and leather, to the world's economy. Most manufactured goods were imported, primarily from Britain. This created a dependent economy in which Latin American prosperity depended on other nations' paying high prices for its raw materials. What made this dependence even more precarious was that most Latin American nations depended on one or two products for their export earnings. When prices for these products fell or collapsed, as they did during the Great Depression of the 1930s, Latin America had little else to trade, and its prosperity plummeted. The table below shows the main products of the principal Latin American countries between the 1820s and 1930.

ARGENTINA	animal products (meat, leather, wool), grain	**ECUADOR**	bananas
BOLIVIA	tin, silver	**MEXICO**	silver, cattle, oil
BRAZIL	coffee, sugar, rubber	**PERU**	nitrates, silver
CHILE	copper	**URUGUAY**	animal products (meat, leather)
COLOMBIA	coffee, cattle	**VENEZUELA**	coffee, cattle

elected president, his return to office was anticlimactic. He was elderly and past his prime. When a member of his staff became involved in the assassination of a journalist, the military demanded that Vargas resign. Instead, he took his own life in 1954.

In the decade after Vargas's death, Brazil remained a democracy, although an unstable one. The government began to undertake vast projects such as the costly construction of the new capital of Brasília, begun in 1957. The rapid growth of cities and the expansion of a working class radicalized political life. The political system could not readily accommodate itself to the concerns of workers and the urban poor. Poverty and illiteracy plagued both the cities and the countryside.

By the early 1960s, when President João Goulert (1918–1977) took office, Brazilian political life was in turmoil. Goulert's predecessors, including Vargas, had attempted to balance interests and political forces. However, Goulert committed himself to the left. In 1964, he announced his support for land reform, which was anathema to conservatives. Goulert also questioned the authority of the military hierarchy. In March 1964, the military, claiming to protect Brazil from communism, seized control of the government, ending its post–World War II experiment with democracy.

SUMMARY

Economic Dependence In the 1820s, Latin America threw off Spanish and Portuguese rule. But the traditional elites—landowners, military officers, the Church—remained in control. A series of strongmen called *caudillos* dominated most Latin American republics. Nor did independence bring economic prosperity. Because Latin American economies remained dependent on producing agricultural commodities for export, foreign nations, particularly Britain, dominated Latin American economic life. When commodity prices collapsed during the Great Depression, Latin American economies were devastated. The crisis did, however, lead to the beginnings of manufacturing in many Latin American countries in an effort to avoid dependence on imports.

Argentina After independence, Buenos Aires came to dominate Argentina economically and politically. Agricultural exports, the growth of industry, and large-scale European immigration contributed to a strong export economy. However, urban social discontent and the growth of nationalism in the 1930s led to military intervention in politics and the corporatist dictatorship of Juan Perón from 1946 to 1956.

Mexico In the first decades after independence Mexico was politically and economically unstable. Mexico lost half its territory to the United States and was invaded by France in the 1860s. The long-lasting dictatorship of Porfirio Díaz brought political stability but led to increasing discontent. The Mexican Revolution that began in 1911 produced cautious social and economic reform under the one-party rule of the PRI, the Institutional Revolutionary Party, which remained in power until the end of the century.

Brazil Brazil was a stable constitutional monarchy after independence until 1889. It also retained slavery until 1888. The establishment of a republic did not change Brazil's economic dependence on coffee exports, however, and the collapse of coffee prices in 1929 led to the dictatorship of Getulio Vargas. Although politically repressive, Vargas instituted social reforms and promoted industrial development, which continued to expand in the decade after his death in 1954.

IMAGE KEY

for pages 598–599

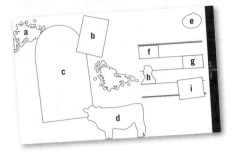

a. Coffee beans
b. Eva Perón
c. Diego Rivera, *Orgy-Night of the Rich*, 1926
d. A black bull
e. Mexican felt hat
f. South American painting, *De Indio y Mestiza Nace Coyote*
g. Porters carrying bags of coffee
h. General Juan Manuel de Rosas
i. Brazilian overseer punishing a slave

REVIEW QUESTIONS

1. What was the condition of the Latin American economies after independence? What role did their economies play in the worldwide economy that developed in the nineteenth century?

2. Did the structure of Latin American societies change after independence? What role did the traditional elites play in the economic and political life of their nations? What was the condition of the mass of the population?

3. How did European and U.S. investment in Latin America affect the region?

4. Why did Latin American nations find it difficult to develop stable regimes? What role did the military play?

5. How did European immigration affect Argentina? Why was Juan Perón able to hold power?

6. How did the Vargas regime change the Brazilian economy? Why did Brazilian democracy end in a military coup in 1964?

KEY TERMS

caudillo (p. 605)
debt peonage (p. 602)
Estado Novo (p. 613)
import substitution (p. 605)

La Reforma (p. 609)
mestizos (p. 603)
mulattos (p. 603)
nacionalismo (p. 607)

neocolonial economy (p. 605)
Perónism (p. 607)
positivism (p. 603)
PRI (p. 611)

 For additional study resources for this chapter, go to:
www.prenhall.com/craig/chapter27

An Indian artist's painting of British officer James Todd (ca. 1880) riding in a ceremonial procession on a royal elephant. "Col. James Todd on elephant Indian painting" c. 1880. E.T. Archive, Victoria and Albert Museum.

K. ATA TURK

28

INDIA, THE ISLAMIC HEARTLANDS, AND AFRICA
The Encounter with the Modern West
1800–1945

HOW DID British rule affect the Indians?

WHAT ROLE did Gandhi play in ending British rule in India?

WHY DID Islamic reform movements arise during the eighteenth century?

WHAT WERE the three typical Islamic reactions to Western encroachment?

WHAT WERE the main Islamic reform movements in nineteenth-century Africa?

HOW DID Africans react to European colonialism?

IMAGE KEY
Image Key for pages 616–617
is on page 634.

The encroachment of the European nations on the rest of the world from the late fifteenth century onward brought radical changes. In the West itself, spiritual and material disruption accompanied the Renaissance, the Reformation, the Enlightenment, and the Industrial and Scientific Revolutions. The effects of these watershed European developments on the Indian, Asian, and African worlds came more rapidly, in greater concentration, and with less preparation than they had in the West.

*To call these complex processes of "modernization" does not reflect the acute differences between the relatively lengthy and gradual processes of change in western Europe and the more rapid and disruptive changes that European imperialism and colonialism brought to other parts of the world. The very concept of "modernity" has been appropriated by the West. Western dominance has led it to a specific and novel notion of modernity: namely, as a special set of ideas and institutions that evolved in Europe between the Renaissance and the early twentieth century and was then gradually exported to, or imposed upon, other societies. The expression **"the impact of modernity"** refers to how the introduction of "modern" Western civilization affected traditional cultures.*

The consequences of the spread of Western culture have been so massive that today non-Western peoples are often merely its passive recipients. The American or European view of the world often portrays the West as the active, creative, dominant force in recent history, as though the rest of the world were some monolithic, archaic entity.

As parochial as such chauvinistic generalizations are, the impingement of the West has been a major element in the recent history of African, Asian, and Indian civilizations. Yet in all of these "Third World" areas, Western modernity entered cultures that had ancient and highly developed traditions of their own. These traditions did not simply melt away on the arrival of the westerners. Islamic, Hindu, and other regions of the Third World maintained continuity with the past. Much of the history of the twentieth-century Asian and African societies hit hardest by the new "modernity" has been shaped by their peoples' realization of the importance of their own traditions.

impact of modernity   The effect of western political, economic, and social ideas and institutions on traditional societies.

THE INDIAN EXPERIENCE

BRITISH RULE

HOW DID British rule affect the Indians?

I n the eighteenth century, Britain became the dominant naval and commercial power in the Southern Seas. In India by the early nineteenth century, the British had built the largest European colonial empire in the Afro-Asian world. India was the "jewel in the crown" of that empire.

BUILDING THE EMPIRE: THE FIRST HALF OF THE NINETEENTH CENTURY

As we saw in Chapter 23, before the British crown asserted direct rule over India in 1858, the British wielded effective imperial control through the East India Company. Those areas not annexed were recognized as independent princely states. They retained their status only so long as they remained faithful to Britain. The India that resulted was a polyglot mixture of tributary states and provinces that the British administered directly.

The economic impact of Company rule was extensive. The need for ever higher revenues squeezed peasants. In addition, demand for Indian indigo, cotton, and opium in the China and British trade also slacked off in the 1830s, and famines brought widespread suffering.

Company rule also affected the physical face of India. Company policies encouraged settled agriculture and small commodity production at the expense of the nomadic and pastoralist cultures of North and central India. British "pacification" involved the clearing of land to deny natural cover to military enemies and the often forced settlement of peasants in new regions. Early in the nineteenth century, European loggers caused extensive deforestation as, after 1840, did the tracts leveled for tea and coffee plantations in Assam and the Bengal hills. This ecological destruction was part of the transformation of India into a more homogeneous peasant farming society that provided a better base for colonial administration.

The Indians were by no means passive in the face of this exploitation. The first half of the nineteenth century saw almost constant revolt in one place or another. The revolts included peasant movements of noncooperation, Muslim farm workers' attacks on British and Hindu estate owners, grain riots, tribal revolts, and other actions. They culminated in the Indian Revolt of 1857.

The immediate trigger of the Revolt was the concern among Bengal troops that animal grease on newly issued rifles exposed them to ritual pollution. Behind this issue, however, lay other grievances, including the addition of Sikhs, Gurkhas, and lower-caste soldiers to the army; deteriorating economic conditions; outrage at excessive tax rates; and anger at the 1856 British annexation of the princely state of Awadh. One can also see in the revolt the desire to rebuild a pre-British political order in North India. The revolt was not an all-India affair. It centered on Delhi, where the last Mughal emperor joined in the rebel cause.

The British eventually won the day. With their forces augmented by Sikhs from the Panjab and Gurkhas from Bengal, they overcame the divided Indian opposition. By the end of 1857, the revolt was broken, often with great brutality. In 1858, the East India Company was dissolved, and India came under direct rule of the British Crown.

The "Mutiny" of 1857 was not a nationalist revolution. Still, it highlighted resentment of the burdens of foreign domination that were to grow increasingly oppressive for Indians of all regions and religions over the ensuing ninety years of Crown rule (the "**raj**").

BRITISH-INDIAN RELATIONS

The overall impact of British presence on the Indian masses was brutal but impersonal and largely economic. India was effectively integrated into Britain's economy, becoming a market for British goods, providing Britain with raw materials and other products, and helping Britain maintain a healthy balance of trade.

British cultural imperialism was never a major nor even an official policy of the East India Company. Nonetheless, the British-Indian relationship had a paternalistic and patronizing dimension, both before and after the events of 1857. The ethos of the British rulers included the understanding that they had the task of governing an inferior "race" that could not handle the job by itself. Even Indians whose university degrees or army training were impeccable by British standards were never accepted as equals. From army to civil-service ranks, the upper echelon of command was British.

Despite this unequal relationship, British ideas influenced a small but powerful Indian elite in both their business and political life and their manners and customs. Conversion to Christianity was rare, but Christian and secular values associated with the European Enlightenment influenced Hindu and Muslim educated classes.

In the nineteenth century, probably the most influential member of the Indian elite to engage the British on their own ground was Ram Mohan Roy (1772–1833). Roy, a Bengali Hindu, rose to the top of the native ranks of East India Company service and became a strong voice for reform, both of Hindu life and of British colonial policy. Roy

20.4
Lord William Bentinck, Comments on Ritual Murder and the Limits of Religious Toleration

raj   The years from 1858 to 1947 during which India was governed directly by the British Crown.

Faces of the raj. A tennis party at the Residency, Kapurkala, Panjab, ca. 1894.

Hulton/Corbis-Bettmann

was a modernist who wanted to meld the best of European-Christian morality and thought with the best of Hindu piety and thought. He opposed autocratic and unfair British legal and commercial practices and campaigned in India and England to reform the Company's India policies. He studied the Christian scriptures and the great thinkers of European civilization and drew upon these sources in his Hindu reform efforts. His public campaigns for education, political involvement, and social progress and against the "backward" practices and ideas of many of his Hindu compatriots alienated most of the leading Hindu thinkers of his age, but twentieth-century Indians have often seen him as a visionary.

If many Indians sought to acquire British ways and join the British in business and administration, many more resented their subordinate status. The anti-imperial sentiment that blossomed into the nationalist movement at the end of the nineteenth century extended to the grass-roots level—among tribal groups, peasant farmers, and workers. Whatever their status, the distrust and animosity most Indians felt continued to grow.

FROM BRITISH RAJ TO INDEPENDENCE

THE BURDEN OF CROWN RULE

WHAT ROLE did Gandhi play in ending British rule in India?

The Revolt of 1857 had numerous consequences beyond the transfer of the administration of India to the British Crown. The bloody conflict exacerbated mutual fear and hatred. Before the revolt, the British had maintained a largely native army under British officers. After the revolt, they tried to maintain a ratio of at least one British to three Indian soldiers. The army was financed by Indian, not British, revenues. This imposed a huge economic burden on India, diverting one-third of its annual revenues to pay for its own occupation.

British economic policies and accelerating population growth put great strains on India's poor. Cheap British goods were exchanged for Indian raw materials and the products of its home industries, harming Indian craft industries and forcing multitudes into poverty or onto the land. Industrialization, which might have provided work for India's unemployed masses, was avoided. Finally, many peasants lost their hereditary lands because of other British policies, forcing thousands to emigrate to Britain's dominions in South Africa, where they worked as indentured servants.

The Revolt of 1857 also created a poisonous distrust of Indians within the British colonial administration. "**Cantonments**" segregating white masters from natives became the rule in Indian cities. Despite the intentions expressed in royal statements and the opening of the civil service, at least nominally, to Indian candidates, the raj discouraged equality between Indian and Britisher.

INDIAN RESISTANCE

cantonments The segregation of areas in which Europeans lived in British-ruled India from those areas inhabited by native Indians.

Indians soon took up political activism. Late in the nineteenth century, they founded the institutions that would help overcome regionalism, build national feeling, and end colonial rule. In 1885, Indian modernists formed The Indian National

Congress. The Muslim League developed as a counterbalance to the Hindu-dominated Congress. The League ultimately worked for, and gained, a separate independent Muslim state, Pakistan. Erratic British policies strengthened the desire for independence.

Besides the British themselves, Indian internal divisions were the major obstacle to independence. These divisions included the many language groups and subject princely states of the subcontinent. These, however, were not even the most critical divisions. For much of British rule, every Indian politician was first a representative of his own region or state and second an Indian nationalist. Furthermore, the Indian elite had little in common with the masses beyond antagonism to foreign rule, making unified resistance difficult. Conflict among Hindus, Muslims, Sikhs, and Jains also impeded concerted political action.

Yet a nationalist movement took root. Three principal elements within the independence movement led to the creation of India and Pakistan in 1947.

The first consisted of those in the National Congress who sought gradual reform and progress toward Indian self-governance, or *swarāj*. (See "Gandhi on Passive Resistance and Swarāj".) This position did not preclude opposition to the British, but it did mean trying to change the system from within. Among the proponents of this approach were the spiritual and political genius Mohandas K. Gandhi (1869–1948) and his follower Jawaharlal Nehru (1889–1964), who became the first prime minister of India. Gandhi was the principal Indian leader after World War I and directed the all-India drive that finally forced the British out. Himself an English-trained lawyer, Gandhi drew not only on his own Hindu (and Jain and Buddhist) heritage, but also on the ideas of Western liberal and Christian thinkers. In the end, Gandhi became a world figure.

The second element consisted of the militant Hindu nationalists, whose leader, the extremist B. G. Tilak (1856–1920), stressed the use of Indian languages and a revival of Hindu culture and learning. Tilak also subscribed to an anti-Muslim, Hindu communalist vision of Indian "self-governance." The Hindu extremists looked to a return to traditional Indian values and self-sufficiency. Their ideas still influence Indian political life, as the resurgence of Hindu extremist groups in recent years and communal strife, especially with Muslims, are unhappy testimony.

Muslims made up the third element. The subcontinent held many divergent regional and sectarian Muslim constituencies. Their leaders could be brought to make common cause only by the fear that, as a minority, Muslims stood to lose what power they had in a Hindu-majority, all-India state. Muslims had been slower than the Hindus to take up British ideas and education and thus lagged behind the Hindu intelligentsia in numbers and influence with the British or other Indians.

HINDU-MUSLIM FRICTION

In the twentieth century, the rift between Muslims and Hindus in the subcontinent grew wider. In the end, the great Indo-Muslim poet and thinker, Muhammad Iqbal (1873–1938), and

India	
1772–1833	Ram Mohan Roy, Hindu reformer
1857–1858	Revolt, or "Mutiny," followed by direct Crown rule as a British colony
1885	Indian National Congress formed
1869–1948	Mohandas K. Gandhi
1873–1938	Muhammad Iqbal
1876–1949	Muhammad Ali Jinnah
1889–1964	Jawaharlal Nehru
1947	Independence and partition

27.2
Gandhi and Nehru: "Two Utterly Different Standpoints": Jawaharal Nehru

The "Great Soul," "Mahatma" Mohandas K. Gandhi, father of the modern state of India.

UPI/Corbis-Corbis-Bettmann

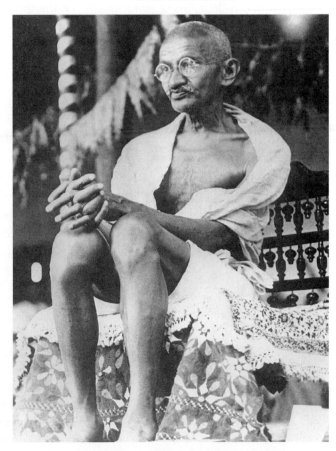

· HISTORY'S VOICES ·

GANDHI ON PASSIVE RESISTANCE AND SWARĀJ

 andhi's powerful thinking and prose were already evident in his Hind Swarāj, *or* Indian Home Rule *of 1909. This work was to remain his basic manifesto. The following excerpts reflect important points in his philosophy.* Swadeshī *refers to reliance only on what one produces at home (rather than on foreign goods).*

HOW DOES Gandhi relate the ideas of passive resistance and *swarāj* to his theory of Indian self-rule? What are the advantages and disadvantages of his strategy for effecting political and social change? How does this document compare with others concerned with movements of independence and nationalism?

Passive resistance is a method of securing rights by personal suffering; it is the reverse of resistance by arms. When I refuse to do a thing that is repugnant to my conscience, I use soul-force. For instance, the government of the day has passed a law which is applicable to me. I do not like it. If by using violence I force the government to repeal the law, I am employing what may be termed body-force. If I do not obey the law and accept the penalty for its breach, I use soul-force. It involves sacrifice of self.

Everybody admits that sacrifice of self is infinitely superior to sacrifice of others. Moreover, if this kind of force is used in a cause that is unjust, only the person using it suffers. He does not make others suffer for his mistakes. . . .

. . . The real meaning of the statement that we are a law-abiding nation is that we are passive resisters. When we do not like certain laws, we do not break the heads of law-givers but we suffer and do not submit to the laws. . . .

If man will only realize that it is unmanly to obey laws that are unjust, no man's tyranny will enslave him. This is the key to self-rule or home-rule. . . .

Let each do his duty. If I do my duty, that is, serve myself, I shall be able to serve others. Before I leave you, I will take the liberty of repeating:

1. Real home-rule is self-rule or self-control.
2. The way to it is passive resistance: that is soul-force or love-force.
3. In order to exert this force, *Swadeshī* in every sense is necessary.
4. What we want to do should be done, not because we object to the English or because we want to retaliate, but because it is our duty to do so. Thus, supposing that the English remove the salt-tax, restore our money, give the highest posts to Indians, withdraw the English troops, we shall certainly not use their machine-made goods, nor use the English language, nor many of their industries. It is worth noting that these things are, in their nature, harmful; hence we do not want them. I bear no enmity towards the English but do towards their civilization.

In my opinion, we have used the term *Swarāj* without understanding its real significance. I have endeavored to explain it as I understand it, and my conscience testifies that my life henceforth is dedicated to its attainment.

From *Sources of Indian Tradition* edited by William Theodore de Bary. Copyright © 1958 by Columbia University Press. Reprinted with permission of the publisher.

the "founder of Pakistan," Muhammad Ali Jinnah (1876–1949), helped move Muslims to separatism.

The independence of India and Pakistan from Western domination was only achieved with violence. Blood was spilled in the long battle with the British, in communal violence between Hindus and Muslims that accompanied partition in 1947, and in the still festering dispute over Kashmir between India and Pakistan. Still, the victory of 1947 gave the peoples of the subcontinent, Indians and Pakistanis, at last a sense of participation in the world of nations on their own terms instead of on those dictated by a foreign power. The British left a legacy of unity and egalitarian and democratic ideals that Indian nationalists turned to their own uses.

THE ISLAMIC EXPERIENCE

ISLAMIC RESPONSES TO DECLINING POWER AND INDEPENDENCE

The eighteenth century saw the weakening of the great Muslim empires and the increasing ascendancy of the West. The diverse Islamic peoples and states were thrust into a struggle for survival. The decline of Islamic preeminence was also the result of internal problems.

By the eighteenth century, the largest Muslim empires had declined from their heydays in the sixteenth and seventeenth centuries. They had grown decentralized, were less stable economically and politically, and were increasingly dominated by entrenched hereditary elites, including those among the gentry, palace guards, military castes, local princes, urban guilds, and even religious leaders (the *ulama*) and the Sufi orders.

During the eighteenth century, reform movements sought to revive Islam as a comprehensive guide for living and to purify it from the more stultifying developments in Islamic societies during the preceding centuries. Most of these movements emphasized inner piety and a puritanical stress on external practice.

The most famous of these movements was that of the Wahhabis, the followers of Ibn Abd al-Wahhab (1703–1792) in Arabia. It sought to combat excesses of popular and Sufi piety to break the stranglehold of the *ulama*'s conformist interpretations of legal and religious issues. The only authorities were to be the Qur'an and the traditions of the Prophet. Allied with a local Arab prince, Sa'ud, the Wahhabi movement swept much of the Arabian peninsula. It was crushed in the early nineteenth century by the Ottomans. It finally saw victory under a descendant of Sa'ud at the onset of this century and has become the guiding ideology of Saudi Arabia.

Other Muslim reform movements reflected similar revivalist and even militantly pietist responses to Islamic decadence and decline. This call continues to rally movements from Africa to Indonesia. In Islamic societies everywhere in recent times, it has provided a response to the challenge of Western-style "modernity" and a model for cultural and religious life.

WHY DID Islamic reform movements arise during the eighteenth century?

WESTERN POLITICAL AND ECONOMIC ENCROACHMENT

From the late 1700s until World War II, the political fortunes of Islamic states were increasingly dictated from outside by Western powers. Western governments extracted capitulations favorable to their own interests from indigenous governments in exchange for promises of military protection or other considerations. These capitulations took the form of treaty clauses granting commercial concessions, special protection, and "extraterritorial" legal status to European merchant enclaves. Such concessions had originally been reciprocal and had served the commercial purposes of Muslim rulers and some merchants as well as Western traders. However, they eventually provided Western powers with pretexts for direct intervention in Ottoman, Iranian, Indian, and African affairs. The Ottoman Empire suffered from internal disunity; its provincial rulers, or *pashas,* were virtually independent. This, combined with the economic problems facing all the agrarian societies of Asia and Africa, made it easy for the Western

WHY WAS it easy for Western powers to encroach on the Islamic world during the nineteenth century?

powers—with their industrializing economies and militaries—to take control. Repeated Ottoman diplomatic and military defeats made that once, great imperial power "the sick man of Europe" after 1800; similar weakness allowed westerners to control Indian and Iranian states.

Napoleon Bonaparte's (1769–1821) unsuccessful invasion of Egypt in 1798 heralded a new era of European imperialism and colonialism in the region. By this date, the British had already wrested control over India and the Persian Gulf from the French; they now became the preeminent European power in the eastern Mediterranean as well. The Russians presented the most serious nineteenth-century challenge to Britain's colonial empire. Russia sought to gain as much territory and influence in the Iranian and Central Asian regions as possible. Afghanistan, an independent kingdom established by Ahmad Shah Durrani (r. 1737–1773), acted as a buffer that prevented Russia from penetrating southwestward into British India. In the Iranian and Ottoman regions, however, Russia and Britain—with French involvement—struggled with each other for supremacy. The Crimean War of 1854–1856 (see Chapter 34) was one result of this conflict.

THE WESTERN IMPACT

Beyond the overt political and commercial impact of the West, Western political ideology, culture, and technology proved critical factors for change in Islamic societies. Outside of India, this effect was most strongly felt in Egypt, Lebanon, North Africa, and Turkey. The Islamic states least and last affected by Western "modernity" were Iran, Afghanistan, and the Central Asian khanates.

The rulers of Iran from 1794 to 1925 were the Qajar shahs, whose absolutist reign was not unlike that of the Safavids. However, the Qajars did not claim, as had the Safavids, to descent from the Shi'ite *imams*. Under Qajar rule, the *ulama* of the Shi'ite community became less strongly connected with the state apparatus. This period also saw the emergence of a Shi'i traditionalist doctrine that encouraged all Shi'ites to choose a **mujtahid**—a qualified scholarly guide—from among the *ulama* and follow his religious-legal interpretations. As a result, the *ulama* were often the chief critics of the government (not least for its attempts to admit Western influences) and exponents of the people's grievances.

A demonstration of *ulama* power occurred when in 1890 the Qajar Shah granted a fifty-year monopoly on tobacco sales to the British. In 1891, the *ulama* decreed a tobacco boycott to protest the concession. This popular action was supported by modernist-nationalist opponents of the Qajar regime who had strong connections to Iran's commercial, or **bazaari**, middle classes. It forced the Shah to rescind the concession.

Subject as it was to the machinations of outsiders, such as Russia, Britain, and France, Iran felt the impact of Western ideas, especially in the latter half of the century, when younger Iranian intellectuals began to warm to Western liberalism. As in other Islamic countries, the seeds of secular nationalism were being sown where religious sentiments had held sway. It worked with a desire among larger sectors of the populace for a voice in government. An uneasy alliance of Iranian modernists with conservative *ulama* proved, on occasion, an effective counterforce to Qajar absolutism, as in the tobacco boycott and in the early stages of the effort to force the Qajars to accept a constitution in 1906–1911. Yet such alliances did not bridge the inherent ideological divisions of the two groups.

HOW DID Iran react to the West during the nineteenth century?

mujtahid A Shi'ite religious-legal scholar.

bazaari The Iranian commercial middle class.

ISLAMIC RESPONSES TO FOREIGN ENCROACHMENT

As the Iranian case shows, Western impingement on the Islamic world in the nineteenth and twentieth centuries elicited varied responses. Every people or state had a different experience. Yet we can point to at least three typical styles of reaction: (1) a tendency to emulate and adopt Western ideas and institutions; (2) the attempt to join Western innovations with traditional Islamic institutions; and (3) a traditionalist rejection of things Western in favor of either the status quo or return to a purified Islamic community.

WHAT WERE the three typical Islamic reactions to Western encroachment?

EMULATION OF THE WEST

A strategy of emulation is exemplified in the career of the virtually independent Ottoman viceroy Muhammad Ali (ca. 1769–1849), pasha of Egypt from 1805 to 1849. He set out to rejuvenate Egypt's agriculture, to introduce modern industry, to modernize the army with European help, and to introduce European education and culture in government schools. Although he did not bring Egypt to a position of power equal to the European states, and his successors' financial and political catastrophes led the British to occupy Egypt (1882–1922), Muhammad Ali did set his country on the path to becoming a modern national state. Hence he is rightly called "the father of modern Egypt."

Efforts to appropriate Western experience and success were made by several Ottoman sultans and viziers after the defeat of the Turks by Russia in 1774. Most notable were the reforms of Selim III (r. 1762–1808), Mahmud II (r. 1808–1839), and the so-called Tanzimat, or beneficial "legislation" era from about 1839 to 1880. Selim made serious efforts at economic as well as administrative and military reform. Mahmud's reforms were much like those of Muhammad Ali. Most important were his destruction of the Janissary corps, his tax and bureaucratic reforms, and his encouragement of Western military and educational methods. Like Muhammad Ali, he was less interested in promoting European enlightenment ideas about citizen rights and equity than in building a stronger, more modern government.

The Tanzimat reforms, introduced by several liberal Ottoman ministers of state, continued the efforts of Selim and Mahmud. They were intended to bring the Ottoman state into line with ideals espoused by the European states, to give European powers less cause to intervene in Ottoman affairs, and to regenerate confidence in the state.

The nineteenth-century Ottoman reforms failed to save the empire. Nevertheless, they paved the way for the rise of Turkish nationalism, the "Young Turk" revolution of 1908, and the nationalist revolution of the 1920s that produced modern Turkey.

The creation of the Turkish republic out of the ashes of the Ottoman state after World War I is probably the most extreme example of an effort to modernize and nationalize an Islamic state on a Western model. This state was largely the child of Mustafa Kemal (1881–1938), known as "Atatürk" ("father of the Turks"), its first president (1922–1938). Atatürk's major reforms ranged from the introduction of a European-style

Islamic Lands

1703–1792	Ibn Abd al-Wahhab
1737–1773	Rule of Ahmad Shah Durrani, founder of modern Afghanistan
1794–1925	Qajar shahs of Iran
1798	Invasion of Egypt by Napoleon Bonaparte
1805–1849	Rule of Muhammad Ali in Egypt
ca. 1839–1880	Era of the Tanzimat reforms of the Ottoman Empire
1839–1897	Jamal al-Din al-Afghani
1845–1905	Muhammad Abduh
1882–1922	British occupation of Egypt
1908	"Young Turk" revolution
1922–1938	Mustafa Kemal, "Atatürk" in power

Kemal Atatürk (right) giving instruction in the Latin alphabet. This 1928 photograph reflects the personal engagement of Mustafa Kemal in the many reform efforts he instituted.

Historical Pictures Collection/Stock Montage Inc.

code of civil law to the abolition of the caliphate, Sufi orders, Arabic script, and the Arabic call to prayer. These changes constituted a radical attempt to secularize an Islamic state and to separate religious from political and social institutions. Nothing quite like it has ever been repeated. Despite some adjustments and even reversals of Atatürk's measures, Turkey has maintained its independence, reaffirmed its commitment to democratic government, and emerged with a unique but still distinctly Islamic identity.

INTEGRATION OF WESTERN AND ISLAMIC IDEAS

The attempt to join modernization with traditional Islamic institutions and ideas is exemplified in the thought of famous Muslim intellectuals, such as Jamal al-Din al-Afghani (1839–1897), and Muhammad Abduh (1845–1905). These thinkers argued for a progressive Islam rather than a materialist Western secularism as the best answer to life in the modern world. Afghani is best known for his emphasis on the unity of the Islamic world, or "**pan-Islamism**," and on a populist, constitutionalist approach to political order.

PURIFICATION AND REVIVAL OF ISLAM

A third kind of Muslim reaction to Western domination has focused on recourse to Islamic values and ideals to the exclusion of "outside" forces. This approach includes reformist revivalism like Wahhabism and the kind of conservatism often associated with Sunni or Shi'ite "establishment" *ulama*, as in Iran since 1979. The conservative spirit has often been the target of revivalist reformers who see in it the worst legacy of medieval Islam. Still, both conservative and revivalist Muslim thinkers look for answers to the questions facing Muslims in the modern world within, not outside, the Islamic tradition.

NATIONALISM

Nationalism is a product of modern history. Nationalist movements in the Islamic world have been either stimulated by Western models or produced in reaction to Western exploitation and colonial occupation. Indeed, the often arbitrary or artificial division of the colonial world by European administrators has frequently produced national units where none had existed—notably in Africa, but also in Syria, Jordan, Iraq, and Central Asia. In Turkey in the 1920s, nationalism took a secularist form; in Libya, Iran, and elsewhere since the 1970s and 1980s, it has taken an Islamic-revivalist form. As an Afro-Asian phenomenon, it will reappear in the next section and in Chapter 35.

pan-Islamism The movement that advocates that the entire Muslim world should form a unified political and cultural entity.

THE AFRICAN EXPERIENCE

Between 1800 and 1945, virtually every part of Africa changed, but nowhere more than sub-Saharan Africa. With the exception of South Africa below the Transvaal, tropical and southern Africa came under major influence and finally colonial control from outside only after 1880. Before then, internal developments—demographic and power shifts and then the rise of Islamic reform movements—overshadowed the European presence in the continent.

NEW STATES AND POWER CENTERS

SOUTHERN AFRICA

In the south, below the Limpopo River, the first quarter of the nineteenth century saw devastating internal warfare, depopulation, and forced migrations of many Bantu peoples in what is known as the *mfecane*, or "crushing" era. Likely brought on by a population explosion and economic competition, the *mfecane* was marked by the rise of military states among the northern Nguni-speaking Bantu. Its result was a period of warfare and chaos; depopulation; and the creation of multitribal, multilingual Bantu states in modern Zimbabwe, Mozambique, Malawi, Zambia, and Tanzania.

The Nguni warrior-king Dingiswayo formed the first of the new military states between circa 1800 and 1818. The most important state was formed by his successor, Shaka, leader of the Nguni-speaking Zulu nation and kingdom (ca. 1818–1828). Shaka's brutal military tactics led to the Zulu conquest of a vast dominion in southeastern Africa and the depopulation of some 15,000 square miles. Refugees fled north into Sotho-speaking Bantu territory or south to put increasing pressure on the southern Nguni peoples. Chaos ensued north and south of Zululand and even in the high veld above the Orange River.

The net result was the creation of diverse states. Some people tried to imitate the military state of Shaka; others fled to the mountains; others even went west into the Kalahari. The most famous of these was Lesotho, the Sotho kingdom of King Mosheshwe, which survived as long as he lived (from the 1820s until 1870). Mosheshwe defended his people from the Zulu and held off the Afrikaners, missionaries, and British. After his death, the latter groups became Lesotho's chief predators.

The new state-building spawned by the *mfecane* was nullified by Boer expansion and British annexation of the Natal province (1843). These developments stemmed from the **Great Trek** of Boer *voortrekers*, which took place between 1835 and 1843. This migration brought about 6,000 Afrikaners from the eastern Cape Colony northeastward into the more fertile regions of southern Africa, Natal, and the high veld above the Orange River. It resulted in the creation after 1850 of two Afrikaner republics: the Orange Free State between the Orange and Vaal Rivers and the South African Republic north of the Vaal.

EAST AND CENTRAL AFRICA

In East and East Central Africa, external trade resulted in the formation of strong states. In the Lakes region, peoples such as the Nyamwezi to the east of Lake Tanganyika

WHAT NEW states arose in Africa during the early nineteenth century?

mfecane A period of widespread warfare and chaos among Bantu peoples in east-central Africa during the early nineteenth century.

Great Trek The migration between 1835 and 1847 of Boer pioneers (called *voortrekkers*) north from British-ruled Cape Colony to establish their own independent republics.

Southern Africa

ca. 1800–1818	Dingiswayo, Nguni Zulu king, forms new military state
1800–1825	The *mfecane* among the Bantu of southeastern Africa
1795	British take Cape Colony from the Dutch
ca. 1818–1828	Shaka's reign as head of the Nguni state; major warfare, destruction, and expansion
ca. 1825–1870	Sotho kingdom of King Mosheshwe in Lesotho region
1835–1843	Great Trek of Boers into Natal and north onto the high veld beyond the Orange
1843	British annexation of Natal province
1852–1860	Creation of the Orange Free State and South African Republic

Mosheshwe, king and founder of Lesotho.
Not all of the Bantu peoples followed
the militaristic example of Shaka.
Mosheshwe, prince of a subtribe of the
Sotho Bantus, fought off Zulu attacks
and led his people to a mountain stronghold in southern Africa, where, through
diplomacy and determination, he founded a small nation that has endured to
the present. The kingdom became the
British protectorate of Basutoland in
1868. In 1966 it achieved independence as the kingdom of Lesotho under
Mosheshwe's great-grandson, King
Mosheshwe II.

Courtesy of the Library of Congress

WHAT WERE the main
Islamic reform movements in
nineteenth-century Africa?

and the Baganda west of Lake Victoria gained regional power
from as early as the late eighteenth century through trade
with the Arab–Swahili eastern coast and the eastern Congo to
the west. This east–west commerce involved slaves; ivory; copper; and, from the outside, Indian cloth, firearms, and manufactured goods.

WEST AFRICA

In West Africa, the slave trade was replaced by European demand for palm oil and gum arabic by the 1820s. In the first
half of the century, *jihad* (holy struggle) movements of the
Fulbe (or Fulani) and others shattered the stability of the
western savannah and forest regions from modern Senegal
and Ghana through southern Nigeria. Wars and dislocation
resulted in the rise of regional kingdoms, such as those of
Asante and Dahomey (modern Benin). These eventually succumbed to internal dissension and the colonial activities of
Britain and France later in the century.

ISLAMIC REFORM MOVEMENTS

The vitality of Islam was a significant agent of change in sub-Saharan Africa
before the European rush for colonies in the 1880s. It is still a factor. In
1800, Islam was already well established from West Africa across the
Sudan to the Red Sea and along the East African coast. Islam was the law of the
land in states such as the sultanate of Zanzibar on the eastern coast and the waning Funj sultanate on the Blue Nile in the eastern Sudan. But in many "Islamic"
states in Africa, the rural populace were still semi- if not wholly pagan; and even
the urban elites were only nominally Muslim.

The nineteenth century is notable for the militant Islamic revivalist and reform movements of *jihad*, which fixed and spread Islam as a lasting part of the
African scene. The most important *jihad* movement was led by a Fulbe Muslim
scholar from Hausa territory in the central Sahel. Usman Dan Fodio (1754–1817)
was influenced by the reformist ideas that spread throughout the Muslim world
in the eighteenth century. Shortly after 1804, he gathered an army and conquered
most of the Hausa lands of northern and central Nigeria, bringing an explicitly Islamic order to the area. Dan Fodio left behind a sultanate centered on the new
capital of Sokoto and governed by one of his sons, Muhammad Bello, until 1837.
The Fulbe became the ruling class in the Hausa regions, and Islam spread into the
countryside, where it still predominates.

Other nineteenth-century reform movements had similar success in
spreading a revivalist, reformist Islamic message among the masses. Most notable were the Sanusi of Libya and the eastern Sahara (after about 1840) and
the Mahdist uprising of the eastern Sudan (1880s and 1890s). The Libyan
movement provided the focus for resistance to the Italian invasion of 1911.
The Sudanese Muhammad Ahmad (1848–1885) condemned the corruption of
basic Muslim ideals and declared himself the awaited deliverer, or Mahdi, in
1881. He led the northern Sudan in rebellion against Ottoman-Egyptian control. His successor governed the Sudan until the British destroyed the young
Islamic state in 1899.

INCREASING EUROPEAN INVOLVEMENT

Muslim reform movements were not the only important developments in Africa during the nineteenth century. Another was the growing involvement of Europe, which led to European domination of the continent. Before the mid-1800s, the penetration of white outsiders had been limited largely to coastal areas, although their slave trade had had significant effects inland (see Chapter 17). This changed as trading companies, explorers, missionaries, and then colonial troops and governments moved into Africa. Ironically, the elimination of the slave trade (primarily through Britain's efforts) was accompanied by increased European exploration and Christian missionizing, which ushered in imperial and colonial ventures that were to have even more disastrous consequences than slaving for Africa's future.

WHAT WAS the "scramble for Africa"?

EXPLORATION

The nineteenth-century European explorers—mostly English, French, and German—uncovered for westerners the "secrets" of Africa: the sources and courses of the Niger, Nile, Zambezi, and Congo Rivers; natural wonders such as Mount Kilimanjaro and Lake Tanganyika; and fabled places like Timbuktu, the once, great Berber trading gateway and center of Islamic learning. The history of European exploration is one of fortune hunting, self-promotion, violence, and mistakes, but also of patience and perseverance, bravery and dedication.

The explorers stimulated European interest and opened the way for traders, missionaries, and finally soldiers and governors from the Christian West. One of the greatest explorers was Dr. David Livingstone (1813–1873), who was a missionary dedicated to Africa and its peoples as few other westerners have been.

CHRISTIAN MISSIONS

The late nineteenth century saw an influx of Christian missionaries, both Protestant and Catholic (by 1900, perhaps as many as 10,000). The missionaries came to know the African peoples far better than did the explorers. Their accounts of Africa contained chauvinistic and misleading descriptions of the "degraded" state of African culture and religion, but they brought real knowledge of and interest in Africa to Europe. Their schools also brought some alphabetic culture and literacy to the African tribal world. Although their settlements, often in remote areas, provided European governments with convenient pretexts for intervention, the missionaries themselves were more often idealists than opportunists. Half of those who went into the tropical regions succumbed to diseases, such as malaria, yellow fever, and sleeping sickness. If they were often paternalistic and instruments of the imperialism of their home countries, they also sought to

A missionary visit to a Zulu Kraal. The 19th-century European-American enthusiasm for working toward "the evangelization of the world in our time" found one of its major outlets in missionary efforts in Africa.

Kyrkans Internationella AV-tjanst/Uppsala/Cooperative Creamery Association

Central Sudan

1754–1817	Usman Dan Fodio, Fulbe leader of major Islamic *jihad*
1810	Dan Fodio founds Islamic sultanate in lands of former Hausa states of northern and central Nigeria
1817–1837	Reign at Sokoto of Muhammad Bello, son of Dan Fodio

QUICK REVIEW

Key Factors in "Scramble for Africa"

◆ Popular and commercial interest in Africa spurred by exploration

◆ Intra-European competition for power and prestige

◆ Technological and material superiority of Europe

scramble for Africa The late nineteenth-century takeover of most of Africa by European powers.

provide Africans with medicine and education. Through the ideals of their faith, they provided Africans—sometimes inadvertently—with a weapon of principle to use against their European exploiters. African Christian churches, for example, played a leading role in resisting apartheid in South Africa, despite white Christian oppression and collusion with racism in that country and elsewhere in Africa (see Chapter 35). As this discussion suggests, the role of Africans in the European domination of Africa was neither simple nor wholly positive.

THE COLONIAL "SCRAMBLE FOR AFRICA"

Before 1850, the only significant European attempts to take African territory were in South Africa and Algeria. In South Africa, as we have noted, the Boers came into conflict with Bantu tribes on their Great Trek. The French invaded Algeria in 1830, settled Europeans on choice farmlands, and waged war on native resistance fighters (1830–1847). Over most of the continent, however, the European presence was felt with real force only from the 1880s. Yet by World War I, all of Africa except Ethiopia and Liberia was divided arbitrarily into a patchwork of European colonial administrations (see Map 28–1).

This takeover was supported by mounting European popular and commercial interest fueled by the publicity given African exploration and missionary work. The European desire for the markets and resources of Africa, together with intra-European competition for power and prestige, pushed one European state after another to lay claim to whatever segments of Africa they could.

What made this wholesale takeover possible was the superior power the West commanded. In particular, European technical expertise opened up the interior of the continent. Except for the Nile and the Niger, the great African rivers have impassable waterfalls near the sea. Steamboats above the falls and railroads around them provided access to the African interior and opened its riches to exploitation.

Britain and France were the colonial vanguard. The British had the largest involvement. On one axis, it ranged from their South African holdings (begun when they took the Cape Colony from the Dutch in 1795) to their protectorate in Egypt (from 1882). On another axis, it extended from trading interests in West Africa to colonies such as Sierra Leone and Gambia, to protectorate rule, as in the Niger districts after 1885, and to a Zanzibar-based sphere of influence in East Africa.

The British preferred "indirect" to "direct" colonial administration. Their rule was only slightly more enlightened than that of the French, who carved out a colonial empire under their direct control. The French had long had government-supported trading outposts in West Africa. Tunisia and the Ivory Coast became French protectorates in the 1880s; Dahomey was bloodily annexed in 1894; and the colony of French Equatorial Africa was proclaimed in 1910.

Beginning in the mid-1880s, the European powers began to seek mutual agreement to their claims on segments of Africa. Leopold II of Belgium (r. 1865–1909) and Otto von Bismarck (1815–1898) in Germany established their claims to parts of South, Central, and East Africa. France and England set about consolidating their African interests. Italy took African colonial territory in Eritrea, Somaliland, and Libya. But the Italian design on Ethiopia was thwarted when Ethiopia defeated an Italian invasion in 1896. The Italians eventually conquered Ethiopia in 1935. The "**scramble for Africa**" was over by the outbreak of World War I. In the aftermath of the war, Germany lost its African possessions to other colonial

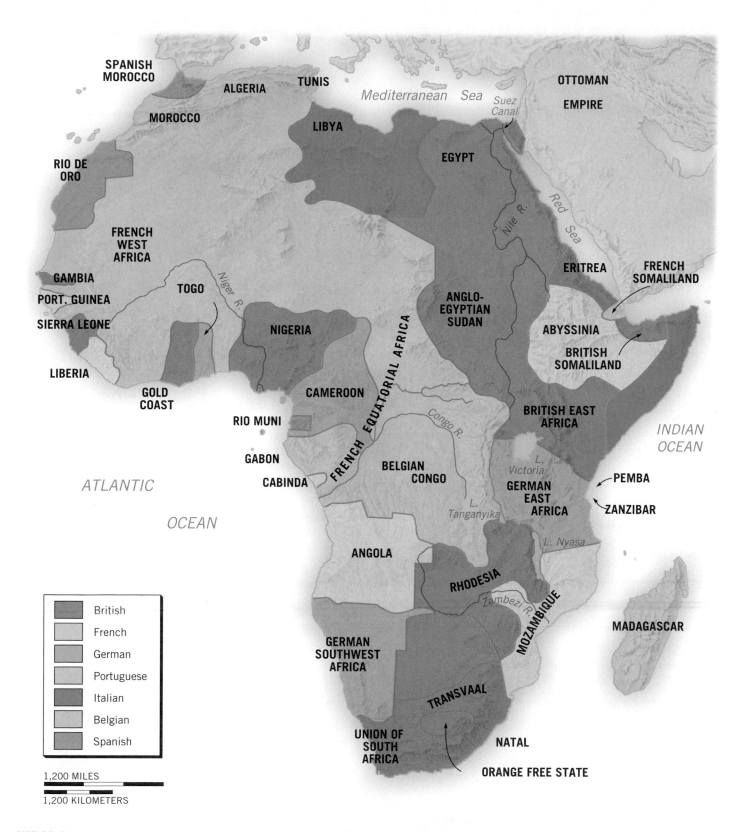

MAP 28-1

Partition of Africa, 1880–1914. By 1914 the only countries in Africa that remained independent were Liberia and Abyssinia (Ethiopia). The occupying powers included most large European states.

WHICH EUROPEAN countries had the largest African possessions?

OVERVIEW

COLONIALISM, 1815–1914

Between the end of the Napoleonic Wars and the outbreak of World War I, European powers, the United States, and Japan extended their rule over much of the Near East, Africa, Asia, and the Pacific. The imposition of foreign rule was often the result of conquest, but it also occurred through purchase or the imposition of a "protectorate" in which a local ruler kept his title but ceded real power, especially over foreign affairs, defense, and finances, to colonial advisors or officials. By 1914, except for the Latin American republics, only Liberia and Abyssinia (Ethiopia) in Africa, the Ottoman Empire in the Near East, and Iran, Afghanistan, Thailand, and China had escaped some form of colonial rule. The table below lists the countries and territories that the Western powers and Japan acquired or dominated as protectorates between 1815 and 1914. In addition, older possessions, such as British India and the Portuguese colonies of Angola and Mozambique, were also increased during these hundred years.

NEAR EAST AND NORTH AFRICA

Britain	Aden (in Yemen), Bahrain, Cyprus, Egypt, Kuwait, Oman, Qatar, United Emirates
France	Algeria, Morocco, Tunisia
Italy	Rhodes, Libya

AFRICA

Belgium	Congo (Zaire)
Britain	Botswana, Ghana, Kenya, Lesotho, Malawi, Nigeria, Somaliland, Sudan, Swaziland, Uganda, Zambia, Zanzibar, Zimbabwe, Zululand (in South Africa)
France	Benin, Burkina Faso, Central African Republic, Chad, Congo, Djibouti, Ivory Coast, Madagascar, Mali, Mauretania, Niger
Germany	Burundi, Cameroons, Namibia, Rwanda, Tanganyika (Tanzania), Togo
Italy	Eritrea, Somalia

ASIA

Britain	Brunei, Hong Kong, Malaysia, Myanmar (Burma), Nepal, Papua, Singapore
France	Cambodia, Laos, Vietnam
Germany	New Guiana, Tientsin (in China)
Japan	Korea, Okinawa, Taiwan
Netherlands	Acheh
Russia	Amur Territories (from China), Central Asia, Chechnya
United States	Philippines

PACIFIC

Britain	Fiji, Tonga, Solomons
France	New Caledonia, Tahiti
Germany	Carolines, Marianas
United States	Guam, Hawaii, Midway, Wake

powers. Europe's colonies in Africa did not gain independence (see Chapters 33 and 35) until after World War II beginning in the 1950s.

European colonial rule in Africa is one of the uglier chapters of modern history. The paternalistic attitudes of late-nineteenth-century Europe and America amounted to racism when applied in Africa. The regions with large-scale white settlement produced the worst exploitation at the expense of vastly greater native populations. The worst legacy of the European presence was the white racist state of modern South Africa, which only ended in 1994. No Western nation can have a clear conscience about its involvement in Africa.

Colonial Africa

1830	French invasion of Algeria
1890	British protectorate in Zanzibar
ca. 1880	French protectorate in Tunisia and Ivory Coast
1880s–1890s	Mahdist uprising in eastern Sudan
1882	British protectorate in Egypt
1894	French annexation of Dahomey
1910	French colony of Equatorial Africa

AFRICAN RESISTANCE TO COLONIALISM: THE RISE OF NATIONALISM

20.6
Rudyard Kipling

HOW DID Africans react to European colonialism?

African states were not, however, passive objects of European manipulation. Astute native rulers sought to use the European presence to their own advantage. Some, like the Bagandan king Mutesa in the 1870s (in what is today Uganda), succeeded for some time. Direct armed resistance was doomed (even Ethiopia's) because of European technological superiority. Nevertheless, such resistance was widespread. In the end, however, other factors brought an end to most foreign rule on African soil.

The most prominent factor was the rise of nationalism across Africa, especially after World War I. However little the colonial partition of Africa reflected native divisions, it still influenced nationalist movements and the eventual shape of African states. The "national" consciousness of the diverse peoples of a given colonial unit was fueled by common opposition to foreign rule, use of a common European tongue, and the assimilation of European thought and culture by an educated native elite. These elites were educated in mission schools and foreign universities. Their ranks increased in the early twentieth century. From them came the leaders of Africa's nationalist movements between the two world wars and of Africa's independent nations after World War II.

The severest indigenous critiques of the Western treatment of Africa often drew on Western religious and political ideals. The process culminated in the creation of over forty self-governing African nations after 1945 (see Chapter 35). African independence movements were based on modern nationalist models from Europe and America rather than ancient ones derived from native tradition. The nationalist and independence movements sought to eject the colonial intruders, not to return to an earlier status quo. Their aim was to take over and run for themselves the Western institutions that colonialism had introduced. This legacy from the West is still visible today.

SUMMARY

Western Encroachment   The century and a half following the French Revolution was a bleak one for the Indian subcontinent, Africa, and the Islamic societies. For centuries there had been a rough balance in material and intellectual culture, commerce, and political stability among the major cultural regions of the world.

IMAGE KEY
for pages 616–617

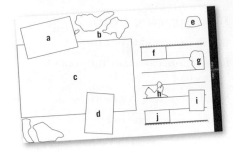

a. Caravan with ivory

b. Tea leaves

c. *Col. James Todd on elephant,* Indian painting ca. 1880

d. Kemal Ataturk

e. Fez

f. Sepoy cavalry attacking British infantry at the Battle of Cawnpore in 1857

g. Mahatma Gandhi

h. Imam Shamil of Dagestan

i. Page from a 19th century Koran, Morocco

j. Bugandan Kabaka Mutesa I and members of his court

Suddenly, over 150 years, the European sector of the global community came to dominate the rest of the world.

The Middle East, Africa, Iran, Central Asia, India, and Indonesia-Malaysia, along with Central and South America—what is today referred to as "the Third World" of "developing nations"—were most drastically affected by European imperialism and colonialism. Regardless of indigenous developments in these regions, the decisive development of this era was unprecedented domination by a single segment of the global community. Western dominance, sometimes positive, often sordid and ugly, was by no means synonymous with "progress," as westerners have often liked to think. Nevertheless, it has been a hallmark of the "modern" age in most of Asia, Africa, and South America.

Indigenous Reactions The vitality of so many of the cultures and traditions that bore the brunt of the Western onslaught has been striking. Arab, Iranian, Indian, African, and other encounters with Western material and intellectual domination produced different responses and initiatives. These have borne full fruit in political, economic, and intellectual independence only since 1945; however, most began much earlier, some even well before 1800. For example, modern Islamic reform and resurgence began in the eighteenth century, although it has become a major global factor only in recent years. Indian national consciousness also developed from the eighteenth century onward in response to British domination, even though it led to national union and independence only after World War II.

One result of the imperial-colonial experience almost everywhere has been the sharpening of cultural self-consciousness and self-confidence among those peoples most negatively affected by Western dominance. The imperial-colonial experiences of the Third World nations may well prove to have been not only ones of misery and reversal, but also of transition to positive development and resurgence, despite the looming economic, educational, and demographic problems that plague many of them.

REVIEW QUESTIONS

1. Why was India called the "jewel in the crown" of the British Empire? What kind of policies did the British follow in government and economics?

2. What kinds of political activism against British rule were there in India after 1800? What success did they have?

3. How was the Islamic world internally divided after 1800? How did those divisions influence the coming of European powers?

4. How did nationalism affect European control in south Asia, Africa, and the Middle East?

5. What were the three main interests of Europeans in the "Dark Continent"? Why were native Africans unable to stop the "scramble for Africa"?

6. What was the role of African nationalism in resisting foreign control?

KEY TERMS

bazaari   (p. 624)

cantonments   (p. 620)

Great Trek   (p. 628)

impact of modernity   (p. 618)

mfecane   (p. 627)

mujtahid   (p. 624)

pan-Islamism   (p. 626)

raj   (p. 619)

scramble for Africa   (p. 630)

 For additional study resources for this chapter, go to:
www.prenhall.com/craig/chapter28

Japan's first foreign mission headed by Prince Iwakura, Ambassador Extraordinary and Plenipotentiary, leaving Yokohama for the U.S. and Europe, Dec. 23, 1871.

Coll. Ministry of Foreign Affairs, Tokyo, Japan.

29

MODERN EAST ASIA

WHAT WERE the most serious threats to Manchu rule in the nineteenth century?

WHO WERE the key figures in the revolution of 1911?

WHY DID the communists win the Chinese Civil War?

WHAT ROLE did the Chōshū and Satsuma play in the overthrow of Tokugawa rule?

WHAT POWERS did the Meiji Constitution give to the emperor?

WHY DID Japan set out to build a modern economy?

IMAGE KEY
Image Key for pages 636–637 is on page 661.

From the mid-nineteenth century, the West was the expanding, aggressive, imperialistic force in world history; it was the trigger for change throughout the world. But the response to the Western impact depended on internal forces in each country. Japan and China were both relatively successful in their responses, for neither became a colony.

The two countries' governing elites were educated in Confucianism, which was just secular enough to crumble in the face of the more powerful secularism of nineteenth-century science and the doctrines associated with it. In both countries, one of the "breakdown products" of the Confucian sociopolitical identity was a strong new nationalism.

But in most other respects, modern Japan and China could hardly be more different. The coming of Commodore Matthew Perry (1794–1858) in 1853–1854 precipitated rapid change in Japan. The old Tokugawa regime collapsed, and the Japanese built a modern state. Economic growth followed. By 1900, Japan had defeated China and was about to defeat Russia. After the Great Depression, Japan, like Italy and Germany, became an aggressive and militarized state and was defeated in World War II. But after the war, Japan reemerged more stable and productive, and with a stronger parliamentary government than ever before.

In contrast, the hold of tradition in China was remarkable. But in one sense, its strength was China's weakness, for only after the overthrow of Manchu rule in 1911 was China willing to begin the modernization that Japan had started in 1868. Even then it was unsuccessful. Along with warlordism, new ills arose from the rending of the very fabric of the dynastic pattern. That China "failed" during this modern century is the view held by the Chinese themselves.

MODERN CHINA (1839–1949)

China's modern century was not the century in which it became modern, but the one in which it encountered the modern West. Its first phase, from the Opium War to the fall of the Ch'ing or Manchu dynasty (1911), was little affected by Western impact. Only during the decade before 1911 did the Confucian tradition begin to be discarded in favor of new ideas from the West. The second phase, from 1911 to the establishment of a communist state in 1949, was a time of turmoil: decades of warlord rule; war with Japan; and then four years of civil war.

21.1
Lin Tse-hsu [Lin Zexu], Letter of Moral Admonition to Queen Victoria

WHAT WERE the most serious threats to Manchu rule in the nineteenth century?

CLOSE OF MANCHU RULE

THE OPIUM WAR

The eighteenth-century three-country trade—British goods to India, Indian cotton to China, and Chinese tea to Britain—was in China's favor. Then the British replaced cotton with Indian opium, and by the 1820s, the balance of trade was reversed.

To check the evil of opium and the outflow of silver, the Chinese government banned opium in 1836. In 1839, the government sent Lin Zeun (1785–1850) to Canton to superintend the ban. He destroyed a six-month supply of opium belonging to foreign merchants, leading to a confrontation with the British.

War broke out in November 1839. For the next two years, the British fought battles and attempted negotiations. The Chinese troops were ineffective. The war was finally ended in August 1842 by the Treaty of Nanking, the first of the **"unequal treaties."**

The treaty gave Britain the island of Hong Kong and a huge indemnity. It also opened five ports: Canton, Shanghai, Amoy, Ningpo, and Foochow. British merchants and their families could reside in the ports and engage in trade; Britain

"unequal treaties"   Agreements imposed on China in the nineteenth century by European powers, the United States, and Japan that granted their citizens special legal and economic privileges on Chinese soil.

could appoint a consul for each city; and British residents were subject to British, not Chinese, law. In 1844, similar treaties followed with the United States and France.

After the signing of the British treaty, Chinese imports of opium increased, but other kinds of trade did not grow as much as had been hoped. Western merchants blamed the lack of growth on Chinese officials. They also complained that Canton remained closed to trade. The Chinese authorities were incensed by the export of coolies to work in Cuba and Peru. A second war broke out in 1856, and the British captured Beijing in 1860. New treaties provided for indemnities, the opening of eleven new ports, the stationing of foreign diplomats in Beijing, the propagation of Christianity anywhere in China, and the legalization of the opium trade.

Meanwhile, the Russians were encroaching on China's northern frontier. In 1858, China ceded the north bank of the Amur to Russia, and in 1860, China gave Russia the Maritime Province between the Ussuri River and the Pacific. China still claims these lands.

REBELLIONS AGAINST THE MANCHU

More serious threats to Manchu rule were the **Taiping**, Nian, and Muslim **rebellions** that convulsed China between 1850 and 1873. The torment and suffering they caused were unparalleled in world history. China's population dropped by 60 million.

The Taipings were begun by Hong Xinguan (1814–1864), a schoolteacher from the southern province of Guangdong. Influenced by Protestant tracts, Hung announced that he was the younger brother of Jesus and that God had told him to rid China of Manchus, Confucians, Daoists, and Buddhists. Like earlier rebels, the Taipings combined moral reform, religious fervor, and a vision of egalitarian society. The Taipings were soon joined by peasants, miners, and workers. The fighting spread until the Taipings controlled most of the Yangzi basin and had entered 16 of the 18 Chinese provinces. Their army numbered close to a million.

The other rebellions were of lesser note. The Nian were located north of the Taipings along the Huai River. They were organized in secret societies and raided the countryside. Eventually they built an army, collected taxes, and ruled 100,000 square miles. A longer revolt was of Muslims against Chinese in the southwest and the northwest. These rebellions took advantage of the weakened state of the dynasty. They occurred in areas that had few officials and no Ch'ing military units.

Against the rebellions, the imperial forces proved helpless: In 1852, the court sent Zeng Guofan (1811–1872) to south-central China to organize a local army. Tseng, a product of the Confucian examination system, saw the Manchu government, of which he was an elite member, as the upholder of morality and the social order, and Chinese rebels as would-be destroyers of that order. He recruited members of the gentry as officers. They were Confucian, and as landlords had the most to lose from rebel rule. They recruited soldiers from their local areas and stopped the Taipings' advance.

In 1860, when the British and French occupied Beijing, a reform government began internal changes, adopted a policy of cooperation with the Western powers, and put Zeng in charge of suppressing all the rebellions. Zeng appointed able officials to raise regional armies. Foreigners and Shanghai merchants gave their support. The Taipings collapsed when Nanking was captured in 1864. The Nian were suppressed by 1868 and the Muslim rebellion was put down five years later. Scholar-officials, relying on local gentry, had saved the dynasty.

QUICK REVIEW

Rebellions

◆ Taiping: Led by Hung Xinguan (1814–1864), the Taiping assembled an army of close to a million men

◆ Nien: Located along the Huai River, the Nien came to control a 100,000 square mile area

◆ Muslim rebellions: Muslim revolt against Chinese in southwest and northwest, areas where China had few officials and little military presence

Taiping rebellion   A nineteenth-century revolt against China's Manchu dynasty that was inspired by quasi-Christian ideas and that led to enormous suffering and destruction before its collapse in 1868.

The empress dowager Cixi (1835–1908), who manipulated the levers of power at the Manchu court in Beijing.

Hulton Picture Library/Corbis-Bettmann

treaty ports Chinese ports ruled by foreign consuls where foreigners enjoyed commercial privileges and immunity from Chinese laws.

SELF-STRENGTHENING AND DECLINE (1874–1895)

In view of the dynasty's advanced stage of administrative decentralization, the Chinese resiliency and capacity to rebuild in the two decades after the suppression of the rebellions were impressive. But if we ask how effective China's response was to the West, or if we compare China's progress with that of Japan, then China during the same decades looks almost moribund. Historians often call these years the period of "self-strengthening," yet China was relatively weaker at the end of the period than at the start.

The Court at Beijing China's inability to act effectively is explained partly by the situation at the court. Prince Gong (1833–1898) and the empress dowager (1835–1908) were coregents for the young emperor. Prince Kung was a man of ideas. In 1861, he established a new office to handle the court's relations with foreign diplomats in Beijing. The following year, he established a school to train Chinese in foreign languages. However, outmaneuvered by the empress dowager, he was ousted in 1884.

The empress dowager had produced the only male child of the former emperor. She had no conception of how to reform China; her single goal was power. She acquired it by forging a political machine of conservative bureaucrats, military commanders, and eunuchs, and by maintaining a balance between the court and the regional governor-generals. The result was a court just able to survive but too weak to govern effectively.

Regional Governments The most vital figures during these decades were a handful of able governors-general. Each had an army and was in charge of two or three provinces. They were loyal to the dynasty that they had restored in the face of almost certain collapse and were allowed great autonomy.

Their first task was reconstruction. Millions were hungry or homeless. The leaders' response was massive and effective. Just as they had mobilized the gentry to suppress the rebellions, now they obtained their cooperation in rebuilding. They set up refugee centers, reduced taxes in the devastated Yangzi valley, reclaimed lands gone to waste, began water-control projects, and built granaries. By the early 1890s, well-being had been restored to Chinese society.

Their second task was self-strengthening—the adoption of Western arms and technology. They built arsenals and shipyards, a telegraph company, railways, and cotton mills. The formula applied in running these enterprises was "official supervision and merchant operation." The major decisions were made by scholar-officials, but day-to-day operations were left to the merchants.

Treaty Ports The **treaty ports**, of which there were 14 by the 1860s, were little islands of privilege and security, under the rule of foreign consuls, where capital was safe from confiscation, trade was free, and "squeeze" (extortion by officials) was the exception. Foreign companies naturally located in the ports, as did Chinese merchants who were also attracted by these conditions. Well into the twentieth century, the foreign concessions (treaty-port lands leased in perpetuity by foreigners) remained the vital sector of China's modern economy.

The effects of the treaty ports and of Western imperialism on China were largely negative. Under the low tariffs mandated by the treaties, Chinese industries had little protection from imports. Native cotton spinning was almost destroyed by imports of yarn. Chinese tea lost ground to Indian tea and Chinese silk to Japanese silk. China found few products to export. The level of foreign trade stayed low, and China's interior markets were affected only slightly.

By the 1870s, the foreign powers had reached an accommodation with China. They counted on the court to uphold the treaties; in return, they became a prop for the dynasty. By 1900, for example, the court's revenues from customs fees were larger than those from any other source. The fees were collected by the Maritime Customs Service, an efficient and honest treaty-port institution headed by an Irishman. In 1895, the Maritime Customs Service had 700 Western and 3,500 Chinese employees.

THE BORDERLANDS: THE NORTHWEST, VIETNAM, AND KOREA

China's other foreign relations were with fringe lands that China claimed by right of past conquest or as tributaries. The tributaries were the mirrors in which China saw reflected its own self-image as a universal empire. During the late nineteenth century, this image was strengthened in the northwest but dealt a fatal blow in Vietnam and Korea.

The Northwest   In the northwest, China confronted imperial Russia. Caught between them, the independent nomadic tribes were rendered impotent. By 1878, China had reconquered Chinese Turkestan, which was renamed Xinjiang, or the "New Territories." A treaty signed with Russia in 1881 restored most of the Ili region in western Mongolia to Chinese control. The victories strengthened court conservatives who wished to take a stronger stance toward the West.

Vietnam   Vietnam had retained its independence from China since 935. It saw itself as an independent state but used the Chinese writing system, modeled its laws and government on those of China, and traded with China. China simply saw Vietnam as a tributary.

During the 1840s, the second emperor of the Nguyen dynasty, which had begun in 1802, moved to reduce French influences and suppress Christianity. Thousands were killed, including French and Vietnamese priests. The French responded by seizing Saigon and Cochin China in 1859, establishing a protectorate over Cambodia in 1864, and taking Hanoi in 1882. China in 1883 sent troops to aid its tributary, but after a two-year war with France China was forced, in 1885, to abandon its claims to Vietnam. By 1893, France had brought together Vietnam, Cambodia, and Laos to form the Federation of Indochina, which remained a French colony until 1940.

Korea   Unlike Vietnam, Korea saw itself as a tributary of China on Chinese terms. The Korean ruler styled himself as a king and not an emperor.

During the last decades of the long (1392–1910) Choson dynasty, the Korean state was weak. It hung on to power in part by enforcing a policy of seclusion almost as total as that of Tokugawa Japan, winning it the name of the Hermit Kingdom. Its only foreign ties were with China and Japan. In 1876, Japan "opened" Korea to international relations, using much the same tactics that Perry had used against Japan. Japan then contended with China for influence in Korea.

In 1893, a popular religious sect unleashed a rebellion against the Seoul government. When the government requested Chinese help to suppress the rebellion, China sent troops, but Japan sent more, and in 1894, war broke out between China and Japan. Taiwan became Japan's first colony. The defeat convinced many in China that basic changes were inevitable.

An American view of the "Open Door." The combination of high self-esteem and anti-foreignism at the turn of the century was not a Chinese monopoly.

Gorbis-Bettmann

QUICK REVIEW

Korea in the Late Nineteenth Century

◆ Tributary of China

◆ The Korean state was weak in the last decades of the nineteenth century

◆ After 1876 Japan contended with China for influence in Korea

FROM DYNASTY TO WARLORDISM (1895–1926)

China was ruled by officials who had mastered the Confucian classics. This intellectual formation was resistant to change. For most officials living in China's interior, the foreign crises of the nineteenth century were "coastal phenomena," soon forgotten. Few officials realized the magnitude of the foreign threat.

China's defeat by Japan in 1895 came as a shock. The response within China was a new wave of reform proposals. The most influential thinker was Kang Yonwei(1858–1927), who described China as "enfeebled" and blamed the "conservatives." They did not understand, Kang argued, that Confucius himself had been a reformer who had invented the idea of a golden age to persuade the rulers of his own age to adopt his ideas. History was evolutionary—a march forward from absolute monarchy to constitutional monarchy to democracy. Kang's reinterpretation of Confucianism removed a major barrier to the entry of Western ideas into China.

In 1898, the emperor himself became sympathetic to Kang's ideas and launched "one hundred days of reform." He took as his models Peter the Great (r. 1682–1725) and the Japanese Meiji Emperor (r. 1867–1912). Edicts were issued to reform China's schools, railroads, police, laws, military, bureaucracy, post offices, and examination system. But conservative resistance was nationwide. At court, the empress dowager regained control and ended the reforms. Kang fled to Japan. One reformer was executed.

The response of the Western powers to China's 1895 defeat was to define spheres of interest, which usually consisted of a leasehold along with railway rights and commercial privileges. Russia gained a leasehold at Port Arthur; Germany acquired one in Shantung. Britain got the New Territories adjoining Kowloon at Hong Kong. New ports and cities were opened to foreign trade. The United States was in a weaker position, so it enunciated an "open-door" policy: equal commercial opportunities for all powers and the preservation of the territorial integrity of China.

There was in China at this time a religious society known as the **Boxers**. They rebelled first in Shandoug in 1898, and, gaining court support, entered Beijing in 1900. There followed a two-month siege of the foreign legation quarter. The rebellion was fueled by pent-up resentments against decades of foreign encroachments. Eventually an international force captured Beijing, and the Russians occupied Manchuria.

The defeat of the Boxers convinced even conservative Chinese leaders of the futility of clinging to old ways. A more powerful reform movement began, with the empress dowager in its vanguard. But the dynasty could not control the movement and eventually was bypassed.

Educational reforms began in 1901. Women were admitted to newly formed schools. In place of Confucianism, the instructors taught science, mathematics, geography, and an anti-imperialist version of Chinese history. Western doctrines, such as classical economics, liberalism, socialism, anarchism, and social Darwinism, were introduced into China. By 1906, there were 8,000 Chinese students in Japan, which became a hotbed of Chinese reformist and revolutionary societies. (See "Chen Duxin's 'Call to Youth' in 1915.")

Military reforms were begun by Yuan Shikai (1859–1916), whose New Army drew on Japanese and Western models. Young men from gentry families, spurred by patriotism, joined the New Army as officers. Their loyalty was to their commanders and their country, not to the dynasty.

In 1905, the examination system was abolished; officials were to be directly recruited from the schools and those who had studied abroad. Provincial

Boxers   A nationalistic Chinese religious society that attacked foreigners and their encroachments on China in the late nineteenth century.

• HISTORY'S VOICES •

CHEN DUXIN'S "CALL TO YOUTH" IN 1915

truggle, *natural selection, and organic process are the images used by Chen Duxin. How different from those of Confucianism!*

HOW DOES Chen's "Call to Youth" relate to the political conditions in China in 1915?

The Chinese compliment others by saying, "He acts like an old man although still young." Englishmen and Americans encourage one another by saying, "Keep young while growing old." Such is one respect in which the different ways of thought of the East and West are manifested. Youth is like early spring, like the rising sun, like trees and grass in bud, like a newly sharpened blade. It is the most valuable period of life. The function of youth in society is the same as that of a fresh and vital cell in a human body. In the processes of metabolism, the old and the rotten are incessantly eliminated to be replaced by the fresh and living. . . . According to this standard, then, is the society of our nation flourishing, or is it about to perish? I cannot bear to answer. As for those old and rotten elements, I shall leave them to the process of nat-

ural selection. . . . I only, with tears, place my plea before the young and vital youth, in the hope that they will achieve self-awareness, and begin to struggle.

What is the struggle? It is to exert one's intellect, discard resolutely the old and the rotten, regard them as enemies and as the flood or savage beasts, keep away from their neighborhood and refuse to be contaminated by their poisonous germs. Alas! Do these words really fit the youth of our country? I have seen that, out of every ten youths who are young in age, five are old in physique; and out of every ten who are young in both age and physique, nine are old in mentality. Those with shining hair, smooth countenance, a straight back and a wide chest are indeed magnificent youths! Yet if you ask what thoughts and aims are entertained in their heads, then they all turn out to be the same as the old and rotten, like moles from the same hill. . . . It is the old and rotten air that fills society everywhere. One cannot even find a bit of fresh and vital air to comfort those of us who are suffocating in despair.

Reprinted by permission of the publisher from *China's Response to the West* by Ssu-Yu Teng and John K. Fairbank, Cambridge, MA: Harvard University Press. Copyright © 1954, 1979 by the President and Fellows of Harvard College.

assemblies were formed in 1909, and a consultative assembly was established in Beijing in 1910.

These changes sparked the 1911 revolution. It began with an uprising in Szechwan province against a government plan to nationalize the main railways. The key figures were:

1. Gentry who stood to lose their investments in the railways.
2. Ch'ing military commanders, who declared their provinces independent.
3. Sun Zhongshan (1866–1925), a republican revolutionary. He organized the Revolutionary Alliance in Tokyo in 1905 and was associated with the Nationalist Party (Guomindang) formed in 1912.
4. Yuan Shih-k'ai, who arranged for the last child emperor to abdicate, for Sun to step aside, and for himself to become president of the new Republic of China.

In 1916, Yuan proclaimed a new dynasty with himself as emperor. The idea of another dynasty, however, met opposition from all quarters. Yuan died in June 1916. China then fell into the hands of warlord armies. The years until the late twenties were a time of agony for the Chinese people. Yet they were also in a time of intense intellectual ferment.

CULTURAL AND IDEOLOGICAL FERMENT: THE MAY FOURTH MOVEMENT

WHAT WAS the May Fourth Movement?

A period of freedom and vigorous experimentation with new doctrines began in 1914 and extended into the 1920s. It is called the May Fourth Movement after an incident in Beijing in 1919 in which thousands of students protested the settlement at Versailles that awarded former German possessions in Shandoug to Japan. The nationalist fervor that led the students to demonstrate in the streets changed the complexion of Chinese thought. Leading thinkers began to judge ideas in terms of their value in solving China's problems.

During the May Fourth era, the center of advanced thought was Beijing. Ideas propounded there quickly spread to the rest of China, especially to its urban centers. Protest demonstrations against imperialist privilege broke out in Shanghai, Wuhan, and Guangzhou, as they had in the capital. Nationalism and anti-imperialist sentiment were stronger than liberalism, although most thinkers spoke of democracy. Only members of an older generation of reformers, appalled by the slaughter of World War I and what they saw as Western materialism, advocated a return to traditional philosophies.

After the Russian Revolution of 1917, Marxism-Leninism entered China. The Leninist definition of imperialism as the last crisis stage of capitalism put the blame for China's ills on the West and offered "feudal" China the possibility of leapfrogging over capitalism to socialism. Marxist study groups formed in Beijing and other cities. In 1919, a student from Hunan, Mao Tse-tung, who had worked in the Beijing University library, returned to Changsha to form a study group. The Chinese Communist Party was formed in Shanghai in 1921; Zhou Enlai (1898–1976) formed a similar group in Paris the same year.

NATIONALIST CHINA

GUOMINDANG UNIFICATION OF CHINA AND THE NANKING DECADE (1927–1937)

WHY DID the communists win the Chinese Civil War?

Sun Yat-sen had fled to Japan during the 1913–1916 rule by Yuan Shih-k'ai. He returned to Guangzhou in 1916, but he was a poor organizer, and his **Guomindang (KMT)**—or Nationalist Party—made little headway. From 1923, Sun began to receive Soviet support. He reorganized his party on the Leninist model, with an executive committee on top of a national party congress, provincial and county organizations, and local party cells.

Since 1905, Sun had enunciated his "three principles of the people": nationality, livelihood, and rights. Sun's nationalism was now directed against Western imperialism. The principle of people's livelihood was defined in terms of equalizing land holdings and nationalizing major industries. By "people's rights" Sun meant democracy, although he argued that it must be preceded by a preparatory period of single-party dictatorship. Sun sent his loyal lieutenant Jiang Jieshi(1887–1975) to the Soviet Union for study. Chiang returned after four months with a cadre of Russian advisers and established a military academy at Whampoa south of Guangzhou in 1924. Sun died in 1925. By 1926, the Whampoa Academy had graduated several thousand officers, and the KMT army numbered almost 100,000. The KMT had become the major political force in China.

The growth of the party was spurred by changes within Chinese society. Industries arose in the cities. Labor unions were organized. New ventures were begun outside the treaty ports. A politically conscious middle class developed.

Guomindang (KMT) China's Nationalist Party, founded by Sun Zhongshan.

The quicksilver element in cities was the several million students. In May 1925, students demonstrated in Shanghai. Police in the international settlement fired on the demonstrators. The incident inflamed national and anti-imperialist feelings. Strikes and boycotts of foreign goods were called throughout China.

Under these conditions the Chinese Communist Party (CCP) also grew and was influential in student organizations, labor unions, and even within the KMT. Sun had permitted CCP members to join the KMT as individuals, but had enjoined them from organizing CCP cells within it. Moscow approved of this policy. It felt that the CCP was too small to accomplish anything on its own.

By 1926, Jiang Jieshi felt ready to march against the warlords. He worried about the growing communist strength, however, and before setting off he ousted the Soviet advisers and CCP members from the KMT offices in Guangzhou. The march north began in July. By the spring of 1927, Jiang's army had reached the Yangzi, defeating warlord armies as it advanced.

After entering Shanghai in April 1927, Jiang carried out a sweeping purge of the CCP. Many were killed. The surviving CCP members fled to the mountainous border region of Hunan and Kiangsi to the southwest and established the "Jiangxi Soviet." Jiang's army took Beijing and gained the nominal submission of most northern Chinese warlords during 1928. Most foreign powers recognized the KMT regime as the government of China.

Jiang Jieshi (1887–1975) as a young revolutionary officer.

Brown Brothers

Jiang Jieshi was the key figure in the government. He believed in military force. He was unimaginative, strict, and incorruptible. Jiang venerated Sun Zhongshan and his three "people's principles." But where Sun was a revolutionary, Jiang was conservative and, though a Methodist, often appealed to Confucian values. The New Life Movement begun by Jiang in 1934 was an attempt to revitalize these values.

Jiang's power rested on the army, the party, and the bureaucracy. The army was dominated by the Whampoa clique, which was loyal to Chiang, and by officers trained in Japan. After 1927, German advisers reorganized Chiang's army along German lines with a general staff system. The larger part of KMT revenues went to the military, which was expanded into a modernized force of 300,000. Whampoa graduates also controlled the secret military police and used it against communists and any others who opposed the government. The KMT was a dictatorship under a central committee. Jiang became president of the party in 1938.

The densely populated central and lower Yangzi provinces were the area of KMT strength. The party, however, was unable to control the outlying areas occupied by warlords, communists, and Japanese. Warlords ruled some areas until 1949. In 1931, Jiang attacked the Jiangxi Soviet. In 1934, the communists were forced to flee to the southwest and then to Shensi province in northwestern China in the epic "**Long March**." During this march Mao Zedong wrested control of the CCP from the Moscow-trained, urban-oriented leaders and established his unorthodox view that a Leninist party could base itself on the peasantry.

The Japanese had held special rights in Manchuria since the Russo-Japanese War of 1905. When Chiang's march north and Chinese nationalism threatened the Japanese position, Japan's Kwantung Army engineered a military coup in 1931 and

Long March   The flight of the Chinese communists from their Nationalist foes to northwest China in 1934.

Modern China

1839–1842	Opium War
1850–1873	Taiping and other rebellions
1870s–1880s	Self-strengthening movement
1894–1895	Sino-Japanese War
1898	One hundred days of reform
1898–1900	Boxer Rebellion
1911	Republican revolution overthrows Ch'ing dynasty
1912–1916	Yuan Shih-k'ai president of Republic of China
1916–1928	Warlord era
1919	May Fourth incident
1924	Founding of Whampoa Military Academy
1926–1928	March north and Guomindang reunification of China
1934–1935	Chinese Communists' Long March to Yenan
1937–1945	War with Japan
1945–1949	Civil war and the establishment of the People's Republic of China

in 1932 proclaimed the independence of Manchukuo, their puppet state. In the years that followed, Japanese forces moved south as far as the Great Wall. Chinese nationalism demanded that Jiang resist. Jiang, well aware of the disparity between his armies and those of Japan, said that the internal unification of China must take precedence. In 1937, however, a full-scale war with Japan broke out, and China's situation changed.

WAR AND REVOLUTION (1937–1949)

The war with Japan began in July 1937 as an unplanned clash at Beijing and then quickly spread. Beijing and Tianjin fell to Japan within a month, Shanghai was attacked in August, and Nanking fell in December. During the following year, the Japanese took Guangzhou and set up puppet regimes in Beijing and Nanking. In 1940, the leader of the left wing of the KMT and many of his associates joined the Japanese puppet government. Japan proclaimed its "New Order in East Asia." It expected Jiang to submit. Instead, in 1938 he relocated his capital to Chongging, far to the west, and was joined by thousands of Chinese.

Jiang's stubborn resistance won admiration from all sides. But the withdrawal to Chongging cut the KMT off from most of the Chinese population; programs for modernization ended; and the KMT's former tax revenues were lost. Inflation increased geometrically and exacerbated the already widespread corruption.

The United States sent advisers and military equipment to strengthen Jiang's forces after the start of the Pacific War. However, Jiang wanted not to fight the Japanese but to husband his forces for a postwar confrontation with the Communists. Within his own army a gap appeared between officers and men. Conditions in the camps were primitive, food poor, and medical supplies inadequate. The young saw conscription almost as a death sentence. Jiang's unwillingness to commit his troops against the Japanese also meant that the surge of anti-Japanese patriotism was not converted to popular support for the KMT.

For the communists, the Japanese occupation was an opportunity. Headquartered at Yenan, they began campaigns to promote literacy and self-sufficiency. Soldiers farmed so as not to burden the peasants. The CCP abandoned its earlier policy of expropriating lands in favor of reductions in rents and interest. They took only those offices needed to ensure their control and shared the rest with the KMT and other parties. They expanded village councils to include tenants. But they also strengthened their party internally.

Party membership expanded from 40,000 in 1937 to 1.2 million in 1945. Schools were established in Yenan to train party cadres. Orthodoxy was maintained by a rectification campaign. Those tainted by impure tendencies were made to repent at public meetings. Mao's thought was supreme. To the Chinese at large, Mao represented himself as the successor to Sun Zhongshan, but within the Communist Party he presented himself as a theoretician in the line of Marx (1818–1883), Engels (1820–1895), Lenin (1870–1924), and Stalin (1879–1953).

The communists learned to operate at the grass-roots level. They infiltrated Japanese-controlled areas and KMT organizations and military units. CCP armies were built up from 90,000 in 1937 to 900,000 in 1945. These armies were supplemented by a rural people's militia and by guerrilla forces. The Yanan leadership and its party, army, and mass organizations possessed a cohesion, determination, and morale that were lacking in Chongqing.

But the strength of the Chinese communists as of 1945 should not be overstated. When the war in the Pacific ended in 1945, China's future was unclear. Even the Soviet Union recognized the KMT as the government of China and expected it to win the postwar struggle. The Allies directed Japanese armies to surrender to the KMT forces in 1945. The United States flew Jiang's troops to key eastern cities. His armies were by then three times the size of the communists' and far better equipped.

A civil war broke out immediately. Efforts by U.S. General George Marshall (1880–1959) to mediate were futile. Until the summer of 1947, KMT armies were victorious—even capturing Yanan. But the tide turned in July as CCP armies went on the offensive in north China. In January 1949, Beijing and Tientsin fell. A few months later all of China was in communist hands. Many Chinese fled with Jiang to Taiwan or escaped to Hong Kong. In China, apprehension was mixed with anticipation. The feeling was widespread that the future of China was once again in the hands of the Chinese.

MODERN JAPAN (1853–1945)

OVERTHROW OF THE TOKUGAWA *BAKUFU* (1853–1868)

From the seventeenth century into the nineteenth, the natural isolation of the islands of Japan was augmented by its policy of seclusion, making Japan into a little world of its own. The 260-odd domains were the states of this world, the *bakufu* in Edo was its hegemon, and the imperial court in Kyoto provided a religious sanction for the *bakufu*-domain system. Then at mid-century, the American ships of Commodore Perry came and forced Japan to sign a treaty opening it to foreign intercourse. Fourteen years later, the entire *bakufu*-domain system collapsed, and a group of talented leaders seized power. Seclusion, like the case of a watch, had been necessary to preserve the Tokugawa political mechanism. With the case removed, the inner workings flew apart.

Little changed during the first four years after Perry. The break came in 1858 when the *bakufu*, ignoring the imperial court's disapproval, was persuaded to sign a commercial treaty with the United States. Some daimyo, who wanted a voice in national policy, criticized the treaty as contravening the hallowed policy of seclusion. Younger samurai, frustrated by their exclusion from office, started a movement to "honor the emperor." The *bakufu*, in turn, responded with a purge. But in 1860, the head of the *bakufu* council was assassinated by extremist samurai. His successors lacked the nerve to continue his tough policies.

In 1861, two domains, Chōshū and Satsuma, emerged to heal the breach between the *bakufu* and the court. First, Chōshū officials proposed a policy that favored the *bakufu* but made concessions to the court. Next, Satsuma advocated a policy that made further concessions and ousted Chōshū as "the friend of the court." In response, the moderate reformist government of Chōshū adopted the pro-emperor policy of its extremist faction and, in turn, ousted Satsuma. Satsuma then seized the court in 1863 in a military coup.

Several points may be noted about the 1861–1863 diplomatic phase of domain action: (1) Even after 250 years of *bakufu* rule, several domains could still act when the opportunity occurred. (2) The two domains that acted first and most of

24.6
"From the Countryside to the City" (May 1949): Mao Zedong

WHAT ROLE did the Chōshū and Satsuma play in the overthrow of Tokugawa rule?

After delivering President Fillmore's letter in 1853, Commodore Perry confers with *bakufu* officials.

Historical Pictures Collection/Stock Montage Inc.

the others that followed had many samurai and substantial financial resources. (3) Both Satsuma and Chōshū had fought against the Tokugawa in 1600 and remembered an earlier independence. (4) By 1861–1863, the new politics had opened decision making to middle-ranking samurai officials in a way that would have been impossible before 1853.

The 1863 Satsuma coup at the Kyoto court initiated a military phase of politics in which battles would determine every turning point. As long as Satsuma and Chōshū remained enemies, politics stalemated and the *bakufu* continued as hegemon. But when the two domains became allies in 1866, the *bakufu* was overthrown in less than two years.

One factor contributing to this process was the movement for a "union of court and camp"; daimyo campaigned for a new conciliar rule in which they would participate together with the emperor and withdrew support from the *bakufu*. A second feature of the years between 1863 and 1868 was antiforeignism. Extremists assassinated foreigners as well as *bakufu* officials; one of their slogans was "expel the barbarians." A third was the formation of new rifle units, commanded mostly by lower samurai. These units transformed political power in Japan. A fourth development during 1867 and 1868 was a cultural shift in the way Japanese saw themselves. During the Tokugawa era, the Japanese saw themselves as civilized Confucians and much of the rest of the world as barbarians. But in the face of Western gunboats, this view seemed hollow. The West, with its technology, science, and humane laws, was seen as "civilized and enlightened;" China, Japan, and countries like Turkey were seen as half civilized; and other areas were barbarian.

Building the Meiji State (1868–1890)

The idea of a "developing nation" did not exist in the mid-nineteenth century. Yet Japan after the 1868 **Meiji restoration** was just such a nation. (The years from 1868 to 1912 are referred to as the Meiji period, after the name of the emperor.) It was committed to progress, by which it meant achieving wealth and power of the kind possessed by Western industrial nations. There was no blueprint for progress. The government advanced by trial and error. It also demanded that the Japanese people make sacrifices for the sake of the future.

The announcement of the restoration of rule by an emperor was made on January 3, 1868. In the battles that followed, Chōshū and Satsuma troops defeated those of the *bakufu*. Edo surrendered and was renamed Tokyo, the "eastern capital." Edo castle became the imperial palace. A year later, the last *bakufu* holdouts surrendered. At the start the Meiji government was only a small group of samurai leaders from Chōshū, Satsuma, and a few other domains. They have been described, only half humorously, as twelve bureaucrats in search of a bureaucracy. But their vision defined the goals of the new government.

Centralization of Power

Their immediate goal was to centralize political power. By 1871, the young leaders had replaced the domains with prefectures controlled from Tokyo. To ensure a break with the past, each new prefectural governor was chosen from samurai of other regions.

Having centralized political authority, about half of the most important Meiji leaders went abroad for a year and a half to study the West. On their return to Japan in 1872, they discovered that officials were planning war with Korea. They quashed the plan, insisting that priority be given to domestic development.

The second goal or task of the Meiji leaders was to stabilize government revenues that, because the land tax was collected mostly in grain, fluctuated with the price of rice. The government converted the grain tax to a money tax. But a third of the revenues still went to pay for samurai stipends, so in 1873 the government raised a conscript army and abolished the samurai class. The samurai were paid off in government bonds; but as the bonds fell during the inflation of the 1870s, most former samurai became impoverished. What had begun as a reform of government finance ended as a social revolution.

Some samurai rebelled. The last and greatest uprising was in 1877. When it was suppressed in 1878, the Meiji government became militarily secure.

Political Parties

Other samurai opposed the government by forming political parties and campaigning for popular rights, elections, and a constitution. They drew heavily on liberal Western models. National assemblies, they argued, were the means used by advanced societies to tap the energies of their peoples. Parties in a national assembly would unite the emperor and the people, thereby curbing the Satsuma-Chōshū clique. Samurai were the mainstay of the early party movement, despite its doctrines proclaiming all classes to be equal. In 1881, the government promised a constitution and a national assembly within ten years. As the date for national elections approached, the parties gained strength, and the ties between party notables and local men of influence grew closer.

The Constitution

The government viewed the party movement with distaste but was not sure how to counter it. Itō Hirobumi (1841–1909), originally from Chōshū, went abroad to shop for a constitution that would serve the needs of the Meiji government. He brought

WHAT POWERS did the Meiji Constitution give to the emperor?

Meiji restoration   The overthrow of the Tokugawa *bakufu* in Japan in 1868 and the transfer, or "restoration," of power to the imperial government under the Emperor Meiji.

The promulgation of the Meiji
Constitution in 1889. The emperor,
standing under the canopy, was declared
"sacred and inviolable." Seated on the
throne, at the left, is the empress.

The Metropolitan Museum of Art, Gift of Lincoln
Kirstein, 1959

home a German jurist to help adapt the conservative Prussian constitution of 1850
to Japanese uses. As promulgated in 1889, the Meiji Constitution granted extensive
powers to the emperor and severely limited the powers of the lower house in the **Diet**
(the English term for Japan's bicameral national assembly).

The emperor was sovereign. According to the constitution, he was "sacred
and inviolable," and in Itō's commentaries this was defined in Shinto terms. The
emperor was given direct command of the armed forces. Yamagata Aritomo
(1838–1922) had set up a German-type general staff system in 1878. The emper-
or had the right to name the prime minister and to appoint the Cabinet. He could
dissolve the lower house of the Diet and issue imperial ordinances when the Diet
was not in session. The Imperial Household Ministry, which was outside the Cabinet, administered the great wealth given to the imperial family during the 1880s—
so that the emperor would never have to ask the Diet for funds. It was understood
that the Meiji leaders would act for the emperor in all of these matters. Finally, the
constitution itself was presented as a gift from the emperor to his subjects.

The lower house of the Diet was given the authority only to approve budgets
and pass laws, and both of these powers was hedged. The previous year's budget
would remain in effect if a new budget was not approved. The appointive House
of Peers, the upper house of the Diet, had to approve any bill to become law. Furthermore, the vote was given only to adult males paying fifteen yen or more in taxes.
In 1890 this was about 5 percent of the adult male population. In sum, Itō's intention was to create not a parliamentary system, but a constitutional system that
included a parliament as one of its parts.

During the 1880s, the government also created institutions to limit the future
influence of the political parties. In 1884, it created a new nobility with which to
stock the future House of Peers. The nobility was composed of ex-nobles and the Meiji
leaders themselves. Itō, born a lowly foot soldier, ended as a prince. In 1885, he established a cabinet system and became the first prime minister. In 1887, Itō established a Privy Council, with himself as its head, to approve the constitution he had
written. In 1888, laws were passed and civil-service examinations instituted to insu-
late the imperial bureaucracy from the tawdry concerns of politicians.

Diet   The bicameral Japanese
parliament.

GROWTH OF A MODERN ECONOMY

The late Tokugawa economy was not markedly different from the economies of other East Asian countries. Almost 80 percent of the population lived in the countryside at close to a subsistence level. Taxes were high, and two-thirds of the land tax was paid in kind. Money had only partially penetrated the rural economy. Japan had not developed factory production with machinery, steam power, or large accumulations of capital.

Early Meiji reforms unshackled the late Tokugawa economy. Occupations were freed, which meant that farmers could trade and samurai could farm. Barriers on roads were abolished, as were the monopolistic guilds. The abolition of domains threw open regional economies. There followed a groundswell of new commercial ventures and traditional agriculturally based industries.

Silk was the wonder crop. The government introduced mechanical reeling, enabling Japan to win markets previously held by the hand-reeled silk of China. Silk production rose from 2.3 million pounds in the post-Restoration era to 93 million in 1929.

A parallel unshackling occurred on the land. The land tax reform of the 1870s created an incentive for growth by giving farmers a clear title to their land and by fixing the tax in money. The freedom to buy and sell land led to a rise in tenancy from perhaps 25 percent in 1868 to about 44 percent at the turn of the century. Progressive landlords bought fertilizer and farm equipment. Rice production rose from 149 million bushels a year during 1880–1884 to 316 million during 1935–1937. More food, combined with a drop in the death rate—the result of better hygiene—led to population growth: from about 30 million in 1868 to 45 million in 1900 to 73 million in 1940. Because the farm population remained constant, the extra hands were available for factory and other urban jobs.

FIRST PHASE: MODEL INDUSTRIES

The modern sector of the economy was the government's greatest concern. It developed in four phases. The first was the era of model industries, which lasted until 1881. With military strength as a major goal, the Meiji government expanded arsenals and shipyards, built telegraph lines, made a start on railroads, developed mines, and established factories. The quantitative output of these early industries was insignificant, however. They were pilot-plant operations that doubled as "schools" for technologists and labor.

Just as important to economic development were banks, post offices, ports, roads, commercial laws, a system of primary and secondary schools, a government university, and so on. They were patterned after European and American examples.

SECOND PHASE: 1880s–1890s

More substantial growth in the modern sector took place during the 1880s and 1890s. It was marked by the appearance of what would later become the great industrial combines known as *zaibatsu*. One of the first industries to benefit was cotton textiles. By 1896, the production of yarn had reached 17 million pounds, and by 1913 it was over 10 times that amount. Production of cotton cloth rose from 22 million square yards in 1900 to 2.7 billion in 1936.

Another area of growth was railroads. Railroads gave Japan an internal circulatory system, opening up hitherto isolated regions. In 1872, Japan had 18 miles of track; in 1894, 2,100 miles; and by 1934, 14,500 miles.

Cotton textiles and railroads were followed during the 1890s by cement, bricks, matches, glass, beer, chemicals, and other private industries. The government created

WHY DID Japan set out to build a modern economy?

zaibatsu   Large industrial combines that came to dominate Japanese industry in the late nineteenth century.

a favorable climate for growth: The society and the polity were stable, the yen was sound, capital was safe, and taxes on industry were low. In every respect, the conditions enjoyed by Japan's budding entrepreneurs differed from those of China.

THIRD PHASE: 1905–1929

Economic growth spurted ahead during World War I. But an economic slump followed the war, and the economy grew slowly during the twenties. One factor was renewed competition from a Europe at peace; another was the earthquake that destroyed Tokyo in 1923. Agricultural productivity also leveled off during the twenties: It became cheaper to import food from the colonies than to invest in new agricultural technology at home.

By the twenties, Japanese society, especially in the cities, was becoming modern. The Japanese were healthier and lived longer. Personal savings rose with the standard of living. Even factory workers drank beer, went to movies, and read newspapers. By 1925, primary school education was universal. Japan had done what no other non-Western nation had even attempted: It had achieved universal literacy. Nevertheless, an immense cultural and social gap remained between the majority who had only a primary school education and the 3 percent who attended university. This gap was a basic weakness in the political democracy of the twenties.

It should also be noted that the costs of growth were sometimes high. Because textiles played a large role in the early phase of Japan's modern economic growth, well into the twentieth century more than half of the industrial labor force was women. They went to the mills after leaving primary school and returned to their villages before marrying. Their working hours were long, their dormitories crowded, and their movements restricted. Some contracted tuberculosis, the plague of late-nineteenth and early-twentieth-century Japan, and were sent back to their villages to die.

FOURTH PHASE: DEPRESSION AND RECOVERY

A Japanese bank crisis in 1927, followed by the worldwide Great Depression in 1929, plunged Japan into unemployment and suffering. The political consequences were enormous. Yet most of Japan recovered by 1933, more rapidly than any other industrial nation.

The recovery was fueled by an export boom and military procurements. During the 1930s, the production of pig iron, raw steel, and chemicals doubled. By 1937, Japan had a merchant fleet of 4.5 million tons, the third largest and the newest in the world. The quality of Japan's manufacturers also rose. The outcry in the West against Japanese exports at this time was not so much because of volume—a modest 3.6 percent of world exports in 1936—but because Japanese products had become competitive in terms of quality.

THE POLITICS OF IMPERIAL JAPAN (1890–1945)

Parliaments began in the West and have worked better there than in the rest of the world. Even so cautious a constitution as that of Meiji had no precedent outside the West at the time. How are we then to view the Japanese political experience after 1890?

One view is that because Japanese society was not ready for constitutional government, the militarism of the thirties was inevitable. From the perspective of an ideal democracy, Japanese society had many weaknesses: a small middle class, weak trade unions, an independent military under the emperor, a strong emperor-centered nationalism, and so on. But these weaknesses did not prevent the Diet from growing in importance, nor did they block the transfer of power from the bureaucratic

QUICK REVIEW

Development of the Japanese Economy

◆ First Phase (–1881): Development of model industries
◆ Second Phase (1880s–1890s): Emergence of the zaibatsu and growth of the railroads
◆ Third Phase (1905–1929): Slow economic growth and modernization of Japanese society
◆ Fourth Phase (1929–1937): Depression and recovery

WHY DID Japan join the imperialist scramble for colonies?

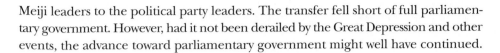

Meiji leaders to the political party leaders. The transfer fell short of full parliamentary government. However, had it not been derailed by the Great Depression and other events, the advance toward parliamentary government might well have continued.

FROM CONFRONTATION TO THE FOUNDING OF THE SEIYŪKAI (1890–1900)

In 1890, the Meiji leaders—sometimes called *oligarchs,* the few who rule—were concerned with nation building, not politics. They saw the cabinet as serving the emperor and nation above the ruck of partisan interests. They viewed the political parties as ineffective and irresponsible. They saw the lower house of the Diet as a place to let off steam without interfering in the government's work of building a new Japan. But the oligarchs had miscalculated: The authority of the lower house to approve or turn down the budget made it more powerful than they had intended. This involved the oligarchs, willy-nilly, in the political struggles.

The first act of the parties in the new 1890 Diet was to slash the government's budget. Prime Minister Yamagata had to make concessions to get part of the cut restored. This pattern continued for 10 years. Rising costs meant that the previous year's budget was never enough. The government tried to intimidate and bribe the parties, but failed. The opposing political parties maintained their control of the lower house. They also had the support of the voters, mostly well-to-do landowners, who opposed the government's heavy land tax.

In 1900, Itō Hirobumi formed a new party, called the Rikken Seiyūkai, or "Friends of Constitutional Government." It was composed of ex-bureaucrats associated with Itō and of politicians from the Liberal Party that Itagaki Taisuke (1837–1919) had formed in 1881. For most of the next 20 years it was the most important party in Japan, providing parliamentary support for successive governments through its control of the lower house. This arrangement was satisfactory to both sides: Prime ministers got the Diet support necessary for the government to function smoothly. The party politicians got cabinet posts and pork barrel legislation with which to reward their supporters.

THE GOLDEN YEARS OF MEIJI

The years before and after the turn of the century represented the culmination of what the government had striven for since 1868. Economic development was under way. Japan got rid of extraterritoriality in 1899 and regained control of its own tariffs in 1911. However, it was international events that won Japan recognition as a world power.

The first event was a war with China in 1894–1895 over Korea. From its victory, Japan secured Taiwan, the Pescadores Islands, the Kwantung Peninsula in southern Manchuria, an indemnity, and a treaty giving it the same privileges in China as those enjoyed by the Western powers (see Map 29–1). Russia, however, with French and German support, forced Japan to give up the Kwantung Peninsula, which included Port Arthur. Three years later, Russia took Kwantung for itself.

The second event was Japan's participation in 1900 in the international force that relieved the Boxers' siege of the foreign legations in Peking. A third development was the Anglo-Japanese Alliance of 1902. For Britain, this alliance ensured Japanese support for its East Asian interests and warded off the likelihood of a Russian-Japanese agreement over spheres of influence in Northeast Asia. For Japan, the alliance meant it could fight Russia without fear of intervention by a third party.

The fourth event was the war with Russia that began in 1904. Japanese armies drove the Russians from their railway zones in Manchuria and seized Mukden in March 1905. The Russians sent their Baltic fleet to join the battle, but it was annihilated by

MAP EXPLORATION

Interactive map: To explore this map further, go to **http://www.prenhall.com/craig2/map29.1**

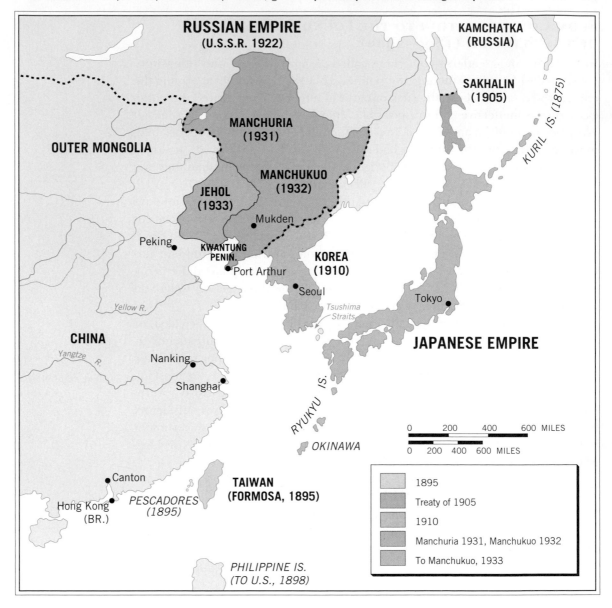

MAP 29–1

Formation of the Japanese Empire. The Japanese Empire grew in three stages: the Sino-Japanese War of 1894–1895, the Russo-Japanese War of 1904–1905, and Japanese conquests in Manchuria and northern China after 1931.

WHY WAS Japan able to build an empire on the Asian mainland?

24.2
Japanese Imperialism

Admiral Tōgō (1847–1934) at the Straits of Tsushima. After months of war, both countries were worn out, and Russia was plagued by revolution. President Theodore Roosevelt (1858–1919) proposed a peace conference at Portsmouth, New Hampshire. The resulting treaty gave Japan the Russian lease in the Liaotung Peninsula, the Russian railway in south Manchuria, the southern half of Sakhalin, and a recognition of Japan's "paramount interest" in Korea, which was annexed in 1910.

Japan joined the imperialist scramble for colonies because it wanted equality with the great Western powers, and military power and colonies were the best credentials. Enthusiasm for empire was shared by political party leaders, most liberal thinkers, and conservative leaders alike.

RISE OF THE PARTIES TO POWER

The founding of the Seiyūkai by Itō in 1900 ended a decade of confrontation between the Diet and the government. The aging oligarch Itō found it intolerable to deal with party politicians, who, unlike the bureaucrats, neither obeyed him nor paid him the respect that he thought his due. In 1903, he relinquished the presidency of the party to Saionji Kinmochi (1849–1940), who passed the post to Hara Takashi (1856–1921) in 1914. With Hara, the office found the man.

Hara was an outsider. Born a generation after the founding fathers of the Meiji state, he helped Itō to found the Seiyūkai and was the most able politician in Japan. His goals for Japan centered on the expansion of national wealth and power and were no different from those of Itō or Yamagata. But he felt that they should be achieved by party government, not oligarchic rule, and worked to expand the power of his party. The years between 1905 and 1921 were marked by the struggle between these two alternative conceptions of government.

The struggle can be represented as a rising curve of party strength and a descending curve of oligarchic influence. The rising curve had two vectors: a buildup of the Seiyūkai party machine that enabled it to win elections and maintain itself as the majority (or plurality) party in the Diet, and the strengthening of the Diet vis-à-vis other elites within the government in Tokyo. For the former, Hara obtained campaign funds from moneyed interests. He also promoted pork barrel legislation. Constituencies that supported Seiyūkai candidates got new schools, bridges, dams, roads, or even railroad lines. Hara was even willing to call on the police and local officials to aid Seiyūkai election campaigns.

In co-opting other governmental elites, the Seiyūkai had mixed success. The party increased its representation in the Cabinet and gained some patronage appointments in the bureaucracy, although most bureaucrats remained professionals and resisted the intrusion of political appointees. The House of Peers and the Privy Council, which ratified treaties, remained independent bodies. The Seiyūkai had no success in penetrating the military services.

The descending curve of weakening oligarchic control reflected the aging of the "men of Meiji." In 1900, Itō was the last oligarch to become prime minister. From 1901 to 1912, Katsura Tarō (1847–1913), a Chōshū general and Yamagata's protégé, and Saionji, Itō's protégé, took turns in the post. Both had Seiyū-kai support. The oligarchs were also weakened by changes within the elites. A younger generation of officers in the military services chafed at the continuing domination by the old cliques. In the civil bureaucracy, younger officials who had graduated from the Law Faculty of Tokyo Imperial University were achieving positions of responsibility. They saw the bureaucracy as an independent service and resisted oligarchic control almost as much as they resisted that of the parties.

The oligarchs maintained their power to act for the emperor in appointing prime ministers. With the deaths of Itō in 1909 and Yamagata in 1922, this vital function was taken over by Saionji and, later, by ex-prime ministers.

As the rising and descending curves approached each other, the political parties advanced. Several turning points were critical. One came in 1912. When the army's demands for a larger budget were refused, it withdrew its minister, causing Saionji's cabinet to collapse. Katsura tried to govern using imperial decrees in place of Diet support. This infuriated the parties, and even the Seiyūkai withdrew its support. Massive popular demonstrations broke out. Katsura was forced to resign in 1913. The lower house had defeated an oligarchic prime minister.

The curves finally crossed in 1918 when Hara became prime minister. It was the first time a politician who was not a Meiji founding father or a protégé of one had obtained the post. He enacted reforms but did nothing to remedy the parliamentary shortcomings of the Meiji Constitution.

A third development was the wave of liberalism that began during World War I and culminated in the period of party governments from 1924 to 1932. Joining the Allies in World War I, Japan had been influenced by democratic thought from England and America. Scholars discussed revising the Meiji Constitution. Labor unions were organized, at first liberal and often Christian, and later Marxist. A social movement was launched to improve conditions in Japan's industrial slums and to pass social and labor legislation. Japan's second political party, the Kenseikai, which had been out of power since 1916, grew steadily more liberal and adopted several of the new social causes as its own, such as universal manhood suffrage. When Hara cut the tax qualification for voting from 10 to 3 yen—a considerable extension of the franchise—the Kenseikai criticized the change as insufficient.

In 1924, the Kenseikai and the Seiyūkai formed a coalition government. For the next eight years, the presidents of one or the other of the two major parties were appointed as prime ministers.

The cabinets (1924–1926) of Katō Kōmei are considered the peak of parliamentarianism in prewar Japan. Blunt, cold, and haughty, Katō was respected, if not liked. He was an Anglophile who advocated a British model of government. His ministry passed universal manhood suffrage, increased academic appointments to the House of Peers, and cut the military budget. He also enacted social and labor legislation. In effect, he legalized the moderate socialist movement and outlawed revolutionary socialism. Katō's cabinet brought Japan close to a true parliamentary government.

MILITARISM AND WAR (1927–1945)

The future of Japan's parliamentary coalition seemed assured during the mid-1920s. The economy was growing; society was stable; the party leaders were experienced. Japan's international position was secure. By a decade later, however, the party leaders had lost the gains of 35 years. By 1945, Japan had been defeated in a devastating war and was occupied by foreign troops for the first time in its history. How did this come about?

Simply put, a small shift in the balance of power among the governmental elites established by the Meiji Constitution had produced a major change in Japan's foreign policy. The parties had been the obstreperous elite between 1890 and 1926 and had advanced by forcing the other elites to compromise. From the late 1920s, the military became the obstreperous elite and did the same. Beginning in 1932, military men replaced party presidents as prime ministers. In 1937, Japan went to war with China; and by the end of 1941, Japan was allied with Germany and Italy and had gone to war with the United States.

From their inception, the military services in Japan had been constructed on different principles from Japan's civilian society. Soldiers were not samurai. Universal conscription had put the new military on a changed footing. But the armed services had their own schools, which inculcated the values of discipline, bravery, loyalty, and obedience. The military saw themselves as the heirs of those who had founded the modern Japanese state and the guardians of Japanese tradition. They contrasted their loyalty to the emperor and their concern for all Japanese with the pandering to special interests by the political parties.

They resented their diminished national stature during the 1920s, when military budgets were cut and the prestige of a military career declined. But even during the liberal 1920s there had been no change in the constitutional position of the services. The general staffs remained directly responsible to the emperor. With the passing of the Meiji oligarchs, this meant they were responsible to no one but themselves.

A Crisis in Manchuria   The new multilateral treaties (the 1924 Washington Conference and the 1930 London Conference) that replaced the earlier system of bilateral treaties (such as the Anglo-Japanese Alliance) recognized the existing colonies of the victors in World War I but opposed new colonial ventures. Japan's position in Manchuria was ambiguous. Because Japan maintained its rule through a tame Chinese warlord, Manchuria was not, strictly speaking, a colony. But because Japan had gained its special position in Manchuria at the cost of 100,000 lives in the 1905 Russo-Japanese War, it saw its claim to Manchuria as similar to that of Western nations to their colonies.

From the late 1920s, the Kuomintang unification of China and the blossoming of Chinese nationalism threatened Japan's special position. Japanese army units tried to block the march north and murdered the Manchurian warlord when he showed signs of independence. In this crisis, the party government in Tokyo equivocated, hoping to preserve a status quo that was crumbling before its eyes. The army saw Manchuria as a buffer between the Soviet Union and the Japanese colony of Korea. In 1931, the army provoked a crisis, took over Manchuria, and proclaimed it an independent state in 1932. When the League of Nations condemned Japan, Japan withdrew from the League in 1933.

The Great Depression   Japan's government acted effectively to counter the Depression, as noted earlier, but the recovery came too late to help the political parties. By 1936, political trends that had begun during the worst years of the Depression had become irreversible.

The Depression galvanized the political left and right. The political left was composed mainly of socialist moderates, who won eight Diet seats in 1928 and 37 in 1937. Supported by unionists and white-collar workers, they would reemerge as an even stronger force after World War II. The radical left consisted of many little Marxist parties led by intellectuals and of the Japanese Communist Party. Although small and subject to governmental repression, the radical parties were influential in intellectual and literary circles during the twenties and thirties.

The Radical Right and the Military   The political right in pre–World War II Japan is difficult to define. Most Japanese, even socialists, were imbued with an emperor-centered nationalism. During the 1930s, however, a new array of right-wing organizations went beyond the usual nationalism to challenge the status quo. Civilian ultranationalists used Shinto myths and Confucian values to attack Western liberalism in Japan's urban society. Some bureaucrats looked to the example of Nazi Germany and argued for the exclusion of party politicians from government. Military officers envisioned a "defense state" guided by themselves. They argued for military expansion and an autarchic colonial empire insulated from the uncertainties of the world economy. Young officers of the revolutionary right advocated "direct action" against the elites of the parliamentary coalition. They called for a second restoration of imperial power.

Modern Japan

Overthrow of Tokugawa *Bakufu*

1853–1854	Perry obtains Treaty of Friendship
1858	*Bakufu* signs commercial treaty
1861–1863	Chōshū and Satsuma mediate
1866	Chōshū defeats *bakufu* army
1868	Meiji Restoration

Nation Building

1868–1871	Shaping a new state
1873–1878	Social revolution from above
1877–1878	Satsuma rebellion
1889	Meiji Constitution promulgated
1890	First Diet session

Imperial Japan

1894–1895	Sino-Japanese War
1900	Seiyūkai formed
1904–1905	Russo-Japanese War
1910	Korea annexed

Era of Party Government

1918	Hara becomes prime minister
1924	Katō becomes prime minister Universal manhood suffrage passed

Militarism

1931	Japan takes Manchuria
1937	War with China
1941	Japan attacks Pearl Harbor
1945	Japan surrenders

Tōjō Hideki (1884–1948), prime minister at the time of the attack on Pearl Harbor in 1941 and one of the chief figures in the rise of Japanese militarism.

Corbis-Bettmann

The last group precipitated political change. On May 15, 1932, junior army and navy officers attacked the Seiyūkai offices, the Bank of Japan, and the Tokyo police headquarters, and murdered Prime Minister Inukai. The attack occurred at the peak of right-wing agitation and the pit of the Depression. Saionji decided that it would be unwise to appoint another party president as the new prime minister; and chose instead a moderate admiral. For the next four years, cabinets were led by moderate military men, but with party participation. These cabinets satisfied neither the parties nor the radical young officers.

During 1936 and 1937, Japanese politics continued to drift to the right. In the election of February 1936, the opposition overturned the Seiyūkai-dominated Diet with the slogan, "What shall it be, parliamentary government or Fascism?" A week later, young officers attempted a coup in Tokyo. They killed cabinet ministers and occupied the Diet and other government buildings. They wanted their army superiors to form a new government. Saionji and other men about the emperor stood firm; the navy opposed the rebellion; and within three days it was suppressed. It was the last "direct action" by the radical right in prewar Japan. The ringleaders were tried and executed, and generals sympathetic to them were retired. The officers in charge of the purge within the army were tough-minded elitist technocrats. They included General Tōjō Hideki (1884–1948), who would lead Japan into World War II.

But the services interfered more than ever in the formation of cabinets. From 1936 on, moderate prime ministers gave way to more outspokenly militaristic figures.

Opposition to militarism remained substantial nonetheless. In the 1937 election, the two major centrist parties, which had joined in opposition to the government, won 354 Diet seats. The Japanese people were more level-headed than their leaders. But the centrists' victory proved hollow. The Diet could not oppose a government in wartime, and by summer, Japan was at war in China.

The Road to Pearl Harbor   Between the outbreak of the war with China and World War II, in the Pacific, there were three critical junctures. The first was the decision in January 1938 to strike a knockout blow at the Nationalist Party (KMT) government. The war had begun as an unplanned skirmish between Chinese and Japanese troops in the Beijing area but had quickly spread. The Japanese army's leaders disagreed on whether to continue. Many held that the only threat to Japanese interests in Korea and Manchuria was the Soviet Union, and that a long war in China was foolish. But as the Japanese armies advanced, the general staff argued that the only way to end the war was to convince the Nationalists that fighting was hopeless. The army occupied most of the cities and railroads of eastern China, but Jiang Jieshi refused to give in. A stalemate ensued that lasted until 1945. China was never a major theater of the war in the Pacific.

The second critical decision was the signing of the **Tripartite Pact** with Germany and Italy in September 1940. Japan had long admired Germany. In 1936, it had joined Germany in the Anti-Comintern Pact directed against international communism. It also wanted an alliance with Germany against the Soviet Union. Germany insisted, however, that any alliance would also have to be directed against the United States and Britain. The Japanese disagreed. The Japanese navy saw the American Pacific fleet as its only potential enemy and was not willing to risk being dragged into a German war. When Japanese troops battled Russian troops in an undeclared mini-war from May to September 1939 on the Mongolian border, sentiment rose in favor of an alliance with Germany, but then Germany "betrayed" Japan by signing a nonaggression pact with the Soviet Union. For a time Japan decided to improve

Tripartite Pact   The alliance between Japan and Nazi Germany and Fascist Italy that was signed in 1940.

OVERVIEW

JAPANESE MILITARISM AND GERMAN NAZISM

Militarism took hold in Japan in the 1930s during the same years when the Nazis seized power in Germany. Japan and Germany became allies, and both countries embarked on campaigns of aggression that led to the outbreak of World War II, first in Europe, then in Asia. In the eyes of many Americans, Japanese militarism seemed the same as German Nazism. Yet a comparison between militarist Japan and Nazi Germany shows major differences as well as similarities.

Similarities Between Japan and Nazi Germany	1. Elitist academic bureaucracies and strong military traditions. 2. Authoritarian family systems. 3. Weak parliamentary traditions. 4. Badly hurt by the Great Depression. 5. Sought to solve their problems through territorial expansion. 6. Thought of themselves as "have-not," victim nations. 7. Persecution of socialists and liberals. 8. Creation of authoritarian regimes.
Differences Between Japan and Nazi Germany	1. Japan was more homogeneous than Germany. It had no Catholic-Protestant, north versus south divide. 2. Japan's socialist movement was much weaker than Germany's, and it did not frighten the Japanese middle class. 3. The Great Depression and runaway inflation did not destroy the Japanese middle class as they did in Germany. 4. No mass totalitarian party like the Nazis existed in Japan. 5. Because the German Reichstag was stronger than the Japanese Diet, the Nazis came to power by winning elections and then by abolishing them. In Japan the antimilitarist parties continued to win elections throughout the 1930s, but the militarists took power anyway through intimidation and by waging undeclared war in China. Moreover, Japan continued to hold parliamentary elections during the war. 6. Anti-Semitism and racism were integral to Nazism. Although there were racist components to Japanese militarism, the Japanese military were not anti-Semitic and never instituted mass murder in pursuit of a racist ideology as the Nazis did. 7. Japan had no Hitler. In Japan power was exercised in the name of the emperor, and militarist leaders came and went. In 1944 the emperor's advisors dismissed General Tōjō Hideki, the prime minister who had brought Japan into World War II, and replaced him with a moderate leader.

its relations with the United States, but America insisted that Japan get out of China. By the late spring of 1940 German victories in Europe—the fall of Britain appeared imminent—again led military leaders in Japan to favor an alliance with Germany.

When Japan signed the Tripartite Pact, it had three objectives: to isolate the United States, to inherit the Southeast Asian colonies of the countries defeated by Germany in Europe, and to improve its relations with the Soviet Union through the good offices of Germany. The last objective was reached when Japan signed a neutrality pact with the Soviet Union in April 1941. Two months later, Germany attacked the Soviet Union without consulting its ally, Japan. It compounded this second "betrayal" by asking Japan to attack the Soviet Union in the east. Japan waited and watched. When the German advance was stopped short of Moscow, Japan decided to honor the neutrality pact and turn south. This decision marked, in effect, the end of Japan's participation in the Axis. Thereafter, it fought its own war in Asia. Yet instead of deflecting American criticism as intended, the pact, by linking Japan to Germany, led to a hardening of America's position on China.

The third and fatal decision was to go to war with the United States. In June 1940, following Germany's defeat of France, Japanese troops had moved into northern French Indochina. The United States retaliated by limiting strategic exports to Japan. When Japanese troops took southern Indochina in July 1941, the United States embargoed all exports to Japan; this cut Japanese oil imports by 90 percent. The navy's general staff argued that oil reserves would last only two years; after that the navy would lose its capability to fight. Its general staff pressed for the capture of the oil-rich Dutch East Indies. But it was too dangerous to move against Dutch and British colonies in Southeast Asia with the United States on its flank in the Philippines. The navy, therefore, planned a preemptive strike against the United States, and on December 7, 1941, it bombed Pearl Harbor. The Japanese decision for war wagered Japan's land-based air power, shorter supply lines, and what it saw as greater will power against American productivity. The navy's chief of staff compared the war with the United States to a dangerous operation that might save the life of a critically ill patient. In the end, the war left Japan defeated and in ruins.

Summary

Modernization of Japan From the late nineteenth century, most countries wanted to become modern. They coveted the wealth and power that science and industry had produced in the West. They did not wish to become Western, for that would have denied them their own cultural identity. However, it was difficult to separate what was modern from what was merely recent Western.

We note three stages in Japan's development as the world's first non-Western modernizer. First, even before its contact with the modern West, it had some of the *preconditions* needed to adopt modern technology: a fairly high literacy, an ethic of duty and hard work, a market economy, a shift from religious to secular thought, an adequate bureaucracy, and political orientations resembling nationalism. These preconditions provided a base for an "external modernization."

Second, after 1868 Japan *Westernized.* The Meiji leaders introduced a wide range of new institutions. Japanese thinkers brought in modern ideas and values. Third, Japan began to *assimilate* the ideas and institutions it had borrowed from the West.

Japan may serve as a useful model in that its modernization has gone further than that in any other non-Western country. We note the absence of comparable preconditions in India or the Islamic world. Even after the end of colonialism, countries in these areas had to create the necessary preconditions while borrowing the new technologies. That difficulty explains their limited success. In Africa the dearth of preconditions was even more pronounced.

Chinese Traditionalism In comparison to most of the non-Western world, the Chinese tradition was advanced. Like Japan, it had already achieved many of the preconditions for modernization: a high level of literacy, a belief in education as the means for advancement, the ingredients for shaping a modern nationalism, a family system that adapted well to small enterprises, and a market economy. But when it came to borrowing Western ideas and institutions, the government by Confucian literati that had long been China's outstanding asset became its greatest liability. It took decades to topple the dynasty and to advance beyond Confucian ideas.

Guomindang versus CCP Then, in the maelstrom of the May Fourth Movement, intellectual changes occurred at a furious pace. But in the chaos following the breakdown of the ancient regime, doctrines alone could not provide a stable polity. Nationalism was the common denominator of most Chinese thought. Sun Yat-sen appealed to it. The Kuomintang drew on it at the Whampoa Academy, during the march north, and in founding their government. Yet other groups could also appeal to nationalism, and eventually the Chinese Communist Party (CCP) won out.

Chinese Communism It is beguiling to view the CCP cadres as a new class of literati operating the machinery of a monolithic, centralized state, with the teachings of Marx and Lenin replacing those of Confucius, and local party organization replacing the Confucian gentry. But this interpretation is too simple. Communism stressed science, materialism, and class conflict. It broke with the Chinese past.

Communism itself was also modified in China. Marx had predicted that socialist revolutions would break out in advanced economies where the contradictions of capitalism were sharpest. Lenin had shifted the emphasis from spontaneous revolutions by workers to the small but disciplined revolutionary party, the vanguard of the proletariat. He thereby changed communism into what it has been ever since: a movement capable of seizing power only in backward nations. Mao Tse-tung slightly modified Lenin's ideas by theorizing that "progressive" peasants were a part of the proletariat. But in practice, he virtually ignored city workers and relied on China's villages for recruits for his armies, who were then indoctrinated using Leninist techniques. Despite its low level of technology, the People's Liberation Army—the communist equivalent of a "citizen's army," was formidable. It was also modern in the sense that it did not loot and despoil the areas it occupied.

Yet, the organizational techniques that were so effective in creating a party and army would prove less so for economic development. It soon became clear that mass mobilization was no substitute for individual incentives.

IMAGE KEY

for pages 636–637

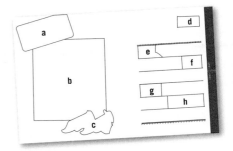

a. Field marshal Oyama's infantrymen confront Russians troops
b. Japan's first foreign mission headed by Pince Iwakura
c. Shoes for bound feet
d. Japanese flag
e. The empress dowager Tz'u-hsi
f. Chinese president Sun Yat Sen
g. Perry expedition to Japan
h. Promulgation of the Meiji Constitution in 1889

REVIEW QUESTIONS

1. Which had the greater impact on China, the Opium War or the Taiping Rebellion?

2. How did the Ch'ing (or Manchu) dynasty recover from the Taiping Rebellion? Why did the recovery not prevent the overthrow of the dynasty in 1911?

3. Did the May Fourth Movement prepare the way for the nationalist revolution and communist revolutions?

4. After the Meiji restoration, what steps did Japan's leaders take to achieve their goal of "wealth and power"?

5. What were the strengths and weaknesses of Japan's prewar parliamentary institutions? What led to the sudden rise of militarism during the thirties?

KEY TERMS

Boxers (p. 642)
Diet (p. 650)
Kuomintang (KMT) (p. 644)
Long March (p. 645)

Meiji restoration (p. 649)
Taiping rebellion (p. 639)
treaty ports (p. 640)
Tripartite Pact (p. 658)

unequal treaties (p. 638)
zaibatsu (p. 651)

  For additional study resources for this chapter, go to:
www.prenhall.com/craig/chapter29

Industrialization

HOW DID the advent of industrialization in the ninetieth and early twentieth centuries shape the art of those countries that industrialized? Did artists view industrialization as a negative or a positive force?

The industrial revolution began in Britain in the eighteenth century. By the mid-nineteenth century factories, coal-fired machines, and railroads had spread throughout Western Europe, and also the eastern portion of the United States. By the later nineteenth-century industrialization and railroad building advanced in the United States, and also in Japan, which had become the most industrialized non-Western power in the world by the 1930s. Industry was understood to be about power, not only the power machines generated and artists celebrated, but also the power of political and military domination.

◀ **Power Loom Weaving of cotton cloth in a textile mill; colored engraving, 1834**. Industrialization began in the cloth industry because cloth was the most important manufactured product in the world from ancient times to the dawn of the modern era. Early factory owners often employed women, whose labor came cheaper than that of men. Factory women worked long hours and were subject to close supervision designed to ensure that their morals would not suffer in the factory setting.
The Granger Collection

▲
Shōsai Ikkei, "Picture of Steam Engine Traffic at Shiodome," 1872.

In stark contrast to China, Japan's strategy for dealing with Western imperialism in nineteenth-century Asia was to compete with the West head-on as an imperial and an industrial power. To do this, Japan imported, copied and, ultimately, improved on Western technology. In this image we see the great symbol of nineteenth-century technology, the railroad, as well as modern, Western-style buildings and, in the distance, modern ships in the harbor.

Courtesy of the Library of Congress. Gift of Mrs E. Crane Chadbourne; 1930

Diego Rivera, "Detroit Industry," Mural, North Wall, 1933.

As industrialization spread from the cloth industry to all forms of manufacture, it became an increasingly masculine enterprise, both because it became a mainstay of male employment in the West but also because its association with power and war meant that it was imagined as largely masculine. In this image we see strong, upright American men at work manufacturing the premier symbol of American industry, the automobile.

Diego Rivera (1886–1957). "Detroit Industry". North Wall, 1933. © 2003 Banco de Mexico Diego Rivera & Frida Kahlo Museums Trust. Av. Cinco de Mayo No. 2, Col. Centro, Del. Cuauhtemoc 06059, Mexico, D.F. Reproduction authorized by the Instituto Nacional de Bellas Artes y Literatura. Photograph © 2001 The Detroit Institute of Art/Bridgeman Art Library

▼

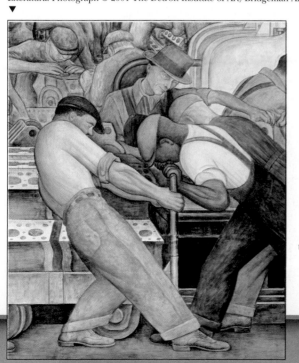

▲
Kazimir Malevich, "The Knife Grinder," 1912.

Technology seemed to those who experienced industrialization to speed life up to a dizzying rate. Although some found the new emphasis on speed and motion that accompanied industry disorienting, many in the early twentieth century celebrated it, and none more than the futurists. Futurism began in Italy, where it is closely associated with the rise of fascism, which also celebrated speed and power. Cubo-Futurism, which this image illustrated, was a Russian creation, product of the advent of industrialization in Russia, and influenced by both Cubism and the new photographic techniques emerging in this period.

Kazimir Severonic Malevich, Russian, 1878–1935. The Knife Grinder. (Principle of Glittering). 1912–1913. Oil on canvas. 79.5 × 79.5 cm (31 5/16 × 31 5/16 in.) Yale University Art Gallery. Gift of Collection Societe Anonyme

PART 7 ◆ GLOBAL CONFLICT AND CHANGE

EUROPE

▲ American World
War II poster

1914–1918	World War I
1917	Bolsheviks seize power, Russia
1919	Versailles Settlement
1922	Mussolini seizes power, Italy
1925	Locarno Pact
1933	Hitler comes to power
1936	Spanish Civil War begins
1938	Munich Conference
1939	World War II begins

1944	D-Day
1945	World War II ends
1948	Berlin blockade and airlift
1949	NATO treaty; Russia detonates atomic bomb
1953	Death of Stalin
1955	Warsaw Pact
1956	Soviets crush Hungarian revolt
1957	EEC founded
1958	Charles de Gaulle comes to power in France

◄ Pablo Picasso, Guernica, 1937

NEAR EAST / INDIA

1947	Indian Independence; creation of Pakistan
1948	Assassination of Mahatma Gandhi
1949	State of Israel founded
1953	Mosaddeq overthrown in Iran
1954–1970	Abdel Nasser leads Egypt
1956	Suez Crisis

1922	British leave Egypt
\1922–1938	Mustafa Kemal first president of Turkey
1928	The Muslim Brotherhood founded by Hasan Al-Banna

Mao Tse-tung ►
with Nikita Khrushchev

EAST ASIA

1916–1928	Warlord era in China
1919	May 4th Movement in China
1925	Universal male suffrage in Japan
1928–1937	Nationalist government in China at Nanking
1931	Japan occupies Manchuria
1937–1945	Japan at war with China

1941	Japan attacks Pearl Harbor
1945	Japan surrenders after U.S. atomic bombs
1945–1949	Civil War in China; People's Republic founded
1950	N. Korea invades S. Korea
1952	U.S. ends occupation of Japan
1953–1972	Double-digit growth in Japan
1955	Liberal-Democratic Party formed in Japan
1959–1960	Sino-Soviet split

AFRICA

| 1919 | W.E.B. DuBois holds first Pan-African Congress in Paris |
| 1935 | Mussolini invades Ethiopia |

1942–1945	World War II engulfs North Africa
1955–1962	Wars of independence in French Algeria
1956	Sudan gains independence from Britain and Egypt
1956	Morocco and Tunisia gain independence from France
1957	Ghana an independent state under Kwame Nkrumah

THE AMERICAS

1917	U.S. enters World War I
1929	Wall Street Crash; the Great Depression begins
1930–1945	Vargas dictatorship in Brazil
1932	F.D. Roosevelt elected U.S. president
1938	Mexico nationalizes oil

1941	U.S. enters World War II
1945	Death of F.D. Roosevelt
1946	Perón elected president in Argentina
1954	U.S. Supreme Court outlaws segregation
1955	Perón overthrown
1956	Montgomery bus boycott
1959	Fidel Castro comes to power in Cuba

◄ Fidel Castro

1960	Paris Summit Conference collapses after U-2 incident
1961	Berlin Wall erected
1964	Khrushchev replaced as Soviet prime minister by Kosygin; as party secretary by Brezhnev
1968	Soviets invade Czechoslovakia
1972	British Impose direct rule on Northern Ireland
1972	Israeli Olympic athletes killed by Arab terrorists
1974	End of military rule in Greece
1974	Portuguese dictatorship deposed; democratic reforms begin

1977	Brezhnev president of USSR
1979	Margaret Thatcher becomes British prime minister
1980	Solidarity Movement in Poland
1981	Crackdown against Solidarity
1984–1985	Bitter strikes by miners in England
1984	Mikhail Gorbachev introduces *glasnost* in USSR

▲ *Opening of the Berlin Wall, 1989*

1989	Berlin Wall demolished
1990	Germany unified
1991	Failed coup in Soviet Union; Yeltsin emerges as leader of Russia
1991	Major replaces Thatcher as England's prime minister
1993	Czechoslovakia divides into two republics
1995	Dayton Peace Accords end war in Bosnia
1999	NATO military campaign against Serbia
2000	Putin elected president of Russia; overthrow of Milŏsevic in Yugoslavia

1966	Indira Gandhi becomes prime minister of India
1967	Israeli-Arab June War
1969	Golda Meir becomes prime minister of Israel
1969	Arafat elected P.L.O. chairman
1971	India-USSR friendship treaty
1973	Arab-Israeli October War
1972	Independence for Bangladesh
1973	OPEC oil embargo

1977	Menachem Begin becomes prime minister of Israel
1978	Iranian revolution under Khomeini's leadership
1979	Egyptian-Israeli Peace Treaty
1979	Iran takes U.S. hostages
1979	Soviets invade Afghanistan
1980–1988	Iran-Iraq War
1981	Hostages released in Iran
1981	Egypt's Sadat assassinated; succeeded by Hosni Mubarak
1982	Israel invades Lebanon
1984	Indira Gandhi assassinated

1989	Soviets leave Afghanistan
1989	Death of Khomeini
1990	Central Asian States become independent on fall of USSR
1990–1991	Gulf War
1991	Indian prime minister Rajiv Ghandi assassinated

Oil wells left burning ▶ by Iraqi troops in Kuwait

1959–1975	Vietnam War
1965–1976	Cultural Revolution devastates China
1968	Death of Ho Chi Minh, president of North Vietnam
1971	Lin Piao killed in China
1972	President Nixon visits China
1973	Economic growth slows in Japan

▲ *Life in China during Cultural Revolution*

1976	Death of Mao Tse-tung
1978–1989	New Economic policies of Teng Hsiao-p'ing in China
1978–1989	Vietnam occupies Cambodia
1980s	Double-digit economic growth in South Korea and Taiwan

Tienanmen Square ▶

1988	Japan's GNP second in world
1989	Vietnam pledges to withdraw from Cambodia
1989	China crushes pro-democracy demonstrations in Beijing
1991–1992	Political scandals and plummeting stock market in Japan
1992	Kim Young Sam, civilian party leader, elected S. Korean president

1960	Belgian Congo granted independence as Zaire
1963	Kenya becomes an independent republic
1964	Zanzibar, the Congo, and Northern Rhodesia (Zambia) become independent republics
1965	Revolution in Kenya
1967–1970	Nigerian Civil War
1974	Drought and famine in Africa
1974	Emperor Haile Selassie of Ethiopia is deposed
1974–1975	Portugal grants independence to Guinea, Angola, Mozambique, Cape Verde

1980	Southern Rhodesia (Zimbabwe) gains independence from Britain
1984	Bishop Desmond Tutu awarded Nobel Peace Prize
1985	U.S. economic sanctions against South Africa result in more repression

1989	Conservative Botha government resigns in South Africa; DeKlerk becomes president
1992	Nelson Mandela freed from prison in South Africa
1994	Nelson Mandela elected president of South Africa

Nelson Mandela ▶

1960	Kennedy elected president
1962	Cuban Missile Crisis
1963	Kennedy assassinated
1964	Passage of Civil Rights Act
1965	U.S. expands Vietnam commitment
1968	Martin Luther King and Robert Kennedy assassinated; campus unrest
1968	Nixon elected
1970	Allende elected in Chile
1972	Nixon visits China and USSR; is reelected president
1973	Watergate scandal breaks
1973	Perón reelected, Argentina
1973	Chile's Allende overthrown
1974	Nixon resigns presidency

1979	Revolution in Nicaragua and El Salvador
1980	Iran hostage crisis
1980	Reagan elected president
1982	War between Argentina and Great Britain over Islas Malvinas (Falkland Islands)
1983	Argentine military government overthrown; elected government restored
1983	End of Mexican oil boom
1988	Major arms agreement between U.S. and USSR

1991	Gulf War
1992	Clinton elected president
1994	Revolt in Chiapas, Mexico
1998	Pope visits Cuba
2001	Terrorist attack on the World Trade Center in New York City and the Pentagon in Washington, D.C.

John Singer Sargent, *Gassed,* 1918–1919.
Gassed, by the American painter John Singer Sargent, has been compared with ancient Greek friezes depicting mythical battles, but where as Greek sculpture always portrayed an element of heroism along with death and suffering, Sargent's painting reveals only the horror of battle.

Imperial War Museum, London

30

IMPERIALISM AND WORLD WAR I

WHAT WAS the New Imperialism?

WHAT WERE the two alliance systems that faced each other in Europe before 1914?

WHAT CAUSED the outbreak of World War I in 1914?

WHY WERE the Bolsheviks able to seize power in Russia?

WHY DID the Versailles settlement leave Germany bitter?

IMAGE KEY
Image Key for pages 666–667
is on page 686.

WHAT WAS the New

Imperialism?

During the second half of the nineteenth century, Europe exercised unprecedented control over the rest of the world. The Americas, Australia, and New Zealand almost became part of the European world as streams of European immigrants populated them. Africa was divided among European nations (see Chapter 28), and Europe imposed its power across Asia (see Map 30–1 and Chapter 29). By 1900, European dominance had brought every part of the globe into a single world economy.

But these developments helped to foster competition and hostility among the great powers of Europe and to bring on a terrible war. The frenzy for imperial expansion that seized Europeans in the late nineteenth century did much to destroy its peace, prosperity, and dominant place in the world.

THE "NEW IMPERIALISM"

The explosive developments in nineteenth-century science, technology, industry, agriculture, transportation, communication, and weapons enabled a few Europeans (and Americans) to impose their will on other peoples many times their number. The growth of national states permitted the European nations to deploy their response in the most effective way. The Europeans also believed that their civilization and way of life were superior to all others. This gave them a confidence and often a cultural arrogance that fostered the expansionist mood.

After 1870, the European states swiftly spread their control over about a fifth of the world's land area and a tenth of its population. The movement has been called the **New Imperialism**.

THE NEW IMPERIALISM

Imperialism can be defined as extending a nation's power by some form of power over foreign peoples. The usual pattern of the New Imperialism was for the European nation to invest capital in the "backward" country and thereby to transform its economy and culture. To guarantee their investments, the European states would establish different degrees of political control ranging from full annexation as a colony, to protectorate status (whereby the local ruler was controlled by the dominant European state), to "spheres-of-influence" status (whereby the European state received special privileges without direct political involvement).

MOTIVES FOR THE NEW IMPERIALISM

There is still no agreement about the motives for the New Imperialism. Economic motives certainly played a part, but the new colonies were never major markets for European goods and investments. It is not even clear that control of them was profitable. Some advocates of imperialism argued that the European nations had a responsibility to bring the benefits of their superior civilization and Christianity to the people of "backward" lands, but few people were influenced by such arrogant arguments, although many shared the assumptions behind them. Nor did the new colonies attract many European emigrants. Most of them went to the Americas and Australia.

Strategic and prestige considerations seem to have been more important in bringing on the New Imperialism. Thus, the completion of the Suez Canal in 1869 made Egypt vital to the British because it sat astride the shortest route to India. When Egypt's stability was threatened in the 1880s, the British established a protectorate. Then, to protect Egypt, they advanced into the Sudan.

Other European nations equated status (Britain was the model) with the possession of colonies. They sought colonies as evidence of their own importance.

New Imperialism The extension in the late nineteenth and early twentieth centuries of Western political and economic dominance to Asia, the Middle East, and Africa.

This explains much of the scramble for Africa (see Chapter 29). In Asia, the emergence of Japan as a great power with claims on China and Korea frightened the other powers, and they pressed feverishly for concessions in China.

By 1900, most of the world had thus come under the control of the industrialized West. The greatest remaining vulnerable area was the Ottoman Empire, but its fate was tied up with European developments (see Map 30–1).

EMERGENCE OF THE GERMAN EMPIRE

FORMATION OF THE TRIPLE ALLIANCE (1873–1890)

Prussia's victories over Austria and France and its creation of the German Empire in 1871 revolutionized European diplomacy. The sudden appearance of a powerful new state posed problems.

The balance of power created at the Congress of Vienna was altered radically. Britain and Russia retained their position. Austria, however, had lost ground and was threatened by nationalism within the Austro-Hungarian Empire. French power and prestige were badly damaged by the Franco-Prussian War and the German annexation of Alsace-Lorraine. The French were both afraid of Germany and resentful of their loss of territory and of France's traditional dominance in western Europe.

BISMARCK'S LEADERSHIP (1873–1890)

Until 1890 Otto von Bismarck (1815–1898) continued to guide German policy. He insisted after 1871 that Germany wanted no further territorial gains, and he meant it. He wanted to avoid a war that might undo his achievement. He tried to assuage France by cultivating friendly relations and supporting its colonial aspirations. He also prepared for the worst. If France could not be conciliated, it must be isolated. Bismarck sought to prevent an alliance between France and any European power— especially Austria or Russia—that would threaten Germany with a war on two fronts.

War in the Balkans   Bismarck's first move was to establish the Three Emperors' League in 1873. It brought together the three great conservative empires of Germany, Austria, and Russia. The league collapsed when Russia went to war with Turkey in 1877. The tottering Ottoman Empire was preserved chiefly by the competing aims of those powers who awaited its demise. Ottoman weakness encouraged its Slavic subjects in the Balkans to rebel.

When Russia entered the fray, it created an international crisis. The Russians hoped to gain control of Constantinople. Russian intervention also reflected the influence of the **Pan-Slavic movement,** which sought to bring all the Slavs, even those under Austrian or Ottoman rule, under the protection of Holy Mother Russia.

The Ottoman Empire was forced to sue for peace. The Treaty of San Stefano of March 1878 was a Russian triumph. The Slavic states in the Balkans were freed of Ottoman rule, and Russia obtained territory and an indemnity. But the terms of the Russian victory alarmed the other great powers. Austria feared that the new Slav states and the increase in Russian influence would threaten its own Balkan provinces. The British were alarmed by the possible Russian control of Constantinople. Disraeli (1804–1881) was determined to resist, and British public opinion supported him.

Congress of Berlin   Disraeli sent a fleet to Constantinople, and Britain and Austria forced Russia to agree to an international conference at which the provisions of San Stefano would be reviewed by the other great powers. The resulting Congress

WHAT WERE the two alliance systems that faced each other in Europe before 1914?

QUICK REVIEW

Bismarck's Goals
- No additional German territorial expansion
- Tried to cultivate frienship with France
- Sought to prevent alliance between France and any other European power that would threaten Germany on two fronts

Pan-Slavic movement   The movement to create a nation or federation that would embrace all the Slavic peoples of Eastern Europe.

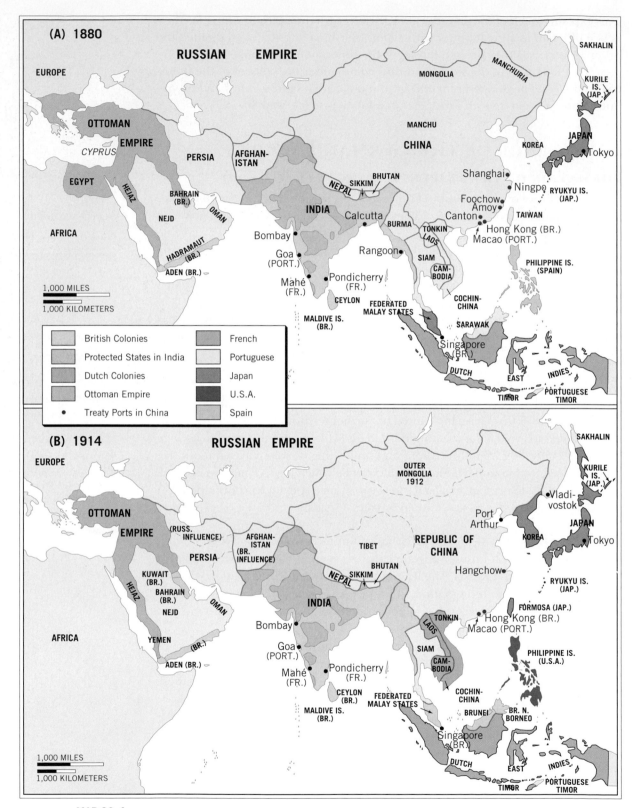

MAP 30–1
Asia 1880–1914. As in Africa, the late nineteenth century saw imperialism spread widely and rapidly in Asia. Two new powers, Japan and the United States, joined the British, French, and Dutch in extending control both to islands and to the mainland and in exploiting an enfeebled China.

HOW DID the new Japanese Empire affect the balance of power in Asia?

of Berlin met in June and July of 1878 under the presidency of Bismarck.

The decisions of the Congress were a blow to Russian ambitions. Bulgaria lost two-thirds of its territory. Austria-Hungary was given Bosnia and Herzegovina to "occupy and administer" under formal Ottoman rule. Britain received Cyprus, and France gained permission to occupy Tunisia. These were compensations for the gains that Russia was permitted to keep. Germany asked for nothing, but the Russians were angry. The Three Emperors' League was dead.

The south Slavic states of Serbia and Montenegro resented the Austrian occupation of Bosnia and Herzegovina. The south Slavic question, no less than the estrangement between Russia and Germany, was a threat to the peace of Europe.

German Alliances with Russia and Austria   Bismarck could ignore the Balkans, but not Russia. He concluded a secret treaty with Austria in 1879. This Dual Alliance provided that if either Germany or Austria were attacked by Russia, the ally would help the attacked party. If either was attacked by someone else, each promised at least to maintain neutrality. The treaty was renewed every five years until 1918.

Bismarck never allowed the alliance to drag Germany into Austria's Balkan quarrels. He made it clear to the Austrians that Germany would never attack Russia.

Bismarck expected the Austro-German negotiations to frighten Russia into seeking closer relations with Germany, and he was right. By 1881, he had renewed the Three Emperors' League on a firmer basis.

Bismarck and the young Kaiser William II meet in 1888. The two disagreed over many issues, and in 1890 William dismissed the aged chancellor.

German Information Center

The Triple Alliance   In 1882, Italy, annoyed by the French preemption of Tunisia, asked to join the Dual Alliance. Bismarck was now allied with three of the great powers and friendly with Great Britain, which held aloof from all alliances. France was isolated. Although the Three Emperors' League was allowed to lapse, the Triple Alliance (Germany, Austria, and Italy) was renewed for another five years in 1887. To restore German relations with Russia, Bismarck negotiated the Reinsurance Treaty that same year, in which both powers promised to remain neutral if either was attacked. However, a change in the German monarchy overturned Bismarck's system.

In 1888, William II (r. 1888–1918) came to the German throne. Like many Germans of his generation, he was filled with a sense of Germany's destiny as the leading power of Europe. To achieve a "place in the sun," he wanted a navy and colonies like Britain's. These aims, of course, ran counter to Bismarck's policy. In 1890, William dismissed Bismarck.

During Bismarck's time, Germany was a force for European peace. This position would not have been possible without its great military power. But it also required a statesman who could exercise restraint and understand what his country needed and what was possible.

FORGING THE TRIPLE ENTENTE (1890–1907)

Franco-Russian Alliance   After Bismarck's retirement, his system of alliances collapsed. His successor refused the Russian request to renew the Reinsurance Treaty, which he considered incompatible with the Austrian alliance. Political isolation and the need for foreign capital then drove the Russians toward France. The French, who were even more isolated, were glad to pour capital into Russia if it would help produce security against Germany. In 1894, the Franco-Russian alliance was signed.

Britain and Germany   Britain now became the key to the international situation. Colonial rivalries pitted the British against the Russians in Central Asia and against the French in Africa. Traditionally, Britain had also opposed Russian control of Constantinople and French control of the Low Countries. There was no reason to think that Britain would soon become friendly to its traditional rivals or abandon its friendliness toward the Germans. Yet within a decade of William II's accession, Germany had become the enemy in the minds of the British. The problem lay in Germany's foreign and naval policies.

At first Germany tried to win the British over to the Triple Alliance, but when Britain clung to "splendid isolation," Germany sought to demonstrate its worth as an ally by making trouble for Britain. The Germans began to exert pressure against Britain in Africa by barring British attempts to build a railroad from Capetown to Cairo. They also openly sympathized with the Boers of South Africa in their resistance to British expansion.

In 1898, William's dream of a German navy began to achieve reality with the passage of a naval law providing for nineteen battleships. In 1900, a second law doubled that figure. The architect of the new navy, Admiral Alfred von Tirpitz (1849–1930), proclaimed that Germany's naval policy was aimed at Britain. As the German navy grew and German policies seemed to become more threatening, the British abandoned their traditional policies.

Entente Cordiale   In 1902, Britain concluded an alliance with Japan to help defend British interests in the Far East against Russia. Next, Britain in 1904 made a series of agreements with the French, collectively called the Entente Cordiale. It was not a formal treaty and had no military provisions, but it settled all outstanding colonial differences between the two nations. The Entente Cordiale went far toward aligning the British with Germany's great potential enemy.

First Moroccan Crisis   In March 1905, William II landed at Tangier and challenged the French predominance there in a speech in favor of Moroccan independence. Germany's chancellor, Prince Bernhard von Bülow (1849–1929), intended to show France how weak it was and how little it could expect from Britain; he also hoped to gain colonial concessions.

The Germans might have achieved their aims, but they demanded an international conference to exhibit their power. The conference met in 1906 at Algeciras in Spain. Austria sided with its German ally, but Spain, Italy, and the United States voted with Britain and France. The French were confirmed in their position in Morocco, and German bullying had driven Britain and France closer together. Sir Edward Grey (1862–1933), the British foreign secretary, without making a firm commitment, authorized conversations between the British and French general staffs. By 1914, French and British military and naval plans were so mutually dependent that the two countries were effectively, if not formally, allies.

British Agreement with Russia   Hardly anyone believed that Britain and Russia could ever be allies. The Russo-Japanese war of 1904–1905 made such a development seem even less likely because Britain was allied with Russia's enemy. But defeat and the Russian Revolution of 1905 left Russia weak and reduced British apprehensions. The British were also concerned that Russia might drift into the German orbit.

QUICK REVIEW

First Moroccan Crisis

◆ March 1905: William II implies Germany has a role in furthering Moroccan independence

◆ Germany hoped to weaken relationship between France and Great Britain

◆ 1906: conference in Algeciras confirms France's claims in Morocco

With French support, in 1907 an agreement settled Russo-British quarrels in Central Asia and Persia and opened the door for wider cooperation. The Triple Entente, an informal but powerful association of Britain, France, and Russia, was now ranged against the Triple Alliance. Because Italy was unreliable, Germany and Austria-Hungary stood surrounded by two great land powers and Great Britain.

William II and his ministers had turned Bismarck's nightmare of the prospect of a two-front war with France and Russia into a reality and had added Britain to the hostile coalition. Bismarck's alliance system had been intended to maintain peace, but the new one increased the risk of war and made the Balkans, where Austrian and Russian ambitions clashed, a likely spot for it.

WORLD WAR I

THE ROAD TO WAR (1908–1914)

Except for the Greeks and the Romanians, most of the inhabitants of the Balkans were Slavs and felt a kinship with one another and with Russia. For centuries they had been ruled by Austrians, Hungarians, or Turks, and the nationalism that characterized late-nineteenth-century Europe made many of them eager for liberty or at least autonomy. The more radical among them longed for a union of the south Slavic, or Yugoslav, peoples in a single nation led by independent Serbia. They hoped to detach all the Slavic provinces (especially Bosnia, which bordered on Serbia) from Austria. Serbia was to unite the Slavs at the expense of Austria, as Piedmont had united the Italians and Prussia the Germans.

In 1908, modernizing reformers called the Young Turks overthrew the Ottoman government. This threatened to revive the empire and precipitated a series of Balkan crises that would lead to world war.

The Bosnian Crisis   In 1908, Austria and Russia decided to act before Turkey became stronger. They agreed to call an international conference in which each of them would support the other's demands. Russia would agree to the Austrian annexation of Bosnia and Herzegovina, and Austria would support Russia's request to open the Dardanelles to Russian warships.

Austria, however, declared the annexation unilaterally before any conference was called. The British, concerned about their own position in the Mediterranean, rejected the Russian demand. The Russians were furious. The Serbs were enraged by the annexation of Bosnia. The Russians were too weak to do anything but accept the new situation. The Germans were unhappy because Austria's action threatened their relations with Russia. But Germany felt so dependent on the Dual Alliance that it assured Austria of its support. To an extent, German policy was being made in Vienna. It was a dangerous precedent. At the same time, the failure of Britain and France to support Russia strained the Triple Entente and made it harder for them to oppose Russian interests again if they wanted to retain Russian friendship.

Second Moroccan Crisis   The second Moroccan crisis, in 1911, emphasized the French and British need for mutual support. When France sent an army to Morocco to put down a rebellion, Germany took the opportunity to extort colonial concessions in the French Congo by sending the gunboat *Panther* to the port of Agadir in Morocco, allegedly to protect German citizens there. As in 1905, the Germans went too far.

Anglo-German relations had already been deteriorating, chiefly because of the naval race. The British now mistakenly believed that the Germans meant to turn Agadir into a naval base on the Atlantic. The crisis passed when France yielded bits of the Congo and Germany withdrew from Morocco. The main result was to draw

WHAT CAUSED the outbreak of World War I in 1914?

The Austrian Archduke Franz Ferdinand and his wife in Sarajevo on June 28, 1914; in the photo above. Later in the day the royal couple were assassinated by young revolutionaries trained and supplied in Serbia, igniting the crisis that led to World War I. Moments after the assassination the Austrian police captured one of the assassins, shown in the photo below.

Brown Brothers

Britain closer to France. Plans were formulated for a British expeditionary force to help defend France against German attack, and the British and French navies agreed to cooperate.

The Balkan Wars After the second Moroccan crisis, Italy feared that France would move into Ottoman Libya. Consequently, in 1911 Italy attacked the Ottoman Empire to forestall the French, and obtained Libya and the Dodecanese Islands in the Aegean. The Italian victory encouraged the Balkan states to try their luck. In 1912, Bulgaria, Greece, Montenegro, and Serbia attacked the Ottoman Empire and won easily. The Serbs and the Bulgarians then quarreled about the division of Macedonia, and in 1913, Turkey and Romania joined Greece and Serbia against Bulgaria, which lost much of what it had gained since 1878.

The Austrians were determined to limit Serbian gains and prevent the Serbs from obtaining a port in Albania on the Adriatic. An international conference sponsored by Britain in early 1913 resolved the matter in Austria's favor and called for an independent kingdom of Albania. But Austria felt humiliated by the public airing of Serbian demands and in October unilaterally forced Serbia to withdraw from Albania. Russia again let Austria have its way.

The lessons learned from this affair influenced behavior in the final crisis of 1914. The Russians had, as in 1908, been embarrassed by their passivity, and their allies were now more reluctant to restrain them. The Austrians were determined not to accept an international conference again. They and their German allies had seen that better results might be obtained from a threat of force.

SARAJEVO AND THE OUTBREAK OF WAR (JUNE–AUGUST 1914)

The Assassination On June 28, 1914, a Bosnian nationalist killed the Austrian Archduke Francis Ferdinand (1863–1914), heir to the throne, and his wife in the Bosnian capital of Sarajevo. The assassin was a member of a conspiracy hatched by a political terrorist society. The chief of intelligence of the Serbian army had helped plan the crime. Even though his role was unknown at the time, it was generally believed that Serbian officials were involved.

Germany and Austria's Response The assassination was condemned throughout Europe. To those Austrians who had long favored an attack on Serbia as a solution to the empire's Slavic problem, the opportunity seemed irresistible. But Count Stefan Tisza (1861–1918), speaking for Hungary, resisted. Count Leopold Berchtold (1863–1942), the Austro-Hungarian foreign minister, knew that German support would be required if Russia should decide to protect Serbia and to persuade the Hungarians to accept a war. The question of peace or war, therefore, had to be answered in Berlin.

William II and Chancellor Theobald von Bethmann-Hollweg (1856–1921) promised German support for an attack on Serbia. They urged the Austrians to move swiftly, while the other powers were still angry at Serbia. They also indicated that a failure to act would be evidence of Austria-Hungary's uselessness as an ally. Therefore, the Austrians determined to attack Serbia. They hoped, with the protection of Germany, to avoid a general European conflict, but were prepared to risk one. The Germans also knew that they risked a general war, but hoped to "localize" the fight between Austria and Serbia.

These calculations proved to be incorrect. Bethmann-Hollweg hoped that the Austrians would strike while the outrage of the assassination was still fresh. He also hoped that German support would deter Russian involvement. Failing that, he was prepared for a continental war that would bring rapid victory over France and allow a full-scale attack on the Russians, who were always slow to bring their strength into action. The German chancellor convinced himself that the British would stand aloof.

However, the Austrians were slow to act. They did not even deliver their deliberately unacceptable ultimatum to Serbia until July 24, when the general hostility toward Serbia had begun to subside. Serbia returned a conciliatory answer, but the Austrians were determined not to turn back. On July 28 they declared war on Serbia, even though they could not field an army until mid-August.

The Triple Entente's Response   The Russians responded angrily to the Austrian demands on Serbia. The government ordered partial **mobilization**—the placing of its armed forces on a war footing—to pressure Austria to hold back its attack on Serbia.

Mobilization of any kind, however, was generally understood to be equivalent to an act of war. It was especially alarming to General Helmuth von Moltke (1848–1916), head of the German general staff. Russian mobilization could upset the delicate timing of Germany's battle plan—the **Schlieffen Plan**, which required an attack on France first—and would endanger Germany. From this point on, Moltke pressed for war. The pressure of military necessity became irresistible.

The western European powers were not eager for war. But the French gave the Russians the same assurances that Germany had given its ally. The British worked hard for another conference of the powers, but Austria would not hear of it. The Germans privately supported the Austrians but were publicly conciliatory in the hope of keeping the British neutral.

When Bethmann-Hollweg realized that if Germany attacked France, Britain would fight, he tried to persuade the Austrians to negotiate, but the Austrians could not retreat without losing their own self-respect and that of the Germans.

On July 30, Austria ordered mobilization against Russia. Russia and Germany then ordered general mobilization. The Schlieffen Plan went into effect. The Germans invaded Belgium on August 3, which violated the treaty of 1839, in which the British had guaranteed Belgian neutrality. This undermined sentiment in Britain for neutrality and united the nation against Germany. Germany then invaded France. On August 4, Britain declared war on Germany.

The Great War had begun. Europe would never be the same.

Coming of World War I

1871	End of the Franco-Prussian War; creation of the German Empire; German annexation of Alsace-Lorraine
1873	Three Emperors' League (Germany, Russia, and Austria-Hungary)
1875	Russo-Turkish War
1878	Congress of Berlin
1879	Dual Alliance between Germany and Austria
1881	Three Emperors' League is renewed
1882	Italy joins Germany and Austria in Triple Alliance
1888	William II becomes German emperor
1890	Bismarck dismissed
1894	Franco-Russian alliance
1898	Germany begins to build battleship navy
1902	British alliance with Japan
1904	Entente Cordiale between Britain and France
1904–1905	Russo-Japanese War
1905	First Moroccan crisis
1907	British agreement with Russia
1908–1909	Bosnian crisis
1911	Second Moroccan crisis; Italy attacks Turkey
1912–1913	First and Second Balkan wars
1914	Outbreak of World War I

mobilization   The placing of a country's military forces on a war footing.

Schlieffen Plan   Germany's plan for achieving a quick victory in the West at the outbreak of World War I by invading France through Belgium and Luxembourg.

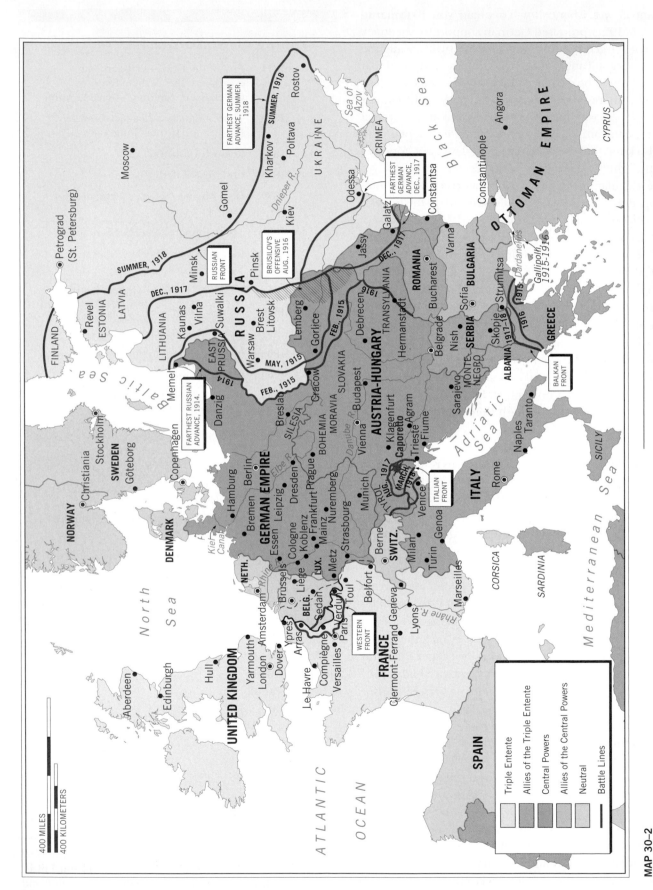

MAP 30–2
World War I in Europe   Despite the importance of military action in the Far East, in the Arab world, and at sea, the main theaters of activity in World War I were in the European areas shown here.

WHICH REGIONS were most affected by military action?

STRATEGIES AND STALEMATE (1914–1917)

Throughout Europe jubilation greeted the outbreak of war. No general war had been fought since Napoleon, and the horrors of modern warfare were not yet understood. The dominant memory was of Bismarck's swift and decisive campaigns, in which costs and casualties were light and the rewards great.

Both sides expected to take the offensive and win a quick victory. The Triple Entente powers—or the Allies, as they came to be called—had superior numbers and financial resources as well as command of the sea. Germany and Austria, the Central Powers, had the advantages of internal lines of communication and of having launched their attack first.

The War in the West   After 1905, Germany's war plan was the one developed by Count Alfred von Schlieffen (1833–1913), chief of the German general staff from 1891 to 1906. It aimed to sweep through Belgium to the Channel, then wheel to the south and east to envelop the French and crush them against the German fortresses in Lorraine. In the east, the Germans planned to stand on the defensive against Russia until France had been beaten, a task they thought would take only six weeks.

The execution of his plan, however, was left to Helmuth von Moltke, a gloomy and nervous man, who made enough tactical mistakes to cause it to fail by a narrow margin. As a result, the French and British were able to stop the Germans at the Battle of the Marne in September 1914.

Thereafter, the war in the west became one of position. Both sides dug in behind a wall of trenches protected by barbed wire that stretched from the North Sea to Switzerland. Machine-gun nests made assaults dangerous. Both sides, nonetheless, attempted massive attacks initiated by artillery bombardments of unprecedented force and duration. Still, the defense always prevented a breakthrough.

The War in the East   In the east, the Russians advanced into Austrian territory and inflicted heavy casualties, but Russian incompetence and German energy soon reversed the situation. General Erich Ludendorff (1865–1937), under the command of the elderly Paul von Hindenburg (1847–1934), destroyed or captured an entire Russian army at the Battle of Tannenberg. In 1915, the Central Powers drove into the Baltic states and western Russia, inflicting over two million casualties. Russian confidence was shaken.

Both sides sought new allies. Turkey and Bulgaria joined the Central Powers. Italy joined the Allies in 1915 after they agreed to give it *Italia Irredenta* (i.e., the Trentino, the South Tyrol, Trieste, and some of the Dalmatian Islands) from Austria after victory. Romania joined the Allies in 1916 but was quickly driven from the war. In the Far East, Japan honored its alliance with Britain and overran the German colonies in China and the Pacific.

In 1915, the Allies undertook to break the deadlock in the fighting by going around it. The idea came chiefly from Winston Churchill (1874–1965), First Lord of the British

22.4
The Perversion of Technology: War in "No Man's Land"

Italia Irredenta   Meaning "unredeemed Italy." Italian-speaking areas that had been left under Austrian rule at the time of the unification of Italy.

MAP EXPLORATION

Interactive map: To explore this map further, go to **http://www.prenhall.com/craig2/map30.3**

MAP 30–3
The Western Front 1914–1918.   This map shows the crucial Western Front in detail.

IF THE Germans had captured Paris, what effect would this have had on the war?

Women munitions workers in England. The First World War demanded more from the civilian populations than had previous wars, resulting in important social changes. The demands of the munitions industries and a shortage of men (so many of whom were in uniform) brought many women out of traditional roles at home and into factories and other war work.

Hulton Getty Picture Collection/Tony Stone Images

Admiralty. He proposed to attack the Dardanelles and capture Constantinople. This policy would knock Turkey from the war and ease communication with Russia. Success depended on daring leadership, but the attack was inept. Before the campaign was abandoned, the Allies lost almost 150,000 men.

Return to the West   Both sides turned back to the west in 1916. Erich von Falkenhayn (1861–1922), who had succeeded Moltke in September 1914, sought success by an attack on the French stronghold of Verdun. It failed. The Allies in turn launched a major offensive along the River Somme in July. The only result was enormous casualties on both sides.

The War at Sea   As the war continued, control of the sea became more important. The British imposed a strict blockade to starve out the enemy, regardless of international law. The Germans responded with submarine warfare to destroy British shipping and starve the British. They declared the waters around the British Isles a war zone, where even neutral ships would not be safe. Both policies were unwelcome to neutrals, and especially to the United States. But the sinking of neutral ships by German submarines was both more dramatic and offensive than Britain's blockade.

In 1915, the British liner *Lusitania* was torpedoed by a German submarine. Among the 1,200 drowned were 118 Americans. President Woodrow Wilson (1856–1924) protested, and the Germans desisted rather than further anger the United States. This development gave the Allies a considerable advantage. The German fleet that had cost so much money and had caused so much trouble played no significant part in the war.

America Enters the War   In December 1916, President Wilson attempted to bring about a negotiated peace. But neither side would give up its hopes for total victory. The war seemed likely to continue until one or both sides reached exhaustion. Two events early in 1917 changed the situation. On February 1, the Germans announced the resumption of unrestricted submarine warfare, which led the United States to declare war on Germany on April 6.

One of the deterrents to an earlier American intervention had been the presence of autocratic tsarist Russia among the Allies. Wilson could conceive of the war only as an idealistic crusade "to make the world safe for democracy." That problem was resolved in March 1917 by a revolution in Russia that overthrew the tsarist government.

23.1
The Bolshevik Seizure of Power
(November–December 1917)

WHY WERE the Bolsheviks able to seize power in Russia?

THE RUSSIAN REVOLUTION

The March Revolution in Russia was neither planned nor led by political faction. It was the result of the collapse of the monarchy's ability to govern. Military and domestic failures produced massive casualties, hunger, strikes, and disorganization. All political factions were discontented.

In early March 1917, strikes and demonstrations erupted in Petrograd, as Saint Petersburg had been renamed. The ill-disciplined troops in the city refused to fire on the demonstrators, and the tsar abdicated on March 15. The Duma formed a provisional government composed chiefly of Constitutional Democrats with Western sympathies. The various socialists also began to organize the workers into councils called *soviets*. They became estranged as the Constitutional Democratics failed to control the army or purge "reactionaries" from the government.

The provisional government decided to continue the war against Germany, but a new offensive in the summer of 1917 collapsed. Disillusionment with the war, shortages of food and other necessities, and the demand for land reform undermined the government, even after its leadership had been taken over by the moderate socialist Alexander Kerensky (1881–1970).

Ever since April the Bolsheviks had been working against the provisional government. The Germans had rushed V. I. Lenin (1870–1924) in a sealed train from his exile in Switzerland to Petrograd in the hope that he would cause trouble for the revolutionary government. The Bolsheviks demanded that all political power go to the soviets, which they controlled. They attempted a coup, but it failed. Lenin fled to Finland, and his chief collaborator, Leon Trotsky (1877–1940), was imprisoned.

An abortive right-wing countercoup gave the Bolsheviks another chance. Trotsky, released from prison, led the powerful Petrograd Soviet. Lenin returned in October and insisted that the time was ripe to take power. On November 6, the Bolsheviks seized power.

The victors moved to fulfill their promises and to assure their own security. The provisional government had decreed an election for late November to select a Constituent Assembly. The Social Revolutionaries won a large majority over the Bolsheviks. When the assembly gathered in January, the Red Army, controlled by the Bolsheviks, dispersed it. All other political parties ceased to function in any meaningful fashion. The Bolshevik government nationalized the land and turned it over to its peasant proprietors. Factory workers were put in charge of their plants. Banks were seized for the state, and the debt of the tsarist government was repudiated. The property of the church was also seized.

The Bolsheviks signed an armistice with Germany in December 1917. On March 3, 1918, they accepted the Treaty of Brest-Litovsk, by which Russia yielded Finland, Poland, the Baltic states, and the Ukraine. Some territory in the Transcaucasus region went to Turkey. The Bolsheviks also agreed to pay an indemnity. These terms were a high price to pay for peace, but the Bolsheviks needed time to impose their rule on Russia.

Until 1921, the Bolsheviks confronted massive domestic resistance. A civil war erupted between the

Petrograd Munitions workers demonstrating in 1917.

Rla-Novosti/Sovfoto/Eastfoto

The Allies promoted Arab efforts to secure independence from Turkey in an effort to remove Turkey from the war. Delegates to the peace conference of 1919 in Paris included British Colonel T.E. Lawrence, who helped lead the rebellion, and representatives from the Middle Eastern region. Prince Feisal, the third son of King Hussein, stands in the foreground of this picture; Colonel T. E. Lawrence is in the middle row, second from the right; and Brigadier General Nuri Pasha Said of Baghdad is second from the left.

Corbis-Bettmann

• HISTORY'S VOICES •

LENIN ESTABLISHES HIS DICTATORSHIP

fter the Bolshevik coup in October, elections for the Constituent Assembly were held in November. The results gave a majority to the Social Revolutionary Party and embarrassed the Bolsheviks. Using his control of the Red Army, Lenin closed the Constituent Assembly in January 1918, after it had met for only one day, and established the rule of a revolutionary elite and his own dictatorship. Here is the crucial Bolshevik decree.

WHAT REASONS does Lenin give for closing the legitimately elected Constituent Assembly? What other reasons might he have had? What were the soviets? Did they have a legitimate claim to the monopoly of political power? Was the dissolution of the assembly a temporary or permanent measure? What defense can be made for the Bolsheviks' action? Is it enough to justify that action?

. . . The Constituent Assembly, elected on the basis of lists drawn up prior to the October Revolution, was an expression of the old relation of political forces which existed when power was held by the compromisers and the Cadets. When the people at that time voted for the candidates for the Socialist-Revolutionary Party, they were not in a position to choose between the Right Socialist-Revolutionaries, the supporters of the bourgeoisie, and the Left Socialist-Revolutionaries, the supporters of Socialism. Thus, the Constituent Assembly, which was to

have been the crown of the bourgeois parliamentary republic, could not become an obstacle in the path of the October Revolution and the Soviet power.

The October Revolution, by giving the power to the Soviets, and through the Soviets to the toiling and exploited classes, aroused the desperate resistance of the exploiters, and in the crushing of this resistance it fully revealed itself as the beginning of the socialist revolution . . . the majority in the Constituent Assembly which met on January 5 was secured by the party of the Right Socialist-Revolutionaries, the party of Kerensky, Avksentyev and Chernov. Naturally, this party refused to discuss the absolutely clear, precise and unambiguous proposal of the supreme organ of Soviet power, the Central Executive Committee of the Soviets, to recognize the program of the Soviet power, to recognize the "Declaration of Rights of the Toiling and Exploited People," to recognize the October Revolution and the Soviet power. . . .

The Right Socialist-Revolutionary and Menshevik parties are in fact waging outside the walls of the Constituent Assembly a most desperate struggle against the Soviet power. . . .

Accordingly, the Central Executive Committee resolves: The Constituent Assembly is hereby dissolved.

Text excerpt from "Lenin, Draft Decree on the Dissolution of the Constituent Assembly" in *A Documentary History of Communism*, Vol. 1, R. V. Daniels, ed. Copyright © University Press of New England, pp. 71–72. Reprinted by permission of the editor.

White Russians Those Russians who opposed the Bolsheviks (the "Reds") in the Russian Civil War of 1918–1921.

"Red" Russians supporting the revolution and the **"White" Russians**, who opposed the Bolsheviks and received aid from the Allies. In the summer of 1918, the tsar and his family were murdered. However, led by Trotsky, the Red Army overcame the opposition. By, 1921, Lenin and his supporters were in firm control. (See "Lenin Establishes His Dictatorship.")

END OF WORLD WAR I

MILITARY RESOLUTION

WHY DID the Versailles settlement leave Germany bitter?

The Treaty of Brest-Litovsk brought Germany to the peak of its success. In 1918, it decided to gamble everything on a last offensive. But the German army could not get beyond the Marne. Germany was exhausted. The Allies, on the other hand, were bolstered by the arrival of American troops in ever increasing numbers.

They launched a counteroffensive that was irresistible. As the Austrian fronts in the Balkans and Italy collapsed, the German high command knew that the end was imminent but wanted peace to be made before the army could be thoroughly defeated in the field, so that the responsibility should fall on civilians. The army therefore allowed a new government to be established on democratic principles to seek peace. The new government, under Prince Max of Baden (1867–1928), asked for peace on the basis of the **Fourteen Points** that President Wilson had declared as the American war aims. These were idealistic principles, but Wilson insisted that he would deal only with a democratic German government that spoke for the German people.

The disintegration of the German army forced William II to abdicate on November 9, 1918. The Social Democratic Party proclaimed a republic to prevent the establishment of a soviet government under the control of their Leninist wing. Two days later this republican, socialist-led government signed an armistice and accepted German defeat. The German people were, in general, unaware that their army had been defeated. No foreign soldier stood on German soil. Many Germans expected a mild settlement. The real peace embittered the German people, many of whom came to believe that Germany had been stabbed in the back by republicans and socialists at home.

The casualties on all sides came to about 10 million dead and twice as many wounded. The financial resources of the European states were badly strained. The victorious Allies, formerly creditors to the world, became debtors to the new American colossus.

The old international order, moreover, was dead. Russia was ruled by a Bolshevik dictatorship that preached world revolution. Germany was in chaos. Austria-Hungary had disintegrated. These kinds of change stirred the colonial empires ruled by the European powers; they would never again be as secure as they had seemed before the war. Europe was no longer the center of the world, free to interfere when it wished or to ignore the outer regions if it chose. Its easy confidence in progress was shattered by four years of horrible war. The memory of that war shook the nerve of the victorious Western powers in the postwar world.

SETTLEMENT AT PARIS

The Peacemakers   The representatives of the victorious states gathered at Versailles and other Parisian suburbs in the first half of 1919. Wilson speaking for the United States, David Lloyd George (1863–1945) for Britain, Georges Clemenceau (1841–1929) for France, and Vittorio Emanuele Orlando (1860–1952) for Italy made up the Big Four. Japan also had an important part in the discussions.

Wilson's idealism came into conflict with the war aims of the victorious powers and with the secret treaties that had been made before and during the war. The British and French people had been told that Germany would be made to pay for the war. Romania had been promised Transylvania at the expense of Hungary. Italy and Serbia had competing claims in the Adriatic. During the war, the British had encouraged Arab hopes of an independent Arab state carved out of the Ottoman Empire; those plans conflicted with the Balfour Declaration (1917), in which the British also seemed to accept Zionism and to promise the Jews a national home in Palestine. Both of these plans conflicted with an Anglo-French agreement to divide the Near East between themselves.

22.6
The Balfour Declaration

Fourteen Points   President Woodrow Wilson's (1856–1924) idealistic war aims.

OVERVIEW

CASUALTIES OF THE MAJOR BELLIGERENTS IN WORLD WAR 1

During World War I, Europeans turned the vast military and industrial power they had created in the nineteenth century against themselves. The result was an unprecedented slaughter that killed millions of soldiers and sailors and wounded many millions more. These casualties represented not only a waste of human life and talent but also the loss of consumers and producers. So traumatic were the losses that most Europeans were horrified at the prospect of another war. (In percentage terms, the French dead alone were the equivalent of the total populations—every man, woman, and child—of the states of Massachusetts, Connecticut, and Rhode Island.) The casualties of World War I help explain why the leaders of Britain and France sought to avoid another by adopting a policy of appeasement toward Hitler's demands in the late 1930s. No responsible statesman, they believed, would inflict another such slaughter on the nations of Europe.

Country	Killed	Wounded	Total Killed as Percentage of Population
Austria-Hungary	1.1 million	3.62 million	1.9
Belgium	38,000	44,000	0.5
Britain	723,000	1.16 million	1.6
Bulgaria	88,000	152,000	1.9
France	1.4 million	2 million	3.4
Germany	2 million	4.2 million	3.0
Italy	578,000	947,000	1.6
Romania	250,000	120,000	3.3
Russia	1.8 million	1.45 million	1.1
Serbia	278,000	138,000	5.7
Turkey	804,000	400,000	3.7
United States	114,000	205,000	0.1

The national goals of the victors presented further obstacles to an idealistic "peace without victors." France was eager to achieve a settlement that would permanently weaken Germany and preserve French political and military superiority. Italy sought to acquire *Italia Irredenta*; Britain looked to its imperial interests; Japan pursued its own advantage in Asia; and the United States insisted on freedom of the seas, which favored American commerce, and on its right to maintain the Monroe Doctrine.

Finally, the peacemakers of 1919 faced a world in turmoil. The greatest immediate threat appeared to be Bolshevism. While Lenin and his colleagues were distracted by civil war, the Allies landed small armies in Russia to help overthrow the Bolshevik regime. Communist governments were established in Bavaria and Hungary. Berlin also experienced an abortive communist uprising. The Allies were so worried that they supported the suppression of these communist movements by right-wing forces. They even permitted an army of German volunteers to fight the Bolsheviks in the Baltic states. But fear of Germany remained the chief concern for France, and traditional interests governed the policies of the other Allies.

The Peace   The Paris settlement consisted of five separate treaties between the victors and the defeated powers. The Soviet Union (as Russia was now called) and Germany were excluded from the peace conference. The Germans were simply presented with a treaty and compelled to accept it. The principle of national self-determination was violated often, as was unavoidable. The undeserved adulation accorded Wilson on his arrival turned into equally undeserved scorn. He had not abandoned his ideals but had given way to the irresistible force of reality.

The League of Nations   Wilson put great faith in the new **League of Nations**. Its covenant was an essential part of the peace treaty. The league was not intended as an international government but as a body of sovereign states that agreed to pursue common policies. If war threatened, the members promised to submit the matter to an international court or the League Council. Refusal to abide by this agreement would justify league intervention in the form of economic or military sanctions.

But the league had no armed forces. Action required the unanimous consent of its council, consisting of Britain, France, Italy, the United States, Japan, and four other states that had temporary seats. The league was generally seen as a device to ensure the security of the victorious powers. The exclusion of Germany and the Soviet Union further undermined the league's claim to evenhandedness.

Provisions of the covenant that dealt with colonial areas and disarmament were ineffective. Members of the league remained fully sovereign and pursued their national interests.

Germany   In the west, the main territorial issue was the fate of Germany (see Map 30–2). The French would have liked to set up the Rhineland as a buffer state, but Lloyd George and Wilson would not permit that. But France did receive Alsace-Lorraine and the right to work the coal mines of the Saar for 15 years. Germany west of the Rhine, and 50 kilometers east of it, was to be a demilitarized zone; Allied troops could stay on the west bank for 15 years. The treaty also provided that Britain and the United States would guarantee to aid France if it were attacked by Germany. Such an attack was made more unlikely by the permanent disarmament of Germany. Its army was limited to 100,000 men; its fleet was all but eliminated; and it was forbidden to have war planes, submarines, tanks, heavy artillery, or poison gas. As long as these provisions were observed, France would be safe.

The East   The settlement in the east ratified the collapse of the empires that had ruled it for centuries. Germany lost part of Silesia, and East Prussia was cut off from the rest of Germany by a corridor carved out to give the revived state of Poland access to the sea. The Austro-Hungarian Empire disappeared. Most of its German-speaking people in the small Republic of Austria were forbidden to unite with Germany. The Magyars occupied the much-reduced kingdom of Hungary.

The Czechs of Bohemia and Moravia joined with the Slovaks and Ruthenians to form Czechoslovakia, which also included several million unhappy Germans. The southern Slavs were united in the kingdom of Serbs, Croats,

League of Nations The association of sovereign states set up after World War I to pursue common policies and avert international aggression.

MAP 30–4

World War I peace settlement in Europe and the Middle East. The map of central and eastern Europe, as well as that of the Middle East, underwent drastic revision after World War I. The enormous territorial losses suffered by Germany, Austria-Hungary, the Ottoman Empire, Bulgaria, and Russia were the other side of the coin represented by gains for France, Italy, Greece, and Romania and by the appearance, or reappearance, of at least eight new independent states from Finland in the north to Yugoslavia in the south. The mandate system for former Ottoman territories outside Turkey proper laid foundations for several new, mostly Arab, states in the Middle East.

HOW DID the disappearance of Austria-Hungary create problems for the future of Central Europe?

and Slovenes, or Yugoslavia. Italy gained the Trentino and Trieste. Romania gained Transylvania from Hungary and Bessarabia from Russia. Bulgaria lost territory to Greece and Yugoslavia. Finland, Estonia, Latvia, and Lithuania became independent states, and much of Poland was carved out of formerly Russian soil.

The old Ottoman Empire also disappeared. The new republic of Turkey was limited to little more than Constantinople and Asia Minor. Palestine and Iraq came under British control and Syria and Lebanon under French control as mandates under the purely theoretical authority of the League of Nations. Germany's former colonies in Africa and the Pacific were divided among the victors.

Reparations   Before the armistice, the Germans promised to pay compensation "for all damages done to the civilian population of the Allies and their property." However, France and Britain were eager to have Germany pay the full cost of the war. No sum was fixed at the conference. Germany was to pay $5 billion annually until 1921, when a final figure would be set, which Germany would have to pay within 30 years. The French calculated that either Germany would be bled into impotence or refuse to pay and justify French intervention.

To justify these huge **reparation** payments, the Allies inserted the notorious **war guilt clause** into the treaty, which placed the responsibility for the war solely on Germany. The Germans bitterly resented the charges but had to accept the treaty as it was written by the victors without negotiation. The German government led by the Social Democrats and the Catholic Center Party signed the treaty. These parties formed the backbone of the German Republic, but they never overcame the stigma of accepting the treaty.

EVALUATION OF THE PEACE

Few peace settlements have been more attacked than the Treaty of Versailles, but many of the attacks on it are unjustified. Germany was neither dismembered nor ruined. Reparations were scaled down, and until the Great Depression of the 1930s, the German economy recovered. The attempt at achieving self-determination for nationalities was less than perfect, but it was the best Europe had ever accomplished.

The peace, nevertheless, was unsatisfactory. The elimination of the Austro-Hungarian Empire, however inevitable, created serious problems. Economically it was disastrous, for it separated raw materials from manufacturing areas and producers from their markets. Poland and especially Czechoslovakia contained unhappy German minorities. Disputes over territories in eastern Europe promoted further tension. The peace also rested on a defeat that Germany did not admit. The Germans believed they had been cheated, not defeated.

Finally, the peace failed to accept reality. Germany and Russia must inevitably play an important part in European affairs, yet they were excluded from the settlement and from the League of Nations. Given the many discontented parties, the peace was not self-enforcing; yet no satisfactory machinery for enforcing it was established. The league was never a serious force for this purpose. It was left to France, with no guarantee of support from Britain and no hope of help from the United States, to defend the new arrangements. France was simply not strong enough for the task if Germany were to rearm. The Treaty of Versailles was neither conciliatory enough to remove the desire for change, nor harsh enough to make another war impossible.

reparations   The requirement incorporated into the Versailles Treaty that Germany should pay for the cost of World War I.

war guilt clause   Clause of the Versailles Treaty, which assigned responsibility for World War I solely to Germany.

SUMMARY

The New Imperialism European imperialism in the last part of the nineteenth century brought the Western countries into contact with most of the world. By 1914, European nations had divided Africa among themselves and controlled large parts of Asia and the islands of the Pacific. Much of the Middle East was under the nominal control of the Ottoman Empire, which was in its death throes and under European influence. The Monroe Doctrine made Latin America a protectorate of the United States. Japan had become an imperial power at the expense of China and Korea.

World War I The emergence of a new, powerful German state at the center of Europe upset the old balance of power. Bismarck, however, preserved the peace for as long as he remained in power. The new German emperor, William II, abandoned the policy of restraint and sought more power and influence for his country. The result was a system of alliances that divided Europe into two armed camps. What began as yet another Balkan War involving the European powers became a world war that influenced the rest of the world. As the terrible war of 1914–1918 dragged on, the real motives that had driven the European powers to fight gave way to public affirmations of the principles of nationalism and self-determination.

The Peace Settlement The peoples under colonial rule took these statements seriously and sought to win their own independence and nationhood. For the most part they were disappointed by the peace settlement. The British and French Empires were larger than ever. The Americans added to the islands they controlled in the Pacific. Japanese imperial ambitions were rewarded at the expense of China.

However, the old imperial nations, especially Britain and France, had paid an enormous price in lives, money, and will for their victory in the war. Colonial peoples pressed for the rights that were proclaimed as universal by the West but denied to their colonies; influential minorities in the countries that ruled them sympathized with colonial aspirations for independence. Tension between colonies and their ruling nations was a cause of instability in the world created by the Paris treaties of 1919.

IMAGE KEY

for pages 666–667

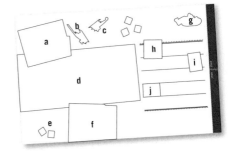

a. The sinking of the Lusitania
b. British Biplane
c. A red triplane with the German iron cross
d. *Gassed* by John Singer Sargent
e. Dice containing the flags of France, Britain, Belgium, Japan, and Russia
f. Gas shells
g. Renault Tank, 1917
h. American cartoon from 1882 depicting John Bull (England) as the octopus of imperialism
i. Bismarck and Kaiser William II in 1888
j. Alexander Gerasimov *Lenin at the Tribune* 1930

REVIEW QUESTIONS

1. What role did Bismarck envisage for the new Germany after 1871?

2. Why did Britain abandon "splendid isolation"?

3. How did developments in the Balkans lead to the outbreak of World War I? Did Germany want a general war?

4. Why did Germany lose World War I? Was Versailles too harsh or too conciliatory? How might it have been improved?

5. Why was Lenin successful in establishing Bolshevik rule in Russia? What role did Trotsky play?

KEY TERMS

Fourteen Points   (p. 681)
Italia Irredenta   (p. 677)
League of Nations   (p. 683)
mobilization   (p. 675)

New Imperialism   (p. 668)
Pan-Slavic movement   (p. 669)
reparations   (p. 685)
Schlieffen Plan   (p. 675)

war guilt clause   (p. 685)
White Russians   (p. 680)

 For additional study resources for this chapter, go to:
www.prenhall.com/craig/chapter30

Hitler's mastery of the techniques of mass politics and propaganda—including huge staged rallies like this one in 1938—was an important factor in his rise to power.

Bildarchiv Preubischer Kulturbesitz

31

DEPRESSION, EUROPEAN DICTATORS, AND THE AMERICAN NEW DEAL

WHAT FACTORS made the Great Depression so severe and longlasting?

HOW DID Stalin gain and keep power in the Soviet Union?

WHY DID the Fascists achieve power in Italy?

WHAT ROLE did terror play in Nazi Germany?

HOW DID FDR's policies affect the role of the federal government?

IMAGE KEY

Image Key for pages 688–689
is on page 708.

In the two decades that followed the Paris Settlement, the western world saw a number of experiments in politics and economic life. Two broad factors accounted for these experiments. First, the war, the Russian Revolution, and the peace treaty had transformed the political face of Europe. The new regimes that emerged in the wake of the collapse of the monarchies of Germany, Austria-Hungary, and Russia faced economic dislocation and nationalistic resentments.

Second, the Great Depression caused political instability and economic crisis. In Europe this often produced authoritarian regimes. In the United States it led to an increased role for the federal government.

AFTER VERSAILLES: DEMANDS FOR REVISION AND ENFORCEMENT

The Paris settlement fostered resentments that counted among the chief political factors in Europe for the next two decades. The arrangements for reparations led to endless haggling. National groups in eastern Europe felt that injustice had been done to them and demanded border adjustments. The victorious powers, especially France, often believed that the treaty was being inadequately enforced. Too many political figures were willing to fish in these troubled international waters for domestic votes.

TOWARD THE GREAT DEPRESSION IN EUROPE

WHAT FACTORS made the Great Depression so severe and long-lasting?

Three factors combined to bring about the severity and the extended length of the **Great Depression**. First, a financial crisis stemmed directly from the war and the peace settlement. To this was added a crisis in the production and distribution of goods in the world market. Finally, these difficulties were exacerbated because no major western European country or the United States provided responsible economic leadership.

FINANCIAL TAILSPIN

France was determined to collect reparations from Germany. The United States was no less determined that its allies repay the wartime loans it had extended to them. German reparations were to provide the means of repaying these debts.

The quest for payment of German reparations caused one of the major diplomatic crises of the 1920s; the crisis itself resulted in further economic upheaval. In early 1923, the Allies—and France in particular—declared Germany to be in default of its reparation payments. On January 11, French troops occupied the Ruhr mining and manufacturing district. The **Weimar Republic** ordered passive resistance. Confronted with this tactic, the French ran the German mines and railroads. The Germans paid, but Britain became more sympathetic to Germany. The cost of the Ruhr occupation, moreover, damaged the French economy.

The political and economic turmoil of the Ruhr invasion led to international attempts to ease the German payment of reparations. The most famous of these were the Dawes Plan of 1924 and the Young Plan of 1929, both devised by Americans. At the same time, American investment capital was pouring into Europe. However, the crash of Wall Street in October 1929—the result of unregulated speculation—saw the loss of large amounts of money. Thereafter, little American capital was available for investment in Europe.

In May 1931, the Kreditanstalt collapsed. It was a primary lending institution for much of central and eastern Europe. The German banking system then came

Great Depression A prolonged worldwide economic downturn that began in 1929 with the collapse of the New York Stock Exchange.

Weimar Republic The German democratic regime that existed between the end of World War I and Hitler's coming to power in 1933.

under severe pressure. As the German difficulties increased, U.S. president Herbert Hoover (1874–1964) announced in June 1931 a one-year moratorium on all payments of international debts. The Hoover moratorium was a prelude to the end of reparations. In the summer of 1932, the Lausanne Conference, in effect, ended the era of reparations.

PROBLEMS IN AGRICULTURAL COMMODITIES

The 1920s witnessed a contraction in the market demand for European goods. The difficulty arose from agriculture. Better methods of farming and more extensive transport facilities all over the globe vastly increased the quantity of grain. Wheat prices fell to record lows. This decreased the income of European farmers, while the cost of the industrial goods they used rose. Consequently, they had great difficulty paying off their debts. These problems were especially acute in central and eastern Europe and abetted farmers' disillusionment with liberal politics.

One of the last American soldiers killed on the Western Front in November 1918. The carnage of World War I was one of the main causes of European weakness and instability in the 1920s and 1930s.

American Stock/Archive Photos

Outside Europe similar problems affected producers of wheat, sugar, coffee, rubber, wool, and lard. The people who produced these goods in underdeveloped nations could no longer make enough money to buy finished goods from industrial Europe. Commodity production had outstripped world demand.

The result was stagnation and depression for European industry. Coal, iron, and textiles had depended largely on international markets. Unemployment spread from these industries to those producing consumer goods. Unemployment in Britain and Germany during the 1920s had created "soft" domestic markets. The policies of reduced spending with which the governments confronted the Depression further weakened domestic demand. By the early 1930s the Depression was feeding on itself.

DEPRESSION AND GOVERNMENT POLICY

The Depression did not mean absolute economic decline or total unemployment. However, the economic downturn made people insecure. Even the employed often seemed to make no progress, and their anxieties created discontent.

The governments of the late 1920s and the early 1930s were not well suited to confront these problems. The electorates demanded action. The government response depended largely on the severity of the Depression in a particular country and on the self-confidence of its political system.

Great Britain and France undertook moderate political experiments. In 1924, the Labour Party in Great Britain established itself as a viable governing party. Under the pressure of the Depression, the Labour prime minister Ramsay MacDonald (1866–1937) organized a National Government, which was a coalition of the Labour, Conservative, and Liberal Parties. It remained in power until 1935, when a Conservative ministry led by Stanley Baldwin (1867–1947) replaced it.

The most important French political experiment was the **Popular Front** Ministry, which came to office in 1936. It was composed of socialists, radicals, and communists—the first time that socialists and communists had cooperated in a ministry. It addressed major labor problems in the French economy, but by 1938 the Popular Front was at an end.

The political experiments of the 1920s and 1930s that reshaped world history involved a Soviet government in Russia, a Fascist regime in Italy, and a Nazi dictatorship in Germany.

Popular Front A government of all left-wing parties that took power in France in 1936 to enact social and economic reforms.

THE SOVIET EXPERIMENT

HOW DID Stalin gain and keep power in the Soviet Union?

The Bolshevik Revolution in Russia led to the most durable of all twentieth-century authoritarian governments. The Communist Party of the Soviet Union retained power from 1917 until the end of 1991, and it influenced the history of much of the world like no other single factor. Unlike the Italian fascists or the German national socialists, the bolsheviks seized power violently through revolution. Their leaders long felt insecure about their hold on the country. The Communist Party was not a mass party nor a nationalistic one. The bolsheviks confronted a much less industrialized economy than that in Italy or Germany. They believed in and practiced the collectivization of economic life attacked by the right-wing dictatorships. The Marxist-Leninist ideology was broader than the nationalism of the fascists and the racism of the Nazis. Communism was an exportable commodity. The communists regarded their government and their revolution as epoch-making events in the development of humanity. Fear of communism and determination to stop its spread were leading political forces in western Europe and the United States for most of the rest of the century and would influence their relationships to much of the rest of the world. (See "A Communist Woman Demands a New Family Life.")

WAR COMMUNISM

Within months of the revolution, a new secret police, known as *Cheka*, appeared. Throughout the Russian civil war Lenin had declared that the Bolshevik Party, as the vanguard of the revolution, was imposing the dictatorship of the proletariat. Under the economic policy of **"War Communism,"** the revolutionary government confiscated the banks, the transport facilities, and heavy industry. The state also requisitioned grain and shipped it from the countryside to feed the army and the cities.

"War Communism" helped the Red Army defeat its opponents. The revolution had survived and triumphed. The policy, however, generated domestic opposition. Many Russians were no longer willing to make the sacrifices demanded by the central party bureaucrats. In 1920 and 1921, strikes occurred. Peasants resisted the requisition of grain. In March 1921, the navy mutinied. Each of these incidents suggested that the proletariat itself was opposing the dictatorship of the proletariat. Also, by late 1920 it had become clear that revolution would not sweep across the rest of Europe. The Soviet Union was a vast island of revolutionary socialism in a sea of worldwide capitalism.

THE NEW ECONOMIC POLICY

Lenin made a strategic retreat. In March 1921, he outlined the **New Economic Policy**, or **NEP**. Apart from "the commanding heights" of banking, heavy industry, transportation, and international commerce, private economic enterprise was allowed and peasants could farm for a profit. The countryside became more stable, and a secure food supply seemed assured for the cities. Similar free enterprise flourished within light industry and retail trade. The revolution seemed to have transformed Russia into a land of small farms and private shops and businesses.

STALIN VERSUS TROTSKY

The NEP had caused sharp disputes within the Politburo, the highest governing committee of the Communist Party. These frictions increased when Lenin suffered a stroke in 1922 and died in 1924. An intense struggle for leadership of the party

War Communism The economic policy adopted by the Bolsheviks during the Russian Civil War to seize the banks, heavy industry, railroads, and grain.

New Economic Policy (NEP) A limited revival of capitalism, especially in light industry and agriculture, introduced by Lenin in 1921 to repair the damage inflicted on the Russian economy by the Civil War and War Communism.

◆ HISTORY'S VOICES ◆

A COMMUNIST WOMAN DEMANDS A NEW FAMILY LIFE

While Lenin sought to consolidate the Bolshevik Revolution against internal and external enemies, there existed within the young Soviet Union a vast utopian impulse to change and reform virtually every social institution that had existed before the revolution or that communists associated with capitalist society. Alexandra Kollontai (1872–1952) was a spokesperson of the extreme political left within the early Soviet Union. There had been much speculation on how the end of bourgeois society might change the structure of the family and the position of women. In this passage written in 1920, Kollontai states one of the most idealistic visions of this change. During the years immediately after the revolution, extreme rumors circulated in both Europe and America about sexual and family experimentation in the Soviet Union. Statements such as this fostered such rumors. Kollontai herself later became a supporter of Stalin and a Soviet diplomat.

WHY DID Kollontai see the restructuring of the family as essential to the establishment of a new kind of Communist society? Would these changes make people loyal to that society? What changes in society does the kind of economic independence she seeks for women presuppose? What might childhood be like in this society?

There is no escaping the fact: the old type of family has seen its day. It is not the fault of the Communist State, it is the result of the changed conditions of life. The family is ceasing to be a necessity of the State, as it was in the past; on the contrary, it is worse than useless, since it needlessly holds back the female workers from more productive and far more serious work. . . . But on the ruins of the former family we shall soon see a new form rising which will involve altogether different relations between men and women, and which will be a union of affection and comradeship, a union of two equal members of the Communist society, both of them free, both of them independent, both of them workers. No more domestic "servitude" of women. No

more inequality within the family. No more fear on the part of the woman lest she remain without support or aid with little ones in her arms if her husband should desert her. The woman in the Communist city no longer depends on her husband but on her work. It is not her husband but her robust arms which will support her. There will be no more anxiety as to the fate of her children. The State of the Workers will assume responsibility for these. Marriage will be purified of all its material elements, of all money calculations, which constitute a hideous blemish on family life in our days. . . .

The woman who is called upon to struggle in the great cause of the liberation of the workers—such a woman should know that in the new State there will be no more room for such petty divisions as were formerly understood: "These are my own children, to them I owe all my maternal solicitude, all my affection; those are your children, my neighbour's children; I am not concerned with them. I have enough to do with my own." Henceforth the worker-mother, who is conscious of her social function, will rise to a point where she no longer differentiates between yours and mine; she must remember that there are henceforth only our children, those of the Communist State, the common possession of all the workers.

The Workers' State has need of a new form of relation between the sexes. The narrow and exclusive affection of the mother for her own children must expand until it embraces all the children of the great proletarian family. In place of the indissoluble marriage based on the servitude of woman, we shall see rise the free union, fortified by the love and mutual respect of the two members of the Workers' State, equal in their rights and in their obligations. In place of the individual and egotistic family there will arise a great universal family of workers, in which all the workers, men and women, will be, above all, workers, comrades.

From *Communism and the Family* by Alexandra Kollontai, as reprinted in Rudolf Schlesinger, ed. and trans., *The Family in the USSR*, London: Routledge and Kegan Paul, 1949, pp. 67–69. Reprinted by permission.

commenced. Two factions emerged. One was led by Trotsky; the other by Joseph Stalin (1879–1953), who had become general secretary of the party in 1922.

The struggle was fought over the question of Russia's path toward industrialization and the future of the communist revolutionary movement. Trotsky, speaking for what became known as the left wing, urged rapid industrialization and looked to voluntary collectivization of farming by poor peasants as a means of increasing agricultural production. Trotsky further argued that the revolution in Russia could succeed only if new revolutions took place elsewhere.

A right-wing faction opposed Trotsky. Stalin was its manipulator. This group pressed for the continuation of Lenin's NEP.

Stalin was the ultimate victor. His power lay in his command of bureaucratic and administrative methods. He mastered the crucial details of party structure, including admission and promotion. He had the support of the lower levels of the party when he clashed with other leaders.

In 1924, Stalin enunciated, in opposition to Trotsky, the doctrine of "socialism in one country." Russian success did not depend on the fate of the revolution elsewhere. Stalin thus nationalized the previously international scope of the Marxist revolution. By 1927, Trotsky had been ousted from the party. In 1929, he was expelled from Russia and was eventually murdered in 1940 by one of Stalin's agents. With the removal of Trotsky, Stalin was firmly in control of the Soviet state.

DECISION FOR RAPID INDUSTRIALIZATION

During the Depression, the Soviet Union registered tremendous industrial advance. As usual in Russia, the direction and impetus came from the top. Stalin far exceeded the tsars in the coercion and terror he brought to the task. Russia achieved its economic growth during the 1930s only at the cost of millions of human lives.

Through 1928, Lenin's NEP had steered Soviet economic development. A few farmers, the *kulaks*, had become prosperous. During 1928 and 1929, they and other farmers withheld grain from the market because prices were too low. Food shortages in the cities caused unrest. Stalin came to a momentous decision. Russia must industrialize rapidly to match the power of the West. Agriculture must be collectivized to produce sufficient grain for food and export and to free peasant labor for the factories. This program, which basically embraced Trotsky's earlier economic position, unleashed a second Russian revolution.

Agricultural Policy In 1929, Stalin ordered party agents to confiscate hoarded wheat. As part of the general plan to collectivize farming, the government undertook to eliminate the *kulaks* as a class. A *kulak*, however, soon came to mean any peasant who opposed Stalin's policy. In the countryside, peasants at all levels of wealth resisted stubbornly. They wreaked their vengeance on the policy of **collectivization** by slaughtering more than 100 million horses and cattle between 1929 and 1933. The situation in the countryside amounted to open warfare.

As many as 10 million peasants were killed, and millions of others were sent to labor camps. Because of the turmoil, there was famine in 1932 and 1933. Yet Stalin persevered. Peasants had their lands incorporated into large collective farms. The state controlled the machinery for these units.

The government now had primary direction over the food supply. The peasants could no longer determine whether there would be stability or unrest in the cities. Stalin and the Communist Party had won the battle of the wheat fields, but the problem of producing enough grain still plagues the former Soviet Union.

collectivization The bedrock of Stalinist agriculture, which forced Russian peasants to give up their private farms and work as members of collectives, large agricultural units controlled by the state.

By the mid-1930s Stalin's purges had eliminated many leaders and other members from the Soviet Communist Party. This photograph of a meeting of a party congress in 1936 shows a number of the surviving leaders with Stalin, who sits fourth from the right in the front row. To his left is Vyacheslav Molotov, long-time foreign minister. The first person on the left in the front row is Nikita Khrushchev, who headed the Soviet Union in the late 1950s and early 1960s.

Itar-Tass/Sovfoto/Eastfoto

Five-Year Plans   The revolution in agriculture had been undertaken for the sake of industrialization. The increased grain supply was to feed the labor force and provide exports to finance the imports required for industrial development. The industrial achievement of the Soviet Union between 1928 and World War II was one of the most striking accomplishments of the twentieth century. Russia made a more rapid advance toward economic growth than any other nation in the western world has ever achieved during a similar period of time. Soviet industrial production rose approximately 400 percent between 1928 and 1940. Few consumer goods were produced. The labor for this development was supplied internally. Capital was raised from the export of grain, even at the cost of internal shortage. The technology was borrowed from industrialized nations.

The organizational vehicle for industrialization was a series of five-year plans first begun in 1928. The State Planning Commission, or Gosplan, set goals of production and organized the economy to meet them. Coordinating all facets of production was difficult and complicated. A vast program of propaganda was undertaken to sell the five-year plans to the Russian people. The industrial labor force became subject to regimentation similar to that being imposed on the peasants. The accomplishment of the three five-year plans probably allowed the Soviet Union to survive the German invasion.

Many non-Russian contemporaries looked at the Soviet economic experiment uncritically. While the capitalist world lay in the throes of the Depression, the Soviet economy had grown at an unprecedented pace. These observers seemed to have had little idea of the social cost of the Soviet achievement. Millions had been killed or uprooted. The suffering and human loss during those years will probably never be known; it far exceeded anything described by Marx and Engels in relation to nineteenth-century industrialization in western Europe.

THE PURGES

Stalin's decisions to industrialize rapidly and to move against the peasants aroused internal political opposition because they were departures from the policies of Lenin. In 1933, Stalin began to fear that he would lose control over the party apparatus. These fears were probably paranoid. Nevertheless, they resulted in the **Great Purges**, among the most mysterious and horrendous political events of this century.

On December 1, 1934, Sergei Kirov (1888–1934), the popular party chief of Leningrad (formerly Saint Petersburg), was assassinated. In the wake of the shooting, thousands of people were arrested, and still more were expelled from the party and sent to labor camps. It now seems certain that Stalin himself authorized Kirov's assassination to forestall any threat from him.

The purges after Kirov's death were just the beginning. Between 1936 and 1938, spectacular show trials were held in Moscow. Previous high Soviet leaders publicly confessed political crimes and were executed. Their confessions were palpably false. Other leaders and party members were tried in private and shot. Thousands of people received no trial at all. It is inexplicable why some were executed, others sent to labor camps, and still others left unmolested. After the civilian party members had been purged, important officers, including heroes of the civil war, were killed. The exact numbers of executions and imprisonments are unknown but ran into the millions.

The scale of the political turmoil was unprecedented. The Russians themselves did not comprehend what was occurring. The only rational explanation is found in Stalin's concern for his own power. The purges created a new party structure absolutely loyal to him.

Despite the violence and repression, the Soviet experiment found many sympathizers. The Soviet Union after the Bolshevik seizure of power had fostered Communist Parties subservient to Moscow throughout the world. Others who were not members of these parties sympathized with what they believed were the goals of the Soviet Union. During at least the first fifty years of its existence, the Soviet Union managed to capture the imagination of some intellectuals around the globe who hoped for a utopian egalitarian transformation of society. During much of the 1930s, the Soviet Union also appeared as an enemy to the fascist experiments in Italy and Germany. The Marxist ideology championed by the Soviet Union appeared to many people living in the European colonial empires as a vehicle for freeing themselves. The Soviet Union welcomed and trained many such anti-colonial leaders. With what is now known about Soviet repression, it is difficult to understand the power its presence exercised over many people's political imaginations, but that attraction was a factor in world politics from the 1920s through at least the early 1970s.

23.4
Nadezhda Mandelstam, Hope
Against Hope

Great Purges The imprisonment and execution of millions of Soviet citizens by Stalin between 1934 and 1939.

THE FASCIST EXPERIMENT IN ITALY

The first authoritarian political experiment in western Europe that arose in part from fears of the spread of bolshevism occurred in Italy. The general term *fascist*, which has been used to describe the various right-wing dictatorships that arose between the wars, was derived from the Italian fascist movement of Benito Mussolini (1883–1945).

WHY DID the Fascists achieve
power in Italy?

The governments regarded as fascist were antidemocratic, anti-Marxist, antiparliamentary, and frequently anti-Semitic. They hoped to hold back the spread of bolshevism, which seemed a real threat at the time. They sought a world that would be safe for the middle class and small farmers. **Fascism** rejected the political ideas of the French Revolution and of liberalism. Their adherents believed that parliamentary politics and parties sacrificed national greatness to petty party disputes. They wanted to overcome the class conflict of Marxism and the party conflict of liberalism by consolidating all classes within the nation for great national purposes. Fascist governments were usually single-party dictatorships rooted in mass political parties and characterized by terrorism and police surveillance.

Mussolini poses with supporters the day after the Black Shirt March on Rome intimidated the King of Italy into making him Prime Minister.

Bildarchiv Preussischer Kutturbesitz

RISE OF MUSSOLINI

The Italian *Fasci di Combattimento* ("Band of Combat") was founded in 1919 in Milan. Most of its members were veterans who felt that the sacrifices of World War I had been in vain. They resented Italy's failure to gain the city of Fiume at the Paris conference. They feared socialism, inflation, and labor unrest.

Their leader or *Duce*, Benito Mussolini, had been active in Italian socialist politics but broke with the socialists in 1914 and supported Italian entry into the war. He then established his own paper, *Il Popolo d'Italia*, and was wounded in the army. As a politician, Mussolini was an opportunist. He could change his ideas and principles to suit any occasion. Action for him was always more important than thought. His goal was political survival.

Many Italians were dissatisfied with the parliamentary system. They felt that Italy had not been treated as a great power at the peace conference or received the territories it deserved. The main spokesman for this discontent was the extreme nationalist writer Gabriele D'Annunzio (1863–1938). In 1919, he captured Fiume with a force of patriotic Italians. The Italian army drove him out, but this made the parliamentary ministry seem unpatriotic.

Between 1919 and 1921, Italy was also wracked by social turmoil. Numerous strikes occurred, and workers occupied factories. Peasants seized land. Parliamentary government seemed incapable of dealing with this unrest. Many Italians believed that a communist revolution might break out.

Mussolini first supported the factory occupations and land seizures, but soon reversed himself. He had discovered that many upper-class and middle-class Italians who were pressured by inflation and feared property loss had no sympathy for the workers or peasants. They wanted order. Consequently, Mussolini and his fascists took direct action in the face of the government inaction. They terrorized socialist supporters, attacked strikers and farm workers, and protected strikebreakers. Conservative land and factory owners were grateful. The government ignored these crimes. By early 1922, the fascists controlled the local government in much of northern Italy.

fascism   Political movements that tend to be antidemocratic, anti-Marxist, antiparliamentary, and often anti-Semitic. Fascists were invariably nationalists and exhalted the nation over the individual. They supported the interests of the middle class and rejected the ideas of the French Revolution and nineteenth-century liberalism. The first fascist regime was founded by Benito Mussolini (1883–1945) in Italy in the 1920s.

Duce   Meaning "leader." Mussolini's title as head of the Fascist Party.

In 1921, Mussolini and 34 of his followers had been elected to the Chamber of Deputies. The fascist movement now had hundreds of thousands of supporters. In October 1922, the fascists, dressed in their characteristic black shirts, began a march on Rome. King Victor Emmanuel III (r. 1900–1946) refused to authorize using the army against them, which ensured a fascist seizure of power. The Cabinet resigned. On October 29, the king telegraphed Mussolini in Milan and asked him to become prime minister. The next day Mussolini arrived in Rome by train and, as head of the government, greeted his followers when they entered the city.

Technically, Mussolini had come into office by legal means. The monarch had the power to appoint the prime minister. Mussolini, however, had no majority in the Chamber of Deputies. Behind the legal facade lay the months of terrorist intimidation and the threat of the fascists' October march.

THE FASCISTS IN POWER

23.5
The Rise of Benito Mussolini

Mussolini, who had not expected to be appointed prime minister, succeeded because of the impotence of his rivals, his use of his office, his power over the masses, and his ruthlessness. On November 23, 1922, the king and Parliament granted Mussolini dictatorial authority for one year to restore order. Wherever possible, Mussolini appointed fascists to office. In 1924, Parliament changed the election law so that the party that gained the largest popular vote (with at least 25 percent) received two-thirds of the seats in the chamber. Coalition government, with all its compromises and hesitations, would no longer be necessary. In the election of 1924, the fascists won complete control of the Chamber of Deputies. They used that majority to end legitimate parliamentary life. Laws permitted Mussolini to rule by decree. In 1926, Italy was transformed into a single-party, dictatorial state.

One domestic initiative brought Mussolini significant political dividends and respectability. Through the Lateran Accord of February 1929, the Roman Catholic Church and the Italian state made peace with each other. The agreement recognized the pope as the temporal ruler of Vatican City. The Italian government agreed to pay an indemnity to the papacy for confiscated land. The state also recognized Catholicism as the religion of the nation, exempted church property from taxes, and allowed church law to govern marriage.

GERMAN DEMOCRACY AND DICTATORSHIP

THE WEIMAR REPUBLIC

WHAT ROLE did terror play in Nazi Germany?

The Weimar Republic was born from the defeat of the imperial army, the revolution of 1918, and the hopes of German Liberals and Social Democrats. Its name derived from the city of Weimar where its constitution was written in August 1919. While the constitution was being debated, the republic, headed by the Social Democrats, accepted the hated Versailles Treaty. Although its officials had signed only under duress, the republic was permanently associated with the national disgrace. Throughout the 1920s, the government was required to fulfill the economic and military provisions imposed by the Paris settlement. Nationalists and military figures whose policies had brought on the tragedy and defeat of the war blamed the young republic and the socialists for its results. In Germany, the desire to revise the treaty was related to a desire to change the form of government.

The Weimar Constitution was an enlightened document. It guaranteed civil liberties and provided for direct election, by universal suffrage, of the **Reichstag** and the president. It also, however, contained structural flaws that eventually allowed it to be overthrown. A complicated system of proportional representation made it rel-

Reichstag The German parliament, which existed in various forms, until 1945.

atively easy for small political parties to gain seats in the Reichstag, which resulted in instability. The president appointed and removed the chancellor, the head of the cabinet. Article 48 allowed the president, in an emergency, to rule by decree. This permitted a possible presidential dictatorship.

In March 1920, a right-wing putsch, or armed insurrection, erupted in Berlin. It failed, but only after government officials had fled the city. In the same month, strikes took place in the Ruhr, and the government sent in troops. Such extremism from both the left and the right would haunt the republic. In May 1921, the Allies presented a reparations bill for 132 billion gold marks. The German government accepted this preposterous demand only after new Allied threats. Throughout the early 1920s, there were assassinations or attempted assassinations of republican leaders. Violence was the hallmark of the first five years of the republic.

Invasion of the Ruhr and Inflation   Inflation brought on the major crisis of this period. The war and postwar deficit spending generated an immense rise in prices. The value of German currency fell. By early 1921, the German mark traded against the American dollar at a ratio of 64 to 1, compared with a ratio of 4.2 to 1 in 1914. The German financial community contended that the mark could not be stabilized until the reparations issue had been solved. Meanwhile, the government kept issuing paper money, which it used to redeem government bonds.

The French invasion of the Ruhr in January 1923, to secure the payment of reparations, and the German response of passive economic resistance produced cataclysmic inflation. Unemployment spread, creating a drain on the treasury and reducing tax revenues. The printing presses had difficulty providing enough paper currency to keep up with the daily rise in prices. Money was literally not worth the paper it was printed on. Stores were unwilling to exchange goods for the worthless currency, and farmers hoarded produce.

The values of thrift and prudence were undermined. Middle-class savings, pensions, insurance policies, and investments in government bonds were wiped out. Debts and mortgages could not be paid off. Speculators made fortunes, but to the middle class and the lower middle class, the inflation was another trauma coming hard on the heels of military defeat and the peace treaty. This social and economic upheaval was behind the later German desire for order and security at almost any cost.

Hitler's Early Career   In 1923, Adolf Hitler (1889–1945) made his first significant appearance on the German political scene. The son of a minor Austrian customs official, his hopes of becoming an artist had been dashed in Vienna. Hitler absorbed the rabid German nationalism and extreme anti-Semitism that flourished there. He came to hate Marxism, which he associated with Jews. During World War I, Hitler fought in the German army, was wounded, rose to the rank of corporal, and won the Iron Cross for bravery. The war gave him his first sense of purpose.

Major Political Events of the 1920s and 1930s

1919	August, Constitution of the Weimar Republic promulgated
1920	Putsch in Berlin
1921	March, Lenin initiates his New Economic Policy
1922	October, fascist march on Rome leads to Mussolini's assumption of power
1923	January, France invades the Ruhr November, Hitler's Beer Hall Putsch
1924	Death of Lenin
1925	Locarno Agreements
1928	Kellogg-Briand Pact; first five-year plan launched in USSR
1929	January, Trotsky expelled from USSR February, Lateran Accord between the Vatican and the Italian state October, New York stock market crash November, Stalin's power affirmed
1930	March, Bruning government begins in Germany September, Nazis capture 107 seats in German Reichstag
1931	August, National Government formed in Britain
1932	March 13, Hindenberg defeats Hitler for German presidency May 31, Franz von Papen forms German Cabinet July 31, German Reichstag election November 6, German Reichstag election December 2, Kurt von Schleicher forms German Cabinet
1933	January 30, Hitler made German chancellor February 27, Reichstag Fire March 5, Reichstag election March 23, Enabling Act consolidates Nazi power
1934	June 30, Blood purge of the Nazi Party August 2, Death of Hindenburg December 1, Assassination of Kirov leads to the beginning of Stalin's purges
1936	May, Popular Front government in France July–August, Most famous of public purge trials in Russia

23.6
Adolf Hitler

After the conflict, Hitler settled in Munich and became associated with a small nationalistic, anti-Semitic party that in 1920 adopted the name of National Socialist German Workers Party, better known as the **Nazis**. The group paraded under a red banner with a black swastika. Its program called for the repudiation of the Versailles Treaty, the unification of Austria and Germany, the exclusion of Jews from German citizenship, agrarian reform, the prohibition of land speculation, the confiscation of war profits, state administration of the giant cartels, and the replacement of department stores with small retail shops.

The "socialism" that Hitler and the Nazis had in mind had nothing to do with traditional German socialism. It meant not state ownership of the means of production but the subordination of all economic enterprise to the welfare of the nation. It often implied protection for small economic enterprises. The Nazis discovered that their social appeal was to the lower middle class, which found itself squeezed between big business and socialist labor unions. The Nazis tailored their message to this troubled economic group.

The Nazi Stormtroopers, or **SA** *(Sturm Abteilung)*, were organized under the leadership of Captain Ernst Roehm (1887–1934). The Stormtroopers were the chief Nazi instrument for terror and intimidation before the party controlled the government. The existence of such a private party army was a sign of the potential for violence in the Weimar Republic and of contempt for the republic.

The social and economic turmoil following the French occupation of the Ruhr and the German inflation gave the Nazis an opportunity for direct action against the Weimar Republic. By this time, Hitler dominated the Nazi Party. On November 9, 1923, Hitler and a band of followers, accompanied by General Erich Ludendorff (1865–1937), attempted an unsuccessful putsch at a beer hall in Munich. The local authorities crushed the rising, and 16 Nazis were killed. Hitler and Ludendorff were tried for treason. The general was acquitted. Hitler made himself into a national figure. In his defense, he condemned the republic, the Versailles Treaty, and the Jews. He was sentenced to five years in prison but spent only a few months in jail before being paroled. During this time, he dictated *Mein Kampf* ("My Struggle"). Another result of the brief imprisonment was his decision to seize political power by legal methods.

The Stresemann Years   Gustav Stresemann (1878–1929) was primarily responsible for the reconstruction of the republic and its achievement of a sense of self-confidence. Stresemann abandoned the policy of passive resistance in the Ruhr. With the aid of banker Hjalmar Schacht (1877–1970), he introduced a new German currency. The rate of exchange was one trillion of the old German marks for one new Rentenmark. Stresemann also moved against challenges from both the left and the right. He supported the crushing of both Hitler's abortive putsch and smaller communist disturbances. In late November 1923, after four months as chancellor, he became foreign minister, a post he held until his death in 1929.

In 1924, the Weimar Republic and the Allies renegotiated the reparation payments. French troops left the Ruhr in 1925. The same year, Field Marshal Paul von Hindenburg (1847–1934), a military hero and a conservative monarchist, was elected president and governed in strict accordance with the constitution. The prosperity of the latter 1920s seemed to reconcile conservative Germans to the republic. Foreign capital flowed into Germany, and employment improved smartly. Giant industrial combines spread.

In foreign affairs, Stresemann pursued a conciliatory course. He fulfilled the provisions of the Versailles Treaty but attempted to revise it by diplomacy. He

Nazis   The German Nationalist Socialist Party.

SA   The Nazi parliamentary forces, or stormtroopers.

Mein Kampf   Meaning "My Struggle." Hitler's statement of his political program, published in 1924.

accepted the settlement in the west but aimed to recover German-speaking territories lost to Poland and Czechoslovakia and possibly to unite with Austria, chiefly by diplomatic means.

Locarno   These developments gave rise to the Locarno Agreements of October 1925. Foreign ministers Austen Chamberlain (1863–1937) for Britain and Aristide Briand (1862–1932) for France accepted Stresemann's proposal for a fresh start. France and Germany accepted the western frontier established at Versailles. Britain and Italy agreed to intervene against the aggressor if either side violated the frontier or if Germany sent troops into the demilitarized Rhineland. No such agreement was made about Germany's eastern frontier, but the Germans made arbitration treaties with Poland and Czechoslovakia, and France strengthened its alliances with those countries. France supported German membership in the League of Nations and agreed to withdraw its occupation troops from the Rhineland in 1930, five years earlier than specified at Versailles.

The Locarno Agreements brought new hope to Europe. Chamberlain, Briand, and Stresemann received the Nobel Peace Prize. The spirit of Locarno was carried even further when the leading European states, Japan, and the United States signed the Kellogg-Briand Pact in 1928, renouncing "war as an instrument of national policy." The joy and optimism were not justified. France had merely recognized its inability to coerce Germany without help. Britain had shown its unwillingness to uphold the settlement in the east. Germany was not reconciled to the eastern settlement.

In both France and Germany, moreover, the conciliatory politicians represented only a part of the nation. In Germany especially, most people continued to reject Versailles and regarded Locarno as only an extension of it. Despite these problems, war was by no means inevitable. Europe, aided by American loans, was returning to prosperity. German leaders like Stresemann would certainly have continued to press for change, but not through force, much less a general war. Continued prosperity and diplomatic success might have won the loyalty of the German people for the Weimar Republic and moderate revisionism, but the Great Depression of the 1930s brought new forces to power.

DEPRESSION AND POLITICAL DEADLOCK

The outflow of foreign, and especially American, capital from Germany that began in 1928 undermined the prosperity of the Weimar Republic. The resulting economic crisis brought parliamentary government to a halt. In 1928, a coalition of center parties and the Social Democrats governed. When the Depression struck, the coalition partners differed sharply on economic policy, and the coalition dissolved in March 1930. President von Hindenburg appointed Heinrich Brüning (1885–1970) as chancellor. Lacking a majority in the Reichstag, the new chancellor governed through emergency presidential decrees. The Weimar Republic had become a presidential dictatorship.

German unemployment rose from 2,258,000 in March 1930 to over 6,000,000 in March 1932. The economic downturn and the parliamentary deadlock worked to the advantage of extremists. In the election of 1928, the Nazis had won only 12 seats in the Reichstag and the communists 54. In the election of 1930, Nazis won 107 seats and the communists, 77.

The power of the Nazis in the streets also rose. The unemployment fed thousands of men into the Stormtroopers, which had almost one million members in 1933. The SA attacked communists and Social Democrats. For the Nazis, politics meant the capture of power through terror and intimidation as well as through

In this painting, which reflects the mood of social and political disillusionment that prevailed in much of Europe in the 1920s, George Grosz satirized conservative and rightmring groups in Weimar Germany, including the army, the courts, the newspapers, and the Nazi Party.

Bildarchiv Preussischer Kulturbesitz

elections. Decency and civility in political life vanished. Nazi rallies resembled religious revivals. They paraded through the streets and the countryside. They gained powerful supporters in the business, military, and newspaper communities. Some intellectuals were also sympathetic. The Nazis transformed this discipline and enthusiasm born of economic despair and nationalistic frustration into electoral results.

HITLER COMES TO POWER

For two years, Brüning governed with the confidence of Hindenburg. The economy did not improve, and the political situation deteriorated. In 1932, the 83-year-old president stood for reelection. Hitler ran against him and Hindenburg won. But Hitler got 36.8 percent of the final vote. The vote convinced Hindenburg that Brüning had lost the confidence of conservative Germans. In May 1932, he appointed Franz von Papen (1878–1969) chancellor. Papen was one of a small group of extremely conservative advisers on whom Hindenburg had become dependent. With the continued paralysis in the Reichstag, their influence over the president amounted to control of the government.

Papen and the circle around the president wanted to draw the Nazis into cooperation with them without giving Hitler effective power. The government needed the popular support on the right that only the Nazis seemed able to generate. The Hindenburg circle decided to convince Hitler that the Nazis could not come to power on their own. Papen removed the ban on Nazi meetings that Brüning had imposed and called a Reichstag election for July 1932. The Nazis won 230 seats and polled 37.2 percent of the vote. Hitler would only enter the Cabinet if he were made chancellor. Hindenburg refused. Another election was called in November. The Nazis gained only 196 seats, and their percentage of the popular vote dipped to 33.1 percent.

In early December 1932, Papen resigned, and General Kurt von Schleicher (1882–1934) became chancellor. People were now afraid of civil war between the extreme left and the far right. Schleicher tried to fashion a coalition of conservatives and trade unionists. The Hindenburg circle did not trust Schleicher's motives, which have never been clear. They persuaded Hindenburg to appoint Hitler chancellor. To control him, Papen was named vice chancellor, and other traditional conservatives were appointed to the Cabinet. On January 30, 1933, Adolf Hitler became the chancellor of Germany.

Hitler had come into office by legal means. The proper procedures had been observed. This permitted the civil service, courts, and other government agencies to support him in good conscience. He had forged a rigidly disciplined party structure and had mastered the techniques of mass politics and propaganda. His support appears to have come from across the social spectrum. Pockets of resistance appeared among Roman Catholic voters in the country and small towns. Otherwise, support for Hitler was strong among farmers, veterans, and the young, who had suffered from the insecurity of the 1920s and the Depression. Hitler promised them security, effective government in place of petty politics, and a strong, restored Germany.

There is little evidence that business contributions made any crucial difference to the Nazis' success. Hitler's supporters were frequently suspicious of business and giant capitalism. They wanted a simpler world in which small property would be safe from both socialism and large-scale capitalist consolidation. These people looked to Hitler and the Nazis rather than to the Social Democrats because the latter never appeared sufficiently nationalistic. The Nazis won out over other conservative nationalistic parties because, unlike those conservatives, the Nazis addressed the problem of social insecurities.

Hitler's mastery of the techniques of mass politics and propaganda—including huge staged rallies like this one in 1938—was an important factor in his rise to power.

Bildarchlv Preussischer Kulturbesitz

HITLER'S CONSOLIDATION OF POWER

Once in office, Hitler moved swiftly to consolidate his control. This process had three facets: the capture of full legal authority, the crushing of alternative political groups, and the purging of rivals within the Nazi Party itself. On February 27, 1933, a mentally ill Dutch Communist set fire to the Reichstag building in Berlin. The Nazis turned the incident to their own advantage by claiming that the fire proved the existence of a communist threat to the government. To the public, this seemed plausible. Under Article 48, Hitler suspended civil liberties and arrested communists or alleged communists. This decree was not revoked for as long as Hitler ruled Germany.

In early March, another Reichstag election took place. The Nazis still received only 43.9 percent of the vote. However, the arrest of communist deputies and the fear aroused by the fire meant that Hitler could control the Reichstag. On March 23, 1933, the Reichstag passed an Enabling Act, which permitted Hitler to rule by decree. Thereafter, there were no legal limits on his power. The Weimar Constitution was never formally repealed.

Hitler understood that he and his party had come to power because his potential opponents had stood divided between 1929 and 1933. To prevent them from regrouping, Hitler outlawed or undermined any German institutions that might have served as rallying points for opposition. By the close of 1933, all major institutions of potential opposition—trade unions, other political parties, the federal state governments—had been eliminated.

The final element in Hitler's personal consolidation of power involved the Nazi Party itself. Ernst Roehm, the commander of the SA, was a possible rival to Hitler. The German officer corps, whom Hitler needed to rebuild the army, were jealous of the SA. To protect his own position and to shore up support with the army, Hitler ordered the murder of key SA officers, including Roehm. Between June 30 and July 2, 1934, more than 800 people were killed, including the former chancellor Kurt von Schleicher and his wife. The German army, which might have prevented the murders, did nothing. On August 2, 1934, President Hindenburg died, and the offices of chancellor and president were combined. Hitler was now the sole ruler of or *Führer* of Germany and of the Nazi Party.

THE POLICE STATE

Terror and intimidation had helped propel the Nazis to office. As Hitler consolidated his power, he oversaw the organization of a police state. The chief vehicle of police surveillance was the **SS** *(Schutzstaffel),* or security units, commanded by Heinrich Himmler (1900–1945). This group was a more elite paramilitary organization than the larger SA. In 1933, the SS had approximately 52,000 members. It was the instrument that carried out the blood purges of the party in 1934. By 1936, Himmler had become head of all police matters in Germany.

The police character of the Nazi regime was all-pervasive, but the people who most consistently experienced its terror were the Jews. Anti-Semitism had been a key plank of the Nazi program—anti-Semitism based on biological racial theories stemming from late-nineteenth-century thought rather than from religious discrimination. Before World War II, the Nazi attack on the Jews went through three stages. In 1933, the Nazis excluded Jews from the civil service and attempted to enforce boycotts of Jewish businesses. The boycotts won little public support. In 1935, the Nuremberg Laws robbed German Jews of their citizenship. All persons with at least one Jewish grandparent were defined as Jews. The professions and major occupations were closed to Jews. Marriage and sexual intercourse between Jews and non-Jews were prohibited. Legal exclusion and humiliation of the Jews became the norm.

The persecution of the Jews increased again in 1938. In November, under orders from the Nazi Party, thousands of Jewish stores and synagogues were destroyed. The Jewish community itself had to pay for the damage that occurred on this **Kristallnacht** because the government confiscated the insurance money. In both large and petty ways, the German Jews were harassed. This persecution allowed the Nazis to inculcate the rest of the population with the concept of a master race of pure German "Aryans" and also to display their own contempt for civil liberties.

After the war broke out, Hitler decided in 1942 to destroy the Jews in Europe. It is thought that over six million Jews, mostly from eastern Europe, died as a result of that decision, unprecedented in its scope and implementation.

WOMEN IN NAZI GERMANY

The Nazis believed in separate social spheres for men and women. Men belonged in the world of action, women in the home. The two spheres should not mix. Respect for women should arise from their function as wives and mothers.

These attitudes conflicted with the social changes that German women, like women elsewhere in Europe, had experienced during the first three decades of the twentieth century. German women had become much more active and assertive. They worked in factories or were independently employed, and had begun to enter the professions. Under the Weimar constitution, they voted. Throughout the Weimar period, there was also a lively discussion of women's emancipation. For the Nazis, these developments were signs of cultural weakness.

The Nazis' point of view was supported by women of a conservative outlook and women who followed traditional roles as housewives. In a period of high unemployment, the Nazi attitude also appealed to many men because it discouraged women from competing with them in the workplace. Such competition had begun during World War I, and many Nazis considered it symptomatic of the social confusion that had followed the German defeat.

Führer Meaning "leader." The title taken by Hitler when he became dictator of Germany.

SS The chief security units of the Nazi state.

Kristallnacht Meaning "crystal night" because of the broken glass that littered German streets after the looting and destruction of Jewish homes, businesses, and synagogues across Germany on the orders of the Nazi Party in November 1938.

OVERVIEW

POLITICAL TYRANNY OF THE 1920S AND 1930S

Although political tyranny was not new to Europe, several factors in the 1920s and 1930s combined to give dictators of the right and the left unique power. The regimes set up by Mussolini in Italy, Stalin in Russia, and Hitler in Germany shared the following characteristics:

1. well-organized political parties
2. nationalism
3. programs that promised to cure social, political, and economic frustrations and end the pettiness of everyday politics
4. a monopoly over mass communications and propaganda
5. highly effective instruments of terror and police power
6. real or imagined national, class, or racial enemies who could be demonized to whip up mass support
7. command over modern technology and its capacity for immense destruction

The Nazi discussion of the role of women was also rooted in Nazi racism. It was the special task of German mothers to preserve racial purity. Hitler championed this view of women. They were to breed strong sons and daughters for the German nation. Nazi journalists often compared the role of women in childbirth to that of men in battle. Each served the state in particular gender roles. In both cases, the good of the nation was superior to that of the individual.

The Nazis also attacked feminist outlooks. Women were encouraged to bear many children, because the Nazis believed the declining German birth rate was the result of emancipated women who had spurned their natural roles as mothers. The Nazis sponsored schools that taught women how to rear children.

The Nazis also saw women as educators of the young and thus the protectors of German cultural values. Through cooking, dress, music, and stories, mothers were to instill a love for the nation. As consumers for the home, women were to buy German goods and avoid Jewish merchants.

The Nazis realized that in the midst of the Depression many women would need to work, but the party urged them to pursue employment that the Nazis considered natural to their character. These tasks included agriculture, teaching, nursing, social work, and domestic service. Nonetheless, the percentage of women employed in Germany changed little from the Weimar to the Hitler years: It was 37 percent in 1928 and in 1939. Thereafter, because of the war, many more women were recruited into the German workforce.

THE GREAT DEPRESSION
AND THE NEW DEAL IN THE UNITED STATES

The United States emerged from World War I as a world power. However, it retreated from that role when the Senate refused to ratify the Versailles Treaty and failed to join the League of Nations. In 1920, Warren Harding (1865–1923) became president and urged a return to what he termed "normalcy," which meant minimal involvement abroad and conservative economic policies at home. Business interests remained in the ascendent, and the federal government took a relatively inactive role in national life, especially under Harding's successor, Calvin Coolidge (1872–1933).

HOW DID FDR's policies affect the role of the federal government?

The Great Depression brought unprecedented unemployment to the United States. In 1930 unemployed workers were photographed standing outside the Municipal Lodging House in New York City.

Corbis-Bettmann

The first seven or eight years of the decade witnessed remarkable American prosperity. New electrical appliances such as the radio, phonograph, washing machine, and vacuum cleaner appeared on the market. Real wages rose for many workers. Industry grew at a robust rate. Automobile manufacturers assumed a major role in national economic life. Factories became mechanized. Engineers and efficiency experts were the heroes of the business world. The stock market boomed. This activity stood in marked contrast to the economic dislocations of Europe.

The material prosperity appeared, however, in a divided society. Segregation remained a basic fact of life for black Americans. The Ku Klux Klan, which sought to terrorize blacks, Roman Catholics, and Jews, enjoyed a resurgence. The Prohibition Amendment of 1919 (repealed in 1933) forbade the manufacture and transport of alcoholic beverages. In the wake of this divisive national policy, major criminal operations arose to supply liquor and disrupt civic life. Many immigrants came from Mexico and Puerto Rico. They settled in cities where their labor was desired but where they were often not welcomed or assimilated. Finally, the wealth of the nation was concentrated in too few hands.

ECONOMIC COLLAPSE

In March 1929, Herbert Hoover became president, the third Republican in as many elections. On October 29, 1929, the New York stock market crashed. The other financial markets also went into a tailspin. During the next year the stock market continued to fall. The banks that had loaned people money with which to speculate in the market suffered great losses.

The financial collapse of 1929 triggered the Great Depression in America, although there were other underlying domestic causes. Manufacturing firms had not made sufficient capital investment. The disproportionate amount of profits going to about 5 percent of the U.S. population undermined the purchasing power of other consumers. Agriculture was in trouble. Finally, the economic difficulties in Europe and Latin America, which predated those in the United States, meant foreigners were less able to purchase American products.

The most pervasive problem of the Great Depression was unemployment. Joblessness hit unskilled workers first but then worked its way up the job ladder to touch factory and white-collar workers. As unemployment spread, small retail businesses suffered. In the major American manufacturing cities, hundreds of thousands of workers could not find jobs. The price of corn fell so low in some areas that it was not profitable to harvest it. By the early 1930s, banks began to fail, and people lost their savings.

The federal government was not equipped to address the emergency. There was no tradition of federal action to alleviate economic distress. President Hoover organized economic conferences and encouraged the Federal Reserve to make borrowing easier. He supported the ill-advised Hawley-Smoot Tariff Act of 1930, which hoped to protect American industry by a high tariff barrier. Hoover believed relief was a matter for local government and voluntary organizations; however, many local relief agencies had run out of money by 1931.

NEW ROLE FOR GOVERNMENT

The election of 1932 was one of the most crucial in American history. The Democrat Franklin Delano Roosevelt (1882–1945), who was known as "FDR," promised "a new deal for the American people." He overwhelmingly defeated Hoover, and quickly redirected federal policy toward the Depression.

Roosevelt had been born into a moderately wealthy New York family and was a distant cousin of Theodore Roosevelt (1858–1919). After serving in World War I as Assistant Secretary of the Navy, in 1920 he ran as the Democratic vice presidential candidate. The next year, however, he was struck with polio and his legs became paralyzed, but he went on to be elected governor of New York in 1928. As president he attempted to convey to the nation the same kind of optimistic spirit that had informed his own struggle of the 1920s.

Roosevelt's first goal was to give the nation a sense that the federal government was meeting the economic challenge. The first hundred days of his administration became legendary. He immediately closed all the banks and permitted only sound institutions to reopen. Congress rapidly passed a new banking act and then enacted the Agricultural Adjustment Act and the Farm Credit Act to aid the farmers. To provide jobs, Roosevelt sponsored the Civilian Conservation Corps. The Federal Emergency Relief Act funded state and local relief agencies. To restore confidence, Roosevelt began making speeches, known as "fireside chats," to the American people.

Roosevelt's most ambitious program was the National Industrial Recovery Act (NIRA), which established the National Recovery Administration (NRA). This agency attempted to foster codes written by various industries to regulate wages and prices to monitor competition and thus protect jobs and assure production.

The NIRA and other New Deal legislation, such as the Wagner Act of 1935, which established the National Labor Relations Board and the Fair Labor Standards Act of 1938, provided a larger role in the American economy for organized labor. It became easier for unions to organize. Union membership grew, and American unionism took on a new character. Most unions had been organized by craft and were affiliated with the American Federation of Labor (AFL). In the 1930s, however, whole industries composed of workers in various crafts were organized in a single union. The most important of these organizations were the United Mine Workers and United Automobile Workers. These new unions organized themselves into the Congress of Industrial Organizations (CIO). The CIO and the AFL merged in the 1950s. These strong industrial labor organizations introduced a new force into the American economic scene.

In 1935, the U. S. Supreme Court declared the NRA unconstitutional. Thereafter, Roosevelt deemphasized centralized economic planning. The number of federal agencies increased, but they operated in general independence from each other.

Through New Deal legislation, the federal government was far more active in the economy than it had ever been. The government itself attempted to provide relief for the unemployed in the industrial sector. The major institution of the relief effort was the Works Progress Administration. Created in 1935, the WPA began a massive program of public works.

The programs of the New Deal years also involved the federal government directly in economic development rather than turning such development over to private enterprise. Through the Tennessee Valley Authority (TVA), the government became directly involved in the economy of the four states of the Tennessee River valley. The TVA built dams and then produced and sold hydroelectricity. Never had the government undertaken so extensive an economic role. Another

During the Great Depression; Franklin Delano Roosevelt (right) replaced Herbert Hoover (left) as president of the United States. FDR's aggressive recovers, program was intended to give America a "New Deal."

Corbis-Bettmann

major new function for the government was providing security for the elderly, through the establishment of the Social Security Administration in 1935.

In one area of American life after another, it was decided that the government must provide personal economic security. These actions established a mixed economy in the United States—that is, one in which the federal government would play an active role alongside the private sector.

Yet the New Deal did not solve the unemployment problem. In the late 1930s, the economy began to falter again. Only the entry of the nation into World War II brought the U.S. economy to full employment.

The experience of the United States under the New Deal stood in marked contrast to the economic and political experiments in Europe. Many business people found Roosevelt too liberal and his policies too activist. Nonetheless, the New Deal preserved capitalism in a democratic setting, where, again in contrast to Europe, there was free political debate—much of it critical of the administration. The United States had demonstrated that a nation with a vast industrial economy could confront its gravest economic crisis and still preserve democracy.

SUMMARY

Postwar Problems The Versailles settlement left much of Europe dissatisfied. In the 1920s there were endless wrangles over reparations between Germany and the Allied powers. After World War I, Europe never recovered its prewar prosperity or stability. The onset of the Great Depression in 1929 caused severe problems in both Europe and the United States and led to the Nazi seizure of power in Germany and FDR's New Deal in the United States.

The Soviet Union The Bolsheviks had expected communist revolutions to break out across Europe. When that did not happen, they were forced to consolidate their regime within Russia. Lenin's New Economic Policy gave the state control over heavy industry, transportation, and international commerce but allowed for small-scale private enterprise and peasant farms. Stalin abandoned this policy to push for rapid industrialization. He abolished private enterprise, collectivized agriculture, and eliminated his opponents in a series of purges in which millions were imprisoned or killed. Despite the violence and oppression, Marxist parties around the world were subservient to the Soviet Union as the world's only communist state and the enemy of fascism.

Fascist Italy Benito Mussolini came to power in Italy in 1922. Many Italians were dissatisfied with the terms of the Versailles Treaty and frightened by the social unrest that followed World War I. Mussolini promised order and a strong state. Although he achieved power by legal means, he soon transformed Italy into a single-party dictatorship. In 1929 he came to terms with the Catholic Church by negotiating the Lateran Accord, which recognized the pope as the independent ruler of Vatican City.

Nazi Germany The postwar Weimar Republic in Germany was buffeted by social, political, and financial instability. Many Germans refused to accept Germany's defeat in World War I or the terms of the Versailles Treaty. Rampant inflation destroyed the savings of the middle class. The Great Depression brought financial collapse and massive unemployment. Many Germans looked to Adolf Hitler and the Nazi Party for solutions. Once Hitler came to power in 1933, he quickly established a one-party dictatorship based on police terror,

IMAGE KEY
for pages 688–689

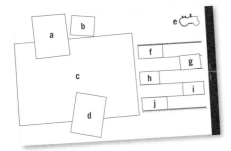

a. *Symbol of Work* Poster, USSR, 1930-1934
b. Volkswagen on German Reich Stamp, 1939
c. Hitler rally, 1938
d. WPA poster
e. Tractor
f. Protest marchers on the Jarrow Crusade
g. Cheka credentials
h. Benito Mussolini
i. George Grosz painting whuch satirized conservative and right-wing groups in Weimar Germany
j. WPA workers

propaganda, and the cult of himself as supreme leader. The Jews, in particular, were persecuted. Hitler also formed an alliance with the German army and began a program of rapid rearmament.

The United States The United States emerged from World War I as a world power, but retreated into isolation during the 1920s. The shallow prosperity of the 1920s ended in the Great Depression. Franklin Delano Roosevelt's New Deal greatly expanded the power of the federal government in social and economic affairs and preserved capitalism in a democratic setting.

REVIEW QUESTIONS

1. Why was the Great Depression more severe and why did it last longer than previous economic downturns?

2. How did Stalin achieve supreme power in the Soviet Union? Why did he decide that Russia had to industrialize rapidly? Why did this require the collectivization of agriculture? Was the policy a success? How did it affect the Russian people? What were the causes of the great purges?

3. Why was Italy unstable after World War I? How did Mussolini achieve power? What were the characteristics of the fascist state?

4. Why did the Weimar Republic collapse in Germany? Which groups in Germany supported Hitler and why were they pro-Nazi? How did he consolidate his power?

5. Why did the U.S. economy collapse in 1929? How did Roosevelt combat the Depression?

KEY TERMS

collectivization (p. 694)

Duce (p. 697)

fascism (p. 697)

Führer (p. 704)

Great Depression (p. 690)

Great Purges (p. 696)

Kristallnacht (p. 704)

Mein Kampf (p. 700)

Nazis (p. 700)

New Economic Policy (NEP) (p. 692)

Popular Front (p. 691)

Reichstag (p. 698)

SA (p. 700)

SS (p. 704)

War Communism (p. 692)

Weimar Republic (p. 690)

  For additional study resources for this chapter, go to:
www.prenhall.com/craig/chapter31

World War II resulted in the near-total destruction of the Jews of Europe, victims of the Holocaust spawned by Hitler's racial theories of the superiority and inferiority of particular ethnic groups. Hitler placed special emphasis on the need to exterminate the Jews, to whom he attributed particular wickedness. This picture shows a roundup of Jews in Warsaw, where there was a large Jewish population, ultimately on their way to concentration or death camps.

Corbis-Bettmann

32

WORLD WAR II

WHAT WERE the main events between 1933 and 1939 that led to World War II?

WHY WAS 1943 the turning point in World War II?

HOW DID war affect civilians in Germany, France, Britain, and the Soviet Union?

WHY DID cooperation between the Soviet Union and the Western powers break down in 1945?

IMAGE KEY

Image Key for pages 710–711 is on page 729.

WHAT WERE the main events between 1933 and 1939 that led to World War II?

The more idealistic survivors of World War I, especially in the United States and Britain, thought of it as "the war to end all wars" and "a war to make the world safe for democracy." Only thus could they justify the slaughter, expense, and upheaval. Yet only 20 years after the peace treaties, a second great war broke out that was more truly global than the first. In this war, the democracies would be fighting for their lives against militaristic, nationalistic, authoritarian, and totalitarian states in Europe and Asia. Britain and the United States would be allied with the Communist Soviet Union. The defeat of the militarists and dictators would lead to a Cold War in which the European states became second-class powers, subordinate to the Soviet Union and the United States.

THE ROAD TO WAR (1933–1939)

The Nazi destruction of political opposition meant that German foreign policy lay in Hitler's hands. From first to last, Hitler's racial theories and goals were central in his thought. He intended to bring the entire German people (*Volk*), understood as a racial group, together into a single nation. The new Germany would include all the Germanic parts of the old Habsburg Empire, including Austria. This virile nation would need more space to live (***Lebensraum***), which would be taken from the Slavs, a lesser race. The new Germany would be purified by the removal of the Jews, the most inferior race in Nazi theory. The plan required the conquest of Poland and the Ukraine to settle Germans and provide badly needed food. However, neither *Mein Kampf* nor later statements of policy were blueprints for action. Hitler exploited opportunities as they arose. But he never lost sight of his goal, which would almost certainly require a major war.

DESTRUCTION OF VERSAILLES

When Hitler came to power, Germany was weak. The first problem was to shake off the fetters of Versailles and make Germany a formidable military power. In October 1933, Germany withdrew from an international disarmament conference and from the League of Nations. These acts were merely symbolic, but in March 1935, Hitler renounced the disarmament provisions of the Versailles Treaty with the formation of a German air force. Soon he reinstated conscription, which aimed at an army of half a million men.

His path was made easier because the League of Nations was ineffective. In September 1931, Japan occupied Manchuria. China appealed to the league, which condemned the Japanese for resorting to force. But the powers would not impose sanctions. Japan withdrew from the league and kept Manchuria.

The league condemned Hitler's decision to rearm Germany, but took no steps to prevent it. France and Britain met with Mussolini in June 1935 to form the so-called Stresa Front and agreed to maintain the status quo in Europe by force if necessary. But Britain was desperate to maintain superiority at sea. Contrary to the Stresa accords, Britain soon made a separate naval agreement with Hitler, allowing him to rebuild the German fleet to 35 percent of the British navy.

ITALY ATTACKS ETHIOPIA

The Italian attack on Ethiopia in October 1935 made the impotence of the League of Nations and the timidity of the Allies even clearer. Using a border incident as an excuse, Mussolini's intent was to avenge a humiliating defeat that the Italians had suffered in 1896 and perhaps to divert Italians from fascist corruption and Italy's economic troubles.

The League of Nations voted economic sanctions and imposed an arms embargo. But Britain and France were afraid of alienating Mussolini, so they refused

Lebensraum "Living space," The Nazi plan to colonize and exploit Eastern Europe.

MAP EXPLORATION

Interactive map: To explore this map further, go to **http://www.prenhall.com/craig2/map32.1**

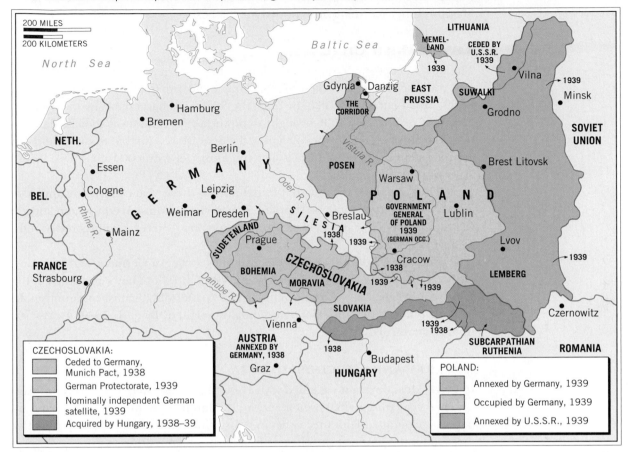

MAP 32–1

Partitions of Czechoslovakia and Poland, 1938–1939.   The immediate background of World War II is found in the complex international drama unfolding on Germany's eastern frontier in 1938 and 1939. Germany's expansion inevitably meant the victimization of Austria, Czechoslovakia, and Poland. With the failure of the Western powers' appeasement policy and the signing of a German-Soviet pact, the stage for the war was set.

HOW DID the failure of appeasement lead to war?

to place an embargo on oil, the one economic sanction that could have prevented Italian victory. Nor did the British prevent the movement of Italian troops and munitions through the Suez Canal. This wavering policy was disastrous. The League of Nations and collective security were discredited, and Mussolini turned to Germany.

REMILITARIZATION OF THE RHINELAND

On March 7, 1936, Hitler took his greatest risk yet, sending a small armed force into the demilitarized Rhineland. This was a breach of the Versailles Treaty and of the Locarno Agreements. It also removed an important element of French security. Yet Britain and France made only a feeble protest.

A Germany that was rapidly rearming and had a defensible western frontier presented a new problem to the western powers. Their response was **"appeasement."** It was based on the assumption that Germany had real grievances,

appeasement   The Anglo-French policy of making concessions to Germany in the 1930s to avoid a crisis that would lead to war. It assumed that Germany had real grievances and Hitler's aims were limited and ultimately acceptable.

that Hitler's goals were limited, and that the correct policy was to make concessions before a crisis could lead to war. Behind this approach was the horror of another war. As Germany armed, the French huddled behind their defensive wall, the Maginot Line, and the British hoped for the best.

THE SPANISH CIVIL WAR

The new European alignment that found the western democracies on one side and the fascist states on the other was made clearer by the Spanish Civil War, which broke out in July 1936. In 1931, the Spaniards had established a republic. Elections in February 1936 brought to power a government of the left. The defeated groups, especially the falangists, the Spanish version of fascists, would not accept defeat at the polls. In July, General Francisco Franco (1892–1975) led an army against the republic.

Thus began a civil war that lasted almost three years. Germany and Italy aided Franco with troops and supplies. The Soviet Union sent equipment and advisers to the republicans. Leftists from Europe and America volunteered to fight against fascism.

The civil war, fought on ideological lines, brought Germany and Italy closer together, leading to the Rome-Berlin **Axis** Pact in 1936. They were joined in the same year by Japan in the Anti-Comintern Pact, ostensibly against communism. In western Europe, the appeasement mentality reigned. By early 1939, the fascists had won control of Spain.

AUSTRIA AND CZECHOSLOVAKIA

In 1934, Mussolini, not yet allied with Hitler, had frustrated a Nazi coup in Austria by threatening military intervention. In March 1938, the new diplomatic situation encouraged Hitler to try again. Mussolini made no objection, and Hitler marched into Vienna to the cheers of his Austrian sympathizers.

The *Anschluss*, or union of Germany and Austria, had great strategic significance. Czechoslovakia was now surrounded by Germany on three sides. It was allied both to France and the Soviet Union but contained about 3.5 million ethnic Germans who lived in the Sudetenland near the German border. Supported by Hitler, they agitated for privileges and autonomy within the Czech state. The Czechs made concessions; but Hitler's motivation was to destroy Czechoslovakia.

The French, as usual, deferred to British leadership. The British prime minister Neville Chamberlain (1869–1940) was determined not to allow Britain to go to war again. In September 1938, German intervention seemed imminent. Chamberlain sought to appease Hitler at Czech expense and avoid war. But Hitler wanted the immediate occupation of the Sudetenland by the German army.

MUNICH

France and Britain prepared for war. At the last moment, Mussolini proposed a conference of Germany, Italy, France, and Britain. It met on September 29 at Munich. Hitler received almost everything he had demanded. The Sudetenland became part of Germany, thus depriving the Czechs of any chance of self-defense. In return, the rest of Czechoslovakia was spared. Hitler promised, "I have no more territorial demands to make in Europe." Chamberlain told a cheering crowd that "I believe it is peace for our time."

Soon, however, Poland and Hungary tore bits of territory from Czechoslovakia, and the Slovaks demanded autonomy. Finally, on March 15, 1939, Hitler broke his

Axis The alliance between Nazi Germany and fascist Italy. Also called the Pact of Steel.

Anschluss Meaning "union." The annexation of Austria by Germany in March 1938.

promise and occupied Prague, putting an end to Czech independence. Munich remains an example of short-sighted policy that helped bring on a war in disadvantageous circumstances as a result of the very fear of war and the failure to prepare for it.

Hitler's occupation of Prague discredited appeasement in Britain. Poland was the next target of German expansion. In the spring of 1939, the Germans put pressure on Poland to restore the formerly German city of Danzig and allow a railroad and a highway through the Polish Corridor to connect East Prussia with the rest of Germany. When the Poles would not yield, the pressure mounted. On March 31, Chamberlain announced a Franco-British guarantee of Polish independence. Hitler did not take the guarantee seriously. He knew that both countries were unprepared for war and that much of their populations opposed war for Poland.

Moreover, France and Britain could not get effective help to the Poles. The only way to defend Poland was to bring Russia into the alliance against Hitler, but a Russian alliance posed problems. Each side was suspicious of the other. The French and British were hostile to communism, and since Stalin's purge of the officer corps of the Red Army, they questioned Russia's military abilities. Besides, both Poland and Romania were suspicious of Russian intentions—with good reason. As a result, western negotiations with Russia were slow and cautious.

On September 29–30, 1938, Hitler met with the leaders of Britain and France at Munich to decide the fate of Czechoslovakia. The Allied leaders abandoned the small democratic nation in a vain attempt to appease Hitler and avoid war. Hitler sits in the center of the picture. To his right is British Prime Minister Neville Chamberlain.

Ullstein Bilderdienst

THE NAZI-SOVIET PACT

The Russians resented being left out of the Munich agreement and were annoyed by the low priority that the west seemed to give to negotiations with Russia. They feared, rightly, that the western powers meant them to bear the burden of the war against Germany. As a result, they opened negotiations with Hitler, and on August 23, 1939, the world was shocked to learn of a Nazi-Soviet nonaggression pact. Its secret provisions divided Poland between them and allowed Russia to annex the Baltic states and take Bessarabia from Romania. Communist parties in the west changed their line overnight from advocating resistance to Hitler to a policy of peace and quiet.

The Nazi-Soviet Pact sealed the fate of Poland. On September 1, 1939, the Germans invaded Poland. Two days later, Britain and France declared war on Germany. World War II had begun.

 25.1
Adolf Hitler, The Obersalzberg Speech

WORLD WAR II (1939–1945)

GERMAN CONQUEST OF EUROPE

The speed of the German victory over Poland astonished everyone, and the Russians hastened to collect their share of the booty before Hitler could deprive them of it. On September 17 they invaded Poland from the east, dividing the country with the Germans. They then absorbed Estonia, Latvia, and Lithuania. In November 1940, the Russians invaded Finland, but the Finns fought back and retained their independence.

Meanwhile, the western front was quiet. The French remained behind the Maginot Line. Britain imposed the traditional naval blockade. Cynics in the west

WHY WAS 1943 the turning point in World Warr II?

OVERVIEW

THE COMING OF WORLD WAR II IN EUROPE, 1933–1939

Date	Event
January 1933	Hitler comes to power in Germany
October 1933	Germany withdraws from the League of Nations
March 1935	Hitler announces German rearmament
October 1935	Mussolini attacks Ethiopia
March 1936	Germany remilitarizes the Rhineland
July 1936	Outbreak of Spanish Civil War
October 1936	Formation of Rome-Berlin Axis
March 1938	Hitler occupies Austria
September 1938	Munich Conference dismembers Czechoslovakia
March 1939	Hitler occupies Prague. End of Czech independence Britain and France guarantee Poland Franco wins the Spanish Civil War
April 1939	Mussolini occupies Albania
May 1939	Germany and Italy conclude a military alliance
August 1939	Nazi-Soviet Pact
September 1939	Hitler invades Poland. Britain and France declare war.

called it the phony war, but in April 1940, the Germans invaded Denmark and Norway. A month later, a combined land and air attack struck the Low Countries. The Dutch surrendered in a few days, and the Belgians less than two weeks later. The British and French armies in Belgium were forced to flee to the English Channel to seek escape from the beaches of Dunkirk. Over 200,000 British and 100,000 French soldiers were saved, but valuable equipment was abandoned.

The Maginot Line ran from Switzerland to the Belgian frontier. Hitler's swift advance through Belgium therefore circumvented France's main line of defense. The French army, poorly led, collapsed. Mussolini attacked France on June 10, though without success. Less than a week later, the French government, under the ancient hero of Verdun, Henri Philippe Pétain (1856–1951), asked for an armistice.

The terms of the armistice, signed June 22, 1940, allowed the Germans to occupy more than half of France, including the Atlantic and English Channel coasts. To prevent the French from fleeing to North Africa to continue the fight, Hitler left southern France unoccupied. Pétain set up a dictatorial regime at the resort city of Vichy and collaborated with the Germans to preserve as much autonomy as possible. The French were too stunned to resist. Many thought that Hitler's victory was certain and saw no alternative to collaboration. A few, notably General Charles de Gaulle (1890–1969), fled to Britain and organized the French National Committee of Liberation, or "Free French." As expectations of a quick German victory faded, French resistance arose.

MAP 32–2
Axis Europe 1941.   On the eve of the German invasion of the Soviet Union, the Germany-Italy Axis bestrode most of western Europe by annexation, occupation, or alliance—from Norway and Finland in the north to Greece in the south and from Poland to France. Britain, the Soviets, a number of insurgent groups, and, finally, the United States had before them the long struggle of conquering this Axis "fortress Europe."

WHAT WERE the strengths and weaknesses of Germany's territorial position in 1941?

BATTLE OF BRITAIN

Hitler expected the British to come to terms. Any chance that the British would consider terms disappeared when Winston Churchill (1874–1965) replaced Chamberlain as prime minister in May 1940.

Churchill established a close relationship with the American president Franklin D. Roosevelt. In 1940 and 1941, before the United States was at war, America sent military supplies and even convoyed ships across the Atlantic to help the British survive.

As Britain remained defiant, Hitler was forced to contemplate an invasion, which required control of the air. The German air force (*Luftwaffe*) destroyed much of London, and about 15,000 people were killed. But the Royal Air Force (RAF), aided by the newly developed radar, inflicted heavy losses on the *Luftwaffe*. Hitler was forced to abandon his plans for invasion.

GERMAN ATTACK ON RUSSIA

Operation Barbarossa, the code name for the invasion of Russia, was aimed at knocking Russia out of the war before winter could set in. Success depended in part on an early start, but here Hitler's Italian alliance proved costly. Mussolini had launched an attack against the British in Egypt and also invaded Greece. But in North Africa the British counter attacked and drove into Libya, and the Greeks repulsed the Italians. In March 1941, the British sent help to the Greeks, and Hitler was forced to divert his attention to the Balkans and to Africa. General Erwin Rommel (1891–1944) soon drove the British back into Egypt. In the Balkans, the German army occupied Yugoslavia and crushed Greek resistance, but the price was a delay of six weeks for Barbarossa. This proved to be costly the following winter.

Operation Barbarossa was launched against Russia on June 22, 1941, and it almost succeeded. Stalin panicked. By November, the German army stood at the gates of Leningrad, on the outskirts of Moscow, and on the Don River. A German victory seemed imminent.

But the Germans could not deliver the final blow before winter struck the German army, which was not equipped to face it. In November and December, the Russians counterattacked. The *Blitzkrieg* had turned into a war of attrition.

HITLER'S EUROPE: THE HOLOCAUST

The demands of war and Hitler's defeat prevented him from fully carrying out his plans. But the measures he took before his death give evidence of a regime unmatched in history for planned terror and inhumanity. Hitler regarded the conquered lands merely as a source of plunder and slave labor. But the most horrible aspect of the Nazi rule in Europe arose from the inhumanity inherent in Hitler's racial doctrines. He considered the Slavs *Untermenschen*, subhuman creatures like beasts. In Poland, the upper and professional classes were jailed, deported, or killed, and harsh living conditions were imposed. In Russia, things were even worse. Hitler spoke of his Russian campaign as a war of extermination. The SS formed extermination squads to elminate 30 million Slavs to make room for the Germans. Some six million Russian prisoners of war and civilians may have died under Nazi rule.

Hitler meant to make Europe *Judenrein* ("free of Jews"). Eventually he decided on the "final solution of the Jewish problem": extermination. The Nazis built extermination camps in Germany and Poland and killed millions of men, women, and children just because they were Jews. Before the war was over, six million Jews had died in what is called the **Holocaust**. (See "An Observer Describes the Mass Murder of Jews in Ukraine.")

AMERICA'S ENTRY INTO THE WAR

The war took on global proportions in 1941. On Sunday morning, December 7, 1941, even while Japanese representatives were negotiating in Washington, Japan launched an air attack on Pearl Harbor, Hawaii, the chief American naval base in the Pacific (see Chapter 29) The next day, the United States and Britain declared war on Japan. Three days later, Germany and Italy declared war on the United States.

QUICK REVIEW

Operation Barbarossa

- June 22, 1941: surprise invasion of Soviet Union by Germany (Operation Barbarossa) launched
- Germany advanced rapidly in the early stages of the campaign
- German failure to deliver a decisive blow delayed victory until winter set in, turning the tide in the Soviet's favor

---

Luftwaffe   The German air force in World War II.

Blitzkrieg   Meaning "lightning war." The German tactic early in World War II of employing fast-moving, massed armored columns supported by airpower to overwhelm the enemy.

Holocaust   The Nazi extermination of millions of European Jews between 1940 and 1945. Also called the "final solution to the Jewish problem."

THE TIDE TURNS

Its potential power was enormous, but America was ill prepared for war. The army was tiny, inexperienced, and poorly supplied. American industry was not ready for war. By the summer of 1942, the Japanese Empire stretched from the Aleutian Islands south almost to Australia, and from Burma east to the Gilbert Islands in the mid-Pacific (see Map 32–3).

In the same year, the Germans almost reached the Caspian Sea. In Africa, Rommel drove the British back toward the Suez Canal. Relations between the democracies and their Soviet ally were not close; German submarines were threatening British supplies.

The tide turned at the Battle of Midway in June 1942. American planes destroyed four Japanese aircraft carriers. Soon American Marines landed on Guadalcanal in the Solomon Islands and began to reverse the momentum of the war. Japan was checked sufficiently to allow the Allies to concentrate their efforts first in the West.

Allied Landings in Africa, Sicily, and Italy   In November 1942, an Allied force landed in French North Africa. Even before that landing, the British Field Marshal Bernard Montgomery (1887–1976), after stopping Rommel at El Alamein, had begun a drive to the west. The American general Dwight D. Eisenhower (1890–1969) pushed eastward through Morocco and Algeria. The German army was trapped in Tunisia and crushed. In July and August 1943, the Allies took Sicily. Mussolini was driven from power, the Allies landed in Italy, and Marshal Pietro Badoglio (1871–1956), the leader of the new Italian government, declared war on Germany. German resistance in Italy was tough and determined, but the need to defend it further strained the Germans' energy and resources.

Stalingrad   The Russian campaign became especially demanding. In the summer of 1942, the Germans resumed the offensive. Their goal was the oil fields near the Caspian Sea, and they got as far as Stalingrad on the Volga. Hitler was determined to take the city and Stalin to hold it. The Battle of Stalingrad raged for months. The Russians lost more men than the Americans lost in combat during the entire war, but their defenses prevailed. Hitler overruled his generals and would not allow a retreat. An entire German army was lost.

Stalingrad marked the turning point of the Russian campaign. Thereafter, as German resources dwindled, the Russians advanced westward inexorably.

Strategic Bombing   In 1943, the Allies also gained ground in production and logistics. The industrial might of the United States came into play. New technology and tactics began eliminating the submarine menace. In the same year, the American and British air forces began massive bombardments of Germany by night and day. In 1944, the Americans introduced long-range fighters that could protect the bombers and allow accurate missions by day. By 1945, the Allies could bomb at will.

DEFEAT OF NAZI GERMANY

On June 6, 1944 (D-Day), Allied troops landed in Normandy (see Map 32–2). By September, France had been liberated. In December, the Germans launched a counterattack called the Battle of the Bulge through the Forest of Ardennes. It was their last gasp. The Allies recovered and crossed the Rhine in March 1945. German resistance crumbled. There could be no doubt that the Germans had lost the war on the battlefield.

In the east, the Russians were within reach of Berlin by March 1945. Because the Allies insisted on unconditional surrender, the Germans fought on until May. Hitler committed suicide in an underground hideaway in Berlin on May 1, 1945. The Russians occupied Berlin. The Third Reich had lasted only a dozen years.

QUICK REVIEW

Key Battles
- June 6, 1944 (D day): Allied forces land in Normandy
- December 1944: Germans inflict heavy losses at the Battle of the Bulge but fail to halt Allies advance
- May 1945: Soviet troops capture Berlin

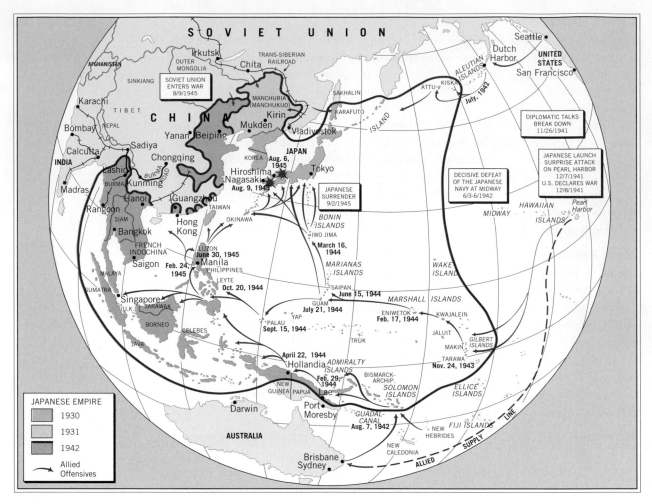

MAP 32–3

The war in the Pacific.   As in Europe, the Allies initially had trouble recapturing areas that the Japanese had quickly seized early in the war. The map shows the initial expansion of the Japanese and the long struggle of the Allies to push them back to their homeland and defeat them.

WHAT WAS the American strategy for defeating Japan in World War II?

FALL OF THE JAPANESE EMPIRE

The war in Europe ended on May 8, 1945. By then victory over Japan was in sight. The Japanese attack on the United States had been a calculated risk. The longer the war lasted, the greater the impact of American superiority in industry and human resources. Beginning in 1943, American forces began a campaign of "island hopping," selecting places strategically located along the enemy supply line. Relentlessly, they moved northeast toward the Japanese homeland. American bombers destroyed Japanese industry and disabled the Japanese navy. But the Japanese government, dominated by a military clique, refused to surrender.

The Americans made plans for an assault on the Japanese homeland, which, they calculated, would cost huge casualties. At this point, science and

•HISTORY'S VOICES•

AN OBSERVER DESCRIBES THE MASS MURDER OF JEWS IN UKRAINE

fter World War II some German officers and officials were put on trial at Nuremberg by the victorious powers for crimes they were charged with having committed in the course of the war. The following selections from the testimony of a German construction engineer who witnessed the mass murder of Jews at Dubno in the Ukraine on October 5, 1942, reveal the brutality with which Hitler's attempt at a "final solution of the Jewish problem" was carried out.

WHY DID the German government commit these atrocities? Why were they directed chiefly at Jews? Was there a cost to Germany in pursuing such a policy? Why did ordinary Germans participate?

On October 5, 1942, when I visited the building office at Dubno, my foreman told me that in the vicinity of the site, Jews from Dubno had been shot in three large pits, each about 30 metres long and 3 metres deep. About 1,500 persons had been killed daily. All the 5,000 Jews who had still been living in Dubno before the pogrom were to be liquidated. As the shooting had taken place in his presence, he was still much upset.

Thereupon, I drove to the site accompanied by my foreman and saw near it great mounds of earth, about 30 metres long and 2 metres high. Several trucks stood in front of the mounds. Armed Ukrainian militia drove the people off the trucks under the supervision of an SS man. The militiamen acted as guards on the trucks and drove them to and from the pit. All these people had the regulation yellow patches on the front and back of their clothes, and thus could be recognized as Jews.

My foreman and I went directly to the pits. Nobody bothered us. Now I heard rifle shots in quick succession from behind one of the earth mounds. The people who had got off the trucks—men, women and children of all ages—had to undress upon the orders of an S.S. man, who carried a riding or dog whip. They had to put down

their clothes in fixed places, sorted according to shoes, top clothing and underclothing. I saw a heap of shoes of about 800 to 1,000 pairs, great piles of underlinen and clothing.

Without screaming or weeping, these people undressed, stood around in family groups, kissed each other, said farewells, and waited for a sign from another SS man, who stood near the pit, also with a whip in his hand. During the fifteen minutes that I stood near I heard no complaint or plea for mercy. I watched a family of about eight persons, a man and a woman both about fifty with their children of about one, eight and ten, and two grown-up daughters of about twenty to twenty-nine. An old woman with snow-white hair was holding the one-year-old child in her arms and singing to it and tickling it. The child was cooing with delight. The couple were looking on with tears in their eyes. The father was holding the hand of a boy about ten years old and speaking to him softly; the boy was fighting his tears. The father pointed to the sky, stroked his head, and seemed to explain something to him.

At that moment the SS man at the pit shouted something to his comrade. The latter counted off about twenty persons and instructed them to go behind the earth mound. Among them was the family which I have mentioned. I well remember a girl, slim and with black hair, who, as she passed close to me pointed to herself and said "23." I walked around the mound and found myself confronted by a tremendous grave. People were closely wedged together and lying on top of each other so that only their heads were visible. Nearly all had blood running over their shoulders from their heads. Some of the people shot were still moving. Some were lifting their arms and turning their heads to show that they were still alive. The pit was already two-third full. I estimated that it already contained about 1,000 people.

From the *Nuremberg Proceedings*, as quoted in Louis L. Snyder, *Documents of German History.* © 1958 by Rutgers, The State University, pp. 462–464. Reprinted by permission of Rutgers University Press.

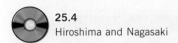
25.4
Hiroshima and Nagasaki

technology presented the Americans with another choice. Since early in the war a secret program had been working to use atomic energy for military purposes.

On August 6, 1945, an American plane dropped an atomic bomb on the city of Hiroshima. More than 70,000 of its 200,000 residents were killed. Two days later, the Soviet Union declared war on Japan and invaded Manchuria. The next day, a second atomic bomb fell on Nagasaki. The Japanese were still prepared to face an invasion, but Emperor Hirohito (r. 1926–1989) forced the government to surrender on August 14. Even then, the Cabinet made the condition that Japan could keep its emperor. President Harry S. Truman (1884–1972), who had come to office on April 12, 1945, on the death of Franklin D. Roosevelt, accepted the condition. Peace was formally signed on September 2, 1945.

THE COST OF WAR

World War II was the most terrible war in history. Military deaths are estimated at 15 million, and at least as many civilians were killed. If deaths linked indirectly to the war are included, 40 million may have died. Most of Europe and parts of Asia were devastated. Yet the end of the war brought little opportunity for relaxation. The dawn of the Atomic Age made people conscious that another major war might destroy humanity. Everything depended on the conclusion of a stable peace, but the victors soon quarreled.

THE DOMESTIC FRONTS

HOW DID war affect civilians in Germany, France, Britain, and the Soviet Union?

World War II represented an effort of total war by all the belligerents. One result was the carnage that occurred in the fighting. Another was an unprecedented organization of civilians on the various home fronts. Each domestic effort and experience was different, but few escaped the impact of the conflict. Shortages, propaganda, and new political developments were ubiquitous.

GERMANY: FROM VICTORY TO DEFEAT

Hitler had expected to defeat all his enemies by rapid strokes, or *blitzkrieg*. Such campaigns would scarcely have affected Germany's society and economy. During the first two years of the war, Hitler demanded few sacrifices from the German people. Spending on domestic projects continued; food was plentiful; the economy was not on a full wartime footing. The failure to knock out the Soviet Union changed everything. Germany had to mobilize for total war, and the government demanded major sacrifices.

A great expansion of the army and military production began in 1942. Albert Speer (1905–1981) guided the economy, and Germany met its military needs instead of making consumer goods. German businesses aided the growth of wartime production. Between 1942 and late 1944, the output of military products tripled; but as the war went on, the army absorbed more men from industry, hurting the production of even military goods.

Beginning in 1942, everyday products became scarce. The standard of living fell. Food rationing began in April 1942, and shortages were severe until the Nazi government seized food from occupied Europe. To preserve their own home front, the Nazis passed on the suffering to their defeated neighbors.

By 1943, there were serious labor shortages. The Nazis required German teenagers and the elderly to work in the factories, and many women joined them. To achieve total mobilization, the Germans closed retail businesses, made more

The Allied campaign of aerial bombard-ment did terrible damage to German cities. This photograph shows the devas-tation it delivered to the city of Cologne on the Rhine.

UPI/Corbis-Bettmann

women do compulsory service, shifted non-German domestic workers to wartime industry, moved artists and entertainers into military service, closed theaters, and reduced basic public services. Finally, the Nazis forced thousands of people from conquered lands to labor in Germany.

Hitler assigned women a special place in the war effort. The celebration of moth-erhood continued, with an emphasis on the mothers of military figures. Films por-trayed ordinary women who became brave and patriotic during the war and remained faithful to their soldier husbands. The government portrayed other wartime activities of women as the natural fulfillment of their maternal roles. As air raid wardens they protected their families; as workers in munitions plants they aided their sons on the front lines. Women working on farms were feeding their soldier sons and husbands; as housewives they were helping to win the war by managing their households fru-gally. Finally, by their faithful chastity, German women were protecting racial purity.

The war years also saw an intensification of political propaganda. The Nazis believed that weak domestic support had led to Germany's defeat in World War I, and they were determined that this would not happen again. Propaganda Minister Josef Goebbels (1897–1945) used radio and films to boost the Nazi cause. Movies demon-strated German military might. As the German armies were checked on the battle-field, especially in Russia, propaganda became a substitute for victory. The propaganda also aimed to frighten the German population about the consequences of defeat.

After May 1943, when the Allies began their major bombing offensive over Ger-many, one German city after another endured bombing, fires, and destruction. But the bombing did not undermine German morale—on the contrary, it may have con-firmed the fear of defeat by such savage opponents and increased German resistance.

World War II brought increased power to the Nazi party. Every area of the economy and society came under its influence or control. The Nazis were determined that they, rather than the German officer corps, would profit from the new authority flowing to the central government because of the war effort. Throughout the war years there was little serious opposition to Hitler or his ministers. In 1944, a small group of army officers attempted to assassinate Hitler; they failed, and had no significant popular support.

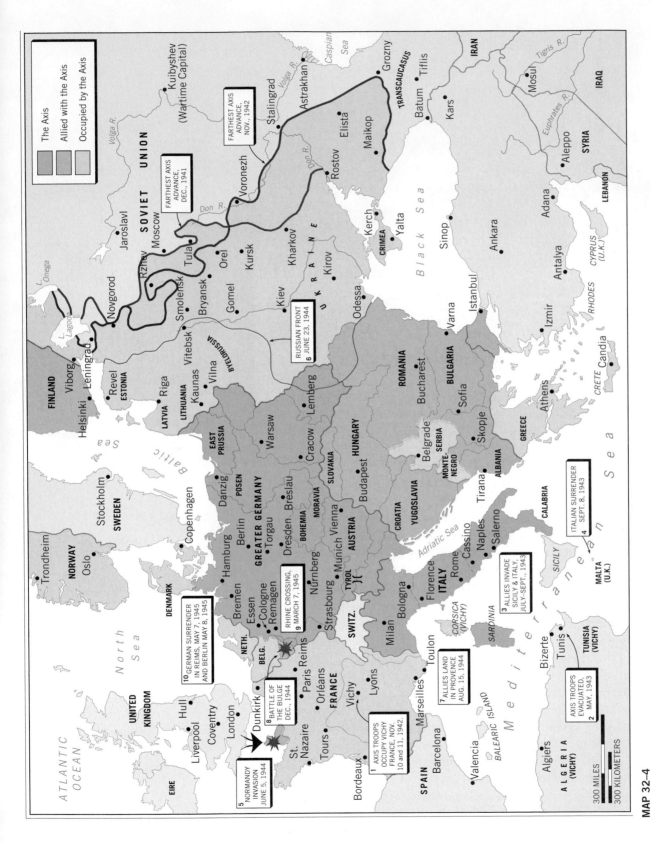

MAP 32–4

Defeat of the Axis in Europe, 1942-1945. Here we see some major steps in the progress toward Allied victory against Axis Europe. From the south through Italy, the west through France, and the east through Russia, the Allies gradually conquered the continent to bring the war in Europe to a close.

WHY WAS it important for the Allies to force the Germans to fight on more than one front?

The war brought great changes to Germany, but what transformed the country afterward was the experience of defeat accompanied by destruction, invasion, and occupation. A new state with new political structures emerged.

FRANCE: COLLABORATION AND RESISTANCE

In France, the Vichy government cooperated with the Germans for a variety of reasons. Some collaborators believed that the Germans were sure to win. A few sympathized with the ideas and plans of the Nazis. Many conservatives regarded the French defeat as a judgment on what they saw as the corrupt Third Republic. But most of the French were not active collaborators and remained demoralized by defeat.

Many conservatives and extreme rightists saw the Vichy government as a device to reshape the French national character and halt the decadence they associated with liberalism. The Roman Catholic clergy gained status under Vichy. The church supported Pétain; his government supported religious education. Vichy adopted the church's views of the importance of family and spiritual values. Divorce was made difficult; large families were rewarded.

The Vichy regime embraced a chauvinistic nationalism. It persecuted foreigners who were not regarded as genuinely French. The chief victims were French Jews. Anti-Semitism was not new in France. Even before Germany undertook Hitler's "final solution" in 1942, the French had begun to remove Jews from government, education, and publishing. In 1941, the Germans began to intern Jews living in occupied France. In 1942, they began deporting Jews, ultimately over 60,000, to the extermination camps. The Vichy government made no protest, and its own anti-Semitic policies facilitated the process.

Serious internal resistance to the German occupiers and the Vichy government developed only late in 1942. The Germans attempted to force young French people to work in German factories; some fled and joined the Resistance, but the total number of resisters was small. Many were deterred by fear. Some disliked the violence that resistance entailed. So long as it appeared that the Germans would win the war, moreover, resistance seemed imprudent and futile. In all, less than 5 percent of the adult French population appear to have been involved.

By early 1944, an Allied victory appeared inevitable, and the Vichy government was clearly doomed. Only then did an active resistance assert itself. From Algiers on August 9, 1944, the Committee of National Liberation declared the authority of Vichy illegitimate. French soldiers joined in the liberation of Paris and established a government for Free France. On October 21, 1945, France voted to adopt a new constitution as the basis of the Fourth Republic.

GREAT BRITAIN: ORGANIZATION FOR VICTORY

On May 22, 1940, Parliament gave the government emergency powers. The government could institute compulsory military service, food rationing, and economic controls.

Churchill and the British war cabinet mobilized the nation. By the end of 1941, British production had already surpassed Germany's. Factory hours were extended, and women were brought into the work force in great numbers. Unemployment disappeared, and the working classes had more money to spend than they had enjoyed for many years.

The bombing "blitz" conducted by the *Luftwaffe* against British cities from 1940 to 1941 was the most immediate and dramatic experience of the war for the British people. Many homes were destroyed; families removed their children to the countryside; more than 30,000 people were killed. This toll was much smaller than the number of Germans killed by Allied bombing. In England as in Germany, however, the bombing seems to have made the people more determined.

Winston Churchill cheered and encouraged the British people. They had to make many sacrifices: Transportation facilities were strained; food, clothing, and gasoline for civilians were in short supply.

The British established their own propaganda machine. The British Broadcasting Company (BBC) sent programs to every country in Europe to encourage resistance. At home the government used the radio to unify the nation. Soldiers heard the same programs as their families.

For most of the population the standard of living actually improved during the war, as did the general health of the nation. These gains should not be exaggerated, but many connected them with the active involvement of the government in the economy and the lives of the citizens. This wartime experience may have contributed to the Labour Party's victory in 1945; many feared that Conservative rule would revive the economic misery of the 1930s.

THE SOVIET UNION: "THE GREAT PATRIOTIC WAR"

No nation suffered more deaths or destruction during World War II than the Soviet Union. Perhaps 16 million people were killed. Hundreds of cities and towns and well over half of the industrial and transportation facilities of the country were devastated.

In the decade before the war, Stalin had already made the Soviet Union a highly centralized nation (see Chapter 31). The country was thus on what amounted to a wartime footing long before the conflict erupted.

Soviet propaganda differed from that of other nations. Because the Soviet government distrusted the loyalty of its citizens, it confiscated radios. Instead, loudspeakers broadcast to the people. Soviet propaganda emphasized Russian patriotism: The struggle was called "The Great Patriotic War."

Stalin even made peace with the Russian Orthodox Church. He hoped that this would give him more support at home and make the Soviet Union more popular in eastern Europe where the Orthodox church predominated.

Within occupied portions of the Soviet Union, resistance arose against the Germans. The swiftness of the German invasion had stranded thousands of Soviet troops, some of whom escaped and carried on irregular warfare behind enemy lines. Stalin supported partisan forces for two reasons: He wanted to cause difficulty for the Germans; and the Soviet-sponsored resistance reminded the peasants in the conquered regions that the Soviet government had not disappeared. Stalin feared that the peasants' hatred of the communist government might lead them to collaborate with the invaders.

As the Soviet armies reclaimed the occupied areas and then moved across eastern and central Europe, the Soviet Union established itself as a world power second only to the United States. Stalin had been a reluctant belligerent, but he emerged a major victor. The war and the extraordinary patriotic effort and sacrifice it generated consolidated the power of Stalin and the party more effectively than had the political and social policies of the 1930s.

PREPARATIONS FOR PEACE

The split between the Soviet Union and its wartime allies that followed the war should cause no surprise. As the self-proclaimed center of world communism, the Soviet Union was dedicated to the overthrow of the capitalist nations. The western allies were no less open about their hostility to communism and its chief purveyor, the Soviet Union.

Although cooperation against a common enemy and strenuous propaganda helped improve western feeling toward the Soviet ally, Stalin remained suspi-

WHY DID cooperation between the Soviet Union and the Western powers break down in 1945?

cious and critical of the western war effort. Likewise, Churchill never ceased planning to contain the Soviet advance into Europe. Roosevelt seems to have hoped that the Allies could continue to work together after the war. But even he was losing faith by 1945. Differences in historical development and ideology, as well as traditional conflicts over power and influence, dashed hopes of a satisfactory peace settlement and continued cooperation.

The close cooperation between Prime Minister Winston Churchill of Britain and President Franklin Roosevelt of the United States greatly helped assure the effective cooperation of their two countries in World War II.

UPI/Corbis-Bettmannn

THE ATLANTIC CHARTER

In August 1941, even before America entered the war, Roosevelt and Churchill had agreed to the Atlantic Charter. A broad set of principles in the spirit of Wilson's Fourteen Points, it provided a theoretical basis for the peace they sought. When Russia and the United States joined Britain in the war, the three powers entered a military alliance, leaving political questions aside. In Moscow in October 1943, their foreign ministers reaffirmed earlier agreements to fight on until the enemy surrendered unconditionally and to continue cooperating after the war in a united-nations organization.

TEHRAN

The first meeting of the three leaders took place at Tehran, the capital of Iran, in 1943. Western promises to open a second front in France the next summer (1944) and Stalin's agreement to join in the war against Japan (when Germany was defeated) created an atmosphere of goodwill in which to discuss a postwar settlement. Stalin wanted to retain what he had gained in his pact with Hitler and to dismember Germany. Roosevelt and Churchill made no firm commitments. The most important decision was for the western allies to attack Germany from Europe's west coast. This decision meant, in retrospect, that Soviet forces would occupy eastern Europe and control its destiny. At Tehran in 1943, the western allies did not foresee this clearly, for the Russians were still fighting deep within their own frontiers.

But by August 1944, Soviet armies were in sight of Warsaw, which had risen in expectation of liberation. But the Russians allowed the Polish rebels to be annihilated. The Russians also gained control of Romania and Hungary. Alarmed by these developments, Churchill went to Moscow and met with Stalin in October. They agreed to share power in the Balkans on the basis of Soviet predominance in Romania and Bulgaria, western predominance in Greece, and equality of influence in Yugoslavia and Hungary. But the Americans were hostile to such un-Wilsonian devices as "spheres of influence."

The three powers agreed on Germany's disarmament and denazification and on its division into four zones of occupation by France and the Big Three (the USSR, Britain, and the United States). Churchill, however, began to balk at Stalin's plan to dismember Germany and to his demands for $20 billion in reparations and forced labor. These matters caused dissension in the future.

Eastern Europe remained a problem. Everyone agreed that the Soviet Union deserved neighboring governments that were friendly, but the West insisted that they also be independent and democratic. However, Stalin knew that freely elected governments in Poland and Romania would not be safely friendly to Russia. He had already established a subservient government in Poland. Under pressure, Stalin agreed to include some Poles friendly to the West. He also promised self-determination and free democratic elections. He probably thought it worth endorsing some meaningless principles as the price of continued harmony. In any case, he soon violated these agreements.

This photograph shows the "Big Three" at Potsdam. By the summer of 1945 only Stalin remained of the original leaders of the major Allies. Roosevelt and Churchill had been replaced by Harry Truman and Clement Attlee.

Corbis-Bettmann

25.6
The Charter of the United Nations

YALTA

The next meeting of the Big Three was at Yalta in the Crimea in February 1945. The western armies had not yet crossed the Rhine. The war with Japan continued, and no atomic explosion had yet taken place. Roosevelt, faced with an invasion of Japan and heavy losses, was eager to bring the Russians into the Pacific war.

As a true Wilsonian, Roosevelt also suspected Churchill's determination to maintain the British Empire. The Americans thought that Churchill's plan to set up British spheres of influence in Europe would encourage the Russians to do the same and lead to war. To encourage Russian participation in the war against Japan, Roosevelt and Churchill made extensive concessions to Russia in Asia. Again in the tradition of Wilson, Roosevelt wanted a United Nations. Soviet agreement on these points seemed well worth concessions elsewhere.

POTSDAM

The Big Three met for the last time in the Berlin suburb of Potsdam in July 1945. Much had changed. Germany was defeated, and news of a successful atomic weapon reached the American president during the meetings. President Truman had replaced Roosevelt; and Clement Attlee (1883–1967), leader of the Labour Party, replaced Churchill during the conference. Progress on undecided questions was slow.

Russia's western frontier was moved far into what had been Poland and German East Prussia. In compensation, Poland was moved about a hundred miles west, at the expense of Germany. The Allies agreed that Germany would be divided into occupation zones until the final peace treaty was signed, and the country remained divided until the end of the Cold War more than forty years later.

A Council of Foreign Ministers was established to draft peace treaties for Germany's allies. Disagreements made the job difficult, and it was not until February 1947 that Italy, Romania, Hungary, Bulgaria, and Finland signed treaties. The Russians signed their own agreements with the Japanese in 1956.

SUMMARY

The Coming of War The second great war of the twentieth century (1939–1945) grew out of the unsatisfactory resolution of the first. In retrospect, the two wars appear to some people to be one continuous conflict, with the two main periods of fighting separated by an uneasy truce. To others, that point of view distorts the situation by implying that the second war was the inevitable result of the first and its inadequate peace treaties.

The latter opinion seems more sound. Whatever the flaws of the treaties of Paris, the world suffered an even more terrible war than the first as a result of failures of judgment and will on the part of the victorious democratic powers.

The United States, which had become the wealthiest and potentially the strongest nation in the world, disarmed almost entirely and withdrew into foolish isolation; it could play no important part in restraining the ambitious dictators who would bring on the war. Britain and France refused to face the threat posed by the Axis powers until the most deadly war in history was required to put it down. If the victorious democracies had remained strong, responsible, and realistic, they could have remedied whatever injustices or mistakes arose from the treaties without endangering the peace.

World War II The second war itself was plainly a world war. The Japanese occupation of Manchuria in 1931 was a precursor. Italy attacked Ethiopia in 1935. Italy, Germany, and the Soviet Union intervened in the Spanish Civil War (1936–1939). Japan attacked China in 1937. These developments revealed that aggressive forces were on the march around the globe and that the defenders of the world order lacked the will to stop them. The formation of the Axis among Germany, Italy, and Japan guaranteed that the war would be fought around the world. There was fighting and suffering in Asia, Africa, the islands of the Pacific, and Europe. The use of atomic weapons brought the struggle to a close, but what are called conventional weapons did almost all the damage. The survival of civilization was threatened even without the use of nuclear devices.

This was ended not with unsatisfactory peace treaties but with no treaty at all in the European area where it had begun. The world quickly split into two unfriendly camps: the western led by the United States, and the eastern led by the Soviet Union. This division hastened the liberation of former colonial territories.

IMAGE KEY
for pages 710–711

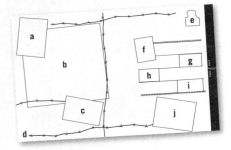

a. Allied war poster
b. A roundup of Jews in Warsaw on their way to concentration or death camps
c. Nazi party membership book with a photograph of the member
d. Barbed wire
e. Atom bomb–Hiroshima, World War II
f. An American propaganda poster from World War II
g. Soviet troops during the Battle of Stalingrad, World War II
h. A Jewish refugee girl
i. Big Three Conference - Winston Churchill, Franklin Delano Roosevelt, Josef Stalin
j. Japanese World War II poster for aircraft Identification

REVIEW QUESTIONS

1. What were Hitler's foreign policy aims?

2. Why did Britain and France adopt a policy of appeasement in the 1930s? What were its main features?

3. Why did Hitler invade Russia? Why did the invasion fail?

4. What was the significance of American intervention in the war? Why did the United States drop atomic bombs on Japan?

5. What was Hitler's "final solution" to the Jewish problem? Why did Hitler want to eliminate Slavs as well?

KEY TERMS

Anschluss (p. 714)
appeasement (p. 713)
Axis (p. 714)

Blitzkrieg (p. 718)
Holocaust (p. 718)
Lebensraum (p. 712)

Luftwaffe (p. 718)

For additional study resources for this chapter, go to:
www.prenhall.com/craig/chapter32

WE INSIST!
MAX ROACH'S – FREEDOM NOW SUITE

CANDID

FEATURING ABBEY LINCOLN
COLEMAN HAWKINS, OLATUNJI

MISSILE EQUIPMENT
MARIEL PORT FACILITY
4 NOVEMBER 1962

4 MISSILE TRANSPORTERS

FUEL TRAILERS

HAVEL

Some thousand people stand around a huge euro symbol
in a park in Frankfurt's banking district in Germany,
Friday, Jan. 1, 1999. AP/Wide World Photos

33

THE WEST SINCE WORLD WAR II

WHAT WERE the causes of the Cold War?

WHAT MAJOR trends have marked European society since World War II?

WHAT ARE the main themes that have characterized postwar America?

WHY DID communist regimes collapse so easily in Eastern Europe in 1989?

HOW DID the West respond to the collapse of Yugoslavia?

WHAT PROBLEMS has Europe faced since the fall of communism?

IMAGE KEY

Image Key for pages 730–731 is on page 753.

WHAT WERE the causes of the Cold War?

Since the conclusion of World War II, Europe's influence on the world scene has been transformed. The destruction of the war itself left Europe incapable of exercising the kind of power it had formerly exerted. The Cold War between the United States and the Soviet Union made Europe a divided and contested territory. Furthermore, Europeans soon began to lose control of their overseas empires.

The decision by the United States to take an activist role in world affairs touched every aspect of the postwar world. American domestic politics and foreign policy became intertwined as in no previous period of American history.

Like virtually every other part of the world, Europe experienced the impact of American culture through military alliances, trade, tourism, and popular entertainment. Europeans also began to build structures for greater economic cooperation.

While Western Europe enjoyed increased democratization and unprecedented prosperity, Eastern Europe experienced economic stagnation and Soviet domination. Yet from the late 1970s onward, there were political stirrings in the east. These culminated in 1989 with revolutions throughout Eastern Europe and in 1991 with the collapse of communist government in the Soviet Union itself. For over a decade since those events, Europeans have been seeking to forge a new political direction.

THE COLD WAR ERA

The tense relationship between the United States and the Soviet Union that dominated world history during the second half of the twentieth century originated in the closing months of World War II.

The split arose from basic differences of ideology and interest. The Soviet Union's attempt to extend its control westward into Europe and southward into the Middle East was a continuation of the policy of tsarist Russia. It had been Britain's traditional role to restrain Russian expansion into these areas; the United States inherited that task as Britain's power waned. The alternative was to permit a major increase in power by a huge, traditionally hostile state. That state, dedicated in its official ideology to the overthrow of nations like the United States, was governed by Stalin (1879–1953), an absolute dictator, with a proven record for horrible cruelties. Few nations would take such risks.

However, the Americans made no attempt to roll back Soviet power where it already existed, even though American military forces were the greatest in their history, American industrial power was unmatched, and America had a monopoly on atomic weapons. In less than a year from the war's end, the Americans reduced their forces in Europe from 3.5 million to half a million. The speedy withdrawal was fully in accord with America's peacetime goals. These goals included support for self-determination, autonomy, and democracy in the political sphere; and free trade, freedom of the seas, no barriers to investment, and the Open Door in the economic sphere. As the strongest, richest nation in the world, the United States would benefit from an international order based on such goals.

However, the Soviets saw American resistance to their expansion as a threat to their security and their legitimate aims. American objections over Poland and other states were seen as attempts to undermine regimes friendly to Russia and encircle the Soviet Union with hostile neighbors.

The growth in France and Italy of Communist parties taking orders from Moscow led the Americans to believe that Stalin was engaged in a worldwide plot to subvert capitalism and democracy. We do not know for certain if these suspicions were justified, but most people in the West considered them plausible.

EARLY COLD WAR CONFLICT

The new mood of hostility among the former allies appeared quickly. In February 1946, both Stalin and his foreign minister, Vyacheslav Molotov (1890–1986), publicly spoke of the Western democracies as enemies. A month later, Churchill (1874–1965) delivered a speech in Fulton, Missouri, in which he spoke of an Iron Curtain dividing a free and democratic West from an East under totalitarian rule. In this atmosphere, difficulties grew.

The attempt to deal cooperatively with the problem of atomic energy was an early victim of the Cold War. The United States continued to develop its own atomic weapons in secrecy, and the Russians did the same. By 1949, the Soviet Union had exploded its own atomic bomb, and the race for nuclear weapons was on.

The resistance of westerners to what they perceived as Soviet intransigence and communist subversion took clearer form in 1947. Since 1944, civil war had been raging in Greece between the royalist government restored by Britain and insurgents supported by the communist countries. In 1947, Britain informed the United States that it was financially no longer able to support the Greeks. On March 12, President Truman (1884–1972) asked Congress to provide funds to support Greece and Turkey, which was also under Soviet pressure. Congress complied. In what became known as the Truman Doctrine, the American president advocated a policy of supporting "free people who are resisting attempted subjugation by armed minorities or by outside pressures," by implication anywhere in the world.

For Western Europe, where the menacing growth of communist parties was fueled by postwar poverty and hunger, the Americans devised the European Recovery Program. Named the Marshall Plan after George C. Marshall (1880–1959), the secretary of state who introduced it, this program provided broad economic aid to European states on condition only that they work together. The Soviet Union forbade its satellites to take part.

The Marshall Plan helped restore prosperity to Western Europe and set the stage for its unprecedented economic growth. It also led to the establishment there of solid democratic regimes.

Stalin's answer was to replace all multiparty governments behind the Iron Curtain with thoroughly communist regimes under his control. He also organized in 1947 the Communist Information Bureau (Cominform) dedicated to spreading revolutionary communism throughout the world.

In February 1948, a brutal display of Stalin's policy took place in Prague. The communists expelled the democratic members of what had been a coalition government and murdered the foreign minister. Czechoslovakia was brought fully under Soviet rule.

These Soviet actions increased America's determination to make its own arrangements in Germany. The Russians dismantled German industry in the eastern zone, but the Americans tried to make Germany self-sufficient, which meant restoring its industrial capacity. To the Soviets the restoration of a powerful industrial Germany was unacceptable.

When the Western powers agreed to go forward with a separate constitution for the western sectors of Germany in February 1948, the Soviets walked out of the joint Allied Control Commission. Berlin, although well within the Soviet zone, was governed by all four powers. The Soviets sealed the city off by closing all railroads and highways to West Germany. Their purpose was to drive the Western powers out of Berlin.

The Western allies responded to the Berlin Blockade with an airlift of supplies that lasted almost a year. In May 1949, the Russians were forced to reopen access to Berlin. The incident hastened the separation of Germany into two states,

26.1
The Soviet Victory: Capitalism versus Communism (February 1946): Joseph Stalin

26.2
"An Iron Curtain Has Descended Across the Continent" (March 1946): Sir Winston Churchill

Cold War   The ideological and geographical struggle between the United States and its allies and the USSR and its allies that began after World War II and lasted until the dissolution of the USSR in 1989.

Marshall Plan   The U.S. program, named after Secretary of State George C. Marshall, that provided economic aid to Europe after World War II.

The Allied airlift in action during the Berlin Blockade. Every day for almost a year Western planes supplied the city until Stalin lifted the blockade in May 1949.

Bildarchiv Preussischer Kulturbesitz

which prevailed for 40 years. West Germany became the German Federal Republic in September 1949, and the eastern region became the German Democratic Republic a month later.

NATO AND THE WARSAW PACT

Meanwhile, Western Europe was coming closer together. The Marshall Plan encouraged international cooperation. In April 1949, Belgium, the Netherlands, Luxembourg, France, Britain, Italy, Denmark, Norway, Portugal, and Iceland signed a treaty with Canada and the United States that formed the North Atlantic Treaty Organization (NATO) for mutual assistance in case of attack. NATO formed the West into a bloc. A few years later West Germany, Greece, and Turkey joined the alliance (see Map 33–1).

Unlike the NATO states, the states of Eastern Europe were under direct Soviet domination through local communist parties controlled from Moscow and overawed by the Red Army. The Warsaw Pact of May 1955, which included Albania, Bulgaria, Czechoslovakia, East Germany, Hungary, Poland, Romania, and the Soviet Union, merely gave formal recognition to a system that already existed. Europe stood divided into two unfriendly blocs.

CRISES OF 1956

The events of 1956 had considerable significance both for the Cold War and for what they implied about the realities of European power in the postwar era.

Suez   In July 1956, President Gamal Abdel Nasser (1918–1970) of Egypt nationalized the Suez Canal. Britain and France feared that this action would imperil their supplies of oil in the Persian Gulf. In October 1956, war broke out between Egypt and Israel. The British and French intervened; however, the United States refused to support them. The Soviet Union protested vehemently. The Anglo-French forces had to be withdrawn, and control of the canal remained with Egypt. The Suez intervention proved that without the support of the United States, the nations of Western Europe could no longer impose their will on the rest of the world.

Poland   Developments in Eastern Europe demonstrated similar limitations on independent action among the Soviet bloc nations. When the prime minister of Poland died, the Polish Communist Party refused to choose a successor selected by Moscow. Considerable tension developed. In the end, Wladyslaw Gomulka (1905–1982) emerged as the new communist leader of Poland. He proved acceptable to the Soviets because he promised to keep Poland in the Warsaw Pact. However, he halted the collectivization of Polish agriculture and improved relations with the Polish Roman Catholic Church.

Uprising in Hungary   Hungary provided the second trouble spot for the Soviet Union. In late October, fighting erupted in Budapest. A new ministry headed by Imre Nagy (1896–1958) was installed. Nagy was a communist who sought an independent position for Hungary. Unlike Gomulka, he called for Hungarian withdrawal from the Warsaw Pact. Soviet troops deposed Nagy, who was later executed, and imposed Janos Kadar (1912–1989) as premier.

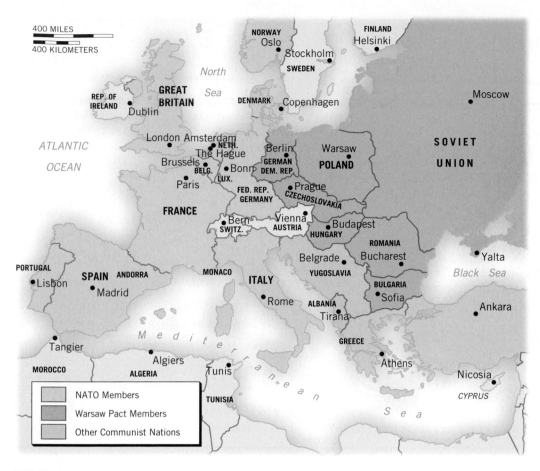

MAP 33–1
Major Cold War European alliance systems.   The North Atlantic Treaty Organization, which includes both Canada and the United States, stretches as far east as Turkey. By contrast, the Warsaw Pact nations were the contiguous Communist states of Eastern Europe, with the Soviet Union, of course, as the dominant member.

WHY DID NATO and the Warsaw Pact emerge and become rivals after World War II?

THE COLD WAR INTENSIFIED

The events of 1956 ended the era of fully autonomous action by the European nation-states. The two superpowers had demonstrated the new political realities. After 1956, the Soviet Union began to talk about "peaceful coexistence" with the United States. In 1959, tensions relaxed sufficiently for Soviet Premier Nikita Khrushchev (1894–1971) to tour the United States. A summit meeting was scheduled for May 1960 in Paris, and American President Dwight D. Eisenhower (1890–1969) was to go to Moscow.

Just before the gathering, the Soviet Union shot down an American U-2 aircraft that was flying reconnaissance over Soviet territory. Khrushchev refused to take part in the summit conference, and Eisenhower's trip to the Soviet Union was canceled.

In fact, the Soviets had long been aware of the American flights. They chose to protest at this time for two reasons. Khrushchev had hoped that the leaders of Britain, France, and the United States would be so divided over the future of Germany that a united Allied front would be impossible. The divisions did not arise, so the conference would have been of little use to him. Second, by 1960 the Communist world had become split between the Soviets and the Chinese, who accused

OVERVIEW

MAJOR DATES OF THE COLD WAR

Cooperation between the West and the Soviet Union did not survive the end of World War II. It was replaced by the Cold War, more than 40 years of mutual rivalry and suspicion that extended around the globe as the United States and the Soviets jockeyed for predominance in Europe, Asia, Africa, and Latin America.

1946	Stalin describes the Western democracies as enemies. Churchill delivers his "Iron Curtain" speech.		1961	Berlin Wall erected
			1962	Cuban Missile Crisis
1947	The United States intervenes in the Greek civil war under the Truman Doctrine.		1963	Soviet-American Test Ban Treaty
			1965	Massive U.S. involvement in Vietnam begins
1948	Berlin Blockade		1968	Soviet invasion of Czechoslovakia
1949	Formation of NATO		1973	United States withdraws from Vietnam
1950	Outbreak of Korean War		1975	Helsinki Accords
1953	Death of Stalin. End of the Korean War		1979	Soviet invasion of Afghanistan
1954	France withdraws from Indochina		1980	Solidarity founded in Poland
1955	Formation of Warsaw Pact		1985	Reagan-Gorbachev summit
1956	Suez Crisis. Hungarian Revolution		1987	U.S.-Soviet Arms Limitation Treaty
1959	Castro takes power in Cuba		1989	Fall of communist regimes in Eastern Europe
1960	U–2 Incident. Paris Summit collapses		1991	End of the Soviet Union

the Russians of lacking revolutionary zeal. Khrushchev's action was an attempt to show the hard-line attitude of the Soviet Union toward the capitalist world.

The abortive Paris conference opened the most difficult period of the Cold War. Throughout 1961, thousands of refugees from East Germany had fled to West Berlin. To stop this outflow, in August 1961 the East Germans erected a concrete wall along the border between East and West Berlin that remained until November 1989.

A year later, the Cuban missile crisis brought the most dangerous days of the Cold War. The Soviet Union placed missiles in Cuba, a nation friendly to Soviet aims lying less than a hundred miles from the United States. The United States blockaded Cuba, halted the shipment of new missiles, and demanded the removal of existing installations. After a tense week, the Soviets backed down and the crisis ended.

DETENTE AND AFTERWARD

In 1963, the two powers concluded a Nuclear Test Ban Treaty. This agreement marked the start of a detente, or lessening in tensions, between the United States and the Soviet Union that intensified during the presidency of Richard Nixon (1913–1994). This policy involved trade agreements and mutual reduction of strategic armaments. But the Soviet invasion of Afghanistan in 1979 hardened relations between Washington and Moscow, and the US Senate refused to ratify the Strategic Arms Limitation Treaty of 1979.

However, President Ronald Reagan (b. 1911) and Soviet leader Mikhail S. Gorbachev (b. 1931) held a friendly summit meeting in 1985, the first East-West summit in six years. Other meetings followed. In December 1987, the United

States and the Soviet Union agreed to dismantle over 2,000 medium- and shorter-range missiles. The treaty provided for mutual inspection. This action represented the most significant agreement since World War II between the two superpowers.

Thereafter, the political upheavals in Eastern Europe and the Soviet Union overwhelmed the issues of the Cold War. The Soviet Union abandoned its support for communist governments in Eastern Europe. By the close of 1991, the Soviet Union itself had collapsed. The Cold War was over.

EUROPEAN SOCIETY IN THE SECOND HALF OF THE TWENTIETH CENTURY

The sharp division of Europe into a democratic west and communist east for most of the second half of the twentieth century makes generalizations about social and economic developments difficult. Prosperity in the west contrasted with shortages in the eastern economies, which were managed to benefit the Soviet Union. Most of the developments discussed in this chapter have taken place in Western Europe.

TOWARD WESTERN EUROPEAN UNIFICATION

Since 1945, the nations of Western Europe have taken unprecedented steps toward economic cooperation. The process is not completed. The collapse of the Soviet Union and the emergence of new free governments in Eastern Europe have further complicated it.

The Marshall Plan and NATO gave the involved countries new experience in working with each other and demonstrated the gains from cooperative action. In 1950, France, West Germany, Italy, Belgium, the Netherlands, and Luxembourg organized the European Coal and Steel Community. Its success reduced suspicions about the concept of coordination and economic integration.

In 1957, through the Treaty of Rome, the six members of the Coal and Steel Community agreed to form a new organization: the **European Economic Community**, or Common Market. The members sought to achieve the eventual elimination of tariffs, a free flow of capital and labor, and similar wage and social benefits in all the participating countries. The chief institution of the EEC was a High Commission composed of technocrats.

The Common Market was a stunning success. By 1968, all tariffs among the six members had been abolished. Trade and labor migration among the members grew steadily. Moreover, nonmember states began to seek membership. In 1973, Great Britain, Ireland, and Denmark became members, and Spain, Portugal, Greece, Sweden, Finland, and Austria were eventually admitted.

In 1988, the leaders of the Community decided to create a virtual free-trade zone throughout the Community. In 1991, the Treaty of Maastricht called for a unified currency and a strong central bank. The European Community was renamed the **European Union**.

However, as the prospect of unity becomes imminent, the people of Europe have begun to raise issues about the democratic nature of the emerging political entity they are being asked to join. They are clearly in favor of closer cooperation, but they are unwilling to see it set forth only by politicians and bureaucrats. They want a wider European market to be genuinely free and not overregulated.

The most striking element of the expanding momentum of economic cooperation is the common currency, called the **Euro**. In 1999, the currencies of Austria, Belgium, Finland, France, Germany, Ireland, Italy, Luxembourg, the

---

WHAT MAJOR trends have marked European society since World War II?

European Economic Community (EEC) The economic association formed by France, Germany, Italy, Belgium, the Netherlands, and Luxembourg in 1957. Also known as the Common Market.

European Union The new name given to the EEC in 1993. It included most of the states of Western Europe.

Euro The common currency created by the EEC in the late 1990s.

Netherlands, Portugal, and Spain were fixed according to the value of the Euro. In 2002, their national currencies and that of Greece were replaced by new coins and notes denominated in the Euro. Such a common currency is unprecedented in European history. In 2003, a panel of the European parliament also published a draft Constitution for a united Europe.

QUICK REVIEW

Western Europe's Consumer Society

◆ Western Europe's economy emphasized consumer goods in the second half of the twentieth century

◆ Soviet bloc economies focused on capital investments and the military

◆ Discrepancy in Western and Eastern European standards of living caused resentment in the East

A Consumer Society

The consumer orientation of the Western European economy emerged as one of the most important characteristics differentiating it from Eastern Europe. Those differences produced important political results. Throughout the Soviet Union and Eastern Europe, economic planning favored capital investment and military production. Those nations produced inadequate food for their people and few and shoddy consumer goods.

Yet people in the East grew increasingly aware of the discrepancy between their lifestyle and that of the West. They saw Western consumerism clearly linked to democratic governments, free societies, and economic policies that favored the free market. Thus the expansion of consumerism in the West, deplored by many, helped generate the discontent that brought down the communist governments of Eastern Europe and the Soviet Union.

The Movement of Peoples

Many people have migrated from, to, and within Europe during the past half century.

External Migration In the decade and a half after 1945, approximately a half million Europeans each year settled elsewhere in the world. Many of these migrants were educated city dwellers.

Decolonization in the postwar period contributed to an inward flow of European colonials and non-European inhabitants of the former colonies to Europe. This influx has caused social tension and conflict. In Great Britain, for example, during the 1980s there were clashes between the police and non-European immigrants. France has had similar difficulties. Moreover, large Islamic populations now exist in several European nations and have become political factors in France and Germany.

Internal Migration The major motivation for internal migration from the late 1950s onward was economic opportunity. The prosperous nations of northern and Western Europe had jobs that paid good wages and provided excellent benefits. Thus, there was a flow of workers from the poorer countries of Turkey, Greece, Yugoslavia, Italy, Spain, and Portugal into the wealthier countries of France, West Germany, Switzerland, and the Benelux nations. The establishment of the EEC in 1957 facilitated this movement.

The migration of workers into northern Europe snowballed after 1960. Several hundred thousand workers would enter France and Germany each year. They were usually welcomed during years of prosperity, and resented when economies began to slow in the mid-1980s. In Germany during the early 1990s, they were attacked.

In the late 1980s, politics again became a major factor in European migration. With the collapse of the communist governments of Eastern Europe in 1988 and 1989, people from all over Eastern Europe have migrated to the West. The civil war in the former Yugoslavia has also created many refugees. However, the new migrants are generating resentment. Several nations have taken steps to restrict migration.

NEW PATTERNS FOR WOMEN

Since World War II, the work patterns and social expectations of women have changed markedly. In all social ranks, women have begun to assume larger economic and political roles. They have entered the professions and are filling major managerial positions.

New Work Patterns   In the late twentieth century, the work pattern of European women has displayed much more continuity than it did in the nineteenth century. Single women enter the work force after their schooling and continue to work after marriage. The number of married women in the work force has risen sharply. Both middle-class and working-class married women have sought jobs outside the home. They might withdraw from the work force to care for young children but return when the children begin school.

In Europe, as in the United States, women have gained access to new roles and opportunities. Geraldine Bridgewater was the first woman to hold a seat on the London Stock Exchange.

Liaison Agency, Inc

Several factors created this new pattern, but women's increasing life expectancy is one of the most important. The lengthening life span has meant that child rearing occupies much less of women's lives. Women throughout the Western world have new concerns about how they will spend those years when they are not rearing children. The age at which women have decided to bear children has risen. In urban areas, childbearing occurs later and the birthrate is lower than elsewhere.

Many women have begun to limit the number of children they bear or to forgo childbearing altogether. Both men and women continue to expect to marry. But the new careers open to women and the desire of couples for a higher standard of living have contributed to a declining birthrate.

Women in the New Eastern Europe   Many paradoxes surround the situation of women in Eastern Europe now that it is no longer governed by communists. Under communism women generally enjoyed social equality as well as a broad spectrum of government benefits. Well over 50 percent of women worked in these societies both because they could and because it was expected of them. There were, however, no significant women's movements since they, like all independent associations, were frowned on.

The new governments of the region are free, but have shown little concern toward women's issues. Economic difficulties may endanger the funding of various health and welfare programs that benefit women and children, like the extensive maternity benefits they used to enjoy. Moreover, the high proportion of women in the work force could leave them more vulnerable than men to the region's economic troubles.

POSTWAR AMERICA

Three major themes have characterized the postwar American experience—opposition to the spread of communism, expansion of civil rights to blacks and other minorities at home, and a determination to achieve economic growth.

WHAT ARE the main themes that have characterized postwar America?

TRUMAN AND EISENHOWER ADMINISTRATIONS

The foreign policy of President Harry Truman was directed against communist expansion in Europe and East Asia (see Chapter 34). Domestically, the Truman administration tried to continue the New Deal. However, Truman encountered opposition from conservative Republicans, who in 1947 passed the Taft-Hartley Act, which limited labor-union activity. Truman won the 1948 election against great odds. Through policies he termed the Fair Deal, he sought to extend economic security.

Those efforts, however, were frustrated by fears of a domestic communist menace fanned by Senator Joseph McCarthy (1909–1957) of Wisconsin. That development, a frustration with the war in Korea, and perhaps the natural weariness of the electorate after 20 years of Democratic Party government, led to the election of war hero Dwight Eisenhower in 1952.

The Eisenhower years now seem a period of calm. Eisenhower ended the Korean War. The country was generally prosperous. The president was less activist than either Roosevelt or Truman had been.

Beneath the apparent quiet, however, stirred forces that would lead to the disruptions of the 1960s.

CIVIL RIGHTS

In 1954, the U.S. Supreme Court, in *Brown v. Board of Education of Topeka,* declared racial segregation unconstitutional. Shortly thereafter, the Court ordered the desegregation of schools. For the next 10 years, the struggle over school integration and civil rights for black Americans stirred the nation. Southern states attempted to resist desegregation. American blacks began to protest it. In 1955, Reverend Martin Luther King, Jr. (1929–1968) organized a boycott in Montgomery, Alabama, against segregated buses that marked the beginning of the use of civil disobedience to fight racial discrimination in the United States. The civil rights struggle continued well into the 1960s. The greatest achievements of the movement were the Civil Rights Act of 1964, which desegregated public accommodations, and the Voting Rights Act of 1965, which cleared the way for blacks to vote. Black citizens were brought nearer to the mainstream of American life than they had ever been.

However, much remained undone. In 1967, race riots occurred in American cities. Those riots, followed by the assassination of Martin Luther King, Jr., in 1968, weakened the civil rights movement. Furthermore, as other groups, particularly Latino Americans, began to raise issues on behalf of their own communities, racial relations became more complicated. Black Americans and other minorities continue to lag behind white Americans economically.

NEW SOCIAL PROGRAMS

The advance of the civil rights movement in the late 1950s and early 1960s represented the cutting edge of a new advance of political liberalism. In 1960, John F. Kennedy (1917–1963) narrowly won the presidential election. He attempted unsuccessfully to expand medical care under the social security program, but the reaction to his assassination in 1963 allowed his successor, Lyndon Johnson (1908–1973), to press for activist legislation. Johnson's domestic program, known as the War on Poverty, established major federal programs to create jobs and provide job training. It also added new entitlements to the social security program, including Medicare, which provides medical services for the elderly and disabled. Johnson's drive for what he termed the Great Society ended the era of major federal initiatives that had begun under Franklin Roosevelt. By the late 1960s, the electorate had become more conservative.

THE VIETNAM WAR AND DOMESTIC TURMOIL

Johnson's activist domestic vision was overshadowed by the U.S. involvement in Vietnam (see Chapter 34). By 1965, Johnson had decided to send American troops to Vietnam. This policy led to the longest of American wars. At home, the war and the draft provoked large-scale protests on the streets and on college campuses. The Vietnam War divided the nation as had no conflict since the Civil War.

Lyndon Johnson decided not to seek reelection in 1968. Richard Nixon led the Republicans to victory. His election marked the beginning of an era of American politics dominated by conservative policies. Perhaps the most important act of his administration was to establish diplomatic relations with the People's Republic of China. Although half of the casualties in the Vietnam War occurred under Nixon's administration, he concluded the war in 1972. That same year he was reelected, but the Watergate scandal began to erode his administration.

The clash between protesting students and the Ohio National Guard at Kent State University was the most violent moment in the protests against the U.S. involvement in Vietnam.

AP/Wide World Photos

THE WATERGATE SCANDAL

On the surface, the Watergate scandal involved only the burglary of the democratic party national headquarters by White House operatives in 1972. The deeper issues related to presidential authority and the right of the government to intrude into the lives of citizens. In 1973, Congress established a committee to investigate the scandal. Testimony revealed that President Nixon had recorded conversations in the White House. In the summer of 1974, the newly released tapes showed that Nixon had ordered federal agencies to try to cover up White House participation in the burglary. After this revelation, Nixon resigned.

The Watergate scandal further shook public confidence in the government. It was also a distraction from the major problems facing the country, especially inflation, which had resulted from fighting the war in Vietnam while expanding federal domestic expenditures. The administrations of Gerald Ford (1974–1977; b. 1913) and Jimmy Carter (1977–1981; b. 1924) battled inflation and high interest rates without success.

THE TRIUMPH OF POLITICAL CONSERVATISM

In 1980, Ronald Reagan was elected president by a large majority and reelected four years later. Reagan was the first fully ideological conservative to be elected in the postwar era. He sought to reduce the role of the federal government in American life through major tax cuts. This plus vastly increased defense spending produced the largest fiscal deficit in American history, but inflation was controlled, and the economy expanded.

In 1988, George H. W. Bush (b. 1924) was elected to succeed Reagan. In the summer of 1990, in response to the invasion of Kuwait by Iraq, he initiated the largest mobilization of American troops since the Vietnam War and forged a worldwide coalition, which forced Iraq out of Kuwait in 1991.

But Bush stumbled in the face of serious economic problems. In 1992, the Democratic nominee, Governor William (Bill) Clinton (b. 1946) of Arkansas, won the election.

Saddam Hussein upon capture by U.S. troops in Iraq in December 2003.

Crobis/Bettmann

29.7
"We Wage a War to Save Civilization Itself" (2001): George W. Bush

WHY DID Gorbachev seek to change the Soviet Union?

In 1994, the Republic Party won majorities in both houses of Congress in an election that marked a major conservative departure in American political life. This Congress continued the conservative redirection of federal policy that had begun under Ronald Reagan.

President Clinton and a Republican dominated Congress were reelected in 1996, but scandals plagued both parties. Because of a personal sexual scandal and allegations of perjury, President Clinton was impeached in 1998 but acquitted in early 1999 by the Senate. In terms of policy, Clinton was seen as moving the Democractic party into a more conservative stance.

The presidential election of 2000 between Texas governor George W. Bush (the son of the former president) and Vice President Al Gore was the closest in modern American history. Gore won a majority of the popular vote, but failed to win a majority in the electoral college. The pivotal electoral votes depended on which candidate carried Florida, where the final vote count was disputed for more than a month after the November election. After complicated legal disputes over how, or indeed whether, to recount the Florida vote, the U.S. Supreme Court voted 5 to 4 to halt the recount, which resulted in Bush being declared the winner in Florida and thus in the presidential election as well.

The 2000 election had also left the U.S. Senate evenly divided between Democrats and Republicans. Early in 2001, however, Senator James Jeffords of Vermont, a Republican, declared himself an Independent and voted with the Democrats to organize the Senate, thus giving them control of the Senate.

On September 11, 2001, a surprise terrorist attack on New York City and Washington, D.C., transformed the political life of the United States. In October 2001, the United States began a war against terrorism. U.S. forces overran the forces of the extremist Islamic Taliban regime in Afghanistan, which had tolerated the presence of Islamic terrorists. In April 2003 a U.S.-led coalition overthrew the regime of Saddam Hussein in Iraq. (Saddam was subsequently captured in december 2003).

THE SOVIET UNION TO 1989

The major themes of Soviet history after 1945 were the rivalry with the United States for world leadership, the rivalry with China for the leadership of communist nations, the effort to sustain Soviet domination of Eastern Europe, and a series of unsuccessful attempts to reform the Stalinist state, which ended in 1991 with the collapse of the Soviet Union.

The Soviet Union emerged from World War II as a major world power, but Stalin did not modify the repressive regime he had fostered. The central bureaucracy grew. Heavy industry was still favored at the expense of consumer goods. Agriculture remained troubled. Stalin's authority was unchallenged. He solidified Soviet control over Eastern Europe.

THE KHRUSHCHEV YEARS

Stalin died on March 6, 1953. No single leader immediately replaced him, but by 1956, Nikita Khrushchev (1894–1971) became premier, but without the extraordinary powers of Stalin.

In 1956, at the Twentieth Congress of the Communist Party, Khrushchev denounced Stalin and his crimes. The speech shocked party circles and opened the way for limited internal criticism of the Soviet government. (See "Khrushchev Denounces the Crimes of Stalin: The Secret Speech")

• HISTORY'S VOICES •

KHRUSHCHEV DENOUNCES THE CRIMES OF STALIN: THE SECRET SPEECH

n 1956, Khrushchev denounced Stalin in a secret speech to the Party Congress. The New York Times published a text of that speech smuggled from Russia.

WHAT ARE the specific actions on the part of Stalin that Khrushchev denounced? Why does Khrushchev pay so much attention to Stalin's creation of the concept of an "enemy of the people"? Why does Khrushchev draw a distinction between the actions of Stalin and those of Lenin?

Stalin acted not through persuasion, explanation, and patient cooperation with people, but by imposing his concepts and demanding absolute submission to his opinion. Whoever opposed this concept or tried to prove his viewpoint and the correctness of his position was doomed to removal from the leading collective [group] and to subsequent moral and physical annihilation. . . .

Stalin originated the concept of "enemy of the people." This term automatically rendered it unnecessary that the ideological errors of a man or men engaged in a controversy be proved; this term made possible the usage of the most cruel repression violating all norms of revolutionary legality, against anyone who in any way disagreed with Stalin, against those who were only suspected of hostile intent, against those who had bad reputations.

This concept "enemy of the people" actually eliminated the possibility of any kind of ideological fight or the making of one's views known on this or that issue, even those of a practical character. In the main, and in actuality, the only proof of guilt used, against all norms of current legal science, was the "confession" of the accused himself; and, as a subsequent probing proved, "confessions" were acquired through physical pressures against the accused. . . .

Lenin used severe methods only in the most necessary cases, when the exploiting classes were still in existence and were vigorously opposing the revolution, when the struggle for survival was decidedly assuming the sharpest forms, even including civil war.

Stalin, on the other hand, used extreme methods and mass repressions at a time when the revolution was already victorious, when the Soviet State was strengthened, when the exploiting classes were already liquidated and Socialist relations were rooted solidly in all phases of national economy, when our party was politically consolidated and had strengthened itself both numerically and ideologically. It is clear that here Stalin showed in a whole series of cases his intolerance, his brutality and his abuse of power. Instead of proving his political correctness and mobilizing the masses, he often chose the path of repression and physical annihilation, not only against actual enemies, but also against individuals who had not committed any crimes against the party and the Soviet Government. . . .

The New York Times, June 5, 1956, pp. 13–16.

Under Khrushchev, intellectuals were somewhat freer to express their opinions. In economic policy, Khrushchev made moderate efforts to decentralize economic planning, but the consumer sector improved only marginally. The ever growing defense budget and the space program made major demands on the nation's productive resources.

Khrushchev redirected Stalin's agricultural policy. The Soviet Union could not feed its own people. Khrushchev removed the most restrictive regulations on private cultivation, but the agricultural problem continued to grow.

By 1964, Communist Party leaders had concluded that Khrushchev had tried to do too much too soon and had done it poorly. His foreign policy, culminating in the backdown over the Cuban missile crisis, appeared a failure. On October 16, 1964, Khrushchev was forced to resign. Leonid Brezhnev (1906–1982) emerged as his successor.

BREZHNEV

The Soviet government became more repressive after 1964. Intellectuals enjoyed less freedom. Jewish citizens of the Soviet Union were harassed.

The internal repression gave rise to a dissident movement. A few Soviet citizens dared to criticize the regime for violating the human rights provisions of the 1975 Helsinki Accords. The dissidents included the Nobel Prize–winning physicist Andrei Sakharov (1921–1989). The Soviet government responded with more repression.

In foreign policy, the Brezhnev years witnessed attempts both to reach accommodation with the United States and to continue to expand Soviet influence and maintain Soviet leadership of the communist movement. Growing spending on defense sqeezed the consumer side of the economy.

In December 1979, the Soviet Union invaded Afghanistan for reasons that still remain unclear. The Afghanistan invasion exacerbated tensions with the United States and tied the hands of the Soviet government in Eastern Europe. Soviet hesitation to react to events in Poland during the 1980s stemmed in part from the military committment in Afghanistan and from the condemnation the invasion provoked from Western European communists and from many governments. The Soviet government also lost support at home as its army became bogged down and suffered steady losses.

SOLIDARITY IN POLAND

In July 1980, the Polish government raised meat prices. The result was strikes across the country. In August, a strike at the Lenin shipyard at Gdansk spread to other shipyards, transport facilities, and factories. The strikers, led by Lech Walesa (b. 1944), refused to negotiate through the government-controlled unions. The Gdansk strike ended on August 31 after the government promised the workers the right to organize an independent union, Solidarity. Less than a week later the Polish communist head of state was replaced.

In the summer of 1981, for the first time in any European communist state, secret elections for the Polish party congress permitted real choices among the candidates. Poland remained a communist state, but real debate was temporarily permitted within the party congress. This experiment ended in December 1981. General Wojciech Jaruzelski (b.1923) became head of the party, and martial law was declared.

GORBACHEV ATTEMPTS TO REDIRECT THE SOVIET UNION

By the time of Brezhnev's death in 1982, the Soviet system seemed incapable of meeting the needs of its people or pursuing a successful foreign policy. But no observers expected rapid change in the Soviet Union or its satellites.

However, in 1985, Mikhail S. Gorbachev (b. 1931) came to power and immediately set about making the most remarkable changes that the Soviet Union had witnessed since the 1920s. His reforms unleashed forces that within seven years would force him to retire and end both communist rule and the Soviet Union itself.

Initially, Gorbachev and his supporters challenged the way the party and bureaucracy managed the Soviet government and economy. Under the policy of *perestroika*, or restructuring, they proposed major economic and political reforms. The centralized economic ministries were streamlined. By early 1990, Gorbachev had even begun to advocate private ownership of property. He and his advisers considered policies to move the economy rapidly toward a free market. However, the

perestroika　Meaning "restructuring." The attempt in the 1980s to reform the Soviet government and economy.

Soviet economy, instead of growing, stagnated and even declined. Shortages of food, consumer goods, and housing became chronic. Old-fashioned communists blamed these results on the abandonment of centralized planning, while democratic critics blamed them on overly slow reform.

Gorbachev also allowed public criticism of Soviet history and Soviet Communist Party policy. This development was termed *glasnost*, or openness. In factories, workers were permitted to criticize party officials and the economic plans of the party and the government. Censorship was relaxed and free expression encouraged. Dissidents were released from prison. In 1988, a new constitution permitted contested elections. After real political campaigning, the Congress of People's Deputies was elected in 1989 and then formally elected Gorbachev as president.

The Soviet Union was a vast empire of diverse nationalities. Some had been conquered under the tsars; others had been seized by Stalin. Glasnost quickly brought to the fore the discontents of all such peoples. Gorbachev proved inept in addressing these ethnic complaints.

glasnost Meaning "openness." The policy initiated by Mikhail Gorbachev (MEEK-hail GORE-buh-choff) in the 1980s of permitting open criticism of the policies of the Soviet Communist Party.

1989: Year of Revolutions in Eastern Europe

In 1989, Soviet domination and communist rule in Eastern Europe ended. None of these revolutions could have taken place without the refusal of the Soviet Union to intervene militarily as it had done in 1956 and 1968. For the first time since the end of World War II, the peoples of Eastern Europe could shape their own political destiny. Once they realized the Soviets would stand back, thousands of citizens denounced Communist Party domination and asserted their desire for democracy.

The generally peaceful character of most of these revolutions was not inevitable. It may have resulted from the shock with which the world responded to the violent repression of prodemocracy protesters in Beijing's Tiananmen Square in May 1989. The Communist Party officials of Eastern Europe and the Soviet Union clearly decided that they could not offend world opinion with a similar attack.

WHY DID communist regimes collapse so easily in Eastern Europe in 1989?

The collapse of Communist Party governments in Eastern Europe and the Soviet Union was the most important political event of the closing years of the twentieth century. It was accompanied by the destruction of the public symbols of those governments. Throughout the region gigantic statues of Communist Party leaders were torn down. Here, Hungarians explore a toppled statue of Lenin.

Sygma

SOLIDARITY REEMERGES IN POLAND

During the mid-1980s, Poland's government relaxed martial law. By 1984, leaders of Solidarity began again to work for free trade unions and democratic government. New dissenting organizations emerged. Poland's economy continued to deteriorate. In 1988, new strikes occurred. This time the communist government failed to reimpose control. Solidarity was legalized.

Jaruzelski, with the tacit consent of the Soviet Union, promised free elections to parliament. When elections were held in 1989, the communists lost overwhelmingly to Solidarity candidates. On August 24, 1989, after negotiating with Lech Walesa, Jaruzelski named Tadeusz Mazowiecki (b. 1927) the first non-Communist prime minister of Poland since 1945. The appointment was made with the express approval of Gorbachev.

President Václav Havel of the Czech
Republic led the revolution that overthrew the Communist government of his
nation and has since become a powerful
advocate of political democracy and
moderation in Eastern Europe.

Giles Bassignac/Liaison Agency, Inc

29.1
A United Germany in a United
Europe (June 5, 1990):
Helmut Kohl

HUNGARY MOVES TOWARD INDEPENDENCE

Hungary had for some time shown the greatest national economic independence of the Soviet Union in Eastern Europe.
The Hungarian government had emphasized the production
of food and consumer goods. In early 1989, as events unfolded in Poland, the Hungarian communist government
permitted independent political parties and free travel between Hungary and Austria, opening the first breach in the
Iron Curtain. Thousands of East Germans then moved
through Hungary and Austria to West Germany.

In May 1989, Premier Janos Kadar (1912–1989) was
voted from office by the parliament. In October, Hungary
promised free elections. By 1990, a coalition of democratic
parties governed the country.

GERMAN REUNIFICATION

In the autumn of 1989, demonstrations erupted in East German cities. The streets filled with people demanding an end to
Communist Party rule.

Gorbachev told the leaders of the East German Communist Party that the Soviet Union would no longer support
them. They resigned, making way for a younger generation of
Communist Party leaders who promised reforms. They convinced few East Germans, however. In November 1989, the
government of East Germany ordered the opening of the Berlin
Wall, and thousands of East Berliners crossed into West Berlin.
By early 1990, the communist government of East Germany
had been swept away.

The citizens of the two Germanies were determined to reunify. By February
1990, reunification had become a foregone conclusion, accepted by the United
States, the Soviet Union, Great Britain, and France.

THE VELVET REVOLUTION IN CZECHOSLOVAKIA

Late in 1989, in "the velvet revolution," communist rule in Czechoslovakia unrav-
eled. In November, under popular pressure from street demonstrations and well-
organized political opposition, the Communist Party began to retreat from office. The
patterns were similar to those occurring elsewhere. The old leadership resigned, and
younger communists replaced them. The changes they offered were inadequate.

The popular new Czech leader was Václav Havel (b. 1936), a playwright of international standing whom the government had imprisoned. Havel and his group,
which called itself Civic Forum, negotiated changes with the government that included
an end to the political dominance of the Communist Party and the inclusion of non-
Communists in the government. In late December 1989, Havel was elected president.

VIOLENT REVOLUTION IN ROMANIA

The most violent upheaval of 1989 occurred in Romania, where President Nico-
lae Ceausescu (1918–1989) had governed without opposition for almost a quarter century. Romania was a corrupt, one-party state with total centralized economic
planning. Ceausescu, who had long been at odds with the Soviet government,

maintained his Stalinist regime in the face of Gorbachev's reforms. He was supported by a loyal security force.

On December 15, troubles erupted in the city of Timisoara in western Romania. The security forces fired on demonstrators, and casualties ran into the hundreds. By December 22, Bucharest was in full revolt. Fighting broke out between the army, which supported the revolution, and the security forces. Ceausescu and his wife attempted to flee the country but were captured and executed on December 25. His death ended the fighting. The provisional government in Bucharest announced the first free elections since the end of World War II.

THE COLLAPSE OF THE SOVIET UNION

Gorbachev believed that the Soviet Union could no longer afford to support communist governments in Eastern Europe. He was beginning to realize that the Communist Party within the Soviet Union was also going to lose power.

WHY DID the Soviet Union collapse?

RENUNCIATION OF COMMUNIST POLITICAL MONOPOLY

In early 1990, Gorbachev formally proposed that the Soviet Communist Party abandon its monopoly of power. After intense debate, the Central Committee abandoned the Leninist position that only a single elite party could act as the vanguard of the revolution and forge a new Soviet society.

Gorbachev confronted challenges from three major political forces by 1990. One group—considered conservative in the Soviet context—wanted to maintain the influence of the Communist Party and the Soviet army. They were disturbed by the country's economic stagnation and disorder. They appeared to have significant support. During late 1990 and early 1991, Gorbachev, who himself seems to have been disturbed by the nation's turmoil, began to appoint members of this group to government posts. In other words, Gorbachev seemed to be making a strategic retreat. He apparently believed that these more conservative forces could give him the support he needed against opposition from a second group, led by Boris Yeltsin (b. 1931), who wanted to move quickly to a market economy and a more democratic government. In 1990, Yeltsin was elected president of the Russian Republic, the most important of the Soviet Union's constituent republics. That position gave him a firm political base from which to challenge Gorbachev's authority and increase his own.

The third force was regional unrest, especially from the three Baltic republics of Estonia, Latvia, and Lithuania. During 1989 and 1990, the parliaments of the Baltic republics tried to increase their independence, and Lithuania actually declared itself independent. Discontent also arose in the Soviet Islamic republics in central Asia. Gorbachev sought to negotiate new constitutional arrangements between the republics and the central government but failed. That may have been the most important reason for the rapid collapse of the Soviet Union.

THE AUGUST 1991 COUP

The turning point came in August 1991 when the conservative forces that Gorbachev had brought into the government attempted a coup. Armed forces occupied Moscow, and Gorbachev himself was placed under house arrest in the Crimea. Yeltsin denounced the coup and asked the world for help.

MAP 33–2

The Commonwealth of Independent States. In December 1991 the Soviet Union broke up into its fifteen constituent republics. Eleven of these are now loosely joined in the Commonwealth of Independent States. Not in the CIS are Estonia, Latvia, Lithuania, and Georgia.

WHAT DOES the breakup of the Soviet Union say about the importance of nationalism in the modern world?

Within two days the coup collapsed. Gorbachev returned to Moscow, but in humiliation, having been victimized by the groups he had turned to for support. From that point on, Yeltsin steadily became the dominant political figure in the nation. The Communist Party, compromised by its participation in the coup, collapsed. On December 25, 1991, the Soviet Union ceased to exist, Gorbachev left office, and the Commonwealth of Independent States came into being.

THE YELTSIN YEARS

As president of Russia, Boris Yeltsin was head of the largest and most powerful of the new states, but by 1993 he faced serious problems. Opposition to Yeltsin personally and to his economic and political reforms grew in the Russian Parliament. Its members were mostly former communists who wanted to slow or halt the movement toward reform. In September 1993, Yeltsin suspended Parliament, which responded by deposing him. The military, however, backed Yeltsin and surrounded the Parliament building. On October 4, 1993, after pro-Parliament rioters rampaged through Moscow, Yeltsin ordered tanks to attack the Parliament building, crushing the revolt.

These actions consolidated Yeltsin's position and authority. The major Western powers supported him. The crushing of Parliament left Yeltsin far more dependent on the military. And the country's continuing economic problems bred unrest. In the December 1993 parlimentary elections, radical nationalists made an uncomfortably strong showing. In 1994 and again after 1999, the central government has found itself at war in the province of Chechnya. In December 1999, Yeltsin, who suffered from poor health, resigned and was succeeded as president by Vladimir Putin. Putin was elected to a full term in April 2000, promising strong leadership.

Putin renewed the war against the rebels in Chechnya, which has resulted in heavy casualties and enormous destruction there, but has also strengthened Putin's political support in Russia itself. After the terrorist attacks on the United States, Putin extended cooperation with the American assault on Afghanistan largely because the Russian government was afraid that Islamic extremism would spread beyond Chechnya to other regions in Russia and to the largely Muslim nations that bordered Russia in Central Asia and the Caucasus.

The internal situation in Russia remains uncertain. Putin has moved to concentrate power again in the hands of the executive in Moscow, but Russia remains more democratic than it ever was under the Soviet system. Yet the economy continues to stagnate, and corruption is rife. Foreign investment remains modest. Observers both inside and outside Russia see it as a nation in decline with many of its most basic economic, social, and educational systems in decay. For the next decade or longer, Russia may resemble Mexico during the 1920s and 1930s, when that country endured almost two decades of political instability in the wake of its revolution and had to finance itself by selling off its natural resources, mainly oil, to foreign buyers.

THE COLLAPSE OF YUGOSLAVIA AND CIVIL WAR

Yugoslavia was created after World War I. Its borders included six major national groups—Serbs, Croats, Slovenes, Montenegrins, Macedonians, and Bosnians (Muslims)—among whom there have been ethnic disputes for centuries. The Croats and Slovenes are Roman Catholic and use the Latin alphabet. The Serbs, Montenegrins, and Macedonians are Eastern Orthodox and use the Cyrillic alphabet. The Bosnians are Islamic. Most members of each group reside in a region with which they are associated historically—Serbia, Croatia, Slovenia, Montenegro, Macedonia, and Bosnia-Herzegovina—and these regions constituted individual republics within Yugoslavia. Many Serbs, however, lived outside Serbia proper.

Yugoslavia's first communist leader, Marshal Tito (1892–1980), had acted independently of Stalin in the late 1940s and pursued his own foreign policy. He muted ethnic differences by encouraging a cult of personality around himself and

HOW DID the West respond to the collapse of Yugoslavia?

by complex power sharing. After his death, economic difficulties undermined the central government, and Yugoslavia dissolved into civil war.

In the late 1980s, the old ethnic differences came to the fore again in Yugoslav politics. Nationalist leaders—most notably Slobodan Milošević (b. 1941) in Serbia and Franjo Tudjman (1922–1999) in Croatia—gained authority. The Serbs contended that Serbia did not exercise sufficient influence in Yugoslavia and that Serbs living in Yugoslavia but outside Serbia encountered discrimination, especially from Croats. Ethnic tension and violence soon resulted. During the summer of 1991, in the wake of the changes in the former Soviet bloc nations, Slovenia and Croatia declared independence from the central Yugoslav government and were recognized by the European community.

From this point on, violence escalated. By June 1991, full-fledged war had erupted between Serbia and Croatia. At its core, however, the conflict was ethnic; as such, it highlights the potential for violent ethnic conflict within the former Soviet Union.

The conflict took a new turn in 1992 as Croatian and Serbian forces determined to divide Bosnia-Herzegovina. The Muslims in Bosnia—who had lived alongside Serbs and Croats for generations—soon became crushed between the opposing forces. The Serbs in particular, pursuing a policy called "ethnic cleansing," a euphemism redolent of some of the worst horrors of World War II, killed or forcibly moved many Bosnian Muslims.

The United Nations attempted unsuccessfully to mediate the conflict and imposed sanctions, which had little influence. But in 1995, NATO forces carried out strategic air strikes. Later that year, under the leadership of the United States, the leaders of the warring forces completed a peace agreement in Dayton, Ohio, which recognized an independent Bosnia. The terms of the agreement were enforced by the presence of NATO troops.

The situation in the former Yugoslavia remained dangerous and deadly. During 1997 and 1998, Serbia moved against ethnic Albanians living in its province of Kosovo. In 1999, NATO again undertook air strikes against Serbian forces, and forced Serbia to withdraw from Kosovo. In 2000, a popular revolution swept the non-democratic government of Yugoslavia. In 2003 the two remaining Yugoslav republics, Serbia and Montenegro, each become autonomous.

PROBLEMS IN THE WAKE OF THE COLLAPSE OF COMMUNISM

WHAT PROBLEMS has Europe faced since the fall of communism?

The collapse of communism has presented Europe with new problems and opportunities. The opportunities include the possibility of establishing democratic governments and market economies throughout the region. They also include the restoration of civil liberties in countries where they have not been known for over a half century. If the countries of the former Soviet bloc reorganize their economies successfully, their citizens may come to enjoy the kinds of consumer goods—and the standard of living they make possible—that have long been available in Western Europe. Realizing these opportunities, however, will require enormous patience. Such patience may be in short supply. Already in Poland, Lech Walesa in 1995 lost the presidential election to a former communist. In other parts of Eastern Europe, former Communists have become a major political force.

The problems in the new political and economic situation are enormous. Unemployment is widespread throughout the former Soviet Union and Eastern Europe. The plants and factories that the Communist governments had built are obsolete and have caused some of the worst environmental problems in the world. These nations also now recognize that by the standards of Western Europe, they are poor. Thousands of people are migrating from Eastern to Western Europe to look for work. In western countries, however, the migrants have encountered resentment, opposition, and violence.

The nations of Western Europe, facing considerable public resentment over the costs already incurred from the collapse of Communism, are hesitant to send economic aid to the east. This is especially true in Germany, where the costs of unification have been high. Western Europeans are also grappling with another issue: How should the former Communist economies relate to the European Union?

The political challenges of the collapse of Communism are no less great than the economic. Civil war has ravaged Yugoslavia. The potential for ethnic violence threatens the former Soviet Union, where nuclear weapons are still available. The Czechs and the Slovaks, unable to establish a unified state, divided Czechoslovakia into two separate nations in 1993. The liberty made possible by the end of the Communist governments has thus far tended to be used in pursuit of ethnic goals, leading to domestic political turmoil. The key question is whether democratic governments can survive or whether they will succumb to illiberal alternatives.

Under these rapidly changing conditions, NATO has expanded its membership to include Poland, the Czech Republic, and Hungary. Yet the exact purpose of NATO remains ill defined. Although initially reluctant to settle the civil war in the former Yugoslavia, NATO eventually assumed the role of internal peacekeeper in the new Europe.

THE WEST SINCE 1945

The history of the West since the end of World War II has been full of paradoxes. Europe, which gave birth to Western civilization and remained its center until the war, has declined in world influence. During the four decades immediately after the war, the United States and the Soviet Union replaced Western Europe as the major powers on the world scene. But they did so in conflict with each other.

The Cold War dominated political struggles throughout the world for more than half a century. It divided Europe between the NATO and Warsaw Pact alliances and forced nations outside Europe to side with one or the other of the superpowers.

In the later 1980s, however, the Cold War unexpectedly ended as the Soviet Union and the nations of Eastern Europe experienced enormous internal political changes. These changes have opened a new epoch of Western history. The United States has emerged from the Cold War as the single remaining superpower. Western Europe stands on the brink of new unity, but its peoples and governments are hesitant to press the process too far too rapidly. Eastern Europe and the former Soviet Union are experiencing economic turmoil and political uncertainty.

A new world order is emerging in which regional conflict will pose many of the gravest dangers. It remains to be seen whether the United States will be able to maintain its position of leadership in the West or whether Western Europe will take a more independent course. It also remains to be seen whether Europe, in response to economic pressures and the turmoil in the east, withdraws somewhat from world involvement during the next decade.

Summary

The Cold War U.S.-Soviet cooperation did not survive World War II. After 1945 Europe was divided into a Soviet-dominated zone in the east (the Warsaw Pact) and a U.S.-led zone in the west (NATO). U.S.-Soviet rivalry played itself out around the world from the 1950s to the 1980s, although gradually a spirit of détente arose between the two powers, especially under President Ronald Reagan and Soviet leader Mikhail Gorbachev. The Cold War ended with the collapse of communist rule in Eastern Europe in 1989 and the disappearance of the Soviet Union in 1991.

Postwar European Society Since World War II, European society has been marked by a rise in prosperity and consumerism, more rights and opportunities for women, and moves toward political and economic unification symbolized by the adoption of a common currency, the Euro, in 2002 and the publication of a draft constitution for a united Europe in 2003.

The United States The major themes in postwar American history were opposition to Communism at home and abroad, the expansion of civil rights to African Americans, and economic prosperity. Politically, the relatively liberal years from the late 1950s through the 1970s were succeeded by a growing conservatism especially under the presidencies of Ronald Reagan, George Bush, and George W. Bush. Even the Democratic President Bill Clinton was more a centrist than a liberal. After the terrorist attacks of September 11, 2001, the United States embarked on a war on terrorism that led to wars in Afghanistan and Iraq.

Eastern Europe The failure of the Communist regimes in Eastern Europe and the Soviet Union to produce economic prosperity or political liberalization led to their growing unpopularity. Soviet economic difficulties led Mikhail Gorbachev to institute liberal reforms that led to the collapse of the communist rule first in Eastern Europe, then in the Soviet Union itself. The disappearance of the Soviet Union led to independence for much of the former Soviet empire. Russia itself has experienced social, economic, and political turmoil under presidents Boris Yeltsin and Vladimir Putin.

In the former Yugoslavia, the end of communist rule led to dismemberment and civil war. In the 1990s the NATO powers, led by the United States, intervened to halt the fighting and end a pattern of ethnic atrocities.

REVIEW QUESTIONS

1. What were the causes of the Cold War? What was the effect of the Cold War on Europe?

2. How did the outcome of World War II affect Europe's position in the world? What were the factors behind the movement toward European unification?

3. What were the chief characteristics of Western European society in the decades since 1945? What was the experience of Eastern Europe during the same period and why was it different?

4. Did the Soviet economy between 1945 and 1990 meet the needs of the Soviet people? What were the causes for the collapse of the Soviet Union? What role did Gorbachev play in that process?

5. Why did communist rule collapse in Eastern Europe? Why was it a relatively bloodless revolution? What problems has the collapse of Communist rule led to?

6. Why did the old Yugoslavia break apart and slide into civil war? How did the West respond to this crisis?

KEY TERMS

Cold War   (p. 733)

Euro   (p. 737)

European Economic Community
   (p. 737)

European Union   (p. 737)

glasnost   (p. 745)

Marshall Plan   (p. 733)

perestroika   (p. 744)

 For additional study resources for this chapter, go to:
www.prenhall.com/craig/chapter33

IMAGE KEY

for pages 730–731

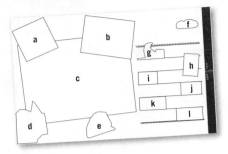

a. Jazz record by Coleman Hawkins with explicit civil rights message

b. Cuban missile site

c. Huge euro symbol in a park in Frankfurt's banking district in Germany

d. Teenager holding poster of Vaclav Havel and Czech flag

e. Piece of the Berlin Wall

f. "Solidarity" graffiti

g. Construction worker building Berlin Wall, 1961

h. European Union Headquarters building in Brussels

i. Martin Luther King, Jr.

j. A demonstration in Prague

k. Woman walks through the ruins of church in Sarajevo.

l. Toppled statue of Vladimir Lenin in the former Soviet Union

In May 1989, tanks rolled in to Tienanmen Square in China's capital, Beijing, to crush demonstrations by students demanding democratic government. Note the single figure (lower left) who for a time blocked the advance of the tanks. We do not know if this student was slain along with hundreds of fellow protesters. AP/Wide World Photos

34

EAST ASIA: THE RECENT DECADES

HOW DID the postwar occupation change Japan politically?

WHY DID Mao launch the Cultural Revolution?

HOW DO U.S. and Chinese policies toward Taiwan differ?

HOW DID South Korean and North Korean postwar developments differ?

HOW DID the collapse of the Soviet Union affect Vietnam?

IMAGE KEY

Image Key for pages 754–755 is on page 767.

The history of East Asia since the end of World War II (see Map 34–1) may be divided into two phases. In the first, from 1945 to 1980, several East Asian nations became Communist but achieved only a small improvement in the conditions of their peoples. In stark Contrast, the nations that used a mixture of state guidance and market-oriented economies made the region as a whole the most dynamic in the postwar world.

The second phase of postwar East Asian history was the eighties and nineties. During the eighties, those nations that had prospered earlier continued to grow. But during the nineties, a recession rippled through East Asia and growth halted or slowed.

The most marked change occurred in China, which, even while maintaining a communist dictatorship, introduced many features of a market economy. The result was explosive growth and social change.

JAPAN

By early 1945, Japan was poor, hungry, and ill-clothed. Cities were burnt out, factories scarred by bombings; shipping had been sunk, railways were dilapidated, and trucks and cars were scarce. On August 15, 1945, the emperor broadcast Japan's surrender to the Japanese people. They expected a harsh and vindictive occupation, but when they found it constructive, their receptivity to new democratic ideas and their repudiation of militarism led one Japanese writer to label the era "the second opening of Japan."

THE OCCUPATION

General Douglas MacArthur was the Supreme Commander for the Allied Powers in Japan, and the occupation forces were mostly American. The chief concern of the first phase of the occupation was demilitarization and democratization. Civilians and soldiers abroad were returned to Japan and the military was demobilized. Wartime leaders were brought to trial for "crimes against humanity." Shinto was disestablished as the state religion, labor unions were encouraged, and the holding companies of **zaibatsu** combines were dissolved. Land reform expropriated landlord holdings and sold them to landless tenants at a fractional cost.

The new constitution, written by MacArthur's headquarters and passed into law by the Japanese Diet, fundamentally changed Japan's polity in five respects:

1. A British-style parliamentary state was established along with an American-style independent judiciary and a federal system of prefectures with elected governors.

2. Women were given the vote.

3. The rights to life, liberty, the pursuit of happiness, a free press, and free assembly were guaranteed.

4. Article 9, the no-war clause, stipulated, "The Japanese people forever renounce war as a sovereign right of the nation."

5. The constitution defined a new role for the emperor as "the symbol of the state deriving his position from the will of the people with whom resides sovereign power."

The Japanese people accepted the new constitution and embraced democracy with uncritical enthusiasm. To create a climate in which the new democracy could flourish, the occupation in its second phase turned to Japan's economic recovery. It dropped plans to deconcentrate big business further, encouraged the Japanese government to

HOW DID the postwar occupation change Japan politically?

zaibatsu Groups of Japanese companies, or "trusts," that had a common ownership and dominated the economy of prewar Japan.

Women, newly enfranchised, voting in postwar Japan.
UPI/Corbis-Bettmann

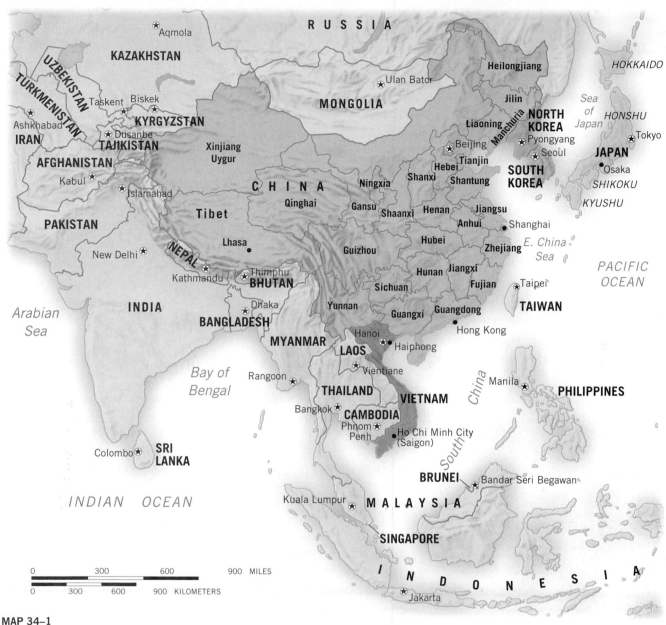

MAP 34–1
Contemporary Asia.

WHICH NATIONS in East Asia are the most prosperous in the early twenty-first century?

curb inflation, and cracked down on communist unions. The United States also gave Japan $2 billion in economic aid.

When Japan regained its sovereignty in April 1952, the changeover was hardly noticeable in the daily life of the Japanese people. On the same day as the peace treaty, Japan signed a security treaty with the United States which became the cornerstone of Japan's minimalist defense policy. (See "The Occupation of Japan.")

PARLIAMENTARY POLITICS

Japan's postwar politics can be divided into three periods. The first, from 1945 to 1955, was the continuation of prewar party politics as modified to fit the new political environment. Two conservative parties, the Liberals and the Democrats,

• HISTORY'S VOICES •

THE OCCUPATION OF JAPAN

here are occupations, and then there are occupations. Former Prime Minister Yoshida Shigeru presents his view.

IS THIS an objective appraisal, or an attempt by Yoshida to justify his own role in the Allied Occupation?

There are some now in Japan who point to similarities between the Allied, and predominantly American, Occupation of Japan, and our Occupation of Manchuria, China and other countries of Asia—the idea apparently being that, once an Occupation régime has been established, the relationship between victors and vanquished is usually found to be the same. I regret that I cannot

subscribe to this opinion. Japan's Occupation of various Asian countries, carried out by Army officers of no higher rank than colonel and more often by raw subalterns, became an object of hatred and loathing among the peoples of the occupied countries, and there is none to dispute that fact. The Americans came into our country as our enemies, but after an Occupation lasting little less than seven years, an understanding grew up between the two peoples which is remarkable in the history of the modern world.

Criticism of Americans is a right accorded even to Americans. But in the enumeration of their faults we cannot include their Occupation of Japan.

From *The Yoshida Memoirs*, Yoshida Shigeru. Copyright © 1961 Heineman Books, p. 60.

---

and the Japanese Socialist Party emerged. For most of this first decade, the Liberals held power.

In the long second period from 1955 to 1993, the Liberal Democratic Party **(LDP)**, which was formed by a merger of the two conservative parties, held power and the Japanese Socialist Party was the permanent opposition.

The LDP became identified as the party that was rebuilding Japan and maintaining Japan's security through close ties with the United States. Despite the cozy relationships that developed between the LDP and business, periodic scandals, and a widespread distrust of politicians, the Japanese people voted to keep it in power. Rule by a single party for such a long period provided for an unusual continuity in government policies.

A third era of politics began with the 1993 election, in which established parties lost ground. The LDP lost its majority in the lower house of the Diet. But since other smaller conservative parties gained, the change inaugurated an era of conservative multiparty politics. The biggest loser in the election was the Japanese Socialist Party, which ended the socialists' role as the major opposition party.

ECONOMIC GROWTH

The extraordinary story of the economic rise of East Asia after World War II began with Japan. Several factors explain this growth. An infrastructure of banking, marketing, and manufacturing skills had carried over from prewar Japan. The international situation was also favorable: oil was cheap, access to raw materials and export markets was easy, and American sponsorship gained Japan early entry into international organizations. A rate of savings close to 20 percent helped reinvestment.

A revolution in education contributed as well. By the early 1980s, almost all middle school graduates went on to high school, and almost 40 percent of high school graduates went on to higher education. This upgrading of human capital and channeling of its best minds into productive careers let Japan tap the huge backlog of technology

LDP   The Liberal Democratic Party. A conservative party that has dominated postwar Japanese politics.

that had developed in the United States during and after the war years. After "improvement engineering," Japan sold its products to the world.

Another factor was an abundance of high-quality, cheap labor. The government also aided manufacturers with tariff protection, foreign exchange, and special depreciation allowances. Industries engaged in advanced technologies benefited from cheap loans, subsidies, and research products of government laboratories. Critics who spoke of "Japan Inc." as though Japan were a single gigantic corporation overstated the case, but government was more supportive of business than it was regulative.

By 1973, the Japanese economy had become "mature." Double-digit growth gave way to 4 percent growth. Smokestack industries declined while service industries, pharmaceuticals, specialty chemicals, scientific equipment, computers, and robots grew. Japan's trade began to generate huge surpluses. The surpluses were generated mainly by the appetite of world markets for Japanese products, but they were also a result of protectionist policies that led to demands from the United States and Europe that they be abolished.

Even slower growth, or no growth at all, characterized the nineties. Banks and individuals retrenched. Unemployment rose from the usual 1.5 to 4.4 percent, and hidden unemployment was higher. But exports continued to boom, and Japan's favorable balance of trade remained large. Like other countries in Asia, Japan hoped to export its way out of recession.

Whatever the future may hold, the economic weight of Japan in Asia is huge. The second largest economy in the world after the United States, the Japanese economy is half again as large as the combined economies of most of the rest of Asia.

Alternatively, Japan may be viewed as a "Western" economy and compared to France and Germany. Japan's economy is larger than that of France and Germany combined, and its per capita product is greater. Of course, land, food, and clothing are so expensive in Japan that the per capita product does not simply equate with standard of living. Still, the important fact is that Japan achieved its present affluence through the peaceful development of human resources in a free society.

An almost completely automated assembly line at Nissan Motors' Zama factory. The high cost of labor in Japan makes such robot-intensive production economical.

Reuters/Susumu Takahashi/Archive Photos

SOCIETY AND CULTURE

The triple engines of change in postwar Japan were occupation reforms, economic growth, and a rapid expansion of higher education. Taken together, one might have expected them to produce deep cultural strains and social dislocations. Yet the ability of the society—the family, the school, the office, and the workshop—to absorb the strains and to lend support to the individual was impressive. Lifetime employment gave workers and salaried employees a feeling of security. The divorce rate was less than one-third of that in the United States. Infant mortality was the lowest in the world and longevity the highest. Japan also had far less crime. By most objective measures the society was stable and healthy.

CHINA

Civil war in China ended in 1949 as the last troops of Chiang Kai-shek fled to Taiwan. The People's Republic of China was proclaimed in October. In the decade that followed, the Soviet model was adopted for the government, the army, the economy, and higher education.

Areas inhabited by Tibetans, Uighur Turks, Mongols, and other minorities were occupied by the Chinese army and settled by Chinese immigrants. The Communist

WHY DID Mao launch the Cultural Revolution?

OVERVIEW

GROSS DOMESTIC PRODUCTS OF JAPAN AND OTHER ASIAN COUNTRIES IN THE YEAR 2000 (IN BILLIONS OF DOLLARS)

China	1,264	Japan	4753
India	474		
South Korea	457		
Australia	378		
Taiwan	310		
Russia	251		
Indonesia	153		
Thailand	122		
Singapore	92		
Malaysia	89		
Philippines	75		
Pakistan	61		
New Zealand	50		
Bangladesh	37		
Vietnam	31		
Sri Lanka	16		
Myanmar	7		
Total:	3867	Total Japan:	4753

brainwashing The Communist practice of forced indoctrination of individuals in Marxist thought followed by confession of errors, repentance, and reacceptance by society. It was particularly favored in China under Mao.

Great Leap Forward Mao's disastrous attempt to modernize the Chinese economy in 1958.

Party held the key levers of power in the government, army, and security forces. Mao was chairman of the party and head of state. The Soviet Union sent financial aid as well as engineers and planners.

Rural society underwent two fundamental changes: land redistribution and then collectivization. In the early fifties, hundreds of thousands of landlords were killed and their holdings redistributed to the landless. Subsequently, all lands were seized by the state and collectivized.

During the early fifties, intellectuals and universities also became a target for thought reform. The Chinese slang term was "**brainwashing**." This involved study and indoctrination in Marxism, group pressures to produce an atmosphere of insecurity and fear, followed by confession, repentance, and reacceptance by society. The indoctrination was intended to strengthen party control and mobilize human energies on behalf of the state.

In 1958, Mao abandoned the Soviet model in favor of a mass mobilization to unleash the productive energies of the people, called the **Great Leap Forward**. The results were disastrous. Between 1958 and 1962, 20 to 30 million Chinese reportedly starved to death.

Sino-Soviet relations also deteriorated. Disputes arose over borders. China was dissatisfied with Soviet aid. The Soviet Union condemned the Great Leap Forward as "leftist fanaticism" and resented Mao's view of himself, after Stalin's death, as the foremost exponent of world communism. In 1960, the Soviet Union halted economic aid and withdrew its engineers from China. Each country deployed about a million troops along their mutual border.

The years between 1960 and 1965 saw conflicting trends. The failure of the Great Leap Forward led some Chinese leaders to turn away from Mao's reckless radicalism toward more moderate policies. Mao remained head of the party but had to give up his post as head of state. Yet even as the government moved toward realistic goals and stable bureaucratic management, a new mass movement was also begun to transform education.

The Great Proletarian Cultural Revolution (1965–1976)

In 1965, Mao again emerged to dominate Chinese politics. He feared that the Chinese revolution—his revolution—would end up as a Soviet-style bureaucratic communism run for the benefit of officials. So he called for a new revolution to create a truly egalitarian culture.

Obtaining army support, Mao urged students and teenagers to form bands of Red Guards. Universities were shut down as student factions fought. Teachers were beaten, imprisoned, and humiliated. Books were burned and art destroyed. Homes were ransacked for foreign books and Chinese who had studied abroad were persecuted. Red Guards beat to death persons viewed as reactionaries. High officials were purged.

Eventually Mao tired of the violence and near anarchy. In 1968 and 1969 he called in the army. Violence came to an end. Worsening relations with the Soviet Union also made China's leaders desire greater stability at home. When President Nixon proposed a renewal of ties, China responded. Nixon visited Beijing in 1972, opening a new era of diplomatic relations.

The second phase of the **Cultural Revolution** between 1969 and 1976 was moderate only in comparison with what had gone before. On farms and in factories, ideology was still a substitute for economic incentives. Universities reopened, but students were admitted by class background. The so-called Gang of Four, which included Mao's wife and was abetted by the aging Mao, revived class struggle.

China After Mao

Political Developments   Mao's death in 1976 brought immediate changes. The Gang of Four and their radical supporters were arrested. In their place, Deng Hsiao-p'ing (Deng Xiaoping, 1904–1997) emerged as the dominant figure in Chinese politics. Teng ousted his enemies, rehabilitated those purged during the Cultural Revolution, and put his supporters in power. After the lunacy of the Cultural Revolution, a "normal" Communist Party dictatorship was a relief. The people could now enjoy a measure of security and material improvement. There continued, however, a tension between the determination of the ruling party to maintain its grip on power and its desire to obtain the benefits of liberalization.

Universities returned to normal in 1977. Entrance examinations were reinstituted, purged teachers returned to their classrooms, and scholars were sent to study in Japan and the West. Students began to demand still greater freedoms with the hope that they would lead to political democracy.

The new spirit came to a head in April and May of 1989, when hundreds of thousands of students, workers, and people from all walks of life demonstrated for democracy in Tiananmen Square in Beijing and in dozens of other cities. The

QUICK REVIEW

Sino-Soviet Relations

◆ 1958: Mao abandons Soviet economic model in favor of Great Leap Forward

◆ Disputes over borders and Chinese dissatisfaction with Soviet aid led to deteriorating relations

◆ 1960: Soviet Union halts economic aid and withdraws engineers

Cultural Revolution   A movement launched by Mao between 1965 and 1976 against the Soviet-style bureaucracy that had taken hold in China. It involved widespread disorder and violence.

The Chinese Cultural Revolution of the 1960s. Marchers hold a banner of Mao Tse-tung.

Archive Photos

29.4
Deng Xiaoping, A Market Economy for Socialist Goals

government sent in tanks and troops. Hundreds of students were killed, and leaders who did not escape abroad were jailed. The event defined the political climate in China for the decade that followed: freedom was allowed in most areas of life, but no challenge to Communist Party rule was tolerated.

Economic Growth Developments in the economy were more promising. Deng's great achievement in the years after 1978 was to demonstrate in China the superiority of market incentives to central planning.

In China's villages, as the farm household became the basic unit of production, grain production rose but agriculture still had problems. Because the government bought up 30 percent of farmers' grain output at an artificially low price, farmers living near cities abandoned grain production in favor of specialty crops such as fruit or the feedgrain required by China's rising consumption of meat. China already imported some of its food, and there were gloomy estimates of more serious food shortages after the turn of the century.

State-operated enterprises, which often ran at a loss and employed twice the labor needed to run them efficiently, were a constant drain on China's state-owned banks. As the free market sector grew faster, their share of production declined. Finally, the government announced that "state ownership" would give way to "public ownership." The costs of such privatization would be high—defaulted loans, bankruptcies, unemployed workers, and a sudden rise in pensioners, but the drain on the state budget would end.

The main driver of the new economy was the free market sector. After 1980, the Chinese economy grew faster than any other Asian economy. Exports skyrocketed.

The factors that fueled this growth were clear: China used tariffs to shield its markets, while making use of cheap labor to flood foreign markets with goods and build up its currency reserves.

Social Change During the Mao years, farmers had been tied to their collective or village. Cities were closed to those without residence permits. City dwellers were members of "units" that provided their members with jobs, housing, food, child care, medical services, and pensions. Party cadres exercised near total control over the unit's members. Block organizations reported any infractions of "socialist morality" to the authorities.

Under Deng, controls were loosened. The "unit" diminished in importance as food became widely available in free markets and apartments were sold to their inhabitants on easy terms. As workers with higher salaries began to provide for their own needs, life became freer and more enjoyable. The market economy placed a premium on individual decisions and initiatives.

The new prosperity and changing mores became increasingly evident. By the nineties, Chinese designers were holding fashion shows in Shanghai and Beijing. Young people associated freely. The "household treasures" of the sixties, radios and bicycles, gave way to stoves and refrigerators, washing machines and color televisions. Motorbikes and privately owned cars competed in crowded streets with the flow of bicycles. Private restaurants opened, and travel for pleasure became commonplace.

But the new wealth was unevenly distributed. The more successful entrepreneurs bought houses, cars, microwaves, computers, and cell phones. They traveled abroad and sent their children to private schools. But many barely scraped by, and in the hinterlands, poverty and hardship remained the rule.

China's Relations with the World From the fifties to the seventies, China isolated itself from the rest of the world. During the eighties, trade ties with the non-Communist world led China to look outward and adopt more moderate policies. In the nineties,

China emerged as the military and political heavyweight of East Asia, though Japan remained, even in recession, the predominant economic power.

China's relations with the United States were difficult. U.S. military alliances with Japan, South Korea, Taiwan, and the non-Communist nations of Southeast Asia were the main countervailing force to Chinese hegemony in the region. From the 1980s, trade with the United States was vital to China's economic growth, and it became more so during the mid-nineties as the rest of East Asia slipped into recession. Despite areas of contention, the United States worked to better relations, hoping that a deeper Chinese engagement with the United States and the rest of the world would lead to a freer Chinese society.

TAIWAN

Taiwan is a mountainous island less than a hundred miles off the coast of central China. A little larger than Massachusetts, it has a population of 22 million. Originally a remote and backward part of the Ch'ing Empire, it became a Japanese colony in 1895. The Japanese colonial government suppressed opium and bandits, eradicated epidemic diseases, built roads and railroads, reformed the land system, and improved agriculture. It also introduced mass education and light industries.

Anticolonial feelings rose slowly, but the Taiwanese were happy to see the Japanese leave in 1945. Guomindang officials however, looted the economy and ruled harshly. By the time Chiang Kai-shek and two million more military and civilian mainlanders fled to the island in 1949, its economy and society were in disarray. Taiwanese hated their new rulers and even compared them unfavorably to the Japanese.

In the mid-1950s, order was restored, and rapid economic growth followed. By the late nineties, Taiwan had the healthiest economy in recession-ridden Asia.

Taiwan's politics was authoritarian until Jiang Jieshi died in 1976. Taiwan then moved toward representative government. In 1987, martial law ended and opposition parties were permitted.

In 1996, Li Denghui, a native Taiwanese, was elected president in what was, as he put it, "the first free election in 5000 years of Chinese history."

Ever since 1949, the communist government in Beijing had claimed that Taiwan was a province of China controlled by a "bandit" government. It did not rule out taking Taiwan by force and refused diplomatic ties with any nation maintaining such ties with Taiwan. From the outbreak of the Korean War in 1950 until 1979, Taiwan was a protégé of the United States. In 1979, however, the United States broke off relations with Taipei and recognized Beijing as the sole government of a China that included Taiwan. But the United States continued to trade with Taiwan and to sell it arms. Both China and the United States are apprehensive about Taiwan. China worries that a democratically elected government will give Taiwan a claim to legitimacy, and speaks of taking back the island. The United States feels it could not see this prosperous and democratic state it had helped to create be forcibly taken over by China.

KOREA

Korea became a Japanese colony in 1910. Annexation was followed by changes designed to make Korea into a model colony. A land survey and land tax reform clarified land ownership. Infectious diseases dropped, and the population grew from 14 million in 1910 to 24 million in 1940. Attendance at schools became widespread. New money was issued and banks established. A huge investment

Student activists construct a 'Goddess of Democracy and Freedom,' taking the Statue of Liberty as their model. The goddess was in place in Tiananmen Square shortly before tanks drove students from the square in June 1989.

Reuters/Ed Nachtrieb/Archive Photos

HOW DO U.S. and Chinese policies toward Taiwan differ?

HOW DID South Korean and North Korean postwar developments differ?

26.6
General Douglas Mac Arthur, Report to Congress, April 19, 1951: "Old Soldiers Never Die"

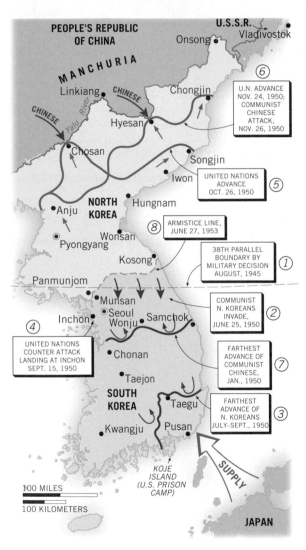

MAP 34–2
Korea, 1950–1953. This map indicates the major developments in the bitter three-year struggle that followed the North Korean invasion of South Korea in 1950.

WHY DID the Korean War end in stalemate?

was made in roads, railways, telegraph lines, hydroelectric power, nitrogenous fertilizer plants, and mining. Koreans who studied at Japanese universities brought new knowledge back to Korea. By the 1930s a modern culture was forming in Korea's cities.

Nonetheless, the colonial government was authoritarian. Its goal was to make Korea a subordinate part of Imperial Japan. Any benefits to the Koreans were incidental. Education was given in Japanese. In government, banking, or industry, Koreans were relegated to the lower echelons. The colonial regime suppressed all nationalist movements and political opposition. The police were brutal. Koreans were pressured to adopt Japanese names, drafted to fight in Japan's wars, and sent to labor in Japan. The legacy of colonial rule in Korea was an animosity that has persisted to this day.

NORTH AND SOUTH

With Japan's defeat in 1945, U.S. forces occupied Korea south of the 38th parallel and Soviet troops occupied the north. Two separate states developed. In the south, the United States settled for the anti-Communist government of Syngman Rhee (1875–1965), a long-term nationalist leader whose party won the May 1948 election. Many of Rhee's officials and officers had served the Japanese. His government was strongly supported by conservative Koreans and those who had fled the north.

In the north, the Russians established a communist government under Kim Il-Sung (1912–1994) in 1948 and withdrew its troops from North Korea. The United States also withdrew its troops from the south.

CIVIL WAR AND U.S. INVOLVEMENT

On June 25, 1950, North Korea invaded the south. The North Korean leader had received Stalin's permission for the invasion and a promise from Mao to send Chinese troops if the United States entered the war. His plan was for a quick victory, but the United States saw the invasion as an act of aggression by world Communism. It rushed troops from Japan to South Korea and obtained United Nations backing.

During the first months of the war, the unprepared American and South Korean forces were driven southward into a small area around Pusan (see Map 34–2). But then, amphibious units landed at Inchon and drove deep into North Korea. China then sent in "volunteers" to rescue the beleaguered North Koreans and pushed the overextended UN forces back to a line close to the 38th parallel. The war ended with an armistice on July 27, 1953.

RECENT DEVELOPMENTS

North Korea remained a closed, authoritarian state with a planned economy. It stressed heavy industry, organized its farmers in collectives, and controlled education and the media. Shortages of food, clothing, and other necessities were chronic. The cult of personality surrounding "the great leader" Kim Il-Sung developed beyond that of even Stalin or Mao. His son, "the beloved leader" Kim Jong-il (b. 1942), succeeded his father in 1994—the only hereditary succession in a communist state.

In South Korea, Rhee was forced to retire in 1960. There followed 27 years of rule by two generals, Park Chung-hee and Chun Doo-hwan. Their rule was semi-authoritarian: Opposition parties were legal and active but their leaders were often jailed. Park and Chun promoted economic growth. They supported business and expanded higher education, emphasizing science and technology. Labor was disciplined, hard-working, and cheap. The United States gave large amounts of aid and provided an open market for Korean exports. These factors produced double-digit growth. By the 1990s, South Korea had moved into the ranks of developed nations.

Industrialization and urbanization produced an affluent and educated middle class that resented authoritarian rule. In 1987, Chun agreed to step down, and a free and direct election was held. Although Chun's hand-picked successor, Roh Tae-woo, became president, most Koreans saw the election as an opening to democracy. This was confirmed four years later when Kim Young-sam, a moderate politician, was elected as president.

Korean international relations have changed only slowly. South Korea's primary ties were with the United States, its long-time ally, which guaranteed its defense. The country's economic weight in the world grew with its trade.

In 2003 it was the world's eleventh largest economy. North Korea's principal ties were with the Soviet Union and China. But with the collapse of the Soviet Union, Russia lost interest in its former ally. China, too, established diplomatic relations with South Korea in 1992. Since then, trade between the two nations has flourished. North Korea was increasingly an orphan. Its future is unclear.

VIETNAM

THE COLONIAL BACKDROP

The Nguyen dynasty that reunited Vietnam in 1802 proved no match for France. France completed its conquest of Vietnam and Cambodia by 1883 and added Laos in 1893.

In many ways, Indochina was a classic case of colonialism: people of one race and culture, for the sake of economic benefits and national glory, controlling and exploiting a people of another race and culture in a far-off land. To obtain access to the country's natural resources, the French built harbors, roads, and a railway. They established rubber and tea plantations, introduced modern mining technology to extract coal, and built breweries, rice and paper mills, and glass and cement factories. Native workers were paid low wages. In the south, 3 percent of landowners owned 45 percent of the land and received 60 percent of the crop. Rice consumption by peasants declined. Over 80 percent of the population was illiterate.

Under the French, only clandestine opposition parties survived. The most skilled organizer of such parties was Ho Chi Minh (1892–1969), who founded the Indochinese Communist Party in 1930. Shortly before the outbreak of the Pacific War, the Japanese occupied Vietnam. Ho, who in 1941 had formed the **Viet Minh** (League for the Independence of Vietnam) as a popular front organization to resist the Japanese, proclaimed the Democratic Republic of Vietnam in 1945. Since then, the history of Vietnam can be seen in terms of three cycles of war followed by two decades of peace.

THE ANTICOLONIAL WAR

The first war lasted from 1946 to 1954. On one side was the Viet Minh, led by Ho. It was controlled by Communists but also included representatives of nationalist parties. On the other side were the French and their conservative Vietnamese allies. The French lost a major battle at Dien Bien Phu in 1954 and departed in defeat.

A conference at Geneva divided the country into a Communist north and a non-Communist south. In the south, Ngo Dinh Diem, a non-Communist nationalist, established the Republic of Vietnam.

THE VIETNAM WAR

The second cycle of war was from 1959 to 1975 and involved the United States. Fighting began with guerrilla warfare in the south and eventually became a full-scale war between the north and the south. The north received material aid from

HOW DID the collapse of the Soviet Union affect Vietnam?

27.7
Views of a Viet Cong Official
27.8
An American Prisoner of War

Viet Minh The Communist-dominated popular front organization formed by Ho Chi Minh to establish an independent Vietnamese republic.

MAP EXPLORATION

Interactive map: To explore this map further, go to
http://www.prenhall.com/craig2/map34.3

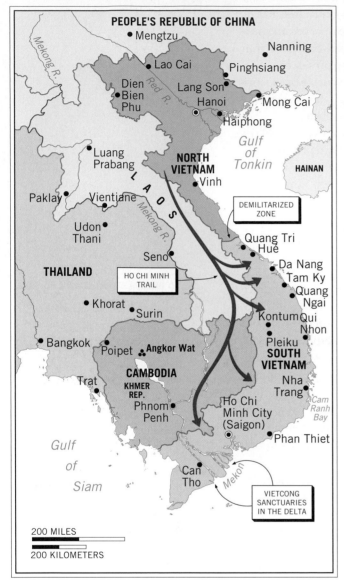

MAP 34–3
Vietnam and its Southeast Asian neighbors. The map identifies important locations involved in the war in Vietnam.

WHICH SURROUNDING countries were most affected by the Vietnam War?

Khmer Rouge   Meaning "Red Cambodia." The radical Communist movement that ruled Cambodia from 1975 to 1978.

the Soviet Union and China. The south was aided by the United States, whose forces increased to over half a million in 1969. Despite such massive support, South Vietnam—and the United States—lost the war.

In January 1973, a ceasefire was arranged in Paris, and two months later the last U.S. troops left. Fighting broke out anew between north and south; the South Vietnamese forces collapsed in 1975, and the country was reunited under the Hanoi government in the north.

WAR WITH CAMBODIA

Vietnam's third cycle of war was with its neighbor, Cambodia. Pol Pot (1926–1998) and the Communist **Khmer Rouge** ("Red Cambodia") had come to power in 1975. His government evacuated cities and towns, abolished money and trade, banned Buddhism, and killed an estimated one million persons, roughly 15 percent of the total population.

Clashes occurred between Khmer Rouge troops and Vietnamese troops along their common border. Historically, Vietnam was Cambodia's traditional enemy, as China was Vietnam's. In 1978, Vietnam occupied much of Cambodia, and the next year, set up a puppet government.

In its international relations, the unified Vietnam of 1975 became an ally of the Soviet Union. Relations with China, never good, worsened. In 1979, China invaded four northern provinces. Vietnamese troops repelled the invaders, but losses were heavy on both sides.

RECENT DEVELOPMENTS

The collapse of the Soviet Union destroyed Vietnam's primary international relationship. Vietnam's leaders also became aware that victories in wars were hollow so long as their people remained destitute.

In 1989, Vietnam withdrew from its costly occupation of Cambodia, and by the mid-nineties, Vietnam's relations with China improved. In 1995, Vietnam joined ASEAN (Association of Southeast Asian Nations) and reestablished diplomatic relations with the United States.

At home, the Communist Party–dominated government monopolized political power, controlled the army, police, and media, and supported a large sector of state-run industries. But it also encouraged the growth of a market economy, and the production of consumer goods grew. Between 1991 and 1996, the economy achieved an average growth of over 8 percent and received more offers of foreign investment than it could absorb.

But all was not rosy. Foreign investors were drawn to Vietnam by cheap labor but often encountered shortages, delays, red tape, and financial bottlenecks. Inflation was high. About 70 percent of labor was still employed in agriculture, and in the countryside barter was common. The gap in standard of living between urban and rural Vietnamese grew. In 2003, the per capita income of Vietnam was $240, less than one-hundredth of Singapore's. It was still unclear where the balance would be struck between communist conservatives and reformers in the government.

SUMMARY

Japan The U.S.-led occupation after World War II established a democratic government and set Japan on the way to its remarkable postwar prosperity. By the twenty-first century, Japan had the second largest economy in the world. Politically, the conservative Liberal Democratic Party has remained dominant despite recent electoral losses. Socially Japan has remained stable and healthy with the world's highest longevity rate.

China Communist rule was established in 1949. Until his death in 1976, Mao Zsedong remained in control of China. Mao broke with the Soviet Union in the 1950s and launched the disastrous Cultural Revolution in 1965. After his death, China opened its economy to free-market reforms. The result has been surging economic growth and rising prosperity. Politically, however, the Communist Party has blocked democratic reform, even using force in 1989 to crush pro-democratic demonstrations.

Taiwan The Nationalist Chinese set up a separate state in Taiwan under U.S. protection after their defeat in the Chinese civil war in 1949. Since then Taiwan has evolved into a prosperous democratic state. The Chinese government, however, insists that Taiwan is an integral part of China. The future of Taiwan could lead to conflict between the United States and China.

Korea The postwar occupation of Korea by the Soviets and the United States led to its division into the communist state of North Korea and the pro-Western South Korea. This division survived the Korean War of 1950–1953. The prosperity of democratic South Korea contrasts with the poverty and hunger of North Korea. Although contacts between the two Koreas have increased, the North remains suspicious and largely closed to the world.

Vietnam From the end of World War II until the 1970s, Vietnam was almost continuously involved in war, first against the reimposition of French colonial rule, then against the United States and its South Vietnamese allies. North Vietnam's victory over the South in 1975 reunified the country, but Vietnam remains poor and the communist government has resisted political or economic liberalization.

IMAGE KEY

for pages 754–755

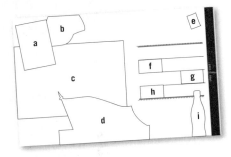

a. Cover of a Japanese comic book

b. Vietnam map

c. A Chinese man blocking a line of tanks in Tiananmen Square in 1989

d. National meeting to commemorate the 91st birth anniversary of late-president Kim Il-Sung

e. Mao Tse-Tung's little red book

f. Young Chinese children march in the streets while carrying red banners

g. An F-14 Tomcat

h. South Korean President Kim Dae-jung, right and North Korean leader Kim Jong II

i. Prototype of bottle for selling Coca-Cola in China

REVIEW QUESTIONS

1. Is postwar Japan better understood in terms of a return to the liberalism of the 1920s, or as a fresh start based on occupation reforms?

2. Is China after 1949 better understood as an outgrowth of its earlier history, or in the context of a comparison with the Soviet Union and other communist states?

3. What background factors shaped Korea and Vietnam in the period after World War II?

4. How did the Cold War affect the postwar histories of Korea and Vietnam?

KEY TERMS

brainwashing (p. 760)   **Khmer Rouge** (p. 766)   *zaibatsu* (p. 756)
Cultural Revolution (p. 761)   **LDP** (p. 758)
Great Leap Forward (p. 760)   **Viet Minh** (p. 765)

  For additional study resources for this chapter, go to:
www.prenhall.com/craig/chapter34

The globalization of the world economy has sparked hostile political reaction. Numerous groups attend the World Trade Organization meetings to protest the development of previously untouched parts of the world, resulting in perceived environmental damage and in expanding wealth for the developed nations and frequent unemployment and poverty elsewhere. AP/Wide World Photos

35

THE EMERGING NATIONS OF AFRICA, ASIA, AND LATIN AMERICA SINCE 1945

WHAT ARE the two main developments that have occurred in the postcolonial world since 1945?

WHAT ARE the most serious problems that Africa faces in the twenty-first century?

HOW DID the creation of the State of Israel affect the history of the modern Middle East?

HOW HAS the growth of Hindu nationalism affected Indian politics?

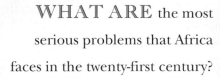

WHERE IN Latin America did the major attempts to establish revolutionary governments occur?

HOW WERE Argentina, Brazil, and Mexico able to sustain stable civilian governments since the 1980s?

IMAGE KEY
Image Key for pages 768–769 is on page 789.

WHAT ARE the two main developments that have occurred in the postcolonial world since 1945?

The post–World War II decades have witnessed the end of the age of Western colonialism and sharp challenges to European and superpower imperialism. This waning of colonial and imperial dominance must, however, be set within a larger historical perspective. Since the sixteenth century the various non-European portions of the globe had been drawn steadily into the European sphere of economic and political influence. Those areas to be treated here—Africa, the Middle East, Southwest and Southeast Asia, and Latin America—were the regions not only influenced but often subjected, exploited, and colonized by European powers. The period of colonialism that began in earnest in the seventeenth century was a relatively brief episode in world history. The last significant colonial holdings were given their independence within two decades after World War II.

THE POSTCOLONIAL ERA

It could be argued that with the passing of **apartheid** South Africa, the postcolonial era has also ended. What we shall witness in the future are waves of economic growth, such as that of the early 1990s in much of East Asia; the forging of dramatic new political alignments, both regional and transregional; and internal struggles in country after country to build political systems that allow the development of civil society and limit the destructive domination of oligarchic or dictatorial regimes.

Since 1945, two distinct developments have occurred in the postcolonial world. The first—in a process that is generally termed *decolonization*—is the emergence of the various parts of Africa and Asia from the direct administration of foreign powers, and the organization of those previous colonial dependencies into independent states (see Map 35–1).

The second development has been the forging of new relationships between the emerging nations and the Western nations and superpowers. These relationships have been of three kinds. First, until the recent breakup of the Soviet Union, its rivalry with the United States manifested itself on every continent and added to the tensions and turmoil of the era. New, emerging nations tended to be under the patronage of one or the other superpower (or, less often, that of China). Second, the character of the world economy, including issues of both trade and resource allocation, has led to new modes of economic interdependence. Third, the ideas of civil society and participatory government have gained ground.

AFRICA, THE MIDDLE EAST, AND ASIA

Throughout the Afro-Asian world, except for much of East Asia, the dominant notes of postwar history have been independence and self-determination. Today the Afro-Asian world encompasses nearly a hundred sovereign states, whereas before 1939 there were only 12. The rise of new nationalisms in these areas goes back to the nineteenth century, but it was only after World War II that nationalist movements emerged forcefully and found themselves strong enough—and their colonial masters weak (or receptive) enough—to win independence. Ironically, what came to define a "country" or a "nation" was less a communal affinity than the arbitrary boundaries of colonial administrations. As the colonial administrations themselves had been the principal targets of liberation and nationalist agitation, pre-independence boundaries naturally provided the geographical frameworks for most new nation-states.

apartheid "Apartness," the term referrig to racist policies enforced by the white-dominated regime that existed in South Africa from 1948 to 1992.

MAP EXPLORATION

Interactive map: To explore this map further, go to **http://www.prenhall.com/craig2/map35.1**

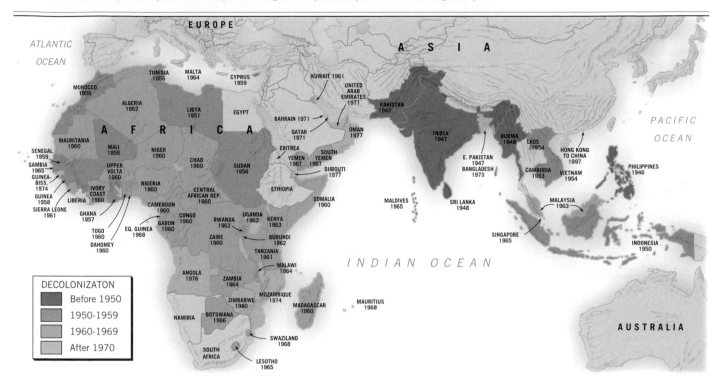

MAP 35–1

Decolonization since World War II.   The Western powers' rapid retreat from imperialism after World War II is graphically shown on this outline map covering half the globe—from West Africa to the Southwest Pacific.

HOW DID colonialism affect the political boundaries of postcolonial Africa?

The difficulties and instability these new states have faced are clear evidence of how little the older colonial powers really did for human development and self-governance in the countries they profited from and ruled. Few of the new nations have had the educational, technological, commercial, and political bases for self-sufficiency. Driving almost all other problems has been that of spiraling over-population, which has typically outpaced indigenous food production and even natural resources. Latin American and the Afro-Asian "Third World" peoples (including China, but not Japan) now make up about three-quarters of the world's population, which is approaching five billion.

In the waning decades of colonial rule and in the subsequent postcolonial era, the small elites of the former colonies have commonly been educated abroad, usually in Europe, America, and the former Soviet Union. Politically, socially, and economically, they have been too cut off from the masses of their own people to be able to lead their new independent states well. The absence of a well-educated middle class has exacted a high price. Populist movements have foundered on internal rivalries and lack of modern political experience. Class differences have pitted one group against another. Tribal or other groups have found it hard to pull together with rival groups. For many of the new nations, the price of independence has been high—in bloodshed; political, ethnic, and religious strife; economic and social chaos; and continuing inequities in the distribution of wealth.

Yet there have also been hopeful signs. Some of these states have made progress in combatting illiteracy, poverty, disease, and authoritarianism. Some have been able to develop a sense of cultural, political, or religious continuity with their precolonial pasts without retreating from the realities of modern challenges. Most African and Asian peoples can now pursue their own course into the twenty-first century. Even if that course is difficult, at least it is not one forced on them by foreign armies and bureaucracies.

POSTCOLONIAL AFRICA

Nowhere is the dramatic continuity between often arbitrary colonial territories and emergent independent states clearer than in Africa. Most of its modern nations are direct inheritors of their colonial predecessors' boundaries, and the former colonial capitals have become the new national capitals, even though the colonial frontiers had little to do with the boundaries of traditional tribal territories or indigenous states. If nationalism was a European export to the rest of the world, Africa provides striking examples of how attractive it can be as a motive for supra-tribal and transregional state formation.

African nationalism can be dated generally to the period between the two world wars, when regional opposition to colonial occupation began to be replaced by larger-scale movements. World War II proved a catalyst for African nationalism, both among Africans themselves and for Europe, which was largely disposed to renounce white supremacy theories and give up its colonial empires after the war.

THE TRANSITION TO INDEPENDENCE

In 1950, apart from Egypt, only Liberia, Ethiopia, and white-controlled South Africa were sovereign states. By 1980, no African state (with the exception of two tiny Spanish holdings on the Moroccan coast) was ruled by a European state, although South Africa and Namibia continued to be white dominated.

The actual transition from colonial administrative territories to independent national states was less fraught with conflict and bloodshed than one might have expected. The most protracted and bloody wars of independence from European overlords were the guerrilla struggles fought in French Algeria from 1955 to 1962; in Portuguese Angola and Mozambique from 1961 to 1975; and in Zaire (formerly the Belgian Congo), Zambia (formerly Northern Rhodesia), and Zimbabwe (formerly Southern Rhodesia) from 1960 to 1980. Usually, however, the transfer of power was relatively peaceable.

The same cannot be said of the internal conflicts that often arose after colonial withdrawal. Much of the instability in emergent African states has been a legacy of both the colonial powers' minimal efforts to prepare their subjects for self-government and the haphazard nineteenth-century division of the continent into often arbitrary colonial units. The establishment of new African governments often succeeded only after substantial civil strife.

Few African states had the numbers of educated and experienced native citizens that were needed to staff the apparatuses of a sovereign country, and this alone made for difficult times after independence. Corruption and military coups were rife; the attempt to implement planned economies on a socialist model often brought economic catastrophe; and tribal and regional revolts at times led to civil war.

Most dangerous and costly were the separatist struggles, civil wars, and border clashes between new states that grew out of the independence struggles. The Nigerian civil war of 1967–1970, in which more than one million people died, was

WHAT ARE the most serious problems that Africa faces in the twenty-first century?

27.4
Kwame Nkrumah, I Speak of Freedom: A Statement of African Ideology

QUICK REVIEW

African Independence

◆ By 1980, no African state was ruled by a European state

◆ Transition to independent states was less bloody than expected

◆ Internal conflicts since independence have led to instability and violence

a bloody example (see next section). However, these conflicts tended to ratify the postcolonial state divisions that had almost always kept to the old colonial boundaries (instead of regional or tribal/linguistic divisions within these units).

Every African state has had a different history in the half century since World War II; here we shall look at two cases: Nigeria and South Africa.

THE NIGERIAN CASE

Nigeria is the most populous state in Africa, with about 100 million inhabitants. It was formed when the British joined their protectorates of Northern and Southern Nigeria in 1914. Nigeria achieved independence in 1960 and ratified a republican constitution in 1964 that federated the three major provincial regions—the Eastern, Western, and Northern—under a national government based in Lagos, the former British administrative capital. Nigeria's largest ethnic and linguistic groups are the major ones of the same three regions or provinces: Igbo (Ibo) in the Eastern, Yoruba in the Western, and Hausa and Fulani in the Northern. The official language is English.

Nowhere was the aftermath of independence bloodier than in Nigeria, which was, at its inception, the most potentially successful state in independent Africa. The three-province federation soon proved to be unworkable, and a 1966 coup brought a military government into power. Its leader, an Ibo, was assassinated within seven months, and Lt. Colonel Yakubo Gawon (b. 1934) took over amid ethnic unrest that ended in massacres in the fall of 1966. Gawon's government subdivided the three provinces into states, but in May 1967, the Eastern Province's assembly empowered its leader, Lt. Colonel Odumegwu Ojukwu (b. 1933), to form the independent state of Biafra out of the three states of the Eastern Province. Ojukwu was an Ibo nationalist but aspired to control lands beyond those of the Ibos—especially the off-shore oil reserves of the Eastern Province. The new Biafran state gained recognition from several African states; and arms and support from France, South Africa, and Portugal. Worldwide propaganda depicted Biafra as a small, brave, mostly Christian country fighting for its survival.

The ensuing two and one-half years saw a bloody civil war. The larger federal forces slowly chipped away at first the non-Ibo regions, then the Ibo heartland of the Biafran state. Famine was a major cause of casualties, and the estimated death toll soared above a million by the time the Biafrans surrendered in January 1970. Out of this brutal conflict, however, came a sense of Nigerian unity, along with a major role for the military in Nigerian politics. The struggle also contributed to the development of African diplomacy and of international aid efforts in Africa.

Gawon was overthrown by another commander in 1975. In the ensuing 25 years, Nigeria has been plagued by political instability, with its leadership passing usually from one military ruler to another. The regime of General Sani Abacha (1993–1998) was especially brutal.

Abacha died in June 1998. Civilian rule was restored in 1999 but ethnic and religious violence soon broke out between Northerns and Southerns, Muslims and Christians.

All of this offers little promise. A great opportunity for successful transition to economic and political independence and leadership of less well-endowed African countries has been squandered.

THE SOUTH AFRICAN CASE

One of the most tragic chapters in the history of modern Africa has finally been closed: that of white minority rule in South Africa, with its radical separation of white from nonwhite peoples in all areas of life as official government policy for

In an act of brutal repression that shocked world opinion, Nigeria's military regime executed playwright and environmental activist henule "Ken" Saro-Wiwa in 1995

Jaques M. Chenet/Liaison Agency, Inc.

QUICK REVIEW

Nigeria
- Achieved independence in 1960
- Collapse of three-province federation led to dictatorship and civil war
- Brutality, instability, and corruption have marked Nigerian government since 1975

nearly 50 years. In the rest of East and southern Africa, minority white-settler governments tried in vain in the postwar period to put down African independence movements. Only in South Africa did they manage, until the 1990s, to sustain a white supremacist state.

From the time the Afrikaner-led National Party (NP) came to power in 1948, the Union of South Africa was governed according to the racist policy of *apartheid* ("apartness"). Until the dismantling of this policy after 1991, the country's white minority (in 1991, 5.4 million persons) ran the country. Its 31 million blacks, 3.7 million "coloreds" (of mixed blood), and 1 million Indians were kept strictly segregated—treated, at best, as second-class citizens or, in the case of blacks, as noncitizens or even nonhumans. This system was maintained by repression, to quell dissent and enforce apartheid laws.

The history of apartheid and its passing is a bloody but triumphant one. In part as a result of worldwide opposition, South Africa saw itself become isolated from the 1960s onward. Meanwhile, the rest of Africa—including other white-run states like Rhodesia (now Zimbabwe)—progressed to majority, African rule. In 1961, South Africa withdrew from the British Commonwealth of Nations. In the sixties and seventies, the government created three tiny "independent homelands" for blacks inside the country, allowing the white minority to treat blacks as immigrant "foreigners" in the parts of South Africa where most had to work. The international community refused to recognize the homelands, or "Bantustans." South Africa's isolation was further dramatized when two anti-apartheid black leaders, the Zulu chief Albert Luthuli in 1960 and the Anglican archbishop Desmond Tutu in 1984, were awarded the Nobel Prize for their work against apartheid.

By 1978, when Pieter Botha (b. 1916) came to power, apartheid was failing: The homelands were economic and political catastrophes; the country was in a recession; skilled whites were emigrating; and South Africa was becoming an international pariah. In the 1980s, internal opposition to apartheid grew.

Beginning in 1986, many nations imposed economic sanctions against the government. Anti-apartheid movements in the United States and elsewhere had convinced companies and individuals to divest themselves of investments in South Africa. Strikes by black workers in 1987 led the government to give virtually unlimited power to its security forces, but the violence created support in the West for a trade embargo of South Africa.

In June 1988, more than two million black workers went on strike to protest new repressive labor laws and a ban on political activity by trade unions and anti-apartheid groups. President Botha resigned in August 1989. His replacement, F. W. de Klerk (b. 1936) (also of the NP, but younger and more ready for accommodation), began to dismantle white-only rule and the official structures of apartheid. In February 1990, de Klerk announced radical changes, and a series of landmark government actions followed: the lifting of the ban on the African National Congress (ANC), the main anti-apartheid organization; the release of ANC leader Nelson Mandela after 27 years of imprisonment; and the repeal of the Separate Amenities Act, the legal basis for segregation in public places. In 1991, the race registration law was repealed. In March 1992, a whites-only referendum voted to grant constitutional equality to all races. The NP government under de Klerk's leadership also negotiated with the ANC leader Mandela, and despite terrorist attempts from both black and white extremists to derail the talks, the two leaders brought their own and 18 other parties of both sides to

28.2
"The Struggle Is My Life"
(1961): Nelson Mandela

On May 10, 1994, Nelson Mandela was sworn in as president of South Africa, bringing an end to the apartheid, white minority government that had imprisoned him for 27 years.

David Brauchli/AP/Wide World Photos

endorse an interim constitution, which was to be implemented once national elections could be held in which all citizens of South Africa would be enfranchised. (Mandela and de Klerk shared the Nobel Peace Prize for 1993.)

The elections were held in April 1994. The ANC won 63 percent of the vote, and the NP 20 percent, thus relegating apartheid to the slag heap of history. The nonracial constitution of December 1996 offers a new basis for the future, but the new state faces huge problems: one of the world's most extreme income inequalities; insufficient education and economic infrastructure; rampant black poverty; high unemployment; militant extremist groups; inadequate public services in much of the country; potentially severe water supply and water quality problems; and difficulties in attracting foreign investment. The obstacles will, however, no longer include a state system that holds the majority of the population in bondage.

While the new independent states of Africa have been anything but models, nevertheless Africa did not revert to tiny tribal and regional political units. However, some struggles—such as those in the Sudan, Somalia, Rwanda, Sierra Leone, Congo, and Liberia—are still ongoing, their human consequences catastrophic, and their ultimate outcomes not clear.

THE AFRICAN FUTURE

Most African states have not achieved peace and prosperity. On the other hand, the last 50 years have seen radical change and development. The prospects for government stability are not entirely bleak. Economic problems loom large, but even here progress is being made. In any case, every African state is different; each faces unique problems and must draw on its unique resources. Probably the most serious problems are those with which almost all of Africa's new nations have to contend: overpopulation, poverty, disease, famine, lack of professional and technical expertise, and general economic underdevelopment. In particular, the explosive growth of new urban centers at the expense of rural areas has brought disruptive changes in the continent's traditionally agrarian-based societies, age-old family and tribal allegiances, religious values, and sociopolitical systems. The challenge for African nations in the twenty-first century is to build a truly civil society and achieve economic health and political stability in the face of internal divisions, exploding population growth, and world-market competition.

THE POSTCOLONIAL MIDDLE EAST AND CENTRAL ASIA

The lands still dominated or marked by Islamic culture and containing either Muslim majority populations or large Muslim minorities stretch from North and West Africa to the Philippines.

Since 1945, six major developments have affected these widespread regions: (1) the emergence of new national states and international alignments, (2) the creation of the state of Israel, (3) the increase in importance of oil, (4) a resurgence of religious, political, and social Islamic reform movements, (5) the Iranian Revolution, and (6) the collapse of Soviet control in Central Asia.

NEW NATIONS IN THE MIDDLE EAST

Saudi Arabia, Iraq, and Egypt obtained sovereign status after World War I, and Lebanon and Syria during World War II. Yet these states only became truly independent of European control after World War II. Others soon followed: Jordan in 1946; Libya in 1951; Morocco and Tunisia in 1956; Algeria in 1962; and, by 1971,

HOW DID the creation of the State of Israel affect the history of the modern Middle East?

the two Yemens and the Arabian Gulf states. Political instability and autocratic rule have been constants in most of these states. All share the Arabic language and the Muslim faith (although Lebanon has many Druze and Christians), but attempts to create pan-Arab alliances or federations have been abortive. Historical, regional, and national factors give each country a distinctive character. The oil wealth and strategic importance of the region have attracted foreign interest and interference, further complicating relations among the Arab states and between them and the rest of the world.

Turkey dates its existence from the 1920s rather than the 1950s. It represents a modernist republican experiment that has managed to allow a civil society and a democratically elected government to be the norm. It has, however, been plagued with ongoing intervention from the military, which has repeatedly deposed existing elected, governments. Turkey, along with Israel, is still the most economically advanced Middle Eastern country. With the creation of new Turkic-language-speaking states in Central Asia after the breakup of the Soviet Union, Turkey is making a bid to strengthen its ties there.

THE ARAB-ISRAELI CONFLICT

Nowhere has the presence of the superpowers and Europe been more sharply felt than in the 1948 creation of the state of Israel in the former British mandate territory of Palestine, intended as a national homeland for the Jewish people. This event was the achievement of the world Zionist movement founded in 1897 by Theodor Herzl (1860–1904) in Europe (see Chapter 25). The British Balfour Declaration of 1917 had already favored a national homeland for the Jews in Palestine. But the potential for difficulties was great.

The interwar years saw growing communal conflict. Immigration of Jews, largely from eastern Europe, increased until Britain tried in 1936 to restrict it, which prevented many European Jews from escaping the Holocaust. Because of the Nazi attempt to exterminate European Jewry, after the war the Zionist movement received a tremendous boost from the Allied nations.

The concept of return to the Holy Land had a long history in the Jewish religion. However, for centuries, the land had been the home of Arabic-speaking Palestinians, who were without voice in the matter. The Palestinians have not been able to see why they should be persecuted, whether because of another people's historic religious attachment to the land or to pay for Europe's sins against the Jews. On the other hand, Jews themselves rightly felt the desperate need for a homeland where they might be safe and to which Jews everywhere might flee from future persecutions.

In 1945, Britain found itself beset in Palestine by Jews seeking to settle there and by Jewish terrorist organizations. In 1947, the British washed their hands of the problem, and the United Nations called for partition into a Jewish and an Arab state. The existing Arab states refused to accept the UN resolution, but in May 1948, the independent state of Israel was proclaimed. This declaration led to the Israeli-Arab war of 1948–1949, in which Syria, Lebanon, Jordan, Egypt, and Saudi Arabia attacked Israel but lost to the better-armed and more resolute Israelis, ceding much territory designated by the UN for a Palestinian state.

Since then there has been, at best, an armed truce between Israel and its neighbors. The Arab nations and the Palestinian people displaced by the new state have generally not wanted to accept Israel's right to exist, and Israel (with the support of the United States) has taken aggressive measures to ensure its survival. The most serious military confrontations were the Suez crisis of 1956; the 1967 June

27.5
Israel's Proclamation of Independence

War, when Israel attacked and occupied the Sinai, the Golan Heights, and the West Bank (of the Jordan River); the October War of 1973 in which the Egyptians staged a surprise attack on Israel in the Sinai that ended in a standoff; and the Israeli invasions of Lebanon in 1978 and 1982.

Even in periods without overt war, bloodshed has become commonplace. Arab terrorism grew out of Palestinian frustration. **The Palestine Liberation Organization (PLO)** and more radical groups carried on determined guerrilla battles within and along Israel's borders for decades.

Simultaneously, the frustrations of an embattled Israel have made it ready to meet terrorist atrocities with preemptive military actions and reprisals. Israel has responded to terrorist attacks and civilian resistance such as the Intifada, or Arab uprising, in the occupied territories with air and commando raids and punitive measures against the Arab populations in the occupied territories.

Arab states have supported guerrilla groups attacking Israel and long refused to deal directly with Israel to reach a Middle East solution. Egypt was the first notable exception to this policy. In the late 1970s, under President Anwar Sadat (1918–1981), and through the mediation of U.S. President Jimmy Carter (b. 1924), Egypt entered into direct negotiations with Israel's prime minister Menachem Begin (1913–1994). The two countries reached an agreement—the Camp David Accords—in 1978, and in 1979 signed a formal peace treaty. Sadat was assassinated in 1981 by Egyptian Muslim extremists, but the treaty has held up under his successor, Husni Mubarak (b. 1928). Nonetheless, the cycle of violence has continued even as peace initiatives have increased.

Added to this bleak history is the ugly legacy of hate instilled in many on both sides over the past 50 years. Many Muslims have come to label all Jews as oppressors and enemies, making virtually no distinction among them. Many Israelis and some Jews around the world have similarly vilified all Arabs and Muslims. In many ways, Arab-Israeli and Muslim-Jewish relations are at an all-time low. The human crisis is far from over, even if peace were to arrive tomorrow.

Some events of recent years have given at least faint hope for an eventual resolution to the conflict. In 1991, in the wake of the Gulf War that followed Iraq's invasion of Kuwait, the parties to the Arab-Israeli conflict began peace negotiations, which led to the September 1993 Middle East Peace Agreement. This raised hopes for a negotiated settlement and the creation of a secular Palestinian state alongside the Jewish state of Israel.

Although parts of the West Bank and Gaza have been turned over to the PLO, there have been fits and starts in the process and ongoing danger that it might break down altogether. Jordan and Egypt agreed in 1994 to a peace treaty with Israel, but other Arab states—notably Syria—have still not been willing to come to an accord with Israel. Extremists on both sides have tried to derail the peace initiative. In November 1995 another Jewish Israeli extremist assassinated Prime Minister Yitzhak Rabin for trying to make peace and to allow the eventual creation of a circumscribed Palestinian state. Then, in the run-up to the Israeli elections of May 29, 1996, called in the wake of Rabin's death, Arab extremists carried out a series of savage bombings on buses and in crowded shopping areas. The subsequent victory in the elections of a Likud conservative hardliner, Benjamin Netanyahu (b. 1949), over Rabin's Labor successor, Shimon Peres, by a margin of less than 1 percent of the vote, cast new uncertainty on peace prospects.

The leadership on both sides proved not to be up to serious progress on a peaceable settlement. The Netanyahu regime repeatedly took hardline stands and even provocative actions such as the determined expansion of Jewish West Bank settlements. To the latter end, new roads and building projects were implemented to divide

Palestine Liberation Organization (PLO)   A political and cultural movement formed by Arab Palestinians to work for the creation of an independent Palestinian state.

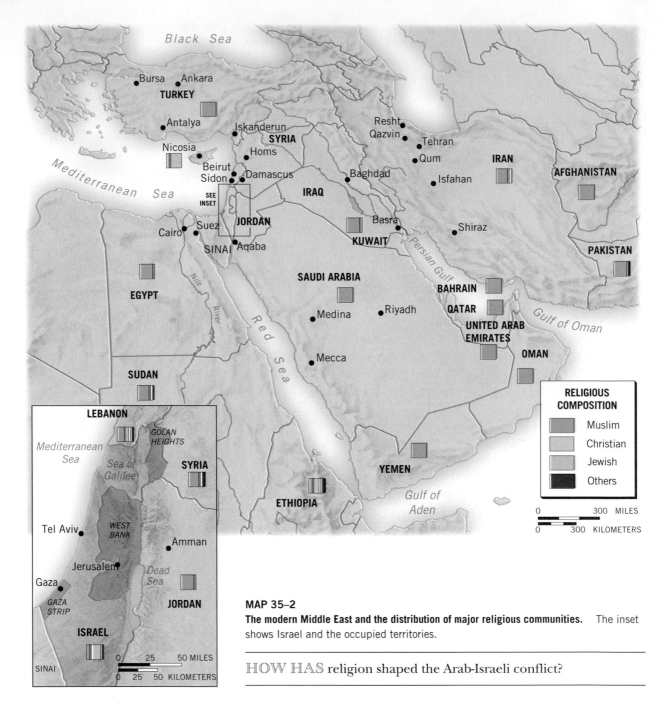

MAP 35–2
The modern Middle East and the distribution of major religious communities.   The inset shows Israel and the occupied territories.

HOW HAS religion shaped the Arab-Israeli conflict?

further the Palestinian population in the occupied territories. Other actions included curtailment of water supplies to Palestinian areas and public declarations of Israel's determination to retain all of Jerusalem and much of the territories even in the face of international censure. Nor did the Palestinian Authority created by the 1993 peace agreement prove any better. It grew steadily more corrupt, ineffective, and out of touch with its constituencies, and the suffering of the masses in the West Bank and Gaza in particular only grew steadily worse after the agreement. Despite the efforts of the Palestinian and Israeli security forces, Arab guerrillas of the extremist wing of the resistance organization Hamas have been able to slaughter Israeli civilians in daylight bombings (such as those in October 1998) in a sustained effort to torpedo the already shaky **"peace process."** These terrorist attacks have led Israel often to seal its borders, resulting in the loss of livelihood for thousands of Arabs in the occupied territories who

peace process   Efforts, chiefly led by the United States, to broker a peace between the State of Israel and the PLO.

normally work in Israel proper, and this has exacerbated the already dire plight of Gaza in particular, keeping thousands of Arab families in poverty and starvation and in turn feeding the extremist resistance groups.

The Netanyahu era ended after a scandal involving the prime minister himself, and in March 2000, Ariel Sharon became prime minister. Sharon is the former army general charged with responsibility for the camp massacres by Christian militias operating in the 1982–1983 Israeli invasion of south Lebanon. His government has been marked by an increasing escalation of violence on both sides. Palestinian terrorist suicide bombings continue apace, and Sharon has responded with violent attacks and assassinations of Palestinians identified by Israel as leaders of the West Bank resistance and terrorist initiatives. At this writing, strong efforts have been made to blame Arafat's Palestinian Authority and even to depose the often hapless leader himself. Two Arab suicide attacks (largely unrelated to events in Palestine) on the World Trade Center in New York and the Pentagon in Washington on September 11, 2001, offered only a further pretext on all sides for escalation of the violence in the ensuing months. As this edition goes to press, the possibility of peace of any kind in Israel and the occupied territories seems tenuous.

On September 11, 2001 a terrorist attack targeted the World Trade Center Towers in New York City. In this photograph the first of the twin towers is in flames as the second plane heads directly toward the second tower. In a very brief time both towers collapsed with the loss of approximately 3,000 lives.

Masatomo Kuriya, Corbis/Sygma

MIDDLE EASTERN OIL

The oil wealth of the Arab and Iranian world has been another significant factor in its recent history. Since Saudi Arabia's first oil production in 1939, the world demand for oil has soared. Oil has become a major bargaining chip in international diplomacy for Arab and other oil-rich Third World states—such as Venezuela, Nigeria, Iran, and Indonesia. In the Arab countries of North Africa and especially of Arabia and the Gulf, oil production and wealth have changed every aspect of life. Oil has propelled formerly peripheral countries of the Sahara or the Arabian deserts into major roles in international banking and finance. Oil also has boosted the damaged self-confidence of the Arab world after a century and a half of Western domination. A testimony to the global importance of Middle Eastern oil was the willingness of the United States and European nations to form a coalition with Arab countries and commit massive forces to expel Iraq from Kuwait in 1991.

ISLAMISM AND POLITICS

The increase in the global importance of the oil-producing states of the Middle East has coincided with efforts to revive pristine Muslim values and standards and to reform Muslim societies. In the spirit, and often in the footsteps, of earlier Muslim resurgents, many Muslims have sought to return to the "fundamentals" of Islamic life, faith, and society. They see this **Islamic fundamentalism** as a means of rejuvenation, of social and economic as well as political justice, and of defense against Western secularist values. A great part of the appeal of Islamist groups is their willingness and ability to address the needs of the underclasses. Islamic groups have provided social services such as housing, medical care, education, and jobs, under the banner of a just, moral Muslim societal ideal. The political actions of "Islamist reformism" range from revolutionary action (Iran) to democratic participation (Turkey) to complete political quietism

Islamic fundamentalism A movement among many Muslims to return to the "fundamentals" of Islamic faith, life, and society.

A Kuwaiti looks at one of the more than six hundred oil wells left burning by Iraqi troops as they retreated during the Gulf War in 1991. The willingness of the United States and Europe to commit massive forces to expel Iraq from Kuwait reflects the global importance of the region's oil wealth.

Will Burgess/Reuters/Corbis-Bettmann

(the Tablighi international revivalist movement begun in Pakistan). Whether these movements will bring lasting change to Islamic societies is an open question.

The background to modern Islamist reform lies in the European expansion over much of the globe since the late 1400s. This expansion brought far more social and political change than religious or even cultural change to the Islamic world. It saw the emergence globally of European-style nationalism and the idea of the nation-state; of post-Enlightenment ideals of individual liberties and rights and representative government; and of the concept of religious faith and affiliation as a private, "religious" matter and citizenship as a public, "secular" matter. Such ideas proved revolutionary in the Islamic world.

The twentieth century in Islamic parts of the world presented a checkered history of autocratic governments. Experiments with European-style parliamentary government have only rarely taken hold, nor have either liberal democratic or Marxist-Socialist political and social ideals. Even so, until recently, little of the political discourse in Islamic lands has given serious attention to specifically *Islamic* alternatives.

With the rise and postcolonial independence of numerous national states and the flourishing of diverse nationalisms, politics became often theoretically as well as actually divorced from Islamic religious tradition and its norms in overt ways that it had not been before. Where leaders had previously claimed Muslim faith and allegiance, some came to espouse secular ideologies and virtually ignored religion except as a political weapon. And used as a weapon it was: Islamic religious allegiance has commonly been invoked to bolster a ruler's claim to legitimacy and often to cloak in pious garb more mundane objectives.

In short, the twentieth century saw no realization of an "ideal" Islamic state in which religious and political authority are conjoined. If anything, the gap widened between Islamic norms and ideals on the one hand and political and social realities on the other. Even the postrevolutionary Islamic Republic of Iran saw a clear division between political necessity and reality and religious values and standards.

When we look at the Islamist movements of recent decades, we find that the calls for a congruence of religion and politics in the Islamic world trace less to some kind of ideal model of a religious state or so-called **theocracy** than to a need for social and political justice, such as that which Islam has always demanded. The cries for a new "jihad" of Muslims are aimed much less often outward than inward at domestic tyrants, corruption, and injustice. Indeed, perhaps the most international and influential of contemporary Islamic revivalist or reform movements, that of the Tabligh-i Jama'at, is explicitly apolitical in its tenets; it looks to convert the individual person of faith to true submission (*islam*) rather than lip service: Reform of the world begins with oneself.

IRAN

Iran was ruled from 1925 to 1941 as a monarchy by a former army commander, Reza Khan, who had come to power by military takeover and governed under the old Persian title Shah Reza Pahlavi. He attempted to introduce modernist reforms, not unlike those of Atatürk (1881–1938). By the time Russian and British forces deposed Reza in 1941 and installed his son, Muhammad Reza, as shah, the power of the Shi'ite religious leaders, or *ulama*, had been muted and a strong, centralized state established. The son, like his father, sought to ground the legitimacy of Pahlavi rule on the ancient, preIslamic dynasties of greater Iran, especially the Achaemenids (see Chapter 4). He continued his father's secularist state building from the end of World War II until 1978.

In the 1960s, Muhammad Reza Shah was finally forced by popular opposition to institute land reform and other socialist or populist reforms. However, his repressive measures against the leftist and especially the religious opposition alienated the Iranian masses. His reign failed to narrow the gap between them and the wealthy elites.

theocracy A state ruled by religious leaders who claim to govern by divine authority.

Finally, in 1978, religious leaders and secularist revolutionaries joined forces to end the Shah's regime with a revolution fueled by Shi'ite feeling and symbolism. In 1979, the constitution of a new Islamic republic was adapted under the guidance of the major Shi'ite religious leader, or **ayatollah**, Ruhollah Khomeini (Khumayni, 1902–1989). Subsequent years have seen a protracted war with Iraq (1980 to 1988) and the institution of repressive and violent measures against enemies of the regime not unlike those used under the Shah. Still, the new state—with religious leaders exercising a degree of influence over politics not seen since early Safavid times in the sixteenth century—has survived. Khomeini and his successor, Hashemi Rafsanjani (b. 1934) had to struggle to find a new formula for combining Muslim values and norms with twentieth-century *Realpolitik*, and this will continue to challenge their successors.

The successor to Rafsanjani, Mohammad Khatami, was elected in 1997 by a resounding majority. Khatami, a moderate cleric with a reputation as a relative liberal, has tried to steer Iran on a moderate and more liberal course but has encountered opposition from the conservative religious establishment.

CENTRAL ASIA

North of Iran, 40 million Central Asian Muslims predominate in the south-central reaches of the former USSR, and 30 million or more Muslims live in Chinese Central Asia. They have had to sustain their traditions in the face of Russian and Chinese imperialism. In the 1980s, both Soviet and Chinese Muslims appeared to be asserting themselves. The 1979 Soviet occupation of Afghanistan reflected the potential importance of this movement. The withdrawal of Soviet forces from Afghanistan in 1988 looked surprisingly like the U.S. withdrawal from South Vietnam. It was soon followed by the collapse of the Soviet Union in 1990 into the loosely connected Commonwealth of Independent States (CIS). Suddenly the Central Asian Islamic republics of the former USSR found themselves effectively independent states, yet with little of the infrastructure to manage such a transition successfully. The great challenge is whether they can attain political viability without being destroyed by economic collapse or ethnic or regional conflict. Islamist reformism will surely play a role in these states, but so can civil-society ideals of democratic governance and free-market economies.

"Ayatollah Khomeini, who until his death in 1989, was the spiritual leader of the world's shiite Muslims. His call for Iranians to rise up against western-style modernization led to his exile in 1963, but by 1979 dissatisfaction with the shah was so great that the shah was forced to flee and Khomeini returned triumphant. Khomeini's view that the purpose of government is to apply the law of God exerts a powerful influence throughout the Muslim world".

Corbis/Bettmann

ayatollah   A major Shi'ite religious leader.

SOUTH AND SOUTHEAST ASIA

Five major southern and Southeast Asian nations—India, Pakistan, Bangladesh, Indonesia, and Malaysia—that together contain well over half of all Muslims in the world, came into being after World War II. India, a largely Hindu state, and Pakistan, a largely Muslim state, gained independence in 1947. Much of their subsequent history has involved mutual antagonism. The two states have still not resolved their differences, including their conflicting claims to Kashmir. Their rivalry has been exacerbated recently by a new round of sabre-rattling, this time a nuclear one, when both India and Pakistan carried out underground nuclear tests in 1998.

Indonesia and Malaysia, the two largest states of Southeast Asia, have long histories that link them to the wider Islamic world, to Indian culture and religion, and to China.

PAKISTAN AND BANGLADESH

The architect and first president of Pakistan, Muhammad Ali Jinnah (1876–1948), oversaw the creation of a Muslim state in the two predominantly Muslim areas of northwest India and East Bengal. In 1971, East Pakistan seceded and became the new Islamic nation of Bangladesh. However, the main political division in the subcontinent remains that between India and Pakistan.

HOW HAS the growth of Hindu nationalism affected Indian politics?

Pakistan's groping efforts to create a fully Islamic society and to solve its massive economic problems have been hampered by periodic lapses into military dictatorship, the latest in 1999. Pakistan, like most Asian societies, faces enormous economic and demographic challenges. The Pakistanis must try to create a modern economic and political system that will meet their physical needs while allowing them to maintain their commitment to remain an Islamic society. Overpopulation, poverty, and a massive military are all major obstacles to Pakistan's progress.

INDIA

India has been directed for most of its existence by the Congress Party, first under Jawaharlal Nehru (1889–1964), who developed India's famous theory of political neutrality vis-à-vis world alignments. He was able to make some headway in reducing the communal hatreds, religious zealotry, and regional tensions of the postpartition era and in the huge task of economic development. Hindi and English were set as the national languages, with fourteen major regional languages, recognized for regional official use. Nehru's resolute opposition to caste privilege also helped to improve equality of citizenship.

Nehru's daughter, Indira Gandhi (1917–1984; prime minister, 1966–1977, 1980–1984; no familial relation to Mohandas Gandhi), carried on most of her father's policies and managed to steer a tricky course of neutralism during the Cold War. India's 1971 victory over Pakistan and the subsequent creation of Bangladesh to replace East Pakistan cemented her political control; this war and the development, with Russian help, of an atomic bomb confirmed India as the major power in South Asia. After her efforts to assume virtual dictatorial power, in 1977 she and the Congress Party were ousted by the voters for three years. She was reelected prime minister and served until her efforts to quell Sikh separatism brought about her assassination in 1984.

Indira Gandhi's son, Rajiv Gandhi (1944–1991), was elected prime minister after her, but charges of corruption led to his party's temporary fall, and in May 1991 he was also assassinated. From the 1990s on, Congress Party rule has alternated with governments dominated by a coalition of Hindu nationalists.

India's problems remain large. Poverty and disease remain widespread. Separatist movements based on regional linguistic affinity, such as that of the Tamil peoples of the south, or religious affinity, such as that of the Sikhs of the Punjab, have pulled at the unity of the Indian state. Industrialization and agricultural modernization have made great strides, yet the neutralizing force of runaway population growth has not been countered. India's population is now about one billion and growing at nearly 2 percent per year. The growing strength of militant Hindu nationalists and fundamentalists and new outbreaks of communal violence between Hindus and the large Muslim minority pose serious threats to stability. As the world's largest functioning democracy, India will be an important model of representative government and pluralistic society if it succeeds in staying together and reducing its overpopulation and mass poverty.

LATIN AMERICA SINCE 1945

During the last half century, the nations of Latin America have experienced divergent paths of political and economic change. Their leaders have tried to alleviate their people's dependence on the more developed nations. At best, these efforts have had mixed results; at worst, they have led to repression and tragedy.

Before World War II, the states of Latin America had been economically dependent on the United States and western Europe. Beginning in the 1950s, Latin America became an arena for confrontations between the United States and the Soviet Union.

QUICK REVIEW

Nehru Dynasty

◆ Jawaharlal Nehru (1889–1964): first prime minister of India

◆ Indira Gandhi (1917–1984): daughter of Nehru, prime minister of India (1966–1977)

◆ Rajiv Gandhi (1944–1991): son of Indira Gandhi, prime minister of India (1984-1989)

HOW HAS Latin America changed since 1945?

• HISTORY'S VOICES •

LOURDES ARIZPE DISCUSSES THE SILENCE OF PEASANT WOMEN

Lourdes Arizpe, a Mexican anthropologist, wrote extensively on the plight of peasant women in the 1970s. In this passage she discusses how the lives and history of Mexican peasant women are shrouded in silence. Though her remarks are directed toward the situation in Mexico, they may well apply to peasant women in other cultures as well.

WHAT ARE the factors that Arizpe cites as leading to the historical silence of peasant women? Why does she believe it is important for such women to learn to speak with their own voices? How do the stereotypes of Mexican peasant women both contribute to the silence and arise from the silence? Why does she believe peasant women to be the most marginalized of all women?

History has imposed a greater silence on peasant women than on any other social group. Perhaps it is the solitude of the plains or the obligatory circumspection of their gender or merely political repression, but circumstances combine to force them to live in a secret world. Doubtless there are those who would assert that their tie to nature leads them to express themselves with actions rather than words. But the male peasant lives in the natural world without being silenced.

Silence, when not deliberate (although, how can we be sure it isn't?) could be anger or wisdom or, simply, a gesture of dignity. When there is no one worth talking to, I stay silent. If someone doesn't want to recognize my existence, I stay silent. In the spectrum of invisibility that history has imposed on women, perhaps the most invisible of the invisibles have been the peasants.

When direct expression is not permitted, the possibility of knowledge is lost and we fill that disturbing vacuum with phantoms. It is therefore not surprising that the Mexican mentality is filled with myths and stereotypes about peasant women. There is the submissive Indian woman who is a product of condescending maternalism; the wild woman both fantasized about and feared by men; the brazen hussy of melodramatic soap operas; the fainthearted but treacherous small-town woman invented by the urban mind. Silence is also created by everyone's desire to hear what they want to hear rather than listen to what women are trying to say.

Today it seems that everyone mouths concerns about peasant women without any sincere interest.

. . . What is important today is to create opportunities for peasant women to speak.

From Lourdes Arizpe, "Peasant Women and Silence," translated by Laura Beard Milroy in *Women's Writing in Latin America: An Anthology* by Sara Castro-Klarén, Sylvia Malloy, and Beatriz Sarlo. Copyright © 1992 by Westview Press. Reprinted by permission of the author.

During this era attempts were made to expand the industrial base and agricultural production of the various national economies. The financing came from U.S. and Western European banks or from Soviet subsidies. Enormous debts were contracted that made Latin American economies virtual prisoners to the fluctuations of world interest rates and international banks or to Soviet subsidies. These new relationships, however, did not alter the underlying character of most Latin American economies, which remain exporters of agricultural commodities and mineral resources.

A culture of poverty continues to be the most dominant social characteristic of the area. Migration into the cities from the countryside has caused urban overcrowding and slums inhabited by the desperately poor. The standards of health and nutrition have often fallen. The growth of service industries in the cities has also fostered the emergence of a professional, educated middle class that often wants to imitate the lifestyle of their social counterparts in the United States and Western Europe. This new professional middle class has displayed little taste for radical politics, social reform, or revolution. They and the more traditional elites were willing, especially during the 1960s and 1970s, to support military governments pledged to maintain the status quo.

Political events in Latin America led to the establishment of authoritarian governments of both the left and the right and to a retreat from the model of parliamentary democracy. Only Mexico, Colombia, Venezuela, and Costa Rica remained parliamentary states throughout this period. Elsewhere, two paths of political development were followed. In Cuba and Nicaragua, and briefly in Chile, revolutionary socialist governments with close ties to the Soviet Union were established. Elsewhere, often in response to the fear of revolution or communism, military governments held power, sometimes punctuated with brief interludes of civilian rule. Such were the situations in Chile, Brazil, Argentina, Bolivia, Peru, and Uruguay. Governments of both the left and the right engaged in political repression.

These political changes fostered new roles for the military and the Roman Catholic Church. Latin American armies have played key political roles since the Wars of Independence. But since World War II, they have frequently assumed the direct government of nations rather than using indirect influence. Many Roman Catholic priests and bishops have protested inequalities and attacked political repression. Certain Roman Catholic theologians have combined traditional Christian concern for the poor with Marxist ideology to formulate what is called a **liberation theology**. This Latin American theological initiative has been attacked by the Vatican.

Since the 1980s, Latin America has changed significantly. Several nations have moved toward democratization and free-market economies. This marks a sharp departure from the 1930s and 1940s, when the state itself was seen as largely responsible for economic development. Yet in most nations, the military keeps a watchful eye on democratic developments and possible disorder. The end of the Cold War brought to a close one source of external political challenge, but the internal social problems of these nations continue to raise difficulties for their governments. In several nations, drug-producing cartels have challenged the authority of governments themselves. (See Lourdes Arizpe Discusses the Silence of Peasant Women.)

liberation theology   The effort by certain Roman Catholic theologians to combine Marxism with traditional Christian concern for the poor.

WHERE IN Latin America did the major attempts to establish revolutionary governments occur?

REVOLUTIONARY CHALLENGES

There were three major attempts among the nations of Latin America to establish revolutionary governments pursuing major social and economic change. They occurred in Cuba in 1959, in Chile in 1970, and in Nicaragua in 1979. Each involved a Marxist political organization and a close relationship with the Soviet Union. The establishment of these governments provoked active resistance by the United States and opposition from traditional elites.

THE CUBAN REVOLUTION

Cuba had remained a colony until the Spanish-American War of 1898. Thereafter, it achieved independence within a sphere of U.S. influence that took the form of economic domination and military intervention. The governments of the island were ineffective and corrupt. During the 1950s, Fulgencio Batista (1901–1973), a dictator supported by the United States, ruled Cuba.

Historically, Cuba had been politically restive. On July 26, 1953, Fidel Castro Ruz (b. 1926), the son of a wealthy landowner, and others attacked a government army barracks. The revolutionary movement that he thereafter came to lead in exile took its name from that date: the Twenty-Sixth of July Movement. In 1956, Castro and a handful of followers landed in Cuba. They took refuge in the Sierra Maestra mountains and attacked Batista's forces. Batista fled Cuba on New Year's Day in 1959. In January, Castro arrived in Havana as the revolutionary victor.

Castro undertook the most extensive political, economic, and social reconstruction seen in recent Latin American history. He rejected parliamentary democracy and governed Cuba in an authoritarian manner. The revolutionary government carried out major land redistribution. Both small landowners and large state farms were established.

The Cuban Revolution spurned an industrial economic model and concentrated on the agricultural sector. Sugar preserved its leading role, and the Cuban economy remained monocultural. The sugar industry depended on large Soviet subsidies and on the Soviet-bloc nations for its market. In that respect, the Cuban economy did not escape the cycle of external dependence.

In foreign affairs, the Cuban Revolution was characterized by a sharp break with the United States and a close relationship with the Soviet Union. Castro aligned himself with the Cuban Communist Party and with the Soviet bloc. The United States was hostile toward Castro and toward the presence of a communist state less than a hundred miles from Florida. In 1961, the United States and Cuban exiles launched the unsuccessful Bay of Pigs invasion. The close Cuban relationship to the Soviet Union led to the missile crisis of 1962, the most dangerous incident of the Cold War. In the late 1970s and the 1980s, a dialogue of sorts was undertaken between Cuba and the United States, but mutual distrust continues.

With the collapse of the Soviet Union and the end of the Cold War, the future of Castro's Cuba has become uncertain. Cuba remains the only state closely associated with the former Soviet bloc that has not experienced political or economic reform. The subsidies that flowed from the Soviet Union to support the Cuban economy, however, have ended, creating a shortage of consumer goods. The Marxist political and economic ideology stands discredited throughout the world, but the aging Castro's leadership remains intact. Cuba must confront the need for a successor to Castro. It also must confront the need for economic reform and find a new role in a Latin American order in which the issues of the Cold War are no longer relevant. One hint of new direction came in 1998 when the Castro government permitted a highly publicized visit from Pope John Paul II.

Throughout the Cold War, Cuba assumed an importance far greater than its size might suggest. After 1959, it served as a center for the export of communist revolution and it sent troops to Angola in the late 1970s. The U.S. government sought to prevent the establishment of a second Cuba in Latin America. That goal led to intervention in other revolutionary situations and to support for authoritarian governments in Latin America.

Ernesto "Che" Guevara, the charismatic Argentine-born revolutionary, who played a key role in the Cuban revolution of 1959. In the 1960's Guevara was a leader of the struggle for militant international solidarity and he attempted to foment socialist revolutions in the Congo and in Bolivia, where he was killed in 1967.

Roberto & Osvaldo Salas/Getty Images, Inc.–Liaison

CHILE

Until the 1970s, Chile was the most enduring model of parliamentary democracy in Latin America. During the 1960s, however, Chilean politics became polarized. Unemployment rose alarmingly. There was labor unrest and popular resentment of the economic domination of Chile by large U.S. corporations.

The situation came to a head in 1970 when Salvador Allende (1908–1973), the candidate of the left-wing political coalition and a Marxist, was elected president. His coalition did not control the Chilean congress, nor did it have the support of the military. The center and right-wing political groups took a watch-and-wait attitude. Allende nationalized some businesses. Other policies were blocked in the congress, and Allende had to govern by decree. By this device he began to expropriate foreign property, much of which belonged to U.S. corporations. This policy frightened the Chilean owners of small and medium-sized businesses, but did not satisfy workers. Inflation ballooned. Harvests were poor.

In the autumn of 1973, Allende found himself governing a nation in turmoil without significant domestic political support and with many foreign enemies. He proved unwilling to make political compromises or to change his policies.

The army became hostile. The government of the United States was disturbed by the prospect of a Marxist nation on the western coast of South America. The Nixon administration supported the discontent within the Chilean army. In mid-September 1973, an army coup overthrew Allende, who was killed in the presidential palace.

Thereafter, for 15 years Chile was governed by a military junta under General Augusto Pinochet (b. 1915). The military government pursued a close relationship with the United States and resisted Marxism in the hemisphere. It established a state-directed free-market economy and reversed the expropriations of the Allende years. There was also harsh political repression.

In a referendum held in late 1988, Chileans rejected Pinochet's bid for another term as president. Democratization was relatively smooth. Civilian rule has included efforts to investigate the political repression of the Pinochet years. Thousands of cases of torture and murder have been revealed. The Chilean government itself moved slowly, not wishing to revisit the most controversial era of the nation's history.

The Sandinista Revolution in Nicaragua

In the summer of 1979, a Marxist guerrilla force, the **Sandinistas**, overthrew the corrupt dictatorship of the Somoza family in Nicaragua. The Somozas had governed Nicaragua as their personal preserve since the 1930s with support from the United States. The Sandinistas established a collective government that pursued social and economic reform and reconstruction. The movement—with Roman Catholic priests on its leadership council—epitomized the new political and social forces in Latin America. However, the revolutionary government confronted significant domestic political opposition and military challenge from the contra guerrilla movement.

The government of the United States, particularly under the Reagan administration (1981–1989), was hostile toward the Sandinistas. It provided both direct and indirect aid to the opposition guerrillas. The U.S. government feared the spread of Marxist revolutionary activity in Central America, a fear reinforced by the close ties between the revolutionary government and the Soviet Union. For the United States, the Sandinista government represented in Central America a problem analogous to that of Cuba a generation earlier.

Sandinista rule came to a relatively quick end. In early 1990, after a negotiated peace settlement with the contras, they lost the presidential election to an opposition coalition and relinquished power peacefully.

Sandinistas   The Marxist guerrilla force that overthrew the Somoza dictatorship in Nicaragua in 1979.

Pursuit of Stability

rgentina, Brazil, and Mexico offer those examples of how Latin American governments have sought to achieve stability.

HOW WERE Argentina, Brazil, and Mexico able to sustain stable civilian governments since the 1980s?

Argentina

In 1955, the Argentine army revolted against the Perón dictatorship, and Juan Perón (1895–1974) went into exile. Two decades of economic stagnation and social unrest followed. In 1973, Perón was recalled from exile in a desperate attempt to restore stability, but died about a year later.

By 1976, the army had undertaken direct rule. There was widespread repression; thousands of citizens disappeared, never to be heard of again. In April 1982, General Leopoldo Galtieri (b. 1926) launched a disastrous invasion of the Islas Malvinas (Falkland Islands). Argentina was defeated by Britain, and the military junta discredited.

In 1983 civilian rule was restored, and Argentina set out on the road to democratization. Under President Raul Alfonsín (b. 1927), many of the former military figures responsible for the years of repression received prison sentences. Alfonsín also sought to turn more real political authority over to the Argentine congress. Argentina has provided the most extensive example in Latin America of the restoration of democratic practices after military rule. Peaceful elections and transitions of governments have occurred for two decades despite serious economic difficulties.

BRAZIL

In 1964, the military assumed the direct government of Brazil and did not fully relinquish it until the mid-1980s. The military government stressed order and used repression to maintain it. The army itself, however, was divided. Many officers were concerned that the corruption of everyday politics would undermine the army's reputation and esprit de corps. Consequently, within the army itself, certain forces sought to restore a more democratic government. In 1985, civilian government returned under the military's watchful eye.

The military government fostered denationalized industrial development. Non-Brazilian corporations were invited to spearhead the drive toward industrialization. Brazil opted for an industrialism guided and dominated from the outside. One result was a massive foreign debt, the servicing and repayment of which have become perhaps Brazil's most important national problem. Brazil also became the major industrialized nation in Latin America. The question now is how the social changes wrought by industrialism, such as growing urbanization, will receive political accommodation. In Brazil, as in Argentina, economic and social pressures have spawned conditions ripe for political agitation. It was just that possibility that led both the traditional and the new professional elites to support authoritarian government in the past.

MEXICO

Institutionally, Mexico has undergone few political changes since World War II. In theory, the government continued to pursue the goals of the revolution. Power remained in the control of the Partido Revolucionario Institucional (PRI).

Yet shifts had occurred under this apparently stable surface. The government retreated from some of the aims of the revolution and appeared conservative when compared to Marxist states. In the early 1950s, certain large landowners were exempted from the expropriation and redistribution of land. The Mexican government maintained relations with Cuba and the other revolutionary regimes of Latin America but also resisted Marxist doctrines in Mexico. When necessary, it arrested malcontents.

Mexico experienced an oil boom from 1977 to 1983, but the world oil glut burst that bubble. The aftermath revealed the absence of stable growth. Like so many other states in the region, Mexico amassed large foreign debts and thus surrendered real economic independence.

In 1988, the PRI encountered a challenge at the polls. Opposition candidates received much of the vote in a hotly contested election. The PRI remained in power but with the knowledge that it would not be able to dominate the political scene as it had done. Thereafter, the leadership began to decentralize the party. President Carlos Salinas moved to privatize economic enterprise. He also favored free-trade agreements. The most important of these was the North American Free Trade Agreement (NAFTA), which created a vast free-trade area including Mexico, Canada, and the United States. In 1991, Salinas made new accommodations with the Roman Catholic Church, thus moving away from the traditional anticlericalism of Mexican politics. By 1991, the PRI appeared to have regained its former political ascendancy.

However, in 1994 Mexico underwent political shocks. Troops had to quell armed rebellion in Chiapas. During the election of that year the leading candidate was assassinated and party members were charged with complicity in the deed. Party corruption received increased publicity. Early in 1995, Mexico suffered a major economic downturn, and only loans from the United States saved the economy. Ernesto Zedillo, elected president in 1994, blamed Salinas and his family for the situation, and the corruption of the Salinas government became public. The government faced further unrest in Chiapas, growing power among drug lords, and turmoil within the governing party itself. In 2000, the PRI lost the election for the presidency although it has remained the most powerful party in the Mexican legislature.

CONTINUITY AND CHANGE IN RECENT LATIN AMERICAN HISTORY

What is most striking about the history of the past four decades in Latin America is its tragic continuity with the region's previous history. Revolution has brought moderate social change, but at the price of authoritarian government, economic stagnation, and dependence on foreign powers. Real independence has not been achieved. Throughout the region for much of the period, parliamentary democracy has been fragile; it was the first element of national life to be sacrificed to the conflicting goals of socialism, economic growth, or resistance to revolution.

The recent trends toward democratization and market economics may, however, mark a break in that pattern. The region could enjoy healthy economic growth if inflation can be contained and investment fostered. The challenge will be to see that the fruits of any new prosperity are shared in a way that prevents resentment and turmoil. Furthermore, as in the past, economic turmoil far from Latin America may harm it. Each time such turmoil has occurred, the governments of Latin America, like the current government of Mexico, have found themselves economically dependent upon either the United States or Europe.

SUMMARY

The Postcolonial World Since 1945 the European colonial empires have disappeared from Africa and Asia and have been replaced by a multitude of independent states. These states have had to adjust their political and economic relations first to one or other of the superpowers during the Cold War and then, since the disappearance of the Soviet Union, to the West.

Africa Independent Africa has faced severe problems: overpopulation, poverty, the absence of an educated middle class, tribal and class conflict, arbitrary boundaries, disease, economic dependence, and political instability. While Nigeria has remained mired in ethnic and religious strife and has experienced a succession of military dictatorships, South Africa has emerged as a stable, multi-ethnic democracy with the end of white rule in the 1990s. The challenge for Africa as a whole is to build a truly civil society and achieve economic health and political stability.

The Middle East Oil and Muslim reaction to the creation of the State of Israel have dominated the history of the Middle East since the 1940s. While the possession of vast deposits of oil has made some Middle Eastern governments wealthy, it has not led to the creation of prosperous democratic societies. The existence of Israel has inflamed the Middle East for more than five decades. Although efforts by the United States to sponsor an Arab-Israeli peace have made some progress, the cycle of terror and retaliatory violence has persisted, and it is unclear whether a lasting peace between Israel and its neighbors can be achieved or a viable Palestinian state created.

Rising Islamic fundamentalism, although not a monolithic movement, has proved increasingly disruptive to the region and the entire Islamic world.

In Iran, the election of a relatively liberal government has met with increasing opposition from the conservative religious establishment.

India and Pakistan Pakistan remains poor and under military rule. India is the world's largest democracy but rising Hindu nationalism has provoked clashes with the large Muslim minority. India and Pakistan remain divided over the future of Kashmir.

Latin America Most Latin American countries remain politically and economically dependent on the United States. Except in Cuba, no revolutionary movement was able to overturn the traditional structure of Latin American society. Despite social and economic problems, Argentina and Brazil have managed to move from military to rule to stable democratic, civilian government. In Mexico, the long dominance of the PRI ended in 2000.

IMAGE KEY

for pages 768–769

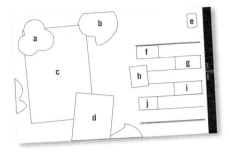

a. Badges supporting Nelson Mandela for the presidency of South Africa
b. Petri Dish containing heavy crude oil
c. Young women raise their arms during a protest against the World Trade Organization in Seattle, Washington
d. Page from *As Safir* newspaper of the 1982 massacre at the Palestinian refugee camps
e. Oil barrel
f. President Jomo Kenyatta with English Prince Andrew and Queen Elizabeth during Kenyan Independence ceremonies in 1963
g. Rwandan refugees
h. Yasser Arafat
i. Golden Temple at Amritsar, India
j. Che Guevara

REVIEW QUESTIONS

1. What factors contributed to the spread of decolonization in sub-Saharan Africa? Why were the newly independent states so fragile?

2. Why was the apartheid regime in South Africa dismantled in the 1990s?

3. How was the State of Israel created?

4. How has Muslim fundamentalism affected the various Muslim nations? Is Muslim fundamentalism a monolithic movement?

5. Why are the nations of Latin America still economically dependent on the United States and Western Europe? How did the superpower rivalry of the Cold War affect Latin America?

KEY TERMS

apartheid (p. 770)
ayatollah (p. 781)
Islamic fundamentalism (p. 779)

liberation theology (p. 784)
Palestine Liberation Organization (PLO) (p. 777)

peace process (p. 778)
sandinistas (p. 786)
theocracy (p. 780)

 For additional study resources for this chapter, go to:
www.prenhall.com/craig/chapter35

Imperialism and Race in Modern Art

HOW HAVE the experiences of imperialism, and race influenced modern and contemporary art, in both style and technique?

The second half of the nineteenth century witnessed the "second wave" of European imperialism. The United States and Japan also participated in the frenzy of the industrialized powers to obtain the labor and natural resources of other regions. The colonizers focused their attention on regions such as China, the African interior, and the Pacific Islands, that were not yet firmly ensconced in older colonial empires.

The colonial experience had an important legacy in Western and non-Western art alike, in terms of providing artistic themes, but also in the influence of Western techniques in painting and sculpture on indigenous artists. The result was often a fruitful and imaginative blending of styles and techniques that in turn have greatly influenced Western artists.

Paul Gauguin, "Where do we come from? What are we? Where are we going?" (1897), Oil on canvas.
Gauguin was one of the last French impressionist painters of the late nineteenth century. Like colonists, he imagined the people of French Tahiti as a kind of "noble savage" among whom he would find the primitive, spiritually pure lifestyle he sought. Race thus is central to his depiction of the Tahitians, but always in an idealized vision of peace and simplicity.
Museum of Fine Arts, Boston, Mass./A.K.G., Berlin/Super Stock
▼

José Clemente Orozco, "Cortés y Malinzin," (1926), fresco.

Orozco, in his fresco of the great Spanish conquistador Hernan Cortés and Cortés' Indian translator and concubine, Malinzin, deals with themes of race, conquest and gender in a much less idealized way than Gauguin. Both the style and theme of this work reflect the often uneasy but creative mixing of Western and Indian genes and culture that characterizes Mexico's *mestizo* society.

Photography: Angel Hurtado, Art Museum of the Americas, OAS. © Orozco Valladares Family. Reproduction authorized by the Instituto Nacional de Bellas Artes

Penny Siopis, "Cape of Good Hope— A History Painting," 1989–1990.

As in the image of Cortés, the naked female form, signifying the violated body of the colonized people, is at the heart of Penny Siopis's conception of the experience of South African blacks under white rule. Siopis's figure literally embodies the suffering of all black South Africans, but also their dignity and patience, in stark contrast to the decadent, voyeuristic whites presumably viewing the painting.

Courtesy of the University of the Witwatersand, Jahannesburg, South Africa

Taguchi Beisaku, "Strange-looking Manchurian Horsemen on an Expedition to Observe the Japanese Camp in the Distance near Sauhoku (Sokako)" 1894.

Japan also entered the race for colonial possessions in the last decade of the nineteenth century. Two wars, one with China (1894–1895) and the other with Russia (1904–1905), resulted in the 1905 Treaty of Portsmouth that earned Japan control of Manchuria, hegemony over Korea, and outright annexation of Sakhalin Island. In this Japanese painting from the period, we see two Manchurian horsemen portrayed as barbaric and ghoulish.

Taguchi Beisaku, Japanese, 1684-1903. Stranger-looking Manchurian horsemen on an expedition to observe the Japanese camp in the distance near Sauhoku (Sokako) Japanese, Meiji era probably published late 1894. Woodblock print; ink and color on paper. Vertical oban triptych: 37 × 71.2 cm (14 9/16 × 28 1/16 in.) Courtesy, Museum of Fine Arts, Boston. Jaen S. and Frederic A. Sharf Collection 2000.255. Reproduction with permission. © 2003 Museum of Fine Arts, Boston. All Rights Reserved

GLOSSARY

absolutism Term applied to strong centralized continental monarchies that attempted to make royal power dominant over aristocracies and other regional authorities.

Acropolis The religious and civic center of Athens. It is the site of the Parthenon.

Afrikaans The new language, derived from Dutch, that evolved in the seventeenth-and eighteenth-century Cape Colony.

agape Meaning "love feast." A common meal that was part of the central ritual of early Christian worship.

agora The Greek marketplace and civic center. It was the heart of the social life of the polis.

agricultural revolution The innovations in farm production that began in the eighteenth century and led to a scientific and mechanized agriculture.

amir/emir An Islamic military commander.

Amitabha The Buddhist Lord of the Western Paradise, or Pure Land.

Annam The Chinese term for Vietnam.

Anschluss Meaning "union." The annexation of Austria by Germany in March 1938.

anti-Semitism Prejudice, hostility, or legal discrimination against Jews.

apartheid "Apartness," the term referring to racist policies enforced by the white-dominated regime that existed in South Africa from 1948 to 1992.

apostolic primacy The doctrine that the popes are the direct successors to the Apostle Peter and as such heads of the church.

appeasement The Anglo-French policy of making concessions to Germany in the 1930s to avoid a crisis that would lead to war. It assumed that Germany had real grievances and Hitler's aims were limited and ultimately acceptable.

Areopagus The governing council of Athens, originally open only to the nobility. It was named after the hill on which it met.

Arianism The belief formulated by Arius of Alexandria (ca. 280–336 C.E.) that Jesus was a created being, neither fully man nor fully God, but something in between.

aristocratic resurgence Eighteenth-century aristocratic efforts to resist the expanding power of European monarchies.

Aryans The Indo-European speakers who invaded India and Iran in the second and first millenia B.C.E.

assignats Government bonds based on the value of confiscated church lands issued during the early French Revolution.

Atman-Brahman The unchanging, infinite principle of reality in Indian religion.

Atomists School of ancient Greek philosophy founded in the fifth century B.C.E. by Leucippus of Miletus and Democritus of Abdera. It held that the world consists of innumerable, tiny, solid, indivisible, and unchangeable particles called atoms.

Augustus The title given to Octavian in 27 B.C.E. and borne there–after by all Roman emperors.

Ausgleich Meaning "compromise." The agreement between the Habsburg Emperor and the Hungarians to give Hungary considerable administrative autonomy in 1867. It created the Dual Monarchy, or Austria-Hungary.

Axis The alliance between Nazi Germany and fascist Italy. Also called the Pact of Steel.

ayan Ottoman notables.

ayatollah A major Shi'ite religious leader.

Bakufu "Tent government." The military regime that governed Japan under the shōguns.

bazaari The Iranian commercial middle class.

bhakti Hindu devotional movements.

bishop Originally a person elected by early Christian congregations to lead them in worship and supervise their funds. In time, bishops became the religious and even political authorities for Christian communities within large geographical areas.

Black Death The bubonic plague that killed millions of Europeans in the fourteenth century.

Black Legend The argument that Spanish treatment of native Americans was uniquely inhumane.

Blitzkrieg Meaning "lightning war." The German tactic early in World War II of employing fast-moving, massed armored columns supported by airpower to overwhelm the enemy.

bodhisattva A "Buddha to be" who postpones his own nirvana until he has helped all other beings become enlightened.

Bolsheviks Meaning the "majority." Term Lenin applied to his faction of the Russian Social Democratic Party. It became the Communist Party of the Soviet Union after the Russian Revolution.

Boxers A nationalistic Chinese religious society that attacked foreigners and their encroachments on China in the late nineteenth century.

boyars The Russian nobility.

Brahmanas Texts dealing with the ritual application of the Vedas.

brainwashing The Communist practice of forced indoctrination of individuals in Marxist thought followed by confession of errors, repentance, and reacceptance by society. It was particularly favored in China under Mao.

Bronze Age The name given to the earliest civilized era, c. 4000 to 1000 B.C.E. The term reflects the importance of the metal bronze, a mixture of tin and copper, for the peoples of this age for use as weapons and tools.

caliphate The true line of succession to Muhammad.

calpulli The wards into which the Aztec capital, Tenochtitlan, was divided.

cantonments The segregation of areas in which Europeans lived in British-ruled India from those areas inhabited by native Indians.

catholic Emancipation The grant of full political rights to Roman Catholics in Britain in 1829.

Catholic Meaning "universal." The body of belief held by most Christians enshrined within the church.

caudillo Latin American strongman, or dictator, usually with strong ties to the military.

censor Official of the Roman republic charged with conducting the census and compiling the lists of citizens and members of the Senate.

Censorate The branch of the imperial Chinese government that acted a watchdog, reporting instances of misgovernment directly to the emperor and remonstrating when it considered the emperor's behavior improper.

Chartism The first large-scale European working-class political movement. It sought political reforms that would favor the interests of skilled British workers in the 1830s and 1840s.

chiaroscuro The use of shading to enhance naturalness in painting and drawing.

chicha A maize beer brewed by the *mamakuna* for the Inca elite.

chun-tzu The Confucian term for a person who behaves ethically, in harmony with the cosmic order.

civilization A form of human culture marked by urbanism, metallurgy, and writing.

Cold War The ideological and geographical struggle between the United States and its allies and the USSR and its allies that began after World War II and lasted until the dissolution of the USSR in 1989.

collectivization The bedrock of Stalinist agriculture, which forced Russian peasants to give up their private farms and work as members of collectives, large agricultural units controlled by the state.

conquistadores Meaning "conquerors." The Spanish conquerors of the New World.

Consulate French government dominated by Napoleon from 1799 to 1804.

Convention French radical legislative body from 1792 to 1794.

corvée A French labor tax requiring peasants to work on roads, bridges, and canals.

Council of Nicaea The council of Christian bishops at Nicaea in 325 C.E. that formulated the Nicene Creed, a statement of Christian belief that rejected Arianism in favor of the doctrine that Christ is both fully human and fully divine.

Counter-Reformation The sixteenth-century reform movement in the Roman Catholic Church in reaction to the Protestant Reformation.

Creoles Persons of European descent who were born in the Spanish colonies.

Crusades Religious wars directed by the church against infidels and heretics.

Cultural Revolution A movement launched by Mao between 1965 and 1976 against the Soviet-style bureaucracy that had taken hold in China. It involved widespread disorder and violence.

culture The ways of living built up by a group and passed on from one generation to another.

cuneiform A writing system invented by the Sumerians that used a wedge-shaped stylus, or pointed tool, to write on wet clay tablets that were then baked or dried (*cuneus* means "wedge" in Latin). The writing was also cut into stone.

Curia The papal government.

daimyo Japanese territorial lord.

debt peonage A system that forces agricultural laborers (peons) to work and live on large estates until they have repaid their debts to the estate's owner.

debt peonage The requirement that laborers remain and continue to work on a hacienda until they had paid their debts to the owner for goods bought from him on credit.

deism A belief in a rational God who had created the universe, but then allowed it to function without his interference according to the mechanisms of nature and a belief in rewards and punishments after death for human action.

Delian League An alliance of Greek states under the leadership of Athens that was formed in 478–477 B.C.E. to resist the Persians.

demesne The part of a manor that was cultivated directly for the lord of the manor.

devshirme The system under the Ottoman Empire that required each province to furnish a levy of Christian boys who were raised as Muslims and became soldiers in the Ottoman army.

dharma Moral law or duty.

Diet The bicameral Japanese parliament.

Diet of Worms The meeting of the representative (diet) of the Holy Roman Empire presided over by the Emperor Charles V at the Germain city of Worms in 1521 at which Martin Luther was ordered to recant his ninety-five theses. Luther refused and was declared outlaw although he was protected by the Elector of Saxony and other German princes.

divine right of kings The theory that monarchs are appointed by and answerable only to God.

domestic or putting-out system of textile production Method of producing textiles in which agents furnished raw materials to households whose members spun them into thread and then wove cloth, which the agents then sold as finished products.

Duce Meaning "leader." Mussolini's title as head of the Fascist Party.

Duma The Russian parliament, after the revolution of 1905.

dynastic cycle The term used to describe the rise, decline, and fall of China's imperial dynasties.

empiricism The use of experiment and observation derived from sensory evidence to construct scientific theory or philosophy of knowledge.

enclosures The consolidation or fencing in of common lands by British landlords to increase production and achieve greater commercial profits. It also involved the reclamation of waste land and the consolidation of strips into block fields.

encomienda The grant by the Spanish crown to a colonist of the labor of a specific number of Indians for a set period of time.

Enlightenment The eighteenth-century movement led by the *philosophes* that held that change and reform were both desirable through the application of reason and science.

Epicureans   School of philosophy founded by Epicurus of Athens (342–271 B.C.E.). It sought to liberate people from fear of death and the supernatural by teaching that the gods took no interest in human affairs and that true happiness consisted in pleasure, which was defined as the absence of pain.

equestrians   Literally "cavalrymen" or "knights." In the earliest years of the Roman Republic, those who could afford to serve as mounted warriors.

Estado Novo   The "new state" based on political stability and economic and social progress supposedly established by the dictator Getulio Vargas after 1937.

Etruscans   A people of central Italy who exerted the most powerful external influence on the early Romans.

Eucharist   Meaning "thanksgiving." The celebration of the Lord's Supper. Considered the central ritual of worship by most Christians. Also called Holy Communion.

Euro   The common currency created by the EEC in the late 1990s.

European Economic Community (EEC)   The economic association formed by France, Germany, Italy, Belgium, the Netherlands, and Luxembourg in 1957. Also known as the Common Market.

European Union   The new name given to the EEC in 1993. It included most of the states of Western Europe.

Fabians   British socialists in the late nineteenth and early twentieth century who sought to achieve socialism through gradual, peaceful, and democratic means.

family economy   The basic structure of production and consumption in preindustrial Europe.

fascism   Political movements that tend to be antidemocratic, anti-Marxist, antiparliamentary, and often anti-Semitic. Fascists were invariably nationalists and exhalted the nation over the individual. They supported the interests of the middle class and rejected the ideas of the French Revolution and nineteenth-century liberalism. The first fascist regime was founded by Benito Mussolini (1883–1945) in Italy in the 1920s.

fealty   An oath of loyalty by a vassal to a lord, promising to perform specified services.

feudal society   The social, political, military, and economic system that prevailed in the Middle Ages and beyond in some parts of Europe.

fief   Land granted to a vassal in exchange for services, usually military.

Fourteen Points   President Woodrow Wilson's (1856–1924) idealistic war aims.

Führer   Meaning "leader." The title taken by Hitler when he became dictator of Germany.

Gentry   In China, a largely urban, landowning class that represented local interests and functioned as quasi-bureaucrats under the magistrates.

ghazis   Warriors who carried Islam by force of arms to pagan groups.

ghettos   Separate communities in which Jews were required by law to live.

glasnost   Meaning "openness." The policy initiated by Mikhail Gorbachev in the 1980s of permitting open criticism of the policies of the Soviet Communist Party.

Glorious Revolution   The largely peaceful replacement of James II by William and Mary as English monarchs in 1688. It marked the beginning of constitutional monarchy in Britain.

Golden Horde   Name given to the Mongol rulers of Russia from 1240 to 1480.

Grand Mufti   The chief religious authority of the Ottoman Empire. Also called "the Shaykh of Islam."

Great Depression   A prolonged worldwide economic downturn that began in 1929 with the collapse of the New York Stock Exchange.

Great Leap Forward   Mao's disastrous attempt to modernize the Chinese economy in 1958.

Great Purges   The imprisonment and execution of millions of Soviet citizens by Stalin between 1934 and 1939.

Great Reform Bill (1832)   A limited reform of the British House of Commons and an expansion of the electorate to include a wider variety of the propertied classes. It laid the groundwork for further orderly reforms within the British constitutional system.

Great Schism   The appearance of two and at times three rival popes between 1378 and 1415.

Great Trek   The migration between 1835 and 1847 of Boer pioneers (called *voortrekkers*) north from British-ruled Cape Colony to establish their own independent republics.

guild   An association of merchants or craftsmen that offered protection to its members and set rules for their work and products.

hacienda   Large landed estates in Spanish America.

hadith   A saying or action ascribed to Muhammad.

Haji   The pilgrimage to Mecca that all Muslims are enjoined to perform at least once in their lifetime.

Harappan   Term used to describe the first civilization of the Indus Valley.

Hegira   The flight of Muhammad and his followers from Mecca to Medina in 622 C.E. It marks the beginning of the Islamic calendar.

heliocentric theory   The theory, now universally accepted, that the earth and the other planets revolve around the sun. First proposed by Aristarchos of Samos (310–230 B.C.E.).

Helots   Hereditary Spartan serfs.

hieroglyphics   The complicated writing script of ancient Egypt. It combined picture writing with pictographs and sound signs. Hieroglyph means "sacred carvings" in Greek.

Hindu   Term applied to the diverse social, racial, linguistic, and religious groups of India.

Holocaust   The Nazi extermination of millions of European Jews between 1940 and 1945. Also called the "final solution to the Jewish problem."

Holy Roman Empire   The revival of the old Roman Empire, based mainly in Germany and northern Italy, that endured from 870 to 1806.

home rule The advocacy of a large measure of administrative autonomy for Ireland within the British Empire between the 1880s and 1914.

hoplite phalanx The basic unit of Greek warfare in which infantrymen fought in close order, shield to shield, usually eight ranks deep.

Huguenots French Calvinists.

humanism The study of the Latin and Greek classics and of the Church Fathers both for their own sake and to promote a rebirth of ancient norms and values.

humanitas The Roman name for a liberal arts education.

The Iliad and the Odyssey, The Epic poems by Homer about the "Dark Age" heroes of Greece who fought at Troy. The poems were written down in the eighth century B.C.E. after centuries of being sung by bards.

imams Islamic prayer leader.

impact of modernity The effect of western political, economic, and social ideas and institutions on traditional societies.

imperator Under the Roman Republic, it was the title given to a victorious general. Under Augustus and his successors, it became the title of the ruler of Rome, meaning "emperor."

imperium In ancient Rome, the right to issue commands and to enforce them by fines, arrests, and even corporal and capital punishment.

Import substitution The replacement of imported goods with those manufactured domestically.

Indo-European A widely distributed language group that includes most of the languages spoken in Europe, Persian, Sanskrit, and their derivatives.

Indo-Greeks Bactrian rulers who broke away from the Seleucid Empire to found a state that combined elements of Greek and Indian civilizations.

indulgences Remission of the temporal penalty of punishment in purgatory that remained after sins had been forgiven.

Industrial Revolution Mechanization of the European economy that began in Britain in the second half of the eighteenth century.

Islam Meaning "submission." The religion founded by the prophet Muhammad.

Islamic fundamentalism A movement among many Muslims to return to the "fundamentals" of Islamic faith, life, and society.

Italia Irredenta Meaning "unredeemed Italy." Italian-speaking areas that had been left under Austrian rule at the time of the unification of Italy.

jacobins The radical republican party during the French Revolution that displaced the Girondins.

Jains An Indian religious community that teaches compassion for all beings.

Janissaries Elite Ottoman troops who were recruited through the *devshirme*.

jatis The many subgroups that make up the Hindu caste system.

jihad "Struggle in the path of God." Although not necessarily implying violence, it is often interpreted to mean holy war in the name of Islam.

July Monarchy The French regime set up after the overthrow of the Bourbons in July 1830.

Junkers The noble landlords of Prussia.

Ka'ba A black meteorite in the city of Mecca that became Islam's holiest shrine.

Kabuki A realistic form of Japanese theater similar to English Elizabethan drama.

Kalahari A large desert in southwestern Africa that partially isolates southern Africa from the rest of he continent.

kamikaze "Divine winds" which sank a portion of the invading Mongol fleet in Japan in 1281.

karma The Indian belief that every action has an inevitable effect. Good deeds bring good results; evil deeds have evil consequences.

Khmer Rouge Meaning "Red Cambodia." The radical Communist movement that ruled Cambodia from 1975 to 1978.

kleindeutsch Meaning "small German." The argument that the German-speaking portions of the Habsburg Empire should be excluded from a united Germany.

Kristallnacht Meaning "crystal night" because of the broken glass that littered German streets after the looting and destruction of Jewish homes, businesses, and synagogues across Germany on the orders of the Nazi Party in November 1938.

Kuomintang (KMT) China's Nationalist Party, founded by Sun Yat-sen.

La Reforma the nineteenth-century Mexican liberal reform movement that opposed Santa Ana's dictatorship and sought to foster economic progress, civilian rule, and political stability. It was strongly anti-clerical.

laissez-faire French phrase meaning "allow to do." In economics, the doctrine of minimal government interference in the working of the economy.

latifundia Large plantations for growing cash crops owned by wealthy Romans.

LDP The Liberal Democratic Party. A conservative party that has dominated postwar Japanese politics.

League of Nations The association of sovereign states set up after World War I to pursue common policies and avert international aggression.

Lebensraum Meaning "living space," The Nazi plan to colonize and exploit Eastern Europe.

Legalism The Chinese philosophical school that argued that a strong state was necessary in order to have a good society.

levée en masse The French revolutionary conscription (1792) of all males into the army and the harnessing of the economy for war production.

liberalism In the nineteenth century, support for representative government dominated by the propertied classes and minimal government interference in the economy.

liberation theology The effort by certain Roman Catholic theologians to combine Marxism with traditional Christian concern for the poor.

Logos Divine reason, or fire, which according to the Stoics, was the guiding principle in nature.

Long Count   A Mayan calendar that dated from a fixed point in the past.

Long March   The flight of the Chinese communists from their Nationalist foes to northwest China in 1934.

Luftwaffe   The German air force in World War II.

madrasa   An Islamic college of higher learning.

Magna Carta   The "Great Charter" limiting royal power that the English nobility forced King John to sign in 1215.

Magna Graecia   Meaning "Great Greece" in Latin, it was the name given by the Romans to southern Italy and Sicily because there were so many Greek colonies in the region.

Magyars   The majority ethnic group in Hungary.

Mahabharata **and** *Ramayana*   The two classical Indian epics.

Mahayana   The "Great Vehicle" for salvation in Buddhism. It emphasized the Buddha's infinite compassion for all beings.

manakuna   Inca women who lived privileged but celibate lives and had important economic and cultural roles.

Mandate of Heaven   The Chinese belief that Heaven entrusts or withdraws a ruler's or a dynasty's right to govern.

Manichaeism   A dualistic and moralistic view of reality in which good and evil, spirit and matter warred with each other.

mannerism   A style of art in the mid to late sixteenth century that permitted artists to express their own "manner" or feelings in contrast to the symmetry and simplicity of the art of the High Renaissance.

manor   Village farms owned by a lord.

Marshall Plan   The U.S. program, named after Secretary of State George C. Marshall, that provided economic aid to Europe after World War II.

Marxism   The theory of Karl Marx (1818–1883) and Friedrich Engels (1820–1895) that history is the result of class conflict, which will end in the inevitable triumph of the industrial proletariat over the bourgeoisie and the abolition of private property and social class.

Meiji restoration   The overthrow of the Tokugawa *bakufu* in Japan in 1868 and the transfer, or "restoration," of power to the imperial government under the Emperor Meiji.

Mein Kampf   Meaning "My Struggle." Hitler's statement of his political program, published in 1924.

Mensheviks   Meaning the "minority." Term Lenin applied to the majority moderate faction of the Russian Social Democratic Party opposed to him and the Bolsheviks.

mercantilism   Term used to describe close government control of the economy that sought to maximize exports and accumulate as much precious metals as possible to enable the state to defend its economic and political interests.

Mesoamerica   The part of North America that extends from the central part of modern Mexico to Central America.

Mesopotamia   Modern Iraq. The land between the Tigris and Euphrates Rivers where the first civilization appeared around 3000 B.C.E.

Messiah   The redeemer whose coming Jews believed would establish the kingdom of God on earth. Christians considered Jesus to be the Messiah (Christ means Messiah in Greek).

mestizos   Persons of mixed Native American and European descent.

Mexica   The Aztecs name for themselves.

mfecane   A period of widespread warfare and chaos among Bantu peoples in east-central Africa during the early nineteenth century.

Minoan   The Bronze Age civilization that arose in Crete in the third and second millennia B.C.E.

mita   The Inca system of forced labor in return for gifts and ritual entertainments.

Mitimaqs   Communities whom the Incas forced to settle in designated regions for strategic purposes.

mobilization   The placing of a country's military forces on a war footing.

monotheism   The worship of one universal God.

Moors   The Spanish and Portuguese term for Muslims.

Mughals   Descendants of the Mongols who established an Islamic empire in India in the sixteenth century with its capital at Delhi.

mujtahid   A Shi'ite religious-legal scholar.

mulattos   Persons of mixed African and European descent.

Mycenaean   The Bronze Age civilization of mainland Greece that was centered at Mycenae.

"mystery" religions   The cults of Isis, Mithra, and Osiris, which promised salvation to those initiated into the secret or "mystery" of their rites.

nacionalismo   A right-wing Argentine nationalist movement that arose in the 1930s and resembled European fascism.

National Studies   A Japanese intellectual tradition that emphasized native Japanese culture and institutions and rejected the influence of Chinese Confucianism.

nationalism   The belief that one is part of a nation, defined as a community with its own language, traditions, customs, and history that distinguish it from other nations and make it the primary focus of a person's loyalty and sense of identity.

Nazis   The German Nationalist Socialist Party.

neocolonial economy   An economic relationship between a former colonial state and countries with more developed economies in which the former colony exports raw materials to and imports manufactured goods from the more developed nations.

Neolithic Revolution   The shift beginning 10,000 years ago from hunter-gatherer societies to settled communities of farmers and artisans. Also called the Age of Agriculture, it witnessed the invention of farming, the domestication of plants and animals, and the development of technologies such as pottery and weaving. "Neolithic" comes from the Greek words for "new stone."

Neo-Taoism   A revival of Taoist "mysterious learning" that flourished as a reaction against Confucianism during the Han dynasty.

New Economic Policy (NEP)   A limited revival of capitalism, especially in light industry and agriculture, introduced by Lenin in 1921 to repair the damage inflicted on the Russian economy by the Civil War and War Communism.

New Imperialism   The extension in the late nineteenth and early twentieth centuries of Western political and economic dominance to Asia, the Middle East, and Africa.

Nilotic Africa   The lands along the Nile River.

Nirvana In Buddhism the attainment of release from the wheel of *karma*.

Nō play A highly stylized form of Japanese drama in which the chorus provides the narrative line as in classical Greek plays.

oba Title of the king of Benin.

Obsidian A hard volcanic glass that was widely used in Mesoamerica.

Old Regime Term applied to the pattern of social, political, and economic relationships and institutions that existed in Europe before the French Revolution.

orthodox Meaning "holding the right opinions." Applied to the doctrines of the Catholic Church.

orthopraxy The correct practice of a religion.

Ottoman Empire The imperial Turkish state centered in Constantinople that ruled large parts of the Balkans, North Africa, and the Middle East until 1918.

padishah Meaning "emperor." One of the titles of the Ottoman monarchs.

Paleolithic Age The earliest period when stone tools were used, from about 1,000,000 to 10,000 B.C.E. From the Greek meaning "old stone."

Palestine Liberation Organization (PLO) A political and cultural movement formed by Arab Palestinians to work for the creation of an independent Palestinian state.

Panhellenic ("all-Greek") The sense of cultural identity that all Greeks felt in common with each other.

pan-Islamism The movement that advocates that the entire Muslim world should form a unified political and cultural entity.

Pan-Slavic movement The movement to create a nation or federation that would embrace all the Slavic peoples of Eastern Europe.

Papal States Territory in central Italy ruled by the pope until 1870.

parlement French regional court dominated by hereditary nobility. The most important was the Parlement of Paris, which claimed the right to register royal decrees before they could become law.

patricians The hereditary upper class of early Republican Rome.

peace process Efforts, chiefly by the United States, to broker a peace between the State of Israel and the PLO.

Peloponnesian Wars The protracted struggle between Athens and Sparta to dominate Greece between 465 and Athens' final defeat in 404 B.C.E.

peninsulares Persons born in Spain who settled in the Spanish colonies.

peninsulares Native-born Spaniards who immigrated from Spain to settle in the Spanish colonies.

perestroika Meaning "restructuring." The attempt in the 1980s to reform the Soviet government and economy.

Perónism An authoritarian, nationalist movement founded in Argentina in the 1940s by the dictatore Juan Perón.

pharaoh The god-kings of ancient Egypt. The term originally meant "great house" or palace.

Pharisees The group that was most strict in its adherence to Jewish law.

philosophes The eighteenth-century writers and critics who forged the new attitudes favorable to change. They sought to apply reason and common sense to the institutions and societies of their day.

Phoenicians The ancient inhabitants of modern Lebanon. A trading people, they established colonies throughout the Mediterranean.

pipiltin Aztec bureaucrats and priests.

pirs Shi'ite holy men.

plantation economy The economic system stretching between Chesapeake Bay and Brazil that produced crops, especially sugar, cotton, and tobacco, using slave labor on large estates.

plebeians The hereditary lower class of early Republican Rome.

plenitude of power The teaching that the popes have power over all other bishops of the church.

pochteca Aztec merchants.

pogroms Organized riots against Jews in the Russian Empire.

polis The basic Greek political unit. Usually, but incompletely, translated as "city-state," the Greeks thought of the *polis* as a community of citizens theoretically descended from a common ancestor.

polytheism The worship of many gods.

Popular Front A government of all left-wing parties that took power in France in 1936 to enact social and economic reforms.

populares Roman politicians who sought to pursue a political career based on the support of the people rather than just the aristocracy.

positivism the philosophy of Auguste Comte that science is the final, or positive, stage of human intellectual development because it involves exact descriptions of phenomena, without recourse to unobservable operative principles, such as gods or spirits.

Pragmatic Sanction The legal basis negotiated by the Emperor Charles VI (r. 1711–1740) for the Habsburg succession through his daughter Maria Theresa (r. 1740–1780).

PRI The Institutional Revolutionary Party, which emerged from the Mexican revolution of 1911 and governed Mexico until the end of the twentieth century.

Proletarianization The process whereby independent artisans and factory workers lose control of the means of production and of the conduct of their own trades to the owners of capital.

Ptolemaic system The pre-Copernican explanation of the universe, which placed the Earth at the center of the universe.

Punic Wars Three wars between Rome and Carthage for dominance of the western Mediterranean that were fought from 264 B.C.E. to 146 B.C.E.

Pure Land Buddhism A variety of Japanese Buddhism that maintained that only faith was necessary for salvation.

puritans English Protestants who sought to "purify" the Church of England of any vestiges of Catholicism.

Qanun Ottoman administrative law.

Quechua The Inca language.

quipu Knotted string used by Andean peoples for recordkeeping.

Qur'an Meaning "a reciting." The Islamic bible, which Muslims believe God revealed to the prophet Muhammad.

racism The pseudoscientific theory that biological features of race determine human character and worth.

raj The years from 1858 to 1947 during which India was governed directly by the British Crown.

Raja An Indian King.

Ramadan The month each year when Muslims must fast during daylight hours.

Reconquista The Christian reconquest of Spain from the Muslims from 1000 to 1492.

Reformation The sixteenth-century religious movement that sought to reform the Roman Catholic Church and led to the establishment of Protestantism.

regular clergy Monks and nuns who belong to religious orders.

Reichstag The German parliament, which existed in various forms, until 1945.

Reign of Terror The period between the summer of 1793 and the end of July 1794 when the French revolutionary state used extensive executions and violence to defend the Revolution and suppress its alleged internal enemies.

Renaissance The revival of ancient learning and the supplanting of traditional religious beliefs by new secular and scientific values that began in Italy in the fourteenth and fifteenth centuries.

reparations The requirement incorporated into the Versailles Treaty that Germany should pay for the cost of World War I.

repartimiento A labor tax in Spanish America that required adult male native Americans devote a set number of days a year to Spanish economic enterprises.

revisionism The advocacy among nineteenth-century German socialists of achieving a humane socialist society through the evolution of democratic institutions, not revolution.

SA The Nazi parliamentary forces, or stormtroopers.

Sahara The world's largest desert. It extends across Africa from the Atlantic to the eastern Sudan. Historically, the Sahara has hindered contact between the Mediterranean and sub-Saharan Africa.

Sahel An area of steppe and semidesert that borders the Sahara.

samsara The endless cycle of existence, of birth and rebirth.

samurai Professional Japanese warriors.

Sandinistas The Marxist guerrilla force that overthrew the Somoza dictatorship in Nicaragua in 1979.

sans-culottes Meaning "without breeches." The lower-middle classes and artisans of Paris during the French Revolution.

satraps Governors of provinces in the Persian Empire.

savannah An area of open woodlands and grassy plains.

Schlieffen Plan Germany's plan for achieving a quick victory in the West at the outbreak of World War I by invading France through Belgium and Luxembourg.

Scholasticism Method of study based on logic and dialectic that dominated the medieval schools. It assumed that truth already existed; students had only to organize, elucidate, and defend knowledge learned from authoritative texts, especially those of Aristotle and the Church Fathers.

Scientific Revolution The sweeping change in the scientific view of the universe that occurred in the West in the sixteenth and seventeenth centuries.

scramble for Africa The late nineteenth-century takeover of most of Africa by European powers.

secular clergy Parish clergy who did not belong to a religious order.

serfs Peasants tied to the land they tilled.

Shahanshah "King of kings," the title of the Persian ruler.

Shari'a Islamic religious law.

Shensi banks Private commercial banks in China under the Manchus.

Shi-a The minority of Muslims who trace their beliefs from the caliph Ali who was assassinated in 661 C.E.

Shinto "The way of the gods." The animistic worship of the forces of nature that is the indigenous religion of Japan.

Shōgun A military official who was the actual ruler of Japan in the emperor's name from the late 1100s until the mid-nineteenth century.

Silk Road Trade route from China to the West that stretched across Central Asia.

Sophists Professional teachers who emerged in Greece in the mid-fifth century B.C.E. who were paid to teach techniques of rhetoric, dialectic, and argumentation.

soviets Workers' and soldiers' councils formed in Russia during the Revolution.

spinning jenny A machine invented in England by James Hargreaves around 1765 to mass-produce thread.

SS The chief security units of the Nazi state.

Steppe peoples Nomadic tribespeople who dwelled on the Eurasian plains from eastern Europe to the borders of China and Iran. They frequently traded with or invaded more settled cultures.

Stoics A philosophical school founded by Zeno of Citium (335–263 B.C.E.) that taught that humans could only be happy with natural law.

streltsy Professional troops who made up the Moscow garrison. They were suppressed by Peter the Great.

studia humanitatis During the Renaissance, a liberal arts program of study that embraced grammar, rhetoric, poetry, history, philosophy, and politics.

stupa A Buddhist shrine.

suffragettes British women who lobbied and agitated for the right to vote in the early twentieth century.

Sufi A movement within Islam that emphasizes the spiritual and mystical.

sultan A Muslim royal title that means "authority."

Sunna Meaning "tradition." The dominant Islamic group.

Swahili A language and culture that developed from the interaction of native Africans and Arabs along the East African coast.

symposion The carefully organized drinking party that was the center of Greek aristocratic social life. It featured games, songs, poetry, and even philosophical disputation.

Table of Ranks An official hierarchy established by Peter the Great in imperial Russia that equated a person's social position and privileges with his rank in the state bureaucracy or army.

taille The direct tax on the French peasantry.

Taiping rebellion A nineteenth-century revolt against China's Manchu dynasty that was inspired by quasi-Christian ideas and that led to enormous suffering and destruction before its collapse in 1868.

Taoism   A Chinese philosophy that teaches that wisdom lies in becoming one with the *Tao*, the "way," which is the creative principle of the universe.

Tennō   "Heavenly emperor." The official title of the emperor of Japan.

tetcutin   Subordinate Aztec lords.

tetrarchy   Diocletian's (r. 306–337 C.E.) system for ruling the Roman Empire by four men with power divided territorially.

theocracy   A state ruled by religious leaders who claim to govern by divine authority.

Theravada   The "Way of the Elders." A school of Buddhism that emphasized the monastic ideal.

Thermidorean Reaction   The reaction against the radicalism of the French Revolution that began in July 1794. Associated with the end of terror and establishment of the Directory.

Third Estate   The branch of the French Estates General representing all of the kingdom outside the nobility and the clergy.

three-field system   A medieval innovation that increased the amount of land under cultivation by leaving only one-third fallow in a given year.

tlatoani   An Aztec ruler.

transubstantiation   The doctrine that the entire substances of the bread and wine are changed in the Eucharist into the body and blood of Christ.

treaty ports   Chinese ports ruled by foreign consuls where foreigners enjoyed commercial privileges and immunity from Chinese laws.

Trekboers   White livestock farmers in Cape Colony.

tribunes   Roman officials who had to be plebeians and were elected by the plebeian assembly to protect plebeians from the arbitrary power of the magistrates.

Tripartite Pact   The alliance between Japan and Nazi Germany and Fascist Italy that was signed in 1940.

ulama   "Persons with correct knowledge." The Islamic scholarly elite who served a social function similar to the Christian clergy.

Umma   The Islamic community.

"unequal treaties"   Agreements imposed on China in the nineteenth century by European powers, the United States, and Japan that granted their citizens special legal and economic privileges on Chinese soil.

Upanishads   Vedic texts most concerned with speculation about the universe.

Urdu-Hindi   A language that combines Persian-Arabic and native Indian elements. Urdu is the Muslim version of the language. Hindi is the Hindu version.

uzama   An order of hereditary chiefs in Benin.

varnas   The four main classes that form the basis for Hindu caste relations.

vassal   A person granted an estate or cash payments in return for accepting the obligation to render services to a lord.

Vedas   The sacred texts of the ancient Aryan invaders of India. The Rig Vedas are the oldest materials in the Vedas.

vernacular   The everyday language spoken by the people as opposed to Latin.

Viet Minh   The Communist-dominated popular front organization formed by Ho Chi Minh to establish an independent Vietnamese republic.

War Communism   The economic policy adopted by the Bolsheviks during the Russian Civil War to seize the banks, heavy industry, railroads, and grain.

war guilt clause   Clause of the Versailles Treaty, which assigned responsibility for World War I solely to Germany.

water frame   A water-powered device invented by Richard Arkwright to produce a more durable cotton fabric. It led to the shift in the production of cotton textiles from households to factories.

Weimar Republic   The German democratic regime that existed between the end of World War I and Hitler's coming to power in 1933.

White Russians   Those Russians who opposed the Bolsheviks (the "Reds") in the Russian Civil War of 1918–1921.

yangban   Elite Korean families of the Choson period.

zaibatsu   Groups of Japanese companies, or "trusts," that had a common ownership and dominated the economy of prewar Japan.

zaibatsu   Large industrial combines that came to dominate Japanese industry in the late nineteenth century.

Zen   A form of Buddhism, which taught that Buddha was only a man and exhorted each person to attain enlightenment by his or her own efforts.

Zionism   The movement to create a Jewish state in Palestine (the Biblical Zion).

Zoroastrianism   A quasi-monotheistic Iranian religion founded by Zoroaster (ca. 628–551 B.C.E.) who preached a message of moral reform and exhorted his followers to worship only Ahura Mazda, the Wise Lord.

SUGGESTED READINGS

Chapter 1

General Prehistory

V. GORDON CHILDE, What Happened in History (1946). A pioneering study of human prehistory and history before the Greeks from an anthropological point of view.

M. EHRENBERG, Women in Prehistory (1989). An account of the role of women in early times.

D. C. JOHNSON AND M. R. EDEY, Lucy: The Beginning of Mankind (1981). An account of the African origins of humans.

CHARLES L. REDMAN, The Rise of Civilization (1978). An attempt to use the evidence provided by anthropology, archaeology, and the physical sciences to illuminate the development of early urban society.

Near East

M. E. AUBER, The Phoenicians and the West (1996). A new study of an important sea-going people who served as a conduit between East and West.

BEN-TOR, ED., The Archaeology of Ancient Israel (1992). A useful and up-to-date survey.

H. CRAWFORD, Sumer and the Sumerians (1991). A discussion of the oldest Mesopotamian civilization.

HENRI FRANKFORT, Ancient Egyptian Religion: An Interpretation (1948). A brief but masterful attempt to explore the religious conceptual world of ancient Egyptians in intelligible and interesting terms.

HENRI FRANKFORT, ET AL., Before Philosophy (1949). A brilliant examination of the mind of the ancients from the Stone Age to the Greeks.

ALAN GARDINER, Egypt of the Pharaohs (1961). A sound narrative history.

W. W. HALLO AND W. K. SIMPSON, The Ancient Near East: A History (1971). A fine survey of Egyptian and Mesopotamian history.

THORKILD JACOBSEN, The Treasures of Darkness: A History of Mesopotamian Religion (1976). A superb and sensitive recreation of the spiritual life of Mesopotamian peoples from the fourth to the first millennium B.C.E.

J. N. POSTGATE, Early Mesopotamia (1992). An excellent study of Mesopotamian economy and society from the earliest times to about 1500 B.C.E., helpfully illustrated with drawings, photos, and translated documents.

JAMES B. PRITCHARD, ED., Ancient Near Eastern Texts Relating to the Old Testament (1969). A good collection of documents in translation with useful introductory material.

D. B. REDFORD, Akhenaten (1987). A study of the controversial religious reformer.

W. F. SAGGS, Everyday Life in Babylonia and Assyria, rev. ed. (1987). A new edition of a classic work.

W. F. SAGGS, The Might That Was Assyria (1984). A history of the northern Mesopotamian Empire and a worthy companion to the author's account of the Babylonian Empire in the south.

B. G. TRIGGER ET AL., Ancient Egypt: A Social History (1982).

JOHN A. WILSON, Culture of Ancient Egypt (1956). A fascinating interpretation of the civilization of ancient Egypt.

India

D. P. AGRAWAL, The Archaeology of India (1982). A fine survey of the problems and data. Detailed, but with excellent summaries and brief discussions of major issues.

B. AND R. ALLCHIN, The Birth of Indian Civilization: India and Pakistan Before 500 B.C. (1968). A one-volume summary of prehistoric India from an archaeological perspective.

W. T. DE BARY ET AL., COMP., Sources of Indian Tradition (1958; 2nd rev. ed., 2 vols., New York, 1988). A fine anthology of original texts in translation from all periods of Indian civilization.

A. L. BASHAM, The Wonder That Was India, 2nd rev. ed. (1963). Chapters 1 and 2 provide a readable and carefully done introduction to ancient India through the Aryan culture. Still the classic survey.

E. C. L. DURING CASPERS, "Sumer, Coastal Arabia and the Indus Valley in Protoliterate and Early Dynastic Eras," JESHO 22, 2 (1979): 121–135.

C. CHAKRABORTY, Common Life in the Rigveda and Atharvaveda—An Account of the Folklore in the Vedic Period (1977). An interesting attempt to reconstruct everyday life in the Vedic period from the principal Vedic texts.

D. D. KOSAMBI, Ancient India: A History of Its Culture and Civilization (1965). The most readable survey history of India to the fourth century C.E. See Chapters 2–4 on prehistoric, Indus, and Aryan culture.

W. D. O'FLAHERTY, The Rig Veda: An Anthology (1981). An excellent selection of Vedic texts in prosaic but very careful translation, with helpful notes on the texts.

J. E. SCHWARTZBERG, ED., A Historical Atlas of South Asia (1978). The definitive reference work for historical geography. Includes chronological tables and substantive essays.

R. L. SINGH, ED., India: A Regional Geography (1971). An excellent reference source for each of the major regions of the subcontinent.

China

K. C. CHANG, The Archeology of Ancient China, 4th ed. (1986). The standard work on the subject.

K. C. CHANG, Art, Myth, and Ritual, The Path to Political Authority in Ancient China (1984). A study of the relation between shamans, gods, agricultural production, and political authority during the Shang and Chou dynasties.

K. C. CHANG, Shang Civilization (1980).

D. HAWKES, Ch'u Tz'u, The Songs of the South (1985). Chou poems from the southern state of Ch'u, superbly translated.

C. Y. HSU, Ancient China in Transition: An Analysis of Social Mobility 722–222 B.C. (1965). A study of the Eastern Chou dynasty.

C. Y. HSU, Western Chou Civilization (1988).

D. N. KEIGHTLEY, The Origins of Chinese Civilization (1983).

M. E. LEWIS, Sanctioned Violence in Early China (1990).

X. Q. LI, Eastern Zhou and Qin Civilizations (1986). This work includes fresh interpretations based on archaeological finds.

Americas

R. L. BURGER, *Chavín and the Origins of Andean Civilization* (1992). A lucid and detailed account of the rise of civilization in the Andes.

M. D. COE, *America's First Civilization* (1968). Examines the earliest civilizations of Mesoamerica.

L. S. CRESSMAN, *Prehistory of the Far West: Homes of Vanished Peoples* (1977). Examines the earliest history of native Americans in the Pacific Northwest.

V. W. FITZHUGH AND A. CROWELL, *Crossroads of Continents: Cultures of Siberia and Alaska* (1988). Covers the area where the immigration from Eurasia to the Americas began.

R. FORD, ED., *Prehistoric Food Production in North America* (1985). Examines the origins of agriculture in the Americas.

D. HEYDEN AND P. GENDREP, *Precolumbian Architecture of Mesoamerica* (1975). A discussion of the architecture of Mesoamerica.

P. D. HUNT, *Indian Agriculture in America: Prehistory to the Present* (1987). Includes a discussion of preconquest agriculture.

J. D. JENNINGS, ED., *Ancient South Americans* (1983). Articles on Andean prehistory.

S. MASUDA, I. SHIMADA, AND C. MORRIS, *Andean Ecology and Civilization* (1985). Includes coverage of the earliest civilizations in the Andes.

C. MORRIS AND A. VON HAGEN, *The Inka Empire and Its Andean Origins* (1993). An overview of Andean civilization with excellent illustrations.

M. MOSELEY, *The Incas and Their Ancestors: The Archaeology of Ancient Peru* (1992). An overview of Peruvian archaeology.

J. A. SABLOFF, *The New Archaeology and the Ancient Maya* (1990). A lively account of recent research in Maya archaeology.

Chapter 2

China

H. G. CREEL, *What Is Taoism? And Other Studies in Chinese Cultural History* (1970).

W. T. DE BARY ET AL., *Sources of Chinese Tradition* (1960). A reader in China's philosophical and historical literature. It should be consulted for the later periods as well as for the Chou.

H. FINGARETE, *Confucius—The Secular as Sacred* (1998).

Y. L. FUNG, *A Short History of Chinese Philosophy*, ed. by D. Bodde (1948). A survey of Chinese philosophy from its origins down to recent times.

A. GRAHAM, *Disputers of the Tao* (1989).

D. HAWKES, *Ch'u Tz'u: The Songs of the South* (1985).

D. C. LAU, trans., *Lao-tzu, Tao Te Ching* (1963).

D. C. LAU, trans., *Confucius, The Analects* (1979).

F. W. MOTE, *Intellectual Foundations of China* (1971).

B. I. SCHWARTZ, *The World of Thought in Ancient China* (1985).

A. WALEY, *Three Ways of Thought in Ancient China* (1956). An easy yet sound introduction to Confucianism, Taoism, and Legalism.

A. WALEY, *The Book of Songs* (1960).

B. WATSON, trans., *Basic Writings of Mo Tzu, Hsun Tzu, and Han Fei Tzu* (1963).

B. WATSON, trans., *The Complete Works of Chuang Tzu* (1968).

H. WELCH, *Taoism, The Parting of the Way* (1967).

India

A. L. BASHAM, *The Wonder That Was India*, rev. ed. (1963). Still unsurpassed by more recent works. Chapter VII, "Religion," is a superb introduction to the Vedic Aryan, Brahmanic, Hindu, Jain, and Buddhist traditions of thought.

W. N. BROWN, *Man in the Universe: Some Continuities in Indian Thought* (1970). A penetrating yet brief reflective summary of major patterns in Indian thinking.

W. T. DE BARY ET AL., *Sources of Indian Tradition* (1958). 2 vols. Vol. I, *From the Beginning to 1800*. ed. and rev. by Ainslie T. Embree (1988). Excellent selections from a variety of Indian texts, with good introductions to chapters and individual selections.

P. HARVEY, *An Introduction to Buddhism* (1990). Chapters 1–3 provide an excellent historical introduction.

T. J. HOPKINS, *The Hindu Religious Tradition* (1971). A first-rate, thoughtful introduction to Hindu religious ideas and practice.

J. M. KOLLER, *The Indian Way* (1982). A useful, wide-ranging handbook of Indian thought and religion.

W. RAHULA, *What the Buddha Taught*, 2nd ed. (1974). A readable introduction to Buddhist thought from a Theravadin viewpoint, with primary-source selections.

R. H. ROBINSON AND W. L. JOHNSON, *The Buddhist Religion*, 3rd ed. (1982). An excellent first text on the Buddhist tradition, its thought and development.

R. C. ZAEHNER, *Hinduism* (1966). One of the best general introductions to central Indian religious and philosophical ideas.

Israel

BRIGHT, *A History of Israel* (1968), 2nd ed. (1972). One of the standard scholarly introductions to biblical history and literature.

W. D. DAVIES AND L. FINKELSTEIN, eds., *The Cambridge History of Judaism*. Vol. I, *Introduction: The Persian Period* (1984). Excellent essays on diverse aspects of the exilic period and later.

J. NEUSNER, *The Way of Torah: An Introduction to Judaism* (1979). A sensitive introduction to the Judaic tradition and faith.

L. W. SCHWARZ, ed., *Great Ages and Ideas of the Jewish People* (1956). Especially the first section, "The Biblical Age," by Yehezkel Kaufmann.

Greece

BURNET, *Early Greek Philosophy* (1963). Stresses the rational aspect of Greek thought and its sharp break with mythology.

F. M. CORNFORD, *From Religion to Philosophy* (1912). Emphasizes the elements of continuity between myth and religion on the one hand and Greek philosophy on the other.

B. FARRINGTON, *Greek Science* (1953). A lively interpretation of the origins and character of Greek scientific thought.

G. B. KERFERD, *The Sophistic Movement* (1981). An excellent description and analysis.

J. LEAR, *Aristotle: The Desire to Understand* (1988). A brilliant yet comprehensible introduction to the work of the philosopher.

J. M. ROBINSON, *An Introduction to Early Greek Philosophy* (1968). A valuable collection of the main fragments and ancient testimony to the works of the early philosophers, with excellent commentary.

G. VLASTOS, *The Philosophy of Socrates* (1971). A splendid collection of essays illuminating the problems presented by this remarkable man.

G. VLASTOS, *Platonic Studies*, 2nd ed. (1981). A similar collection on the philosophy of Plato.

G. VLASTOS, *Socrates, Ironist and Moral Philosopher* (1991). The results of a lifetime of study by the leading interpreter of Socrates in our time.

Chapter 3

The Rise of Greek Civilization

A. R. BURN, *Persia and the Greeks*, 2nd ed. (1984). A thorough narrative and analysis of the conflict between the Persians and the Greeks down to 479 B.C.E.

J. B. BURY AND R. MEIGSS, *A History of Greece*, 4th ed. (1975). A thorough and detailed one-volume narrative history.

P. CARTLEDGE, *Sparta and Lakonia* (1979).

J. CHADWICK, *The Mycenaean World* (1976). A readable account by a man who helped decipher Mycenaean writing.

R. DREWS, *The Coming of the Greeks* (1988). A fine discussion of the Greeks' arrival as part of the movements of the Indo-European peoples.

V. EHRENBERG, *The Greek State* (1964). A good handbook of constitutional history.

J. V. FINE, *The Ancient Greeks* (1983). An excellent survey that discusses historical problems and the evidence that gives rise to them.

M. I. FINLEY, *World of Odysseus*, rev. ed. (1965). A fascinating attempt to reconstruct Homeric society.

P. GREEN, *Xerxes at Salamis* (1970). A lively and stimulating history of the Persian War.

V. D. HANSON, *The Western Way of War* (1989). A brilliant and lively discussion of the rise and character of the hoplite phalanx and its influence on Greek society.

V. D. HANSON, *The Other Greeks* (1995). A revolutionary account of the Greek invention of the family farm and its centrality for the shaping of the *polis*.

S. HOOD, *The Minoans* (1971). A sketch of Bronze Age civilization on Crete.

D. KAGAN, *The Great Dialogue: A History of Greek Political Thought from Homer to Polybius* (1965). A discussion of the relationship between the Greek historical experience and political theory.

W. K. LACEY, *The Family in Ancient Greece* (1984).

J. F. LAZENBY, *The Defense of Greece, 490–479 B.C.* (1993). A new and valuable study of the Persian Wars.

J. F. MCGLEW, *Tyranny and Political Culture in Ancient Greece* (1993). A recent account of political developments in the Archaic period.

O. MURRAY, *Early Greece* (1980). A lively and imaginative account of the early history of Greece to the end of the Persian War.

C. ROEBUCK, *Economy and Society in the Early Greek World* (1984). A valuable study.

B. SNELL, *Discovery of the Mind* (1960). An important study of Greek intellectual development.

A. M. SNODGRASS, *The Dark Age of Greece* (1972). A good examination of the archaeological evidence.

C. G. STARR, *The Economic and Social Growth of Early Greece, 800–500 B.C.* (1977).

EMILY VERMEULE, *Greece in the Bronze Age* (1972). A study of the Mycenaean period.

A. G. WOODHEAD, *Greeks in the West* (1962). An account of the Greek settlements in Italy and Sicily.

W. J. WOODHOUSE, *Solon the Liberator* (1965). A discussion of the great Athenian reformer.

D. C. YOUNG, *The Olympic Myth of Greek Athletics* (1984). A lively challenge to the orthodox view that Greek athletes were amateurs.

Classical and Hellenistic Greece

M. AUSTIN AND P. VIDAL-NAQUET, *The Economic and Social History of Classical Greece* (1977). A combination of documents and explanation.

W. BURKERT, *Greek Religion* (1987). An excellent study by an outstanding student of the subject.

G. CAWKWELL, *Philip of Macedon* (1978). A brief but learned account of Philip's career.

J. K. DAVIES, *Democracy and Classical Greece* (1978). Emphasizes archaeological evidence and social history.

J. R. LANE FOX, *Alexander the Great* (1973). An imaginative account that does more than the usual justice to the Persian side of the problem.

Y. GARLAN, *Slavery in Ancient Greece* (1988). An up-to-date survey.

P. GREEN, *Alexander to Actium: The Historical Evolution of the Hellenistic Age* (1990). A remarkable synthesis of political and cultural history.

C. D. HAMILTON, *Agesilaus and the Failure of Spartan Hegemony* (1991). An excellent biography of the king who was the central figure in Sparta during its domination in the fourth century B.C.E.

N. G. L. HAMMOND, *Philip of Macedon* (1994). A new biography of the founder of the Macedonian Empire.

N. G. L. HAMMOND AND G. T. GRIFFITH, *A History of Macedonia*, Vol. 2, *550–336 B.C.* (1979). A thorough account of Macedonian history that focuses on the careers of Philip and Alexander.

R. JUST, *Women in Athenian Law and Life* (1988). An account of women's place in Athenian society.

D. KAGAN, *The Outbreak of the Peloponnesian War* (1969). Argues that war could have been avoided.

B. M. W. KNOX, *The Heroic Temper: Studies in Sophoclean Tragedy* (1964). A brilliant analysis of tragic heroism.

D. M. LEWIS, *Sparta and Persia* (1977). A valuable discussion of relations between Sparta and Persia in the fifth and fourth centuries B.C.E.

A. A. LONG, *Hellenistic Philosophy: Stoics, Epicureans, Sceptics* (1974). An account of Greek science in the Hellenistic and Roman periods.

R. MEIGGS, *The Athenian Empire* (1972). A fine study of the rise and fall of the empire, making excellent use of inscriptions.

H. W. PARKE, *Festivals of the Athenians* (1977). A fine discussion of the religious practices of the Athenians.

J. J. POLLITT, *Art and Experience in Classical Greece* (1972). A scholarly and entertaining study of the relationship between art and history in classical Greece, with excellent illustrations.

J. J. POLLITT, *Art in the Hellenistic Age* (1986). An extraordinary analysis that places the art in its historical and intellectual context.

M. I. ROSTOVTZEFF, *Social and Economic History of the Hellenistic World*, 3 vols. (1941). A masterpiece of synthesis by a great historian.

D. M. SCHAPS, *Economic Rights of Women in Ancient Greece* (1981).

B. S. STRAUSS, *Athens After the Peloponnesian War* (1987). An excellent discussion of Athens's recovery and of the nature of Athenian society and politics in the fourth century B.C.E.

B. S. STRAUSS, *Fathers and Sons in Athens* (1993). An unusual synthesis of social, political, and intellectual history.

W. W. TARN, *Alexander the Great*, 2 vols. (1948). The first volume is a narrative account, the second a series of detailed studies.

V. TCHERIKOVER, *Hellenistic Civilization and the Jews* (1970). A fine study of the impact of Hellenism on the Jews.

G. VLASTOS, *Socrates, Ironist and Moral Philosopher* (1991). The results of a lifetime of study by the leading interpreter of Socrates in our time.

F. W. WALBANK, *The Hellenistic World* (1981).

Chapter 4

Iran

M. BOYCE, *Zoroastrians: Their Religious Beliefs and Practices* (1979). The most recent survey, organized historically and based on extensive research.

M. BOYCE, ED. AND TRANS., *Textual Sources for the Study of Zoroastrianism* (1984). Well-translated selections from a broad range of ancient Iranian materials.

J. M. COOK, *The Persian Empire* (1983). Survey of the Achaemenid period.

J. CURTIS, *Ancient Persia* (1989). Excellent portfolio of photographs of artifacts and sites, with a clear historical survey of the arts and culture of ancient Iran.

W. D. DAVIES AND L. FINKLESTEIN, ED., *The Cambridge History of Judaism*, Vol. 1 (Introduction; The Persian Period). Good articles on Iran and Iranian religion as well as Judaism.

J. DUCHESNE-GUILLEMIN, TRANS., *The Hymns of Zarathushtra*, trans. by M. Henning (1952, 1963). The best short introduction to the original texts of the Zoroastrian hymns.

R. N. FRYE, *The Heritage of Persia* (1963, 1966). A first-rate survey of Iranian history to Islamic times: readable but scholarly.

R. GHIRSHMAN, *Iran* (1954). Good material on culture, society, and economy as well as politics and history.

W. W. MALANDRA, TRANS. AND ED., *An Introduction to Ancient Iranian Religion: Readings from the Avesta and Achaemenid Inscriptions* (1983). Helpful especially for texts of inscriptions relevant to religion.

India

A. L. BASHAM, *The Wonder That Was India*, rev. ed. (1963). Excellent material on Mauryan religion, society, culture, and history.

A. L. BASHAM, ED., *A Cultural History of India* (1975). A fine collection of historical-survey essays by a variety of scholars. See Part I, "The Ancient Heritage" (Chapters 2–16).

N. N. BHATTACHARYYA, *Ancient Indian History and Civilization: Trends and Perspectives* (1988). Covers Mauryan and Gupta times as well as earlier periods, with chapters on political systems, cities and villages, ideology and religion, and art.

W. T. DE BARY ET AL., COMP., *Sources of Indian Tradition*, 2nd ed. (1958). Vol. I: *From the Beginning to 1800*, ed. and rev. by Ainslie T. Embree (1988). Excellent selections from a wide variety of Indian texts, with good introductions to chapters and selections.

B. ROWLAND, *The Art and Architecture of India: Buddhist/Hindu/Jain*, 3rd rev. ed. (1970). The standard work, lucid and easy to read. Note Part Three, "Romano-Indian Art in North-West India and Central Asia."

V. A. SMITH, ED., *The Oxford History of India*, 4th rev. ed. by Percival Spear et al. (1981), pp. 71–163. A dry, occasionally dated historical survey. Includes useful reference chronologies.

R. THAPAR, *Ashoka and the Decline of the Mauryans* (1973). The standard treatment of Ashoka's reign.

R. THAPAR, *A History of India, Part I* (1966), pp. 50–108. Three chapters that provide a basic survey of the period.

S. WOLPERT, *A New History of India*, 2nd ed. (1982). A basic survey history. Chapters 5 and 6 cover the Mauryans, Guptas, and Kushans.

Greek and Asian Dynasties

A. K. NARAIN, *The Indo-Greeks* (1957. Reprinted with corrections, 1962). The most comprehensive account of the complex history of the various kings and kingdoms.

F. E. PETERS, *The Harvest of Hellenism* (1970), pp. 222–308. Helpful chapters on Greek rulers of the Eastern world from Seleucus to the last Indo-Greeks.

J. W. SEDLAR, *India and the Greek World: A Study in the Transmission of Culture* (1980). A basic work that provides a good overview.

D. SINOR, ED., *The Cambridge History of Early Inner Asia* (1990). See especially Chapters 6 and 7.

Chapter 5

From Republic to Empire

F. E. ADCOCK, *The Roman Art of War Under the Republic* (1940). An analysis of Roman military procedures.

E. BADIAN, *Foreign Clientelae* (1958). A brilliant study of the Roman idea of a client-patron relationship extended to foreign affairs.

E. BADIAN, *Roman Imperialism in the Late Republic*, 2nd ed. (1968).

A. H. BERNSTEIN, *Tiberius Sempronius Gracchus: Tradition and Apostasy* (1978). A new interpretation of Tiberius's place in Roman politics.

J. BOARDMAN, J. GRIFFIN, AND O. MURRAY, *The Oxford History of the Roman World* (1990). An encyclopedic approach to the varieties of the Roman experience.

T. J. CORNELL, *The Beginnings of Rome: Italy and Rome from the Bronze Age to the Punic Wars, c. 1000–264 B.C.* (1995). A consideration of the royal and early republican periods of Roman history.

T. CORNELL AND J. MATTHEWS, *Atlas of the Roman World* (1982). Much more than the title indicates, this book presents a comprehensive view of the Roman world in its physical and cultural setting.

S. DIXON, *The Roman Mother* (1988). Describes the place of women within the Roman family.

R. M. ERRINGTON, *The Dawn of Empire: Rome's Rise to Power* (1972). An account of Rome's conquest of the Mediterranean.

M. GELZER, *Caesar: Politician and Statesman*, trans, by P. Needham (1968). The best biography of Caesar.

E. S. GRUEN, *The Last Generation of the Roman Republic* (1973). An interesting but controversial interpretation of the fall of the Republic.

E. S. GRUEN, *The Hellenistic World and the Coming of Rome* (1984). A new interpretation of Rome's conquest of the eastern Mediterranean.

W. V. HARRIS, *War and Imperialism in Republican Rome, 327–70 B.C.* (1975). An analysis of Roman attitudes and intentions concerning imperial expansion and war.

A. KEAVENEY, *Rome and the Unification of Italy* (1988). The story of how Rome organized her defeated opponents.

A. KEAVENEY, *Lucullus: A Life* (1992). A biography of the famous Roman epicure.

J. F. LAZENBY, *Hannibal's War: A Military History of the Second Punic War* (1978). A careful and thorough account.

M. PALLOTTINO, *The Etruscans*, 6th ed. (1974). Makes especially good use of archaeological evidence.

R. T. RIDLEY, *The History of Rome* (1989). A solid general history.

E. T. SALMON, *The Making of Roman Italy* (1982). The story of Roman expansion on the Italian peninsula.

H. H. SCULLARD, *A History of the Roman World 753–146 B.C.*, 4th ed. (1980). An unusually fine narrative history with useful critical notes.

H. H. SCULLARD, *From the Gracchi to Nero*, 5th ed. (1982). A work of the same character and quality.

D. STOCKTON, *Cicero: A Political Biography* (1971). A readable and interesting study.

L. R. TAYLOR, *Party Politics in the Age of Caesar* (1949). A fascinating analysis of Roman political practices.

G. WILLIAMS, *The Nature of Roman Poetry* (1970). An unusually graceful and perceptive literary study.

Imperial Rome

J. P. V. D. BALSDON, *Roman Women* (1962).

T. BARNES, *The New Empire of Diocletian and Constantine* (1982).

K. R. BRADLEY, *Slavery and Society at Rome* (1994). A study of the role of slaves in Roman life.

P. BROWN, *Augustine of Hippo* (1967). A splendid biography.

P. BROWN, *The World of Late Antiquity, A.D. 150–750* (1971). A brilliant and readable essay.

J. BURCKHARDT, *The Age of Constantine the Great* (1956). A classic work by the Swiss cultural historian.

E. R. DODDS, *Pagan and Christian in an Age of Anxiety* (1965). An original and perceptive study.

A. FERRILL, *The Fall of the Roman Empire, The Military Explanation* (1986). An interpretation that emphasizes the decline in the quality of the Roman army.

A. FERRILL, *Caligula: Emperor of Rome* (1991). A biography of the monstrous young emperor.

E. GIBBON, *The History of the Decline and Fall of the Roman Empire*, 2nd ed., 7 vols., ed. by J. B. Bury (1909–1914). One of the masterworks of the English language.

M. GRANT, *The Fall of the Roman Empire* (1990). A lively, well-written account.

N. HANNESTAD, *Roman Art and Imperial Policy* (1988). An analysis of how the emperors used the arts to further their own and imperial interests.

A. H. M. JONES, *The Later Roman Empire*, 3 vols. (1964). A comprehensive study of the period.

D. KAGAN, ED., *The End of the Roman Empire: Decline or Transformation?* 3rd ed. (1992). A collection of essays discussing the problem of the decline and fall of the Roman Empire.

J. LEBRETON AND J. ZEILLER, *History of the Primitive Church*, 3 vols. (1962). From the Catholic viewpoint.

J. E. LENDON, *Empire of Honor, The Art of Government in the Roman World* (1997). An original and path-breaking interpretation.

H. LIETZMANN, *History of the Early Church*, 2 vols. (1961). From the Protestant viewpoint.

F. LOT, *The End of the Ancient World and the Beginnings of the Middle Ages* (1961). A study that emphasizes gradual transition rather than abrupt change.

E. N. LUTTWAK, *The Grand Strategy of the Roman Empire* (1976). An original and fascinating analysis by a keen student of modern strategy.

R. MACMULLEN, *Paganism in the Roman Empire* (1981).

R. MACMULLEN, *Roman Social Relations, 50 B.C. to A.D. 284 (1981)*.

R. MACMULLEN, *Corruption and the Decline of Rome* (1988). A study that examines the importance of changes in ethical ideas and behavior.

R. W. MATHISON, *Roman Aristocrats in Barbarian Gaul: Strategies for Survival* (1993). An unusual slant on the late empire.

W. A. MEEKS, *The Origins of Christian Morality: The First Two Centuries*. An account of the shaping of Christianity in the Roman Empire.

F. G. B. MILLAR, *The Emperor in the Roman World, 31 B.C.–A.D. 337* (1977). A study of Roman imperial government.

F. MILLAR, *The Roman Empire and Its Neighbors*, 2nd ed. (1981).

A. MOMIGLIANO, ED., *The Conflict Between Paganism and Christianity* (1963). A valuable collection of essays.

H. M. D. PARKER, *A History of the Roman World from A.D. 138 to 337* (1969). A good survey.

M. I. ROSTOVTZEFF, *Social and Economic History of the Roman Empire*, 2nd ed. (1957). A masterpiece whose main thesis has been much disputed.

V. RUDICH, *Political Dissidence Under Nero, The Price of Dissimulation* (1993). A brilliant exposition of the lives and thoughts of political dissidents in the early empire.

E. T. SALMON, *A History of the Roman World, 30 B.C. to A.D. 138* (1968). A good survey.

R. SYME, *The Roman Revolution* (1960). A brilliant study of Augustus, his supporters, and their rise to power.

R. SYME, *The Augustan Aristocracy* (1985). An examination of the new ruling class shaped by Augustus.

L. A. THOMPSON, *Romans and Blacks* (1989).

Chapter 6

P. BOHANNAN AND P. CURTIN, *Africa and Africans*, rev. ed. (1971). An enjoyable and enlightening discussion of African history and prehistory and of major African institutions (e.g., arts, family life, religion).

P. CURTIN, S. FEIERMANN, L. THOMPSON, AND J. VANSINA, *African History* (1978). Probably the best survey history. The relevant portions are chapters 1, 2, 4, 8, and 9.

T. R. H. DAVENPORT, *South Africa: A Modern History*, 3rd rev. ed. (1987). Chapter 1 gives excellent summary coverage of prehistoric southern Africa, the Khoisan peoples, and the Bantu migrations.

B. DAVIDSON, *The African Past* (1967). A combination of primary-source selections and brief secondary discussions trace sympathetically the history of the diverse parts of Africa.

J. D. FAGE, *A History of Africa* (1978). A fine general history. The relevant segment here is Part I, "The Internal Development of African Society" (Chapters 1–5).

P. GARLAKE, *The Kingdoms of Africa* (1978). A lavishly illustrated set of photographic essays that provide a helpful introduction to the various historically important areas of precolonial Africa.

R. W. JULY, *Precolonial Africa: An Economic and Social History* (1975). A very readable, topically arranged study. See especially "The Savannah Farmer," "The Bantu," "Cattle-men," and "The Traders" chapters.

R. W. JULY, *A History of the African People*, 3rd ed. (1980). Part I, "Ancient Africa" covers the precolonial centuries and offers a very readable historical introduction to African civilization.

J. KI-ZERBO, *Methodology and African Prehistory*. Vol. I of *UNESCO General History of Africa* (1981). Useful summary and interpretive articles (but of very uneven quality) treat diverse topics, including sources, languages, geography, and prehistory.

H. LOTH, *Woman in Ancient Africa*. Trans. S. Marnie (1987). An interesting survey of legal, familial, cultural, and other aspects of women's roles.

G. MOKHTAR, *Ancient Civilizations of Africa*. Vol. II of *UNESCO General History of Africa* (1981). As in other volumes, the quality of articles varies greatly. Relevant chapters are 8–16 on Nubia, Meroe, and Aksum; 17–20 on the Saharan region in ancient times; and 22–29 on the early history of sub-Saharan Africa.

R. OLIVER, *The African Experience* (1991). A masterly, balanced, and engaging sweep through African history. The chapters on prehistory and early history are outstanding summaries of the results and implications of recent research.

I. VAN SERTIMA, *Black Women in Antiquity* (1984, 1988). Studies of queens, goddesses, matriarchy, and other aspects of the role and status of women in Egyptian, Ethiopian, and other African societies of the past.

Chapter 7

D. BODDE, *China's First Unifier* (1938). A study of the Ch'in unification of China, viewed through the Legalist philosopher and statesman Li Ssu.

T. T. CH'U, *Law and Society in Traditional China* (1961). Treats the sweep of Chinese history from 202 B.C.E. to 1911 C.E.

T. T. CH'U, *Han Social Structure* (1972).

A. COTTERELL, *The First Emperor of China* (1981).

R. COULBORN, *Feudalism in History* (1965). One chapter interestingly compares the quasi-feudalism of the Chou with that of the Six Dynasties period.

J. K. FAIRBANK, E. O. REISCHAUER, AND A. M. CRAIG, *East Asia: Tradition and Transformation* (1989). A fairly detailed single-volume history covering China, Japan, and other countries in East Asia from antiquity to recent times.

J. GERNET, *A History of Chinese Civilization* (1982). A survey of Chinese history.

C. Y. HSU, *Ancient China in Transition* (1965). On social mobility during the Eastern Chou era.

C. Y. HSU, *Han Agriculture* (1980). A study of the agrarian economy of China during the Han dynasty.

J. LEVI, *The Chinese Emperor* (1987). A novel about the First Ch'in Emperor based on scholarly sources.

M. LOEWE, *Everyday Life in Early Imperial China* (1968). A social history of the Han dynasty.

J. NEEDHAM, *The Shorter Science and Civilization in China* (1978). An abridgment of the multivolume work on the same subject with the same title—minus Shorter—by the same author.

S. OWEN, ED. AND TRANS., *An Anthology of Chinese Literature: Beginnings to 1911* (1996).

I. ROBINET, *Taoism: Growth of a Religion* (1987).

M. SULLIVAN, *The Arts of China* (1967). An excellent survey history of Chinese art.

D. TWITCHETT AND M. LOEWE, EDS., *The Ch'in and Han Empires, 221 B.C.E.–C.E. 220* (1986). (Vol. 1 of *The Cambridge History of China*.)

Z. S. WANG, *Han Civilization* (1982).

B. WATSON, *Ssu-ma Ch'ien, Grand Historian of China* (1958). A study of China's premier historian.

B. WATSON, *Records of the Grand Historian of China*, Vols. 1 and 2 (1961). Selections from the *Shih-chi* by Ssu-ma Ch'ien.

B. WATSON, *The Columbia Book of Chinese Poetry* (1986).

A. WRIGHT, *Buddhism in Chinese History* (1959).

Y. S. YU, *Trade and Expansion in Han China* (1967). A study of economic relations between the Chinese and their neighbors.

Chapter 8

General

P. BOL, *This Culture of Ours* (1992). An insightful intellectual history of the T'ang through the Sung dynasties.

J. CAHILL, *Chinese Painting* (1960). An excellent survey.

J. K. FAIRBANK AND M. GOLDMAN, *China: A New History* (1998). The summation of a lifetime engagement with Chinese history.

F. A. KIERMAN, JR., AND J. K. FAIRBANK, EDS., *Chinese Ways in Warfare* (1974). Chapters by different authors on the Chinese military experience from the Chou to the Ming.

Sui and T'ang

P. B. EBREY, *The Aristocratic Families of Early Imperial China* (1978).

D. MCMULLEN, *State and Scholars in T'ang China* (1988).

S. OWEN, *The Great Age of Chinese Poetry: The High T'ang* (1980).

E. G. PULLEYBLANK, *The Background of the Rebellion of An Lu-shan* (1955). A study of the 755 rebellion that weakened the central authority of the T'ang dynasty.

E. O. REISCHAUER, *Ennin's Travels in T'ang China* (1955). China as seen through the eyes of a ninth-century Japanese Marco Polo.

E. H. SCHAFER, *The Golden Peaches of Samarkand* (1963). A study of T'ang imagery.

SO. TEISER, *The Ghost Festival in Medieval China* (1988). On T'ang popular religion.

D. TWITCHETT, ED., *The Cambridge History of China, III: Sui and T'ang China, 589–906, Part 1* (1979).

G. W. WANG, *The Structure of Power in North China During the Five Dynasties* (1963). A study of the interim period between the T'ang and the Sung dynasties.

A. F. WRIGHT, *The Sui Dynasty* (1978).

Sung

C. S. CHANG AND J. SMYTHE, *South China in the Twelfth Century* (1981). China as seen through the eyes of a twelfth-century Chinese poet, historian, and statesman.

J. GERNET, *Daily Life in China on the Eve of the Mongol Invasion* (1962).

J. W. HAEGER, ED., *Crisis and Prosperity in Sung China* (1975).

R. HYMES, *Statesmen and Gentlemen* (1987). On the transformation of officials into a local gentry elite during the twelfth and thirteenth centuries.

J. T. C. LIU AND P. J. GOLAS, EDS., *Change in Sung China: Innovation or Renovation?* (1969).

M. ROSSABI, *China Among Equals* (1983). A study of the Liao, Ch'in, and Sung Empires and their relations.

W. M. TU, *Confucian Thought, Selfhood as Creative Transformation* (1985).

K. YOSHIKAWA, *An Introduction to Sung Poetry*, trans. by B. Watson (1967).

Yuan

T. T. ALLSEN, *Mongol Imperialism* (1987).

J. W. DARDESS, *Conquerors and Confucians: Aspects of Political Change in Late Yuan China* (1973).

H. FRANKE AND D. TWITCHETT, EDS., *The Cambridge History of China, VI: Alien Regimes and Border States, 710–1368* (1994).

J. D. LANGLOIS, *China Under Mongol Rule* (1981).

R. LATHAM, TRANS., *Travels of Marco Polo* (1958).

H. D. MARTIN, *The Rise of Chingis Khan and His Conquest of North China* (1981).

D. MORGAN, *The Mongols* (1986).

Chapter 9

M. ADOLPHSON, *The Gates of Power: Monks, Courtiers, and Warriors in Premodern Japan* (2000). A new interpretation stressing the importance of temples in the political life of Heian and Kamakura Japan.

C. BLACKER, *The Catalpa Bow* (1975). An insightful study of folk Shinto.

R. BORGEN, *Sugawara no Michizane and the Early Heian Court* (1986). A study of a famous courtier and poet.

D. M. BROWN, ED., *The Cambridge History of Japan: Ancient Japan* (1993). This series of six volumes sums up several decades of research on Japan.

D. BROWN AND E. ISHIDA, EDS., *The Future and the Past* (1979). A translation of a history of Japan written in 1219.

M. COLLCUTT, *Five Mountains* (1980). A study of the monastic organization of medieval Zen.

P. DUUS, *Feudalism in Japan* (1969). An easy survey of the subject.

W. W. FARRIS, *Population, Disease, and Land in Early Japan, 645–900* (1985). An innovative reinterpretation of early history.

W. W. FARRIS, *Heavenly Warriors: The Evolution of Japan's Military, 500–1300* (1992).

W. W. FARRIS, *Sacred Texts and Buried Treasures* (1998). Studies of Japan's prehistory and early history, based on recent Japanese research.

K. F. FRIDAY, *Hired Swords: The Rise of Private Warrior Power in Early Japan* (1991). The interpretation in this book may be compared to that in Farris's *Heavenly Warriors*.

A. E. GOBLE, *Go-Daigo's Revolution* (1996). A provoking account of the 1331 revolt by an emperor who thought emperors should rule.

J. W. HALL, *Government and Local Power in Japan, 500–1700: A Study Based on Bizen Province* (1966). The best book on Japanese history to 1700.

J. W. HALL AND J. P. MASS, EDS., *Medieval Japan* (1974). A collection of topical essays on medieval history.

J. W. HALL AND T. TOYODA, *Japan in the Muromachi Age* (1977). Another collection of essays.

D. KEENE, ED., *Anthology of Japanese Literature from the Earliest Era to the Mid–Nineteenth Century* (1955).

D. KEENE, ED., *Twenty Plays of the Nō Theatre* (1970).

J. M. KITAGAWA, *Religion in Japanese History* (1966). A survey of religion in premodern Japan.

I. H. LEVY, *The Ten Thousand Leaves* (1981). A fine translation of Japan's earliest collection of poetry.

J. P. MASS, *The Development of Kamakura Rule, 1180–1250* (1979).

J. P. MASS AND W. HAUSER, EDS., *The Bakufu in Japanese History* (1985). Topics in *bakufu* history from the twelfth to the nineteenth centuries.

I. MORRIS, TRANS., *The Pillow Book of Sei Shōnagon* (1967). Observations about the Heian court life by the Jane Austen of ancient Japan.

S. MURASAKI, *The Tale of Genji*, trans. by A. Waley (1952). A comparison of this translation with that of Seidensticker is instructive.

S. MURASAKI, *The Tale of Genji*, trans. by E. G. Seidensticker (1976). The world's first novel and the greatest work of Japanese fiction.

R. J. PEARSON ET AL., EDS., *Windows on the Japanese Past: Studies in Archaeology and Prehistory* (1986).

D. L. PHILIPPI, TRANS., *Kojiki* (1968). Japan's ancient myths.

J. PIGGOT, *The Emergence of Japanese Kingship* (1997).

E. O. REISCHAUER, *Ennin's Diary, the Record of a Pilgrimage to China in Search of the Law and Ennin's Travels in T'ang China* (1955).

E. O. REISCHAUER AND A. M. CRAIG, *Japan: Tradition and Transformation* (1989). A more detailed work covering the total sweep of Japanese history from the early beginnings to the present day.

H. SATO, *Legends of the Samurai* (1995). Excerpts from various tales and writings.

D. H. SHIVELY AND W. H. MCCULLOUGH, EDS., *The Cambridge History of Japan: Heian Japan* (1999).

D. T. SUZUKI, *Zen and Japanese Culture* (1959).

H. TONOMURA, *Community and Commerce in Late Medieval Japan* (1992).

R. TSUNODA, W. T. DEBARY, AND D. KEENE, COMPS., *Sources of the Japanese Tradition* (1958). A collection of original religious, political, and philosophical writings from each period of Japanese history. The best reader.

H. P. VARLEY, *Imperial Restoration in Medieval Japan* (1971). A study of the 1331 attempt by an emperor to restore imperial power.

A. WALEY, TRANS., *The Nō Plays of Japan* (1957). Medieval dramas.

K. YAMAMURA, ED., *Cambridge History of Japan: Medieval Japan* (1990).

Chapter 10

Iran

M. BOYCE, *Zoroastrians: Their Religious Beliefs and Practices* (1979). A detailed survey by the current authority on Zoroastrian religious history. See Chapters 7–9.

M. BOYCE, ED. AND TRANS., *Textual Sources for the Study of Zoroastrianism* (1984). A valuable anthology with an important introduction that includes Boyce's arguments for a revision of the dates of Zoroaster's life (to between 1400 and 1200 B.C.E.).

R. N. FRYE, *The Heritage of Persia* (1963). Still one of the best surveys, Chapter 6 deals with the Sasanid era.

R. GHIRSHMAN, *Iran* (1954 [orig. ed. 1951]). An introductory survey of similar extent to Frye, but with differing material also.

R. GHIRSHMAN, *Persian Art: The Parthian and Sasanid Dynasties* (1962). Superb photographs, and a very helpful glossary of places and names. The text is minimal.

GEO WIDENGRAN, *Mani and Manichaeism* (1965). Still the standard introduction to Mani's life and the later spread and development of Manichaeism.

India

A. L. BASHAM, *The Wonder That Was India* (1963). The best survey of classical Indian religion, society, literature, art, and politics.

W. T. DE BARY ET AL., COMP. *Sources of Indian Tradition*, 2nd ed. (1958). Vol. I, *From the Beginning to 1800*, ed. and rev. by Ainslie T. Embree (1988). Excellent selections from a wide variety of Indian texts, with good introductions to the text selections.

S. DUTT, *Buddhist Monks and Monasteries of India* (1962). The standard work. See especially Chapters 3 ("Bhakti") and 4 ("Monasteries Under the Gupta Kings").

D. G. MANDELBAUM, *Society in India* (1972). 2 vols. The first two chapters in Volume I of this study of caste, family, and village relations are a good introduction to the caste system.

B. ROWLAND, *The Art and Architecture of India: Buddhist/Hindu/Jain*, 3rd rev. ed. (1970). See the excellent chapters on Sungan, Andhran, and other early Buddhist art (6–8, 14), the Gupta period (15), and the Hindu Renaissance (17–19).

V. A. SMITH, *The Oxford History of India*, 4th rev. ed. (1981). See especially pages 164–229 (the Gupta period and following era to the Muslim invasions).

R. THAPAR, *A History of India, Part I* (1966), pp. 109–193. Three chapters covering the rise of mercantilism, the Gupta "classical pattern," and the southern dynasties to ca. 900 C.E..

P. YOUNGER, *Introduction to Indian Religious Thought* (1972). A sensitive attempt to delineate classical concerns of Indian religious thought and culture.

Chapter 11

J. ASHTIANI, T. M. JOHNSTONE, J. D. LATHAM, R. B. SERGEANT, AND G. R. SMITH, EDS., *Abbasid Belles Lettres* (1990). A wide-ranging survey of Arabic letters between 750 and 1258 C.E., arranged by genres and major writers.

A. F. L. BEESTON, T. M. JOHNSTONE, R. B. SERGEANT, AND G. R. SMITH, EDS., *Arabic Literature to the End of the Umayyad Period* (1983). The most comprehensive survey of the early Arabic historical, religious, poetic, and other literary sources.

K. CRAGG AND R. MARSTON SPEIGHT, EDS, *Islam from Within: Anthology of a Religion* (1980). One of the best and most sensitive collections of selections from Islamic primary sources.

F. M. DONNER, *The Early Islamic Conquests* (1981). The introduction and first chapter are especially good for an introduction to many important issues in the origin and spread of Islam.

H. A. R. GIBB, *Studies on the Civilization of Islam*, ed. by S. J. Shaw

and W. R. Polk (1962). This volume of selected essays by Gibb has some very helpful general studies on Islamic political order and religion.

H. A. R. GIBB, *Mohammedanism: An Historical Survey* (1970). Despite the offensive title, still the best brief introduction to Islam as a religious tradition.

O. GRABAR, *The Formation of Islamic Art* (1973). A critical and creative interpretation of major themes in the development of distinctively Islamic forms of art and architecture.

G. E. VON GRUNEBAUM, *Classical Islam: A History 600–1258*, trans. by K. Watson (1970), pp. 1–140. A competent, culturally oriented introductory survey of formative developments.

M. G. S. HODGSON, *The Classical Age of Islam* (1974). 3 vols. Vol. I, *The Venture of Islam*. The most thoughtful and comprehensive attempt to deal with classical Islamic civilization as a whole and in relation to contemporaneous non-Islamic cultures.

A. HOURANI, *A History of the Arab Peoples* (1991). A masterly survey of the Arabs down through the centuries and a clear picture of many aspects of Islamic history and culture that extend beyond the Arab world.

B. LEWIS, ED., *Islam and the Arab World* (1976). A large-format, heavily illustrated volume with many excellent articles on diverse aspects of Islamic (not simply Arab, as the misleading title suggests) civilization through the premodern period.

F. RAHMAN, *Major Themes of the Qur'an* (1980). The best introduction to the basic ideas of the Qur'an and Islam, seen through the eyes of a perceptive Muslim modernist scholar.

M. A. SHABAN, *Islamic History: A New Interpretation (1971–76)*. 2 vols. An influential reassessment of the course of Islamic history to 1055 C.E.

D. SOURDEL, *Medieval Islam* (1979). Eng. trans. by W. M. Watt (1983). A brief but excellent survey of the world of medieval Islam with emphasis on social, religious, and political institutions.

Chapter 12

R. BARTLETT, *The Making of Europe, 950–1350* (1992). A study of the way immigration and colonial conquest shaped the Europe we know.

M. BLOCH, *Feudal Society*, Vols. 1 and 2, trans. by L. A. Manyon (1971). A classic on the topic and as an example of historical study.

P. BROWN, *Augustine of Hippo: A Biography* (1967). Late antiquity seen through the biography of its greatest Christian thinker.

P. BROWN, *The Body and Society* (1988). Understanding late antiquity through people's attitudes toward the physical body.

J. H. BURNS, *The Cambridge History of Medieval Political Thought c. 350–c. 1450* (1991).

H. CHADWICK, *The Early Church* (1967). Among the best treatments of early Christianity.

R. H. C. DAVIS, *A History of Medieval Europe: From Constantine to St. Louis* (1972). Unsurpassed in clarity.

K. F. DREW, ED., *The Barbarian Invasions: Catalyst of a New Order* (1970). Collection of essays that focus the issues.

G. DUBY, *The Early Growth of the European Economy: Warriors and Peasants from the Seventh to the Twelfth Century* (1974). Readable, authoritative account of rural society.

H. FICHTENAU, *The Carolingian Empire: The Age of Charlemagne*, trans by Peter Munz (1964). Strongest on the political history of the era.

R. FLETCHER, *The Barbarian Conversion: From Paganism to Christianity* (1998). Up-to-date survey.

F. L. GANSHOF, *Feudalism*, trans. by Philip Grierson (1964). A profound brief analysis of the subject.

P. GEARY, *Before France and Germany* (1988). The medieval evolution of these territories.

A. F. HAVIGHURST, ED., *The Pirenne Thesis: Analysis, Criticism, and Revision* (1958). Excerpts from the scholarly debate over the extent of Western trade in the East during the early Middle Ages.

R. HODGES ET AL., *Mohammed, Charlemagne, and the Origins of Europe* (1982). Good on the society and economy of early medieval Europe.

G. HOLMES, ED., *The Oxford History of Medieval Europe* (1992). Overviews of Roman and northern Europe during the "Dark Ages."

A. HOURANI, *A History of the Arab Peoples* (1991). A comprehensive text that includes an excellent overview of the origins and early history of Islam.

D. KNOWLES, *Christian Monasticism* (1969). Sweeping survey with helpful photographs.

R. KRAUTHEIMER, *Early Christian and Byzantine Architecture* (1965). Makes the developments clear and interesting.

M. L. W. LAISTNER, *Thought and Letters in Western Europe, 500 to 900* (1957). Among the best surveys of early medieval intellectual history.

C. H. LAWRENCE, *Medieval Monasticism* (1989). Comprehensive survey.

J. LECLERCQ, *The Love of Learning and the Desire for God: A Study of Monastic Culture*, trans. by Catherine Misrahi (1962). Lucid, delightful, absorbing account of the ideals of monks.

J. LECLERCQ, F. VANDENBROUCKE, AND L. BOUYER, *The Spirituality of the Middle Ages* (1968). Perhaps the best survey of medieval Christianity, East and West, to the eve of the Protestant Reformation.

C. MANGO, *Byzantium: The Empire of New Rome* (1980).

J. MARTIN, *Medieval Russia 980–1584* (1995). A concise narrative history.

M. McCORMICK, "Byzantium and the West, A.D. 700–900," in *The New Cambridge Medieval History*, Vol. 2: *The Early Medieval West 700–900* (1993). Up-to-date framing of events and political developments.

P. MUNZ, *The Age of Charlemagne* (1971). Penetrating social history of the period.

T. NOBLE, *The Republic of St. Peter* (1988). How the church became an empire.

H. PIRENNE, *A History of Europe*, I: *From the End of the Roman World in the West to the Beginnings of the Western States*, trans. by Bernhard Maill (1958). Comprehensive survey, with now-controversial views on the demise of Western trade and cities in the early Middle Ages.

S. RUNCIMAN, *Byzantine Civilization* (1970). Succinct, comprehensive account by a master.

P. SAWYER, *The Age of the Vikings* (1962). The best account.

R. W. SOUTHERN, *The Making of the Middle Ages* (1973). Originally published in 1953, but still a fresh account by an imaginative historian.

C. STEPHENSON, *Medieval Feudalism* (1969). Excellent short summary and introduction.

A. A. VASILIEV, *History of the Byzantine Empire 324–1453* (1952). The most comprehensive treatment in English.

S. F. WEMPLE, *Women in Frankish Society: Marriage and the Cloister 500–900* (1981). The impact of Christian marriage customs on the Franks.

L. WHITE, JR., *Medieval Technology and Social Change* (1962). Often fascinating account of how primitive technology changed life.

G. WILLS, *Saint Augustine* (1999). Highly readable.

H. WOLFRAM, *The Roman Empire and Its Germanic Peoples* (1997). Challenging, but most rewarding.

Chapter 13

The Islamic Heartlands

C. E. BOSWORTH, *The Islamic Dynasties: A Chronological and Genealogical Handbook* (1967). A handy reference work for dynasties and families important to Islamic history in all periods and places.

J. A. BOYLE, ED., *The Cambridge History of Iran*, Vol. 5, *The Saljuq and Mongol Periods* (1968). Useful and reasonably detailed articles on political, social, religious, and cultural developments.

P. K. HITTI, *History of the Arabs*, 8th ed. (1964). Still a useful English resource, largely for factual detail. See especially Part IV, "The Arabs in Europe: Spain and Sicily."

M. G. S. HODGSON, *The Expansion of Islam in the Middle Periods*, Vol. 2 of *The Venture of Islam*. 3 vols. (1964). The strongest of Hodgson's monumental three-volume survey of Islamic civilization and the only English work of its kind to give the period 945–1500 such broad and unified coverage.

A. HOURANI, *A History of the Arab Peoples* (1991). The newest survey history and the best, at least for the Arab Islamic world.

S. K. JAYYUSI, ED., *The Legacy of Muslim Spain*, 2 vols. (1994). A comprehensive survey of the arts, politics, literature, and society by experts in various fields.

B. LEWIS, ED., *Islam and the Arab World* (1976). A large-format, heavily illustrated volume with many excellent articles on diverse aspects of Islamic (not simply Arab, as the misleading title indicates) civilization through the premodern period.

D. MORGAN, *The Mongols* (1986). A recent and readable survey history.

J. J. SAUNDERS, *A History of Medieval Islam* (1965). A brief and simple, if sketchy, introductory survey of Islamic history to the Mongol invasions.

D. SOURDEL, *Medieval Islam*, trans. by W. M. Watt (1983). The synthetic, interpretive chapters on Islam and the political and social orders (4, 5) and on towns and art (6) are especially helpful.

B. SPULER, *The Muslim World: A Historical Survey*, trans. by F. R. C. Bagley (1960). 3 vols. Volumes I and II are handy references offering a highly condensed chronicle of Islamic history from Muhammad through the fifteenth century.

B. SPULER, *The Mongols in History*, trans. by Geoffrey Wheeler (1971). A short introductory survey of Mongol history, of which Chapters 2–5 are most relevant.

India

W. T. DE BARY ET AL., COMP., *Sources of Indian Tradition*, 2nd ed. (1958). Vol. I, *From the Beginning to 1800*, ed. and rev. by Ainslie T. Embree (1988). Excellent selections from a wide variety of Indian texts, with good introductions to chapters and individual selections.

S. M. IKRAM, *Muslim Civilization in India* (1964). The best short survey history, covering the period 711 to 1857.

R. C. MAJUMDAR, GEN. ED., *The History and Culture of the Indian People*, Vol. VI, *The Delhi Sultanate*, 3rd ed. (1980). A comprehensive political and cultural account of the period in India.

M. MUJEEB, *The Indian Muslims* (1967). The best cultural study of Islamic civilization in India as a whole, from its origins onward.

F. ROBINSON, ED., *The Cambridge History of India, Pakistan, Bangladesh, Sri Lanka, Nepal, Bhutan, and the Maldives* (1989). A very helpful quick reference source with brief but well-done survey essays on a wide range of topics relevant to South Asian history down to the present.

A. WINK, *Al-Hind: The Making of the Indo-Islamic World*, Vol. 1 (1991). The first of five promising volumes to be devoted to the Indo-Islamic world's history. This volume treats the seventh to eleventh centuries.

Chapter 14

B. S. BAUER, *The Development of the Inca State* (1992). An important new work that emphasizes archaeological evidence over the Spanish chronicles in accounting for the emergence of the Inca Empire.

F. F. BERDAN, *The Aztecs of Central Mexico: An Imperial Society* (1982). An excellent introduction to the Aztecs.

R. E. BLANTON, S. A. KOWALEWSKI, G. FEINMAN, AND J. APPEL, *Ancient Mesoamerica: A Comparison of Change in Three Regions* (1981). Concentrates on ancient Mexico.

K. O. BRUHNS, *Ancient South America* (1994). A clear discussion of the archaeology and civilization of the region with emphasis on the Andes.

R. L. BURGER, *Chavín and the Origins of Andean Civilization* (1992). A detailed study of early Andean prehistory by one of the leading authorities on Chavín.

R. M. CARMACK, J. GASCO, AND G. H. GOSSEN, *The Legacy of Mesoamerica: History and Culture of a Native American Civilization* (1996). A survey of Mesoamerica from its origins to the present.

I. CLENDINNEN, *Aztecs: An Interpretation* (1995). A fascinating attempt to reconstruct the Aztec world.

M. D. COE, *Breaking the Maya Code* (1992). The story of the remarkable achievement of deciphering the ancient Maya language.

M. D. COE, *The Maya* (1993). The best introduction.

M. D. COE, *Mexico from the Olmecs to the Aztecs* (1994). A wide-ranging introductory discussion.

G. CONRAD AND A. A. DEMAREST, *Religion and Empire: The Dynamics of Aztec and Inca Expansionism* (1984). An interesting comparative study.

S. D. GILLESPIE, *The Aztec Kings* (1989).

R. HASSIG, *Aztec Warfare.*

J. HYSLOP, *Inka Settlement Planning* (1990). A detailed study.

M. LEÓN-PORTILLA, *Fifteen Poets of the Aztec World* (1992). An anthology of translations of Aztec poetry.

M. E. MILLER, *The Art of Mesoamerica from Olmec to Aztec* (1986). A well-illustrated introduction.

C. MORRIS AND A. VON HAGEN, *The Inka Empire and Its Andean Origins* (1993). A clear overview of Andean prehistory by a leading authority. Beautifully illustrated.

M. E. MOSELY, *The Incas and Their Ancestors: The Archaeology of Peru* (1992). Readable and thorough.

J. A. SABLOFF, *The Cities of Ancient Mexico* (1989). Capsule summaries of ancient Mesoamerican cultures.

J. A. SABLOFF, *Archaeology and the Maya* (1990). A look at changing views of the ancient Maya.

L. SCHELE and M. E. MILLER, *The Blood of Kings* (1986). A rich and beautifully illustrated study of ancient Maya art and society.

R. S. SHARER, *The Ancient Maya*, 5th ed. (1994). A classic. Readable, authoritative, and thorough.

M. P. WEAVER, *The Aztecs, Maya, and Their Predecessors* (1993). A classic textbook.

Chapter 15

L. B. ALBERTI, *The Family in Renaissance Florence*, trans. by R. N. Watkins (1962). A contemporary humanist, who never married, explains how a family should behave.

E. AMT, ED., *Women's Lives in Medieval Europe: A Source-book* (1992). Outstanding collection of sources.

J. W. BALDWIN, *The Scholastic Culture of the Middle Ages: 1000–1300* (1971). Best brief synthesis available.

M. W. BALDWIN, ED., *History of the Crusades, I: The First Hundred Years* (1955). Basic historical narrative.

H. BARON, *The Crisis of the Early Italian Renaissance*, Vols. 1 and 2 (1996). A major work, setting forth the civic dimension of Italian humanism.

G. BARRACLOUGH, *The Origins of Modern Germany* (1963). Penetrating political narrative.

R. BARTLETT, *The Making of Medieval Europe* (1992). Sees the interaction of different cultures as the decisive factor in the creation of west European civilization.

M. BLOCH, *French Rural Society*, trans. by J. Sondheimer (1966). A classic by a great modern historian.

G. BRUCKER, *Renaissance Florence* (1983). Considered the best introduction to the subject.

J. BURCKHARDT, *The Civilization of the Renaissance in Italy* (1867). The old classic that still has as many defenders as detractors.

A. CAPELLANUS, *The Art of Courtly Love*, trans. by J. J. Parry (1941). Translation of this classic along with other documents from the court of Marie de Champagne.

C. CIPOLLA, *Before the Industrial Revolution: European Society and Economy, 1000–1700* (1976). Readable, sweeping account.

R. H. C. DAVIS, *A History of Medieval Europe: From Constantine to St. Louis, Part 2* (1972).

G. DUBY, *The Three Orders: Feudal Society Imagined*, trans. by Arthur Goldhammer (1981). Large, comprehensive, and authoritative.

W. K. FERGUSON, *The Renaissance* (1940). A brief, stimulating summary of the Renaissance in both Italy and northern Europe.

F. GILBERT, *Machiavelli and Guicciardini* (1984). The two great Renaissance historians compared.

E. M. HALAM, *Capetian France 987–1328* (1980). Especially good on politics and heretics.

J. R. HALE, *Europe in the Renaissance* (1994). New, learned survey focusing on social and cultural history.

C. H. HASKINS, *The Renaissance of the Twelfth Century* (1927). Still the standard account.

C. H. HASKINS, *The Rise of Universities* (1972). A short, minor classic.

D. HERLIHY, *Medieval Households* (1985). Sweeping survey of Middle Ages that defends the medieval family against modern caricatures.

D. HERLIHY AND C. KLAPISCH-ZUBER, *Tuscans and Their Families* (1985). Important work based on unique demographic data that gives the reader an appreciation of quantitative history.

J. C. HOLT, *Magna Carta*, 2nd ed. (1992). The famous document and its interpretation by succeeding generations.

J. HUIZINGA, *The Waning of the Middle Ages: A Study of the Forms of Life, Thought, and Art in France and the Netherlands in the Dawn of the Renaissance* (1924). A classic study of "mentality" at the end of the Middle Ages.

D. JENSEN, *Renaissance Europe: Age of Recovery and Reconciliation* (1981). Up-to-date textbook.

R. KIECKHEFER, *Unquiet Souls* (1984). Penetrating and sympathetic study of fourteenth-century religious life.

P. O. KRISTELLER, *Renaissance Thought: The Classic, Scholastic, and Humanist Strains* (1961). A master shows the many sides of Renaissance thought.

G. LEFF, *Paris and Oxford Universities in the Thirteenth and Fourteenth Centuries: An Institutional and Intellectual History* (1968). Very good on debates on Scholasticism.

K. LEYSER, *Medieval Germany and Its Neighbors, 900–1250* (1982). Basic and authoritative.

R. S. LOPEZ AND I. W. RAYMOND, EDS., *Medieval Trade in the Mediterranean World* (1955). An illuminating collection of sources, concentrated on southern Europe.

W. H. MCNEILL, *Plagues and Peoples* (1976). The Black Death in a broader context.

E. MÂLE, *The Gothic Image: Religious Art in France in the Thirteenth Century* (1913). A classic.

L. MARTINES, *Power and Imagination: City States in Renaissance Italy* (1980). Stimulating account of cultural and political history.

H. E. MAYER, *The Crusades*, trans. by John Gilligham (1972). Extremely detailed, and the best one-volume account.

R. I. MOORE, *The Formation of a Persecuting Society: Power and Deviance in Western Europe, 950–1250* (1987). A sympathetic look at heresy and dissent.

J. B. MORRALL, *Political Thought in Medieval Times* (1962). A readable and illuminating account.

T. NOONAN, *Contraception: A History of Its Treatment by the Catholic Theologians and Canonists* (1967). A fascinating account of medieval theological attitudes toward sexuality and sex-related problems.

S. OZMENT, *Ancestors: The Loving Family of Old Europe* (2001). Fluid, insightful, and provocative.

E. PANOFSKY, *Gothic Architecture and Scholasticism* (1951). A controversial classic.

E. PERROY, *The Hundred Years' War*, trans. by W. B. Wells (1965). The most comprehensive one-volume account.

H. PIRENNE, *Medieval Cities: Their Origins and the Revival of Trade*, trans. by Frank D. Halsey (1970). A minor classic.

J. RILEY-SMITH, *The Crusades: A Short History* (1987). Up-to-date, lucid, and readable.

S. SHAHAR, *The Fourth Estate: A History of Women in the Middle Ages* (1983). Readable survey.

Q. SKINNER, *The Foundations of Modern Political Thought I: The Renaissance* (1978). A broad survey, very comprehensive.

B. TIERNEY, *The Crisis of Church and State 1050–1300* (1964). A very useful collection of primary sources on key church-state conflicts.

Part 4 provides the major documents in the clash between Boniface VIII and Philip the Fair.

J. WEISHEIPL, *Friar Thomas* (1980). Biography of Thomas Aquinas that attempts to do justice to the human side of the story as well as to the theological.

S. WILLIAMS, ED., *The Gregorian Epoch: Reformation, Revolution, Reaction* (1964). Variety of scholarly opinion on the significance of Pope Gregory's reign presented in debate form.

P. ZIEGLER, *The Black Death* (1969). A highly readable journalistic account.

Chapter 16

R. ASHCRAFT, *Revolutionary Politics and Locke's Two Treatises of Government* (1986). The most important study of Locke to appear in recent years.

R. H. BAINTON, *Here I Stand: A Life of Martin Luther* (1957). The most readable and positive biography of the reformer.

W. BOUWSMA, *John Calvin. A Sixteenth Century Portrait* (1988). Interpretation of Calvin against background of Renaissance intellectual history.

C. BOXER, *Four Centuries of Portuguese Expansion 1415–1825* (1961). A comprehensive survey by a leading authority.

F. BRAUDEL, *The Mediterranean and the Mediterranean World in the Age of Philip the Second*, vols. 1 and 2 (1976). A widely acclaimed work by a French master.

R. BRIGGS, *Witches and Neighbors: A History of European Witchcraft* (1996). Readable introduction.

K. C. BROWN, *Hobbes Studies* (1965). A collection of important essays.

E. CAMERON, *The European Reformation* (1990). Large synthesis of recent studies, with most attention given to the German Reformation.

J. DELUMEAU, *Catholicism Between Luther and Voltaire: A New View of the Counter Reformation* (1977). Programmatic essay for a new social history of the Counter-Reformation.

A. G. DICKENS, *The Counter Reformation* (1969). A brief narrative with pictures.

A. G. DICKENS, *The English Reformation* (1974). The best one-volume account.

B. DIEFENDORF, *Beneath the Cross: Catholics and Huguenots in Sixteenth Century Paris* (1991). Stresses the primary forces of popular religion in the French wars of religion.

G. DONALDSON, *The Scottish Reformation* (1960). A dependable, comprehensive narrative.

E. DUFFY, *The Stripping of the Altars* (1992). Strongest argument yet that there was no deep reformation in England.

R. DUNN, *The Age of Religious Wars 1559–1689* (1979). An excellent brief survey of every major conflict.

M. DURAN, *Cervantes* (1974). Detailed biography.

J. H. ELLIOTT, *Europe Divided 1559–1598* (1968). A direct, lucid narrative account.

G. R. ELTON, *Reformation Europe 1517–1559* (1966). Among the best short treatments, especially strong on political issues.

H. O. EVENNETT, *The Spirit of the Counter Reformation* (1968). An essay on the continuity of Catholic reform and its independence from the Protestant Reformation.

P. GEYL, *The Revolt of the Netherlands, 1555–1609* (1958). The authoritative survey.

HANS-JÜRGEN GOERTZ, *The Anabaptists* (1996). Best treatment of minority Protestants.

M. GREENGRASS, *The French Reformation* (1987). Summary account, pulling everything together succinctly.

C. HAIGH, *The English Reformation Revised* (1988). Argues that the English Reformation was less revolutionary than historians have traditionally argued.

M. HOLT, *The French Wars of Religion, 1562–1629* (1995). Scholarly appreciation of religious side of story

R. P. HSIA, *The German People and the Reformation* (1989). Collection illustrative of the new social history of the German Reformation.

H. JEDIN, *A History of the Council of Trent*, Vols. 1 and 2 (1957–1961). Comprehensive, detailed, and authoritative.

T. F. JESSOP, *Thomas Hobbes* (1960). A brief biographical sketch.

W. K. JORDAN, *Edward VI: The Young King* (1968). The basic biography.

R. KIECKHEFER, *European Witch Trials: Their Foundations in Popular and Learned Culture 1300–1500* (1976). One of the best treatments of the subject.

R. J. KNECHT, *The French Wars of Religion, 1559–1598* (1989).

A. KORS AND E. PETERS, EDS., *European Witchcraft, 1100–1700* (1972).

P. LASLETT, *Locke's Two Treatises of Government*, 2nd ed. (1970). Definitive texts with very important introductions.

CARTER LINDBERG, *The European Reformations* (1996). New survey with traditional strengths and clarity.

A. MACFARLANE, *The Family Life of Ralph Josselin: A Seventeenth Century Clergyman* (1970). Exemplary family history.

J. MCNEILL, *The History and Character of Calvinism* (1954). The most comprehensive account, very readable.

G. MATTINGLY, *The Armada* (1959). A masterpiece, novel-like in style.

H. C. E. MIDELFORT, *The Mad Princes of Renaissance Germany* (1996).

K. MOXLEY, *Peasants, Warriors, and Wives* (1989). The English Reformation through popular art.

C. G. NAUERT, JR., *Humanism and the Culture of Renaissance Europe* (1995). Lucid up-to-date overview.

J. E. NEALE, *The Age of Catherine de Medici* (1962). A short, concise summary.

J. W. O'MALLEY, *The First Jesuits* (1993). Extremely detailed account of the creation of the Society of Jesus and its original purposes.

S. OZMENT, *The Age of Reform 1250–1550: An Intellectual and Religious History of Late Medieval and Reformation Europe* (1980). Broad, lucid survey.

S. OZMENT, *When Fathers Ruled: Family Life in Reformation Europe* (1983). Effort to portray the constructive side of Protestant thinking about family relationships.

S. OZMENT, *Three Behaim Boys: Growing Up in Early Modern Germany* (1990). Teenagers and young adults in their own words.

S. OZMENT, *The Bürgermeister's Daughter: Scandal in a Sixteenth Century German Town* (1996). A woman's struggle for justice.

S. OZMENT, *Flesh and Spirit: Private Life in Early Modern Germany* (1998). The German family from courtship and marriage to sending a new adult generation into the world.

S. OZMENT, *Ancestors: The Loving Family in Old Europe* (2001). Readable discussion of changing views of the premodern family.

G. PARKER, *The Thirty Years' War* (1984). Large, lucid survey.

J. H. PARRY, *The Age of Reconnaissance* (1964). A comprehensive account of explorations from 1450 to 1650.

E. F. RICE, JR., *The Foundations of Early Modern Europe 1460–1559* (1970). A broad, succinct narrative.

J. H. M. SALMON, ED., *The French Wars of Religion: How Important Were the Religious Factors?* (1967). Scholarly debate over the relation between politics and religion.

J.J. SCARISBRICK, *Henry VIII* (1968). The best account of Henry's reign.

A. SOMAN, ED., *The Massacre of St. Bartholomew's Day: Reappraisals and Documents* (1974). The results of an international symposium on the anniversary of the massacre.

L. SPITZ, *The Religious Renaissance of the German Humanists* (1963). Comprehensive and entertaining.

G. STRAUSS, *Luther's House of Learning: The Indoctrination of the Young in the German Reformation* (1978). Account of Protestant efforts to rear children in the new faith, stressing the authoritarian elements.

G. STRAUSS, ED. AND TRANS., *Manifestations of Discontent in Germany on the Eve of the Reformation* (1971). A rich collection of sources for both rural and urban scenes.

R. H. TAWNEY, *Religion and the Rise of Capitalism* (1947). Advances beyond Weber's arguments relating Protestantism and capitalist economic behavior.

K. THOMAS, *Religion and the Decline of Magic* (1971). Something of a classic on the subject.

E. TROELTSCH, *The Social Teaching of the Christian Churches*, Vols. 1 and 2, trans. by Olive Wyon (1960).

M. WEBER, *The Protestant Ethic and the Spirit of Capitalism*, trans. by Talcott Parsons (1958). First appeared in 1904–1905; it has continued to stimulate debate over the relationship between religion and society.

C. V. WEDGWOOD, *The Thirty Years' War* (1939). Controversial, but basic.

C. V. WEDGWOOD, *William the Silent* (1944). An excellent political biography.

F. WENDEL, *Calvin: The Origins and Development of His Religious Thought*, trans. by Philip Mairet (1963). The best treatment of Calvin's theology.

M. WIESNER, *Working Women in Renaissance Germany* (1986). Sketch of women's opportunities in six German cities.

G. H. WILLIAMS, *The Radical Reformation* (1962). A broad survey of the varieties of dissent within Protestantism.

H. WUNDER, *He Is the Sun, She Is the Moon: Women in Early Modern Germany* (1998). The best book in any language on the subject to date.

Chapter 17

J. ABUN-NASR, *A History of the Maghrib in the Islamic Period* (1987). The most recent North African survey. Pages 59–247 are relevant to this chapter.

D. BIRMINHAM, *Central Africa to 1870* (1981). Chapters from the *Cambridge History of Africa* that give a brief, lucid overview of developments in this region.

P. BOHANNAN AND P. CURTIN, *Africa and Africans*, rev. ed. (1971). Accessible, topical approach to African history, culture, society, politics, and economics.

P. D. CURTIN, S. FEIERMANN, L. THOMPSON, AND J. VANSINA, *African History* (1978). An older, but masterly survey. The relevant portions are chapters 6–9.

R. ELPHICK, *Kraal and Castle: Khoikhoi and the Founding of White South Africa* (1977). An incisive, informative interpretation of the history of the Khoikhoi and their fateful interaction with European colonization.

R. ELPHICK AND H. GILIOMEE, *The Shaping of South African Society, 1652–1820* (1979). A superb, synthetic history of this crucial period.

J. D. FAGE, *A History of Africa* (1978). Still a readable survey history.

M. HISKETT, *The Development of Islam in West Africa* (1984). The standard survey study of the subject. Of the relevant sections (Chapters 1–10, 12, 15), that on Hausaland, which is treated only in passing in this text, is noteworthy.

R. W. JULY, *Precolonial Africa: An Economic and Social History* (1975). Chapter 10 gives an interesting overall picture of slaving in African history.

R. W. JULY, *A History of the African People*, 3rd ed. (1980). Chapters 3–6 treat Africa before about 1800 area by area; Chapter 7 deals with "The Coming of Europe."

I. M. LEWIS, ED., *Islam in Tropical Africa* (1966), pp. 4–96. Lewis's introduction is one of the best brief summaries of the role of Islam in West Africa and the Sudan.

D. T. NIANI, ED. *Africa from the Twelfth to the Sixteenth Century, UNESCO General History of Africa*, Vol. IV (1984). Many survey articles cover the various regions and major states of Africa in the centuries noted in the title.

R. OLIVER, *The African Experience* (1991). A masterly, balanced, and engaging survey, with outstanding syntheses and summaries of recent research.

J. A. RAWLEY, *The Transatlantic Slave Trade: A History* (1981). Impressively documented, detailed, and well-presented survey history of the Atlantic trade; little focus on African dimensions.

A. F. C. RYDER, *Benin and the Europeans: 1485–1897* (1969). A basic study.

JOHN K. THORNTON, *The Kingdom of Kongo: Civil War and Transition, 1641–1718* (1983). A detailed and perceptive analysis for those who wish to delve into Kongo state and society in the seventeenth century.

M. WILSON AND L. THOMPSON, EDS., *The Oxford History of South Africa*, Vol. I., *South Africa to 1870* (1969). Relatively detailed, if occasionally dated, treatment.

Chapter 18

P. BAKEWELL, *A History of Latin America* (1997). A recent accessible survey.

I. BERLIN, *Many Thousands Gone: The First Two Centuries of Slavery in North America* (1998). The most extensive recent treatment emphasizing he differences in the slave economy during different decades.

L. BETHWELL, *The Cambridge History of Latin America*, Vols. 1 and 2 (1984). Excellent essays by leading scholars.

R. BLACKBURN, *The Making of New World Slavery from the Baroque to the Modern 1492–1800* (1997). An extraordinary work.

B. COBO, *History of the Inca Empire* (1979). A major discussion.

G. A. COLLIER, R. I. ROSALDO, AND J. D. WIRTH, *The Inca and Aztec States 1400–1800* (1982). An important collection of advanced essays.

P. D. CURTIN, *The Atlantic Slave Trade: A Census* (1969). Still a basic work.

P. D. CURTIN, *Economic Change in Precolonial Africa: Senegambia on the Eve of the Slave Trade.* (1975) The chapter on slave trading is an illuminating treatment of the topic with respect to one area of Africa.

D. B. DAVIS, *The Problem of Slavery in Western Culture* (1966). A brilliant and far-ranging discussion.

H. L. Gates, Jr. and W. L. Andrews, eds., *Pioneers of the Black Atlantic: Five Slave Narratives from the Enlightenment 1772–1815* (1998). An anthology of autobiographical accounts.

H. A. GEMERY AND J. S. HOGENDORN, EDS., *The Uncommon Market: Essays in the Economic History of the Atlantic Slave Trade* (1979). Useful on trans-Saharan and particular African regions of the Atlantic slave trade.

C. GIBSON, *The Aztecs Under Spanish Rule: A History of the Native Americans of the Valley of Mexico* (1964). An exceedingly interesting book.

C. GIBSON, *Spain in America* (1966). A splendidly clear and balanced discussion.

S. GRUZINSKI, *The Conquest of Mexico: The Incorporation of Indian Societies into the Western World, 16th–18th Centuries* (1993). Interprets the experience of native Americans, from their own point of view, during the time of the Spanish conquest.

L. HANKE, *Bartolomé de Las Casas: An Interpretation of His Life and Writings* (1951). A classic work.

J. HEMMING, *The Conquest of the Incas*, (1970). A lucid account of the conquest of the Inca Empire and its aftermath.

J. HEMMING, *Red Gold: The Conquest of the Brazilian Native Americans, 1500–1760* (1978). A careful account with excellent bibliography.

H. KLEIN, *The Middle Passage: Comparative Studies in the African Slave Trade* (1978). A far-ranging overview of the movement of slaves from Africa to the Americas.

M. LEON-PORTILLA, ED., *The Broken Spears: The Aztec Account of the Conquest of Mexico* (1961). A collection of documents recounting the experience of the Aztecs from their own point of view.

J. LOCKHARDT AND S. B. SCHWARTZ, *Early Latin America: A History of Colonial Spanish America and Brazil* (1983). The standard work.

J. R. McNEIL, *Atlantic Empires of France and Spain: Louisbourg and Havana, 1700–1763* (1985). An examination of imperial policies in terms of two key overseas outposts.

P. MANNING, *Slavery and African Life: Occidental, Oriental, and African Slave Trades* (1990). An admirably concise yet probing and careful economic-historical synthesis of the evidence, with multiple tables and statistics to supplement the magisterial analysis. An indispensable attempt at presenting the "big picture" of African slavery.

S. W. MINTZ, *Sweetness and Power: The Place of Sugar in Modern History* (1985). Traces the role of sugar in the world economy and sugar's impact on world culture.

A. PAGDEN, *Lords of All the World: Ideologies of Empire in Spain, Britain, and France c. 1500–c. 1800* (1955). An effort to explain the imperial thinking of the major European powers.

J. H. PARRY, *Trade and Dominion: The European Overseas Empires in the Eighteenth Century* (1971). A comprehensive account with attention to the European impact on the rest of the world.

J. A. RAWLEY, *The Transatlantic Slave Trade: A History* (1981). Impressively documented, detailed, and well-presented survey history of the Atlantic trade; little focus on African dimensions.

S. B. SCHWARTZ, *Sugar Plantations in the Formation of Brazilian Society: Bahia, 1550–1835* (1985). A broad-ranging study of the emergence of the plantation economy.

I. K. STEELE, *The English Atlantic, 1675–1740s: An Exploration of Communication and Community* (1986). An exploration of culture and commerce in the transatlantic world.

R. L. STEIN, *The French Sugar Business in the Eighteenth Century* (1988). A study that covers all aspects of the French sugar trade.

S. J. STEIN, *Peru's Indian Peoples and the Challenge of Spanish Conquest: Huamanga to 1640* (1933). A work that examines the impact of the conquest of the Inca empire over the scope of a century.

H. THOMAS, *Conquest: Montezuma, Cortés, and the Fall of Old Mexico* (1993). A splendid modern narrative of the event with careful attention to the character of the participants.

J. THORNTON, *Africa and Africans in the Making of the Atlantic World, 1400–1680* (1992). A discussion of the role of Africans in the emergence of the transatlantic economy.

N. WACHTEL, *The Vision of the Vanquished: The Spanish Conquest of Peru Through Indian Eyes, 1530–1570* (1977). A presentation of Incan experience of conquest.

Chapter 19

China

D. BODDE AND C. MORRIS, *Law in Imperial China* (1967). Focuses on the Ch'ing dynasty (1644–1911).

C. S. CHANG AND S. L. H. CHANG, *Crisis and Transformation in Seventeenth Century China: Society, Culture, and Modernity* (1992).

P. CROSSLEY, *Translucent Mirror: History and Identity in Qing Imperial Ideology* (1999).

W. T. DE BARY, *Learning for One's Self: Essays on the Individual in Neo-Confucian Thought* (1991). A useful corrective to the view that Confucianism is simply a social ideology.

M. ELVIN, *The Pattern of the Chinese Past: A Social and Economic Interpretation* (1973). A controversial but stimulating interpretation of Chinese economic history in terms of technology. It brings in earlier periods as well as the Ming, Ch'ing, and modern China.

J. K. FAIRBANK, ED., *The Chinese World Order: Traditional China's Foreign Relations* (1968). An examination of the Chinese tribute system and its varying applications.

H. L. KAHN, *Monarchy in the Emperor's Eyes: Image and Reality in the Ch'ien-lung Reign* (1971). A study of the Chinese court during the mid-Ch'ing period.

P. KUHN, *Soulstealers: The Chinese Sorcery Scare of 1768* (1990).

LI YU, *The Carnal Prayer Mat*, trans. by P. Hanan (1990).

F. MOTE AND D. TWITCHETT, EDS., *The Cambridge History of China: The Ming Dynasty 1368–1644*, Vols. VI (1988) and VII (1998).

S. NAQUIN, *Peking Temples and City Life, 1400–1900* (2000).

S. NAQUIN AND E. S. RAWSKI, *Chinese Society in the Eighteenth Century* (1987).

J. B. PARSONS, *The Peasant Rebellions of the Late Ming Dynasty* (1970).

P. C. PERDUE, *Exhausting the Earth, State and Peasant in Hunan, 1500–1850* (1987).

D. H. PERKINS, *Agricultural Development in China, 1368–1968* (1969).

M. RICCI, *China in the Sixteenth Century: The Journals of Matthew Ricci, 1583–1610* (1953).

W. ROWE, *Hankow* (1984). A study of a city in late imperial China.

G. W. SKINNER, *The City in Late Imperial China* (1977).

J. D. SPENCE, *Ts'ao Yin and the K'ang-hsi Emperor: Bondservant and Master* (1966). An excellent study of the early Ch'ing court.

J. D. SPENCE, *Emperor of China: A Self-Portrait of K'ang-hsi* (1974). The title of this readable book does not adequately convey the extent of the author's contribution to the study of the early Ch'ing emperor.

J. D. SPENCE, *Treason by the Book* (2001). On the legal workings of the Ch'ing authoritarian, bureaucratic state. It reads like a detective story.

L. A. STRUVE, TRANS. AND ED., *Voices from the Ming-Ch'ing Cataclysm* (1993). A reader with translations of Chinese sources.

F. WAKEMAN, *The Great Enterprise* (1985). On the founding of the Manchu dynasty.

Japan

M. E. BERRY, *Hideyoshi* (1982). A study of the sixteenth-century unifier of Japan.

M. E. BERRY, *The Culture of Civil War in Kyoto* (1994). On the Warring States era.

H. BOLITHO, *Treasures Among Men: The Fudai Daimyo in Tokugawa Japan* (1974). A study in depth.

C. R. BOXER, *The Christian Century in Japan, 1549–1650* (1951).

M. CHIKAMATSU, *Major Plays of Chikamatsu*, trans. by D. Keene (1961).

R. P. DORE, *Education in Tokugawa Japan* (1965).

C. J. DUNN, *Everyday Life in Traditional Japan* (1969). A descriptive study of Tokugawa society.

G. S. ELISON, *Deus Destroyed: The Image of Christianity in Early Modern Japan* (1973). A brilliant study of the persecutions of Christianity during the early Tokugawa period.

J. W. HALL AND M. JANSEN, EDS., *Studies in the Institutional History of Early Modern Japan* (1968). A collection of articles on Tokugawa institutions.

J. W. HALL AND J. L. MCLAIN, EDS., *The Cambridge History of Japan: Early Modern Japan* (1991).

J. W. HALL, K. NAGAHARA, AND K. YAMAMURA, EDS., *Japan Before Tokugawa* (1981).

S. HANLEY, *Everyday Things in Premodern Japan: The Hidden Legacy of Material Culture* (1997).

H. S. HIBBETT, *The Floating World in Japanese Fiction* (1959). An eminently readable study of early Tokugawa literature.

M. JANSEN, ED., *The Nineteenth Century*, Vol. 5 in *The Cambridge History of Japan* (1989).

K. KATSU, *Musui's Story* (1988). The life and adventures of a boisterous, no-good samurai of the early nineteenth century. Eminently readable.

D. KEENE, TRANS., *Chushingura, the Treasury of Loyal Retainers* (1971). The puppet play about the forty-seven rōnin who took revenge on the enemy of their former lord.

M. MARUYAMA, *Studies in the Intellectual History of Tokugawa Japan*, trans. by M. Hane (1974). A seminal work in this field by one of modern Japan's greatest scholars.

K. W. NAKAI, *Shogunal Politics* (1988). A brilliant study of Arai Hakuseki's conceptualization of Tokugawa government.

P. NOSCO, ED., *Confucianism and Tokugawa Culture* (1984). A lively collection of essays.

H. OOMS, *Tokugawa Village Practice: Class, Status, Power, Law* (1996).

I. SAIKAKU, *The Japanese Family Storehouse*, trans. by G. W. Sargent (1959). A lively novel about merchant life in seventeenth-century Japan.

G. B. SANSOM, *The Western World and Japan* (1950).

C. D. SHELDON, *The Rise of the Merchant Class in Tokugawa Japan* (1958).

T. C. SMITH, *The Agrarian Origins of Modern Japan* (1959). On the evolution of farming and rural social organization in Tokugawa Japan.

R. P. TOBY, *State and Diplomacy in Early Modern Japan: Asia in the Development of the Tokugawa Bakufu* (1984).

C. TOTMAN, *Tokugawa Ieyasu: Shōgun* (1983).

C. TOTMAN, *Green Archipelago, Forestry in Preindustrial Japan* (1989).

H. P. VARLEY, *The Ō'nin War: History of Its Origins and Background with a Selective Translation of the Chronicle of Ō'nin* (1967).

K. YAMAMURA AND S. B. HANLEY, *Economic and Demographic Change in Preindustrial Japan, 1600–1868* (1977).

Korea

T. HATADA, *A History of Korea* (1969).

W. E. HENTHORN, *A History of Korea* (1971).

KI-BAIK LEE, *A New History of Korea* (1984).

P. LEE, *Sourcebook of Korean Civilization*, Vol. I (1993).

Vietnam

J. BUTTINGER, *A Dragon Defiant, a Short History of Vietnam* (1972).

NGUYEN DU, *The Tale of Kieu* (1983).

N. TARLING, ED., *The Cambridge History of Southeast Asia* (1992).

K. TAYLOR, *The Birth of Vietnam* (1983).

A. B. WOODSIDE, *Vietnam and the Chinese Model* (1988).

Chapter 20

M. S. ANDERSON, *Europe in the Eighteenth Century*, 1713–1783 (1988). A good one-volume introduction to the individual states.

T. M. BARKER, *Army, Aristocracy, Monarchy: Essays in War, Society and Government in Austria, 1618–1780* (1982). Examines the intricate power relationships among these major institutions.

W. BEIK, *Absolutism and Society in Seventeenth-Century France* (1985). An important study that questions the extent of royal power.

J. BLACK, *Eighteenth-Century Europe 1700–1789* (1990). An excellent survey.

R. BONNEY, *Political Change in France Under Richelieu and Mazarin 1624–1661* (1978). An important examination of the emergence of French absolutism.

J. BREWER, *The Sinews of Power: War, Money, and the English State, 1688–1783* (1989). A study that emphasizes the financial power behind British military success.

G. BURGESS, *Absolute Monarchy and the Stuart Constitution* (1996) A new study that challenges many of the traditional interpretative categories.

P. BURKE, *The Fabrication of Louis XIV* (1992). Examines the manner in which the public image of Louis XIV was forged in art.

F. L. CARSTEN, *The Origins of Prussia* (1954). Discusses the groundwork laid by the Great Elector in the seventeenth century.

J. C. D. CLARKE, *English Society, 1688–1832: Social Structure and Political Practice During the Ancien Régime* (1985). An important, controversial work that emphasizes the role of religion in English political life.

L. COLLEY, *Britons: Forging the Nation, 1707–1837* (1992) A major study of the making of British nationhood.

W. DORN, *Competition for Empire, 1740–1763* (1940). Still one of the best accounts of the mid-eighteenth-century struggle.

W. DOYLE, *The Old European Order, 1660–1800* (1992). The most thoughtful treatment of the subject.

P. DUKES, *The Making of Russian Absolutism: 1613–1801* (1982). An overview based on recent scholarship.

R. J. W. EVANS, *The Making of the Habsburg Monarchy, 1550–1700: An Interpretation* (1979). Places much emphasis on intellectual factors and the role of religion.

F. FORD, *Robe and Sword: The Regrouping of the French Aristocracy After Louis XIV* (1953). Remains an important book for political, social, and intellectual history.

P. GOUBERT, *Louis XIV and Twenty Million Frenchmen* (1966). A fine overview of seventeenth-century French social structure.

R. HATTEN, ED., *Louis XIV and Europe* (1976). Covers foreign policy.

D. HIRST, *Authority and Conflict: England 1603–1658* (1986). Scholarly survey integrating history and historiography.

J. M. HITTLE, *The Service City: State and Townsmen in Russia, 1600–1800* (1979). Examines the relationship of cities in Russia to the growing power of the central government.

L. HUGHES, *Russia in the Age of Peter the Great* (1998). A major new account.

H. C. JOHNSON, *Frederick the Great and His Officials* (1975). An excellent recent examination of the Prussian administration.

P. LANGFORD, *A Polite and Commercial People: England 1717–1783* (1989). An excellent survey of mid-eighteenth-century Britain based on the most recent scholarship covering social history as well as politics, the overseas wars, and the American Revolution.

A. LOSSKY, *Louis XIV and the French Monarchy* (1994). The most recent major analysis.

R. K. MASSIE, *Peter the Great: His Life and His World* (1980). A good popular biography.

R. MIDDLETON, *The Bells of Victory: The Pitt-Newcastle Ministry and the Conduct of the Seven Years' War, 1757–1762* (1985). A careful study of the intricacies of eighteenth-century cabinet government that questions the centrality of Pitt's role in the British victory.

J. H. PLUMB, *Sir Robert Walpole*, 2 vols. (1956, 1961). A masterful biography ranging across the sweep of European politics.

J. H. PLUMB, *The Growth of Political Stability in England, 1675–1725* (1969). An important interpretive work.

J. G. A. POCOCK, ED., *Three British Revolutions: 1641, 1688, 1776* (1980). An important collection of essays.

N. V. RIASANOVSKY, *The Image of Peter the Great in Russian History and Thought* (1985). Examines the ongoing legacy of Peter in Russian history.

J. C. RILEY, *The Seven Years' War and the Old Regime in France: The Economic and Financial Toll* (1986). An analysis of pressures that would undermine the French monarchy.

H. ROSENBERG, *Bureaucracy, Aristocracy, and Autocracy: The Prussian Experience, 1660–1815* (1960). Emphasizes the organization of Prussian administration.

D. L. RUBIN, *The Sun King: The Ascendancy of French Culture During the Reign of Louis XIV* (1992). A collection of useful essays.

C. RUSSELL, *The Fall of the English Monarchies, 1637–1642* (1991). A major revisionist account, which should be read with Stone's book.

K. SHARPE, *The Personal Rule of Charles I* (1992). A major narrative work.

L. STONE, *The Causes of the English Revolution 1529–1642* (1972) Survey stressing social history and ruminating over historians and historical method.

G. TREASURE, *Mazarin: The Crisis of Absolutism in France* (1996). An examination not only of Mazarin, but also of the larger national and international background.

D. UNDERDOWN, *Fire from Heaven: Life in an English Town in the Seventeenth Century* (1992). A lively account of how a single English town experienced the religious and political turmoil of the century.

J. WEST, *Gunpower, Government, and War in the Mid–Eighteenth Century* (1991). A study of how warfare touched much government of the day.

J. B. WOLF, *Louis XIV* (1968). Authoritative and readable.

Chapter 21

I. T. BEREND AND G. RANKI, *The European Periphery and Industrialization, 1780–1914* (1982). Examines the experience of eastern and Mediterranean Europe.

J. BLUM, *Lord and Peasant in Russia from the Ninth to the Nineteenth Century* (1961). A thorough and wide-ranging discussion.

J. BLUM, *The End of the Old Order in Rural Europe* (1978). The most comprehensive treatment of life in rural Europe, especially central and eastern, from the early eighteenth through the mid-nineteenth centuries.

F. BRAUDEL, *The Structures of Everyday Life: The Limits of the Possible*, trans. by M. Kochan (1982). A magisterial survey by the most important social historian of our time.

J. CANNON, *Aristocratic Century: The Peerage of Eighteenth-Century England* (1985). A useful treatment based on the most recent research.

G. CHAUSSINAND-NOGARET, *The French Nobility in the Eighteenth Century* (1985). Suggests that culture, not class, was the decisive element in late-eighteenth-century French society.

P. DEANE, *The First Industrial Revolution*, 2nd ed. (1979). A well-balanced and systematic treatment.

J. DE VRIES, *The Economy of Europe in an Age of Crisis, 1600–1750* (1976). An excellent overview that sets forth the main issues.

J. DE VRIES, *European Urbanization 1500–1800* (1984). The most important and far-ranging of recent treatments of the subject.

W. DOYLE, *Venality: The Sale of Offices in Eighteenth-Century France* (1997). Examines the manner in which the phenomenon characterized much of the society.

P. EARLE, *The Making of the English Middle Class: Business, Community, and Family Life in London, 1660–1730* (1989). The most careful study of the subject.

M. W. FLINN, *The European Demographic System, 1500–1820* (1981). A major summary.

F. FORD, *Robe and Sword: The Regrouping of the French Aristocracy After Louis XIV* (1953). An important treatment of the growing social tensions within the French nobility during the eighteenth century.

R. FORSTER AND O. RANUM, *Deviants and the Abandoned in French Society* (1978). This and the following volume contain important essays from the French journal *Annales*.

R. FORSTER AND O. RANUM, *Medicine and Society in France* (1980).

D. V. GLASS AND D.E.C. EVERSLEY, EDS., *Population in History: Essays in Historical Demography* (1965). Fundamental for an understanding of the eighteenth-century increase in population.

P. GOUBERT, *The Ancien Régime: French Society, 1600–1750*, trans. by Steve Cox (1974). A superb account of the peasant social order.

D. HAY ET AL., *Albion's Fatal Tree: Crime and Society in Eighteenth-Century England* (1976). Separate essays on a previously little-explored subject.

D. HAY AND N. ROGERS, *Eighteenth-Century English Society: Shuttles and Swords* (1997). Explores the social experience of the lower orders.

O. H. HUFTON, *The Poor of Eighteenth-Century France, 1750–1789* (1975). A brilliant study of poverty and the family economy.

C. JONES, *Charity and Bienfaisance: The Treatment of the Poor in the Montpellier Region, 1740–1815* (1982). An important local French study.

E. L. JONES, *Agriculture and Economic Growth in England, 1650–1815* (1968). A good introduction to an important subject.

A. KAHAN, *The Plow, the Hammer, and the Knout: An Economic History of Eighteenth-Century Russia* (1985). An extensive and detailed treatment.

H. KAMEN, *European Society, 1500–1700* (1985). A useful one-volume treatment.

P. LASLETT, *The World We Have Lost* (1984). Examination of English life and society before the coming of industrialism.

R. K. MCCLURE, *Coram's Children: The London Foundling Hospital in the Eighteenth Century* (1981). A moving work that deals with the plight of all concerned with the problem.

N. MCKENDERICK, ED., *The Birth of a Consumer Society: The Commercialization of Eighteenth-Century England* (1982). Deals with several aspects of the impact of commercialization.

F. E. MANUEL, *The Broken Staff: Judaism Through Christian Eyes* (1992). An important discussion of Christian interpretations of Judaism.

M. A. MEYER, *The Origins of the Modern Jew: Jewish Identity and European Culture in Germany, 1749–1824* (1967). A general introduction organized around individual case studies.

S. POLLARD, *The Genesis of Modern Management: A Study of the Industrial Revolution in Great Britain* (1965). Treats industrialization from the standpoint of factory owners.

S. POLLARD, *Peaceful Conquest: The Industrialization of Europe, 1760–1970* (1981). A useful survey.

A. RIBEIRO, *Dress in Eighteenth-Century Europe, 1715–1789* (1985). An interesting examination of the social implication of style in clothing.

G. RUDE, *The Crowd in History 1730–1848* (1964). A pioneering study.

G. RUDE, *Paris and London in the Eighteenth Century* (1973).

H. SCHMAL, ED., *Patterns of European Urbanization Since 1500* (1981). Major essays.

L. STONE, *An Open Elite?* (1985). Raises important questions about the traditional view of open access to social mobility in England.

T. TACKETT, *Priest and Parish in Eighteenth-Century France: A Social and Political Study of the Cures in a Diocese of Dauphine, 1750–1791* (1977). An important local study that displays the role of the church in the fabric of social life in the Old Regime.

L. A. TILLY AND J. W. SCOTT, *Women, Work, and Family* (1978). An excellent survey of the issues in western Europe.

D. VALENZE, *The First Industrial Woman* (1995). An elegant work exploring the manner in which industrialization transformed the work of women.

A. VICKERY, *The Gentleman's Daughter: Women's Lives in Georgian England* (1998). Argues that women experienced expanding social horizons in the eighteenth century.

R. WALL, ED., *Family Forms in Historic Europe* (1983). Essays that cover the entire Continent.

C. WILSON, *England's Apprenticeship, 1603–1763* (1984). A broad survey of English economic life on the eve of industrialism.

E. A. WRIGLEY, *Continuity, Chance and Change: The Character of the Industrial Revolution in England* (1988). A major conceptual reassessment.

E. A. WRIGLEY AND R. S. SCHOFIELD, *The Population History of England, 1541–1871: A Reconstruction* (1982). One of the most ambitious demographic studies ever undertaken.

Chapter 22

A. L. BASHAM, ED., *A Cultural History of India* (1975). Part II, "Age of Muslim Dominance," is of greatest relevance here.

S. S. BLAIR AND J. BLOOM, *The Art and Architecture of Islam, 1250–1800* (1994). A fine survey of the period for all parts of the Islamic world.

K. CHELEBI, *The Balance of Truth* (1957). A marvelous volume of essays and reflections by probably the major intellectual of Ottoman times.

M. A. COOK, ED., *A History of the Ottoman Empire to 1730* (1976). Articles from *The Cambridge History of Islam* and *The New Cambridge Modern History*, with a brief introduction by Cook.

W. T. DE BARY ET AL., COMP., *Sources of Indian Tradition*, 2nd ed. (1958). Vol. I, *From the Beginning to 1800*, ed. and rev. by Ainslie T. Embree (1988). Excellent selections from a wide variety of Indian texts, with good introductions to chapters and individual selections.

C. H. FLEISCHER, *Bureaucrat and Intellectual in the Ottoman Empire: The Historian Mustafa Ali (1541–1600)* (1986). A major study of Ottoman intellectual history.

G. HAMBLY, *Central Asia* (1966). Excellent survey chapters (9–13) on the Chaghatay and Uzbek (Shaybanid) Turks.

R. S. HATTOX, *Coffee and Coffee-Houses: The Origins of a Social Beverage in the Medieval Near East* (1985). A fascinating piece of social history.

M. G. S. HODGSON, *The Gunpowder Empires and Modern Times*, Vol. 3 of *The Venture of Islam*, 3 vols. (1974). Less ample than Vols. 1 and 2 of Hodgson's monumental history, but a thoughtful survey of the great post-1500 empires.

P. M. HOLT, ANN K. S. LAMBTON, AND BERNARD LEWIS, *The Cambridge History of Islam*, 2 vols. (1970). A traditional, somewhat compartmentalized history useful for reference. Vol. I has important surveys on the Ottoman Empire and Safavid Iran. Vol. II includes chapters on post-1500 India, Southeast Asia, and Africa.

S. M. IKRAM, *Muslim Civilization in India* (1964). Still the best short survey history, covering the period from 711 to 1857.

H. INALCIK, *The Ottoman Empire: The Classical Age 1300–1600* (1973). An excellent, if dated, survey with solid treatment of Ottoman social, religious, and political institutions.

H. INALCIK, *An Economic and Social History of the Ottoman Empire, 1300–1914* (1994). A masterly survey by the dean of Ottoman studies today.

C. KAFADAR, *Between Two Worlds: The Construction of the Ottoman State* (1995). A readable analysis of theories of Ottoman origins and early development.

N. R. KEDDIE, ED., *Scholars, Saints, and Sufis: Muslim Religious Institutions in the Middle East Since 1500* (1972). A collection of interesting articles well worth reading.

R. C. MAJUMDAR, GEN. ED., *The History and Culture of the Indian People*, Vol. VII, *The Mughal Empire* (1974). A thorough and readable political and cultural history of the period in India.

M. MUJEEB, *The Indian Muslims* (1967). The best cultural study of Islamic civilization in India as a whole, from its origins onward.

G. NECIPOGLU, *Architecture, Ceremonial, and Power: the Topkapi Palace in the Fifteenth and Sixteenth Centuries* (1991). A superb analysis of the symbolism of Ottoman power and authority.

S. A. A. RIZVI, *The Wonder That Was India*, Vol. II (1987). A sequel to Basham's original *The Wonder That Was India*; treats Mughal life, culture, and history from 1200 to 1700.

F. ROBINSON, *Atlas of the Islamic World Since 1500* (1982). Brief, excellent historical essays, color illustrations with detailed accompanying text, and chronological tables, as well as precise maps, make this a refreshing general reference work.

R. SAVORY, *Iran Under the Safavids* (1980). A solid and readable survey.

S. J. SHAW, *Empire of the Gazis: The Rise and Decline of the Ottoman Empire, 1280–1808*, Vol. I of *History of the Ottoman Empire and Modern Turkey* (1976). A solid historical survey with excellent bibliographic essays for each chapter and a good index.

J. O. VOLL, *Islam: Continuity and Change in the Modern World* (1982). Chapter 3 provides an excellent overview of eighteenth-century revival and reform movements in diverse Islamic lands.

Chapter 23

R. ASHCRAFT, *Revolutionary Politics and Locke's Two Treatises of Government* (1986). Relates Locke to the political radicals of his day.

R. P. BARTLETT, *Human Capital: The Settlement of Foreigners in Russia 1762–1804* (1979). Examines Catherine's policy of attracting farmers and skilled workers to Russia.

D. BEALES, *Joseph II: In the Shadow of Maria Theresa, 1741–1780* (1987). The best treatment in English of the early political life of Joseph II.

C. BECKER, *The Heavenly City of the Eighteenth Century Philosophers* (1932). An influential but very controversial discussion.

T. BESTERMANN, *Voltaire* (1969). A biography by the editor of Voltaire's letters.

M. BIAGIOLI, *Galileo Courtier: The Practice of Science in the Culture of Absolutism* (1993). A major revisionist work that emphasizes the role of the political setting on Galileo's career and thought.

D. D. BIEN, *The Calas Affair: Persecution, Toleration, and Heresy in Eighteenth-Century Toulouse* (1960). The standard treatment of the famous case.

R. CHARTIER, *The Cultural Origins of the French Revolution* (1991). A wide-ranging discussion of the emergence of the public sphere and the role of books and the book trade during the Enlightenment.

H. CHISICK, *The Limits of Reform in the Enlightenment: Attitudes Toward the Education of the Lower Classes in Eighteenth-Century France* (1981). An attempt to examine the impact of the Enlightenment on nonelite classes.

I. B. COHEN, *Revolution in Science* (1985). A general consideration of the concept and of historical examples of change in scientific thought.

R. DARNTON, *The Literary Underground of the Old Regime* (1982). Essays on the world of printers, publishers, and booksellers.

I. DE MADARIAGA, *Catherine the Great: A Short History* (1990). A good brief biography.

J. DUNN, *The Political Thought of John Locke: An Historical Account of the "Two Treatises of Government"* (1969). An excellent introduction.

M. A. FINOCCHIARO, *The Galileo Affair: A Documentary History* (1989). A collection of all the relevant documents with an introductory commentary.

J. GAGLIARDO, *Enlightened Despotism* (1967). Remains a useful discussion.

P. GAY, *The Enlightenment: An Interpretation*, 2 vols. (1966, 1969). The most important and far-reaching treatment.

A. GOLDGAR, *Impolite Learning: Conduct and Community in the Republic of Letters, 1680–1750* (1995). A lively survey of the structure of the European intellectual community.

D. GOODMAN, *The Republic of Letters: A Cultural History of the French Enlightenment* (1994). Concentrates on the role of salons.

I. HARRIS, *The Mind of John Locke: A Study of Political Theory in Its Intellectual Setting* (1994). The most comprehensive recent treatment.

M. C. JACOB, *Living the Enlightenment: Freemasonry and Politics in Eighteenth-Century Europe* (1991). The best treatment in English of Freemasonry.

R. KREISER, *Miracles, Convulsions, and Ecclesiastical Politics in Early Eighteenth-Century Paris* (1978). An important study of the kind of religious life that the *philosophes* opposed.

T. S. KUHN, *The Copernican Revolution* (1957). Remains the most influential treatment.

D. LINDBERG AND R. L. NUMBERS, EDS., *Good and Nature: Historical Essays on the Encounter Between Christianity and Science* (1986). The best collection of essays on the subject.

C. A. MACARTNEY, *The Habsburg Empire, 1790–1918* (1971). Provides useful coverage of major mid-eighteenth-century developments.

F. MANUEL, *The Eighteenth Century Confronts the Gods* (1959). A broad examination of the *philosophes'* treatment of Christian and pagan religion.

R. R. PALMER, *Catholics and Unbelievers in Eighteenth-Century France* (1939). A discussion of the opponents of the *philosophes*.

G. RITTER, *Frederick the Great* (trans. 1968). A useful biography.

R. O. ROCKWOOD, ED., *Carl Becker's Heavenly City Revisited* (1958). Important essays qualifying Becker's thesis.

H. M. SCOTT, ED., *Enlightened Absolutism: Reform and Reformers in Later Eighteenth-Century Europe* (1990). A useful collection that incorporates recent scholarship.

S. SHAPIN, *The Scientific Revolution* (1996). An important revisionist survey emphasizing social factors.

J. N. SHKLAR, *Men and Citizens, a Study of Rousseau's Social Theory* (1969). A thoughtful and provocative overview of Rousseau's political thought.

D. SPADAFORA, *The Idea of Progress in Eighteenth Century Britain* (1990). A recent major study that covers many aspects of the Enlightenment in Britain.

L. STEINBRÜGGE, *The Moral Sex: Woman's Nature in the French Enlightenment* (1995). Emphasizes the conservative nature of Enlightenment thought on women.

L. STEWART, *The Rise of Public Science: Rhetoric, Technology, and Natural Philosophy in Newtonian Britain, 1660–1750* (1992). Examines how science became related to public life and economic development.

R. S. WESTFALL, *Never at Rest: A Biography of Isaac Newton* (1981). A very important major study.

A. M. WILSON, *Diderot* (1972). A splendid biography of the person behind the project for the *Encyclopedia* and other major Enlightenment publications.

L. WOLFF, *Inventing Eastern Europe: The Map of Civilization on the Mind of the Enlightenment* (1994). A remarkable study of the manner in which Enlightenment writers recast the understanding of this part of the continent.

N. WOLTERSTORFF, *John Locke and the Ethics of Belief* (1996). The best work on Locke's religious thought.

Chapter 24

R. ANSTEY, *The Atlantic Slave Trade and British Abolition, 1760–1810* (1975). A standard overview that emphasizes the role of religious factors.

B. BAILYN, *The Ideological Origins of the American Revolution* (1967). An important work illustrating the role of English radical thought in the perceptions of the American colonists.

K. M. BAKER, *Inventing the French Revolution: Essays on French Political Culture in the Eighteenth Century* (1990). Important essays on political thought before and during the revolution.

K. M. BAKER AND C. LUCAS, EDS., *The French Revolution and the Creation of Modern Political Culture*, 3 vols. (1987). A splendid collection of important original articles on all aspects of politics during the revolution.

R. J. BARMAN, *Brazil: The Forging of a Nation, 1798–1852* (1988). The best coverage of this period.

C. BECKER, *The Declaration of Independence: A Study in the History of Political Ideas* (1922). Remains an important examination of the political and imperial theory of the Declaration.

J. F. BERNARD, *Talleyrand: A Biography* (1973). A useful account.

L. BETHELL, *The Cambridge History of Latin America*, Vol. 3 (1985). Contains an extensive treatment of independence.

R. BLACKBURN, *The Overthrow of Colonial Slavery, 1776–1848* (1988). A major discussion quite skeptical of the humanitarian interpretation.

T. C. W. BLANNING, ED., *The Rise and Fall of the French Revolution* (1996). A wide-ranging collection of essays illustrating the debates over the French Revolution.

J. BROOKE, *King George III* (1972). The best biography.

R. COBB, *The People's Armies* (1987). The major treatment in English of the revolutionary army.

O. CONNELLY, *Napoleon's Satellite Kingdoms* (1965). The rule of Napoleon and his family in Europe.

E. V. DA COSTA, *The Brazilian Empire* (1985). Excellent coverage of the entire nineteenth-century experience of Brazil.

D. B. DAVIS, *The Problem of Slavery in the Age of Revolution, 1770–1823* (1975). A transatlantic perspective on the issue.

F. FEHÉR, *The French Revolution and the Birth of Modernity* (1990). A wide-ranging collection of essays on political and cultural facets of the revolution.

A. FORREST, *The French Revolution and the Poor* (1981). A study that expands consideration of the revolution beyond the standard social boundaries.

M. GLOVER, *The Peninsular War, 1807–1814: A Concise Military History* (1974). An interesting account of the military campaign that so drained Napoleon's resources in western Europe.

J. GODECHOT, *The Counter-Revolution: Doctrine and Action, 1789–1804* (1971). An examination of opposition to the revolution.

A. GOODWIN, *The Friends of Liberty: The English Democratic Movement in the Age of the French Revolution* (1979). A major work that explores the impact of the French Revolution on English radicalism.

L. HUNT, *Politics, Culture, and Class in the French Revolution* (1986). A series of essays that focus on the modes of expression of the revolutionary values and political ideas.

W. W. KAUFMANN, *British Policy and the Independence of Latin America, 1802–1828* (1951). A standard discussion of an important relationship.

E. KENNEDY, *A Cultural History of the French Revolution* (1989). An important examination of the role of the arts, schools, clubs, and intellectual institutions.

M. KENNEDY, *The Jacobin Clubs in the French Revolution: The First Years* (1982). A careful scrutiny of the organizations chiefly responsible for the radicalizing of the revolution.

M. KENNEDY, *The Jacobin Clubs in the French Revolution: The Middle Years* (1988). A continuation of the previously listed study.

H. KISSINGER, *A World Restored: Metternich, Castlereagh and the Problems of Peace, 1812–1822* (1957). A provocative study by an author who became an American secretary of state.

G. LEFEBVRE, *The Coming of the French Revolution* (trans. 1947). A classic examination of the crisis of the French monarchy and the events of 1789.

G. LEFEBVRE, *Napoleon*, 2 vols., trans. by H. Stockhold (1969). The fullest and finest biography.

J. LYNCH, *The Spanish American Revolutions, 1808–1826* (1986). An excellent one-volume treatment.

P. MAIER, *American Scripture: Making the Declaration of Independence* (1997). Stands as a major revision of our understanding of the Declaration.

G. MASUR, *Simón Bolívar* (1969). The standard biography in English.

S. E. MELZER AND L. W. RABINE, EDS., *Rebel Daughters: Women and the French Revolution* (1992). A collection of essays exploring various aspects of the role and image of women in the French Revolution.

M. MORRIS, *The British Monarchy and the French Revolution* (1998). Explores the manner in which the British monarchy saved itself from possible revolution.

R. MUIR, *Tactics and the Experience of Battle in the Age of Napoleon* (1998). Examines the wars from the standpoint of the soldiers in combat.

H. NICOLSON, *The Congress of Vienna* (1946). A good, readable account.

T. O. OTT, *The Haitian Revolution, 1789–1804* (1973). An account that clearly relates the events in Haiti to those in France.

R. R. PALMER, *Twelve Who Ruled: The Committee of Public Safety During the Terror* (1941). A clear narrative and analysis of the policies and problems of the committee.

R. R. PALMER, *The Age of the Democratic Revolution: A Political History of Europe and America, 1760–1800*, 2 vols. (1959, 1964). An impressive survey of the political turmoil in the transatlantic world.

C. PROCTOR, *Women, Equality, and the French Revolution* (1990). An examination of how the ideas of the Enlightenment and the attitudes of revolutionaries affected the legal status of women.

A. J. RUSSELL-WOOD, ED., *From Colony to Nation: Essays on the Independence of Brazil* (1975). A series of important essays.

P. SCHROEDER, *The Transformation of European Politics, 1763–1848* (1994). A fundamental treatment of the diplomacy of the era.

T. E. SKIDMORE AND P. H. SMITH, *Modern Latin America*, 4th ed. (1997). A very useful survey.

A. SOBOUL, *The Parisian Sans-Culottes and the French Revolution, 1793–94* (1964). The best work on the subject.

A. SOBOUL, *The French Revolution* (trans. 1975). An important work by a Marxist scholar.

D. G. SUTHERLAND, *France, 1789–1825: Revolution and Counterrevolution* (1986). A major synthesis based on recent scholarship in social history.

T. TACKETT, *Religion, Revolution, and Regional Culture in Eighteenth-Century France: The Ecclesiastical Oath of 1791* (1986). The most important study of this topic.

T. TACKETT, *Becoming a Revolutionary: The Deputies of the French National Assembly and the Emergence of a Revolutionary Culture (1789–1790)* (1996). The best study of the early months of the revolution.

J. M. THOMPSON, *Robespierre*, 2 vols. (1935). The best biography.

D. K. VAN KEY, *The Religious Origins of the French Revolution: From Calvin to the Civil Constitution, 1560–1791* (1996). Examines the manner in which debates within French Catholicism influenced the coming of the revolution.

M. WALZER, ED., *Regicide and Revolution: Speeches at the Trial of Louis XVI* (1974). An important and exceedingly interesting collection of documents with a useful introduction.

I. WOLOCH, *The New Regime: Transformations of the French Civic Order, 1789–1820s* (1994). An important overview of just what had and had not changed in France after the quarter century of revolution and war.

G. WOOD, *The Radicalism of the American Revolution* (1991). A major interpretation.

Chapter 25

B. ANDERSON, *Imagined Communities*, rev. ed. (1991). A discussion of the forces that have fostered national identity.

S. AVINERI, *The Making of Modern Zionism: The Intellectual Origins of the Jewish State* (1981). An excellent introduction to the development of Zionist thought.

M. BENTLEY, *Politics Without Democracy, 1815–1914* (1984). A well-informed survey of British development.

R. M. BERDAHL, *The Politics of the Prussian Nobility: The Development of a Conservative Ideology, 1770–1848* (1988). A major examination of German conservative outlooks.

M. D. BIDDIS, *Father of Racist Ideology: The Social and Political Thought of Count Gobineau* (1970). Sets the subject in the more general context of nineteenth-century thought.

J. BLASSINGAME, *The Slave Community* (1975). Emphasizes the manner in which slaves shaped their own community.

D. BLACKBOURN, *The Long Nineteenth Century: A History of Germany, 1780–1918* (1998). An outstanding recent survey.

G. CRAIG, *Germany, 1866–1945* (1978). An excellent survey.

D. G. CREIGHTON, *John A. MacDonald* (1952, 1955). A major biography of the first Canadian prime minister.

D. DONALD, *Lincoln* (1995). Now the standard biography.

M. DUBERMAN, ED., *The Anti-Slavery Vanguard* (1965). Important essays.

T. DUBLIN, *Women at Work: The Transformation of Work and Community in Lowell, Massachusetts, 1826–1860* (1979). The best work on this important setting of early American industrialization.

D. FEHRENBACHER, *The Dred Scott Case* (1978). A brilliant study that goes far beyond the subject of the title.

E. GENOVESE, *Roll Jordan Roll* (1974). The best overview of American slavery.

L. GREENFIELD, *Nationalism: Five Roads to Modernity* (1992). A major comparative study.

E. J. HOBSBAWM, *The Age of Revolution, 1789–1848* (1962). A very comprehensive survey emphasizing the social ramifications of the liberal democratic and industrial revolutions.

E. J. HOBSBAWM, *Nations and Nationalism Since 1780: Programme, Myth, Reality*, rev. ed. (1992). The best recent introduction to the subject.

R. A. KAHN, *The Multinational Empire*, 2 vols. (1950). Remains the basis treatment of the nationalities problem of Austria-Hungary.

W. LACQUER, *A History of Zionism* (1989). The most extensive one-volume treatment.

W. L. LANGER, *Political and Social Upheaval, 1832–1852* (1969). A remarkably thorough survey strong in both social and intellectual history as well as political narrative.

A. J. MAY, *The Habsburg Monarchy, 1867–1914* (1951). Narrates in considerable detail and with much sympathy the fate of the dual monarchy.

F. MCMILLAN, *Napoleon III* (1991). The best recent study.

J. M. MCPHERSON, *The Battle Cry of Freedom: The Civil War Era* (1988). An excellent one-volume treatment.

C. C. O'BRIEN, *Parnell and His Party* (1957). An excellent treatment of the Irish Question.

J. P. PARRY, *The Rise and Fall of Liberal Government in Victorian Britain* (1994). An outstanding study.

M. D. PETERSON, *The Great Triumvirate: Webster, Clay, and Calhoun* (1988). A splendid narrative of American politics from the 1820s through the 1850s.

O. PFLANZE, *Bismarck and the Development of Germany*, 3 vols. (1990). Carries the story from the achievement of unification to the end of Bismarck's career.

A. PLESSIS, *The Rise and Fall of the Second Empire, 1852–1871* (1985). A useful survey of France under Napoleon III.

D. M. POTTER, *The Impending Crisis, 1848–1861* (1976) A penetrating study of the coming of the American Civil War.

J. SHEEHAN, *German History, 1770–1866* (1989). A very long work that is now the best available survey of the subject.

D. M. SMITH, *Cavour* (1984). An excellent biography.

C. P. STACEY, *Canada and the Age of Conflict* (1977, 1981). A study of Canadian foreign relations.

P. STEARNS, *Eighteen Forty-Eight: The Tide of Revolution in Europe* (1974). A good discussion of the social background.

A. B. ULAM, *Russia's Failed Revolutionaries* (1981). Contains a useful discussion of the Decembrists as a background for other nineteenth-century Russian revolutionary activity.

S. WILLENTZ, *Chants Democratic: New York City and the Rise of the American Working Class, 1788–1850* (1984). An important examination of labor and politics.

Chapter 26

I. M. ARONSON, *Troubled Waters: The Origins of the 1881 Anti-Jewish Pogroms in Russia* (1990). The best discussion of this subject.

J. H. BATES, *St. Petersburg: Industrialization and Change* (1976). Impact of industrialization on the capital of imperial Russia.

L. R. BERLANSTEIN, *The Working People of Paris, 1871–1914* (1985). Interesting and comprehensive.

I. BERLIN, *Karl Marx: His Life and Environment*, 4th ed. (1996). A volume that remains an excellent introduction.

P. BRANCA, *Silent Sisterhood: Middle Class Women in the Victorian Home* (1975). A well-researched work.

N. BULLOCK AND J. READ, *The Movement for Housing Reform in Germany and France, 1840–1914* (1985). An important and wide-ranging study of the housing problem.

A. D. CHANDLER, JR., *The Visible Hand: Managerial Revolution in American Business* (1977). The best discussion of the innovative role of American business.

A. CLARKE, *The Struggle for the Breeches: Gender and the Making of the British Working Class* (1995). An examination of the manner in which industrialization made problematical the relationships between men and women.

W. COLEMAN, *Death Is a Social Disease: Public Health and Political Economy in Early Industrial France* (1982). One of the first works in English to study this problem.

J. M. COOPER, JR., *The Warrior and the Priest: Woodrow Wilson and Theodore Roosevelt* (1983). An interesting dual biography.

W. CRONIN, *Nature's Metropolis: Chicago and the Great West, 1848–1893* (1991) The best examination of any major American nineteenth-century city.

J. ELSTER, *An Introduction to Karl Marx* (1985). The best volume to provide a discussion of Marx's fundamental concepts.

P. GAY, *The Dilemma of Democratic Socialism: Eduard Bernstein's Challenge to Marx* (1952). A clear presentation of the problems raised by Bernstein's revisionism.

R. F. HAMILTON, *The Bourgeois Epoch: Marx and Engels on Britain, France, and Germany* (1991). Examines Marx's and Engels's observations against what is known to have been the situation in each nation.

S. C. HAUSE, *Women's Suffrage and Social Politics in the French Third Republic* (1984). A wide-ranging examination of the question.

G. HIMMELFARB, *The Idea of Poverty: England in the Early Industrial Age* (1984). A major work covering the subject from the time of Adam Smith through 1850.

SUGGESTED READINGS **SR-21**

G. HIMMELFARB, *Poverty and Compassion: The Moral Imagination of the Late Victorians* (1991). The best examination of late Victorian social thought.

E. J. HOBSBAWM, *The Age of Capital* (1975). Explores the consolidation of middle-class life after 1850.

L. HOLCOMBE, *Wives and Property: Reform of the Married Women's Property Law in Nineteenth-Century England* (1983). The standard work on the subject.

T. HOPPEN, *The Mid-Victorian Gerneration, 1846–1886* (1998). The most extensive treatment of the subject.

J. T. KLOPPENBERG, *Uncertain Victory: Social Democracy and Progressivism in European and American Thought* (1986). An extremely important comparative study.

L. KOLAKOWSKI, *Main Currents of Marxism: Its Rise, Growth, and Dissolution*, 3 vols. (1978). Especially good on the last years of the nineteenth century and the early years of the twentieth.

P. KRAUSE, *The Battle for Homestead, 1880–1892* (1992). Examines labor relations in the steel industry.

D. LANDES, *The Wealth and Poverty of Nations: Why Some Are So Rich and Some So Poor* (1998). A major international discussion of the subject.

A. H. MCBRIAR, *Fabian Socialism and English Politics, 1884–1918* (1962). The standard discussion.

A. MACLAREN, *Sexuality and Social Order: The Debate over the Fertility of Women and Workers in France, 1770–1920* (1983). Examines the debate over birth control in France.

G. L. MOSSE, *German Jews Beyond Judaism* (1985). Sensitive essays exploring the relationship of Jews to German culture in the nineteenth and early-twentieth centuries.

F. K. PROCHASKA, *Women and Philanthropy in Nineteenth-Century England* (1980). Studies the role of women in charity.

J. RENDALL, *The Origins of Modern Feminism: Women in Britain, France and the United States, 1780–1860* (1985). A well-informed introduction.

T. RICHARDS, *The Commodity Culture of Victorian England: Advertising and Spectacle, 1851–1914* (1990). A study of how consumers were persuaded of their need for new commodities.

P. ROBERTSON, *An Experience of Women: Pattern and Change in Nineteenth-Century Europe* (1982). A useful survey.

H. ROGGER, *Russia in the Age of Modernization and Revolution, 1881–1917* (1983). The best synthesis of the period.

H. ROGGER, *Jewish Policies and Right-Wing Politics in Imperial Russia* (1986). A very learned examination of Russian anti-Semitism.

M. L. ROZENBLIT, *The Jews of Vienna, 1867–1914: Assimilation and Identity* (1983) Covers the cultural, economic, and political life of Viennese Jews.

A. L. SHAPIRO, *Housing the Poor of Paris, 1850–1902* (1985). Examines what happened to working-class housing during the remodeling of Paris.

B. G. SMITH, *Ladies of the Leisure Class: The Bourgeoises of Northern France in the Nineteenth Century* (1981). Emphasizes the importance of the reproductive role of women.

R. A. SOLOWAY, *Birth Control and the Population Question in England, 1877–1930* (1982). An important book that should be read with MacLaren (listed above).

N. STONE, *Europe Transformed* (1984). A sweeping survey that emphasizes the difficulties of late-nineteenth-century liberalism.

S. TRACHTENBERG, *The Incorporation of America: Culture and Society in the Gilded Age* (1982). Studies the manner in which corporate organization affected various aspects of American life outside the realm of business.

A. B. ULAM, *The Bolsheviks: The Intellectual and Political History of the Triumph of Communism in Russia* (1965). Early chapters discuss prewar developments and the formation of Lenin's doctrines.

R. M. UTLEY, *The Indian Frontier and the American West, 1846–1890* (1984). A broad survey of the pressures of white civilization against Native Americans.

A. M. VERNER, *The Crisis of Russian Autocracy: Nicholas II and the 1905 Revolution* (1990). A major study of this crucial event.

J. R. WALKOWITZ, *Prostitution and Victorian Society: Women, Class, and the State* (1980). A work of great insight and sensitivity.

E. WEBER, *Peasants into Frenchmen: The Modernization of Rural France, 1870–1914* (1976). An important and fascinating work on the transformation of French peasants into self-conscious citizens of the nation-state.

M. J. WIENER, *English Culture and the Decline of the Industrial Spirit, 1850–1980* (1981). The best study of the problem.

C. V. WOODWARD, *The Strange History of Jim Crow* (1966). A clear discussion of the imposition of racial segregation in the United States.

Chapter 27

S. ARROM, *The Women of Mexico City, 1790–1857* (1985). A pioneering study.

E. BERMAN, ED., *Women, Culture, and Politics in Latin America* (1990). Useful essays.

L. BETHELL, ED., *The Cambridge History of Latin America*, 8 vols. (1992). The single most authoritative coverage, with extensive bibliographical essays.

V. BULMER-THOMAS, *The Economic History of Latin America Since Independence* (1994). A major study in every respect.

E. B. BURNS, *The Poverty of Progress: Latin America in the Nineteenth Century* (1980). Argues that the elites suppressed alternative modes of cultural and economic development.

E. B. BURNS, *A History of Brazil* (1993). The most useful one-volume treatment.

D. BUSHNELL AND N. MACAULAY, *The Emergence of Latin America in the Nineteenth Century* (1994). A survey that examines the internal development of Latin America during the period.

R. CONRAD, *The Destruction of Brazilian Slavery, 1850–1889* (1971). A good survey of the most important problem in Brazil in the second half of the nineteenth century.

R. CONRAD, *World of Sorrow: The African Slave Trade to Brazil* (1986). An excellent survey of the subject.

E. V. DA COSTA, *The Brazilian Empire: Myths and Histories* (1985). Essays that provide a thorough introduction to Brazil during the period of empire.

H. S. FERNS, *Britain and Argentina in the Nineteenth Century* (1968). Explains clearly the intermeshing of the two economies.

M. FONT, *Coffee, Contention, and Change in the Making of Modern Brazil* (1990). Extensive discussion of the problems of a single-commodity economy.

R. GRAHAM, *Britain and the Onset of Modernization in Brazil* (1968). Another study of British economic dominance.

S. H. HABER, *Industry and Underdevelopment: The Industrialization of Mexico, 1890–1940* (1989). Examines the problem of industrialization before and after the revolution.

G. HAHNER, *Emancipating the Female Sex: The Struggle for Women's Rights in Brazil, 1850–1940* (1990). An extensive examination of a relatively understudied issue in Latin America.

C. H. HARING, *Empire in Brazil: A New World Experiment with Monarchy* (1958). Remains a useful overview.

J. HEMMING, *Amazon Frontier: The Defeat of the Brazilian Indians* (1987). A brilliant survey of the experience of Native Americans in modern Brazil.

R. A. HUMPHREYS, *Latin America and the Second World War*, 2 vols. (1981–1982). The standard work on the topic.

F. KATZ, ED., *Riot, Rebellion, and Revolution in Mexico: Social Base of Agrarian Violence, 1750–1940* (1988). Essays that put the violence of the revolution in a longer context.

A. KNIGHT, *The Mexican Revolution*, 2 vols. (1986). The best treatment of the subject.

S. MAINWARING, *The Catholic Church and Politics in Brazil, 1916–1985* (1986). An examination of a key institution in Brazilian life.

M. C. MEYER AND W. L. SHERMAN, *The Course of Mexican History* (1995). An excellent survey.

M. MORNER, *Adventurers and Proletarians: The Story of Migrants in Latin America* (1985). Examines immigration to Latin America and migration within it.

J. PAGE, *Perón: A Biography* (1983). The standard English treatment.

D. ROCK, *Politics in Argentina, 1890–1930: The Rise and Fall of Radicalism* (1975). The major discussion of the Argentine Radical Party.

D. ROCK, *Argentina, 1516–1987: From Spanish Colonization to Alfonsin* (1987). Now the standard survey.

D. ROCK, ED., *Latin America in the 1940s: War and Postwar Transitions* (1994). Essays examining a very difficult decade for the continent.

R. M. SCHNEIDER, *"Order and Progress": A Political History of Brazil* (1991). A straightforward narrative with helpful notes for further reading.

T. E. SKIDMORE, *Black into White: Race and Nationality in Brazilian Thought* (1993). Examines the role of racial theory in Brazil.

P. H. SMITH, *Argentina and the Failure of Democracy: Conflict Among Political Elites. 1904–1955* (1974). An examination of one of the major political puzzles of Latin American history.

S. J. STEIN AND B. H. STEIN, *The Colonial Heritage of Latin America: Essays on Economic Dependence in Perspective* (1970). A major statement of the dependence interpretation.

D. TAMARIN, *The Argentine Labor Movement, 1930–1945: A Study in the Origins of Perónism* (1985). A useful introduction to a complex subject.

H. J. WIARDA, *Politics and Social Change in Latin America: The Distinct Tradition* (1974). Excellent essays that stress the ongoing role of Iberian traditions.

J. D. WIRTH, ED., *Latin American Oil Companies and the Politics of Energy* (1985). A series of case studies.

J. WOLFE, *Working Women, Working Men: São Paulo and the Rise of Brazil's Industrial Working Class, 1900–1955* (1993). Pays particular attention to the role of women.

J. WOMACK, *Zapata and the Mexican Revolution* (1968). A classic study.

Chapter 28

India

A. AHMAD, *Islamic Modernism in India and Pakistan, 1857–1964* (1967). The standard survey of Muslim thinkers and movements in India during the period.

C. A. BAYLY, *Indian Society and the Making of the British Empire, The New Cambridge History of India*, II.1 (1988). One of several major contributions of this author to the ongoing revision of our picture of modern Indian history since the eighteenth century.

R. GUHA, ED., *Subaltern Studies: Writings on South Asian History and Society* (1982). Essays on the colonial period that focus on the social, political, and economic history of "subaltern" groups and classes (hill tribes, peasants, etc.) rather than the elites of India only.

S. N. HAY, ED., "Modern India and Pakistan," Part VI of Wm. Theodore de Bary et al., eds., *Sources of Indian Tradition*, 2nd ed. (1988). A superb selection of primary-source documents with brief introductions and helpful notes.

D. KOPF, *British Orientalism and the Bengal Renaissance: The Dynamics of Indian Modernization, 1773–1835* (1969). An intriguing study of British-Indian interchange and mutual influence in the heyday of the East India Company.

F. ROBINSON, ED., *The Cambridge Encyclopedia of India, Pakistan, Bangladesh, Sri Lanka, Nepal, Bhutan, and the Maldives* (1989). A fine collection of survey articles by various scholars, organized into topical chapters ranging from "Economies" to "Cultures."

W. C. SMITH, *Modern Islam in India: A Social Analysis* (1943). A Marxist critique. Still the best survey and analysis of Indian Muslim thought from Sayyid Ahmad Khan to the early 1940s.

P. SPEAR, *The Oxford History of Modern India, 1740–1947* (1965). Still a helpful quick reference tool.

M. N. SRINIVAS, *Social Change in Modern India* (1966). An older but highly influential treatment of topics such as "sanskritization," "westernization," and "secularization."

E. STOKES, *The Peasant Armed: The Indian Revolt of 1857* (1986). The basic starting point for study of the revolt. A posthumously edited work on the battles and the involvement of rural districts of North India in what Stokes saw as a "peasant revolt."

S. WOLPERT, *A New History of India*, 2nd ed. (1982). Chapters 14–25. A solid survey and useful quick reference source.

Central Islamic Lands

K. CRAGG, *Counsels in Contemporary Islam* (1965). A brief survey of intellectual trends in the modern Islamic world in the nineteenth and twentieth centuries.

J. J. DONAHUE AND J. L. ESPOSITO, EDS., *Islam in Transition: Muslim Perspectives* (1982). An interesting selection of primary-source materials on Islamic thinking in this century.

D. F. EICKELMAN, *Knowledge and Power in Morocco: The Education of a Twentieth-Century Notable* (1985). A fascinating study of traditional Islamic education and society in the twentieth century through a social biography of a Moroccan religious scholar and judge.

M. G. S. HODGSON, *The Venture of Islam* (1974). Vol. 3, *The Gunpowder Empires and Modern Times*. Although less ample than his first two volumes, this volume still provides a solid interpretive introduction.

A. HOURANI, *Arabic Thought in the Liberal Age, 1798–1939* (1967). The standard work, by which all subsequent scholarship on the topic is to be judged.

N. R. KEDDI, *An Islamic Response to Imperialism* (1968). A brief study of al-Afghani, the great Muslim reformer, with translations of a number of his writings.

N. R. KEDDI, ED., *Religion and Politics in Iran* (1983). A collection of essays with a helpful historical introduction by the editor and varied articles on modern Iran.

M. H. KERR, *Islamic Reform: The Political and Legal Theories of Muhammad Abduh and Rashid Rida* (1966). A fine study of two major Muslim reformers in the colonial period in Egypt.

B. LEWIS, *The Emergence of Modern Turkey*, 2nd ed. (1968). A concise but thorough history of the creation of the Turkish state, including nineteenth-century background.

E. MORTIMER, *Faith and Power: The Politics of Islam* (1982). A fine survey of contemporary Islamic countries by a knowledgeable and thoughtful journalist.

F. RAHMAN, *Islam* (1966). Chapters 12 and 13. These two chapters from a fine introductory survey of Islam by a major modern Muslim historian and thinker deal with reform movements and other modern developments in the Islamic world.

J. C. B. RICHMOND, *Egypt, 1798–1952: Her Advance Towards a Modern Identity* (1977). A basic history, with focus on political change.

S. J. SHAW AND E. K. SHAW, *History of the Ottoman Empire and Modern Turkey* (1977). Vol. II, *Reform, Revolution, and Republic: The Rise of Modern Turkey, 1808–1975*. Detailed and careful analytic and survey history of the modern period.

W. C. SMITH, *Islam in Modern History* (1957). Dated, but still the most penetrating analysis of the dilemmas facing Muslim individuals and states in the twentieth century.

J. O. VOLL, *Islam: Continuity and Change in the Modern World* (1982). Chapters 1–6. An interpretive survey of the Islamic world since the eighteenth century. Its emphasis on eighteenth-century reform movements is especially noteworthy.

Africa

A. A. BOAHEN, *Africa Under Colonial Domination, 1880–1935* (1985). Vol. VII of the *UNESCO General History of Africa*. Excellent chapters on various regions of Africa in the period. Chapters 3–10 detail African resistance to European colonial intrusion in diverse regions.

W. CARTEY AND M. KILSON, EDS., *The Africa Reader: Colonial Africa* (1970). Original source materials give a vivid picture of African resistance to colonial powers, adaptation to foreign rule, and the emergence of the African masses as a political force.

P. CURTIN, S. FEIERMANN, L. THOMPSON, AND J. VANSINA, *African History* (1978). The relevant portions are Chapters 10–20.

B. DAVIDSON, *The African Genius: An Introduction to African Social and Cultural History* (1969). A sensitive analysis of Africa from the standpoint of African rather than European thought and action. Especially interesting are African responses to imperial and colonial penetration.

J. D. FAGE, *A History of Africa* (1978). The relevant chapters, which give a particularly clear overview of the colonial period, are 12–16.

D. FODE AND P. M. KABERRY, EDS., *West African Kingdoms in the Nineteenth Century* (1967). Very useful treatments of the different West African states such as Benin, Asante, and Gonja.

B. FREUND, *The Making of Contemporary Africa: The Development of African Society Since 1800* (1984). A refreshingly direct synthetic discussion and survey that take an avowedly, but not reductive, materialist approach to interpretation.

R. HALLETT, *Africa Since 1875: A Modern History* (1974). Detailed survey of modern African history from the outset of the colonial period.

R. W. JULY, *A History of the African People*, 3rd ed. (1980). The strongest portions of the book are those on the nineteenth and twentieth centuries.

M. A. KLEIN, *Islam and Imperialism in Senegal: Sine-Saloum, 1847–1914* (1968). A first-rate study of the shift in the Serer states of Senegal from traditional authority to that of the colonial French.

A. OGOT AND J. A. KIERAN, EDS., *Zamani: A Survey of East African History*, 2nd rev. ed. (1974). Good material on the nineteenth century and colonial period in the various regions.

A. D. ROBERTS, ED., *The Colonial Moment in Africa: Essays on the Movement of Minds and Materials, 1900–1940* (1986). Chapters from *The Cambridge History of Africa* treating various aspects of the colonial period in Africa, including economics, politics, and religion.

Chapter 29

China

P. M. COBLE, *The Shanghai Capitalists and the Nationalist Government, 1927–1937* (1980).

L. E. EASTMAN, *The Abortive Revolution: China Under Nationalist Rule, 1927–1937* (1974).

L. E. EASTMAN, *Seeds of Destruction: Nationalist China in War and Revolution, 1937–1949* (1984).

M. ELVIN AND G. W. SKINNER, *The Chinese City Between Two Worlds* (1974). A study of the late Ch'ing and Republican eras.

J. W. ESHERICK, *The Origins of the Boxer Rebellion* (1987).

S. ETŌ, *China's Republican Revolution* (1994).

J. K. FAIRBANK AND M. GOLDMAN, *China, a New History* (1998). A survey of the entire sweep of Chinese history; especially strong on the modern period.

J. K. FAIRBANK AND D. TWITCHETT, EDS., *The Cambridge History of China*. Like the premodern volumes in the same series, the volumes on modern China represent a survey of what is known. Volumes 10–15, which cover the history from the late Ch'ing to the People's Republic, have been published, and the others will be available soon. The series is substantial. Each volume contains a comprehensive bibliography.

C. HAO, *Chinese Intellectuals in Crisis: Search for Order and Meaning, 1890–1911* (1987).

W. C. KIRBY, ED., *State and Economy in Republican China* (2001).

P. A. KUHN, *Rebellion and Its Enemies in Late Imperial China: Militarization and Social Structure, 1796–1864* (1980). A study of how the Confucian gentry saved the Manchu dynasty after the Taiping Rebellion.

J. LEVENSON, *Liang Ch'i-ch'ao and the Mind of Modern China* (1953). A classic study of a major Chinese reformer and thinker.

LU HSUN, *Selected Works* (1960). Novels, stories, and other writings by modern China's greatest writer.

E. O. REISCHAUER, J. K. FAIRBANK, AND A. M. CRAIG, *East Asia: Tradition and Transformation* (1989). A more detailed text on east Asian history. Contains ample chapters on Japan and China and shorter chapters on Korea and Vietnam.

H. Z. SCHIFFRIN, *Sun Yat-sen, Reluctant Revolutionary* (1980). A biography.

B. I. SCHWARTZ, *Chinese Communism and the Rise of Mao* (1951). A classic study of Mao, his thought, and the Chinese Communist Party before 1949.

B. I. SCHWARTZ, *In Search of Wealth and Power: Yen Fu and the West* (1964). A fine study of a late-nineteenth-century thinker who introduced Western ideas into China.

J. D. SPENCE, *The Gate of Heavenly Peace: The Chinese and Their Revolution, 1895–1980* (1981). Historical reflections on twentieth-century China.

J. D. SPENCE, *The Search for Modern China* (1990). A thick text that reads well.

S. Y. TENG AND J. K. FAIRBANK, *China's Response to the West* (1954). A fine collection of translations from Chinese thinkers and political figures, with commentaries.

T. H. WHITE AND A. JACOBY, *Thunder Out of China* (1946). A view of China during World War II by two who were there.

Japan

G. C. ALLEN, *A Short Economic History of Modern Japan* (1958).

J. R. BARTHOLOMEW, *The Formation of Science in Japan* (1989). The pioneering English-language work on the subject.

W. G. BEASLEY, *Japanese Imperialism, 1894–1945* (1987).

G. M. BERGER, *Parties Out of Power in Japan, 1931–1941* (1977). An analysis of the condition of political parties during the militarist era.

A. M. CRAIG, *Chōshū in the Meiji Restoration* (1961). A study of the Chōshū domain, a Prussia of Japan, during the period 1840–1868.

P. DUUS, *Party Rivalry and Political Change in Taisho Japan* (1968). A study of political change in Japan during the 1910s and 1920s.

P. DUUS, ED., *The Cambridge History of Japan: The Twentieth Century* (1988). This volume also extends into the post–World War II era.

P. DUUS, *The Abacus and the Sword, the Japanese Penetration of Korea, 1895–1910* (1995). A thoughtful analysis.

S. ERICSON, *The Sound of the Whistle: Railroads and the State in Meiji Japan* (1996).

Y. FUKUZAWA, *Autobiography* (1966). Japan's leading nineteenth-century thinker tells of his life and of the birth of modern Japan.

A. GARON, *The State and Labor in Modern Japan* (1987).

C. N. GLUCK, *Japan's Modern Myths: Ideology in the Late Meiji Period* (1988).

A. GORDON, *The Evolution of Labor Relations in Japan: Heavy Industry, 1853–1955* (1985).

I. HALL, *Mori Arinori* (1973). A biography of Japan's first minister of education.

T. R. H. HAVENS, *The Valley of Darkness: The Japanese People and World War II* (1978).

A. IRIYE, *After Imperialism: The Search for a New Order in the Far East, 1921–1931* (1965). (See also other studies by the same author.)

M. J. JANSEN, ED., *The Cambridge History of Japan: The Nineteenth Century* (1989).

W. JOHNSTON, *The Modern Epidemic: A History of Tuberculosis in Japan* (1995).

D. KEENE, ED., *Modern Japanese Literature, An Anthology* (1960). A collection of modern Japanese short stories and excerpts from novels.

J. W. MORLEY, ED., *The China Quagmire* (1983). A study of Japan's expansion on the continent between 1933 and 1941. (For diplomatic history, see also the many other works by this author.)

R. H. MYERS AND M. R. PEATTIE, EDS., *The Japanese Colonial Empire, 1895–1945* (1984).

T. NAJITA, *Hara Kei in the Politics of Compromise, 1905–1915* (1967). A study of one of Japan's greatest party leaders.

K. OHKAWA AND H. ROSOVSKY, *Japanese Economic Growth: Trend Acceleration in the Twentieth Century* (1973).

G. SHIBA, *Remembering Aizu* (1999). A moving autobiographical account of a samurai youth whose domain lost in the Meiji Restoration.

K. SMITH, *A Time of Crisis: The Great Depression and Rural Revitalization* (2001).

J. J. STEPHAN, *Hawaii Under the Rising Sun* (1984). Japan's plans for rule in Hawaii.

R. H. SPECTOR, *Eagle Against the Sun: The American War with Japan* (1985).

E. P. TSURUMI, *Factory Girls: Women in the Thread Mills of Meiji Japan* (1990).

Chapter 30

L. ALBERTINI, *The Origins of the War of 1914*, 3 vols. (1952, 1957). Discursive but invaluable.

V. R. BERGHAHN, *Germany and the Approach of War in 1914* (1973). A work similar in spirit to both of Fischer's (see below) but stressing the importance of Germany's naval program.

R. BOSWORTH, *Italy and the Approach of the First World War* (1983). A fine analysis of Italian policy.

L. CECIL, *Wilhelm II: Prince and Emperor 1859–1900* (1989). The first part of a projected two-volume history of the Kaiser.

V. DEDIJER, *The Road to Sarajevo* (1966). The fullest account of the assassination that provoked World War I and its Balkan background.

S. B. FAY, *The Origins of the World War*, 2 vols. (1928). The best and most influential of the revisionist accounts.

F. FISCHER, *Germany's Aims in the First World War* (1967). An influential interpretation that stirred a great controversy in Germany and around the world by emphasizing Germany's role in bringing on the war.

F. FISCHER, *War of Illusions* (1975). A long and diffuse book that tries to connect German responsibility for the war with internal social, economic, and political developments.

I. GEISS, *July 1914* (1967). A valuable collection of documents by a student of Fritz Fischer. The emphasis is on German documents and responsibility.

M. GILBERT, *The First World War* (1994). A lively narrative that combines discussion of the battlefields with accounts of the home front.

O. J. HALE, *The Great Illusion 1900–1914* (1971). A fine survey of the period, especially good on public opinion.

M. B. HAYNE, *The French Foreign Office and the Origins of the First World War* (1993). An examination of how professionals in the foreign service influenced French policy.

J. N. HORNE, *Labour at War: France and Britain, 1914–1918* (1991). An examination of a major issue on the home fronts.

J. JOLL, *The Origins of the First World War* (1984). A brief but thoughtful analysis.

P. KENNEDY, *The Rise of the Anglo-German Antagonism 1860–1914* (1980). An unusual and thorough analysis of the political, economic, and cultural roots of important diplomatic developments.

J. M. KEYNES, *The Economic Consequences of the Peace* (1920). The famous and influential attack on the Versailles Treaty.

L. LAFORE, *The Long Fuse* (1965). A readable account of the origins of World War I that focuses on the problem of Austria-Hungary.

W. L. LANGER, *European Alliances and Alignments*, 2nd ed. (1966). A splendid diplomatic history of the years 1871–1890.

W. L. LANGER, *The Diplomacy of Imperialism* (1935). A continuation of the previous study for the years 1890–1902.

B. H. LIDDELL HART, *The Real War 1914–1918* (1964). A fine short account by an outstanding military historian.

D. C. B. LIEVEN, *Russia and the Origins of the First World War* (1983). A good account of the forces that shaped Russian policy.

E. MANTOUX, *The Carthaginian Peace* (1952). A vigorous attack on Keynes's view (see Keynes, above).

J. STEINBERG, *Yesterday's Deterrent* (1965). An excellent study of Germany's naval policy and its consequences.

Z. STEINER, *Britain and the Origins of the First World War* (1977). A perceptive and informed account of the way British foreign policy was made in the years before the war.

A. J. P. TAYLOR, *The Struggle for Mastery in Europe, 1848–1918* (1954). Clever but controversial.

L. C. F. TURNER, *Origins of the First World War* (1970). Especially good on the significance of Russia and its military plans.

S. R. WILLIAMSON, JR., *Austria-Hungary and the Origins of the First World War* (1991). A valuable study of a complex subject.

Chapter 31

W. S. ALLEN, *The Nazi Seizure of Power: The Experience of a Single German Town, 1930–1935*, rev. ed. (1984). A classic treatment of Nazism in a microcosmic setting.

J. BARNARD, *Walter Reuther and the Rise of the Auto Workers* (1983). A major introduction to the new American unions of the 1930s.

K. D. BRACHER, *The German Dictatorship* (1970). A comprehensive treatment of both the origins and the functioning of the Nazi movement and government.

A. BULLOCK, *Hitler: A Study in Tyranny*, rev. ed. (1964). The best biography.

M. BURLEIGH AND W. WIPPERMAN, *The Racial State: Germany 1933–1945* (1991). Emphasizes the manner in which racial theory influenced numerous areas of policy.

R. CONQUEST, *The Great Terror: Stalin's Purges of the Thirties* (1968). The best treatment of the subject to this date.

G. CRAIG, *Germany, 1866–1945* (1978). A major survey.

I. DEUTSCHER, *The Prophet Armed* (1954), *The Prophet Unarmed* (1959), and *The Prophet Outcast* (1963). Remains the major biography of Trotsky.

I. DEUTSCHER, *Stalin: A Political Biography*, 2nd ed. (1967). The best biography in English.

B. EICHENGREEN, *Golden Fetters: The Gold Standard and the Great Depression, 1919–1939* (1992). A remarkable study of the role of the gold standard in the economic policies of the interwar years.

E. EYCK, *A History of the Weimar Republic*, 2 vols. (trans. 1963). The story as narrated by a liberal.

M. S. FAUSOLD, *The Presidency of Herbert Hoover* (1985). An important treatment.

G. FELDMAN, *The Great Disorder: Politics, Economics, and Society in the German Inflation, 1914–1924* (1993). The best work on the subject.

S. FITZPATRICK, *Stalin's Peasants: Resistance and Survival in the Russian Village After Collectivization* (1994). A pioneering study.

P. FUSSELL, *The Great War and Modern Memory* (1975). A brilliant account of the literature arising from World War I during the 1920s.

J. K. GALBRAITH, *The Great Crash* (1979). A well-known account by a leading economist.

R. GELLATELY, *The Gestapo and German Society: Enforcing Racial Policy, 1933–1945* (1990). A discussion of how the police state supported Nazi racial policies.

H. J. GORDON, *Hitler and the Beer Hall Putsch* (1972). An excellent account of the event and the political situation in the early Weimar Republic.

R. HAMILTON, *Who Voted for Hitler?* (1982). An examination of voting patterns and sources of Nazi support.

J. HELD, ED., *The Columbia History of Eastern Europe in the Twentieth Century* (1992). Individual essays on each country.

P. KENEZ, *The Birth of the Propaganda State: Soviet Methods of Mass Mobilization, 1917–1929* (1985). An examination of the manner in which the Communist government inculcated popular support.

B. KENT, *The Spoils of War: The Politics, Economics, and Diplomacy of Reparations, 1918–1932* (1993). A comprehensive account of the intricacies of the reparations problem of the 1920s.

D. LANDES, *The Unbound Prometheus: Technological Change and Industrial Development in Western Europe from 1750 to the Present* (1969). Includes an excellent analysis of both the Great Depression and the few areas of economic growth.

B. LINCOLN, *Red Victory: A History of the Russian Civil War* (1989). An excellent narrative account.

M. MCAULEY, *Bread and Justice: State and Society in Petrograd, 1917–1922* (1991). A study that examines the impact of the Russian Revolution and Leninist policies on a major Russian city.

D. J. K. PEUKERT, *Inside Nazi Germany: Conformity, Opposition, and Racism in Everyday Life* (1987). An excellent discussion of life under Nazi rule.

R. PIPES, *The Unknown Lenin: From the Secret Archives* (1996). A collection of previously unpublished documents that indicated the repressive character of Lenin's government.

P. PULZER, *Jews and the German State: The Political History of a Minority, 1848–1933* (1992). A detailed history by a major historian of European minorities.

L. J. RUPP, *Mobilizing Women for War: German and America Propaganda, 1939–1945* (1978). Although concentrating on a later period, it includes an excellent discussion of general Nazi attitudes toward women.

A. M. SCHLESINGER, JR., *The Age of Roosevelt*, 3 vols. (1957–1960). The most important overview.

D. M. SMITH, *Mussolini's Roman Empire* (1976). A general description of the Fascist regime in Italy.

D. M. SMITH, *Italy and Its Monarchy* (1989). A major treatment of an important neglected subject.

A. SOLZHENITSYN, *The Gulag Archipelago*, 3 vols. (1974–1979). A major examination of the labor camps under Stalin by one of the most important contemporary Russian writers.

R. J. SONTAG, *A Broken World, 1919–1939* (1971). An exceptionally thoughtful and well-organized survey.

A. J. P. TAYLOR, *English History, 1914–1945* (1965). Lively and opinionated.

H. A. TURNER, JR., *German Big Business and the Rise of Hitler* (1985). An important major study of the subject.

H. A. TURNER, *Hitler's Thirty Days to Power* (1996). A narrative of the events leading directly to the Nazi seizure of power.

L. YAHIL, *The Holocaust: The Fate of European Jewry, 1932–1945* (1990). A major study of this fundamental subject in twentieth-century history.

Chapter 32

W. S. ALLEN, *The Nazi Seizure of Power: The Experience of a Single German Town, 1930–1935*, rev. ed (1984). A classic treatment of Nazism in a microcosmic setting.

J. BARNARD, *Walter Reuther and the Rise of the Auto Workers* (1983). A major introduction to the new American unions of the 1930s.

I.T. BEREND, *Decades of Crisis: Central and Eastern Europe Before World War II* (1998). The best discussion of a remarkably troubled region.

M. BURLEIGH AND W. WIPPERMAN, *The Racial State: Germany 1933–1945* (1991). Emphasizes the manner in which racial theory influenced numerous areas of policy.

R. CONQUEST, *The Great Terror: Stalin's Purges of the Thirties* (1968). The best treatment of the subject to this date.

I. DEUTSCHER, *The Prophet Armed* (1954), *The Prophet Unarmed* (1959), and *The Prophet Outcast* (1963). Remains the major biography of Trotsky.

I. DEUTSCHER, *Stalin: A Political Biography*, 2nd ed. (1967). The best biography in English.

M. S. FAUSOLD, *The Presidency of Herbert Hoover* (1985). An important treatment.

G. FELDMAN, *The Great Disorder: Politics, Economics, and Society in the German Inflation, 1914–1924* (1993). The best work on the subject.

S. FITZPATRICK, *Stalin's Peasants: Resistance and Survival in the Russian Village After Collectivization* (1994). A pioneering study.

S. FITZPATRICK, *Everyday Stalinism, Ordinary Life in Extraordinary Times: Soviet Russian in the 1930s* (1999). A major study based on newly available materials.

F. FURET, *The Passing of an Illusion: The Idea of Communism in the Twentieth Century* (1995). A brilliant account of how communism shaped politics and thought outside the Soviet Union.

R. GELLATELY, *The Gestapo and German Society: Enforcing Racial Policy, 1933–1945* (1990). A discussion of how the police state supported Nazi racial policies.

J. A. GETTY AND O. V. NAUMOV, *The Toad to Terror: Stalin and the Self-Destruction of the Bolsheviks, 1933–1939* (1999). A major collection of newly available documents revealing much new information about the purges.

B. HAMANN, *Hitler's Vienna: A Dictator's Apprenticeship* (1999). Probing study of the politics and society of Vienna as experienced by the young Hitler.

R. HAMILTON, *Who Voted for Hitler?* (1982). An examination of voting patterns and sources of Nazi support.

J. HELD, ED., *The Columbia History of Eastern Europe in the Twentieth Century* (1992). Individual essays on each country.

E. HILBERG, *The Destruction of the European Jews*, 3 vols. (1985). The classic account of the political and administrative processes that supported the Holocaust.

P. KENEZ, *The Birth of the Propaganda State: Soviet Methods of Mass Mobilization, 1917–1929* (1985). An examination of the manner in which the Communist government inculcated popular support.

B. KENT, *The Spoils of War: The Politics, Economics, and Diplomacy of Reparations, 1918–1932* (1993). A comprehensive account of the intricacies of the reparations problem of the 1920s.

D. KENNEDY, *Freedom from Fear: The American People in Depression and War, 1925–1949* (1999). A powerful survey.

I. KERSHAW, *Hitler*, 2 vols. (1998, 2000). Now the standard biography.

D. J. K. PEUKERT, *Inside Nazi Germany: Conformity, Opposition, and Racism in Everyday Life* (1987). An excellent discussion of life under Nazi rule.

R. PIPES, *The Unknown Lenin: From the Secret Archives* (1996). A collection of previously unpublished documents that indicated the repressive character of Lenin's government.

P. PULZER, *Jews and the German State: The Political History of a Minority, 1948–1933* (1992). A detailed history by a major historian of European minorities.

L. J. RUPP, *Mobilizing Women for War: German and American Propaganda, 1839–1945* (1978). Although concentrating on a later period, it includes an excellent discussion of general Nazi attitudes toward women.

D. M. SMITH, *Mussolini's Roman Empire* (1976). A general description of the Fascist regime in Italy.

R. J. SONTAG, *A Broken World, 1919–1939* (1971). An exceptionally thoughtful and well-organized survey.

H. A. TURNER, *Hitler's Thirty Days to Power* (1996). A narrative of the events leading directly to the Nazi seizure of power.

D. VITAL, *A People Apart: The Jews in Europe, 1789–1939* (1999). A major survey with excellent discussions of the interwar years.

W. WEBER, *The Hollow Years: France in the 1930s* (1995). Examines France between the wars.

L. YAHIL, *The Holocaust: The Fate of European Jewry, 1932–1945* (1990). A major study of this fundamental subject in twentieth-century history.

Chapter 33

B. S. ANDERSON AND J. P. PINSSER, *A History of Their Own: Women in Europe from Prehistory to the Present*, Vol. 2 (1988). A broad-ranging survey.

T. S. ASH, *The Uses of Adversity* (1989) Important essays on central European culture and politics prior to the events of 1989.

P. BALDWIN, *The Politics of Social Solidarity: Class Bases of the European Welfare State 1875–1975* (1990). An excellent analysis of the political forces that allowed the welfare state to come into being.

I. BANAC, ED., *Eastern Europe in Revolution* (1992). Excellent articles on the events of 1989 and afterward.

J. H. BILLINGTON, *Russia Transformed: Breakthrough to Hope, Moscow, August, 1991* (1992). A thoughtful essay on the attempted coup.

E. BOTTOME, *The Balance of Terror: Nuclear Weapons and the Illusion of Security, 1945–1985* (1986). A review of the issues that dominated the Cold War era.

A. BROWN, *The Gorbachev Factor* (1996). An important commentary by an English observer.

A. N. DRAGNICH, *Serbs and Croats: The Struggle in Yugoslavia* (1992). An introduction to the historical roots of the current struggle.

M. ELLMAN AND V. KONTOROVICH, *The Disintegration of the Soviet Economic System* (1992). An overview of the economic strains that the Soviet Union experienced during the 1980s.

H. FEIS, *From Trust to Terror: The Onset of the Cold War, 1945–1950* (1970). The best general account.

J. L. GADDIS, *What We Know Now* (1997). Examines the Cold War in light of newly released documents.

D. J. GARROW, *Bearing the Cross: Martin Luther King, Jr. and the Southern Leadership Conference 1955–1968* (1986). The best work on the subject.

M. GLENNY, *The Fall of Yugoslavia: The Third Balkan War* (1992). An overview by a British journalist.

B. GWERTZMAN AND M. T. KAUFMAN, *The Collapse of Communism* (1991). A collection of contemporary news accounts.

B. GWERTZMAN AND M. T. KAUFMAN, *The Decline and Fall of the Soviet Empire* (1992). A collection of contemporary news accounts.

D. HOLLOWAY, *The Soviet Union and the Arms Race* (1985). Excellent treatment of internal Soviet decision making.

L. JOHNSON, *Central Europe: Enemies & Neighbors & Friends* (1996). Explores the complexities of relationships in the region.

R. G. KAISER, *Why Gorbachev Happened* (1992). A useful overview.

D. KEARNS, *Lyndon Johnson and the American Dream* (1976). A useful biography.

J. KEEP, *The Last of the Empires: A History of the Soviet Union, 1956–1991* (1995). A clear narrative.

R. F. LESLIE, *The History of Poland Since 1863* (1981). An excellent collection of essays that provide the background for later events in Poland.

F. LEWIS, *Europe: Road to Unity* (1992). A discussion of contemporary Europe by a thoughtful journalist.

R. MALTBY, ED., *Passing Parade: A History of Popular Culture in the Twentieth Century* (1989). A collection of essays on a topic just beginning to receive scholarly attention.

P. H. MERKL, *German Unification in the European Context* (1993). The first major essay on the impact of German unity.

C. MURRAY, *Losing Ground: American Social Policy 1950–1980* (1983). A pessimistic assessment.

P. PULZER, *German Politics, 1945–1995* (1996). An important overview.

L. SCHAPIRO, *The Communist Party of the Soviet Union* (1960). A classic analysis of the most important institution of Soviet Russia.

A. M. SCHLESINGER, JR., *A Thousand Days: John F. Kennedy in the White House* (1965). A biography by an adviser and major historian.

H. SIMONIAN, *The Privileged Partnership: Franco-German Relations in the European Community (1969–1984)* (1985). An important examination of the dominant role of France and Germany in the EEC.

J. STEELE, *Soviet Power: The Kremlin's Foreign Policy—Brezhnev to Andropov* (1983). A broad survey.

D. STOCKMAN, *The Triumph of Politics: The Inside Story of the Reagan Revolution* (1987). A critical memoir by one of Reagan's aides.

G. STOKES, ED., *From Stalinism to Pluralism: A Documentary History of Eastern Europe Since 1945* (1996). An important collection of documents which are not easily accessible elsewhere.

H. A. TURNER, JR., *Germany from Partition to Reunification* (1992). The best and most recent introduction.

M. WALKER, *The Cold War and the Making of the Modern World* (1994). A major survey.

B. WOODWARD AND C. BERNSTEIN, *The Final Days* (1976). A discussion of the Watergate scandal by the reporters who uncovered it.

Chapter 34

China

A. CHAN, R. MADSEN, AND J. UNGER, *Chen Village: A Recent History of a Peasant Community in Mao's China* (1984). An account of the postwar history of a Chinese village.

J. CHANG, *Wild Swans: Three Daughters of China* (1991). An intimate look at recent Chinese society through three generations of women. Immensely readable.

B. M. FROLIC, *Mao's People: Sixteen Portraits of Life in Revolutionary China* (1987).

T. GOLD, *State and Society in the Taiwan Miracle* (1986). The story of economic growth in postwar Taiwan.

M. GOLDMAN AND R. MACFARQUHAR, EDS., *The Paradox of China's Post-Mao Reforms* (1999).

A. IRIYE, *China and Japan in the Global Setting* (1992).

H. LIANG, *Son of the Revolution* (1983). An autobiographical account of a young man growing up in Mao's China.

K. LIEBERTHAL, *Governing China, from Revolution Through Reform* (1995).

B. LIU, *People or Monsters? and Other Stories and Reportage from China After Mao* (1983). Literary reflections on China.

R. MACFARQUHAR AND J. K. FAIRBANK, EDS., *The Cambridge History of China XIV, Emergence of Revolutionary China* (1987), and *XV, Revolutions Within the Chinese Revolution, 1966–1982* (1991).

G. WHITE, ED., *In Search of Civil Society: Market Reform and Social Change in Contemporary China* (1996).

M. WOLF, *Revolution Postponed: Women in Contemporary China* (1985).

ZHANG X. AND SANG Y., *Chinese Lives: An Oral History of Contemporary China* (1987).

Japan

G. BERNSTEIN, *Haruko's World: A Japanese Farm Woman and Her Community* (1983). A study of the changing life of a village woman in postwar Japan.

T. BESTOR, *Neighborhood Tokyo* (1989). A portrait of contemporary urban life in Japan.

G. L. CURTIS, *The Logic of Japanese Politics: Leaders, Institutions, and the Limits of Change* (1999).

R. P. DORE, *City Life in Japan* (1999). A classic, reissued.

R. P. DORE, *Land Reform in Japan* (1959). Another classic.

S. GARON, *Molding Japanese Minds: The State in Everyday Life* (1997).

A. GORDON, ED., *Postwar Japan as History* (1993).

H. HIBBETT, ED., *Contemporary Japanese Literature: An Anthology of Fiction, Film, and Other Writing Since 1945* (1977). Translations of postwar short stories.

Y. KAWABATA, *The Sound of the Mountain* (1970). Sensitive, moving novel by Nobel author.

J. NATHAN, *Sony, the Private Life* (1999). A lively account of the human side of the growth of the Sony Corporation.

D. OKIMOTO, *Between MITI and the Market* (1989). A discussion of the respective roles of government and private enterprise in Japan's postwar growth.

S. Pharr, *Losing Face: Status Politics in Japan* (1996).

E. O. Reischauer, *The Japanese* (1977). The best overall account of contemporary Japanese society and politics.

E. F. Vogel, *Japan as Number One: Lessons for America* (1979). While dated and somewhat sanguine, this remains an insightful classic.

Korea and Vietnam

B. Cumings, *Korea, The Unknown War* (1988).

B. Cumings, *The Origins of the Korean War* (Vol. 1, 1981; Vol. 2, 1991).

B. Cumings, *The Two Koreas: On the Road to Reunification?* (1990).

C. J. Eckert, *Korea Old and New, A History* (1990). The best short history of Korea, with extensive coverage of the postwar era.

C. J. Eckert, *Offspring of Empire: The Koch'ang Kims and the Colonial Origins of Korean Capitalism, 1876–1945* (1991).

G. M. T. Kahin, *Intervention: How America Became Involved in Vietnam* (1986).

S. Karnow, *Vietnam: A History* (revised edition) (1996).

L. Kendall, *Shamans, Housewives, and Other Restless Spirits: Women in Korean Ritual and Life* (1985).

K. B. Lee, *A New History of Korea* (1984). A translation by E. Wagner and others of an outstanding Korean work covering the full sweep of Korean history.

T. Li, *Nguyen Cochinchina: South Vietnam in the Seventeenth and Eighteenth Centuries* (1998).

D. Marr, *Vietnam 1945: The Quest for Power* (1995).

C. W. Sorensen, *Over the Mountains Are Mountains* (1988). How peasant households in Korea adapted to rapid industrialization.

A. Woodside, *Vietnam and the Chinese Model* (1988). Provides the background for Vietnam's relationship to China.

Chapter 35

Africa

B. Davidson, *Let Freedom Come* (1978). A broad-ranging study of modern Africa, using incisive specific examples to support thoughtful analyses of trends and events across the continent since the nineteenth century.

B. Freund, *The Making of Contemporary Africa: The Development of African Society Since 1800* (1984). The final three chapters give excellent treatment of decolonization after 1940, tropical Africa since independence, and southern Africa into the 1980s.

R. W. July, *A History of the African People*, 3rd ed. (1980). Chapters 14–22. The last part of the book provides a careful and clear survey of post–World War I history, including chapters on the various regions of the continent and on topics like nationalism.

A. J. H. Latham, *Africa, Asia, and South America Since 1800: A Bibliographic Guide* (1995). A valuable tool for finding materials on the topics in this chapter.

R. Oliver, *The African Experience* (1991). The closing chapters give a thoughtful and probing overview of postcolonial Africa.

India and Pakistan

W. T. de Bary et al., eds., *Sources of Indian Tradition*, 2nd ed. (1988). The final chapters offer selections from major modern Indian political and literary figures, accompanied by solid introductions.

F. Robinson, ed., *The Cambridge Encyclopedia of India, Pakistan, Bangladesh, Sri Lanka, Nepal, Bhutan, and the Maldives* (1989). A sweeping and detailed reference source for the South Asian world to 1988.

D. E. Smith, *India as a Secular State* (1963). Still pertinent today for the vexed question in South Asia of how to deal with secularism and religion in the political arena.

S. Wolpert, *A New History of India*, 3rd ed. (1988). The closing chapters of this fine survey history are particularly helpful in orienting the reader in postwar Indian history until the mid-1980s.

Islam and the Middle East

J. Esposito, *The Islamic Threat: Myth or Reality* (2nd ed., 1992). A useful corrective to some of the polemics against Islam and Muslims today.

N. R. Keddie, *Roots of Revolution: An Interpretive History of Modern Iran* (1981). Chapters 6–9 focus on Iran from 1941 through the first years of the 1978 revolution and provide a solid overview of history in this era.

T. Mostyn and A. Hourani, eds., *The Cambridge History of the Middle East and North Africa* (1988). A detailed reference source on the entire region to the mid-1980s.

H. Munson, Jr., *Islam and Revolution in the Middle East* (1988). Based on numerous specific studies of recent years, this little book offers a good general picture, especially for students.

P. Sluglett and M. Faroule-Sluglett, eds., *Tuttle Guide to the Middle East* (1992). A superb handbook arranged by country, with useful appendices.

W. C. Smith, *Islam in Modern History* (1957). Old, but still the most thoughtful and comprehensive treatment of issues facing Muslim peoples from the Arab world to India.

Latin America

J. Dominguez, *Cuba: Order and Revolution* (1978). A useful overview. Essential for understanding the background of the present tensions in the area.

C. Fuentes, *A New Time for Mexico* (1996). A commentary by an influential contemporary writer.

P. Lowden, *Moral Opposition to Authoritarian Rule in Chile* (1996). A discussion of Chilean politics from the standpoint of human rights.

S. D. Morris, *Political Reformers in Mexico: An Overview of Contemporary Mexican Politics* (1995). An examination of a rapidly changing scene.

L. H. Oppenheim, *Politics in Chile: Democracy, Authoritarianism, and the Search for Development* (1993). Examines the controversial course of Chilean politics during the last quarter century.

D. K. L. Van Cott, ed., *Indigenous People and Democracy in Latin America* (1994). Examination of an often neglected subject.

H. Wirarda, *Democracy and Its Discontents: Development, Interdependence, and U.S. Policy in Latin America* (1995). A useful overview.

CREDITS

Part 1 Timeline, Page xxxii, top to bottom, left to right: Neg. No. 39686. Photo, Kirschner. Courtesy Dept. of Library Services, American Museum of Natural History; Victory stele of Naram-Sin, King of Akkad, over the mountain-dwelling Lullubi, Mesopotamian, Akkadian Period, c. 2230 B.C. (pink sandstone). Louvre, Paris, France. The Bridgeman Art Library International Ltd; Paul Macapia/Seattle Art Museum; "Fan Ding". Ceremonial food vessel. Shang Dynasty. Bronze. 24 1/2" H. Academia Sinica, Taibei, Twiwan ROC; Archaeological Museum, Amman, Jordan, kingdom. Photograph © Erich Lessing, Art Resource, NY; "Seated Scribe". Dynasty 5, c. 2510–2460 B.C.E.. Painted limestone, height 21' (53 cm). Musee du Louvre, Paris. © Giraudon/Art Resource;

Page 1, top to bottom, left to right: Corbis/Bettmann; Corbis/Bettmann; ©Scala/Art Resource; © Nik Wheeler/CORBIS; Confucius depicted wearing the robes of a scholar of a later age. Collection of the National Palace Museum, Taipei, Taiwan, Republic of China.; Courtesy of the Freer Gallery of Art, Smithsonian Institution, Washington, D.C. (72.1); Clay tablet from the Chaldean period (612 539 B.C.E.) Courtesy of the Trustees of the British Museum. © Copyright The British Museum; Josephus Daniels/Photo Researchers, Inc.; George Holton/Photo Researchers, Inc.

Chapter 1 a. Dorling Kindersley/British Museum; b. © Judith Miller & Dorling Kindersley/Albert Amor; c. Dorling Kindersley Media Library; e. Dorling Kindersley Media Library; f. Dorling Kindersley/British Museum; g. Museum of Natural History; h. Courtesy of The Oriental Institute Museum of The University of Chicago. Photo by Victor J. Boswell; i. Josephine Powell; j. ©Scala/Art Resource; k. Alan Hills; Dorling Kindersley Media Library.

Chapter 2: a. Markowitz Jeffrey; Corbis/Sygma; c. Corbis/Bettmann; d. Corbis/Bettmann; e. Bharath Ramamrutham; Dorling Kindersley Media Library; f. KEREN SU; Getty Images, Inc.—Taxi; g. Corbis/Bettmann; h. Kunsthistorisches Museum Wien.

Part 2 Timeline, Page 46, top to bottom, left to right: Courtesy of the Trustees of the British Museum; Mike Yamashita/Woodfin Camp & Associates; The Natural History Museum, London; Robert & Linda Mitchell Photography.

Page 47, top to bottom, left to right: The Charioteer of Delphi. Dedicated by Polyzalos of Gela for a victory either in 478 or 474 B.C.E.. Greek (Classical). Bronze. Archaelogical Museum, Delphi, Greece. Copyright Nimatallah/Art Resource, NY; Scala/Art Resource; Dale Williams; Giraudon/Art Resource, N.Y.; Female Attendant, North China; Western Han Period, 2nd century B.C.E.. Earthenware with slip and traces of pigment. H: 21 1/2 in. (54.6 cm) 1979.110. The Asia Society, New York: Mr. and Mrs John D. Rockefeller, 3rd Collection.; National Museum, Beijing, China/Erich Lessing/Art Resource, NY; ©Werner Forman Archive/Art Resource, NY. Jos Museum, Nigeria.

Chapter 3 a. © Gianni Dagli Orti/CORBIS; b. Dorling Kindersley; d. Corbis/Bettmann; e. Dorling Kindersley/British Museum; f. Deutches Archaologisches Institut, Athen: Mykon 70; g. Dorling Kindersley/British Museum; h. Courtesy of the Trustees of the British Museum; i. Photograph © Eric Lessing/Art Resource, NY; j. Alison Frantz Photographic Collection, American School of Classical Studies at Athens.

Chapter 4 a. Guy Ryecart; Dorling Kindersley Media Library; b. Gianni Dagli Orti; CORBIS-NY; d. Dorling Kindersley Media Library; e. Werner Forman Archive, Art Resource, NY; f. Corbis/Bettmann; g. CORBIS-NY; h. Oriental Institute Museum, University of Chicago; i. Giraudon; Art Resource, NY; j. The Buddha's Nirvana. Indian Musee. Giraudon/Art Resource, NY.

Chapter 5 a. © The Academy of Natural Science/CORBIS; b. Dorling Kindersley/British Museum; d. Dorling Kindersley; e. Clive Streeter/Dorling Kindersley Media Library; f. Sarcophagus of a Couple. Etruscan, 6th B.C.E.. Terracotta. H: 114 cm. Louvre, Paris, France. Copyright Erich Lessing/Art Resource, NY; g. A Roman Warship. Direzione Generale Musei Vaticani; h. Charitable Foundation, Gemeinnutzige Stiftung Leonard von Matt; i. Gismondi. Reconstruction of a large house and apartments at Ostia. Museo della Civiltà Romana, Rome, Italy. Copyright Scala/Art Resource, NY; j. Hirmer Fotoarchiv; k. Scala/Art Resource; Art Resource, NY.

Chapter 6 a. Pierre Colombel; CORBIS-NY; c. Philip Dowell; Dorling Kindersley Media Library; d. Nigeria, Nok head, 900B.C.-200A.D., Rafin Kura, Nok. Prehistoric West African sculpture from the Nok culture. Terracotta, 36 cms high. ©Werner Forman Archive, Art Resource. National Museum, Lagos, Nigeria; e. The Natural History Museum, London; f. Chris Scarre; g. Mike Yamashita; Woodfin Camp & Associates; h. Werner Forman Archive; Art Resource, NY.

Chapter 7 a. Alan Hills and Geoff Brightling; Dorling Kindersley Media Library; c. Matthew Ward; Dorling Kindersley Media Library; d. Corbis/Bettmann; e. Glen Allison; Getty Images Inc.—Stone Allstock; f. The New York Public Library for the Performing Arts/Art Resource; g. Alan Hills; Dorling Kindersley Media Library; h. "Lintel & Pediment of a Tomb". China, Western Han dynasty, 1st century B.C. Gray earthenware; hollow tiles painted in ink & colors on a whitewashed ground. 73.8 × 204.7 cm. Denman Waldo Ross Collection, & Gift of C.T. Loo. Courtesy Museum of Fine Arts, Boston; CORBIS-NY.

Part 3 Timeline, Page 154, top to bottom, left to right: Kunsthistorisches Museum, Vienna; Bronze equestrian statuette of Charlemagne, from Metz Cathedral, 9th-10th c. 3/4 view. Louvre, Paris, France. Copyright Giraudon/Art Resource, NY; William haranguing his troups for combat with the English army. Detail from the Bayeux tapestry, scene 51. Musee de la Tapisserie, Bayeux, France. Copyright Giraudon/Art Resource, NY; A leaf from a Manichaean Book, Kocho, Temple K (MIK III 6368), 8th-9th century, manuscript painting, 17.2 × 11.2 cm. Museum fur Indische Kunst, Staatliche Museen Preussischer

Kulturbesitz, Berlin; Ewer with carved flower sprays. Porcelain with molded and carved low-relief decoration in grayish-green glaze approx. 1000-12000. Northern Song Dynasty (960–1127) H. 9 5/8 in × W. 5 1/4 in × D. 7 3/4 in, H. 24.5 cm × W. 13.4 cm × D. 19.7 cm. China; Shaan; Copyright Werner Forman/Art Resource, NY; Robert Frerck/Odyssey Productions, Inc.

Page 155, top to bottom, left to right: Lauros-Giraudon/Art Resource, NY; The Nelson-Atkins Museum of Art, Kansas City, Missouri. (Purchase: Nelson Trust) 50-20; Picture Desk, Inc./Kobal Collection; Albert Craig; Werner Forman Archive Bardo Museum, Tunis; Templo Mayor CoyoIxauhqui. Aztec Moon Goddess Stone. Aztec, 15th century. Stone, diameter 11′6″ (3.5 m).

Chapter 8 a. Corbis/Bettmann; c. CORBIS-NY; d. CORBIS-NY; e. Museum of Fine Arts, Boston; f. Worcester Art Museum; g. Dorling Kindersley Media Library.

Chapter 9 a. Corbis/Bettmann; c. Araldo de Luca/Corbis/Bettmann; d. Corbis/Bettmann; e. Tokyo National Museum; f. Corbis/Bettmann; g. "Fan-Shaped Sutra" Tokyo National Museum. Image: TNM Image Archives. Source: **http://TnmArchives.jp/**; h. "Scroll w/depictions of the Night Attach on the Sanjo Palace" from Heiji monogatari emaki, 2nd half of the 13th c. Unknown. Japanese,Kamakura Period.Handscroll; ink & colors on paper.41.3 × 699.7 cm. Fenollosa-Weld C. Courtesy of Museum of Fine Arts, Boston; i. PPS/Pacific Press Service.

Chapter 10 a. Corbis/Bettmann c. J. Kershaw/Dorling Kindersley Media Library; d. J. Kershaw/Dorling Kindersley Media Library; e. Corbis/Bettmann; f. © Hulton-Deutsch Collection/CORBIS; g. Sassanid Art. Bottom of a silver bowl with Sassanid relief work. Leningrad Museum. Corbis-Bettmann; h. Borromeo; Art Resource, NY; i. The Nelson-Atkins Museum of Art, Kansas City, Missouri. (Purchase: Nelson Trust) 50-20; j. Paul Almasy; Corbis/Bettmann; k. J. Kershaw; Dorling Kindersley Media Library.

Chapter 11 b. Bowl. Unidentified. 10th Century, Earthenware painted under glaze H 11.2 × Diam. 39.3 cm. Iran. freer Gallery of Art, Smithsonian Institution, Washington, D.C.: Purchase, F1957.24; c. Folio from a Koran: Sura 21, verses 111-2; Sura 221-2. 9th Century, ink, color, and gold on paechment 28.3 × 39.8 cm. Probably North Africa. Freer Gallery of Art, Smithsonian Intsitution, Washington, D.C.; Purchase, F1945.16; d. Dorling Kindersley Media Library; e. Arabic Manuscript: 30.60 Page from a Koran, 8th-9th century. Kufic script. H: 23.8 × W: 35.5 cm. Courtesy of the Freer Gallery of Art, Smithsonian Institution, Washington, D.C.; f. Werner Forman Archive; Art Resource, NY; g. Library of Congress; h. Scala/Art Resource, NY.

Chapter 12 a. Trinity College, Dublin, Ireland/Rev. Raymond Schoder/SuperStock; c. Book of Kells: St. Matthew, Chi Rho initial. Ca. 800 C.E.. Trinity College, Dublin, Ireland, © Art Resource, NY; d. © Werner Forman/Art Resource, NY; e. Scala/Art Resource, NY; f. Bodleian Library, University of Oxford; g. Giraudon/Art Resource; h. Bronze equestrian statuette of Charlemagne, from Metz Cathedral, 9th-10th c. 3/4 view. Louvre, Paris, France. Copyright Giraudon/Art Resource, NY.

Chapter 13 b. Bowl. Iran, late 12th century. Stone-paste painted over glaze with luster; 7.8 × 17.3 cm. Arthur M. Sackler Gallery,

Smithsonian Institution, Washington, D.C. Gift of Osborne and Gratia Hauge, S1997.113; c. Adam Woolfitt; Corbis/Bettmann; d. Ellen Rooney; Robert Harding World Imagery; e. Geoff Dann; Dorling Kindersley Media Library; f. Clare Arni; Dorling Kindersley Media Library.

Chapter 14 a. Lowell Georgia/NGS Image Collection; b. Siede Preis; Getty Images, Inc.-Photodisc; c. © CONACULTA-INAH-MEX. Authorized reproduction by the Instituto Nacional de Antropologia e Historia; e. Dorling Kindersley Media Library; f. ©Erich Lessing/Art Resource, NY; g. Robert Frerck/Odyssey Productions, Inc.; h. Jeff Greenberg/AGE Fotostock America, Inc.; i. Robert Frerck/Odyssey Productions, Inc.; j. © CONACULTA-INAH-MEX. Authorized reproduction by the Instituto Nacional de Antropologia e Historia; k. Scala/Art Resource, NY; l. © Bettmann/CORBIS.

Chapter 15 a. Dorling Kindersley/The Wallace Collection; b. © Historical Picture Archive/CORBIS; d. Corbis/Bettmann; e. The Granger Collection; f. Scala/Art Resource, NY; g. Geoff Brightling/Dorling Kindersley Media Library; h. Scala/Art Resource, NY; i. Photograph © Erich Lessing/Art Resource, NY; j. Reunion des Musees Nationaux/Art Reesource, NY.

Part 4 Timeline, Page 328, top to bottom, left to right: Elizabeth I (1558–1603) standing on a map of England in 1592. An astute politician in both foreign and domestic policy, Elizabeth was perhaps the most successful ruler of the sixteenth century. By courtesy of the National Portrait Gallery, London; Sultan Muhammad (active ca. 1501–1545), "Allegory of Worldly and Otherworldly Drunkenness". Leaf from a manuscript of a "Divan" by Hafiz, folio 137r. Opaque watercolor, ink and gold on paper. 11 3/8 × 8 1/2 in. (28.9 × 21.6 cm). Promised Gift of Mr. and Mrs. Stuart Cary Welch, Jr. in honor of the students of Harvard University and Radcliffe College. Partially owned by The Metropolitan Museum of Art and The Arthur M. Sackler Museum, Harvard University, 1988. Copyright 1989, Metropolitan Museum of Art; Courtesy of the Freer Gallery of Art, Smithsonian Institution, Washington, DC; The Bridgeman Art Library International Ltd; Corbis/Bettmann.

Page 329, top to bottom, left to right: Giraudon/Art Resource; Francis Wheatley (RA) (1747–1801) "Evening", signed and dated 1799, oil on canvas, 17 1/2 × 21 1/2 in. (44.5 × 54.5 cm), Yale Center for British Art, Paul Mellon Collection B1977.14.118; Trevor Wood/Getty Images Inc.-Stone Allstock; Japan Airlines Photo; Unidentified Artist. The Emperor Ch'ien Lung (1736–1795) as a Young Man. Colors on silk. H. 63-1/2 in. W. 30-1/2 in. ©The Metropolitan Museum of Art, Rogers Fund, 1942. (42.141.8). Photograph ©1980 The Metropolitan Museum of Art; Peter Greenberg; Corbis/Bettmann.

Chapter 16 a. Dorling Kindersley/British Museum; c. Gemalde von Lucas Cranach d. A., 1529, "Dr. Martin Luther and his wife Katharina of Bora". Oil painting on book wood, 36 × 23 cm. Darmstadt, Hessisches Landesmuseum. Bildarchiv Preussisches Kulturbesitz; d. Museu De Marinha, Lisbon, Portugal; e. Picture Collection, The Branch Libraries, The New York Public Library, Astor, Lenox and Tilden Foundations; f. Bibliotheque publique et universitaire, Geneve; g. Le Massacre de la St-Barthelemy, entre 1572 et 1584. Oil on wood, 94 × 154 cm. Musee cantonal des

Beaux-Arts, Lausanne. Photo: J.-C. Ducret, Musee cantonal des Beaux-Arts, Lausanne; h. The Granger Collection, New York.

Chapter 17 a. Dorling Kindersley Media Library; c. Mapungubwe Museum; d. Corbis/Bettmann; e. UN/DPI PHOTO/Jeffrey Fox; f. Cliche Bibliotheque nationale de France—Paris; g. Kal Muller/Woodfin Camp & Associates; h. Courtesy Entwistle Gallery, London.

Chapter 18 a. Dorling Kindersley Media Library; b. Courtesy, American Antiquarian Society; d. Guy Ryecart/Dorling Kindersley Media Library; e. Courtesy of The University of Texas Archives. The UT Institute of Texan Cultures at San Antonio; f. Chas Howson/Dorling Kindersley Media Library; g. Dorling Kindersley Media Library; h. Samuel Scott, "Old Custom House Quay" Collection. V&A IMAGES, THE VICTORIA AND ALBERT MUSEUM, LONDON; i. The Granger Collection; j. Hulton/Corbis/Bettmann; k. Fur traders and Indians: engraving, 1777. c. The Granger Collection, New York; l. Glenbow Museum.

Chapter 19 a. Dorling Kindersley Media Library; c. Box: Carved lacquer box with cover decorated with scene of sages in a garden. Chinese, Yongle (1403–1429). Carved red lacquer over wood. 7.9 × 26.6 cm. China. freer Gallery of Art. Smithsonian Institution, Washington, D.C.: Purchase, F1953.64a; d. Karaori kimono. Middle Edo period, c. 1700. Brocaded silk. Tokyo National Museum; e. Tai Chin, "Fisherman on an Autumn River", (1390–1460). Painting. Ink and color on paper. 18-1/8 × 291-1/4 in. (46 × 740 cm). Courtesy of the Freer Gallery of Art, Smithsonian Institution, Washington, D.C.; f. Albert Craig; g. Melon-shaped Ewer, Stoneware. Koryo Dynasty, ca. 12th century H. 9″ × Diam. 19-1/2″. Korea. The Avery Brundage Collection, Asian Art Museum of San Francisco; h. Roger Phillips/Dorling Kindersley Media Library.

Chapter 20 a. Corbis/Bettmann; b. Dorling Kindersley/State Historical Museum, Moscow; d. Culver Pictures, Inc.; e. Dave King/Dorling Kindersley Media Library; f. Art Resource, NY; g. Art Resource/Musee du Louvre; h. By permission of the Master and Fellows of Sidney Sussex College, Cambridge; i. The Granger Collection; j. The Art Archive/Musee du Chateau de Versailles/Dagli Orti.

Chapter 21 a. Andrew McRobb/Dorling Kindersley Media Library; b. Mary Evans Picture Library Ltd; d. The Bridgeman Art Library International Ltd; e. Dorling Kindersley/The Museum of English Rural Life; f. Claude Joseph Vernet, "Construction of a Road". Louvre, Paris, France. Giraudon/Art Resource, NY; g. Art Resource/Bildarchiv Preussischer Kulturbesitz; h. Francis Wheatley (RA) (1747–1801) "Evening", signed and dated 1799, oil on canvas, 17 1/2 × 21 1/2 in. (44.5 × 54.5 cm), Yale Center for British Art, Paul Mellon Collection B1977.14.118; i. Judaica Collection Max Berger, Vienna, Austria. Photograph © Erich Lessing/Art Resource, NY.

Chapter 22 b. Folio: Lion, Ch'ilin and Dragon set in floral sprays mid 16th Century, ink, color and gold on paper 17.5 × 28.5 cm. Turkey. Freer Gallery of Art, Smithsonian Institution, Washington, D.C.: Purchase, F1948.17; c. Woman with a veil. Riaz Abbasi, Ca. 1590–95 (1565–1635). Opaque watercolor, ink, and gold on paper 34.2 × 21.5 cm. Arthur M. Sackler Gallery, Smithsonian Institution, Washington, D.C.: Lent by The Art and History Trust, LTS1995.2.80; d. Corbis/Bettmann; e. Chris

Hellier/CORBIS; Corbis/Bettmann; f. Suleyman I (Kanuni); Shehzade by Talikizade Suphi. Folio 79a of the Talikizade Shehnamesi, Library of the Topkapi Palace Museum, A3592, photograph courtesy of Talat Halman; g. Victoria & Albert Museum, London; Art Resource, NY; h. Michel Gotin; i. Marit Nieuwland; Omni-Photo Communications, Inc.

Part 5 Timeline, Page 492, top to bottom, left to right: France, 18th c., "Seige of the Bastille, 14 July, 1789". Obligatory mention of the following: Musee de la Ville de Paris, Musee de la Ville de Paris, Musee Carnavalet, Paris, France. Giraudon/Art Resource, NY; Sir Godfrey Kneller, "Sir Isaac Newton". Bildarchiv Preussischer Kulturbesitz.; Corbis/Bettmann; Kitagawa Utamaro (1753–1806), "Mother Bathing Her Son". Print. Color woodblock print, oban, tate-e, nishiki-e, mica 14 7/8″ × 10 1/8″ (37.8 × 25.7 cm.). The Nelson-Atkins Museum of Art, Kansas City, Missouri (Purchase: Nelson Trust). (C) The Nelson Gallery Foundation. All Reproduction Rights Reserved; The Granger Collection, New York.

Page 493, top to bottom, left to right: "Col. James Todd on elephant Indian painting" c. 1880. E.T. Archive, Victoria and Albert Museum; Corbis/Bettmann; Art Resource/Bildarchiv Preussischer Kulturbesitz.

Chapter 23 b. Corbis/Bettmann; c. © Archivo Iconografico, S.A./CORBIS; d. Corbis/Bettmann; e. © Archivo Iconografico, S.A./CORBIS; f. © James A. Sugar/CORBIS; g. Dave King; Dorling Kindersley Media Library h. The Granger Collection; i. Gerard Le Gall; Art Resource/Bildarchiv Preussischer Kulturbesitz; j. Giraudon; Art Resource, NY; k. The Granger Collection; l. © Bettmann/CORBIS.

Chapter 24 a. Dorling Kindersley/The Wallace Collection; b. © Historical Picture Archive/CORBIS; d. North Wind Picture Archives; e. © Bettmann/CORBIS; f. Corbis/Bettmann; g. The Granger Collection; h. The Granger Collection, New York; i. SuperStock, Inc.; j. The Granger Collection, New York; k. Corbis/Bettmann.

Chapter 25 a. Corbis/Bettmann; c. Fort Sumter National Monument; d. Dave King (US); Dorling Kindersley Media Library; e. Library of Congress; f. Getty Images Inc.—PhotoDisc; g. Austrian Archive/Corbis; h. Mary Evans Picture Library Ltd; i. The Granger Collection; j. © Hulton-Deutsch Collection/CORBIS.

Part 6 Timeline, Page 564, top to bottom, left to right: Art Resource/Bildarchiv Preussischer Kulturbesitz; William I of Prussia was declared emperor of Germany in the Hall of Mirrors at Versailles after the defeat of France in the Franco-Prussian War. Otto von Bismarck, the Prussian minister who engineered the unification of Germany, stands in the white uniform toward the right of the picture. Bildarchiv Preussischer Kulturbesitz. Original: Friedrichsruh, Bismarck-Museum; Corbis/Bettmann; Hulton Picture Library/Bettman; Library of Congress.

Page 565, top to bottom, left to right: Art Resource/Bildarchiv Preussischer Kulturbesitz; Shosai Ginko (Japanese, act. 1874–1897), View of the Issuance of the State Constitution in the State Chamber of the New Imperial Palace, March 2, 1889 (Meiji 22), Ink and color on paper, 14 1/8 × 28 3/8 in. "The Metropolitan Museum of Art, Gift of Lincoln Kirstein, 1959 (JP3233-3235) Photograph © The Metropolitan Museum of Art;" Corbis/Bettmann; The Granger Collection.

INDEX

WORLD HISTORY DOCUMENTS CD-ROM

SINGLE PC LICENSE AGREEMENT AND LIMITED WARRANTY

READ THIS LICENSE CAREFULLY BEFORE OPENING THIS PACKAGE. BY OPENING THIS PACKAGE, YOU ARE AGREEING TO THE TERMS AND CONDITIONS OF THIS LICENSE. IF YOU DO NOT AGREE, DO NOT OPEN THE PACKAGE. PROMPTLY RETURN THE UNOPENED PACKAGE AND ALL ACCOMPANYING ITEMS TO THE PLACE YOU OBTAINED THEM.

1. **GRANT OF LICENSE AND OWNERSHIP:** THE ENCLOSED COMPUTER PROGRAMS <<AND DATA>> ("SOFTWARE") ARE LICENSED, NOT SOLD, TO YOU BY PEARSON EDUCATION, INC. PUBLISHING AS PEARSON PRENTICE HALL ("WE" OR THE "COMPANY") AND IN CONSIDERATION OF YOUR PURCHASE OR ADOPTION OF THE ACCOMPANYING COMPANY TEXTBOOKS AND/OR OTHER MATERIALS, AND YOUR AGREEMENT TO THESE TERMS. WE RESERVE ANY RIGHTS NOT GRANTED TO YOU. YOU OWN ONLY THE DISK(S) BUT WE AND/OR OUR LICENSORS OWN THE SOFTWARE ITSELF. THIS LICENSE ALLOWS YOU TO USE AND DISPLAY YOUR COPY OF THE SOFTWARE ON A SINGLE COMPUTER (I.E., WITH A SINGLE CPU) AT A SINGLE LOCATION FOR ACADEMIC USE ONLY, SO LONG AS YOU COMPLY WITH THE TERMS OF THIS AGREEMENT. YOU MAY MAKE ONE COPY FOR BACK UP, OR TRANSFER YOUR COPY TO ANOTHER CPU, PROVIDED THAT THE SOFTWARE IS USABLE ON ONLY ONE COMPUTER.

2. **RESTRICTIONS:** YOU MAY NOT TRANSFER OR DISTRIBUTE THE SOFTWARE OR DOCUMENTATION TO ANYONE ELSE. EXCEPT FOR BACKUP, YOU MAY NOT COPY THE DOCUMENTATION OR THE SOFTWARE. YOU MAY NOT NETWORK THE SOFTWARE OR OTHERWISE USE IT ON MORE THAN ONE COMPUTER OR COMPUTER TERMINAL AT THE SAME TIME. YOU MAY NOT REVERSE ENGINEER, DISASSEMBLE, DECOMPILE, MODIFY, ADAPT, TRANSLATE, OR CREATE DERIVATIVE WORKS BASED ON THE SOFTWARE OR THE DOCUMENTATION. YOU MAY BE HELD LEGALLY RESPONSIBLE FOR ANY COPYING OR COPYRIGHT INFRINGEMENT THAT IS CAUSED BY YOUR FAILURE TO ABIDE BY THE TERMS OF THESE RESTRICTIONS.

3. **TERMINATION:** THIS LICENSE IS EFFECTIVE UNTIL TERMINATED. THIS LICENSE WILL TERMINATE AUTOMATICALLY WITHOUT NOTICE FROM THE COMPANY IF YOU FAIL TO COMPLY WITH ANY PROVISIONS OR LIMITATIONS OF THIS LICENSE. UPON TERMINATION, YOU SHALL DESTROY THE DOCUMENTATION AND ALL COPIES OF THE SOFTWARE. ALL PROVISIONS OF THIS AGREEMENT AS TO LIMITATION AND DISCLAIMER OF WARRANTIES, LIMITATION OF LIABILITY, REMEDIES OR DAMAGES, AND OUR OWNERSHIP RIGHTS SHALL SURVIVE TERMINATION.

4. **LIMITED WARRANTY AND DISCLAIMER OF WARRANTY:** COMPANY WARRANTS THAT FOR A PERIOD OF 60 DAYS FROM THE DATE YOU PURCHASE THIS SOFTWARE (OR PURCHASE OR ADOPT THE ACCOMPANYING TEXTBOOK), THE SOFTWARE, WHEN PROPERLY INSTALLED AND USED IN ACCORDANCE WITH THE DOCUMENTATION, WILL OPERATE IN SUBSTANTIAL CONFORMITY WITH THE DESCRIPTION OF THE SOFTWARE SET FORTH IN THE DOCUMENTATION, AND THAT FOR A PERIOD OF 30 DAYS THE DISK(S) ON WHICH THE SOFTWARE IS DELIVERED SHALL BE FREE FROM DEFECTS IN MATERIALS AND WORKMANSHIP UNDER NORMAL USE. THE COMPANY DOES NOT WARRANT THAT THE SOFTWARE WILL MEET YOUR REQUIREMENTS OR THAT THE OPERATION OF THE SOFTWARE WILL BE UNINTERRUPTED OR ERROR-FREE. YOUR ONLY REMEDY AND THE COMPANY'S ONLY OBLIGATION UNDER THESE LIMITED WARRANTIES IS, AT THE COMPANY'S OPTION, RETURN OF THE DISK FOR A REFUND OF ANY AMOUNTS PAID FOR IT BY YOU OR REPLACEMENT OF THE DISK. THIS LIMITED WARRANTY IS THE ONLY WARRANTY PROVIDED BY THE COMPANY AND ITS LICENSORS, AND THE COMPANY AND ITS LICENSORS DISCLAIM ALL OTHER WARRANTIES, EXPRESS OR IMPLIED, INCLUDING WITHOUT LIMITATION, THE IMPLIED WARRANTIES OF MERCHANTABILITY AND FITNESS FOR A PARTICULAR PURPOSE. THE COMPANY DOES NOT WARRANT, GUARANTEE OR MAKE ANY REPRESENTATION REGARDING THE ACCURACY, RELIABILITY, CURRENTNESS, USE, OR RESULTS OF USE, OF THE SOFTWARE.

5. **LIMITATION OF REMEDIES AND DAMAGES:** IN NO EVENT, SHALL THE COMPANY OR ITS EMPLOYEES, AGENTS, LICENSORS, OR CONTRACTORS BE LIABLE FOR ANY INCIDENTAL, INDIRECT, SPECIAL, OR CONSEQUENTIAL DAMAGES ARISING OUT OF OR IN CONNECTION WITH THIS LICENSE OR THE SOFTWARE, INCLUDING FOR LOSS OF USE, LOSS OF DATA, LOSS OF INCOME OR PROFIT, OR OTHER LOSSES, SUSTAINED AS A RESULT OF INJURY TO ANY PERSON, OR LOSS OF OR DAMAGE TO PROPERTY, OR CLAIMS OF THIRD PARTIES, EVEN IF THE COMPANY OR AN AUTHORIZED REPRESENTATIVE OF THE COMPANY HAS BEEN ADVISED OF THE POSSIBILITY OF SUCH DAMAGES. IN NO EVENT SHALL THE LIABILITY OF THE COMPANY FOR DAMAGES WITH RESPECT TO THE SOFTWARE EXCEED THE AMOUNTS ACTUALLY PAID BY YOU, IF ANY, FOR THE SOFTWARE OR THE ACCOMPANYING TEXTBOOK. BECAUSE SOME JURISDICTIONS DO NOT ALLOW THE LIMITATION OF LIABILITY IN CERTAIN CIRCUMSTANCES, THE ABOVE LIMITATIONS MAY NOT ALWAYS APPLY TO YOU.

6. **GENERAL:** THIS AGREEMENT SHALL BE CONSTRUED IN ACCORDANCE WITH THE LAWS OF THE UNITED STATES OF AMERICA AND THE STATE OF NEW YORK, APPLICABLE TO CONTRACTS MADE IN NEW YORK, EXCLUDING THE STATE'S LAWS AND POLICIES ON CONFLICTS OF LAW, AND SHALL BENEFIT THE COMPANY, ITS AFFILIATES AND ASSIGNEES. THIS AGREEMENT IS THE COMPLETE AND EXCLUSIVE STATEMENT OF THE AGREEMENT BETWEEN YOU AND THE COMPANY AND SUPERSEDES ALL PROPOSALS OR PRIOR AGREEMENTS, ORAL, OR WRITTEN, AND ANY OTHER COMMUNICATIONS BETWEEN YOU AND THE COMPANY OR ANY REPRESENTATIVE OF THE COMPANY RELATING TO THE SUBJECT MATTER OF THIS AGREEMENT. IF YOU ARE A U.S. GOVERNMENT USER, THIS SOFTWARE IS LICENSED WITH "RESTRICTED RIGHTS" AS SET FORTH IN SUBPARAGRAPHS (A)-(D) OF THE COMMERCIAL COMPUTER-RESTRICTED RIGHTS CLAUSE AT FAR 52.227-19 OR IN SUBPARAGRAPHS (C)(1)(II) OF THE RIGHTS IN TECHNICAL DATA AND COMPUTER SOFTWARE CLAUSE AT DFARS 252.227-7013, AND SIMILAR CLAUSES, AS APPLICABLE.

SHOULD YOU HAVE ANY QUESTIONS CONCERNING THIS AGREEMENT OR IF YOU WISH TO CONTACT THE COMPANY FOR ANY REASON, PLEASE CONTACT IN WRITING: LEGAL DEPARTMENT, PRENTICE HALL, 1 LAKE STREET, UPPER SADDLE RIVER, NJ 07450 OR CALL PEARSON EDUCATION PRODUCT SUPPORT AT 1-800-677-6337.